THE WISDOM TEXTS FROM QUMRAN
AND THE DEVELOPMENT
OF SAPIENTIAL THOUGHT

BIBLIOTHECA EPHEMERIDUM THEOLOGICARUM LOVANIENSIUM

CLIX

THE WISDOM TEXTS FROM QUMRAN AND THE DEVELOPMENT OF SAPIENTIAL THOUGHT

EDITED BY

C. HEMPEL, A. LANGE
AND H. LICHTENBERGER

LEUVEN
UNIVERSITY PRESS

UITGEVERIJ PEETERS
LEUVEN – PARIS – STERLING, VA

2002

ISBN 90 5867 243 3 (Leuven University Press)
D/2002/1869/50
ISBN 90-429-1010-0 (Peeters Leuven)
D/2001/0602/33

*All rights reserved. Except in those cases expressly determined by law,
no part of this publication may be multiplied, saved in an automated data file
or made public in any way whatsoever
without the express prior written consent of the publishers.*

Leuven University Press / Presses Universitaires de Louvain
Universitaire Pers Leuven
Blijde-Inkomststraat 5, B-3000 Leuven-Louvain (Belgium)

© 2002, Peeters, Bondgenotenlaan 153, B-3000 Leuven (Belgium)

FOREWORD

The sapiential texts from Qumran considerably enlarge the limited corpus of Israelite or Jewish wisdom texts known before the Dead Sea Scrolls were found. While formerly only Proverbs, Job, Qohelet, Ben Sira, the Wisdom of Solomon, and Pseudo-Phocylides gave testimony of the Israelite-Jewish contribution to ancient near eastern wisdom, the library of Qumran adds at least another seven texts to this corpus: 4QWiles of the Wicked Women (4Q184), 4QSapiential Work (4Q185), 4QWords of the Maskil to All Sons of Dawn (4Q298), the Book of Mysteries (1Q27, 4Q299-301), Instruction (*mûsār l^emebîn*; 1Q26, 4Q415-418.418a.418c.423), 4QInstruction-like Composition B (4Q424), and 4QBeatitudes (4Q525). In addition, several manuscripts were found which might represent further sapiential texts but are too fragmentary today to allow for such a characterization with certainty. Thus, the finds from the Qumran caves have more than doubled the corpus of Israelite-Jewish sapiential literature. The sheer number of new texts, most of which were published only recently, documents beyond any doubt, that in Judaism the end of wisdom was not reached with books like Job, Qohelet, or Ben Sira, but that Jewish wisdom flourished especially in Hellenistic times.

The contributions of the present volume try to interpret the new texts in the context of the history of spaiential thought. In addition, some of the contributions are dedicated to introductory questions or particular interpretative issues. Thus, it is hoped that the volume will make the new material more accessible to wisdom research in the fields of the Ancient Near East, the Hebrew Bible, Ancient Judaism and Early Christianity. It comprises the lectures presented to a research seminar dedicated to the same questions and organized by A. Lange and H. Lichtenberger (Tübingen, 22nd-24th May and 20th-21st June 1998). Additional articles on subjects which were not dealt with at the research seminar for various reasons have been contributed by A. Behringer, C. Böttrich, H.-J. Fabry, D. Harrington, A. Schoors, J. Strugnell, and L. Stuckenbruck.

A number of final publications of the texts discussed here appeared when this volume was in a very advanced stage of editing. In some cases the system of numbering the fragments has been changed in the final editions over against previously available preliminary editions. Some contributors were able to make use of the most up-to-date fragment numbers whereas others still worked with the old numbers. In order to provide the reader with some assistance when it comes to using the references in our volume we have appended at the very end a synopsis of fragment numbers prepared by Mr. A. Behringer. To prevent overloading the footnotes with bibliographical details we have employed standardized short titles throughout and included full bibliographical details in the bibliographies at the end.

A number of institutions have provided financial assistance for this project. The research seminar was funded by the Graduiertenkolleg "Die Bibel – ihre Entstehung und ihre Wirkung" and the "Vereinigung der Freunde der Universität Tübingen (Universitätsbund) e.V." A public lecture by Philip Alexander, also included in this volume, was sponsored by the British Council. The publication of the present volume was supported by the "Vereinigung der Freunde der Universität Tübingen (Universitätsbund) e.V." It is our obligation and our pleasure to express our gratitude and thanks to all donors as well as to the authors of this volume for their contributions. Furthermore we are obliged to Mr. Alexander Behringer who worked on this book as a student assistant and to Mrs. Monika Merkle for her extensive proofreading. Special thanks are also to be given by the Tübingen editors of this volume to Dr. Charlotte Hempel who handled its redaction and compiled its index. Last but not least all editors would like to express their appreciation to the editor of the series Bibliotheca Ephemeridum Theologicarum Lovaniensium, Prof. Dr. Frans Neirynck, and to Mr. Paul Peeters of Uitgeverij Peeters for accepting this volume for publication.

Charlotte Hempel
Meyerhoff Center for Jewish Studies
University of Maryland

Armin Lange
Department of Religious Studies
University of North Carolina at Chapel Hill

Hermann Lichtenberger
Institut für antikes Judentum und hellenistische Religionsgeschichte
Eberhard-Karls-Universität Tübingen

January 2001

TABLE OF CONTENTS

Foreword   VII

I
INTRODUCTORY AND LINGUISTIC QUESTIONS

1. A. LANGE
   Die Weisheitstexte aus Qumran: Eine Einleitung   3
2. J. STRUGNELL
   The Smaller Hebrew Wisdom Texts Found at Qumran:
   Variations, Resemblances, and Lines of Development   31
3. A. SCHOORS
   The Language of the Qumran Sapiential Works   61

II
CONTRIBUTIONS TO SPECIFIC TEXTS

4. E. TIGCHELAAR
   Towards a Reconstruction of the Beginning of 4QInstruction
   (4Q416 Fragment 1 and Parallels)   99
5. H. LICHTENBERGER
   Der Weisheitstext 4Q185 – Eine neue Edition 127

III
THE WISDOM TEXTS FROM QUMRAN
AND THE ANCIENT NEAR EAST

6. H.-P. MÜLLER
   Tun-Ergehens-Zusammenhang, Klageerhörung und Theodizee
   im biblischen Hiobbuch und in seinen babylonischen Parallelen 153
7. H. NIEHR
   Die Weisheit des Achikar und der *musar lammebin* im Vergleich 173

IV
THE WISDOM TEXTS FROM QUMRAN
AND THE HEBREW BIBLE

8. H.-J. FABRY
   Die Seligpreisungen in der Bibel und in Qumran 189

9. G.J. BROOKE
   Biblical Interpretation in the Wisdom Texts from Qumran . . 201

V
THE WISDOM TEXTS FROM QUMRAN AND ANCIENT JUDAISM

10. P.S. ALEXANDER
    Enoch and the Beginnings of Jewish Interest in
    Natural Science 223
11. L.T. STUCKENBRUCK
    4QInstruction and the Possible Influence of Early Enochic
    Traditions: An Evaluation 245
12. D.J. HARRINGTON
    Two Early Jewish Approaches to Wisdom:
    Sirach and Qumran Sapiential Work A 263
13. C. HEMPEL
    The Qumran Sapiential Texts and the Rule Books 277
14. C. BÖTTRICH
    Frühjüdische Weisheitstraditionen im slavischen Henochbuch
    und in Qumran 297
15. J.H. CHARLESWORTH
    The Odes of Solomon and the Jewish Wisdom Texts 323
16. J. DOCHHORN
    »Sie wird dir nicht ihre Kraft geben« - Adam, Kain und der
    Ackerbau in 4Q423 2_3 und Apc Mos 24 351

VI
THE WISDOM TEXTS FROM QUMRAN AND THE NEW TESTAMENT

17. J. FREY
    Flesh and Spirit in the Palestinian Jewish Sapiential Tradition
    and in the Qumran Texts: An Inquiry into the Background of
    Pauline Usage 367
18. A. KLOSTERGAARD PETERSEN
    Wisdom as Cognition: Creating the Others in the Book of
    Mysteries and 1 Cor 1-2 405

APPENDIX

19. A. BEHRINGER
    Synopsis of Fragment Numbers Employed in the Editions of
    the Sapiential Manuscripts from Qumran 435

BIBLIOGRAPHIES AND INDEX

LITERATURE ON THE WISDOM TEXTS FROM QUMRAN	445
OTHER LITERATURE	455
INDEX OF REFERENCES	487

I
INTRODUCTORY AND LINGUISTIC QUESTIONS

DIE WEISHEITSTEXTE AUS QUMRAN

Eine Einleitung

Die Frage nach der Weisheit in Qumran hat trotz des großen öffentlichen und wissenschaftlichen Interesses an den Textfunden vom Toten Meer über lange Jahrzehnte kaum eine Rolle gespielt. Die wenigen Arbeiten zum Thema beschränkten sich fast ausschließlich auf die Untersuchung weisheitlicher Themen, Motive und Formen in nichtweisheitlichen Texten oder kamen über Beschreibungen der vor 1992 veröffentlichten Handschriften kaum hinaus[1]. Lediglich die von J.M. Allegro schon 1968 in *Qumrân Cave 4. I* veröffentlichten und nur einige Fragmente umfassenden Handschriften 4Q184 und 4Q185 (pp. 82-87) fanden ein gewisses Echo in der Forschungsgeschichte[2]. Signifikant ist der Überblick in M. Küchlers großem Buch *Frühjüdische Weisheitstraditionen*. Neben einzelnen Abschnitten aus nichtweisheitlichen Werken nennt er lediglich 1Q26 und weist auf drei damals noch unveröffentlichte Texte hin, nämlich 4Q487, 4Q485 und den größten Weisheitstext aus Höhle 4, 4QInstruction (*mûsar l^emēbîn*) (pp. 98ff.). Als Küchler seine Arbeit im Jahr 1979 vorlegte, war von der Existenz der meisten Weisheitstexte aus Qumran noch so gut wie nichts bekannt.

Dies änderte sich erst, als E. Tov 1992 die ersten Kataloge über die noch unveröffentlichten Handschriften aus den Höhlen 4 und 11 von Qumran vorlegte[3], und B.Z. Wacholder und M.G. Abegg im gleichen Jahr den zweiten Faszikel ihrer *A Preliminary Edition of the Unpublished Dead Sea Scrolls* fertigstellten. Jetzt wurde deutlich, daß man in den Höhlen von Qumran bis zu 40 Handschriften unterschiedlicher Weisheitstexte gefunden hatte. Hinzu kamen Textzeugen der biblischen Bücher Hiob (2QJob, 4QJob^{a-c}, 4QtgJob, 11QtgJob), Prov (4QProv^{a-b}), Koh (4QQoh^{a-b}), Sir (2QSir, MasSir) und Tob (4QTob^{a-e}). Insbesondere die nichtbiblischen Weisheitstexte sind in den letzten Jahren Gegenstand intensiver Diskussion gewesen[4]. Eine alles Material berücksichtigende

---

1. S. die Arbeiten von WORREL, *Concepts of Wisdom*; LIPSCOMB/SANDERS, *Wisdom at Qumran*; KÜCHLER, *Weisheitstraditionen*; NEWSOM, *Sage*; TANZER, *Sages at Qumran*.
2. CARMIGNAC, *Poème allégorique*; GAZOV-GINZBERG, *Double Meaning*; STRUGNELL, *Notes en marge*, pp. 263-273; LICHT, *4Q184*; NEBE, *Lexikalische Bemerkungen*; BURGMANN, *Simon*; LICHTENBERGER, *Weisheitliche Mahnrede*; MOORE, *Personification*; BROSHI, *Wiles*; AMUSSIN, *Pamphlet*; BAUMGARTEN, *Seductress*; TOBIN, *4Q185*.
3. *Unpublished Qumran Texts* (BA 55); *Unpublished Qumran Texts* (JJS 43).
4. Eine leider auf die englische Literatur beschränkte und bis in das Jahr 1997 reichende Forschungsgeschichte zum Thema findet sich bei bei KAMPEN, *Diverse Aspects*.

Arbeit, die die Weisheitstexte im Kontext der nachexilischen und antikjüdischen Weisheitstraditionen verortet, steht jedoch noch aus[5].

1. Die Weisheitstexte aus Qumran – Ein Überblick[6]

Im ursprünglichen Herausgeberteam scheint eine Tendenz bestanden zu haben, Handschriften immer dann als weisheitlich zu kategorisieren, wenn in ihnen weisheitliches Vokabular anzutreffen ist. Dies führte dazu, daß insbesondere eine große Zahl von stark beschädigten Manuskripten den Weisheitstexten zugeordnet wurden. Eine erste Bestandsaufnahme bietet E. Tovs Handschriftenkatalog (*Companion Volume*, pp. 23.35.39.43-45):

1Q26	wisdom apocryphon (Sap. Work A f)
1Q27	Myst
4Q184	Wiles of the Wicked Woman
4Q185	sapiential work
4Q298	crA Words of the Sage to the Sons of Dawn
4Q299-301	Myst^{a-c}
4Q302	pap Praise of God
4Q302a	pap Parable of the Tree
4Q303-304	Meditation on Creation A
4Q305	Meditation on Creation B
4Q307	sapiential frags.?
4Q308	sapiential frags.?
4Q408	sapiential work
4Q410	sapiential work
4Q411	sapiential work
4Q412	sapiential work
4Q413	sapiential work
4Q415-418.423	Sap. Work A
4Q419	Sap. Work B
4Q420-421	Ways of Righteousness
4Q424	sapiential work
4Q425	Sap. Work C
4Q426	sapiential work
4Q472	sapiential work
4Q473	The Two Ways
4Q474	sapiential work
4Q475	sapiential work
4Q476	sapiential work

---

5. Eine erste alle Texte umfassende Darstellung findet sich bei HARRINGTON, *Wisdom Texts from Qumran* (vgl. ID., *Wisdom at Qumran* und KAMPEN, *Diverse Aspects*).

6. Im folgenden bleiben weisheitliche Passagen in nicht weisheitlichen Werken – wie z.B. die weisheitliche Lehrerzählung über die Gefährdung der Ahnfrau in 1QGenAp XIX$_{10}$-XX$_{32}$ (dazu vgl. LANGE, *Wisdom Didactive Narrative*) – unberücksichtigt.

Zusätzlich werden von M. Baillet, E. Puech und E.J.C. Tigchelaar auch 4Q294[7], 4Q486, 4Q487, 4Q498 und 4Q528[9] als weisheitlich charakterisiert.

2. STARK BESCHÄDIGTE HANDSCHRIFTEN

Aus diesen Texten gilt es in einem ersten Arbeitsschritt[10] jene Handschriften auszusortieren, die nicht eigentlich als weisheitlich verstanden werden können oder zu stark beschädigt sind, um sie mit Sicherheit der weisheitlichen Literatur zuordnen zu können[11]. Anschließend werden die verbleibenden Texte intensiver besprochen.

4Q294 Die 23 teilweise oder ganz erhaltenen Buchstaben des einzigen Fragments von 4QSapiential-Didactic Work C erlauben keine sichere Charakterisierung der Handschrift. Das] יהגה יום [(»]er sinnt nach Tag[«) aus Zeile 4 steht Ps 1,2 zwar textlich näher als Jos 1,8[12], aber eine Anspielung auf Jos 1,8 läßt sich bei den wenigen erhaltenen Buchstaben aber trotzdem nicht ausschließen.

4Q302 Die ursprünglich zu zwei verschiedenen Handschriften (4Q302 und 4Q302a) gezählten und aus den Jahren 125-100 v.Chr. stammenden[13] 18 Frag. von 4QpapAdmonitory Parable werden von ihrer Herausgeberin B. Nitzan als Textzeugen eines »discourse or admonition of the *rib* (lawsuit) pattern« charakterisiert[14]. Neben Gattungselementen eines *rîb*-Textes finden sich aber auch typisch weisheitliche Formelemente, wie das Baumgleichnis in 4Q302 2 II und die es einleitende und für die weisheitliche Lehrrede typische Lehreröffnungsformel הבינו נא בזאת החכמים (»erkennt dies, die ihr weise seid«; 2 II₂). Ob es sich um ein weisheitliches Werk handelt, das *rîb*-Elemente nutzt oder umgekehrt, kann wegen der starken Beschädigungen von 4Q302 nicht mehr sicher gesagt werden.

4Q303-305 Die drei 4QMeditation on Creation A-C genannten Fragmente[15] sind für eine sichere Zuweisung zur Weisheitsliteratur zu stark beschädigt. Was sich noch erkennen läßt, sind mit der Schöpfung verbundene Begriffe und Motive.

---

7. TIGCHELAAR, *4QSapiential-Didactic Work C*, pp. 247f.
8. Zu 4Q486, 4Q487 und 4Q498 s. BAILLET, *Qumrân Grotte 4*, pp. 4-10. 73f.
9. PUECH, *Qumrân grotte 4. XVIII*, p. 188.
10. Im folgenden werden die aktuellen Benennungen der einzelnen Handschriften aus der Reihe DJD verwendet.
11. Zu letzteren s. auch den Beitrag von J. STRUGNELL in diesem Band.
12. Vgl. TIGCHELAAR, *4QSapiential-Didactic Work C*, p. 248.
13. NITZAN, *4Q302/302a*, p. 152; EAD., *Admonitory Parable*, p. 126.
14. *4Q302/302a*, pp. 167f.; EAD., *Admonitory Parable*, p. 127.
15. LIM, *Meditation on Creation*, pp. 151-158.

4Q307 Wie schon im Fall von 4Q303-305 machen umfangreiche Textbeschädigungen es auch für 4QText Mentioning a Temple unmöglich, dieser Handschrift noch einen Sinnzusammenhang zu entnehmen[16].

4Q308 Die früher als »sapiential frags.?« bezeichnete Handschrift kann nach Auskunft der letzten Fassung von E. Tovs Handschriften-Katalog nicht mehr lokalisiert werden[17].

4Q408 4QApocryphon of Moses^c? überlappt mit den Handschriften 1Q29 und 4Q376 und sollte daher als eine weitere Handschrift des auch von 1Q22, 1Q29 und 4Q375-376 bezeugten Apocryphon of Moses gewertet werden[18].

4Q410 Die noch erhaltenen, stark beschädigten vier Frag. von 4QVision and Interpretation lassen nur noch eine kurze Visionsbeschreibung mit anschließender Auslegung ($1_{7ff.}$) erkennen[19].

4Q411 Das einzige von 4QSapiential Hymn erhaltene Fragment bezeugt Reste eines weisheitlich geprägten Schöpfungshymnus[20]. Jedoch ist keinesfalls auszuschließen, daß dieser Hymnus Teil einer umfangreicheren Sammlung poetischer Texte oder eines Prosatextes gewesen ist.

4Q412 Auch über Sapiential-Didactic Work A kann wegen des schlechten Erhaltungszustands der Handschrift nicht mehr gesagt werden, als daß »4Q412 seems to be a didactic collection, giving instructions for the life and behaviour of a person, as well as liturgical commands«[21].

4Q413 Von 4QComposition concerning Divine Providence sind nur zwei Frag. erhalten, die mit einer herodianischen Schrift beschrieben sind und zum oberen Ende einer Kol. gehören. Daß der relativ breite rechte Kolumnenrand keine Nahtreste aufweist, spricht dafür, daß das Frag. vom Anfang einer Rolle stammt.

»It is difficult to determine the nature of this work ... The four preserved lines contain an appeal ... exhorting the reader to consider carefully the historical events of the past, which demonstrate that whoever follows God has been rewarded, while whoever did not has failed to survive. This

---

16. Vgl. LIM, *4QText Mentioning a Temple*, p. 255.
17. TOV, *List*, p. 684.
18. Vgl. STEUDEL, *4QApocryphon of Moses^c?*, p. 298.
19. Vgl. STEUDEL, *4QVision and Interpretation*, p. 316.
20. Vgl. STEUDEL, *Sapiential Texts*, p. 159.
21. STEUDEL, *Sapiential Texts*, p. 163.

concept of divine providence is commonly found in other Qumran literary works, such as the *Damascus Document*«[22].

Die Frevler werden dabei in Zeile 3 unter Aufnahme von Jes 11,3 geschildert[23].

Obwohl beide Fragmente weisheitliches Gedankengut und weisheitliche Begrifflichkeit verwenden[24], ist keinesfalls sicher, daß sie ursprünglich zu einem Weisheitstext gehört haben. Insbesondere wegen der inhaltlichen Nähe zu Texten wie der Damaskusschrift[25] könnte 4Q413 auch den Rest einer von weisheitlichem Gedankengut geprägten Einleitung einer Gemeinderegel darstellen[26].

4Q419 Für 4QInstruction-like Composition A kann an dieser Stelle auf die Ausführungen von Harrington verwiesen werden:

»The text once designated Sapiential Work B (4Q419) may not be a wisdom text at all. Of its eleven fragments only two (1 and 8) are substantial. It was related to Sapiential Work A (1Q26; 4Q415-418, 423) on the basis of the phrase from Deuteronomy 15:7 ('if He [God] will shut His hand, the spirit of all flesh will be removed') that appears in both 4Q416 2 ii 2-3 and 4Q419 8 7. But the style and content of the two works are quite different. Fragment 1 of 4Q419 addresses a plural audience, and exhorts them to act according to the Law of Moses, to respect the eternal priesthood chosen from the seed of Aaron, and to avoid the abomination of impurity. Column 2 of fragment 8 uses third person language to talk about God's visitation, which will mean rewards for the righteous and destruction for the wicked: 'to their earth they shall return' (line 8; see Psalm 104:29)«[27].

4Q420-421 Bei den beiden von ihrem Herausgeber T. Elgvin[28] als weisheitlich verstandenen Handschriften 4QWays of Righteousness[a-b] handelt es sich nicht um Textzeugen eines weisheitlichen Werkes, sondern, wie Überlappungen mit 4Q264a belegen, um zwei weitere Handschriften von 4QHalakha B[29].

---

22. E. QIMRON, *4QComposition concerning Divine Providence*, p. 169; vgl. ID., *Divine Providence*, p. 192.
23. Vgl. QIMRON, *Divine Providence*, pp. 191.194; ID., *4QComposition concerning Divine Providence*, p. 171.
24. Zum weisheitlichen Charakter von 4Q413 vgl. auch HARRINGTON, *Wisdom Texts from Qumran*, pp. 64f.
25. Dazu vgl. auch HARRINGTON, *Wisdom Texts from Qumran*, p. 65.
26. Vgl. etwa die Funktion von 4Q420-421 im Text 4QHalakha B.
27. HARRINGTON, *Wisdom Texts from Qumran*, p. 73; zu den besonderen Schwierigkeiten in der Klassifizierung von 4Q419 vgl. auch TANZER, *4QInstruction-like Composition A*, pp. 321f.
28. *Admonition Texts*, pp. 179.184f.; *4Q Ways of Righteousness*, pp. 173.183.
29. TIGCHELAAR, *Sabbath Halakha*.

4Q425 Von 4QSapiential-Didactic Work B fanden sich noch sechs sehr stark beschädigte Fragmente, die in einer hasmonäisch-herodianischen Semikursiven gehalten sind. Es könnte sich um ein weisheitlich-didaktisches Werk mit proverbienartigem Charakter handeln[30], jedoch lassen die umfangreichen Beschädigungen der Handschrift kein eindeutiges Urteil zu.

4Q426 Die 14 sehr stark beschädigten Frag. aus dem späten 2. oder frühen 1. Jh. v.Chr. von 4QSapiential-Hymnic Work A bezeugen evtl. »a sapiential work which ... contained prayer, hymnic, and didactic elements«[31], jedoch läßt die geringe Textmenge kein eindeutiges Urteil zu.

4Q472 Der Text der beiden Frag. des heute 4QEschatological Work B genannten Werkes ist schwer zu beschreiben. T. Elgvin denkt als Thema von Frag. 1 an »the end-time renewal of Israel. God will bring redemption and joy to his elect who now suffer hardships.«[32] Frag. 2 könnte von einer Gruppe von Erwählten handeln. Der Begriff יחד bezeichnet möglicherweise die essenische Gemeinschaft[33].

Der ursprünglich als Frag. 2 der Handschrift 4Q472 zugewiesene Textrest wird heute als eigenständige Handschrift wahrscheinlich halachischer Natur verstanden (4QHalakha C [4Q472a])[34].

4Q473 In Frag. 2 des The Two Ways genannten Werkes findet sich eine an Dtn 11,13-17 und Dtn 27-30 orientierte Zwei-Wege-Motivik[35]. Beide Frag. sind jedoch zu klein, um sie einem bestimmten Genre zuweisen zu können. Die Segnungen und Verfluchungen von Frag. 2 sprechen sogar eher dafür, an einen Text wie 1QS II$_{1-18}$, 1QSb oder 4QBerakhot zu denken.

4Q474 In dem jetzt Text Concerning Rachel and Joseph genannten Werk finden sich keine Hinweise auf einen weisheitlichen Text. Daß Rachel erwähnt (1$_5$) und auf Joseph angespielt wird (1$_2$), könnte eher auf ein parabiblisches Werk deuten[36].

4Q475 Das einzige erhaltene Frag. der Handschrift 4QRenewed Earth »deals with God's eschatological renewal of His people and all the

---

30. So STEUDEL, *Sapiential Texts*, p. 204.
31. STEUDEL, *Sapiential Texts*, p. 211.
32. *4QEschatological Work B*, p. 452.
33. Vgl. ELGVIN, *4QEschatological Work B*, p. 454.
34. S. ELGVIN, *4QHalakha C*, p. 155.
35. Vgl. ELGVIN, *473. 4QThe Two Ways*, p. 293.
36. Vgl. die Überlegungen bei ELGVIN, *4QText Concerning Rachel and Joseph*, pp. 456f.

earth«[37]. Für einen weisheitlichen Charakter spricht im heute noch erhaltenen Textbestand nichts.

4Q476 und **4Q476a** (ursprünglich als eine Handschrift gezählt) sind für eine inhaltliche Charakterisierung zu stark beschädigt, jedoch sprechen die erhaltenen Textreste eher für eine liturgische[38] als eine weisheitliche Charakterisierung.

4Q486, 4Q487 und **4Q498** sind gegen Baillet (*Qumrân Grotte 4*, pp. 4-10.73f.) für eine inhaltliche Charakterisierung zu stark beschädigt.

4Q528 »4QOuvrage hymnique ou sapientiel B« erinnert zwar insbesondere durch das אשריכם כול יראי יהוה (»selig seid ihr alle, die ihr den HERRN fürchtet«; Zeile 5) an weisheitliche Texte, jedoch erlauben die wenigen erhaltenen Zeilen keine eindeutige Zuschreibung des Textes zur weisheitlichen Literatur.

3. DIE WEISHEITSTEXTE AUS QUMRAN – EINE EINLEITUNG

3.1. 4Q184: Wiles of the Wicked Woman

Von dem Wiles of the Wicked Woman genannten Text existieren noch sechs in einer frühherodianischen Schrift gehaltene Fragmente[39]. Von ihnen bietet nur Frag. 1 einen größeren Textzusammenhang. Die fünf kleineren Fragmente tragen zur Interpretation des Werkes kaum etwas bei. Lediglich das מש[פט וחוק] (»[Ge]setz und Gebot[«) in Frag. 5₅ könnte auf die sich dann auch in 1₁₄f. artikulierende Toraweisheit hinweisen. Den Text von Frag. 1 faßt J. Maier pointiert zusammen:

> »The first fragment is of considerable length (eighteen lines) and bears a strong resemblance to *Proverbs* 7 in that it describes a female who is a dangerous seductress of pious men. There is, however, one fundamental difference. In *Proverbs* 7 it is (as in *Prv*. 5 and 6.20-35) indeed the foreign woman who represents a danger for the upright and wise man with, however, an additional connotation: the attitude in favor of the foreign woman is seen as the antithesis of a life lived in accordance with wisdom. Wiles of the Wicked Woman (4Q184), on the other hand, represents the female figure as much more than a temptation to lead a life contrary to the tenets of wisdom; she has become, rather, the personification of an antagonistic group, and the central controversy has evolved into the author's concern for the correct fulfillment of the entire Torah. The implacable nature of the controversy reflected in this work is characterized

---

37. ELGVIN, *4QRenewed Earth*, p. 467.
38. So ELGVIN, *Liturgical Works*, pp. 437f., 445.
39. Zur paläographischen Einordnung s. ALLEGRO, *Wiles*, p. 55; CARMIGNAC, *Poème allégorique*, p. 361; STRUGNELL, *Notes en marge*, p. 263.

by dualistic traits. It is no longer simply a question of morality but that of the right or wrong observance of God's will in general and in its details reflects a symbolism much nearer to the old biblical concept of idolatry as adultery and fornication than to the moralistic attitude of normal wisdom literature«[40].

Ob die von Maier genannte »antagonistic group« allerdings im Sinne einer allegorischen Deutung mit den in CD I und 4QpNah 3-4 II-III kritisierten Pharisäern[41] identifiziert werden darf, hängt davon ab, wann der »Wiles of the Wicked Woman« genannte Text zu datieren ist und von welchem Verfasser er stammt.

Beides ist in Ermangelung im Text erwähnter Realien nur schwer zu beantworten. Die große Nähe zu Prov 7[42] bei gleichzeitiger Verschärfung des ethischen Dualismus und die Verschmelzung weisheitlicher Ethik mit den Geboten der Tora ($1_{14f.}$) rät von einer Datierung wesentlich vor dem 3. Jh. v.Chr. ab. Der Terminus *ante quem* ergibt sich aus der paläographischen Datierung von 4Q184 in das letzte Drittel des 1. Jh. v.Chr. Hinweise auf eine essenische Herkunft des Textes, wie gemeindespezifisches Vokabular etc., finden sich nicht[43].

4Q184 1 dürfte sich vielmehr mit Hilfe der radikalisierten Topik von Prov 7 mit dem Frevel im allgemeinen beschäftigen[44] und ihm mit Hilfe dämonologischer Sprache und Bilder eine dämonenhafte Qualität zuweisen[45]. Damit dürften sich auch andere allegorische Deutungen – etwa auf den Makkabäer Simon[46] oder Rom[47] – als obsolet erwiesen haben[48].

---

40. MAIER, *Wiles of the Wicked Woman*, p. 976.
41. So AMUSSIN, *Pamphlet*; vgl. CARMIGNAC, *Poème allégorique*, pp. 372-374; GAZOV-GINZBERG, *Double Meaning*, pp. 279-284; ZUR, *Parallels*, p. 106; MAIER, *Wiles of the Wicked Woman*, p. 976.
42. Vgl. dazu u.a. LICHT, *4Q184*; NEBE, *Lexikalische Bemerkungen*, pp. 101-103; BROSHI, *Wiles*, pp. 54f.; WHITE CRAWFORD, *Lady Wisdom*, p. 360.
43. Gegen CARMIGNAC, *Poème allégorique*, pp. 362f.; MOORE, *Personification*, p. 506; BROSHI, *Wiles*, p. 54; 4Q184 »reflects the Essene fear of, as well as contempt for, women«.
44. So schon MOORE, *Personification*, pp. 506-519; vgl. GASTER, *Dead Sea Scriptures*, p. 495.
45. Cf. BAUMGARTEN, *Seductress*, pp. 138-143, und WHITE CRAWFORD, *Lady Wisdom*, pp. 360f. Gegen BAUMGARTEN scheint mir aber eine Beschreibung der Hure von 4Q184 als einer »Lilit-like seductress« im Sinne einer dämonischen Gestalt (*ibid.*, p. 143) über die Aussageintention des Textes hinauszugehen.
46. BURGMANN, *Simon*.
47. ALLEGRO, *Wiles*, p. 53.
48. Zur Kritik an den allegorischen Deutungen vgl. etwa BROSHI, *Wiles*, pp. 54.56; VAN DER WOUDE, *Wisdom*, p. 247; HARRINGTON, *Wisdom Texts from Qumran*, p. 33; COLLINS, *Jewish Wisdom*, pp. 114-116.

3.2. 4Q185: Sapiential Work

Die sechs erhaltenen Fragmente von 4Q185 bezeugen den Rest einer ursprünglich wesentlich umfangreicheren weisheitlichen Mahnrede[49], die in einer späthasmonäischen Buchschrift kopiert wurde[50]. Der freie Gebrauch des Tetragramms in 1-2 II_3[51] und die für essenische Texte untypische Verwendung von אלהים in 1-2 I_{14}; III_{13}[52] zeigen, daß es sich um ein mindestens vor 150 v.Chr. anzusetzendes nichtessenisches Werk handelt[53]. Im Text finden sich nach der Art einer Anthologie eine Vielzahl biblischer Anspielungen[54], was vor einer zu frühen Datierung der Werkes warnt. Daher schlägt Tobin einen Ansatz im späten 3. oder frühen 2. Jh. v.Chr. vor[55]. Daß sich jedoch in dem seinerseits schon in das 3. Jh. v.Chr. zu datierenden Werk 4QAdmonition Based on the Flood (4Q370) in II_{5-9} eine Kurzfassung des Textes von 4Q185 1-2 I_{13}–II_3 findet[56], spricht für eine Datierung von 4QSapiential Work in das 3. Jh. v. Chr.

Erhalten sind drei kurze Mahnreden und zwei Seligpreisungen[57]. Die erste Mahnung warnt vor der Vergänglichkeit des Menschen (I_{9-13}), die zweite mahnt, Weisheit aus Gottes geschichtlichem Handeln zu gewinnen (I_{13}–II_3), und die dritte (II_{3-8}) scheint eine Zwei-Wege-Lehre und das Gericht zum Gegenstand zu haben. Anschließend folgt eine Seligpreisung dessen, dem die mit der Weisheit identifizierte Tora gegeben wurde (II_{8-13})[58]. »Das besondere Spezifikum dieses Textes beruht darauf, daß hier nicht allein Israel angeredet wird, sondern sich deutliche Hinweise finden ..., daß auch die Völker in bezug auf die Weisheit/das Gesetz angesprochen sind«[59]. In der zweiten Seligpreisung wird dann derjenige, der die weisheitliche Tora erfüllt, glücklich gepriesen (II_{13}-III_1).

---

49. Zur Gattung s. LICHTENBERGER, *Mahnrede*, pp. 151f.; TOBIN, *4Q185*, p. 145; zum weisheitlichen Charakter des Textes s. auch STRUGNELL, *Notes en marge*, p. 269. Eine Neuedition der Handschrift wurde von LICHTENBERGER in diesem Band vorgelegt.
50. S. STRUGNELL, *Notes en marge*, p. 269; vgl. HARRINGTON, *Wisdom Texts from Qumran*, p. 36.
51. Zur Diskussion über den freien Gebrauch des Tetragramms vgl. STEGEMANN, *Gottesbezeichnungen* und PUECH, *Psaumes*, pp. 80-88.
52. Zur Vermeidung von אלהים in essenischen Texten s. STEGEMANN, *Gottesbezeichnungen*, p. 196; NEWSOM, *Sectually Explicit Literature*, pp. 182f.
53. Vgl. LICHTENBERGER, *Mahnrede*, pp. 161f.; ID., zu 4Q185 im vorliegenden Band; TOBIN, *4Q185*, p. 148; VAN DER WOUDE, *Wisdom*, p. 248.
54. Vgl. LICHTENBERGER, *Mahnrede*, pp. 153f.; TOBIN, *4Q185*, pp. 146f.
55. TOBIN, *4Q185*, p. 152.
56. Vgl. die Überlegungen von NEWSOM, *4QAdmonition Based on the Flood*, pp. 89f.
57. Zum Aufbau vgl. HARRINGTON, *Wisdom Texts from Qumran*, pp. 37f.
58. Mit LICHTENBERGER, *Mahnrede*, p. 152; vgl. WHITE CRAWFORD, *Lady Wisdom*, p. 363. Zur Diskussion, ob sich das Suffix der 3. Pers. Fem. Sing. auf die Weisheit oder die Tora bezieht, s. STRUGNELL, *Notes en marge*, p. 269; KÜCHLER, *Weisheitstraditionen*, pp. 103.105; TOBIN, *4Q185*, p. 145; FABRY, *Makarismus*, p. 367.
59. LICHTENBERGER, *Mahnrede*, p. 153; vgl. VAN DER WOUDE, *Wisdom*, p. 248.

3.3. 4Q298: Words of the Maskil to All Sons of Dawn

Das einzige erhaltene Manuskript von Words of the Maskil to All Sons of Dawn ist in der Geheimschrift Crypt A geschrieben. Nur die Überschrift ist in Quadratschrift gehalten. Sie erlaubt eine paläo-graphische Datierung von 4Q298 in die zweite Hälfte des 1. Jh. v.Chr[60]. Abschreibfehler in den Zeilen 1$_3$ und 3-4 II$_7$ (אהבו statt אהבי) machen eine Vorlage in Quadratschrift wahrscheinlich[61].

Die wenigen erhaltenen Fragmente geben kaum Aufschluß über den Text. Die Überschrift weist das Werk als einen Lehrtext aus: דבר[י] משכיל אשר דבר לכול בני שחר (»Worte eines Unterweisers, die er zu allen Söhnen der Dämmerung spricht«). Dieser lehrhafte Charakter wird durch die Lehreröffnungsformeln in 1-2 I$_{1-3}$; 3-4 II$_{3f.}$ unterstrichen. Vom Vokabular her könnte es sich um einen essenischen Text zur Belehrung von neuen Mitgliedern der Gemeinschaft handeln[62]. Die בני שחר wären dann mit Pfann als im Aufnahmeverfahren befindliche Mitglieder der essenischen Gemeinschaft zu identifizieren, die, um im Bild zu bleiben, aus der Finsternis des nichtessenischen Judentums in das essenische Licht kommen, und daher »Söhne der Dämmerung« genannt werden[63].

Über den weiteren Inhalt des Werkes kann kaum etwas gesagt werden: Die neuen Mitglieder werden aufgefordert, Gerechtigkeit zu verfolgen, חֶסֶד zu lieben und Erkenntnis über die festgelegten Zeiten zu gewinnen (1-2 I$_{2f.}$; 3-4 II$_{4-9}$). Sie sollen Einsicht in das Ende der Ewigkeiten erlangen und die früheren Zeiten betrachten (3-4 II$_{9f.}$).

3.4. 1Q27, 4Q299-301: Das *Book of Mysteries*

Vom *Book of Mysteries* wurden in Qumran vier Handschriften gefunden (1Q27; 4Q299-4Q301), wovon 1Q27 und 4Q299-4Q300 überlappen[64]. Paläographisch können alle Handschriften herodianischen Schrift-

---

60. PFANN, *4Q298*, pp. 213-216; ID./KISTER, *4Q298*, p. 9.
61. S. PFANN, *4Q298*, p. 211; ID./KISTER, *4Q298*, p. 13.
62. So PFANN, *4Q298*, pp. 224f.; ID./KISTER, *4Q298*, pp. 15f.; vgl. HARRINGTON, *Wisdom Texts from Qumran*, pp. 65f.
63. PFANN, *4Q298*, p. 225; ID./KISTER, *4Q298*, p. 17; vgl. KISTER, *4Q298*, p. 238. Vgl. dazu jedoch den Beitrag von CH. HEMPEL im vorliegenden Band.
64. 4Q301 wird von SCHIFFMAN für die Handschrift eines anderen, der Hechalotliteratur zuzurechnenden Werkes gehalten (*Reclaiming the Dead Sea Scrolls*, p. 206; ID., *4QMysteries^b*, p. 205; ID., *4QMysteries^a*, p. 207; ID., *Mysteries*, pp. 31.113f.). Jedoch fällt auf, daß 4Q301 mit den anderen Myst-Handschriften seltene Redewendungen und Lexeme wie שורשי בינה (4Q301 1$_2$; 2b$_1$) und שורש חוכמה (4Q300 1a II-b$_3$) oder ... תומכין (4Q301 1$_2$) und ... תומכי[ן (4Q299 3a II$_9$; 6 II$_4$; 43$_2$; 4Q300 8$_5$) gemeinsam hat und ihnen stilistisch in der Aneinanderreihung rhetorischer Fragen ähnelt (letzteres beobachtet auch SCHIFFMAN, *Mysteries*, p. 42). Sogar die Vorstellung von der verborgenen Weisheit ist – gegen SCHIFFMAN, *Mysteries*, p. 114 – kein Proprium der Handschrift 4Q301, sondern fin-

formen zugeordnet werden[65]. Das im Text verwandte Vokabular legt eine späte Datierung nahe: Die ältesten hebräischen Belege des persischen Lehnwortes רז sind Sir 8,18; 12,11, während das Nomen מוֹלָד sogar erst in der Mischna vorkommt[66]. Für die Datierung des Werkes ist ferner die Anspielung auf Nebukadnezzars Traum (Dan 2) in 4Q300 1a II-b$_1$ von Bedeutung. Das *Book of Mysteries* wäre somit im 2. oder 1. Jh. v.Chr. anzusetzen. Dieser Zeitraum kann durch inhaltliche Bezüge des Werkes zur Zwei-Geister-Lehre (1QS III$_{13}$-IV$_{26}$) weiter eingeengt werden[67]. Da Dualismus und Eschatologie der Zwei-Geister-Lehre als eine Weiterentwicklung des in Myst geäußerten Gedankengutes[68] verstanden werden können, dürfte das *Book of Mysteries* vor der gegen Mitte des 2. Jh. v.Chr. zu datierenden Zwei-Geister-Lehre[69] entstanden sein.

Eine essenische Herkunft wurde für Myst von Rabinowitz[70], Betz[71], Becker[72], Tov[73] und Larson[74] vorgeschlagen. Dagegen spricht: a) in Myst kommen keine zentralen Themen des *yaḥad*, keine *yaḥad*-typische Sprache und auch keine zentralen Figuren aus der Geschichte des *yaḥad* vor, b) die vielen Belege der in essenischen Texten vermiedenen Wurzel חכ[ם, und c) die sich in dem Satz ונ[כבד אל בעם קודשו] (»[und] Gott [wird] sich durch sein heiliges Volk ehren« 4Q301 3a-b$_6$) artikulierende und für essenische Texte untypische gesamtisraelitische Perspektive.

Neben weisheitlichen Gattungen und Themen zeichnet auch das weisheitliche Vokabular des Werkes Myst als einen Weisheitstext aus:

אויל: 4Q299 6 II$_3$
אולת: 1Q27 1 I$_7$
בין: 1Q27 1 I$_3$; 4Q299 8$_5$; 34$_3$; 43$_3$; 46$_2$
בינה: 4Q299 8$_{6f.}$; 4Q300 1a II-b$_2$; 5$_1$; 8$_6$; 4Q301 1$_2$; 2b$_1$
דעה: 1Q27 1 I$_7$; 4Q299 35$_1$; 73$_3$

---

det sich u.a. auch in 4Q300 1a II-b$_{2-5}$ und 4Q300 5$_5$. Mit dem ersten Bearbeiter der 4QMyst-Handschriften, J.T. MILIK, ist 4Q301 daher als eine weitere Handschrift des *Books of Mysteries* anzusehen (zur Sache s. WACHOLDER/ABEGG, *Preliminary Edition 2*, pp. 35ff.; LARSON, *Mysteries*, p. 587).

65. Zur Sache s. SCHIFFMAN, *4QMysteries^b*, p. 205; ID., *4QMysteries^a*, p. 209; ID., *Mysteries*, pp. 33.99.114.

66. Vgl. BARTHÉLEMY/MILIK, *Qumran Cave 1*, p. 104; SCHIFFMAN, *4QMysteries^b*, p. 214, und JASTROW, *Dictionary*, p. 742.

67. Zur Verwandtschaft der Zwei-Geister-Lehre mit Myst s. BECKER, *Heil Gottes*, p. 94, und LANGE, *Weisheit und Prädestination*, pp. 128-130.

68. Zum Dualismus in Myst s. FREY, *Dualistic Thought*, p. 299.

69. Zur Datierung der Zwei-Geister-Lehre s. LANGE, *Weisheit und Prädestination*, p. 130.

70. *Authorship, Audience, and Date*, p. 32; *Sequence and Dates*, p. 185.

71. *Offenbarung*, p. 57.

72. *Heil Gottes*, p. 94.

73. *Letters*, p. 331; *Scribal Markings*, pp. 57f.

74. *Mysteries*, p. 588.

דעת: 4Q299 8$_7$
חכם (Adj.): 4Q299 3a II-b$_4$; 4Q301 2a$_1$
חכמה: 4Q299 3a II-b$_5$; 17 I$_2$; 42$_4$; 4Q300 1a II-b$_{3f.}$; 3$_3$; 5$_5$
כסיל: 4Q301 2a$_1$
כסל (Nomen): 4Q300 1a II-b$_2$
מוסר: 4Q299 30$_4$
ערמה: 4Q299 3a II-b$_5$
פתי (Nomen): 4Q300 8$_4$; 4Q301 1$_3$
שׂכל (Verb): 4Q300 1a II-b$_2$
שׂכל (Nomen): 4Q299 8$_{2.6.8}$; 4Q301 1$_8$

Trotz umfangreicher Textbeschädigungen können im Text noch weisheitliche Gattungen identifiziert werden: So sind mehrere weisheitliche Lehrreden belegt (1Q27 1 I; 4Q299 3a II-b$_9$; 4Q299 6 II; 4Q300 1a II-b; 4Q301 1 und 4Q301 2b)[75], und in 4Q299 6 I ist ein hymnisches Lehrgedicht auf Gott als den Schöpfer des geordneten Kosmos erhalten. Weisheitliche Themen dürften von Myst u.a. in 1Q27 1 II$_{3ff.}$ (Tun-Ergehen-Zusammenhang), 4Q299 8 (epistemologische Erörterung), 4Q299 3a II-b$_{10f.}$; 6 I und 4Q300 1a II-b$_2$ (weisheitliche Urordnung) behandelt werden.

Neben weisheitlichen Lexemen, Gattungen und Inhalten finden sich in Myst auch priesterliche Sprache, Motivik und Themen:

- 1Q27 3$_2$ erwähnt Priester (לו לכוהנׄיׄםׄ; »für ihn, für Priester«).
- 1Q27 6$_{2f.}$ bezeugt zweimal die Wurzel כפר.
- 1Q27 6$_2$ thematisiert in Anspielung auf Lev 5,18 das Ritual zur Sühne versehentlich begangener Sünden.
- Auf Priesterliches könnte auch die Terminologie von 4Q299 3a II-b$_3$ par 4Q300 5$_4$ (וכול מעשה צׄדׄיׄק הטמ[אה; »alles Tun eines Gerechten wird verunrei[nigt«) und 4Q299 70$_3$ (לחול; »für Unheiliges«)[76] hinweisen.
- 4Q299 55$_5$ spricht im Zusammenhang mit dem Dienst im Tempel von der Sühne (...]°° עבו[דת קודשו ולכפרׄ עׄל; »Dien]st seines Heiligtums und um zu entsühnen °° [...«).
- Desweiteren dürften die in 4Q299 69$_2$ erwähnten Urim und Thummim im Zusammenspiel mit dem א]חת בשנה (»ein]mal im Jahr«; 4Q299 69$_1$) auf den Rest einer Schilderung der Yom Kippur-Feier oder eines vergleichbaren Ritus hinweisen[77].
- 4Q299 79$_{6f.}$ erwähnt schließlich »Aaron and the offering of sacrifices«[78].

75. Die für weisheitliche Lehrreden typischen Einleitungsformeln könnten sich noch in folgenden Textresten finden: שמעו תומכי רוׄזיׄ (»hört, die ihr ergreift die Ge[heimnisse der«; 4Q299 3a II-b$_9$);]וׄעתה[(»und nun«; 4Q299 44$_3$);]ׄיכם אשמיׄעׄ[(»]eure, ich will hören lassen«; 4Q299 53$_{11}$); [ועתה פׄ [(»und nun«; 4Q299 80$_2$); אב[יעה רוחי ולמיניכם ... אחלקה דברי אליכםׄ ... (»i]ch will sprudeln lassen meinen Geist, und nach euren Arten meine Worte euch zuteilen[...«; 4Q301 1$_1$).
76. Zu חל im Gegensatz zu קֹדֶשׁ vgl. auch Lev 10,10; 1 Sam 21,5.6; Ez 22,26; 42,20; 44,23; CD VI$_{17f.}$; XII$_{20}$.
77. So SCHIFFMAN, *4QMysteries^a*, p. 251; ID., *Mysteries*, p. 82.
78. ID., *4QMysteries^a*, p. 255; SCHIFFMAN (*ibid.*, pp. 251, 255; *Mysteries*, pp. 82.88)

Ferner bezeugt Myst ein starkes Interesse an Tora und Eschatologie: Zwar findet sich in den erhaltenen Resten des Werkes keine ausgeführte Identifikation von Weisheit und Tora, jedoch nimmt Myst besonders im Kontext priesterlicher Fragen Toravorschriften auf. So ist das $š^eg\bar{a}g\hat{a}$-Opfer (Lev 4-5; Num 15,22-31; vgl. Koh 5,5) in 1Q27 6$_2$ Gegenstand der weisheitlichen Reflexion – wobei der erhaltene Textbestand eine Anspielung auf Lev 5,18 wahrscheinlich macht. Die Erwähnung der Urim und Thummim in 4Q299 69 (s.o.) läßt an Lev 16 denken, und daß in 4Q299 70 חוק und חול kurz aufeinander folgen, könnte auf eine »halachische« Erörterung deuten[79].

Die Eschatologie ist in Myst zumindest an einer Stelle von zentraler Bedeutung, 1Q27 1 I$_{5-7}$ par 4Q300 3$_{4-6}$ schildert die eschatologische Offenbarung der Weisheit und die eschatologische Vernichtung des Frevels[80]:

כי יהיה
5 וזה לכם האות בהסגר מולדי עולה וגלה הרֹשע מפני הצדק כגלוֹת [חושׁ]ך מפני
6 אור וכתום עשׁן ואֹ[י]ננו] עוד כן יתם הרשׁע לעֹד והצדק יגלה כשׁמֹשׁ תכון
7 תבל וכול תומכי רזי פלאֹ אינמה עוד ודעה תמלא תבל ואֹין שׁם לעֹ[ד] אולת

»(5) Und dies soll ihnen das Zeichen sein, daß es so sein wird: Wenn die Kinder des Frevels ausgeliefert werden werden, dann wird der Frevel entschwinden vor der Gerechtigkeit, wie die Finsternis entschwindet vor (6) dem Licht. Und wie Rauch verfliegt und n[icht] mehr ist, so wird der Frevler für immer vergehen[81]. Und die Gerechtigkeit wird offenbart werden, wie die Sonne aufgeht über (7) der Erde. Und alle, die die wunderbaren Geheimnisse festhalten, werden nicht mehr sein. Und Erkenntnis wird die Welt erfüllen, und Torheit wird es dort nimmermehr geben«.

Nach einer Prophezeiung über die endzeitliche Vernichtung der Frevler beschreiben die Zeilen, woran das Eintreffen dieser Prophezeiung zu erkennen ist: »Wenn die Kinder des Frevels ausgeliefert werden werden, dann wird der Frevel entschwinden vor der Gerechtigkeit, wie die Finsternis entschwindet vor dem Licht« (Zeile 5f.). Erst nach dem eschatologischen Untergang des Frevels wird die präexistente weisheitliche Ordnung des Seins verwirklicht werden: »Und wie Rauch verfliegt und n[icht] mehr ist, so wird der Frevler für immer vergehen. Und die

---

bestreitet auf Grund der priesterlichen Thematik von 4Q299 69; 79 die Zugehörigkeit dieser Frag. zu 4Q299. Da priesterliches Gedankengut und Vokabular aber auch an anderen Stellen des Werkes belegt sind, überzeugt das Argument nicht.

79. Ob die weiteren Belege von חוק im Book of Mysteries (4Q299 20$_1$; 61$_2$) auf die Gebote des Sinaigesetzes bezogen werden können, kann wegen starker Textbeschädigungen nicht mehr sicher gesagt werden.

80. Zu Transkription und Übersetzung s. LANGE, *Weisheit und Prädestination*, pp. 96-98.

81. Wörtlich »aufhören«.

Gerechtigkeit wird offenbart werden, wie die Sonne aufgeht über der Erde. Und alle, die die wunderbaren Geheimnisse festhalten, werden nicht mehr sein. Und Erkenntnis wird die Welt erfüllen, und Torheit wird es dort nimmermehr geben« (Zeile 6f.).

Darüber hinaus wird die eschatologische Zerstörung des Frevels und die endzeitliche Inthronisierung Israels in 4Q301 3a-b$_{6ff.}$ thematisiert[82]:

6 [...] ה֯ ונ֯כ֯ב֯[ד הו]א֯ בא֯[ו]ר֯ך אפיו֯[וגדו]ל֯ הוא[ה] ברוב חמתו֯ ונ֯[ה]דר [...]
7 [...]הואה בהמון רחמיו ונורא הואה במזמת אפו נכב֯ד֯ הוא֯[ה...]
8 [...] ב֯ו ובאשר בק֯ץ המשילו ו[י]נ֯כבד אל בעם קודשו ונהדר ה֯[ואה ...]
9 [...] ב֯חירין ונה֯ד֯ר֯[ן] הואה ...קו[ד]שו גדול הואה בברכות[יו...]
10 [...ה]דרם ות[...] ב֯כלונ֯ת [ק֯ץ רשעה ועשות[...]

6 [...]*h* und er wird geehrt um seiner Langmut willen, [und] er ist [groß] in der Fülle [seines] Zorns, [und] er [wird verherrlicht...]
7 [...]ist er wegen des Reichtums[83] seines Erbarmens, aber er wird gefürchtet wegen des Plans seines Zorns. Er wird geehrt [...]
8 [...]*bw* und weil er es am Ende zur Herrschaft einsetzen wird, [und] Gott wird sich durch sein heiliges Volk ehren, und er wird verherrlicht [...]
9 [...]Erwählte und [er] wird verherrlicht[...] sein [Hei]liges. Er ist groß wegen [seiner] Segnungen[...]
10 [...]ihre [Pr]acht *wt*[...]wenn er beendet die Zeit des Frevels und macht[...]

Eschatologisch könnten ferner auch die Zeilen 4Q299 59$_{1-5}$ zu interpretieren sein. Dort werden im Kontext der Wendung במשפט יריב א[ת (»im Gericht wird er streiten m[it«; Zeile 2) Personen erwähnt, die »in allem se[in] Gebot übertreten (בכול עוברי פיה֯ו; Zeile 3) und dem Frevel beistehen« (עוזרי רשעה; Zeile 4)[84].

Myst dürfte somit in einem weisheitlichen Milieu entstanden sein, dessen kultisches Interesse auf eine Nähe zum Tempel deutet[85]. Der Text ist neben priesterlichen Elementen von einer eschatologisch geprägten Toraweisheit bestimmt.

---

82. Zur Sache s. LANGE, *Physiognomie oder Gotteslob*, pp. 287-294.
83. Zur Übersetzung cf. CLINES, *Dictionary* 2, p. 569.
84. Gegen SCHIFFMAN, *4QMysteries^a*, p. 247: »Again we encounter the motif of God's doing justice against those who violate his commandments.«
85. Die ohne nähere Begründung von BARTHÉLEMY/MILIK, *Qumran Cave 1*, p. 103; DUPONT-SOMMER, *Schriften*, pp. 353. 355; BECKER, *Heil Gottes*, p. 94; RUSSELL, *Method and Message*, p. 47, und HENGEL, *Judentum und Hellenismus*, p. 400, vorgenommene Zuordnung von Myst zur Apokalyptik darf nach Bekanntwerden aller Myst-Handschriften aus den oben genannten Gründen als gescheitert gelten (zur Sache vgl. CARMIGNAC, *Apocalyptique*, pp. 26f. und STEGEMANN, *Bedeutung*, p. 513).

3.5. 1Q26; 4Q415-418.418a.418c.423: *mûsār lᵉmēbîn* (4QInstruction; Sap Work A)⁸⁶

Vom *mûsar lᵉmēbîn* wurden in Qumran sieben oder acht Handschriften gefunden: 1QInstruction, 4QInstruction$^{a-e.f?.g}$ (1Q26, 4Q415-418.418a. 418c, 4Q423)⁸⁷. Abgesehen von einigen größeren Fragmenten in 4Q416; 4Q417 und 4Q418 sind alle Handschriften stark beschädigt. »All the manuscripts are written in the Herodian formal hand of the late first century BCE or early first century CE«⁸⁸. Nach mündlicher Auskunft von A. Steudel bewahren nach einer von ihr gemeinsam mit B. Lucassen erstellten materialen Rekonstruktion die Fragmente 4Q416 1 und 4Q417 1 den Beginn ihrer jeweiligen Handschriften. Da 4Q416 1 ein eschatologisches Geschehen schildert (s.u., pp. 20f.), während 4Q417 1 I eine weisheitlichen Lehrrede über die Erkenntnisfähigkeit des מבין bietet, ist davon auszugehen, daß der MLM eine Redaktion erfahren hat. Welchen Umfang diese Redaktion hatte, kann erst nach der Veröffentlichung der materialen Rekonstruktion von Lucassen/Steudel beantwortet werden⁸⁹. Inhaltliche Ähnlichkeiten zwischen 4Q416 1 und 4Q418 69 II auf der einen und 1Q27 1 I auf der anderen Seite erlauben jedoch Spekulationen, ob die in 4Q416 bezeugte Version des MLM etwa zur Abfassungszeit des aus dem gleichen Milieu wie der MLM stammenden Book of Mysteries (zur Sache s.u., p. 25) erstellt worden sein könnte. Bei der von 4Q416 bezeugten Version des MLM würde es sich dann um die jüngere Fassung des Werkes handeln.

In beiden Versionen sind sowohl weisheitliche Formen als auch weisheitliches Vokabular bezeugt: So finden sich in 4Q417 1 I$_{1-18}$ par 4Q418 43.44.45 I; 4Q417 1 I$_{18}$-II$_5$; 4Q418 69 II par 4Q417 5; 4Q418 81 + 81a; 4Q418 103 II und 4Q418 126 II weisheitliche Lehrreden ver-

---

86. Bis vor kurzem trug der Text den vorläufigen Namen Sapiential Work A (cf. TOV/ PFANN, *Companion Volume*, p. 43; REED/LUNDBERG, *Catalogue*, pp. 110-112). Die Herausgeber, D.J. HARRINGTON und J. STRUGNELL, schlagen in ihrer Edition den Namen *mûsar lamēbîn* vor (*Qumran Cave 4. XXIV*, p. 3), wovon sich der englische Kurztitel Instruction herleitet.
87. S. HARRINGTON, *Wisdom Texts from Qumran*, p. 40; STRUGNELL/HARRINGTON/ ELGVIN, *Qumran Cave 4. XXIV*, pp. 1f. HARRINGTON beschreibt in einer früheren Publikation auch 4Q419 als eine MLM-Handschrift (*Wisdom at Qumran*, pp. 139f.); ähnlich ELGVIN, *Admonition Texts*, p. 180; *Reconstruction*, pp. 570-572. Zur unsicheren Identifikation von 4QInstruction^{f}? s. STRUGNELL/HARRINGTON/ELGVIN, *Qumran Cave 4. XXIV*, p. 501.
88. HARRINGTON, *Wisdom Texts from Qumran*, p. 40; vgl. STRUGNELL/HARRINGTON/ ELGVIN, *Qumran Cave 4. XXIV*, pp. 42.76.146f.217.476.501.506f.; ID., *Appendix*, p. 535.
89. Ob sie, wie ELGVIN annimmt (*Wisdom and Apocalypticism*, pp. 226.246), alle eschatologischen und revelatorischen Passagen des Werkes umfaßte, scheint mir jedoch fraglich.

schiedenen Inhalts mit teils stark ausgeprägtem paränetischen Charakter. Lange Paränesen, die größere zusammenhängende Passagen mit Einzelsprüchen kombinieren und bisweilen traktatartige Züge annehmen können, sind in 4Q416 2 I-IV parr 4Q417 2 I-II, 4Q418 7-10 und 4Q418 88 erhalten. Traktate könnten in 4Q418 55 und 4Q418 77 bezeugt sein. Ein großer Teil des MLM kann wegen starker Textzerstörungen keiner Gattung mehr zugeordnet werden.

Den häufigen Gebrauch weisheitlichen Vokabulars in beiden Versionen des MLM mag die folgende Liste illustrieren:

אויל: 4Q417 5_5; 4Q418 58_1; 69 $II_{4.8}$; 4Q418 205_2

אולת: 4Q415 9_6; 4Q416 2 II_3; 4Q417 1 I_7; 4Q418 220_3; 243_2; 4Q423 5_7

בין: 4Q415 $11_{4f.12}$; 4Q416 2 III_{14}; 4_3; 4Q417 1 $I_{1.12.14.18.20.25}$; 2 $II_{10.14}$; 3_3; 4Q418 $2,2a$-$c_{7f.}$; 17_2; 43-45 I_{15}; 46_1; 68_5; 77_3; $81+81a_{15.17}$; $102a+b_3$; 117_2; 122 I_5; 123 $II_{4f.}$; $147_{5f.}$; 158_4; 168_4; 176_3; 189_2; 205_2; $221_{2f.5}$; 227_1; 238_3; 273_1; 4Q418a $7_{2f.}$; 8_2; 10_4; 4Q423 5_6; 7_7

בינה: 4Q416 1_{16}; 2 III_{13}; 4Q417 27_2; 4Q418 $9,9a$-c_{14}; $55_{5f.9}$; 58_2; 69 II_{11}; 73_1; 148 $III_{3.6}$; 163_2; 165_3; 177_4; 193_1; 240_2; 302_3

דעה: 4Q417 1 I_8; 43-45 I_6; 55_5; 4Q418 69 $II_{4.11f.}$

דעת: 4Q416 2 III_{13}; 4Q418 $9,a$-c_{13}; 55_{10}; 69 II_{11}; $81+81a_{15}$; 95_3; 117_1; 148 $II_{5.7}$

חכם (Adj.): 4Q418 $81+81a_{20}$

חכמה: 4Q416 2 II_{12}; 4Q417 1 $I_{6.9}$; 4Q418 8_{13}; $81+81a_{15.19}$; $102a+b_3$; 126 II_5; 137_2; 139_2

מוסר: 4Q416 2 III_{13}; 4Q418 $9,9a$-c_{13}; $169+170_3$; 297_1

משכיל: 4Q416 2 II_{15}; 4Q417 1 I_{25}; 4Q418 8_{15}; 81_{17}; 238_1; 4Q418a 19_2

סכל: 4Q417 20_2

שכל (Verb): 4Q418 43-45 I_1; 69 II_2; 81_{20}; 165_3; 174_3; 197_2; 4Q418a 2_1; 4Q418c 1_7; 4Q423 1-2 $I_{1f.}$; 5_8

שכל (Nomen): 4Q417 20_6; 4Q418 55_{10}; $81+81a_9$; 149_6; 158_6; 4Q423 5_{6-8}

Insbesondere der angemessene Lebenswandel ist ein zentrales Anliegen des MLM (s. z.B. 4Q416 2 I-IV parr 4Q417 2 I-II und 4Q418 7-10; 4Q418 126 II und 127). In die Ermahnungen zu einem solchen Lebenswandel werden mehrfach – für die ältere Weisheit völlig untypisch – Zitate aus und Anspielungen auf den Pentateuch eingeflochten (s. dazu den Beitrag von G.J. Brooke in diesem Band). An Prov 3,19 und Ps 104,24 erinnert der Satz ... וגם לוא נהיו בלוא רצונו ומחו̇ש[בתו (»und sie sind auch nicht entstanden ohne seinen Willen und aus [seiner] Weish[eit...«; 4Q418 126 II_5)[90].

Dieser Umgang des MLM mit autoritativen Schriften läßt ein besonderes Verhältnis des Werkes zur Tora erwarten. So kann es nicht verwundern, daß die weisheitliche Urordnung in 4Q417 1 I (par 4Q418 43-

---

90. Rekonstruktion nach MAIER, *Texte 2*, p. 467; vgl. jetzt auch STRUGNELL/HARRINGTON/ELGVIN, *Qumran Cave 4. XXIV*, 350.

45 I) mit dem Sinaigesetz und einem »Vision der Erklärung« (חזון ההגוֹּה 4Q417 1 I$_{16}$; cf. 1 I$_{17}$) genannten halachischen Werk identifiziert wird. In dem Abschnitt wird begründet, warum ein als מבין bezeichneter weisheitlicher Lehrer[91] Gottes Herrlichkeit, seine machtvollen Taten, seine wunderbaren Geheimnisse und die eigene Bedeutungslosigkeit erkennen kann: Es wird ausgeführt, daß Gott die Welt mit Hilfe dualer Unterscheidungen geordnet und geschaffen hat. Dies wird am Beispiel von Mann und Frau verdeutlicht. Für den Weisen ist Erkenntnis anhand dieser, hier als רז נהיה oder מחשבה bezeichneten dualen Ordnung möglich (4Q417 1 I$_{8-12}$)[92]. In einer zweiten Begründung für die Erkenntnisfähigkeit des מבין legt der MLM dar, daß dem Weisen diese Ordnung auf Grund von zwei Offenbarungen zugänglich ist. Die erste Offenbarung wird in Anspielung auf Ex 32,16 geschildert: »[denn] eingehauen hat er das Ge[b]ot [geb]racht und einschlagen lassen hat er alle Heimsuchung« (]כי ה[בא ח]ו[ר]וֹת החוקים֯ החקיק כול הפקודה֯; 1 I$_{14}$)[93]. Damit ist gesagt: die duale weisheitliche Ordnung der Welt ist dem Weisen in der mosaischen Tora zugänglich.

Auch der zweite Offenbarungsvorgang erfährt mit der »Vision der Erklärung« eine schriftliche Fixierung (4Q417 1 I$_{15-18}$)[94]: Es handelt sich um eine Enosch gegebene Offenbarung. Diese wird als חזון ההגה (»Vision der Erklärung«) bezeichnet und mit dem ספר זכרון (»Buch der Erinnerung«) aus Mal 3,15f. identifiziert (4Q417 1 I$_{15f.}$). In den essenischen Texten von Qumran wird dieser חזון ההגה als ספר ההגו (»Buch der Erklärung«; 1QSa I$_{6f.}$; CD X$_6$; XIII$_{2f.}$; XIV$_{6-8}$) bezeichnet. Daß CD XIV$_8$ das »Buch der Erklärung« mit der Tora parallelisiert, belegt seinen halachischen Charakter und seine autoritative Geltung. Die halachische Natur der »Vision der Erklärung« wird für den MLM durch die Wendung לשמרי דברו (»für jene, die auf sein Wort achten«) bestätigt. Eine Stichwortverknüpfung mit dem kurz vorher erwähnten Sinaigesetz wird durch das חרות in Zeile 15 hergestellt. Laut dem MLM wurde es von Gott eingemeißelt (מחוקק לאל; Zeile 15) bzw. vor ihm geschrieben (כתוב לפניו; ibid.) und erscheint daher als ein himmlisches Buch. חרות und מחוקק zeigen, daß es sich um die himmlischen Tafeln handelt. Neben dem mosaischen Gesetz ist die weisheitliche Ordnung des Seins dem Weisen damit in einer weiteren halachischen Schrift zugänglich, dem Buch Hago. Es dürfte für sich selbst beansprucht haben,

---

91. Zu מבין als Bezeichnung eines Weisheitslehrers s. LANGE, *Weisheit und Prädestination*, pp. 55-57.
92. Zum Begriff רז נהיה s. HARRINGTON, *Raz Nihyeh*.
93. Daß hier auf Ex 32,16 und keinen anderen Vers der Sinaiperikope angespielt wird, zeigt das im AT nur dort bezeugte חרות.
94. Zum Text s. LANGE, *Weisheit und Prädestination*, pp. 50ff.

in der Urzeit Enosch als Offenbarung zumindest eines Teils der himmlischen Tafeln gegeben worden zu sein.

Der schon aus der älteren Weisheit vertraute ethische Dualismus wird zumindest in der jüngeren Version des MLM dualistisch und eschatologisch weiterentwickelt[95]: Besonders deutlich ist dies in 4Q416 1 und 4Q418 69 II greifbar[96]: Die Zeilen 4Q416 1₁₋₉ sind zwar stark beschädigt, die erhaltenen Textreste lassen aber noch Vermutungen über ihren Inhalt zu: Die Wendung מועד במועד (Zeile 3) könnte auf einen kultischen Hintergrund hinweisen – dann wäre »Festzeit um Festzeit« zu übersetzen – oder aber die Abfolge der Jahreszeiten bezeichnen – dann wäre mit Strugnell/Harrington/Elgvin »season by season« (*Qumran Cave 4. XXIV*, p. 82) zu übersetzen. Das וצבא השמים הכין (»und das Heer des Himmels hat er aufgestellt«; Zeile 7) deutet dagegen auf ein himmlisches Geschehen. וכל פקודתהמה (Zeile 9) könnte eschatologisch zu verstehen sein und dann mit »ihre ganze Heimsuchung« wiederzugeben sein, jedoch sind auch die Übersetzungen von Maier (»all ihr Auftrag«, *Texte 2*, p. 430) und García Martínez (»all his commands«, *Dead Sea Scrolls Translated*, p. 383) keinesfalls auszuschließen[97]. Eindeutig eschatologischen Charakter haben erst die Zeilen 10-14. Sie schildern ein endzeitliches Gericht mit kosmischen Dimensionen:

10 בש̇מים ישפוט על עבודת רשעה וכל בני אמת ירצו ע̇[...]
11 קצה ויפחדו ויריעו כל אשר התגללו בה כי שמים יראה̇[ן...]
12 מים ותהמות פחדו ויתערערו כל רוח בשר ובני השמי̇[ם...]
13 [מש]פטה וכל עולה תתם עוד ושלם קץ האמ[ת...]
14 בכל קצי עד כי אל אמת הוא ומקדם שנ̇י[...]

»(10) Im Himmel wird er über den Freveldienst richten, aber alle Söhne der Wahrheit werden wohlgefällig angenommen werden ˙[...] (11) sein (scil. des Frevels?) Ende. Und es werden sich fürchten und schreien alle, die sich in ihm (scil. dem Frevel?) wälzen, denn sie sind solche, die Furcht setzen[...] (12) Wasser und Fluten beben, und aller Geist des Fleisches wird zerstört werden[98], und Söhne des Himme[ls ...] (13) sein (scil. des

---

95. Zum Dualismus im MLM s. Frey, *Dualistic Thought*, pp. 298f.
96. Elgvins Auslegungen von 4Q416 1 und 4Q418 69 II im Kontext des essenischen Dualismus (*Wisdom, Revelation, and Eschatology*, pp. 456-459; *Early Essene Eschatology*, pp. 146-164) basieren im wesentlichen auf seiner materialen Rekonstruktion der Handschriften 4Q416 und 4Q418 (*Reconstruction*, pp. 563-568.570-574). Diese erscheint jedoch nach den Ergebnissen von A. Steudel und B. Lucassen problematisch. Bis zur Veröffentlichung ihrer Arbeit gilt es daher, sich bei der Interpretation von 4Q416 1 und 4Q418 69 ausschließlich auf den Text dieser Fragmente selbst zu beschränken.
97. Zu einer Rekonstruktion von 4Q416 1₁₋₉ s. jetzt auch den Beitrag von E.J.C. Tigchelaar im vorliegenden Band.
98. ויתערערו ist als Hitpalpel von ערר zu verstehen (cf. Jer 51,58). Alternativ könnte es ein Nitpalpel von ערר II sein (»entblößt werden«; so García Martínez, *Dead Sea*

Frevels?) [Ur]teil/[Ger]icht. Und aller Frevel wird dauerhaft enden und die Epoche der Wahrh[eit] wird er vollständig machen[...] (14) in allen Epochen der Ewigkeit. Denn er ist der Gott der Wahrheit und von Urzeit her šny[...]

Die Ausführungen von Zeile 10, daß Gott im Himmel über den Freveldienst richten wird, während er alle Söhne der Wahrheit wohlgefällig aufnimmt (וכל בני אמת ירצו), zeigen, daß die Eschatologie des MLM zumindest in der Version von 4Q416 von einem ethischen Dualismus geprägt ist. Dies wird durch die Hoffnung, aller Frevel werde dauerhaft enden und Gott werde die Epoche der Wahrheit vollständig machen (Zeile 13), erhärtet. Eine kosmische Dimension erhält diese an einem ethischen Dualismus orientierte Eschatologie durch das Motiv vom Beben der Wasser und Fluten (Zeile 12). Mit dem *kî*-Satz in Zeile 14 beginnt eine hymnische Begründung dieses eschatologischen Gerichts, deren Ende nicht mehr erhalten ist. Die Wendung [ע]לרׄ טוב בין צדק להכין (»um Gerechtigkeit festzusetzen zwischen Gut und Bö[se]«; Zeile 15) könnte im Zusammenspiel mit dem מקדם (»von Urzeiten her«) aus Zeile 14 auf Gottes Festsetzen der Ordnung der Welt vor und während der Schöpfung deuten. הואה בשר וׄי[צר] (»ein [Ge]bilde von Fleisch ist er«; Zeile 16) erinnert an die Niedrigkeitsdoxologien der Hodayot. Die Begründung für das eschatologische Gericht könnte also auf die Gerechtigkeit und Wahrhaftigkeit Gottes, sein Festsetzen einer gerechten Seinsordnung und die menschliche Niedrigkeit und Nichtigkeit abheben. Falls im vorhergehenden Kontext himmlische Ordnung und Kult thematisiert sein sollten, erscheint es möglich, daß der begründende Hymnus hierauf zurückgreift und das Gerichtsszenario inkludiert. Auf diese Weise würde dann die Vollkommenheit und Gerechtigkeit der himmlischen Ordnung mit der menschlichen Nichtigkeit kontrastiert.

In 4Q418 69 II finden sich, jeweils auf ein *vacat* folgend, drei Anreden: ועתה אוילי לב (»und nun, ihr Toren des Herzens«; Zeile 4), ואתם בחירי אמת ורודפי (»und ihr Erwählten der Wahrheit und Verfolger von[«; Zeile 10), ואתה בן [מבין] (»und du Sohn eines [Lehrers«; Zeile 15). Sowohl *vacat* als auch Anrede machen deutlich, daß es sich bei 4Q418 69 II$_{4-9.10-15.15ff.}$ um drei eigenständige Abschnitte handelt. Da jede Anrede mit ו eingeleitet wird, dürfte im nicht mehr erhaltenen Text zumindest noch eine weitere Gruppe angesprochen worden sein. Das verknüpfende ו weist die Zeilen 4Q418 69 II$_{?-4}$; 4Q418 69 II$_{4-9}$; 4Q418 69 II$_{10-15}$ und 4Q418 69 II$_{15ff.}$ ferner als Unterabschnitte einer längeren Paränese aus, die verschiedene Adressaten anspricht. Für die Frage nach

Scrolls Translated, p. 383 [zum Bedeutungsspektrum von ערער II im Nitpalpel s. M. JASTROW, *Dictionary*, pp. 1121f.]).

der Bedeutung der Eschatologie im MLM ist die Ermahnung jener, die törichten Herzens sind, von Interesse (4Q418 69 II$_{4-9}$):

4 [...]הֿם ובדעה כול גליהם vacat ועתה אוילי לב מה טוב ללוא
5 [...]מה השקט ללוא היה ומה משפט ללוא נוסד ומה יאנחו מתים על מֿ[...]ם
6 וֿתֿמֿ[...]ל נוצרתם ולשחת עולם תשובתם כי תקֿ°°[...] וֿאֿכֿם[...]
7 מחשכיֿםֿ יצרחו על רובכם וכול נהיה עולם דורשי אמת יעורו למשפטֿ°[...]
8 ישמדו כול אוילי לב ובני עולה לוא ימצאו עוֿדֿ] וכֿ[וֿ]ל מחזיקי רשעה יֿבשֿוּ [...
9 במשפטכם ירוֿעו מוסדי הֿרקיע וירעמו כול צֿ[...]לֿ[...]לֿ אהבֿיֿ[...]

»(4) [...]hm und mit Erkenntnis all ihre Wogen. vacat Und nun, ihr Toren des Herzens, was ist gut ohne (5) [... was] ist Ruhe ohne Werden und was Recht, ohne daß es gegründet wird, und was stöhnen Tote über m[...]m (6) und vollendet[...]l ihr wurdet geformt und zu ewigem Verderben ist eure Rückkehr, denn tq°°[...] (7) dunkle Plätze schreien über eurer Menge und alles wird in Ewigkeit sein. Die nach Wahrheit suchen werden erwachen zum Gericht°[...] (8) und sie werden alle Toren des Herzens ausrotten, und Söhne des Frevels wird man nicht mehr finden, [und al]le die Frevel ergriffen haben werden zuschand[en ...]. Während eures Gerichts werden die Fundamente des Firmaments aufschreien und donnern alle z[...]l[...]l die lieben[...]«

Das eschatologische Gericht dient in diesem Abschnitt als Begründung der Ermahnung jener, die törichten Herzens sind. Die Eschatologie des MLM ist hier von einem ethisch-kosmischen Dualismus geprägt. Die ethische Komponente tritt in den Ermahnungen an die Toren des Herzens zutage, daß ihre Rückkehr zu ewigem Verderben sein werde (Zeile 6), daß jene, die nach Wahrheit suchen, zu ihrem Gericht erwachen würden (Zeile 7), daß alle Toren des Herzens ausgerottet würden, daß man alle Söhne des Frevels nicht mehr finden werde und daß alle, die Frevel ergriffen haben, zu Schande würden (Zeile 8). Die kosmische Komponente wird in den Vorhersagen, dunkle Plätze würden über ihrer Menge schreien (Zeile 7) und während ihres Gerichts würden die Fundamente des Firmaments aufschreien (Zeile 9), deutlich.

Eine letzte besonders auffällige Eigenart des MLM ist mit Harrington das Armenvokabular des Werkes:

»One of the most striking features of the document is its extensive vocabulary with regard to poverty: the nouns *maḥsor* and *rîš / rê(')š*, and the adjectives *rîš* and *'ebyôn*. Yet poverty is presented not so much as an ideal or a more perfect state as it is a symbol of human limitation and mortality. Though this vocabulary appears in other wisdom texts, it is particularly prominent in this work. Another prominent term is *raz nihyāh* (or *nihyeh*). We have been translating it as 'the mysteries of what is to be (or, come)' since in some contexts it appears to refer to the eschatological plan of God«[99].

99. *Wisdom at Qumran*, p. 145.

Daß 1QH^a XVIII$_{29f.}$ (Ed. Sukenik X$_{27f.}$) den in 4Q418 55$_{10}$ erhaltenen Text zitiert[100], und daß 1QH^a X$_{28f.}$ (Ed. Stegemann [Ed. Sukenik I$_{26f.}$]) auf den in 4Q417 1 I$_8$ bezeugten Text anspielt[101], schließt eine Datierung des MLM wesentlich nach der Mitte des 2. Jh. v.Chr. aus. Späte Vokabeln und Konstruktionen wie das persische Lehnwort רז (älteste Belege im Hebräischen sind Sir 8,18; 12,11), das aramäische Lehnwort כשר (die ältesten Belege der Wurzel im Hebräischen sind Est 8,5; Koh 2,21; 5,10; 11,6; Sir 13,4), das Part. Hi. der Wurzel בין (die ältesten Belege im Hebräischen sind 1 Chr 15,22; 2 Chr 34,12; Dan 8,23; Sir 10,1; 38,4; 42,21; 4Q381 45$_1$)[102] und im temporalen Sinn gebrauchtes עם mit Infinitiv (עם התהללו 4Q417 1 I$_{12}$; die ältesten Belege im Hebräischen sind Esr 1,11; Sir 38,23; 40,14) zeigen, daß der MLM nicht wesentlich vor dem 3. Jh. v.Chr. verfaßt worden sein kann. Wird in Rechnung gestellt, daß eine gewisse Zeit vergeht, bevor ein Text zitiert und redaktionell überarbeitet wird, so dürfte der MLM gegen Ende des 3. oder zu Beginn des 2. Jh. v.Chr. anzusetzen sein[103].

Gegen eine mehrfach von Elgvin angenommene[104] und zeitweise auch von Harrington vertretene[105] essenische oder protoessenische Herkunft des MLM spricht, daß sich im Text weder typisch essenisches Vokabular[106] noch essenische *theologumena* finden. Mit Harrington haben dagegen die Ausführungen zu den Eltern und zum Umgang mit der Ehefrau in 4Q416 2 III-IV in den erhaltenen essenischen Texten keine Parallele[107]. Hinzu kommt das Interesse des MLM an finanziellen Fragen in 4Q416 2 II-III par 4Q417 2:

---

100. So zuerst HARRINGTON, *Wisdom at Qumran,* pp. 142f.; vgl. STRUGNELL/ HARRINGTON/ELGVIN, *Qumran Cave 4. XXIV*, p. 2.

101. Vgl. LANGE, *Weisheit und Prädestination*, p. 46.

102. Zu den Belegen der genannten Lemmata im MLM s. jeweils die DJD 34 beigegebene Konkordanz.

103. Vgl. STRUGNELL/HARRINGTON/ELGVIN, *Qumran Cave 4. XXIV*, p. 41: »between Proverbs and Sirach«.

104. *Admonition Texts*, pp. 185f.191f.; *Wisdom, Revelation, and Eschatology*, pp. 443ff.; *Early Essene Eschatology*, pp. 128-134; *Mystery to Come*, pp. 115-118; *Wisdom and Apocalypticism*, pp. 246f. (vgl. auch DIMANT, *Qumran Manuscripts*, p. 43).

105. *Wisdom Texts from Qumran*, pp. 41f.

106. Einzige mögliche Ausnahme ist das in 4Q415 9$_7$; 4Q416 2 III$_{21}$; 2 IV$_5$; 4Q418 103 II$_{8f.}$; 167a+b$_{5f.}$; 199$_1$; 4Q418a 13$_1$ belegte Nomen יחד. Leider sind die Belege 4Q418 167$_{5f.}$; 199$_1$; 4Q418a 13$_1$ wegen Textzerstörungen nicht mehr sicher zu interpretieren. In 4Q415 9$_7$; 11$_4$; 4Q416 2 III$_{21}$; 4Q418 103 II$_{8f.}$ und 167a+b$_{5f.}$ ist יחד – anders als in den essenischen Texten – nie eine Gruppenbezeichnung und in 4Q416 2 IV$_5$ beschreibt es sogar – für den essenischen Sprachgebrauch sehr ungewöhnlich – die Vereinigung mit einer Frau. Der in 4Q408 bezeugte und mit einer gewissen Wahrscheinlichkeit nichtessenische Text zeigt ferner, daß das Lexem zumindest vor der Gründung der essenischen Bewegung auch in nichtessenischen Texten benutzt wurde (zu 4Q408 s.o., p. 4).

107. *Wisdom at Qumran*, p. 144; vgl. STRUGNELL/HARRINGTON/ELGVIN, *Qumran Cave 4. XXIV*, p. 20.

> »The maven (scil. der מבין) is presumed to be involved in loans and standing surety. Thus he is clearly part of the common »secular« society found anywhere in Judaism ... indeed, one can ask whether there is any need to talk of a »community« at all in 4Q415 ff. Instead he may have had an administrative function in a court, or even may have taught his wisdom to an international audience, as several fragments, especially 4Q418 81, suggest«[108].

Gegen einen essenischen Ursprung des MLM spricht auch die Beobachtung Elgvins: »The work does not reflect a hierarchically structured community, as the *yaḥad* does. Only two small passages deal with purity matters or priestly tradition«[109].

Schließlich macht auch der von Strugnell/Harrington/Elgvin geleistete Vergleich von Vokabular und Themen des MLM mit den anderen Texten des Qumran-Korpus[110] einen solchen essenischen Ursprung des MLM unwahrscheinlich:

> »In all the areas where scholarship has proposed finding decisive marks that a work is sectarian (e.g. purity and impurity, the Torah, the community, doxological language, dualism), 4Q415 ff. is clearly distinct from the norm of sectarian vocabulary and thought as found in the 1-11Q texts«[111].
>
> Die verbleibenden sprachlichen Gemeinsamkeiten zwischen beiden Textgruppen sind vor einem »general non-sectarian and post-exilic sapiential Jewish background« zu verstehen[112].

Aufschluß über die Herkunft des MLM geben demgegenüber die Hinweise auf ein für weisheitliche Texte ungewöhnlich starkes kultisches Interesse:
- die Bemerkungen zum Erstlingsopfer (4Q423 3_4 par 1Q26 2_4),
- die Ausführungen zum Auflösen des Gelübdes einer Ehefrau durch ihren Mann (4Q416 2 $IV_{8f.}$ par 4Q418 $10a+b_{9f.}$),
- die Erörterung zur Vermischung unter Aufnahme von Lev 19,19; Dtn 22,9-11 (4Q418 103 III_{6-9}),
- die Belege zu Festen und Kalenderfragen in 4Q416 1_3; 4Q418 118_3,
- die Belege von נדה in 4Q417 4 II_2; 4Q418 20_2,
- die Beschreibung der Erwählung eines/der Gerechten als von Gott mit Hilfe des Losorakels vorherbestimmt (הפיל גורלכה; 4Q418 $81+81a_5$).

Der gegen Ende des 3. oder zu Beginn des 2. Jh. v.Chr. verfaßte MLM dürfte somit am Jerusalemer Tempel zu verorten sein.

---

108. STRUGNELL/HARRINGTON/ELGVIN, *Qumran Cave 4. XXIV*, p. 20.
109. *Early Essene Eschatology*, p. 128.
110. *Qumran Cave 4. XXIV*, pp. 24-30; vgl. STRUGNELL, *Sapiential Work*, passim.
111. *Qumran Cave 4. XXIV*, p. 30.
112. *Loc. cit.*

Exkurs: MLM, Myst und die Zwei-Geister-Lehre

Sowohl das *Book of Mysteries* als auch der *mûsār lᵉmēbîn* teilen viele Besonderheiten. Hier ist nicht nur das für weisheitliche Texte außergewöhnlich starke kultische Interesse der beiden Werke zu nennen, sondern auch die Tatsache, daß sie anders als die meisten Weisheitstexte Vorschriften aus dem Pentateuch zitieren. Ferner sind Parallelen in der Eschatologie beider Werke auffällig: Hier ist besonders auf die endzeitliche Offenbarung und Realisierung der weisheitlichen Urordnung hinzuweisen (s.o., pp. 15ff.20f.). Neben inhaltlichen Parallelen fallen aber auch Gemeinsamkeiten im Vokabular auf. Als Beispiele seien hier die sonst kaum belegten Wendungen רז נהיה (1Q27 1 I$_4$ par 4Q299 2$_4$)[113] und שורשי בינה («Wurzeln der Einsicht»; 4Q418 55$_9$; 4Q301 1$_2$; 2b$_1$; cf. שורש חוכמה 4Q300 1a III-b$_3$) genannt. Beide Werke dürften daher aus dem gleichen, am Tempel zu lokalisierenden weisheitlichen Milieu stammen[114].

Ähnlichkeiten im Vokabular der etwas später zu datierenden Zwei-Geister-Lehre (1QS III$_{13}$-IV$_{26}$ par 4QpapS^c V$_{1-8}$) machen deutlich, daß es sich bei diesem Werk um einen weiteren dem Milieu von MLM und Myst zuzuweisenden Text handelt[115]:

מחשבה bezeichnet sowohl im MLM (4Q417 2 I$_{12}$) als auch in 1QS III$_{15}$; IV$_4$ die präexistente Ordnung von Kosmos und Geschichte, den Plan Gottes.

תולדות benennt sowohl im MLM (4Q418 77$_2$) als auch in der Zwei-Geister-Lehre (1QS III$_{13}$) die menschliche Geschichte.

נחל In der Zwei-Geister-Lehre werden mit Formen der Wurzel נחל die Anteile eines Menschen an den beiden Geistern beschrieben (1QS IV$_{15ff.}$). Eine ähnliche Verwendung findet das Nomen נחלה im MLM: [...]בה לא ינקה כפי נחלתו בהיר (»in ihr soll nicht straflos bleiben, gemäß seinem Anteil am Zwielicht«; 4Q417 2 I$_{24}$); הבט ברז] נהיה וקח מולדי ישע ודע מי נוחל כבוד ועו[ן]ל (»[betrachte das Geheimnis] des Werdens, nimm die Kinder des Heils wahr, und erkenne, wer Erbteil hat, an Herrlichkeit und Frevel«; 4Q416 2 I$_5$ par 4Q417 2 I$_{10f.}$).

---

113. Zu den Belegen der Wendung im MLM s. WACHOLDER/ABEGG/BOWLEY, *Concordance*, p. 331.

114. Zur Verwandtschaft von Myst mit dem *mûsār l'mēbîn* cf. SCHIFFMAN, *4QMysteries^b*, p. 203; ID., *4QMysteries^a*, p. 207f.; ID., *Reclaiming the Dead Sea Scrolls*, p. 206; ID., *Mysteries*, p. 31; ELGVIN, *Admonition Texts*, p. 179; ID., *Wisdom, Revelation, and Eschatology*, pp. 47f.; ID., *Early Essene Eschatology*, pp. 132.153-157; STRUGNELL/HARRINGTON/ELGVIN, *Qumran Cave 4. XXIV*, p. 2.

115. Zur Sache, zum eigenständigen Charakter und zur Datierung der Zwei-Geister-Lehre s. LANGE, *Weisheit und Prädestination*, pp. 126-130.

Inhaltlich erinnert der Topos von der eschatologischen Offenbarung der Weisheit (1QS IV$_{22}$) an die Aussagen von 1QMyst 1 I$_7$[116]. Von der Sache her betont die Zwei-Geister-Lehre die schon im MLM und Myst angelegten dualistischen Tendenzen stärker und stellt die bereits im MLM und Myst angetroffene Eschatologie mehr ins Zentrum.

Die für das weisheitliche Milieu von MLM, Myst und der Zwei-Geister-Lehre charakteristische Kombination von Toraweisheit und Eschatologie findet sich schließlich auch in der zweiten Redaktion des Koheletbuches (Koh 8,5f.; 11,9c; 12,12-14) und der Endredaktion des protomasoretischen Psalters (s. etwa die Rahmenpsalmen 1-2.145-150)[117].

Ein Vorläufer dieses Milieus könnte sich schließlich im Aramaic Levi Document finden, das im 3. Jh. v.Chr.[118] verfaßt wurde und wohl aus priesterlichen Kreisen stammt[119]. Es enthält neben einer langen Reihe kultischer Instruktionen (ALD 13-61) u.a. auch eine weisheitliche Paränese mit einem Lob auf den Weisen (ALD 83ff.). Allerdings unterscheidet sich das ALD darin deutlich von den oben genannten Werken, daß sich in seinem noch erhaltenen Textbestand (1QTLevi, 4QLevi^{a-f}, CLevi, Zusätze zu den TestXII in der Athos-Handschrift Koutloumous 39, BM Add. 17,193) keine eschatologischen Gedanken finden[120].

3.5. 4Q424: 4QInstruction-like Composition B

Die einzige erhaltene Handschrift von Instruction-like Composition B besteht aus zwei größeren (Frag. 1 und 3) sowie zwei kleineren Fragmenten (Frag. 2 und 4). Sie ist in einer »early Herodian rustic semi-formal« Schrift kopiert worden und könnte vom gleichen Schreiber wie 4Q390 stammen[121]. 4Q424 bezeugt eine proverbienartige Sammlung von Kunstsprüchen, die sich mit der praktischen Lebensführung, Gerichtsbarkeit und ähnlichen Dingen beschäftigt. Formal handelt es sich um ermahnende und belehrende Kunstsprüche. Die einzelnen Sprüche scheinen nach thematischen und formalen Kriterien angeordnet worden zu sein:

> »4Q424 is a compendium of wisdom sayings about two types of individuals: men with whom one is not to participate or who are not to be

---

116. Vgl. dazu schon PHILONENKO, *L'apocalyptique qoumrânienne*, p. 213.
117. Dazu vgl. LANGE, *In Diskussion mit dem Tempel*; ID., *Endgestalt*; ID., *Eschatological Wisdom*.
118. Vgl. STONE, *Sectarian Origins*, pp. 247f. Anm. 2; DE JONGE, *Testament of Levi*, pp. 373f.; KUGLER, *Patriarch*, pp. 134f.
119. So HULTGÅRD, *L'eschatologie*, pp. 15-81, cf. auch die Bemerkungen von STONE, *Ideal Figures*, pp. 263-265; GREENFIELD/STONE, *Remarks*, pp. 226f.; ID., *Prayer*, p. 253.
120. So u.a. COLLINS, *The Scepter and the Star*, p. 88.
121. S. TANZER, *4QInstruction-like Composition B*, p. 334.

entrusted with responsibilities and men who represent valued qualities. By far the greater proportion of extant text is concerned with the first category.

Most of the sayings about men with whom one is not to participate or who are not to be entrusted with responsibilities conform to one or two forms:
1. X עם, »with such a person ...« ... A variation of this form found in frg. 1 6-7 is introduced ביד עצל, »into the hand of one who is stupid ...«.
2. איש, »a man who/a man of ...«[122].

Lehreröffnungsformeln oder ähnliche Formelemente, die auf zusammenhängende Lehrreden oder Traktate hinweisen, fehlen im erhaltenen Text von 4Q424 ebenso wie weisheitliche Hymnen. Dieses Fehlen längerer zusammenhängender Textstücke spricht m.E. trotz der zwischen weisheitlichen Texten nicht ungewöhnlichen lexematischen Berührungen[123] dagegen, 4Q424 gemeinsam mit Handschriften wie 1Q26, 4Q415-418a.423 als eine Instruction zu beschreiben[124].

Von der Art her erinnert der Text am ehesten an ältere Spruchsammlungen, wie sie sich in Prov 1-9 oder sogar Prov 10ff. finden[125]. Auf ein relativ hohes Alter der Sammlung könnte neben der Form auch das verwendete Vokabular deuten. So wird beispielsweise die Wurzel דרש ($3_{1.4}$) noch ohne einen Beigeschmack von Schriftauslegung verwendet und משפט (1_9; 2_2; $3_{2.4.8}$) findet sich lediglich im Kontext normaler Gerichtsbarkeit, ohne mit dem mosaischen Gesetz in Verbindung zu stehen oder eschatologisch konnotiert zu sein. Es ist daher keinesfalls auszuschließen, daß die von 4Q424 bezeugte Proverbien-Sammlung nicht erst nach dem Jahr 200 v.Chr.[126] angesetzt werden darf, sondern wesentlich älter ist und aus exilischer oder nachexilischer Zeit stammt.

In diesem Kontext ist schließlich auch auf das Verhältnis von 4Q424 1_3 zu Ez 13,10f. einzugehen:

[...] חיץ יבחר לבנותה ותפל טח קירו גם היאׄ [...] מׄ[סׄתר מפני זרם

»[...] eine (unvermörtelte) Scheidewand wählte er aus, sie zu bauen, und verputzte seine Mauer, doch sie [gibt keinen[127] Sch]utz (wörtlich Versteck) vor strömendem Regen« (4Q424 $1_{3f.}$).

»Darum, ja darum, weil sie mein Volk in die Irre geführt haben, indem sie sagten: Heil! wo doch kein Heil ist – (dies)es aber baut sich eine Wand

---

122. TANZER, *4QInstruction-like Composition B*, p. 335; vgl. BRIN, *4Q424 1-2*, pp. 21f.42; ID., *4Q424 Fragment 3*, p. 271; ID., *Wisdom Issues*, p. 300.
123. Gegen STRUGNELL/HARRINGTON/ELGVIN, *Qumran Cave 4. XXIV*, p. 2, ist die sicher späte und für Myst und den MLM typische Wendung רז נהיה in 4Q424 nicht belegt.
124. Gegen STRUGNELL/HARRINGTON/ELGVIN, *Qumran Cave 4. XXIV*, p. 2; TANZER, *4QInstruction-like Composition B*, 335.
125. Ähnlich auch VAN DER WOUDE, *Wisdom*, p. 249.
126. Gegen BRIN, *4Q424 1-2*, p. 23; ID., *4Q424 Fragment 3*, pp. 217f.
127. Der sich in Z. 4f. anschließende Spruch legt nahe, daß es sich in $1_{3f.}$ um eine negative Aussage handelt.

auf, und siehe, sie bestreichen sie mit Tünche – (11) sage zu den Tünchestreichern '': 'Wenn dann' ein Platzregen kommen wird und '' Hagelsteine fallen und ein Sturmwind losbricht und die Mauer eingestürzt ist, wird man dann nicht zu euch sagen: Wo ist (nun) der Lehmstrich, den ihr angestrichen habt?« (Ez 13,10-12)[128].

Brin[129] geht ohne weitere Begründung davon aus, daß Ez 13,10f. in 4Q424 $1_{3f.}$ zitiert wird, während Harrington es versäumt, überhaupt auf Ez 13,10f. hinzuweisen[130], und Tanzer[131] die Frage nach der gegenseitigen Abhängigkeit ungeklärt läßt. Es fällt jedoch auf, daß das Bild von der trügerisch übertünchten Scheidewand, die keinen Schutz vor stürmischem Regen gewährt, in dem Spruch von 4Q424 $1_{3f.}$ wesentlich allgemeiner verwendet wird als in Ez 13,10-12, wo das Bild die trügerische Sicherheit der Botschaft von Ezechiels prophetischen Gegnern umschreibt[132]. Aus diesem Grund dürften Ez 13,10-12 und 4Q424 $1_{3f.}$ eher auf eine gemeinsame Tradition zurückgreifen, oder aber Ez 13,10-12 die von 4Q424 dokumentierte Sammlung zitieren. In letzterem Fall wäre mit einer exilischen Datierung dieser Proverbien-Sammlung zu rechnen.

3.6. 4Q525: Beatitudes

Von dem heute Beatitudes genannten Werk ist nur eine in einer späthasmonäischen oder frühherodianischen Semikursiven[133] gehaltene Handschrift von 50 stark beschädigten Fragmenten erhalten. Nennenswerte Textmengen bieten nur Frag 2-3, 5, 14, 15. Zusammenhängende Sätze finden sich nur in Frag 2-3 II. Frag 14 II bietet 28 Halbzeilen Text. Der Name des Textes leitet sich von einer Kette von Seligpreisungen in Frag. 2-3 II ab und beschreibt keineswegs das gesamte Werk. Ob in Frag. 1 tatsächlich der Beginn des Werkes erhalten ist[134], muß wegen der geringen Textmenge des Frag. fraglich bleiben.

Der weisheitliche Charakter des von 4Q525 bezeugten Werks ist durch seine Sprache und den Gebrauch weisheitlicher Formen und Themen deutlich dokumentiert:

Weisheitliches Vokabular

אולת: 4Q525 2-3 II_2
בין: 4Q525 5_{10}; 6 II_2; 14 II_{18}; 16_3; 24 II_3

---

128. Text und Übersetzung nach ZIMMERLI, *Ezechiel*, pp. 281f.283f.
129. *4Q424 1-2*, p. 24.
130. *Wisdom Texts from Qumran*, pp. 62f.
131. *4QInstruction-like Composition B*, p. 335.
132. Vgl. LANGE, *Vom prophetischen Wort zur Schriftauslegung*, pp. 146-148.
133. Zur Paläographie von 4Q525 s. PUECH, *Qumrân grotte 4. XVIII*, pp. 116f.
134. So PUECH, *4Q525*, p. 82; ID., *Beatitudes*, p. 353; ID., *Qumrân grotte 4. XVIII*, p. 115.

דעת: 4Q525 1₂; 14 II₁₉
חכם (Adj.): 4Q525 5₈; 23₄
חכמה: 4Q525 1₁f.; 2-3 II₃; 23₆
מוסר: 4Q525 1₂
ערמה: 4Q525 23₅
שכל (Verb): 4Q525 1₂; 5₉

Weisheitliche Gattungen und Themen

Wie schon erwähnt, beginnt der noch lesbare Text von Frag. 2-3 II mit einer Kette von Seligpreisungen. In Aufnahme von Ps 1,2 und 15,2f. wird der Mensch gepriesen, der sein Leben nach der mit der Weisheit identifizierten Tora ausrichtet[135]. Die Paränese von Frag. 5 mahnt dann, die Vorschriften der mit der Weisheit identifizierten Tora einzuhalten. Auch 4Q525 wäre somit der Toraweisheit zuzuordnen. In Frag. 14 II finden sich Reste zweier weisheitlicher Lehrreden, die an einen weisen Lehrer adressiert sein dürften, der in Zeile 18 מבין genannt wird. Die erste Lehrrede reicht bis Zeile 16 und spricht u.a. über die Vorteile der Weisheit und das Weiterwirken weisheitlicher Lehre noch nach dem Tod des Weisen. Die zweite Lehrrede will dem מבין nahelegen, wie er zu lehren hat. Der erhaltene Text betont dabei im wesentlichen die bedächtige Zurückhaltung bei der Unterweisung.

Die Datierung des Werkes ist wegen fehlender Realien schwierig. Der *terminus ante quem* liegt aus paläographischen Gründen zu Beginn der herodianischen Schriftepoche. Für den *terminus post quem* weist Puech in seiner Edition auf die strikte Vermeidung des Tetragramms hin. Es wird auch in Wendungen, die biblisch gerne mit dem Gottesnamen konstruiert werden, durch אל oder אלהים ersetzt. Das Werk dürfte deswegen nach der Mitte des 2. Jh. v.Chr. verfaßt worden sein. Sollten die von Puech angenommenen ideengeschichtlichen Abhängigkeiten früher essenischer Texte wie der Gemeinderegel, der *Hôdāyôt* und der Damaskusschrift von den Beatitudes einerseits, der Beatitudes von Ben Sira (Sir 14,20-27 [-15,2]) andererseits zutreffen, muß der Text zwischen 160 und 140 v.Chr. datiert werden[136]. Der Gebrauch der Gottesbezeichnung אלהים (4Q525 5₁; 5₉.₁₃; 14 II₁₀; 19₃; 21₂; 23₁; 29₃) macht trotz solcher ideengeschichtlichen Abhängigkeiten eine nichtessenische Herkunft des Werkes wahrscheinlich[137].

---

135. Zur Diskussion um die Seligpreisungen in 2-3 II s. PUECH, *Un hymne essénien*; ID., *4Q525*; ID., *Beatitudes*; BROOKE, *Matthew's Beatitudes*; FITZMYER, *Beatitudes*; FABRY, *Makarismus*; ID., im vorliegenden Band; VIVIANO, *Beatitudes*; ID., *Eight Beatitudes*.

136. PUECH, *4Q525*, pp. 90f.; ID., *Beatitudes*, pp. 354.358f.; ID., *Qumrân grotte 4. XVIII*, pp. 117-119; anders BROOKE, *Matthew's Beatitudes*, p. 35 (zwischen 50 v.Chr. und 50 n.Chr.).

137. Gegen DE ROO, *Qumran Sectarian Document*, pp. 345-367. Zur Vermeidung von אלהים in essenischen Texten s. Anm. 52.

4. Resumee

Die vor den Textfunden vom Toten Meer noch unbekannten Weisheitstexte aus der Bibliothek von Qumran stammen, wahrscheinlich mit Ausnahme des in 4Q424 bezeugten Textes, aus der Zeit vom 3. bis zum 1. Jh. v.Chr. Soweit der meist schlechte Erhaltungszustand der Handschriften inhaltliche Beschreibungen noch zuläßt, gehören sie wiederum mit Ausnahme von 4Q424 der sogenannten Toraweisheit an. Damit wird deutlich, daß die vor den Funden von Qumran nur aus Dtn 4,6, den Weisheitspsalmen, Sir und Bar 3,9-4,4 bekannte Identifikation von weisheitlicher Seinsordnung und Tora spätestens ab dem 3. Jh. v.Chr. im antiken Judentum zum dominierenden Element weisheitlichen Denkens geworden ist. Dem entspricht es, daß zumindest der MLM, das *Book of Mysteries*, Beatitudes (4Q525) und Sapiential Work (4Q185) – anders als sonst aus der Weisheitsliteratur bekannt – auf biblische Texte anspielen oder diese zitieren.

Eine zunehmende Dualisierung und Eschatologisierung weisheitlichen Denkens, wie sie vom MLM, Myst und der Zwei-Geister-Lehre dokumentiert werden, deuten für das antike Judentum auf eine zunehmende Affinität der Weisheit zur Apokalyptik hin. Diese Beobachtung wird in den genannten Texten durch die Verschmelzung des Gedankens von einer weisheitlichen Seinsordnung mit geschichtlichen Kategorien zu einem epochalen Weltbild ebenso erhärtet wie durch ihr Interesse an der Engelwelt.

The Department of Religious Studies Armin LANGE
101 Saunders Hall, CB 3225
University of North Carolina at Chapel Hill
Chapel Hill, NC 27599-3225
USA

THE SMALLER HEBREW WISDOM TEXTS FOUND AT QUMRAN

VARIATIONS, RESEMBLANCES, AND LINES OF DEVELOPMENT

In the *General Introduction* to 4Q415ff., to be found in DJD 34 (STRUGNELL, HARRINGTON, & ELGVIN, *Qumran Cave 4*. XXIV, pp. 22-33), you will find an analysis of that work from the point of view of its preferences in vocabulary, together with a comparison of its favourite topics with the topics that would be expected and those which would be unexpected in the Wisdom books of the Bible, both the earlier ones, i.e. Proverbs, the Wisdom Psalms[1], and Job, and the later ones, i.e. Qohelet and Ben Sira. From our study in DJD 34, briefly incorporated into the synopsis appended to the end of this article, we concluded first that there were in 4Q415ff. many lexical preferences and thematic interests that would have been unexpected in Biblical Wisdom, and next that 4Q415ff. was frequently in its language *non-sectarian* and also most probably *pre-sectarian*, though there were occasional coincidences with the thoughts found in the Qumran sect's compositions, especially in the area of eschatology. This conclusion is also supported by many a clear indication that sociologically 4Q415ff. reflected a non-sectarian background, cf. its interests in matrimonial questions, financial transactions, etc., etc., and cf. the absence in it of any mention of a religious community.

About 4Q415ff., which was clearly influential at Qumran (its seven or so copies suggest that it was almost canonical) and a very long work (it is recorded on ca. 4750 cards in the Handwritten Concordance), three further questions should be posed; first, what are, more precisely, the lexicographical, theological, chronological, and sociological contacts between 4Q415ff. and the Biblical Wisdom corpus (but that inquiry we will leave for the moment to others), and (two further questions) how was 4Q415ff. related to the other less extensively preserved Wisdom works copied at Qumran (whether they were in fact of sectarian origin or not)[2] and how

---

1 Since there is considerable uncertainty about which Biblical Psalms should be counted as sapiential, schematically we will use here only the vocabulary of the certainly sapiential Psalm 119 as an example. For a much more nuanced discussion, cf. HURWITZ, *Ḥochmah*.

2. We will use such phrases as "sectarian writings" or "writings (composed at Qumran)" to refer specifically to CD, 1QS, and 1QH, as well as some similar works; we are trying to separate from those sectarian works those which were of an earlier date though they were accepted by the Qumranites; even though such works were congenial to the men of Qumran, they were not in fact composed by them.

were these works related to each other – i.e. questions of trajectories, of schools of Wisdom thought and writings, and of the lines of development between such writings[3].

Since we are posing a question about ideologies, groups and "schools" it is not necessary that every passage examined here should be, *formally* speaking, strictly sapiential (e.g. 4Q185 and 4Q298 are not); after all the formally very different CD, 1QS and 1QH each presents apparent similarities in sapiential thought, language and style, but these need merely attest the general influence of the Wisdom texts and school, or schools, reflected by 4Q415ff., 4Q299ff. and 4Q525. Even those latter three works differ formally in important details from each other (e.g. in the address to an individual or a group) and doctrinally.

First, we should explain how the data are presented in the synopses of the vocabularies of these minor sapiential works, as they are displayed at the end of this article. In the first column you will find a numerical reference to guide you to the entry on each Hebrew word being considered; then comes each word itself, not arranged in alphabetical order but grouped *roughly* into semantic classes[4]. Next comes an indication of the number of the occurrences of each word in 4Q415ff., in relation to the total number of its occurrences in the rest of the 1-11Q non-Biblical texts; 4Q415ff. being much shorter, the normal proportion between occurrences in 4Q415ff. and those in the rest of the 1-11Q non-Biblical corpus will be between 1:7 (i.e. one occurrence in 4Q415ff. to seven occurrences in the non-Biblical texts in the rest of the Qumran concordances) and 1:15 in the same corpus of texts. Next follow vertical columns devoted to the vocabulary of each Wisdom work from caves 4 and 11 which we have selected for study; these columns are arranged under the standard abbreviations for each work[5].

---

3. Giving absolute dates to Wisdom Books and material will usually be hard; in the DJD edition we suggested (though the dust-jacket says the opposite!) that 4Q415ff. and the Law Code preserved at the end of the *Damascus Document* were probably near-contemporaries from the 4th-3rd Century B.C.

4. Adapted from the classes in DJD 34 *ad loc*. A question mark after a word indicates that a word might have belonged to two or more classes; e.g. MŠPṬ could have referred to an eschatological Judgment or to that in an earthly court. At the end of the words listed come a few other non-lexical miscellanea. The summaries of the data on words given in the body of the article are presented differently, including between square brackets the # number under which the word can be found and, after an x, its frequency in a given work.

5. Of the abbreviations first used here, 4Q215b refers to a manuscript with those sapiential fragments that should be separated from 4Q215a [the *Testament of Naphtali*]; 4Q299ff. will refer to 4Q299-300-301 (and 1Q27), the *Book of Mysteries*, while "4Q303ff." groups artificially together 4Q303-4-5. 11QPs^a[col]xviii refers to Psalm 154 and 11QPs^a[col]xxvi to the "*Hymn to the Creator*". As for 4Q420ff., 4Q425 and 4Q426 and a possible redistribution of their fragments cf. our discussion below on

Beneath each siglum is an indication of the preserved extent of that work, as is suggested by the number of cards which contain its text in the preliminary or Handwritten Concordance, and supplemented by the corrected numbers for the texts in 1Q27 and 11Q as found in the 1Q *Konkordanz* of Kuhn and in the 11Q concordances, corrected as is appropriate for those texts which were never entered into the Handwritten Concordance. For various reasons there may be slight discrepancies between the numbers given in that Concordance and those in the DJD concordances, but they will be insignificant[6].

Our selection of the texts to be examined here contains all the certainly sapiential and paraenetic pieces in *Hebrew* found at Qumran. A few more *dubia* might have been considered (e.g. 4Q410, 4Q528), but these would scarcely effect the overall picture. One should note also the presence of considerable sapiential elements in the language of the *Hôdāyôt*, and occasionally in the *Serek ha-Yaḥad;* though we would be dealing here with works in different genres, the vocabulary of 1QH[a] and 1QS is important for this study in that it often shows how sapiential and paraenetic material and vocabulary is incorporated into compositions of different genres; some of which are to be dated to the period of the Qumran community and were certainly composed at Qumran[7].

How then should one interpret the tables of the varying verbal usages of each work and how is one to assess their importance? Since most of the works discussed here are so small, we must follow a different method from the method we employed in 4Q415ff. Many of the words discussed here, whether they were of frequent or of rare occurrence, were in any case quite *commonplace* in the vocabulary of Biblical Hebrew, in that of the Biblical Wisdom texts and in that of 4Q415ff. Again, many of these works were quite short, and the shorter a text is the less certain also our extrapolations and deductions about it must be. Because of this *ordinariness* of the vocabulary in all these manuscripts,

---

those Manuscripts. These texts are principally to be found in the DJD series, esp. vol. 20; in addition, for 4Q184-85 cf. DJD 5, for 11QPs[a] cols. xviii and xxvi cf. DJD 4, and for 4Q525 cf. *DJD* XXV. The texts of 4Q215b and 4Q424 can be found in WACHOLDER & ABEGG, *Preliminary Edition* 2 and 3 or in GARCÍA MARTÍNEZ & TIGCHELAAR, *Study Edition* I and II.

6. *En passant*, note that to compare the lengths of works, we have corrected the data so as to be mutually compatible a) by using regularly the provisional Handwritten Concordance (which includes entries for prepositions, etc.) rather than those of WACHOLDER & ABEGG (*Concordance*) or those of PFANN in the later volumes of DJD, and b) by regularizing similarly the data of KUHN's *Konkordanz*, of DJD 1, 4 and 5, and of YADIN's concordance for 11QT in YADIN, *Temple Scroll*.

7. The various *Testaments*, with their paraenetic material, are usually in Aramaic and cannot be used in our inquiry.

whether they be a) quite short, for instance, with 1-75 entries in the Concordances [i.e., 11QPs^a xxvi, 4Q303ff., 4Q411, 4Q412, 4Q413, 4Q425, but that manuscript is perhaps to be treated as another copy of the same work as 4Q426 and perhaps of 4Q420-1 and 4Q424] or b) somewhat more substantially preserved ones, e.g., with 76-300 entries [i.e., 4Q184, 4Q185, 4Q215b, 4Q298, 4Q302, 4Q420ff, 4Q424, 4Q426, 11QPs^a xviii (Psalm 154)] or even c) quite long ones, e.g., with more than 300 entries [i.e., 4Q299ff., "The Book of Mysteries," and (though a work not quite so long) 4Q525 "Béatitudes"]. In all these works, the *non-occurrence* of a word, or even its occurrence only once, means that it should be ignored as being perhaps merely accidental. In works of whatever length, *multiple occurrences* of a word frequent also in 4Q415ff. might argue for some connection between such a word and 4Q415ff. In general the absence of certain *classes* of words here and in 4Q415ff., e.g. of priestly and sacrificial language or of terms expressing awareness of a (the) community *may* well be significant; but perhaps they did not belong either to the language or the interests of the Biblical Wisdom texts.

It should be noted that some of these works, especially the smaller ones, are clearly sapiential not only in their themes and language (this we will find significant for the similarities to the themes and lexicon of 4Q415ff.) but also for the forms they use, e.g. paraenesis addressed not only to an individual but also to a group, and sometimes by a 1st plural subject but usually by a 1st singular one, or parables, or descriptions of Wisdom or Folly personified. It should be noted that some of the longer fragments are usually composed of one of these forms consistently, but with other works which are only partially preserved the smaller fragments might well have come from sapiential works, but equally well might also not have; if only we had had them in a better state of preservation. However it does not matter how thoroughgoing and uninterrupted was the presence of these sapiential themes, elements and forms; we are interested in the similarity in themes, vocabulary and beliefs attested between 4Q415ff. and these other works, i.e. the possible similarity of their ideologies and of the circles or schools that produced each and influenced or was influenced by the others. A similar question can also be raised about the circles that produced the earlier sectarian parts of CD and 4QD, parts of the sectarian-legal 1QS, and the certainly sectarian 1QH^a – 4QH^{a-f}; each is, in a different way, run through with sapiential language or influenced by it though none of them is, as it stands now, a purely sapiential composition.

Next, how can we use these synopses so as to identify connections of theme and word-use between these works we are studying here, the Biblical Wisdom writings, and 4Q415ff? A first glance at *the divine names used* will show us that YHWH [#26], a name not infrequently used in Psalm 119 [x25], in Proverbs [xca. 8], in Job [x24] and not infrequently in Ben Sira (but *never* in Qohelet or in the sectarian writings from Qumran) is also never found in 4Q415ff. or in the clearly paraenetic works 4Q525 and 4Q299ff. For various reasons, however, it is found with some frequency in 4Q411 [x5] and in 11QPs^a 154 [x3], and also, though less frequently, elsewhere. This may reflect a chronological or a theological development, but in any case it is not a uniform one.

With this we may contrast the use of ᶜLYWN [#27], a word not found in 4Q415ff. or in the Wisdom Psalm 119, in Proverbs, Job, or in Qohelet, but which becomes quite frequent in Ben Sira [x23], as it does also in 4Q525 [x2] and in 11Q Psalm 154 [x4]. 4Q299ff. still reflects the non-use of this word, as do the other texts we are studying; in the later sectarian texts too ᶜLYWN occurs only very rarely.

The use of 'LHYM [#25] as a proper name (not a common noun) should be noted. The word occurred in Proverbs [x3], Job [x11] Qohelet [x7] and Ben Sira [x22]. Not only 4Q302 [x3] but also 4Q525 [x8!] and 4Q185 [x3] (both paraenetic pieces) use it often, but 4Q415ff. and 4Q299ff. seem to avoid the use of it completely, as do the longer sectarian pieces CD, 1QS, and 1QH. In contrast to that name, the related (?) name 'L [#24][8] was used *passim* in Job and Ben Sira, but was avoided, as it would seem, in Proverbs and Qohelet. That name is characteristic of *all* the sectarian writings of Qumran. In the Wisdom writings which we are examining, too, it is used regularly, at least in 4Q215b [x2], 4Q298, 4Q299ff [x5], 4Q302 [x2], 4Q303, 4Q425, 4Q426 and 4Q525 [x5] as it was also, though perhaps less regularly, in 4Q415ff. [x26].

It is at first glance hard to explain these changes in the names used for Wisdom's God in each of these corpora, the Biblical, the sectarian and that of the smaller sapiential works found at Qumran. Can they be explained as examples of a unilinear chronological development (but this can scarcely explain the cases of YHWH and 'L) or as examples of changes in style or in theological belief or fashion in different sapiential schools? It is uncertain whether the divine names in 4Q415ff. and 4Q525 can be set in a single line of development, or whether those works were relatives, either more distant ones or closer kin or even descendants the one of the other.

We can ask another question of our synopsis, whether the vocabulary of each work reflects any special social setting, whether in a community or a sect, especially one like the Qumran community, with its technical terms, its functionaries and the like. It will not be sufficient evidence if

---

8. Is one word to be translated "God"? (or "El") and the other "'Elôhîm"?

a *maskîl*, or personifications of Wisdom or Folly [cf. 4Q184, 11QPs^a 154], addresses a group of the righteous called e.g. "you who pursue righteousness" or "ye who are chosen of/by righteousness" – in such phrases there is no clear sign of any one organized community with its specific officers, structure, and the like. Perhaps phrases such as "folly *has no inheritance* with those who gird themselves with light" [4Q184] show a predestinarian thought more developed than what we found in 4Q415ff., a work that had a developed eschatology but little determinism; determinism, however, is not confined to the thought of Qumran nor even to the period when that community flourished. Occurrences in a work of the word YḤD [#6] do not attest an origin of that work in the specific Qumran *yaḥad*-community; the word is almost always in these texts and in 4Q415ff. not the *noun* meaning "community," but the *adverb* "together" cf. esp. 4Q525 [#6:x6!]. Thus the presence of this word x1 in 4Q184 need not suggest that the text implausibly entitled *"The Wiles of the Wicked Woman"* had anything to do with the Qumran community, whether historically or allegorically; the Lady is as timeless as she was in Proverbs 9,13-18! The presence in a work of some technical terms used elsewhere for the Qumran community would probably argue for Qumran as the social setting of the work and consequently for its date, but such words or phrases occur only rarely in the minor Wisdom Texts which we will be studying, and furthermore they do not seem to belong to the language of the Wisdom *genre*; words like ᶜDH [#7] or ᶜṢH [#9], and even such non-specifically-sectarian group-words as QHL [#10], ᶜM [#8], or YŚR'L [#12], as well as historical names like YᶜQWB [#13], are avoided in these Wisdom Texts as they usually were also in 4Q415ff. We have also noted that 4Q415ff. showed no signs of reflecting a setting in an organized community like that of Qumran nor in the scholastic *bêt-midraš* setting of Ben Sira (though 4Q415ff., like the Qumran compositions and like Ben Sira, all reflect some priestly traditions). The *absence* in these works which we will be examining of community language or concerns will not be significant; it is the absence of those features which would have been characteristic of earlier Biblical Wisdom texts too, and would not suggest any particular affinity with one MS or another; but the *presence* of such features would clearly differentiate the works containing them from 4Q415ff.

PART I

First then, for tidiness' sake, let us group together and examine the shorter fragments; as we saw, because of their shortness much less can be said with any certainty about them.

We have gathered in one column (as 4Q303ff.) the evidence of the brief fragments of 4Q303-304-305. Clearly these were all written by different hands; all of them treat of creation, all have a shared narrative and possibly hymnic style (cf. 11QPs^a col. xxvi), but little vocabulary is shared among all of them except what is to be expected in descriptions of the creation – thus "light" and "darkness" here; not all of these frgg. seem necessarily sapiential in style[9]. Even if the hypothesis that these are fragments of the same literary work be allowed (and even more so if each fragment must be treated in isolation) the brevity of all of them prevents any preciser characterization. The two occurrences of D^{c}T will scarcely help us; as for NPL'WT, it only occurs once here just as it occurred only rarely in the Biblical Wisdom Texts [x5 in Job and x2 in the Wisdom Psalm 119, but not in Proverbs or Qohelet]; likewise it only occurs once in 4Q415ff. and in 4Q185 only once. It becomes more frequently used later, e.g., x5 in Ben Sira and x48 in the principal Qumran texts in various contexts.

The passage on creation, 4Q411, can be compared in its subject matter with 11QPs^a col. xxvi (to be discussed next). In 4Q411 the mixture of first, second, and third person references, used respectively for the teacher, his pupil, and God and/or anything else, strongly suggests that this is a sapiential work, as is suggested also by the presence of several words relating to knowledge and by its use of rhetorical questions. The divine name employed here is only YHWH [#26], which in the Wisdom texts we are studying is only to be found with any frequency here [x5!] and in 11QPs^a 154; it also happens to be the only divine name found once in the other *"Hymn to the Creator"* [1QPs^a col. xxvi] and once in 4Q185. It is not used in the longer texts 4Q415ff., 4Q525, and 4Q299ff. nor regularly in the compositions found at Qumran, though it occurs not infrequently in each of the Biblical Wisdom writings [except Qohelet]. A sectarian origin or any specially close relationship to one of the longer works in the Biblical Wisdom tradition or to those Wisdom works which we are studying can surely be ruled out for 4Q411 as can also any connection with the sectarian compositions originating from Qumran[10].

Together with 4Q411 we should consider and compare another complete but short *"Hymn (?) on Creation,"* in 11QPs^a col. xxvi. This however contains only two of the words especially frequent in 4Q415ff.,

---

9. The sapiential nature of 4Q303 becomes much more apparent in H. JACOBSON's re-edition of it, cf. JACOBSON, *Notes*. Note especially the introductory "Hearken, O ye intelligent ones" (cf. the Synopsis #105 for other works sometimes addressed to a group).

10. On a possible connection with 4Q184 see our discussion of that piece *infra*.

QDWŠ [#32; x2] and 'MT [#64; x2]; the first of these characterizes only a few of our Wisdom texts, but the latter is found spread widely over all the texts we are studying, and occurs also frequently in the 1-11Q sectarian compositions. *Perhaps* the use of the divine name YHWH [#26], found only once but with *no other divine name* occurring here at all, is also significant. That this description of creation comes from some Wisdom school is clear, as is shown by its statement that God "established the world by His Wisdom... and by His Knowledge." This composition seems to have had no special connection with other sectarian writings, as we can see from the lack in it of any language about the community or about purity; but arguments from silence are not very convincing – cf. especially that on YHWH above.

4Q412 is addressed to a single person, although one who is envisaged as situated among a community, cf. especially BQHL RBYM [#10-11; x2]; that expression however should not be taken as employing the technical term HRBYM used of the community at Qumran – here it just means "an assembly of many people" as in QHL RB in Psalm 22, 26; 35, 18; 40, 10-11, and in Ezra 10, 1. The fragments of 4Q412 contain exhortations to hear words of wisdom [x2], as well as commonplace encouragements to life, righteousness [*sic legendum* also in 4Q412 1 6 *bis*] and the praise of God – but none of these features is characteristic uniquely of the Wisdom tradition, whether the Biblical, the Qumranic or that of the works we are studying here. One should notice also that in 4Q412 the Aramaism MLYM [x1 or x2] is used rather than 'MRYM or DBRYM; MLYM occurs also frequently in 4Q298ff. [x2] and in 4Q525 [x3][11]. It is not necessary to see a developed determinism in the statement that God created BRṢWNW (#67). In general, in view of the brevity of 4Q412 nothing distinguishes its fragments from the texts of the longer Wisdom works, 4Q415ff., 4Q299ff. and especially 4Q525, but there is also nothing in it that points to a specifically Qumranic origin.

4Q413, the briefest of all the works we are studying, may be even shorter than it appears to be from the DJD edition by Qimron; it was only by a *hesitant* suggestion of mine, made in 1959, that these two fragments were joined together – their texts indeed seemed able to be fitted harmoniously together, but the script of each seemed very different, even if one were to assume that one of the pieces was badly shrunken.

---

11. Is not the word HWṢY' (in 4Q412 1 4) a *plena scriptio* for the imperative (! as the context suggests), so reading "bring forth words"? We do not have enough of the text of this manuscript to establish how regular its orthographic practices were, and thus whether this is an abnormal spelling for the imperative or an error needing conjecture. One could also read ṢDQ as easily as ṢDYQ in 4Q412 1 4; see #41; x3.

Clearly the larger fragment comes from the beginning of an exhortation, addressed *to a group* (cf. the second person plural), inviting them, in standard sapiential language, to the study of Wisdom. Of its characteristic words, NHLH [#65], PcWLH [#66], and 'MT [#64], each recurs only once here; they could perhaps be predestinarian or determinist in sense, but need not be so; they are certainly very characteristic of 4Q415ff. Thus PcWLH [#66; x9 in 4Q415ff.] occurs only once here, and rarely elsewhere (i.e. 4Q215b, 4Q424, and 4Q426), 'MT [#64: x41 in 4Q415ff.] occurs 3 times in 4Q299ff., 4 times in 4Q420f. and twice in 11QPsa col. xxvi; while NHLH [#65: x1 here, and x35 in 4Q415ff.] occurs twice in 4Q426 and twice in 4Q525[12].

In general because of the limitations deriving from the brevity of this fragment, no connection can be drawn with any confidence between this clearly sapiential composition and any of the other works we are studying.

Part II

4Q184 and 11QPsa 154 are two of the pieces of intermediate length, the former presenting a personification of Dame Folly the seductress while in the latter Lady Wisdom is presented as inviting the righteous to her banquet. The use of such hypostases is frequent in all periods of Hebrew Wisdom literature – one finds Wisdom the harlot leaning out of her window in Proverbs 9,13-18, while Lady Wisdom can be found in Job 28, in Proverbs *passim*, e.g., 8-9, 1-6 – note how there Wisdom's invitation to Her banquet is followed immediately by Folly's invitation to hers –, cf. also 1Baruch 3,9; 4,4, Ben Sira 24, Wisdom 7-9,21, 1Enoch 43, etc.[13]

From the presence of pieces with such hypostases nothing can be deduced, either as to the school from which they come, nor as to their date, whether they be early or late; such pieces occur widely, all over the Wisdom corpus. More significant, one should notice how in all the abundant fragments of 4Q415ff. there is *no trace* at all of the presence of such hypostases (e.g. of Wisdom or Folly) though they are frequently found in many of the other sapiential texts found at Qumran.

How does the vocabulary of each of these two passages containing personifications relate to the general vocabulary of 4Q415ff.? In fact,

---

12. The use of 'L in paleo-Hebrew should of course be disregarded as merely a scribal feature of the fragment, not one characteristic of this text as a literary work.

13. It is frequently difficult to tell whether nouns like HKMH, and the feminine pronouns or suffixes referring to them, indicate the presence of a true hypostasis, e.g. "Lady Wisdom," or only refer to the abstract "wisdom" itself. This uncertainty often makes the translation especially of 4Q525 difficult.

very little; the vocabulary of each is conditioned by the portrait it gives and the circumstances of the scenes it depicts rather than by concerns for theological terminology. Thus in 4Q184, apart from such terms as might be expected in the lamentable scene that is being described, we find that the only terms which that work uses frequently and which also coincide with the vocabulary of 4Q415ff. are ḤWQ [#34] and PŠ^c [#51]; each of these two words occurs twice here, but that is hardly enough to suggest any special closeness to the *thought* of 4Q415ff., where those words are in fact *proportionately* much rarer. Some of the other words which are shared with 4Q415ff., e.g., NḤLH [#65] ṢDQ [#41] and ŠḤR [#45], are rather commonplace. Should one ask if 4Q184, unlike 4Q415ff., could have been composed at Qumran? Scarcely; certain features are indeed noteworthy by their absence in both, e.g., the absence of priestly and purity terminology, the absence of any interest in the specific Qumran community and of the technical terminology relating to it. (Note that in 4Q184's phrase WLHLYṢ YḤD BŠW' the word YḤD is not the noun that refers to the Qumran community, but the adverb which means "together"; as for the references to the group of the Virtuous in ll.14-16, these are too general to be considered as referring to the specific Qumran community.) One detail perhaps deserves attention; the phrase "She is the beginning of the ways of 'WL (iniquity)" clearly alludes to the text in Job 40, 19 about Behemoth, "He/she is the beginning of the ways of 'L (God)," and shows that the author knew that text in Job, but inverted it[14].

Turning to 11QPs^a 154, we should notice in it the frequent divine names YHWH [#26:x3] and 'LYWN [#27:x4] which clearly differentiate 11QPs^a 154 from the language of 4Q415ff. (where each of these names is avoided) and also from the usage of divine names attested in most of the other works we are studying. In 11QPs^a 154, as in 4Q184 with its other portrait of the hypostasized Folly, this scene where Wisdom, personified, invites youths to Her banquet does not have much lexical overlap with 4Q415ff. nor with the Wisdom pieces we are studying in this article; the scene and story is very specific and different from the normal contents of Wisdom literature and consequently so will the

---

14. What it means is unclear, but the coincidence of the phrase T'HL ŠBT in 4Q184 1, 7 with K'HL LŠ[BT in 4Q411 1 ii 10 *could* attest literary dependence (in which direction?), but it may as well be a shared phrase but one once common in Hebrew. Note also that in 4Q184 both frg. 2 and 3 (with their 2nd singular suffixes, and with the word TWRH [#37] otherwise rare in these wisdom texts) should perhaps be placed in another manuscript – why not 4Q525?

language used be. As in 4Q415ff., so also here we find almost no language that belongs to our categories of purity or sacrifice; as for the presence in this text of a communitarian consciousness or of a specific community, we find general references to groups of the wise and the upright and exhortations to unite with them, but these references do not use any of the technical terminology that describes the Qumran sect. Some of the language of knowledge and of eschatology, which is used here (but only rarely), occurs also in Biblical Wisdom texts, as in 4Q415ff. and in the other fragments we will be studying. In this piece we also find specific proper names which refer to Israel and its sacred history, material which is almost never referred to in the earlier Biblical Wisdom texts, in 4Q415ff., or in the other texts which we are studying here.

In the phrase HHBYRW YHD the word YHD [#6] could be an adverb or a noun, but even so it would not necessarily be the Qumranic noun with its precise technical sense. The injunction HHBYRW is noteworthy; it could be translated "join together" or "make an assembly join together;" cf. also the phrase BHBR YHDYW which, though it describes a community of followers of Wisdom, is distinct from the usage of 4Q415ff.; in that work the closely similar phrase in 4Q416 2 iii 21 has a very different meaning, namely that of sexual intercourse. One should note also about the use of YHD that this precise form of the *adverb* (not YHDYW, not YHDW) is unknown elsewhere in 4Q415ff. Other features worth noticing are a) that TWRH [#37] as used here is never found in 4Q415ff.! (while in the corpus we are studying it occurs only once in 4Q525, once in 4Q184 (?), and once in 11QPs^a Syr 154), and also b) that in the theologically important (?) phrase in lines 7-10, the praise of God is equated with the sacrifice of the altar!

To summarize then, 11QPs^a 154 could not have belonged with 4Q415ff. either linguistically or theologically. It might have been contemporaneous with Ben Sira, whose usage of divine names is somewhat similar. The presence of an hypostasis in it tells us very little about its date since hypostases are used at many points in the history of the Wisdom school; some linguistic features in it however seem to belong to late classical Hebrew. Because of its interest in a community (but one described in a fashion terminologically distinct from that of Qumran), we have perhaps been able to say here something a little more specific about the sources and ideology of 11QPs^a 154 than what we could say about 4Q184.

4Q185 is a wisdom instruction[15], an exhortation or parae-nesis addressed to "my sons" or "my people;" it is not clear who is

---

15. Cf. VERSEPUT, *4Q185*.

conceived to be the author or the addressees. The fragments are often hard to decipher in detail but overall the text is an exhortation to pursue God or Wisdom; numerous third feminine singular suffixes (systematically or spasmodically changed by some translators into masculines!) probably refer to wisdom, though some of them might refer to the Law, and even if they refer to wisdom this is not necessarily the personified Wisdom whom we found in 11QPs[a] 154. The language of the piece resembles the "style anthologique" of French scholars. If there were any special relationship with the vocabulary of the other texts that we know, the text here should have been long enough to show it; in fact however the frequent occurrences in 4Q185 of ḤSD [#30: x3] and QDWŠ [#32: x2] would distinguish 4Q185 from their very rare use in 4Q415ff.; cf. also the infrequent uses of ḤWQ [#34: x2], BRYT [#99: x1] and √MLK [#84: x1 or x2]. Furthermore the absence of words from certain semantic fields which are also avoided in 4Q415ff. (e.g., purity) may perhaps be of some significance. Apart from this, from the theological point of view one should perhaps note the frequent proper names drawn from Israel's history and the insistence that Wisdom can be found (especially? or only?) in Israel and can also be found in the study of matters of Israel's history such as the Exodus, topics generally foreign to the Biblical Wisdom tradition and certainly foreign to 4Q415ff.

Under the siglum 4Q215b we have examined the vocabulary of some Wisdom fragments that were once taken to be part of 4Q215a, the *Testament of Naphtali*. The fragments of 4Q215b are written in the same hand as 4Q215a but are probably to be distinguished from it on material grounds; 4Q215b is also somewhat sapiential, but contains also a description, past or future, of the end-time; most of its elements are common to the eschatological picture of Qumran, of Ben Sira, of 4Q415ff. and of the other works that we have been studying. The usage of the following words, some more frequent and others very rare in 4Q215b, e.g., ḤWQ [#34: x1], BRYT [#99:x1] and P‘WLH [#66:x1] differs from that of 4Q415ff.; little however can be concluded from this about 4Q215b's theology or its place in the sapiential tradition. The construct phrases, with BḤYRY followed by e.g. 'MT or ṢDQ, are found also in 4Q415ff. (e.g. 4Q416 69 ii 10) but occurs also in the sectarian writings, e.g., 1QS VIII, 6 or 1QH[a] II, 13. Theologically too, words like QWDŠ [#33:x2] and ḤSD [#30: x1] would be unusual in 4Q415ff., but other rare words (e.g., 'LWHYM [#25: x1] and QṢ "period" [#56: x2]) merely attest here the usage of later Hebrew. In general, then, the vocabulary is that of later Hebrew, or perhaps specifically that of Qumran Hebrew, but in any case it is somewhat different from that of 4Q415ff.

Despite their length, the fragments' language is too ordinary and nondescript to permit a confident dating or theological localization for it.

4Q298 is an exhortation or paraenesis (esoteric, as is shown also by its use of a cryptic script), which is addressed by a *maśkîl* to "all the sons of the dawn [?]". The title "*maśkîl*"[16] was frequently used in works written at Qumran to indicate their *author*, but was *not used* in that way in Biblical Hebrew, in Ben Sira, in 4Q415ff. or in the shorter Wisdom pieces we have been studying. From the esoteric script and from the use of "*maśkîl*," then, its Qumranic or sectarian origins can be concluded.

This work is not extensively preserved. The "sons of the dawn[?]" are exhorted to pay attention to "my (the *maśkîl*'s)" words; the epithets given to the addressees of 4Q298 are not characteristic of, or confined to, the Qumran community although *some* of them do in fact coincide with epithets also used in other Qumran writings[17]. The topics to be studied are especially "the end of the ages... the former things... the appointed times;" these are unexpected subjects, either in Wisdom writings or even in much of the Qumran corpus.

With a not very long text like 4Q298, which is preserved in only 110 cards in the Handwritten Concordance, it is often easier to establish that a fragment differs from the constant usage of 4Q415ff., not that it clearly resembles it. Thus in 4Q298 the use of TKWN [#63:x3] – whatever exactly that means – and also of MŚKYL [#79], ḤSD [#30] and BNY ŠḤR [each of these occurring only once here] perhaps differentiate the vocabulary of this work from that of 4Q415ff. The absence both of the terminology of purity, and of many of the epithets used for the community might seem to differentiate this work from Qumranic works, but its fragments are very short, and other descriptions of the community here, e.g. 'NŠY LBB, YD'YM, and 'NŠY RṢWNW, have good parallels in the certainly sectarian writings from Qumran – while yet others (e.g., RWDPY ṢDQ) are found also in 4Q415ff. Some *perhaps* deterministic

---

16. Our very hesitant suggestion (Cf. STRUGNELL, HARRINGTON, & ELGVIN, *Qumran Cave 4*. XXIV, p. 3) that 4Q415ff. too could have been ascribed to a *maśkîl* would have implied also that that work also was composed at Qumran and therefore would also have implied a Qumran date for it; but that suggestion should almost certainly be withdrawn. The word *maśkîl in this technical sense* does not in fact belong to the vocabulary of 4Q415ff.

17. The verbs in the beginning of this work should *all* be translated as imperatives [*contra* DJD *ad loc.*], cf. frg. 1-2 i 3 WHŠYBW and HBYNW, and not instead spasmodically as indicatives. Thus one should supplement DR[WŠ]W in frg. 1-2 i 3, and correct HṢNYᶜ to HṢNYᶜW in 3-4 ii 5.

words or phrases, frequent or not in 4Q298, e.g., TKWN [#63: x3] and also RṢWN [#67: x1(?)], recur perhaps both in 4Q415ff. and in the deterministic sectarian texts. In such a brief text as this, the rare use here of ṢDQ [#41:x1], used also not infrequently in the Wisdom corpus we are studying (esp. e.g. in 4Q185, 4Q215b, 4Q299ff., 4Q412, 4Q420f., and 4Q525) is of little interest – that is a word that is very common also in Biblical Wisdom texts, in 4Q415ff. and in the sectarian texts of whatever genre which were composed at Qumran.

In sum, there are many words and topics that set this certainly sectarian work apart from 4Q415ff., but which are at home in the Qumran sect. Since 4Q298 is also Qumranic (cf. its date of composition), it can be used to contrast its date with that of the earlier 4Q415ff., and with the other Wisdom texts of uncertain date which we are studying here; can we see if the lexicon and the themes of these latter works attest any detectable typological development?

Although somewhat sapiential in its choice of words, 4Q302 is formally a *rib*-admonition combined with a *parable*, and thus in its *form* distinct from the other works we have under consideration in this article; it is furthermore too short (only 122 Concordance cards) for any clearer characterization or overall description. Apart from its *incipit* (with HBYNW N' BZ'T, and similar exhortations), its vocabulary is not particularly sapiential, and it does not resemble especially closely either that of 4Q415ff., nor that of the other sapiential pieces we are studying here; DJD *ad loc.* suggested a pre-sectarian date of composition for it. Much of the vocabulary of 4Q302, such as the rare QWDŠ [#33], 'M [#8], the proper names YŚR'L [#12:x1] and 'BRHM [x1], and, especially characteristic, the divine name 'LHYM [#25:x1] are found almost never in 4Q415ff., and are also foreign to the language of the sapiential pieces we have been considering. Much of its vocabulary choices are in fact conditioned by the nature and subject matter of the parable itself; they are also somewhat nondescript, and hard to locate or characterize. One might notice in it an interest in politics greater than what we find in 4Q415ff., and perhaps greater than what we find in the other Wisdom texts found at Qumran (one perhaps more at home in Ben Sira), but this characteristic again arises from the subject matter of the parable itself and does not necessarily express any development in the interests of the Wisdom material[18].

4Q420 and 4Q421 (*"Ways of Righteousness"*) contain overlapping texts in mss long enough to allow us to make more reliable arguments

---

18. It might be noticed also that God is sometimes addressed in the third person, sometimes in the second; the literary or dramatic reasons for this are however hard to explain.

from silence about this or that verbal detail. The work contains somewhat ordinary sapiential instructions, some of which seem to relate to the duties of a judge (a topic found also in 4Q415ff.). Although there are references to the people among whom he acts as judge, these do not point to any specific community like that of Qumran.

A section of 4Q421, namely frag. 11(?)-12-13, seems not to contain wisdom sayings, but to treat of sacrificial matters (a topic foreign to earlier Wisdom texts, to 4Q415ff., to Ben Sira, and to most of the smaller Wisdom texts we have been studying). It is however quite likely that these fragments, 4Q421, 11(?) –12 –13, on sacrifice belonged to a different manuscript and work, although one written in the same hand as 4Q421. This proposal became almost a certainty when DJD XXXV was published, with its edition of extensive fragments of a new "halakhic" work, <sit venia verbo>, 4Q264a. The fragments we had proposed to separate from 4Q421 1-10 on formal grounds as containing exclusively legal matter (frgg. 11-13) now appear to be another copy of 4Q264a, the newly published legal work which overlaps with 4Q421 11-12-13, but with *no other* fragments of 4Q420-421.

This situation could be explained in two ways.

a) that 4Q420, 4Q421, and 4Q264a are three copies of the same work, one which combined sapiential and legal matter or

b) that there are two compositions, each surviving in two MSS
    I) the sapiential 4Q420 and 4Q421 1-10, and
    II) a purely legal work consisting of 4Q421 11-12-13 and 4Q264a.

Which proposal should be preferred? 1) The formula 'L YQTL 'YŠ can be found both in legal texts and in sapiential ones. 2) Paleographically the fragments of 4Q421 could derive either from one MS or from two. 3) It is possible (but not likely) that one MS could have contained legal matter (on sacrifices) mixed with *varied* sapiential topics. 4) However the observation that all of 4Q264a attests *exclusively* legal matter and overlaps *only* with frgg. 11-13 of 4Q421 but not with any of the sapiential matter of 4Q420-421 1-10 should be taken as decisively favouring the proposal that two distinct works have been combined under the siglum 4Q421.

The following words, where we have added also an indication of the proportionate frequencies of each in 4Q420f. Compared with the number of its occurrences in 4Q415ff. and in the rest of the Qumran non-Biblical corpus, e.g. MŠPṬ [#36:x3], 'MT [#64:x4], BYNH [#71:x3], ṢDQ [#41:x5], MŚKYL [#79:x3] and HTHLK B [#42:x2], all occur frequently in 4Q415ff., but not disproportionately so[19]. There are no other

---

19. The supplement BYḤD 'L (4Q421 1a i 2-3), proposed in DJD *ad loc.*, would be unlikely since the work otherwise reflects a pre-Qumranic style, cf. the usage of YḤD in 4Q415ff.

clear reflections of Qumran language in 4Q420-421 frgg. 1-10. Of the other words in 4Q420-421 which, though occurring only rarely, overlap with the vocabulary of 4Q415ff. (while other isolated words would not) note ḤPṢ [#93:x1], HWN [#92: x1], ḤBR [#5:x1], and ḤWQ [#34:x1]; especially noteworthy are GWRL [#60:x1] – here and also, rarely, in 4Q415ff. with a non-sectarian sense – and SRK, which would be found though only rarely if it is a verb, but would be sectarian if it were a noun. The sense of L'ŚWT ṢDQH is ambiguous (either "act righteously" or "give alms") but in any case the phrase would not help us to define the date or the background of this work. In Hebrew the Persian and Aramaic loan word PTGM is found only in Wisdom texts, e.g. Qohelet, Ben Sira, and Esther; in these Qumran MSS it occurs only x1, in 4Q420. This could be either an indication of the sapiential character of that work, or just of the lateness of its Hebrew.

Attention should be drawn to a formal feature here; not infrequently clusters of sentences occur each beginning with 'YŠ, followed by a noun or adjective [e.g. 'YŠ N'MN, 'YŠ ᶜNYW (?)] and each concluded by a predicate, usually "he will *xx*" or "thou shalt not *xxx* him." Such sentences (which we will call "'YŠ-sentences") are also found in Job, not infrequently in Proverbs, (cf. *s.v.* W'YŠ) and in Ben Sira (e.g., 10, 4; 16, 12 and in a cluster, at 35, 17-8). There were hardly any traces of such a form in 4Q415ff. (except once in 4Q417 2,7), in 4Q299ff. or in 4Q525, but it occurs frequently (sometimes also in clusters) also in 4Q424 (1,7. 10; 3, 1.3.6.7.8), in 425 1+3, 7, and in 426 1 ii 5; 2,1; 8,3. 4Q420, and 4Q421 seem certainly to be two copies of a work with 'YŠ-sayings (cf. 4Q421 1 a ii-b12.15; 4Q421 10), perhaps the same work.

Whether any of the other three MSS with clusters of with 'YŠ-sayings, 4Q424, 4Q425 and 4Q426, belong to non-overlapping and missing parts of the *same* work could not be proved from formal considerations; it depends on whether sufficient similarities of vocabulary and historical setting can be detected. As in 4Q415ff., in the other works we have been studying there are also no traces of interest in purity, in determinism, in the nation or perhaps (cf. above on the division of 4Q421 into two MSS) not even in sacrificial matters.

4Q424, whose text at the moment is found most easily in Wacholder & Abegg's, *Preliminary Edition* 2, pp. 174-6 or in García Martínez & Tigchelaar, *Study Edition* II, pp. 888-891 is a wisdom text composed almost exclusively of such "'YŠ-sayings" (cf. above on 4Q420-421) and of others of the pattern "Do not *x* with a *Y*." Most of this material seems to give instructions to a person in a position of some authority to avoid certain contacts, or to avoid entrusting others with responsible judicial tasks. This concern with judgment was frequent also in 4Q415ff.; the fragments of 4Q424 likewise do not seem to show any trace of a sectarian background; they give advice of a secular order, and mainly of a judicial nature. There is no reference to God, nor to any Final Judgment; MŠPṬ [#36:x5] is frequently referred to, but the word seems to denote a secular judgment. The only frequently recurring words in 4Q424 are HWN [#92:x3], √YŠR [#39:x2], ḤKMH [#73:x3], 'BYWN [#17:x2], HMŠYL [#85:x3] and √ BYN [#69-71:x2]; none of these except HMŠYL and HWN is especially significant or distinctive, though the frequent HWN points clearly to the secular nature of these instructions.

4Q424 has however linguistic contacts with 4Q415ff. so precise as to suggest that this is a work *derived from* 4Q415ff. or having shared origins with it. We do not rely on the phrase RWDPY DᶜT (424 3 3 cf. 4Q415ff. in 4Q418 69 ii 11) – for that would not be very distinctive – but note especially A) the word 'Ṭ [#80], which is unique here, while it occurs 15 times in 4Q415ff. and *nowhere else* in Hebrew (!), and B) the word MḤSWR [#19] which occurs once here (1,7), and once in 4Q299ff. but 28(!) times in 4Q415ff. – these two words alone demonstrate literary contacts between the three works. In the Bible MḤSWR occurs sporadically, but note its occurrences in Biblical Wisdom Texts, i.e. mainly in Proverbs (x8) and once in Ben Sira: it is not to be found in the texts composed in the Qumran sect. Only one of the occurrences of these two words defines their meaning with any precision; 'WṬ seems to mean 'secret' or 'affair.'

Finally one might perhaps note another stylistic feature reminiscent of those of 4Q415ff., the relative frequency of GM [#103:x2] rather than 'P [#101:x0], a preference characteristic also of 4Q415ff. and perhaps significant in the history of Hebrew.

Of the brief fragments of 4Q425 we should note that, although there were only a few words which both occurred frequently in them and also were especially characteristic of 4Q415ff., in general a) the vocabulary of 4Q425 was that found elsewhere in this sapiential corpus e.g., ḤWQ [#34:x1] and MŠQL [#87:x1]; b) that the phrase 'WYLY LB is found once here, but elsewhere in the Qumran corpus only in 4Q415ff. at 4Q417 18,1; 4Q418 58, 1; 69 ii 4 and 8; 205,2; and c) that "'YŠ-sentences" are present in both 4Q425 and 4Q426 (there being also an almost certain overlap between the texts of 4Q425 and 4Q426); all this suggests that 4Q425 and 4Q426 might well be copies of the same work; this work seems also to share significant formal features with 4Q415ff., especially with 4Q424 and perhaps even with 4Q420-1. The presence of such 'YŠ-sentences, however, would alone be an inadequate argument in favour of identifying 4Q425 [and 4Q426] as texts from the missing parts of 4Q415ff., but might support an identification with 4Q420f.

The same conclusions will hold even more if we treat 4Q426 as part of the same work as 4Q425 (and perhaps 4Q420-421 and 4Q424) and combine at least the vocabularies of 4Q425-6. The vocabulary of 4Q426 is also typical of the corpus of the minor Wisdom texts, as also of the Biblical Wisdom books, cf. RŠ^c [#53:x2+1], ṬWB [#38:x2], 'WṢR [#89:x2], NḤLH [#65:x2; very frequent in 4Q415ff. and 4Q525], BYNH [#71:x2], HTBWNN [#70:x2] and P^{c}WLH [#66: x1] as also are the 'YŠ-sayings, which seem to have occurred five times in 4Q426 and three (?) times in 4Q425. Less expected however, are the references to ṬM'H in 4Q426 [#2:x1] and TW^{c}BH [#54:x2], – unless these should be assigned to another work – and especially the list of the five sons of Shem in 4Q426 12, 3 (again if that fragment really belongs to this manuscript). Both 4Q425 and 4Q426 are didactic and lack any sign of interest in the Qumran community – as does also 4Q424 and perhaps even 4Q420f.

Part III

The title, "the book of mysteries," was given early on to 1Q27 but, now that more extensive fragments of it, i.e., 4Q299ff. [= 1Q27 + 4Q299-300-301], have been identified as parts of the same work, that title seems somewhat less appropriate. The numerous fragments of this work, the longest one we are considering here, make deductions as to any relations of it with 4Q415ff. and with the other minor Wisdom texts somewhat more reliable.

The frequency in 4Q299ff. of the following words, 'BYWN [#17:x2], ḤWQ [#34:x4], ṬWB [#38:x3], KBWD[#31:x4], √NBṬ [#75:x3], ṢDQ [#41:x7], QDWŠ [#32:x3], √ŚKL [#77-9:x4], and HMŠYL [#85:x3] is approximately that found in 4Q415ff.; other words occur in 4Q299ff. proportionately even more frequently than they do in 4Q415ff., e.g. GBWRH [#28:x6], QWDŠ [#33:x7], ṢDQH [#40:x5], MŠPṬ [#36:x12], MŠQL [#87:x2], RZ [#61:x12], ḤKMH [#73:x8] and HWN [#92:x8], while others seem to be somewhat rare in 4Q299ff., though they were very frequent in 4Q415ff., e.g. 'WṬ [#80:x0] and MḤSWR [#19:x1]. Certain words seem to be avoided (intentionally?) in both works, e.g. TWRH [#37:x0]! There are also some words frequent in 4Q299ff. which seem to have been avoided by 4Q415ff. (though it is unclear what was the intention behind this); for other words that are unexpectedly rare or frequent, or somewhat abnormal in their subject matter, cf. 'WR [#58:x6], ḤWŠK [#59:x4], YŚR'L! [#12:x7], but ᶜM [#8:x1], ḤPṢ [#93:x0], TKWN [#63:x2] QṢ [#56:x1] and 'MT [#64:x3].

It is not clear what literary or theological connection the presence here of 4Q415ff.'s very frequent RZ NHYH [#62:x4] suggests; note that the phrase occurs also in 1QS but only once. The presence of the word BRYT [#99, but only once] scarcely suggests dependence on 4Q415ff., since that word was completely absent there also; the total absence of ḤPṢ [#93] in 4Q299ff. would also be hard to explain if that work were related to 4Q415ff., a work where that word is extremely frequent.

One might also note that as in 4Q415ff. there is no trace of interest in cultic purity. Furthermore, does 4Q299ff. have any concern with a (or the) community? Though the work is addressed to groups, none of these are named or described in the terminology of 4Q415ff. or that of those works that clearly refer to the Qumran sect. The eschatological language used here cannot be distinguished from that of 4Q415ff. but possibly deterministic phrases, though not new, are more frequent here, e.g., 'WR [#58], ḤWŠK [#59], RZ [#61]; to the contrary, however, NḤLH [#65:x1] and RṢWN [#67:x1] are rare in this work though very frequent in 4Q415ff.

In view of the substantial extent of the text of each work, we can confidently state that *"The Book of Mysteries"* could not be the same work as 4Q415ff.; even neglecting the differences in linguistic usage and the differences of ideology [e.g. the frequent use of YŚR'L and of ᶜM in 4Q299ff. but not in 4Q415ff.], this is especially clear from the use of the second plural almost without exceptions in 4Q299ff., while in 4Q415ff. only the second singular is found. Some of the similarities of language, of topic, and of social setting, can be neglected as common features of Wisdom writings (e.g., the absence of purity or sacrificial terminology), but others demand at least some type of positive continuity between individual works – but the nature of this continuity, whether ideological or social, is indefinable and probably lost to us in the dark ages of the history of Israelite thought and its schools before the foundation of the Qumran sect.

The clearly sapiential text 4Q525, the next in length of the works we have been examining, should also permit us to reach fairly reliable conclusions about the type of Wisdom represented in it, and about its relations with other Wisdom texts or schools, both those in the Biblical Wisdom books and in the other shorter manuscripts found at Qumran. The lexicographical criteria we have been employing show clearly that 4Q525 had no special and exclusive relationship with 4Q415ff.; as for the blend in it of various forms, some not originally sapiential, and of eschatological (and deterministic[?]) considerations with moral material, such combinations are found not only in 4Q415ff. but also in 4Q299ff. (and probably in many of the shorter works studied above as well).

Is there an increase in the quantity of dualistic material found here over that of the amount of the rarer dualistic material found in 4Q415ff., which might show that this work comes from circles where the dualistic and deterministic material was in process of becoming more abundant? Here however, we risk arguing from silence!

The wisdom instruction in 4Q525 contains little that is "sectually specific" (*ut ita dicam*) whether in its sapiential material (both moral and intellectual) or in that which is eschatological and deterministic. It contains the customary but inexplicable hodge-podge of subjects. It should be noted also that statements made in the second person singular, such as are found constantly in 4Q415ff., alternate here with others addressed to a second person plural, in an alternation that is inexplicable, formally speaking, and which takes place for no obvious reason. As in Ben Sira, 4Q525 has also several passages composed in the first person singular (e.g. among others 23, 1-6); unfortunately at no place is the sectarian title for its author, "*maskîl*", used in the first singular; sometimes indeed (24, 3-5) the figure of Wisdom is intended as the speaker instead. The epithets used for the group addressed, e.g., "seekers after Wisdom," "you who lay hold of *her* laws" etc., have only little in common with the epithets for the virtuous regularly used at Qumran. It is worth noticing that purity language comes only rarely into this composition – it was likewise absent from Biblical Wisdom, from 4Q415ff. and from most of the shorter works we have been studying; the rare mention here of ṬHR[#3:x1] might seem to reflect purity language, but it may be used just metaphorically, not literally.

Lange saw in the presence of frequent allusions at Qumran to purity language a *positive* sign that a work could belong to the Qumran corpus; their *absence*, however, as shown here is capable of many explanations; it need not indicate a non-sectarian origin – it could be that in general such sacrificial and purity considerations were not at home in the Wisdom genre and in its *Formensprache* (cf. STRUGNELL, HARRINGTON & ELGVIN, *Qumran Cave 4*. XXIV, p. 25). The same is true of the absence of the special language used for the community; thus though YḤD [#6:x6] may be used frequently, as in 4Q415ff. it was always (?) used as an adverb, not as the typically Qumranic noun.

As to the lexical preferences of 4Q525, one notes also that 'LHYM[#25:x8] is used twice as often as 'L [#24:x5] – 'LHYM is also not infrequent in Biblical Wisdom texts from Job to Ben Sira. As for the other divine names, YHWH [#26:x0] is completely avoided here as it was also in 4Q415ff.; was this perhaps significant, chronologically or theologically? 'L [#24:x5] is standard in this Wisdom text as it was in 4Q415ff. and in the later Biblical Wisdom texts (but not in Proverbs!); ᶜLYWN [#27], which occurs twice in the fragments of 4Q525, was avoided in 4Q415ff. as it was in *almost* all the other texts we have been examining here – it was rare also in earlier Biblical Wisdom texts, but found more often in Ben Sira and in 11QPsᵃ 154.

A preliminary comparison of the vocabulary of 4Q525 with that of 4Q415ff. shows that 4Q525 contains only a few of the words that were especially characteristic of 4Q415ff. though its vocabulary overlaps considerably with the moral, epistemological and eschatological vocabulary that was commonly used both here and in the other texts we have examined. In several cases where 4Q415ff. used frequently words that were elsewhere somewhat rare in the Qumran corpus, 4Q525 attests these also, whether frequently or not, e.g., ḤWQ [#34:x3], ṢDQ [#41:x3], HTHLK{TMYM}B [#42:x8], NŠMR [#43:x2], ŠWH [#44:x1], ŠḤR [#45:x1], HBYN [#69:x2], HŚKYL [#78:x2], ḤKMH [#73:x4], ḤRPH [#95:x2], ḤYYM [#86:x1], TMYD [#88:x2], the rare GM [#103:x0], Rʿ [#52:x3] and RŠʿ [#53:x2]. Does this suggest a somewhat higher degree of contact (ideological or linguistic) between the two works?

However many other words that are frequent in 4Q415ff. and very characteristic of it are absent in 4Q525; note 'WṬ [#80:x0], MḤSWR [#19:x0], PQWDH [#55:x0], HPṢ [#93:x1], √ MLK [#84:x1], and TWʿBH [#54:x0]. Does this difference indicate a considerable distance in the dates, ideologies or settings of the two works? To the contrary it may be of interest to notice that ʿNWH [#21] is not used in 4Q415ff. (where other synonyms are used) but occurs very frequently in 4Q525; however it is the absence of √ ʿNW [#20-21:x5] in 4Q415ff., not its presence in 4Q525, which needs special explanation against the background of its use in the Wisdom tradition (where we find it everywhere except in Qohelet).

The startling complete absence of TWRH [#37] in 4Q415ff. holds true also for 4Q525 with but one exception (contrast ḤWQ [#34:x3] and MṢWH [#35:x0]); the word has also been absent in most of the other texts we have examined[20].

20. Perhaps one should notice the remark of G.W. NICKELSBURG, *Enochic Wisdom*, pp. 124ff. on the preference in the Enochic writings for revealed Wisdom as an alternative for, or rival to, the Mosaic Torah. One might try to explain this virtual absence of any mention of TWRH and MṢWH in Enochic literature and in Jubilees, because it would have been anachronistic in the light of the pseudepigraphic dates of those works, but such an explanation would not hold for their almost total absence in 4Q415ff.

The rareness of use of NḤLH [#65:x2] may be relevant to the question of the degree of determinism found in this work; some other terms that could relate to dualism and determinism are also very rare in both 4Q415ff. and 4Q525, though others are more frequent in 4Q415ff. than in the other work, e.g. PQWDH [#55], QṢ [#56], √ ŠPṬ [#57], 'MT [#64], PᶜWLH [#66], RṢWN [#67], ḤPṢ [#93], MŠPṬ [#36].

What then can be deduced about the social setting of the Sage in this work? He sits with kings (and priests?) with a crown on his head, and judges, as he did from the days of 4Q415ff. up to the times of Ben Sira. As for any preciser date for this work, nothing can be deduced from the one proverb shared between it and Ben Sira, cf. 4Q525 25,4; in the case of proverbs one can rarely establish any direction of dependence.

Some Conclusions

What significant or suggestive conclusions can be drawn from our preliminary observations on the vocabulary (and sometimes the themes) characteristic of the smaller Wisdom texts? We cannot hope to relate each of them to the others as in one genealogical tree or flow-chart, but some relations can be (at least roughly) observed, a) first by grouping or disassociating the characteristic words of 4Q299ff., 4Q415ff., and 4Q525 (i.e., those frequent in 4Q299ff. but not found in 4Q415ff. and 4Q525, those frequent in 4Q415ff. but not in 4Q299ff. and 4Q525, and those characteristic or frequent in 4Q525 but not in 4Q299ff. and 4Q415ff.); b) by noting the words common to two of these works but not the third; and c) by noting which of the words listed under a) or b) occur also with noteworthy frequency in the other shorter 4Q Wisdom MSS – neglecting in all cases words which occur *only once* as having no certain probative value. (Of course words frequent in all three of our works cannot give us any distinct or useful results). Under a), b), and c) we may have discovered the marks of a school, or at least marks indicating a connection between some of the smaller MSS and one or more of the longer ones. From our synopses of the vocabularies it will also be apparent how large an amount of vocabulary is common to all post exilic wisdom literature and to Ben Sira, and how remote from these vocabularies is that of Qohelet. There are also some other words common to the shorter MSS examined here (e.g., especially 4Q420-1, 4Q424, and 4Q425-6) but not especially characteristic of our three longer works – these we have not examined here, with any precision, but it may be that 4Q420-1, 4Q424, and 4Q425-6 will all turn out to be MSS of the same work.

We can start grouping the MSS by separating those which use only the 2nd person singular (i.e., 4Q415ff. together with 4Q411, 4Q412,

4Q424) from those which use consistently the 2nd person plural (i.e., 4Q299ff. together with 4Q185, 4Q298, 4Q303ff., 4Q413, 4Q420f., 11QPs^a 154). MSS 4Q302, 4Q425-6, and 4Q525 use both persons for no clear reasons.

One might also attempt a grouping of the MSS according to the divine names used in them: 'L [#24] is commonly found in almost all the MSS examined, as it was in 4Q299ff., 4Q415ff. and 4Q525 while 'LWHYM [#25] was frequent in 4Q525 as it was in 4Q185 and 4Q302, but scarcely in 4Q415ff. or 4Q299ff. ᶜLYWN [#27] occurs, though rarely, only in 4Q525 and (frequently) in 11QPs^a 154. As for YHWH [#26] it is found frequently in none of our longer MSS but only in 4Q411 and 11QPs^a 154, while 'DWN [#23] occurs neither in the longer MSS nor in the shorter ones – compare perhaps YHWH in Ps. 154.

Before we turn to the question of the grouping and distribution of characteristic words two further questions of the themes discussed deserve attention. a) In earlier Wisdom literature (but not in Ben Sira) almost no attention is paid to Israel's salvation history and the names belonging to it. This is also true of the works examined here (cf. especially #12-16, save for YŚR'L [#12;x7 in 299ff.!], YᶜQWB [#13:x2 in 4Q215b], and the Exodus [4Q185]). The priestly 4Q415ff. has a different "historical" interest, in Moses, the scoundrelly Korah, and priestly legitimacy. b) Do any of these works show any interest in, or signs of being written in, *a* community, or even in *the* Qumran Community? MŚKYL [#79] which was a title of a functionary at Qumran, not just of a member of the class of wise men or teachers, is probably sufficient to identify 4Q298ff as Qumranic, but none of the other words that we have investigated [YḤD #6, but an adverb in both 4Q415ff. and 4Q525], ḤBR [#5] and RBYM [#11; cf. 4Q412] betray any contacts with Qumran or even a "community consciousness."

In what follows we first note the words characteristic of only one of the 3 larger works, and together with it any other shorter work which also contains the word with some frequency.

a) only in 4Q299ff. (but not 4Q415ff. or 4Q525) do we find names from Israel's history [#12-16]. TKWN [#63; x2] is found in 4Q299ff. and also in 4Q298 [x3], while 'RṢ [#81;x7] recurs not only in 4Q299ff. but also (though rarely) in 4Q215b [x2], 4Q302 [x2], and 4Q426 [x1];

b) only in 4Q525 (but not in the other two longer MSS) we can perhaps note a greater interest in purity and an almost total absence of the word TWRH [#37; only once elsewhere in this corpus, in 11QPs^a 154];

c) in the longest work, 4Q415ff. (but not in 4Q299ff. and 4Q525) we find (as one might expect) the greatest number of these characteristic words, i.e., not 'P [#101] but GM [#103;4Q424], RṢWN [#67], GWRL [#60], ḤPṢ [#93], PᶜWLH [#66], 'WṢR [#89], 'WYLY LB [#90; cf. 4Q425 x1], 'WLT [#91], 'WṬ [#80; cf. 4Q424 x1], RŠ [#22], NDYB [#96], TWᶜBH [#54], ŠQD [#46], and BRYT [#99]. Note the frequent recurrences of GM also in 4Q424 [x2] and of 'WṢR in 4Q426.

As for the words that are both frequent and also shared between two of our three major MSS, notice

a) that there are almost no words frequent in, and common to, 4Q299ff. and 4Q525, without being found also in 4Q415ff.;
b) the words frequent in 4Q299ff. and 4Q415ff. (but not 4Q525) are √ MLK [#84; found also in 4Q426 x2], 'BYWN [#17; found also x2 in 4Q424], GBWRH [#28], KBWD [#31], QDWŠ [#32, found also x2 in 4Q185 and x2 in 11QPsᵃ col. xxvi], QWDŠ [#33, also x2 in 4Q215b], HTBWNN [#70, found also x2 in 4Q426], √ NBṬ [#75], HŚKYL [#78; cf. 4Q420f. x3], ŚKL [#77], BYNH [#71; also x2 in 4Q298, x3 in 4Q420f. and x2 in 4Q426], MŠQL [#87], HWN [#92; also x3 in 4Q424], PŠᶜ [#51; x2 also in 4Q184], PQWDH [#55], ŠPṬ [#57; also x2 in 4Q185], QṢ [#56; x2 in 4Q215b], ML'K [#83], HMŠYL [#85; in 4Q424 x3], 'WR/ḤWŠK [#58-9, more frequently in 4Q299ff. than in 4Q415ff., found also in 4Q184 and 4Q215b, but very rarely in 4Q525], RZ (NHYH) [#61-2; also x1 in 1QS], 'MT [#64; also x4 in 4Q420 f.], √ PTY [#68], 'RṢ [#81; also x2 in 4Q215b, x2 in 4Q302, and x1 in 4Q426];
c) as for the words frequent in and common to 4Q415ff. and 4Q525, note the non-sectarian sense (?) of MŚKYL [#79; also x3 in 4Q420f.], TMYD [#88], ḤRPH [#95], the rare BL [#102], NŠMR [#43], √ ᶜWL [#49-50], ᶜWWN [#48], and NḤLH [#65; also x2 in 4Q426].

It should be noted that the number of words shared between 4Q299ff. and 4Q415ff. is much greater than of those showing any closeness of 4Q525 to 4Q415ff. or of 4Q415ff. to 4Q525; nothing indicates any special closeness of 4Q299ff. to 4Q525. These observations gain in weight in the light of the relative lengths of 4Q415ff., 4Q299ff. and 4Q525.

Does this distance of 4Q525 from the others indicate also a difference in date or rather one of literary genre? Perhaps, if we note that the 2nd singular address in those works is typologically and formally prior to that of the 2nd plural and to the works where singular and plural addressees are mixed together; then 4Q415ff. could be formally the purest (and oldest?) in form, 4Q299ff. would stand next to it, and 4Q525 would be the remotest both in language and *in form*; but which of these three is *chronologically* the first and which the latest can probably not be decided. The clearly Qumranic 4Q298 also has "I" and "You," but so also do 4Q525, 4Q426 (but both of these also with cases of "Thou"), 4Q413, and 4Q185. 4Q415ff. has "Thou" and "I" almost without exception, as also do 4Q411 and 4Q412. If then we place 4Q298 at a lesser distance from 4Q415ff. than was 4Q525, then perhaps 4Q415ff. will be the oldest and 4Q525 the youngest; but the argument is hard to manipulate convincingly.

The further marks of date (e.g., an interest in the Qumran community, a trait which would be important for chronology) will not be of much help, especially for the shorter pieces – these will only rarely be able to be dated; though the divine names used may help us at least to group those fragments – from JEPD onward to the theologians of the 20th century each school stays faithful to the nickname it prefers for its God – yet whether chronological consequences can be drawn from these frequencies is uncertain even in the case of YHWH and ʿLYWN.

Because of what we have called the "ordinariness" of much of the vocabulary of the sapiential works, and the brevity of many surviving texts, it will be of little use to observe which of the shorter works shares the greater number of frequently occurring words with any of our 3 major MSS; a coincidence in one of the smaller MSS with words that (e.g., in longer works like 4Q415ff.) were technical or abnormally frequent (e.g., 'WṬ, MḤSWR, RZ NHYH, ḤPṢ, NḤLH or ŠQD) might point to some ideological or chronological connection, but what that was escapes us. However, from our studies of the contents of each vocabulary, firmer conclusions about the thought and interests of some of these works can occasionally be drawn with some greater confidence.

Harvard University					John STRUGNELL
The Divinity School
45 Francis Avenue
Cambridge, MA 02138
USA

Synopsis of Sapiential Vocabulary

	4Q	184	185	215b	298	299ff.	302	303ff.	411	412	413	420f.	424	425	426	525	11Q	Ps^a	xxvi
		263	162	122	110	1406	130	59	50	73	47	235	250	74	123	654		154 186	74
							Purity and Impurity												
#1 HT' (2:60)	"	1															"	"	
#2 TM' (1:128)	"	1															"	"	
#3 √THR (1:175)	"	1		1										?		1	"	"	
#4 NDH (2:61)	"															1	"	"	
							The Community												
#5 ḤBR (1:10)	"	1															"	"	1
#6 YḤD (0:198)	"	1										1				6	"	"	1
(Here usually adverbial)																			
#7 'DH (0:138)	"					1											"	"	
#8 'M (2:231)	"	1				1											"	"	1
#9 'ŚH (2:133)	"									2			1				"	"	
#10 QHL (0:44)	"									2							"	"	
#11 RB(YM) (0:66)	"		1			1											"	"	1
#12 YŚR'L (0:374)	"		1	2		7										1	"	"	2
#13 Y'QWB (0:59)	"						1										"	"	1
#14 ṢYWN (0:22)	"																"	"	1
#15 YRWŠLYM (0:32)	"														1		"	"	1
#16 YṢḤQ ((0:18)	"		1														"	"	

THE SMALLER HEBREW WISDOM TEXTS FOUND AT QUMRAN

	4Q	184 263	185 162	215b 122	298 110	299ff. 1606	302 130	303ff. 59	411 50	412 73	413 47	420f. 235	424 250	425 74	426 123	525 654	11Q	Ps^a	154 186	xxvi 74
Descriptions of the Group, etc																				
#17 'BYWN (6:28)	"																"	"		
#18 DL (1:6)	"																"	"		
#19 MḤSWR (28:2[!])	"	1															"	"		
#20 'NW / 'NY (0:31)	"					1						1	1			1	"	"	1	
#21 'NWH (0:17)	"																"	"		
#22 RWŠ (11:5)	"				1								1			4	"	"		
Divine Names, Attributes, etc																				
#23 'DWN(Y) (2:70)	"	?															"	"	1	
#24 'L (26:404)	"	1	3	2	1	5	2	1				3		1	3	5	"	"		1
#25 'LHYM (1:367)	"		1	1	1		5									8	"	"	3	
#26 YHWH (0:174)	"																"	"	4	
#27 'LYWN (0:30)	"			1		6			5							2	"	"	1	1
#28 GBWRH (5:116)	"		1	1		7											"	"	1	
#29 HDR (6:44)	"		1			1										4	"	"		
#30 ḤSD (3:110)	"		3	1	1	4		1			1					1	"	"	1	1
#31 KBWD (18:308)	"					3									1	1	"	"	1	2
#32 QDWŠ (8:114)	"		2			7											"	"		
#33 QWDŠ (13:419)	"			2			1					1		1			"	"	1	
The Law																				
#34 ḤWQ (12:150)	"	2		1		4						1	1	1		3	"	"	1	
#35 MṢWH (3:48)	"	1				1						3	5		1		"	"		
#36 MŠPṬ(?)(30:394)	"	1	1		1	12(!)				1						2	"	"		1
#37 TWRH (0:140)	"															1	"	"	1	

									Good and Bad Acts											
	4Q	184 263	185 162	215b 122	298 110	299ff. 1606	302 130	303ff. 59	411 50	412 73	413 47	420f. 235	424 250	425 74	426 123	525 654	11Q	Ps^a	154 186	xxvi 74
#38 TWB (14:96)	"		4			3	3		1			1			2	2	"	"		1
#39 √YŠR (0:45)	"	1			1		1					1	2		2	1	"	"		
#40 ṢDQH (3:140)	"			5	1	5						2					"	"		1
#41 ṢDQ (23:182)	"	4			2	7				3		5	1	1		3	"	"		
#42 HTHLK B etc. (78:139)	"					2	1					1	1			8	"	"		1
#43 NŠMR (8:10)	"					1										2	"	"		
#44 ŠWH (10:7)	"	1														1	"	"		
#45 ŠḤR (11:20)	"				2											1	"	"		
#46 ŠQD (10:3)	"							1	1								"	"		
#47 NʿWH (3:18)	"			1						1						3	"	"		
#48 ʿWWN (4:12)	"					1						1				2	"	"		
#49 ʿWLH (10:58)	"	1				3							1	2	1	1	"	"		
#50 ʿWL (5:60)	"	2	1			3					1			1		1	"	"	1	
#51 PŠʿ (2:74)	"		1			8		1				2				3	"	"	1	
#52 Rʿ (4:120)	"	1		1		1										2	"	"		
#53 RŠʿ (8:26)	"																"	"		
#54 TWʿBH (3:43)	"																"	"		

THE SMALLER HEBREW WISDOM TEXTS FOUND AT QUMRAN

4Q	184	185	215b	298	299ff.	302	303ff	411	412	413	420f.	424	425	426	525	11Q	Ps^a	154	xxvi
	263	162	122	110	1606	130	59	50	73	47	235	250	74	123	654			186	74

Eschatological and Deterministic Language

	184	185	215b	298	299ff.	302	303ff	411	412	413	420f.	424	425	426	525	11Q	Ps^a	154	xxvi
#55 PQWDH (16:20)																"	"		
#56 QṢ (17:148)		2			2?	1										"	"		
#57 √ŠPṬ (9:91)		1			1											"	"		
#58 'WR (3:169)	1		2		4		1									"	"		
#59 HWŠK (0:76)	1				6		1									"	"		
#60 GWRL (2:91)			2		4											"	"		
#61 RZ (13:59)					12						1					"	"		
#62 RZ NHYH (32:4)				3	4									1	1	"	"		
#63 TKWN (0:52)				1	2									2	1	"	"		
#64 'MT (?) (41:228)			1		3			1			4		1		1	"	"	2	
#65 NḤLH (35:47)	1				1					1				1	2	"	"		
#66 P'WLH (9:17)			1							1						"	"		
#67 RṢWN (17:101)		1		1	1				1	1		1				"	"		
#68 PTY (2:27)		1(?)			2											"	"	1	

The Vocabulary of Knowledge, etc.

	184	185	215b	298	299ff.	302	303ff	411	412	413	420f.	424	425	426	525	11Q	Ps^a	154	xxvi
#69 HBYN (25:54)				2	1	1	1			1	1	1			2	"	"		1
#70 HTBWNN (12:22)				1	2					1	3	1		2		"	"	1	
#71 BYNH (15:64)				2	8				1					2		"	"		
#72 MBWNH (6:0)																"	"		
#73 HKMH (10:39)					8			1			2	3			4	"	"	1	
#74 MWSR (4:15)					1										1	"	"		
#75 √NBṬ (7:25)				1	3								1		1	"	"		
#76 'RMH (0:18)																"	"		
#77 ŚKL (noun) (8:45)			1		3		1				1	1	1(?)	1	2	"	"	1	
#78 HŚKYL (10:71)			1		1						3					"	"		
#79 MŚKYL (6:24)			1								3					"	"		
#80 'WT (?) (15:1)												1				"	"		

Miscellanea

4Q	184/263	185/162	215b/122	298/110	299ff/1606	302/130	303ff/59	411/50	412/73	413/47	420f./235	424/250	425/74	426/123	525/654	11Q	Ps^a	154/186	xxvi/74
#81 'RŠ (2:92)		1	2		7									1	1	"	"		1
#82 BHN (3:26)		1	1													"	"		
#83 ML'K (2:92)		1	1													"	"		1
#84 √MLK (4:218)					3		1									"	"		
#85 ḤMŠYL (18:7)				1	7							3	1(?)	2	1	"	"		1
#86 ḤYYM (18:56)					3						1	1	1			"	"		
#87 MŠQL (7:14)					1						1					"	"		
#88 TMYD (11:37)				1	2									2	2	"	"		1
#89 WṢR (3:11)																"	"		
#90 'WYLY LB (4:1)					1	1									1	"	"		
#91 'WLT (6:5)												3	1		1	"	"	1	1
#92 ḤWN (17:84)					8						1	1			1	"	"	1	1
#93 ḤPṢ (22:23)																"	"		
#94 ḤML (4:1)																"	"		
#95 ḤRPH (10:13)															2	"	"		
#96 NDYB (6:11)																"	"		
#97 NŚY' (1:45)					1											"	"		
#98 TBW'H (11:8)					1(?)					1	1(?)					"	"		
#99 BRYT (5:239)					2							2		2	2	"	"		
#100 'Z (28:26)						x		x	x	x	x		x	x	x	"	"	x	
#101 'P (2:40)						x		x	x	x	x	x	x	x	x	"	"		
#102 BL (1:25)						x										"	"		
#103 GM (18:66)							x							x	x	"	"		
#104 "Thou"	?				?											"	"		
#105 "You"		x		x	x											"	"		
#106 "I"		x		x	?											"	"		
#107 "We"											x					"	"		
#108 'L YQTL 'YŠ					x						x	x	x	x	x	"	"	x	

THE LANGUAGE OF THE QUMRAN SAPIENTIAL WORKS

According to B.Z. Wacholder and M.G. Abegg, the Hebrew of the sapiential works of Qumran is by and large classic, though with an admixture of Aramaic[1]. A. Lange suggests that, on linguistic grounds, the *terminus post quem* of these texts is the end of the 3rd and the beginning of the 2nd century B.C[2]. The aim of this article is to test this thesis. The following texts have been thoroughly scrutinized:

1Q26 (1QInstruction)
1Q27 (1QMysteries)
4Q184 (4QWiles of the Wicked Woman)
4Q185 (4QSapiential Work)
4Q299-301 (4QMysteries[a.b.c.])
4Q392 (4QWorks of God)
4Q410 (4QSapiential Work / 4QVision and Its Interpretation)
4Q412 (4QSapiential Work / 4QSapiential-Didactic Work A)
4Q413 (4QSapiential Work / 4QComposition concerning Divine Providence)
4Q415 (4QSapiential Work II[b] / 4QInstruction[a])
4Q416 (4QSapiential Work I[b] / 4QInstruction[b])
4Q417 (4QSapiential Work I[c] / 4QInstruction[c])
4Q418 (4QSapiential Work I[a] / 4QInstruction[d])
4Q419 (4QSapiential Work I[d] / 4QSapiential Work B)
4Q420 (4QSapiential Work IV[a] / 4QWays of Righteousness[a])
4Q421 (4QSapiential Work IV[b] / 4QWays of Righteousness[b])
4Q423 (4QSapiential Work V / 4QInstruction[g])
4Q424 (4QSapiential Work II / 4QSapiential Text)
4Q425 (4QSapiential Work / 4QSapiential-Didactic Work B)
4Q426 (4QSapiential Work II[b] / 4QSapiential-Hymnic Work A)
4Q525 (4QBeatitudes)

1Q26; 4Q415-418; 4Q423 are manuscripts of Sapiential Work A, to which Strugnell and Harrington have given the title *mûsār l[e]mēbîn*, whereas 1Q27 and 4Q299-301 are what remains of the *Book of Mysteries*[3]. Mostly the fragments of these manuscripts are too small and do not contain sufficient text material to identify clauses, let alone sentences, for morphosyntactical and syntactical analysis. Even 4Q299 3a II-b,

---

1. B.Z. WACHOLDER & M.G. ABEGG, *Preliminary Edition*, p. xiv.
2. A. LANGE, *Weisheit und Prädestination*, pp. 47 and 94; cf. for 4Q299-301: ID., *Physiognomie oder Gotteslob*, p. 283: possibly before the *Zwei-Geister-Lehre*, which originated about the end of the 2nd century B.C.
3. A. LANGE, *In Diskussion mit dem Tempel*, pp. 127-134.

which offers more than just scraps of words is too fragmentary for a syntactical analysis. Due to this situation the linguistic study of these texts can only be fragmentary.

I. ORTHOGRAPHY AND PHONETICS

1. Orthography of Consonants

ישחק: 4Q185 1-2 ii 4. In BH this orthography of the name Isaac is limited to Jer 33,26; Amos 7,9.16; Ps 105,9, which are not necessarily late texts.

2. Orthography of Vowels

The examples are classified according to the masoretic vowels.

2.1. Ḥolem

2.1.1. Plene

אדרוש: 4Q416 2 iii 13; תדרוש: 4Q417 28,1; ידרוש: 4Q418 102,4; 126 ii 12; 4Q424 3,1; אסוף (impv.): 4Q423 5,6; אוהב: 4Q416 4,1; 4Q418 122 I 3; 4Q426 4,2; 4Q525 5,12; אוסף (noun): 4Q525 24 ii 7; אורחותיה: 4Q184 1,9 vs. ארחותיך: 4Q424 1,7; אופל: 4Q525 15,1; אורך: 4Q418 137,4; 4Q426 1 i 1; אלוהים: 4Q392 1,3; 4Q525 1,1; 5,8.12; 19,3; 21,2; בור (BH בֹּר): 4Q525 2 ii+3, 3; דובר: 4Q424 3,5; דורש: 4Q301 2b,4; 4Q252 2 ii 2; 4Q417 2 i 6; 4Q418 81,18; 88,6; 126 ii 11; etc.; דרוש (impv.): 4Q416 2 iii 14; 4Q418 81,7; הולכי (part.): 4Q300 8,4; 4Q525 5,10; 20,2; זורה: 4Q424 3,4; חוזק (noun): 4Q301 2a+b,3; חום: 4Q299 5,3; חוקרי (part.): 4Q301 1,2; 2b,1; חושך: 1Q27 i 5; 4Q184 1,4.6; 4Q299 5,2; 6 ii 10; 30,3; 4Q419 8 ii 5 vs. חשך: 4Q392 1,4.6; יודעיכה: 4Q525 14 ii 15; יושבין: 4Q299 97, 1; יותר: 1Q27 ii 3; יחמול: 4Q418 101 ii 4; יטושנה: 4Q525 2 ii+3,5; יכשול: 4Q415 11,9; ימשול: 4Q424 3,6; יעמוד: 4Q417 1 i 16; יעקוב: 4Q418 8,12; יצורו: 4Q525 5,9; ישבות (impf. שבת): 4Q418 126 ii 1; ישכון: 4Q426 11,2; ישמור: 4Q421 4,1; ישפוט: 4Q299 81,2; 4Q416 1, 10 vs. ישפט: 4Q425 6,3; כוהניו: 4Q419 1,3; 4Q525 4,3; כופלים: 4Q392 1,7; לדרוש: 4Q424 3,4; לוא: 1Q27 i 3.4.8.9.11; ii 5.6.8; 4Q299 1,3; 2,2; 3a ii 4.6; 7,5; 8,5; 21,3; 30,4; passim; vs. לא: 4Q300 1b,2.3.4; 8,7; 9,1; 10,3; 4Q392 1,2; לנטור: 4Q300 7,2; לנקום: 4Q299 53,7; לסגור: 4Q418 126 ii 7; לקרוא: 4Q421 8,2; לשונו[ת: 4Q299 66,1; לשפוך: 4Q525 13,3; מושל: 4Q416 2 i 19; 4Q417 1 i 13; 4Q421 1a ii-b,6; 4Q423 5,4; מצוות: 4Q426 1 i 2 (cf. Neh 9,14); נחל (part.): 4Q184 1,8.11; 4Q147 1 i 11; 4Q148 55,6; 4Q525 13,5; נוטר: 4Q299 7,5; נוקם (part.):4Q300 7,2; נושה: 4Q417 1 ii 6.7; עבודה: 4Q299 6 i 3; 68,3; 88,1; 4Q300 1a i 4; 4Q301 1,3; etc. cf. 1-2 Chron, passim; עבור (impv.): 4Q417 1 i 2; עוברי: 4Q299 59,3;

עווֹן: 4Q412 1,3; 4Q418 7,8; 102,5; 4Q525 19,5 vs. עוֹן: 4Q525 2 ii+3,5(?); 14 ii 2; עוֹזרי: 4Q299 59,4; עוֹל (yoke): 4Q421 1a ii-b, 10; עוֹמר: 4Q415 11,2; עוֹפרת: 4Q424 1,5; עוֹרף: 4Q301,14; עוֹשי/עוֹשה/עוֹשׁה: 4Q299 3a ii-b 7.8.11; 59,5; עמוֹק: 4Q300 6,6; פקוֹד (impv.): 4Q423 5,5.6; צרוֹף(impv.): 4Q416 2 iii 13; קוֹדקוֹד: 4Q301 1,4; קוֹדש(ים): 4Q421 13,4; 4Q423 9,3; ראוֹש: 4Q418 126 ii 7; רוֹאש: 4Q525 14 ii 3; רוֹב: 4Q184 1,4; 4Q299 8,6; 4Q301 3a-b,4; 4Q416 2 iii 13; 4Q418 126 ii 9; etc.; רוֹדפי: 4Q299 8,7; 4Q424 3,2; ריאשוֹנים: 4Q413 1-2,4; שוֹכן: 4Q525 24 ii 5; שוֹמעת: 4Q424 3,5; שוֹפט(ים): 4Q299 10,5.7; 4Q423 6,3; 4Q424 3,1; שלוֹש: 4Q412 2,3; תוֹאר: 4Q525 14 i 12; תוֹם (inf. תמם): 1Q27 i 6; 4Q416 3,3; 4Q418 113,1; תוֹמכי (part.): 1Q27 i 7; 4Q299 3a ii-b 9; 6 ii 4; 43,2; 4Q300 8,5; 4Q301 1,2; תחשוֹב: 4Q417 2 ii 15; תעבוֹר: 4Q410 1,2; תעזוֹב: 4Q418 33,2; 183,2; תעזוֹר: 4Q418 178,3; תערוֹב: 4Q418 103 ii 6; תעשוֹק: 4Q418 146,1; תשבוֹת: 4Q417 20,3; תשפוֹך: 4Q525 14 ii 23; תשקוֹט: 4Q416 3,3; יתמוֹכו: 4Q525 2 ii+3,1; מואדה (BH מְאֹד): 4Q415 11,11; 4Q417 3,3; 4Q418 81,5; 4Q525 14 ii 24.26 vs. מאדה: 4Q416 2 ii 16; מאד: 4Q418 123 ii 7

2.1.2. Defective

אבתיו: 4Q185 1-2 ii 14; אזן: 4Q424 3,5; הדות: 4Q412 1,8 (הודות in other Qumran texts)[4]; יבא: 4Q421 12,3; יפקד: 4Q418 123 ii 7; יקפץ: 4Q417 1 i 24 vs. יקפוֹץ: 4Q416 2 ii 2; 4Q417 1 ii 4; 4Q418 8,1; 88,5; 4Q419 8 ii 7; יתם (impf. תמם): 1Q27 i 6; כח: 4Q185 1-2 i 7 vs. כוֹח: 4Q299 21,3; 4Q418 159 ii 3; 4Q423 1 ii 9; 2,3 (cf. Dan 11,6); כשר: 4Q417 1 i 2 vs. כוֹשר: 4Q417 2 i 11; לשן: 4Q299 1,2 vs. לשוֹן: 1Q27 i 10; פעלי און: 4Q418 126 ii 6 (sticks to the biblical orthography); רוֹחתיו: 4Q185 1-2 i 9; שמרי (part.): 4Q417 2 i 16; תעבות: 4Q418 81,2 vs. תוֹעבה in 4Q418 102,5 and BH, with one exception, viz. in Jer 44,4

2.2. *Qameṣ ḥaṭuf*

2.2.1. Plene

אוֹננו/יו: 4Q299 8,6; 4Q413 1-2,3; 4Q423 5,2 vs. אזנים/אוֹזנכה: 4Q418 184,2; 4Q419 6,1; אוֹרחוֹת: 4Q525 15,8; גוֹפרית: 4Q525 15,6; דוֹרשם(impv.+suff.): 4Q418 103 ii 4; עוֹבדם (impv.+suff.): 4Q416 2 iii 17; פוֹעלוֹת: 4Q413 1-2,1; קוֹדקוֹד: 4Q301 1,4; קוֹדשוֹ/כה: 4Q299 53,2; 55,1.5; 4Q301 3a-b,6; 4Q415 1 ii 3; 4Q416 2 ii 6; etc.; גוֹעלוֹ (infin.): 4Q413 1-2,2; שוֹמעכה: 4Q525 14 ii 22; (ב)שוֹפטם: 4Q299 56,2; שוֹרשי: 4Q301 2b,1; 4Q416 2 iii 14; 4Q418 55,9 vs. שרש: 4Q418 278,3; כוֹל: 1Q26,2.7.9; 27 i 1.7.8.9; ii 5.7.10.11; 4Q299 1,5; 3a ii 3.8.10.11.15; 6 I 8.12. etc. vs. כל: 4Q299 6 i 9; 36,1; 67,4; 4Q421 9,3; 4Q423 1 I 5; 2,1.5.6; 4,2; 5,4.5

---

4. Probably a scribal error for הוֹדוֹת according to *4QWays of Righteousness*, p. 165.

2.2.2. Defective

חכמה: 4Q418 8,13; 81,15.19; 87,3; 102,3; 4Q424 3,6.7 vs. חוכמה[5]:
1Q27 i 3; 4Q299 17 i 2; 4Q300 1b,4; 4Q413 1-2,1; 4Q418 139,2;
4Q525 1,1.2; 23,6; etc.; לעבדו ולשמרו: 4Q423 2,2

2.3. Qibbuṣ

2.3.1. Plene

חוקים: 4Q299 61,2; 4Q415 2 ii 3; 4Q416 2 ii 8; 4Q525 2 ii+3 1 vs.
חקים: 4Q418 8,8; לאומים: 1Q27 i 9; סגולה: 4Q299 60,3; אור[ים ותומים:
פקודה: (גְּבוּלֹתֶיךָ); and גְּבֻלֹתֶיךָ 4Q299 78,2 (MT) גבולותיה]: 4Q299 69,2;
4Q416 1,9; 7,2; 4Q417 2 i 7.14; 4Q418 43,5; 68 2.3; 113,2 vs. פקדה:
4Q417 1 i 8

2.3.2. Defective

אחזה: 4Q418 55,12; גברתו: 4Q299 6 i 7 vs. גבורתו/גבורה: 4Q299 6 i 16;
33,4; 53,6; 4Q392 3,3; 4Q417 2 i 13; כלם: 4Q300 11,2; מלמדי
(part.pu.): 4Q300 1b,1; פעלה: 4Q417 2 i 14; 4Q418 69 ii 13; 137,5;
4Q424 3,1 vs. פעולה 4Q418 107,4; 108,2; 130,2; 4Q426 1 ii 4; תבאות:
4Q299 6 ii 14 vs. תבואה in BH

2.4. Ḥireq

ריאשונים: 4Q413 1-2,4; חינם: 4Q421 11,3 vs חנם: 4Q421 12,4

2.5. Ṣere

שית (Seth): 4Q417 2 i 15; עיד: 4Q417 2 i 17

3. Double *yod*

4Q424 2,2: מעיין, "spring"

4. *Yod > aleph*

גואים: 4Q299 10,3

5. *Aleph > he*

4Q417 1 i 23 תשה: a ל"ה instead of a ל"א(תשא); this instance has to be added to the four cases listed in Qimron §100.7[6].

---

5. This plene orthography occurs 13 times in the non-biblical Dead Sea Scrolls, according to E. QIMRON, *Divine Providence*, p. 192; in his opinion the more frequently used defective spelling reflects another pattern, e.g. *hikma* or *hakma*.
6. E. QIMRON, *Hebrew*. Cf. A. CAQUOT, *Sagesse*, p. 9.

6. Redundant *aleph*

כיא: 4Q184 1,9; 4Q299 3a ii-b,6; 6 ii 6; 20,1; 53,5; 54,3; 55,3; 72,3; 4Q417 1 i 10; 4Q421 11,4 vs. כי: 4Q299 3a ii-b,14; 6 ii 7; 42,2; 4Q300 1b,2.3.4; 4Q301 5,3; 4Q415 9,7; 4Q416 2 ii 7

לפיא: 4Q415 11,4 (following after כי)

מיא: 4Q301 2b,3.4

ראש, "poor": 4Q416 2 iii 2; cf. 2 Sam 12,1; Prov 13,23, etc. vs. רש in lines 12.19; 4Q417 1 i 10; 4Q418 254,3 and in 1 Sam 18,23; Prov 22,7, etc. In 4Q416 2 iii 11; 4Q418 9,11; 43,1 ראש is the equivalent of biblical ריש, "poverty"; cf. Prov 30,8.

7. Dropt *aleph*

מוזנים: 4Q418 127,6; 167,2; cf. 1QIsa^a 40,12.15 (in vs. 15 מזנים); vs. מאזנים: 4Q418 207,4

רישון: 4Q421 1a i 4

יוכל: 4Q421 12,2

8. Dropt *he*

לגיש: 4Q419 1,6; *he* of the infinitive hi. is omitted; cf. Qimron §310.145.

9. Discussion

According to Lichtenberger, 4Q185 shows a striking use of defective spelling and our study of the text confirms his statement[7].

Qimron asserts that in the Tiberian tradition a *šwa* before a guttural was pronounced like the vowel of the guttural. This pronunciation is also reflected in the spelling of 4Q413 1-2,1 פּוֹעֲלוֹת instead of פְּעֻלּוֹת, to be pronounced as *puʿullôt*[8]. However, the possibility that this form is a plural cstr. st. of the noun פּוֹעַל (Masoretic פֹּעַל) should not be excluded, even if in BH this plural is פָּעֳלֵי.

4Q525 belongs to the group of texts which show a relatively full orthography and which, according to Tov, have been written at Qumran[9]. Such words as לוא, כול and -כמה are always written *plene*, whereas -כה is used in practically all instances. Also a perusal of the above list will

---

7. H. LICHTENBERGER, *Weisheitliche Mahnrede*, p. 161.
8. Cf. E. QIMRON, *Divine Providence*, pp. 191 and 198-202. A. CAQUOT, *Sagesse*, p. 5: "*pwʿlwt* est une graphie qoumrânienne pour le classique *pᵉʿallôt* (sic!) (Psaumes 17,4)".
9. Cf. E. TOV, *Orthography*.

show the same preference for full spelling[10]. Strange exceptions are תטיב and יטיב for תיטיב and ייטיב in 9,6 and הבן for הבין in 6 ii 2 (cf. PUECH, *Qumrân grotte 4. XVIII*, p. 119). The same can be said about Sapiential Work A (1Q26; 4Q415-418; 4Q423), which has an overwhelming majority of *plene* spellings but is not always consistent in the orthography of a word, e.g. חוקים (4Q415 2 ii 3; 4Q416 2 ii 8) vs. חקים (4Q418 8,8), or יקפוץ (4Q416 2 ii 2; 4Q417 1 ii 4; 4Q418 8,1; 88,5) vs. יקפץ (4Q417 1 i 24). The *Book of Mysteries* shows the same picture. Striking inconsistencies are לשן (4Q299 1,2) vs. לשון (1Q27 i 10), גברתו (4Q299 6 i 7) vs. גבורתו/גבורה (4Q299 6 i 16; 33,4; 53,6). Notice also the difference between לוא in 1Q27; 4Q299 and לא in 4Q300 and the defective spelling of *qibbuṣ* in כלם and מלמדי in 4Q300. Also 4Q425 shows a tendency towards plene writing (cf. ELGVIN, *4QWays of Righteousness*, p. 204), but the preserved text is too limited and so we cannot draw far-reaching conclusions from it. Full orthography is practically the rule in 4Q185; 413; 419; 426; also 4Q421 has a majority of un-masoretic *plene* spellings. 4Q424 has more defective spelling and 4Q392 even more so. Sometimes manuscripts of the same work seem to have slightly different orthographic characteristics.

Orthographic differences do not necessarily betray a different date, for they can be bound to the copyist's personal style. In sum, it is practically impossible to prove on account of orthography that the sapiential works were written before the major Essenian writings and outside Qumran. The manuscripts with a somewhat more defective spelling come close to Qohelet's orthography, which represents a somewhat middle stage in the development of the *plene* writing[11].

II. MORPHOLOGY

1. Pronouns

1.1. *Personal Pronouns*

1.1.1. Separate Pronouns

אני: 1Q26,8

הואה: 4Q299 3a ii-b,12; 65,2; 4Q301 3,4.5.7; 4,4; 6,3; 4Q416 1,16; 4Q417 1 i 5.6; etc.

הוא: 4Q299 8,1.3.8; 23,2; 32,2; 46,3; 79,5; 86,3; 4Q300 6,4; 9,3; 4Q301 2b,2; 4Q392 1,4; 4Q416 1,14; *passim*

---

10. J.C.R. DE ROO, *Qumran Sectarian Document*, p. 346; E. PUECH, in *Qumrân grotte 4. XVIII*, p. 119.
11. Cf. A. SCHOORS, *The Preacher*, pp. 22-33.

היאה: 4Q184 1,8; 4Q299 24,2; 4Q415 9,7; 4Q417 3,5; 4Q421 11,4
היא: 4Q300 1b,4

1.1.2. Pronominal Suffixes
2nd m. sg. כה-: 1Q26,2.4.5.6.7.8; 4Q299 62,4; 4Q410 1,3.4; 4Q412 1,5; 4Q415 1 ii 3
ך-: 4Q416 2 IV 4.7; 6,1; 4Q418 91,1; 95,2
2nd m. pl. כם-: 1Q27 i 5; 4Q299 6 ii 2; 53,3.11; 71,2; 4Q300 1b,2.4; 4Q301 2,2.4; etc.
כמה-: 1Q27 i 8; 4Q300 1b,2; 4Q301 2b,1; 4Q413 1-2,1; 4Q417 2 i 20; etc.
3rd m. sg. הו-: 4Q416 2 ii 18
והי-: cf. Qimron §322.144; this suffix is not found in the texts under discussion.
3rd m. sg. energ. נו-: 1Q27 i 10
3rd m. pl. מה-: 1Q27 i 3.4.7.9; 4Q392 1,8; 4Q415 9,10; 4Q416 1,9; 2 iii 17; 4Q420 2,9; 4Q421 1a ii 8
המה-: 1Q27 i 4; 4Q416 1,8; 2 iii 18; 4,2; 4Q417 1 i 12; 4Q421 13,1
הם-: 4Q299 6 i 6.14; 21,2; 55,6; 79,6; 4Q416 18,4; 4Q417 2 i 7; 4Q421 1a ii 7
ם-: 4Q299 6 i 13; 56,2; 4Q416 2,9; 4Q418 69,13; 4Q419 1,12; 4,2; 8 ii 8

1.1.3. Discussion
In 4Q299 the pronouns and pronominal suffixes almost always appear in the short form; exceptions are 24,2 היאה and 65,2 הואה (cf. *Mysteries*, p. 33). According to L.H. Schiffman (*ibid.*), "though forms similar to those of 𝔐 are in the majority, nevertheless, the two long forms of the pronoun, the case of the long pronominal suffix, spellings like חוכמה, and the tendency towards *scriptio plena* warrant the inclusion of the manuscript [4Q299] within the orthographic system of Qumran Hebrew". As for 4Q300, Schiffman concludes that "the text as preserved does not exhibit features of Qumran orthography (except in the case of כסלכמה frg. 1b,2). However, certain lexical usages are familiar from the sectarian corpus." (*Mysteries*, p. 99). Here again in other works, e.g. Sapiential Work A, the spelling of the pronouns and suffixes (with or without final ה) is not consistent and it does not indicate a relatively older date for the sapiential works.

For the suffixes ending in -מה, cf. the Samaritan pronunciation of the suffixes (BARTHÉLEMY and MILIK, *Qumran Cave I*, p. 104).

1.2. Demonstrative pronouns

F.sg. זות: 4Q420 1a ii-b,1. This spelling seems not to occur in BH, except for a few *Qere*s, and in MH (where זו is currently used) or Qumran. It must be a scribal error.

1.3. Interrogative pronouns

מהיא (4Q299 6 ii 8). This contraction is unknown in BH but is used in Talmudic Aramaic (cf. Jastrow, p. 736).

1.4. Relative pronoun

אשר is fully in use as a relative pronoun: e.g. 4Q419 1,2.4.9; 4Q420 2,6; 4Q421 1a ii-b,8; 6,3; 4Q423 5,2.10; 4Q424 3,5; -ש does not occur. הַ as relative particle in 4Q392 1,8: אנחנו בשר הלוא נשכיל כמה, "we are flesh, which does not understand how many..." (transl. F. García Martínez). Biblical attestations are practically limited to younger texts: Josh 10,24; Dan 8,1; Ezra 8,25; Neh 13,23 (conj.); 1 Chron 26,28; 29,17; 2 Chron 29,36. I have no knowledge of this usage in other Qumran texts.

1.5. Indefinite pronouns

מה אשר: 1Q27 1 i 4; cf. מה־ש in Qoh 1,9; 3,15.22; 6,10; 7,24; 8,7; 10,14 and frequently in the Mishna; to be identified with Aramaic מה די (Dan 2,20.28.29.45; Ezra 7,18; CIS II 199,6-7; 3913, I 4)[12].

2. Nouns

2.1. Formation of Nouns

Qittûl: תכון (1Q27 i 6; 4Q299 6 ii 16; 20,1.2)

2.2. Gender

In 4Q417 2 i 9 ממשלת occurs vs. 4Q418 43,7 ממשל in an identical context.

רוח is masculine in 4Q416 1,12; it is also masculine in Qoh 1,6; 3,19.

2.3. Plural

נצני, pl. cstr. of נץ (4Q525 2 iii 5); cf. Cant 2,12.

2.4. Nominal suffixes

4Q424 1,10 שפתו for שפתיו; 1Q27 1 i 5; 4Q392 1,5.9: מפנו/לפנו; according to Qimron §322.141, there are about 30 cases in Qumran literature and this spelling shows that the suffixes יו- and ו- were pronounced alike (ō or ū).

---

12. Cf. A. SCHOORS, *The Preacher*, pp. 59-60.

3. Verbs

3.1. *Verbal Stems*

3.1.1. Nifal

1Q27 1 i 5 בהסגור ni.inf. In BH הקטול is the inf.abs., but in this text the preposition shows that it is an inf. cstr. Qimron does not mention this form.

3.1.1. Piel

4Q525 5,12 יסיבלו could be pi. of the root סבל written *plene*, as is found sometimes in MH (PUECH, *Qumrân grotte 4. XVIII*, p. 134).

3.2. *Tenses and Modi*

3.2.1. Perfect or Suffix-conjugation

2nd m. sg. -תה: 1Q26,7; 4Q299 71,3; 4Q418 81,19; 83,1; 88,7.8; 103 ii 7; 127 3.4; etc.

2nd m. pl. -תם: 4Q299 70,2; 4Q300 1b,1.2.3; 4Q418 69,6; 162,2

-תמה: 4Q418 55,8

Again the frequency of endings with or without final ה is too scanty to alter the results of the orthographic analysis presented above.

3.2.2. Imperfect or Prefix-conjugation

3rd m. pl.: יתמוכו (4Q525 2 ii+3,1) vs. ידרשו (4Q418 103 ii 5; 131,3)

3rd f. pl.: ישכילו (4Q184 1,13); -ו instead of -נה: according to Qimron §310.128, there are only three cases of the ending -נה in Qumran literature. In MH the form has completely disappeared, but the process of replacing the ending -נה by -ו began already in BH[13].

יחפץ (1Q27 1 i 11) suggests the vocalization יֶחְפָּץ which in BH is used in pausa (with *qames*) versus יַחְפֹּץ.

יבטוח (4Q418 55,4), if correctly read, departs from Masoretic Hebrew, where the imperfect form of roots ending in laryngals has *pataḥ*.

3.2.3. Jussive

Cf. also 3.5.5 on the ל"ה verbs. In hi. the jussive form יַקְטֵל is sometimes used: 4Q424 1,6 אל תפקד; 10 אל תמשל.

3.2.4. Imperative

4Q416 2 iii 15: כבוד impv. qal of כָּבֵד meaning "to honour"? = 4Q418 9,17 כבד, probably pi.[14].

---

13. Cf. E.Y. KUTSCHER, *History*, §59.
14. D.J.A. CLINES, *Dictionary* IV, p. 349.

4Q525 14 ii 18: שמעה, impv. with paragogic -āh
4Q418 81,17 הוסף; 18 הוצא; 4Q525 14 ii 19 הפק; 20 הוצא: impv. hi. as in BH הַקְטֵל. In MH the jussive rarely has the shortened form יַקְטֵל[15]; the grammars do not deal with the question of hi. impv. הקטל vs. הקטיל in MH, nor does Qimron with respect to Qumran Hebrew.

3.3. *The Verb with Suffixes*

Qal impf. יעושקנו: 1Q27 1 i 10; יעוזבנה: 4Q525 2 ii+3,5; cf. similar forms in 1QS VI, 14; X, 13; 1QpHab XII, 5; according to QIMRON §311.13g, these forms have no parallel in any other tradition. In 4Q423 9,2 we even find ידורשוהו, 3rd pl. + suff. 3rd m. sg.; this form is not mentioned in Qimron §311.13 (differently תדרשוה 4Q525 5,5; יזכרוכה 4Q525 14 ii 16).
Qal impf. יטושנה in 4Q525 2 ii+3,5 is a good Qumran form vs. BH יִטְּשֶׁנָּה; cf. Qimron §311.13.
Jussive אל תערבהו, "do not mortgage it" (4Q416 2 ii 18; 4Q424 2,3): not the energic form. Qimron §322.143 has counted 23 instances of the suffix הו- but he does not pay attention to the distinction between indicative and jussive.
4Q418 9,8 has וישיביכה vs. 4Q416 2 iii 9 ישיבכה. The *yod* represents a vowel; this form might be the equivalent of Masoretic Hebrew יְשִׁיבְךָ; cf. the table in Qimron §322.
Also in 4Q525 2 ii+3,2 דורשיה, the *yod* represents a vowel between the participle sg. and the suffix, as in pause in the MT of the Bible (cf. PUECH, *Qumrân grotte 4. XVIII*, p. 124).

3.4. *Passive Participle*

ילוד(ים): 4Q299 28,1-2: either יְלוֹדִים (Exod 1,22; Josh 5,5; 2 Sam 5,14; 12,14; Jer 16,3) or יְלוּדִים (sg. יָלוּד; 1 Kings 3,26-27; Job 14,1; 15,14; 25,4; 1 Chron 14,4). It is not clear how far back in time this distinction between the two forms in MT goes.

3.5. *Weak Verbs*

3.5.1. פ״א

יאוהב 4Q525 10,5: impf. 3rd m. sg. = יֶאֱהַב; digraphs of this type are characteristic of Qumran Hebrew; cf. Qimron §100.5.
יוכל 4Q421 12,2: impf. 3rd m. sg. = יֹאכַל.

---

15. Cf. M.H. SEGAL, *Grammar*, §144; M. PÉREZ FERNÁNDEZ, *Grammar*, p. 122.

3.5.2. הלך and פ״י

Qal impv. הלך: 4Q418 81,6. This form is not attested in the Bible, but there are a few instances of the infin. הלך (Exod 3,19; Num 22,13-14.16; Job 34,23; Qoh 6,8.9) and strong impf. forms (Exod 9,23; Jer 9,3; Ps 58,9; 73,9; Job 14,20; 16,6.22; 20,25; 23,8; Qoh 8,10 [emend.]), whereas Jer 51,50 has the impv. pl. הלכו. In Sir 3,17 (ms. C) we find הלוך, which may be an impv. or an inf. abs. The form seems not to be attested in MH, and Qimron does not mention it with regard to Qumran Hebrew.

Qal impv. רוש: 4Q417 2 i 14; = BH רֵשׁ, impv. of ירש[16]?

Ho. part. מולדי: 1Q27 1 i 5 מולדי עולה, "those born of sin", this form is not found in BH, nor, as it seems, in MH or in Qumran; 4Q416 2 iii 9 מולדיו, "its origins"; מוֹלָד, "issue, descendant, birth" (Keth 72b) is rather a noun; cf. V. Vocabulary, under מולדים.

3.5.3. ע״ע

ידולל 4Q525 15,3: Pol. impf. of דלל, "make low"; according to García Martínez and Tigchelaar "be raised"[17]; this form is *hapax* in Classical Hebrew; cf. CLINES, *Dictionary* II, p. 440.

3.5.4. ע״ו

Ni. impf. תכון: 1Q27 1 i 6, according to Lange; García Martínez and Tigchelaar translate "(the sun which) regulates"; this is impossible, for if it is not ni. the form can only be qal, which has an intransitive meaning only[18].

Hi. impf. cons. ויכן: 4Q525 2 ii+3,4; a good classical impf. cons.

Hi. inf. cstr. הבן: 4Q525 6 ii 2, after the negation לבלתי; a strange defective spelling.

3.5.5. ל״ה

The *forma apocopata* (jussive) is in full use: 4Q416 2 ii 8 אל תרף; 19 אל תשת; iii 8 אל תתאו.

4Q419 1,5-8 ויצו: apocopated form in an impf. cons.

4Q417 1 i 27 יכנו, hi.impf. of √נכה with energic suffix of 3rd m. sg.

3.5.6. היה ni. 1Q26,2; 1Q27 1 i 3.4; 4Q423 3,2; cf. V. Vocabulary, under נהיה.

---

16. F. GARCÍA MARTÍNEZ & E.J.C. TIGCHELAAR, *Study Edition* II, p. 859.
17. F. GARCÍA MARTÍNEZ & E.J.C. TIGCHELAAR, *Study Edition* II, p. 1057.
18. A. LANGE, *In Diskussion mit dem Tempel*, p. 135, n. 85; F. GARCÍA MARTÍNEZ & E.J.C. TIGCHELAAR, *Study Edition* I, p. 67.

4. Adverbs

4Q184 1,16 בל ידרוכו; 4Q413 1-2,3 בל יחיה; in the Qumran texts the negative particle בל is always used before an imperfect tense, whereas in the Bible it occurs before various forms[19].

5. Prepositions

בלוא, "without": 4Q299 7,5; 4Q301 2b,3; 4Q416 2 iii 20; 4Q417 1 i 2; 4Q418 126 ii 5; cf. BH and other Qumran texts.

III. MORPHOSYNTAX

1. Pronouns

1.1. *Reflexive pronominal suffixes*

תכבדכה 1Q26,6: "should you glorify yourself"
ת[גדללכה 1Q26,9: "you will (not) glorify yourself"

This use of suffix pronouns with a reflexive meaning is not attested in BH, unless with prepositions (e.g. with ל: Judg 3,16; with את: Exod 5,19). We find, however, a few instances of reflexive pronouns suffixed to the verb in Sir 7,7.16 (ms. A).

2. Article

The article is not always used where we would expect it, e.g. 4Q418 81,1.12 קודשים. Erratic use of the article is typical of Qohelet, but also in both the Mishna and Qumran literature, the use of the article seems to become more irregular (cf. e.g. MBBath 4,7; Snh 3,3; 1QS III, 19 vs. III, 25; IX, 16 vs. IX, 22)[20].

3. Nouns

3.1. *Plural*

בשפתותיכה 4Q525 14 ii 27: plural instead of dual. The plural is used in later texts, Isa 59,3; Pss 45,3; 59,8[21]; Cant 4,3.11; 5,13; Qoh 10,12, in accordance with a growing decline of the use of the dual[22].

---

19. E. QIMRON, *Divine Providence*, p. 195; cf. CLINES, *Dictionary* II, p. 174.
20. Cf. A. SCHOORS, *The Preacher*, pp. 164-169; PÉREZ FERNÁNDEZ, *Grammar*, p. 26.
21. A pre-exilic date of these two psalms cannot be excluded.
22. A. SCHOORS, *The Preacher*, pp. 71-72.

3.2. *Genitive and Construct State*

A participle in the construct state before a preposition occurs frequently in BH (Joüon-Muraoka §129m). For the texts under consideration, cf. 4Q184 1,9 תומכי בה; 4Q525 11-12,2 תומכי בי.

If it is not a scribal error, חיים עולם in 4Q418 69 ii 13 represents an apposition instead of a construct phrase; compare Dan 12,2: חיי עולם.

4. Verbs

4.1. *Tenses and modes*

4.1.1. Perfect or suffix conjugation

מלטו pi. perf. 3rd m. pl. 1Q27 1 i 4. This cannot be a future tense, *pace* García Martínez. BARTHÉLEMY and MILIK, (*Qumran Cave I*, p. 103), circumvent the problem with the rendering "ils ne savent pas...ni comment sauver leurs âmes du mystère futur". Schiffman's translation is correct: "and they did not save their lives from the mystery that was coming into being"[23].

Stative verbs use the perfect tense to express the present: שנאו (1Q27 i 9; 4Q299 1,1), חפץ (1Q27 i 10; possibly participle); שׂו (1Q27 ii 2;? context unclear); נחה...אור (4Q392 1,5); ידעתה (4Q416,2 iii 5).

4.1.2. Imperfect or prefix conjugation

There are a large number of imperfect forms that have a frequentative force or express the habitual or a general present: 1Q27 i 9-10: יתהלך, יעושקנו; 1Q27 i 11: יחפץ (versus חפץ participle or perfect in line 10), יגזל; (11 עשק and 12 גזל are perfect tenses expressing the past: "that has not oppressed...that has not looted"); 4Q184 1,1-3: תשחד...תוציא...ירדו...תמכו...נעלו...יכין: the change of forms from imperfect to perfect seems to reflect the distinction between frequentative/continuous present action and a present situation which is the result of past action. For a continuous present see also 4Q184 1,7 ותשכון...תאהל; 10 תצעד; 11 ותכשילהו... ותשגהו...תרים...ישכילו...תתיצב...תתעלף 12; תארוב; 4Q418 לוא יעוזבנה ולוא...ולוא יטושנה 5 ירצה 4Q525 2 ii+3,4; יתהלכו 69,14; יפיקו...ימאסו 10 ויתהלכו...יצורו 5,9; ישוחח...יהגה...לוא יגעלנה 6 ישכחנה; יצניעו...יביטו 13 יכרו... יסובלו 12 ימאסו...יטו 11.

בטרם נדבר, "before it is discussed" (4Q300 1 ii 1): perfect tense, whereas in BH the particle is usually followed by the imperfect. But it can also be the pi. impf.1st pl.

---

23. F. GARCÍA MARTÍNEZ, *Dead Sea Scrolls Translated*, p. 399; L.H. SCHIFFMAN, *4QMysteries^a*, p. 211.

4.1.3. Perfect consecutive

וגלה 1Q27 i 5; 4Q300 3,5. The perf. consec. continues the infinitive הסגר which refers to a future event.

ושלם קץ האמת 4Q416 1,13: continues the impf. תתם.

ושב אפו ועבר 4Q417 1 i 15: continues the impf. יראה; ונאספה 4Q417 1 ii 4: *waw apodoseos* after יקפוץ ידו; אם ושבעתה 4Q418 81,19: continues the impf. תמלא; והייתה 4Q418 103 ii 7: continues the impf. יהיה; והייתה...ואותה...ודאבה 4Q418 127,1-3: continues the impf. ושבעתה; תמצא 4Q418 184,3: continues the impf. תשכל.

Because of the lacunary nature of the preserved text, we cannot be sure, but a perf. consec. is possible in 4Q525 14 ii 10 והתענגתה, "and you will delight", and 12 וחלצכה, "and he will deliver you" (cf. PUECH, *Qumrân grotte 4. XVIII*, p. 119)[24].

Often no perf. cons. is used, e.g. יצורו דרכיה ויתהלכו 4Q525 5,9; שמעה לי ושים 4Q525 14 ii 18.

4.1.4. Imperfect consecutive

ו[יגל 4Q299 2,2. The context is too fragmentary to make sure whether this is an impf. cons. or a jussive.

אמרו המשל והגידו 4Q300 1 ii 1. No imperfect consecutive is used. However, there is probably no succession but parallelism: "They utter the parable and relate the riddle".

בחן וינחילנו 4Q299 3a ii-b 14. This seems to be an impf. cons. However, it is possible to syntactically disconnect the two verb forms, translating: "He tested our heart and will give us as an inheritance"[25].

וישימכה 4Q418 81,5; הפיל גורלכה וכבודכה הרבה מואדה וישימכה is the continuation of the perf. הפיל and הרבה.

ויצו...ויתנמו...ויבחר 4Q419 1,5-8; is a row of impf. cons.; this is confirmed by the apocopated form ויצו.

ויתאפק...ויכן...ויתהלך 4Q525 2 ii+3,3-4; are the continuation of the perf. השיג. However, they could also be syndetically connected imperfect forms, which certainly is the case for ירצה. But morphologically the defectively written ויכן should be an impf. cons. After these three impf. cons. forms, the author switches to impf. in order to express continuous action, as it also appears from the adverb תמיד.

4.1.5. Volitives

4.1.5.1. Indirect volitives

והתבוננו 4Q413 1-2,1 (imperative!): continues the impf. אלמדכמה, which, therefore, appears to be a cohortative; translate: "let me teach

---

24. 4Q525 14 ii 16 והייתה is a very doubtful case; in my opinion, it is a conjunctive perfect: "and you were...".

25. F. GARCÍA MARTÍNEZ & E.J.C. TIGCHELAAR, *Study Edition* II, p. 659.

you wisdom that you may understand the ways of man"; cf. Joüon-Muraoka §116.

4.1.6. Infinitive

4.1.6.1. Infinitive absolute

The inf. abs. in the *figura etymologica* occurs in 4Q424 1,9: הליז יליז; 13: בלע יבלעם. QIMRON §310.14 points out that the use of the inf. abs. is rather rare in Qumran Hebrew and that this relative non-usage is typical of late BH and Samaritan Hebrew and culminates in MH, where the inf. abs. completely disappears[26].

4.1.6.2. Infinitive construct

לבלתי 4Q525 6,2; לבלתי הבן 4Q525 2 ii+3,7; לבלתי לכת used as the negation of the infin. as in BH; cf Qimron §400.12.

IV. SYNTAX

1. Word order

1.1. In 4Q184 1,14, ישרים להטות דרך, "in order to turn the upright (from) the path", the object precedes the infinitive, as is the case in the majority of instances in Biblical Aramaic and sometimes in other Aramaic dialects. This order is rare in BH[27]. J. Carmignac found 8 sure and 6 doubtful instances in Qumran, which is more than in BH and which he ascribes to Aramaic influence[28]. Qimron §400.05 concludes that, with so few examples, any conclusion must be tentative.

2. Expansion of verb phrase

2.1. *Direct object (accusative)*

4Q413 1-2,2 את איש. "The use of את before the indefinite object is peculiar"[29].

2.2. *Direct vs. indirect government*

4Q184 often has direct government where the use of a preposition is possible: 1,9-10 משגות עול "lead astray towards wickedness"; 11 באיה "going to her", ירדו שחת "descend to the pit"; 14-15 להטות דרך "to

---

26. Cf. R. POLZIN, *Late Biblical Hebrew*, pp. 43-44; R. MACUCH, *Grammatik*, pp. 258 and 514-516; PÉREZ FERNÁNDEZ, *Grammar*, p. 144.
27. H. BAUER – P. LEANDER, *Grammatik*, §85c-d; T. MURAOKA – B. PORTEN, *Grammar*, p. 308; C. BROCKELMANN, *Grundriß* II, p. 438; cf. J. STRUGNELL, *Notes en marge*, p. 268.
28. J. CARMIGNAC, *L'infinitif*.
29. E. QIMRON, *Divine Providence*, p. 194.

turn from the path", and further מנצור מצוה and in line 16 ולהטות פעמיהם מדרכי צדק, both with preposition.

The use of hi. פרר, "annul", with the preposition על (4Q416 2 iv 9) is unknown in BH.

2.3. Prepositions

4Q413 1-2,4 בינו ב; "The introduction of the object of בין by ב is typical of Qumran Hebrew and LBH"[30].

4Q426 4,2 אוהב ב; cf. Qoh 5,9; this usage could have been influenced by such verbs as חפץ ב and רצה ב[31]. In Qoh the object is "wealth", not a person; in 4Q426 the object itself is unknown, due to the state of the manuscript.

4Q217 2 i 15 מחוקק לאל; as in BH, with verbs in a passive form the preposition ל indicates the agent; cf. *HAL*, p. 485; CLINES, *Dictionary* IV, p. 484[32].

3. Expression of will

The negative adverb אל is used in a nominal clause in 4Q417 1 i 22; 4Q418 7,7; 8,9.

4. Subordination

4.1. Subordinating particles

עד, "until"; 4Q418 2,5: עד ישלם, "until is ended"; however, this reading is doubtful since in 4Q416 1,13 the same sentence reads תתם עוד ושלם קץ האמ[ת, "will end again and the time of truth will be complete"[33].

אשר, "so that"; 4Q416 2 ii 5-6: אשר לוא יקח, "so that he does not take".

בל, "lest": בל ידרוכו, "so that they do not walk" (4Q184,16) (?)[34].

בלוא, "without" (4Q299 8,5); this composite particle is used with the perf. According to Qimron §400.10, it occurs only in 1QH. This is no longer correct, since in the text under discussion we read ומה יתבונן גבר בלוא ידע ולוא שמע, "How can a man understand without knowing, without hearing"; cf. 4Q417 2 ii 14 בלוא צוה, "without commanding".

כן, "as" instead of -כ or כאשר in 4Q185 1-2 ii 14: כן תתן לאבתיו כן ירשנה, "As she was given to his fathers so will he inherit her"[35]. To the best of my knowledge, this is a unique instance.

---

30. E. QIMRON, *Divine Providence*, p. 195.
31. Cf. A. SCHOORS, *The Preacher*, pp. 192-3.
32. Cf. A. LANGE, *In Diskussion mit dem Tempel*, p. 138, n. 93.
33. F. GARCÍA MARTÍNEZ & E.J.C. TIGCHELAAR, *Study Edition* II, pp. 848-9.
34. J.M. ALLEGRO, *Qumran Cave 4*. I, p. 82, reads בל ערוכי[ם].
35. J. STRUGNELL, *Notes en marge*, p. 271.

למה, "lest" instead of פן in 1Q26,5 (cf. BARTHÉLEMY and MILIK *Qumran Cave I*, p. 102); further in 4Q418 88,3; 103 ii 7; possibly in Qoh 5,5; 7,16-17[36]. However, here interrogative למה cannot be excluded[37]. We find פן in 4Q415 2 ii 4; 4Q416 2 iii 4.6.8; 4Q417 1 i 1.10; 4Q418 9,4; 184,3; 188,7; 4Q423 5,1a; 4Q525 14 ii 21.27; 23,7.

4.2. *Temporal clauses*

4.2.1. ב + infinitive

1Q27 i 5 בהסגור מולדי עולה, "When those born of sin are locked up"; 4Q413 1-2,3; 4Q416 2 iii 21; 4Q418 81,4; cf. Qimron §400.03. Forms with *kaph* do not occur, according to Qimron, *loc. cit.*, note 12.

4.2.2. עם + infinitive

4Q417 2 i 12 עם התהלכו may be an instance of עם + infinitive used as a temporal clause, which is found elsewhere in Qumran and even in LBH, but not before Ezra 1,11; Sir 38,23; 40,14; cf. Qimron §400.04. The infinitive then has the 3rd m. sg. suffix. García Martínez seems to treat the form as a perf. 3rd pl.: "while they walk"[38].

4.3. *Conditional clauses*

Several times in 4Q416, the conditional clause preceding the main clause is not introduced with a particle; e.g. 4Q416 2 ii 19-20 (If you lack bread); iii 12 (If you are poor); 20 (If you take a wife).

V. VOCABULARY

אוט, storehouse (?)
4Q417 1 ii 3; 4Q418 79,2; 81,16; 107,4; 126 ii 2.12.13; 127,5; 138,3; 177,8; 4Q423 1 i 5; cf. CLINES, *Dictionary* I, p. 150. Caquot rejects the meaning "storehouse, treasure" and conjectures "indulgence" in 4Q417 1 ii 3, and "slowness" in 4Q418 126 ii 2 (root אטט, cf. לאט in 2 Sam 18,5)[39]. García Martínez and Tigchelaar often leave it untranslated; only in 4Q417 1 ii 3 they render it as "goodness". In his earlier translation García Martínez has "extension" (4Q418 81,16), "lovableness" (4Q418,126 ii 12) and "simply" (4Q418 127,5). To the best of my knowledge, the word is not found outside the Qumran texts.

אוש, fundament
4Q417 2 i 9; cf. CLINES, *Dictionary* I, p. 403. It occurs in other Qumran

---

36. Cf. LXX ἵνα and μήποτε; M. DAHOOD, *Canaanite-Phoenician Influence*, p. 195.
37. Cf. A. SCHOORS, *The Preacher*, pp. 137-8.
38. F. GARCÍA MARTÍNEZ, *Dead Sea Scrolls Translated*, p. 387; A. LANGE, *Weisheit und Prädestination*, p. 47.
39. A. CAQUOT, *Sagesse*, pp. 11 and 26.

texts, e.g. 1QH III, 13.30.35; VII, 4.9; 1QSb III, 20; 4Q286 ii 4; 11QShirShabb V, 7. In 4Q184 1,6-7 the reading באישני is preferable to באישני. Here the noun seems to be a variant of אוש, formed with the ending *ôn*[40]. אוש is not found in BH but it occurs in Jewish Aramaic (BQam 50a).

אט, affair (?)
4Q424 1,6: is this the same as BH אָט? cf. CLINES, *Dictionary* I, p. 202. CAQUOT surmises a transition from ע to א, thus the word would be עט, "stylet, plume". García Martínez and Tigchelaar translate it as "an affair" with a ?[41]. This suggestion deserves attention, because the word refers to something that can be entrusted to somebody.

אייקום, non-existence
4Q185 1-2 i 11; this is an abstract term, which is — almost obviously — absent from BH; compare איכבוד (1 Sam 4,21); אי־נקי (Job 22,30)[42].

אנוש, man
4Q413 1-2,1; 4Q418 8,12; is a good biblical word, showing a high concentration in Job (4,17; 5,17; 9,2; 10,4; 32,8; 33,26; etc.), Sirach (7,11; 10,18; 13,25; 14,1.20; 15,19.20; 32,24; 34,19.27; 37,14; etc.) and Qumran texts (1QH I, 25.32.34; IX, 15; XV, 13; 1QS XI, 10; 4Q184 1,17; etc.). In the Bible it occurs only in poetry, whereas in Qumran it is found in prose as well[43].

ארגמון, purple
4Q525 2 iii 5; BH and 1QM VII, 11 אַרְגָּמָן or אַרְגְּוָן.

ארץ צביו, the land of his delight
4Q299 79,5; cf. Dan 11,16.41; Jer 3,19; Ezek 20,6.27; 25,9. The association of ארץ with צבי occurs in relatively late to late biblical texts.

בוע hi., spring forth
4Q525 2 ii+3,2; cf. 1QH XVI, 18; read as יבועו this could be a neoform of נבע under Aramaic influence, the Aramaic word occurring in the targums, cf. *infra* and CLINES, *Dictionary* II, p. 128. Puech prefers the hi. of נבע, common in BH, e.g. Pss 59,8; 94,4; Prov 15,2.28, for the correct reading is undoubtedly יביעו (*Qumrân grotte 4. XVIII*, p. 124).

---

40. Cf. G.W. NEBE, *Lexikalische Bemerkungen*, pp. 101-2.
41. A. CAQUOT, *Sagesse*, p. 31; F. GARCÍA MARTÍNEZ & E.J.C. TIGCHELAAR, *Study Edition* II, p. 889.
42. H. LICHTENBERGER, *Weisheitliche Mahnrede*, p. 154, n. 21.
43. E. QIMRON, *Divine Providence*, p. 193.

בין (ב)משפט, understand judgment
4Q418 77,3; 4Q424 3,2; this phrase occurs in the Bible only in wisdom literature: Job 32,9; Prov 28,5 (cf. 2,9); cf. also Sir 35,16; 1QS VI, 15; 1QSa, I 5[44].

בעל ריב, opponent (at a lawsuit)
4Q417 1 i 12; 4Q424 3,9. This expression does not occur in the Bible. It appears in 1QH XV, 22-23[45].

ברר, separate
4Q424 3,5[46]; is attested only in Qumran, in CD, in Chron (1 Chron 9,22; 16,41) and in Qoh 9,1; cf. CLINES, *Dictionary* II, p. 276[47].

גוה, exalt (?)
4Q416 2 iii 10: כי יגוה אל ת°°הו, rendered by García Martínez as "for God exalts his…"[48]. The verb is unknown in BH and MH. According to Caquot, it might be a variant of יגאה (pi.)[49]. However, it is preferable to read יגיה, hi. impf. of נגה, "to enlighten" (cf. García Martínez and Tigchelaar, *Study Edition* II, pp. 850-851: "for God will lighten his… on all your paths").

גורל, lot, assigned portion, destiny
4Q418 81,5; 4Q421 1a i 4; this good biblical word is extremely common in Qumran texts, especially in sectarian writings; cf. CLINES, *Dictionary* II, pp. 337-8.

דברי קודש, holy things
4Q421 13,4; 4Q418 188,7; the phrase is not found in the Bible, but it does occur in Qumran: 4Q403 1 i 24; 4Q436 1 i 7; it seems to refer to matters related to the temple (ELGVIN, *4QWays of Righteousness*, p. 201).

דבת דבוב, evil defamation (?)
4Q412 1,3; from the words דִּבָּה "defamation, evil report", which is good BH, and דבב "plead in court, make an accusation" (Aramaism?); the form דבוב "adverse" occurs in MH. An alternative translation to "evil defamation" might be "slander of the slanderer" (taking דבוב as a designation for an evil being)[50]. In my opinion, דבה derives from the

---

44. Cf. G. BRIN, *4Q424 Fragment 3*, p. 278.
45. G. BRIN, *4Q424 Fragment 3*, p. 293.
46. G. BRIN, *4Q424 Fragment 3*, p. 272, reads תכר instead of תבר.
47. A. SCHOORS, *The Preacher*, pp. 95-96.
48. F. GARCÍA MARTÍNEZ, *Dead Sea Scrolls Translated*, p. 384.
49. A. CAQUOT, *Sagesse*, p. 14.
50. A. STEUDEL, *Sapiential Texts*, p. 165.

root דבב; cf. also Caquot: "la médisance d'un médisant": דבוב evokes Aramaic דבבא, "enemy"[51]. CLINES, *Dictionary* II, p. 383 parses the phrase as perf. 2nd m. sg. + inf. abs.: "*you have indeed glided over*, i.e. perh. spread an evil report". Although the context has been poorly preserved, I suggest that reading the phrase as a nominal construction is preferable[52]. In 4Q418 24,1 we may read דובב, but nothing of the context has been preserved.

הבהב, greedy
4Q426 2,1; cf. Prov 30,15: literally, "give, give!" (STEUDEL, *Sapiential Texts*, p. 216), and Hos 8,13; "gift", according to CLINES, *Dictionary* II, p. 485, a meaning which fits especially Hos 8,13. Because the text is too poorly preserved, it is impossible to be positive about the meaning of this word in 4Q426.

הבל, ephemeral, vanity, absurdity
This stock word of Qohelet is found in 4Q184 1,1 and probably in 4Q299 64,3. But besides in Qoh, it occurs frequently in BH.

הגו(י), הגי, meditation, interpretation
4Q417 2 i 16.17; does not occur in BH, whereas we find הגו in Qumran Hebrew: 1QH XI, 2.21; 1QSa I, 7; CD X, 6; XIII, 2; XIV, 8; cf. CLINES, *Dictionary* II, p. 488. According to Lange, who invokes the authority of Ginzberg and others, ספר הגו means "the Book of Interpretation (of scripture)" and חזון הגו "the vision of interpretation"[53].

הורים, (human) origin
4Q416 2 iii 17. The word normally means "parents". With the meaning "origin" it is unknown in biblical and later Hebrew.

היה/הוה, destruction
4Q185 1,8 (הוה); 4Q418 69,5 (היה). In BH this word occurs in the form הוה (Pss 5,10; 38,13; 52,4; 55,12; Job 6,30; etc.), with one exception, viz. Job 6,2 K היתי; in Qumran the orthography is הווה (1QH II, 6.36; III, 33.38; V, 26.31; VI, 21; VII, 4.5;) or הוה (1QH V, 25; VII, 7.11). Cf. CLINES, *Dictionary* II, pp. 502-3.

חזה, see
4Q424 3,3, where it means something like "observe"; the verb is well known in BH, where it is practically restricted to prophetic and poetic

---

51. A. CAQUOT, *Sagesse*, p. 4.
52. Cf. also F. GARCÍA MARTÍNEZ & E.J.C. TIGCHELAAR, *Study Edition* II, p. 841: "defamatory talk".
53. A. LANGE, *Weisheit und Prädestination*, p. 85; L GINZBERG, *Jewish Sect*, pp. 49-51; J.M. BAUMGARTEN, *Qumran Law*, p. 16; C. RABIN, *Zadokite Documents*, p. 50.

verse or elevated language, in which it refers to prophetic vision (Isa 30,10; Ezek 13,16; 21,34; Lam 2,14). Here it indicates "supervision, observation"[54].

חזק לבב, strengthen the heart
4Q421 9,2; in the Bible the expression has the negative meaning "harden somebody's heart", but in Qumran it means positively "strengthen somebody's heart"; cf. 1QM XVI, 13-14; 4Q436 1 i 1.4; 4Q504 1-2 v 8-9.

חרת, engrave
4Q417 2 i 14.15 (חרות). This word is a *hapax* in the MT (Exod 32,16), but it occurs in Sir 45,11 and several times in Qumran (e.g. 1QM XII, 3; 1QS X, 6.8.11; 4QShirShabb[a] 1 i 5.15; 4QShirShabb[c] 4,3; 4QShirShabb[f] 23 ii 3; 4QShir[b] 63 ii 3), always in contact with nomistic terminology[55]. Cf. CLINES, *Dictionary* III, p. 325.

טרף, food
4Q416 2 i 22; 4Q417 1 i 17; ii 2.3; 4Q418 7,15; 81,16; usually meaning "prey", but it occurs with the meaning "food" in BH too, cf. Mal 3,10; Ps 111,5; Job 24,5; Prov 31,15. In 4Q417 1 i 20 טרף hi. means "to feed", as in Prov 30,8; cf. CLINES, *Dictionary* III, p. 376.

ידע, knowledge
4Q424 3,7. This noun is not used anywhere in the Bible. The phrase איש ידע, "a man of knowledge" is similar to איש תבונה elsewhere in the Qumran texts[56]. The formula also occurs in 4Q426 1 ii 5 but A. Steudel thinks that here it could be a participle or perhaps, preferably, an imperfect tense of the verb ידע (cf. *Sapiential Texts*, p. 216); García Martínez and Tigchelaar, too, translate צעדי איש ידע as "the steps of man he will know"[57].

יהוה, YHWH
As in Qohelet, the tetragrammaton does not occur in these wisdom texts, with the exception of 4Q185 1-2 ii 3. According to Lichtenberger, who refers to H. Stegemann, this free use of the tetragrammaton outside a Bible text suggests an early origin of the text; it may point to a date in the 3rd or early 2nd century B.C.[58] In 4Q411 we find the tetra-

---

54. Cf. G. BRIN, *4Q424 Fragment 3*, pp. 280-1.
55. A. LANGE, *Weisheit und Prädestination*, p. 80.
56. G. BRIN, *4Q424 Fragment 3*, p. 290.
57. F. GARCÍA MARTÍNEZ & E.J.C. TIGCHELAAR, *Study Edition* II, p. 893.
58. H. LICHTENBERGER, *Weisheitliche Mahnrede*, p. 162; cf. H. STEGEMANN, *Gottesbezeichnungen*.

grammaton several times (1 ii 2.11.12.13.17) and, according to the editor A. Steudel, this suggests a pre-Qumran origin of the work (*Sapiential Texts*, p. 159). In 4Q299 3a ii-b 12, הואה seems to be a substitute for the tetragrammaton[59].

יותר, advantage, benefit
1Q27 ii 3; cf. Qoh 6,8.11; 7,11 and יתרון in Qoh 1,3; 2,11.13; 3,9; 5,8.15; 7,12; 10,10.11. With adverbial functions the word also occurs in Esther 6,6; Qoh 2,15; 7,16; 12,12; Sir 3,23; 8,13; 10,31 and in MH.

יחד, the Community
4Q184 1,2 and very frequently in Qumran texts. In BH the word never has that concrete meaning; it occurs mostly in an adverbial function meaning "together" and in the late text 1 Chron 12,18 it means something like "unitedness"[60].

יצר רע, evil inclination
4Q417 2 ii 12; cf. 4Q370 I 3; 4Q422 1 i 12; became a popular expression in MH[61]. The noun יצר, meaning "inclination", is also found in Sir 15,14.

כבד אזן, hard of hearing
4Q424 3,4; this phrase does not occur in the Bible; cf. 1QS IV, 11: כבוד אוזן.

כלי, vessel
4Q416 2 ii 21 [חוקקה] כלי חיקקה, "the vessel of your bosom" or "your lawful vessel"; here, the noun is used metaphorically for "wife", as in 1 Thess 4,4; this is unique in BH and Qumran[62]. According to CLINES, *Dictionary* IV, p. 424, it would rather mean "body", yet with the remark that "the body of your statute/bosom" makes reference to one's wife.

כסיל, stupid, fool
4Q301 2,1; as for BH, besides three occurrences in Psalms (49,11; 92,7; 94,8), the word is found in Proverbs and Qohelet only. It occurs also in Sir 20,7.13; 34,20.30 (B); 42,8 and in 4Q381 46,4.

כרה, dig
4Q418 55,3; 4Q424 3,6. In the last instance the object is מחשבות, thoughts; the verb here has the meaning of "plotting, devising", as in

---

59. L.H. SCHIFFMAN, *4QWays of Righteousness*, p. 43.
60. Cf. QIMRON §500.03: *Words Not Attested either in BH or in MH*; S. TALMON, יחד.
61. A. CAQUOT, *Sagesse*, pp. 19-20; cf. M. JASTROW, *Dictionary*, Vol. 2, p. 590.
62. J. STRUGNELL, *Wives and Marriage*, pp. 538-540; A. CAQUOT, *Sagesse*, p. 12.

Prov 16,27: כרה רעה, plotting evil. "It should be noted that all the appearances of the roots כרה and חרש in connection with thoughts and plots appear in the Wisdom literature, something that suits the literary nature of the present document" (i.e. 4Q424)[63].

כשר, suitable, appropriate
4Q417 2 i 11; Aramaic loan, which in BH shows up in Esther 8,5; Qoh 2,21; 5,10 (כשרון); 11,6 and in Sir 13,4 (cf. *TWAT* IV, pp. 383-4)[64]. As is well known, the word became a technical term in MH, meaning "ritually permitted, legal".

לוז, perversity
4Q424 1,8: איש לוז שפתים, "man of perversity of lips" (CLINES, *Dictionary* IV, p. 524), i.e. "a man with twisted lips" (transl. García Martínez[65]); a *hapax* the root of which is לוז, "be devious"; cf. line 9 משפטך הליז יליז בשפתיו, "he will certainly pervert your trial with his lips". Brin reads איש לו שפתים, which he renders as "the man with twisted lips"[66]. In MH we find the verb לוז and the noun לייזה with the meaning "evil talk, suspicion"[67].

לפנים, firstly
4Q525 14 ii 24; this word is good BH with the meaning "formerly, in time past"; with the meaning "first(ly)" (followed by אחר, "afterwards") it occurs only in Sir (4,17; 11,7; 37,8) and Qumran (1QSa II, 20); cf. CLINES, *Dictionary* IV, pp. 563-4.

מבין, understanding person, counsellor/teacher
4Q417 2 i 1.18; 4Q418 123 ii 45; the participle hi. of בין is found only in LBH and Qumran: 1 Chron 15,22; 2 Chron 34,12; Dan 8,23; Sir 10,1; 38,4; 42,21; 1QH VII, 21; X, 20; 4Q381 45,1; 4Q509 12-13 i 3. From 4Q417 2 i 18, it appears that the word is the designation of the sage[68].

מבינה, understanding
4Q417 2 i 10.11; 29 i 7; 4Q418 43,8; does not occur elsewhere; בינה is the usual Hebrew word.

---

63. G. BRIN, *4Q424 Fragment 3*, p. 288.
64. A. LANGE, *Weisheit und Prädestination*, pp. 47 and 64-65; ID., *In Diskussion mit dem Tempel*, p. 130.
65. F. GARCÍA MARTÍNEZ, *Dead Sea Scrolls Translated*, p. 393; ID. & E.J.C. TIGCHELAAR, *Study Edition* I, p. 389.
66. G. BRIN, *4Q424 1-2*, pp. 36-7.
67. Cf. JASTROW, *Dictionary*, p. 706.
68. A. LANGE, *Weisheit und Prädestination*, p. 47; ID., *Wisdom and Predestination*, p. 341, n. 3.

מבנית, building, structure, frame

4Q299 6 i 13; cf. 1QH VII, 4.9; 1QS XI, 8; 4Q403 1 i 41; 4Q405 14-15 i 6; 11Q17 i 5; x 8. In BH only in Job 20,3 by conjecture (*BHS*).

מדהב(ה), hardship, annihilation

4Q416 2 ii 14; 4Q418 176,3 (מדהבה); cf. Isa 14,4 and 1QH III, 25; XII, 18; CD XIII, 9[69]. The word does not occur in MH but was used in Piyyut[70].

מהל, circumcise

4Q525 6,3; due to the fragmentary state of the context, it is not clear whether the phrase רוח מוהלת means "a spirit which circumcises". In BH only מול is used, unless מהל in the phrase סבאך מהול, "your wine is mixed (with water)" (Isa 1,22) is the same root. In MH and JA מהל is the technical term for "circumcise"; cf. Jastrow, *Dictionary*, p. 737.

מודה, much, very?

4Q299 6 ii 15; 4Q418 81,17; 137,4; according to Schiffmann, *Mysteries*, p. 48 this word is a later development of BH מְאֹד; cf. also Qimron §200.11.

מוט hitpol, totter

4Q424 1,4; התמוטט is said of the earth or hills in Isa 24,19; 54,10; and possibly of a ship in Sir 33/36,2. But in the last instance it is metaphorically applied to a person. Here and in other Qumran texts it seems "to refer to individuals who are not straightforward but are ethically unstable"[71]; cf. 4Q525 14 ii 5-8 (another sapiential text); 1QH VI, 21.

מולדים, (time of) birth

4Q299 1,4; 3a ii 13; 5,5; 4Q415 2 ii 9; 4Q417 1 i 11; cf. TgO Gen 40,20 בית ולדא = Heb בית הלדת (Schiffman, *Mysteries*, p. 37). According to T. Elgvin, מולדי ישע (4Q417 1 i 11) can be interpreted as "birth-times/birth-pangs/origins of salvation"; cf. 1QH XX, 8, where מולדי עת carries the meaning "beginnings of the set times". Caquot translates the word with "conditions de naissance" and the phrase in 4Q417 1 i 11

---

69. Cf. A. Caquot, *Sagesse*, p. 12: "malheur". With respect to Isa 14,4, most commentators suggest a reading מרהבה, invoking the testimony of 1QIsa[a], Sym, Th, Syr, Targ, and partly LXX; see e.g. GB, p. 399 and F. Zorell, *Lexicon*, p. 411, where, nevertheless, we find the translations "Bedrängung" and "terror"; in my opinion the versions render the word under discussion as referring to a person and the Qumran reading is not superior to the MT; therefore we should stick to the MT.

70. Cf. E. Ben Yehuda, *Thesaurus*, Vol. 4, p. 2804.

71. G. Brin, *4Q424 1-2*, p. 29.

with "(conditions) salutaires de naissance"⁷². Apart from Qumran, the oldest attestation of the word מולד is in the Mishna⁷³.

מחסור, need
4Q416 1,6; 4Q424 1,8; continually found in the wisdom texts of Qumran as well as eight times in Proverbs (6,11; 11,24; 14,23; 21,5.17; 22,16; 24,34; 28,7).

מלה, word
4Q525 14 ii 23; this noun is derived from the root מלל, "speak". Although it occurs in a possibly pre-exilic context (Ps 19,5; Prov 23,9), both verb and noun are frequently used in post-exilic texts, such as Prov 6,13; Pss 73,10; 106,2; 2 Chron 25,4.26 and especially Job with 36 occurrences. The word is no doubt of Aramaic origin and, as a rule, it is a sign of LBH; it remains in use in MH⁷⁴.

ממשל, dominion, rule
4Q299 6 i 15; cf. 1QS IX, 24; 1QM I 5; this form, as against the feminine ממשלה, occurs in BH in later texts only (Dan 11,3.5; 1 Chron 26,6 [?]). This form of the noun seems not to occur in MH⁷⁵.

מקוה, hope
4Q185 1-2 i 7-8.12. I do not see whence Strugnell has taken the meaning "support", when he translates: "and none to support the indignation of her wrath"⁷⁶. In line 12 he translates the same word with "hope". The word is found with that meaning in Jer 14,8; 17,13; 50,7; Ezra 10,2; 1 Chron 29,15. It is rather common at Qumran in the phrase אין/יש מקוה; cf. Qimron §500.1.

משטמה, animosity, enmity
4Q525 19,4; a technical term in Qumran literature (e.g. 1QM XIII, 11; 1QS III, 23; cf. CD XVI, 5); in BH attested in Hos 9,7-8 only.

משכיל, wise
4Q298 i 1; 4Q417 2 i 25; 4Q421 1a ii 10.12; שכל hi. is very common in BH; the participle, however, is practically restricted to later and mostly sapiential texts (e.g. Pss 14,2; 41,2; 47,8; 53,3; Prov 10,5.19; 14,35;

---

72. T. ELGVIN, *Early Essene Eschatology*, p. 145, n. 50; A. CAQUOT, *Sagesse*, pp. 8-9.
73. Cf. JASTROW, *Dictionary* p. 742; A. LANGE, *In Diskussion mit dem Tempel*, p. 131.
74. Cf. M. WAGNER, *Aramaismen*, pp. 77-8.
75. JASTROW, *Dictionary*, p. 795 mentions ממשל, meaning "parable", but only the plural ממשלות seems to be actually attested in the texts; cf. J. LEVY, *Wörterbuch*, Vol. 3, p. 144.
76. J. STRUGNELL, *Notes en marge*, p. 269.

15,24; 16,20; 17,2; 19,14; 21,2; Job 22,2; Dan 1,4; 11,35; 12,3.10; 2 Chron 30,22). In the title of a number of Psalms, it seems to indicate a literary type or genre (Pss 32; 42; 44; 45; 52; 53; 54; 55; 74; 78; 88; 89; 142). In sectarian texts from Qumran it can mean the knowledgeable (e.g. CD XII, 21; 1QH XX, 11); often, however, it refers to the authoritative teacher, the spiritual guide of the community (1QS III, 13-IV, 26; X, 26-XI, 2; 1QSb III, 22; V, 28), a meaning which is fully developed in the last two chapters of Dan[77].

נבע hi., allow to gush forth, utter
4Q301 1,1 אביעה רוחי, "I will pour out my heart", i.e. I will speak my mind; cf. Prov 1,23. Cf 1QH I, 29: מבע רוח ... ומבעי רוחות, the puff(s) of breath(s)[78]. 4Q525 2 ii+3,2 יביעו: cf. *supra*, under בוע. For MH, cf. JASTROW, *Dictionary*, p. 870.

נג(ו)ע, plague, misfortune
4Q184 1,5: גווע; elsewhere in Qumran נגיע; BH: נֶגַע; this form occurs also in 4Q417 1 i 25; 2 ii 9; 4Q418 7,10; according to Strugnell, "la forme [נגוע] est courante à Qumrân"[79]. Thus, in Qumran literature, the biblical spelling of the word seems to be limited to these wisdom texts.

נהיה, existence, being
1Q26 1,2; 1Q27 1 i 3.4; 4Q415 6,4; 4Q416 2 i 5; iii 9.14.18; 7,3; 4Q417 1 i 11; 2 i 8.18.21; ii 3; 4Q418 5,1; 43,14.16; 77,2.4; 123 ii 4; 172,1; 184,2 all have the expression רז נהיה. The expression occurs about 30 times in the sapiential work represented by 1Q26 and 4Q415-418 and 423 (*mûsār lammēbîn*). It is also found in the *Book of Mysteries*. Next to "the mystery of being", some suggest the translation "The mystery of what is to be", because in some contexts it appears to refer to the eschatological plan of God[80]. According to Wacholder and Abegg the expression translates as "the mystery of what *we shall be*", "the mystery of our being", or, more simply, "the mystery of being"[81]. However, נהיה may also be a participle used as an attribute with רז, which would result in a meaning "a secret/mystery that is happening, i.e.

---

77. Cf. H. KOSMALA, *Maskil*, pp. 239-241; T. ELGVIN, *Wisdom in the Yaḥad*, p. 215; D.J. HARRINGTON, *Wisdom Texts from Qumran*, p. 65.
78. F. GARCÍA MARTÍNEZ & E.J.C. TIGCHELAAR, *Study Edition* I, p. 161.
79. J. STRUGNELL, *Notes en marge*, p. 266; J.M. BAUMGARTEN, *Seductress*, p. 141, n. 28.
80. D.J. HARRINGTON, *Wisdom at Qumran*, p. 145. Cf. BARTHÉLEMY and MILIK, *Qumran Cave I*, p. 104: "'futur' et non 'passé'", with reference to the ni. participle of היה in 1QS III, 15; X, 5; XI, 3/4.9.11.18; CD II, 10; XIII, 8; Sir 42,19; and 48,5 (LXX: ἐσόμενα), where נהיות is parallel to נסתרות; A. CAQUOT, *Sagesse*, p. 9.
81. B.Z. WACHOLDER & M.G. ABEGG, *Preliminary Edition*, p. xii; italics are mine.

that is realized", be it in the past or in the present/future. Where he adopts this parsing, Harrington is still convinced that the expression refers to the future: "the mystery that is to be/come", especially in the *Book of Mysteries* (1Q27; 4Q299-301). In his opinion, it seems to be a body of teaching that concerns behaviour and eschatology[82]. Contrary to this and in the same work, he seems to admit that this same mystery has several aspects: creation or the cosmos, moral behaviour or ethics, God or theology, and eschatology[83]. Parallel with קדמוניות (1Q27 1 i 3) it could refer to the past — but an antithetic parallelism cannot be excluded —, whereas יבוא עליהמה (1Q27 1 i 4) connects it with the future (cf. *TWAT* II, 401-2). This course is adopted by Schiffman: "This term... takes in the entire past, present and future. Therefore we take נהיה as a participle and translate accordingly", e.g. "the mystery of that which was coming into being" (cf. *Mysteries*, p. 37)[84]. Elgvin follows a similar line: "(the mystery which is coming into being, the unfolding mystery), God's mysterious plan for creation and history, for mankind and the redemption of the elect"[85]. According to Lange it is the "Geheimnis des Werdens", which he later describes as a "weisheitliche Urordnung dualen Charakters, die sich im Sinai Gesetz und in einer Enosch gegebenen Vision offenbart, und die... auch kosmologische und eschatologische Züge trägt"[86]. The conclusion of Harrington's article which he expressly devoted to this expression clearly and in a convincing way recapitulates what we know about it: "It seems to be a body of teaching. It could be written or oral. It appears to have some fixed form. It concerns behavior and eschatology... Rather, the *rz nhyh* is more likely an extrabiblical compendium — most likely something like the Maskil's instruction in *1QS* 3,13-4,26. Or ... the 'Book of Meditation' (*1QSa* 1,6-8) ... Or perhaps it may be the 'Book of Mysteries' (*1Q27; 4Q299-301*)"[87]. The phrase together with other typical words found in 1Q27; 4Q299; 4Q300; 4Q415-418, such as הבט or התבונן is lacking in 4Q301, a fact which makes Schiffman doubt that 4Q301 belongs to the same composition (*Mysteries*, p. 113).

---

82. D.J. HARRINGTON, *Wisdom Texts from Qumran*, pp. 48-49 and 71.
83. *Ibid.*, pp. 55 and 83; ID., *Approaches*, p. 35: "These parallels suggest that the 'mystery' concerns creation, ethics, and eschatology".
84. Cf. also J.I. KAMPEN, *Diverse Aspects*, p. 229 and P. WERNBERG-MØLLER, quoted in note 89.
85. T. ELGVIN, *Reconstruction*, p. 560; ID., *Early Essene Eschatology*, p. 134; cf. J.J. COLLINS, *Wisdom Reconsidered*, p. 274: the mystery "seems to encompass the entire divine plan, from creation to eschatological judgment".
86. A. LANGE, *Weisheit und Prädestination*, p. 57; ID., *Wisdom and Predestination*, p. 341, n. 4; ID., *In Diskussion mit dem Tempel*, p. 129.
87. D.J. HARRINGTON, *Raz Nihyeh*, pp. 552-553.

The use of the form נהיה is not limited to the expression רז נהיה; cf. 4Q418 43,2: למה נהיה ומה נהיה; 69,7: כול נהיה עולם "all that was done and happened in history"[88]; 123 ii 3: כול הנהיה. Cf. 4Q180 1,1-2: כל [הויה]ונהיה, "Alles was ist und sein wird" (= 1QS III, 15)[89].

נואל, fool
4Q299 6 ii 13. "This word for a 'fool' appears in some readings in the Geniza manuscripts of Sir 37:19. Only the verbal usage of this root, יאל, occurs in the Bible"[90]. Cf. Num 12,11; Isa 19,13; Jer 5,4; 50,36; cf. CLINES, *Dictionary* IV, p. 71.

נטר, bear a grudge
4Q299 7,5; 4Q300 7,2; this is a root נטר II, *pace HAL*, pp. 656-7, where it is stated that it would act as the root נטר, "guard, keep", in a derived meaning "keep his wrath"; *LVTL*, p. 613 distinguishes between roots I and II[91]. Root I is not a classical BH root, since it occurs only in Cant 1,6; 8,11-12 (cf. Aramaic נטר vs. Hebrew נצר). For the combination of נטר and נקם, cf. Lev 19,18; Nahum 1,2; CD IX, 2-5; 1QS VII, 10-11[92]. נטר II is also used in MH (JASTROW, *Dictionary*, p. 901), although at that time it was probably considered to be the same root as נטר I.

נמאר, wasting, painful
4Q426 9,1; this word, a part. ni. of מאר does not occur in BH, but we find the hi. in Lev 13,51-52; 14,44; Ezek 28,24; for the ni. cf. 1QH V, 28 and a manuscript אסף הרופא (München), mentioned by Ben Yehuda[93].

נעויה, perversity
4Q416 2 i 7; 4Q417 1 i 13; noun derived from the ni. part. of עוה; unknown in BH, which has the participle masculine and feminine נעוה (Prov 12,8; 1 Sam 20,30).

נעלם, dissembler
4Q424 1,4. In the Bible this nominalized participle never refers to a person, whereas in Qumran it often means "hypocrite" (1QH III, 28; IV, 14; VII, 34; 1Q35 i 9)[94].

---

88. T. ELGVIN, *Early Essene Eschatology*, p. 160.
89. A. LANGE, *Weisheit und Prädestination*, p. 279; F. GARCÍA MARTÍNEZ & E.J.C. TIGCHELAAR, *Study Edition* I, p. 371. According to P. WERNBERG-MØLLER, *Manual of Discipline*, p. 68, "BARDTKE's rendering: 'alles Sein und Geschehen' is perhaps preferable because it avoids any specific time-aspect read into the text".
90. L.H. SCHIFFMAN, *4QMysteries*ᵃ, p. 225; cf. *Mysteries*, p. 48.
91. Cf. BEN YEHUDA, *Thesaurus*, p. 3640, where this view is expressed in a less clear way.
92. L.H. SCHIFFMAN, *4QMysteries*ᵇ, p. 219; cf. *Mysteries*, p. 49.
93. BEN YEHUDA, *Thesaurus*, p. 2766.
94. G. BRIN, *4Q424 1-2*, pp. 26-7.

נתר, collapse (?)

4Q424 1,4; ni. perf. [ו]נתר; ni. is not attested in BH, where we find the hi. Ben Yehuda does not know any ni. form[95].

סאון, mud (?)

4Q525 21,6; García Martínez and Tigchelaar translate it with "mud", Puech with "souillure"(*Qumrân grotte 4. XVIII*, p. 158); in BH the only attested meaning is "boot", and it is not mentioned with the meaning "mud" in Ben Yehuda, where it is explained as meaning "noise, din", an allophone of שאון[96].

סוד, foundation (?)

4Q417 2 i 8.20: סוד אמת, "the foundation of truth"; √יסד, cf. Prov 3,19-20; JASTROW, *Dictionary* p. 961[97].

סרך, muster, inscribe

4Q421 1a i 3; in the sectarian writings the verb has this specific meaning (ELGVIN, *4QWays of Righteousness*, p. 187). In Jewish Aramaic the pe. and pa. and in medieval and modern Hebrew the ni. mean "adhere"[98].

עורמה, craftiness, prudence

4Q299 3a ii-b,5. In Qumran this noun is predominantly used in its positive meaning "Klugheit", not in the negative one "Hinterlist, Tücke"[99]. In 4Q299 3a ii-b,5 the nominal phrase is חוכמת עורמת רוע, which reflects the negative meaning: "the wisdom of evil cunningness" (cf. 1QS IV, 11).

עתת, afflict (?)

4Q185 1-2 ii 5. This verb is unknown in Hebrew. Strugnell suggests a possible etymological connection with Arab. *'atta*[100].

פארת/פארה*, beauty, glory

4Q418 81,13. As far as I know this feminine noun does not occur in biblical or later Hebrew. MH has a noun פְּאֵר, the plural of which is פארות[101].

---

95. Cf. W. BAUMGARTNER, *Lexikon*, pp. 695-6; BEN YEHUDA, *Thesaurus*, pp. 3887-90.
96. F. GARCÍA MARTÍNEZ & E.J.C. TIGCHELAAR, *Study Edition* II, pp. 1058-9; BEN YEHUDA, *Thesaurus*, pp. 3897-8.
97. Cf. A. LANGE, *Weisheit und Prädestination*, p. 52.
98. Cf. JASTROW, *Dictionary* pp. 1027-8; BEN YEHUDA, *Thesaurus*, pp. 4219-21.
99. A. LANGE, *Weisheit und Prädestination*, p. 292; H. NIEHR, ערם, p. 392.
100. J. STRUGNELL, *Notes en marge*, p. 271.
101. Cf. JASTROW, *Dictionary* p. 1131; E. BEN YEHUDA, *Thesaurus*, pp. 4805-8; H. LICHTENBERGER, *Weisheitliche Mahnrede*, p. 154, n. 15.

פּוֹתִי, simplicity, foolishness
4Q301 1,3; פתי in 4Q300 8,4; in Prov 1,22 the vocalization is פֶּתִי פּוֹתִי could be a scribal error, a copyist having read it as פֹּתִי, "width". On the other hand, in BH פֶּתִי normally means "simple", whereas the same word with the abstract meaning "simplicity" is a biblical *hapax*. This could be an error, since a *qutl* form would be more apt for an abstract noun.

פחז, recklessness
4Q184 1,15; cf. Sir 41,17 (var. זנות). The root is used in BH but the noun is not; it is, however, found in MH; cf. JASTROW, *Dictionary*, p. 1152.

פלג, divide, distribute
4Q418 55,6; the word does not occur with the meaning "distribute, apportion" in BH and MH, but it does have that meaning in Aramaic[102]. However, in MH the noun פֶּלֶג means "part, share". The Qumran use seems to be an aramaism.

פלס, observe, take heed
4Q424 3,4. In the Bible this word occurs only in Prov 4,26; 5,6.21. It is also found with that meaning in later rabbinical Hebrew[103].

פקודה, visitation (by God)
4Q416 1,9; "très caractéristique du vocabulaire qoumrânien"[104]. The word occurs already with that meaning in BH, e.g. Isa 10,3; Jer 8,12; 10,15; 11,23; 23,12; 46,21; 48,44; 50,27; 51,18; Hos 9,7; Micah 7,4. But the context is very fragmentary, and a meaning "command, assignment" cannot be excluded.

פרי שפה, the fruit of (his) lips
4Q424 1,10; this phrase does not occur in the Bible, but is attested elsewhere in Qumran: e.g. 1QH I, 28.

פתגם, word
4Q420 1a ii-b,2; cf. Qoh 8,11; Esther 1,20; Sir 5,11; 8,9 and BA; a loan word from Persian via Aramaic[105].

צדיק, righteous
It is striking that two phrases with this noun occurring in 4Q299 are also found in Qoh: 4Q299 3a ii-b 3 מעשה צדיק (cf. Qoh 8,14) and 4Q299 3a ii-b 4 חכם וצדיק (cf. Qoh 9,1).

---

102. Cf. J. HOFTIJZER – K. JONGELING, *Dictionary*, Vol. 2, pp. 911-2; JASTROW, *Dictionary*, pp. 1175-6.
103. BEN YEHUDA, *Thesaurus*, p. 4960.
104. A. CAQUOT, *Sagesse*, p. 7.
105. Cf. M. WAGNER, *Aramaismen*, p. 96.

צנע hi., act secretly, carefully

4Q424 1,6; Brin translates the clause לא יצניע מלאכתך as "he will not keep your matter private"¹⁰⁶; according to García Martínez and Tigchelaar it means "he will not deal carefully with your business". Brin's suggestion is supported by MH בצינעה, meaning "secretly" and the meaning "put aside, hide", which is sometimes attached to צנע hi.¹⁰⁷. The root צנע is found in Prov 11,2; Micah 6,8 and several times in Ben Sira: 16,25; 34,22; 35,3; 42,8; further in 1QS IV, 5; VIII, 2.4. In all these contexts it can mean "act humbly, modestly" but also "act carefully".

In 4Q525 5,13 we find יצניעו בה, which García Martínez and Tigchelaar translate as "they humble themselves in her (= wisdom)"¹⁰⁸, but the whole context, which is in a poor state of preservation, allows a rendering "they act carefully".

קץ, appointed time, period

4Q301 3,8; 4Q416 1,11.13.14; 4Q417 2 i 7; 4Q418 69,14; 123 ii 2.4.6; in BH the word only means "end", but in Qumran texts it is commonly used with the meaning it has in the texts cited above; cf. 1QpHab V, 7-8; 1QM I, 8; X, 15; 1QH IX, 24; XIV, 29; 4Q180 i 1; 11QMelch II, 20; CD VI, 10.14; XII, 23; XV, 7.10. It is also used with that meaning in MH¹⁰⁹.

רוח בינה, spirit of discernment

4Q301 4,2; cf. 4Q405 17,3; 4Q418 58,2; 4Q444 2 i 3; 4Q510 1,6; 4Q511 10,6-7; the expression occurs in Isa 29,24 (and cf. Isa 11,2: רוח חכמה ובינה).

רז, mystery

1Q26 2,5; 1Q27 1 i 2.7; 4Q299 3a ii-b,11.15; 5,2; 4Q300 1 i 2; 8,5.7; 4Q415 24,1; 4Q416 2 ii 8; 4Q417 2 i 2.13; 4Q418 177,7a; 190,2; 219,2; and cf. supra, under נהיה; does not occur in BH; found in Sir 8,18; 12,11; Qumran; BA (Dạn 2,18-19.27-30.47; 4,6); JA; MH. It is a Persian loanword which entered into Hebrew via an Aramaic loan and is only found in Hebrew texts dating from the 2nd century B.C. and later (oldest attestations are Sir 8,18; 12,11)¹¹⁰.

---

106. G. BRIN, *4Q424 1-2*, p. 31.
107. JASTROW, pp. 1292-3; BEN YEHUDA, *Thesaurus*, pp. 5556-8.
108. F. GARCÍA MARTÍNEZ & E.J.C. TIGCHELAAR, *Study Edition* II, p. 1055.
109. Cf. JASTROW, *Dictionary*, pp. 1403-4; BEN YEHUDA, *Thesaurus*, pp. 6078-9.
110. A. LANGE, *Weisheit und Prädestination*, p. 47; ID, *In Diskussion mit dem Tempel*, p. 130; D. HARRINGTON, *Raz Nihyeh*, p. 550.

שוב pol., answer

4Q525 14 ii 21; תשובב; in BH and MH the hi. is used. But Puech translates: "Ne reviens pas (sur les propos de tes collègues)" (cf. *Qumrân grotte 4. XVIII*, p. 148). The fragmentary context does not allow us to decide.

שוה, be of value

1Q27 1 ii 2.8; in BH the verb means "be even, equal, alike"; in QH and MH it also means "be of value"[111].

שוע עינים, blind

4Q424 3,3; 4Q425 1+3,7; this form does not occur in BH, but the root שעע, "be smeared", hi. "stick", is used several times in Isaiah in connection with the eyes (Isa 6,10; 29,9; 32,3).

שקה, drink

ישקו (4Q299 6 i 5) can be hi. or qal. Since qal is not used in BH, hi. seems to be preferable. However, here the meaning of the verb is "they shall drink" and the phrase is reminiscent of Ezek 4,11.16: מים במשורה תשתה (ישתו), "water you (they) shall drink by measure". Therefore the form must be qal.

שקל, משקל, weigh, weight

4Q415 11,8; 4Q418 77,3; 127,6; 4Q424 3,1. In the Bible, the metaphoric use of the root is absent but it is found in Sir 6,15; 16,25; 26,15; 1QS IX, 12; 1QH XIV, 26; XVI, 22; and in MH (cf. JASTROW, *Dictionary*, p. 1623)[112].

תוצאות, outcome, consequences

1Q27 1 i 12; 4Q299 1,7; 4Q217 2 i 13; 4Q421 1a ii-b,15; 3,1; 4Q426 7,1. In BH the word means "exits" (Ezek 48,3), "end-points" (Josh 15,4 and *passim*) and "source/origin" (Prov 4,23); in the sapiential texts from Qumran, only 4Q417 2 i 13 offers sufficient context to grasp the meaning of the word. "The addressee is admonished to meditate on these mysteries and reflect on 'their outcome', what derives from them. The word probably carries the same meaning, 'outcome/results of the matter/consequences' in the other sapiential works"[113]. In 4Q426 7,1 we seem to find the singular תוצאת, which is attested only in later Hebrew (STEUDEL, *Sapiential Texts*, p. 220). This meaning is also at-

---

111. JASTROW, *Dictionary*, p. 1532; BEN YEHUDA, *Thesaurus*, pp. 6948-55.
112. G. BRIN, *4Q424 Fragment 3*, pp. 273-4.
113. T. ELGVIN, *Wisdom in the Yaḥad*, p. 216; cf. L.H. SCHIFFMAN, *4QMysteries*[a], p. 211.

tested in later and modern Hebrew (BEN YEHUDA, *Thesaurus*, pp. 7696-7).

תכון, decision, regulation, measure
1Q27 1 i 6; 4Q299 6 ii 16; 20 1.2; 39,2; cf. 1QS V, 3.7; VI, 4,8-9.10.22; VII, 21; VIII, 4.13; IX, 2.3.7.12; 1QpHab VII, 13; meaning "détermination; précision; mesure exacte, fixée; critère, prescription" (BARTHÉLEMY and MILIK, *Qumran Cave I*, p. 105), "that which God has apportioned, measure, lot" (SCHIFFMAN, *Mysteries*, p. 48); cf. the verb תכןin 4Q416 1,2; 4Q424 1,11. "In Biblical Hebrew it [the root תכן] occurs only in poetical texts, all of them dealing with the creation of the world (Isa 40,12-13; Job 28,25; Ps 75,4)... In Qumran texts the verb TKN (Pi'el) occurs in connection with God's activity in the creation of the world, in determining man's mental abilities, and also in connection with man's activity. (1QH^a IX, 17; 1QS I,12-13)"[114]. In 1Q27 1 i 6, Lange parses תכון as a ni. ipf of כון (cf. supra §II.3.5.4). The noun תכון seems to occur in Qumran only (cf. BEN YEHUDA, *Thesaurus*, p. 7742).

תכם, entrails
4Q525 23,1; not attested in BH, but occurring in other Qumran texts, e.g. 1QH IV, 25; XIII, 28; XV, 4; 1QS IV, 20; תכמים according to QIMRON §500.3. The word seems to be attested in Qumran only[115].

תלונה, complaint
4Q424 1,7; tax collector (?); cf. Greek τελώνης; García Martínez and van der Woude have so translated the word (belastingambtenaar)[116]. According to Brin, איש תלונה means "contentious man"[117]. תלונה in the sense of "complaint" occurs in BH (Exod 16,7-9.12; Num 14,27; 17,20.25) and in other Qumran texts (1QS V, 25; 1QH V, 23.30).

תמך, BH "hold, support"; QH also "curb"
1Q27 1 i 7; 4Q301 1,2; MILIK, *Qumran Cave I*, p. 105 translates it by "détenir", which can have the positive meaning "possess" as well as the negative one "keep in detention, curb". Lange is right when he asserts that, contrary to the use of תמך in BH, in 1Q27 1 i 7 תומכי רזי פלא has a negative force[118].

---

114. M.Z. KADDARI, *Root TKN*, pp. 219-20.
115. BEN YEHUDA, *Thesaurus*, p. 7752.
116. F. GARCÍA MARTÍNEZ & A.S. VAN DER WOUDE, *Rollen*, vol. 1, p. 419.
117. G. BRIN, *Wisdom Issues*, p. 310. Cf. also F. GARCÍA MARTÍNEZ & E.J.C. TIGCHELAAR, *Study Edition* II, p. 889.
118. A. LANGE, *Weisheit und Prädestination*, pp. 102-3; ID., *Wisdom and Predestination*, p. 345. Cf. F. GARCÍA MARTÍNEZ & E.J.C. TIGCHELAAR, *Study Edition* I, p. 67: "those who curb the wonderful mysteries".

תקל, stumble; noun: stumbling
4Q525 14 ii 26; is absent from BH, but the noun תקלה is found in Sir 31,7 (34,7) and the verb as well as the noun is frequently used in MH[119]. The root seems to be of Aramaic origin.

VI. Conclusions

As I have stated above most of these texts show a relatively full orthography, notwithstanding the presence of some strange exceptions, and a more defective spelling is limited to 4Q185, 4Q392 and 4Q424. The latter texts come close to Qohelet's orthography, but this is not sufficient proof for dating them to the 3rd century B.C.

The same conclusion goes for the orthography of the personal pronouns and suffixes and the endings (ה)ת- and (ה)תמ- of perf.2m.sg. and pl. Here the *Book of Mysteries* comes closer to the average orthography of the Bible, although 1Q27 has a somewhat more full writing. Some usages recall Qohelet, e.g. the indefinite pronoun מה אשר (Qoh ש־מה), the masculine gender of רוח, the use of אהב with the preposition ב-. The presence of some features is limited to later biblical texts, e.g. ה used as a relative particle. 4Q424, which is known for its relatively defective spelling, sometimes uses the jussive form in hifil, but 4Q418 and 4Q525, with a more full orthography, also show the hi. impv. form הַקְטֵל, while 4Q525 has the hi. impf. cons. ויכן. 4Q416 and 4Q424 also show the jussive in a suffixed form of the type יקטלהו. In 4Q416 and 4Q419 we find apocopated forms of ל"ה. A number of verbs are in, what would be called in the masoretic Bible text, pausal forms: יקטולו, יקטולנו (with suffix), יקטליה or קוטליה, or they have suffixed forms of the type יקוטלני, but all these instances are rather rare when compared to other Qumran texts. That could mean that texts like 1Q27 or 4Q525 are slightly earlier than the bulk of Qumran texts.

Some morphosyntactical peculiarities, such as reflexive pronominal suffixes, erratic use of the article or plural use instead of dual have parallels in Sir and Qoh and other later Bible texts. Consecutive tenses are still in use, but not consistently, and more as *wayyiqtol* than as *weqatal*. By and large this corresponds to what we generally find in the Qumran texts[120]. The two instances of infin. abs. in a *figura etymologica* in a limited context in 4Q424 can be called a rare phenomenon that corresponds to the rather rare use in QH in general.

---

119. JASTROW, *Dictionary* p. 1691; BEN YEHUDA, *Thesaurus*, pp. 7876-7.
120. Cf. A. SÁENZ-BADILLOS, *History*, p. 144.

The one instance of putting the direct object before the infinitive can be an Aramaism. The use of ב with בין and אהב, or of עם with infin. as a temporal clause point to LBH and are even typical of QH.

The most promising data for dating the Qumran wisdom texts might come from the vocabulary. Some good biblical words or expressions are used in Qumran with a new meaning, e.g. מוט, חזק לבב pol., שוה, תוצאות, מחסור, נעלם, קץ. Other words are typical of Qumran texts, e.g. כבד אזן, יצר רע, יחד, חרת, הגי/הגו(י), דברי קודש, גורל, בעל ריב, אוש תכם, תכון, פרי שפה, סרך, (רז) נהיה, משטמה, מבנית. But the question is: Can we date their first appearance in our textual corpora? A number of words appear for the first time in LBH, e.g. פלס (?), פחז ממשל, מבין, יותר, ברר, ארץ צביו. Others are older but show a strikingly higher concentration in LBH, e.g. אנוש, משכיל. As was said above, the limited use of the tetragrammaton could point to an early phase in Qumran literature. Some words appear for the first time in our texts and continue to be used in MH, e.g. סוד, נעויה, מולדים, לוז. There are also a few Aramaisms, which have been borrowed or at least more commonly used in LBH and later, e.g. תקל, רז, פתגם, פלג, מלה, כשר. In sum, an important portion of the vocabulary in the Qumran wisdom texts points to an origin not earlier than LBH. Schiffman is correct when he writes, with regard to 4Q300, that certain lexical usages are familiar from the sectarian corpus[121]. We can also agree with Lange, who states that late words and constructions show that *mûsār lammēbîn* has been written not much earlier than the end of the 3rd century B.C.[122]. But how much later was it written? There is no proof that the texts under consideration have not been written much later than the end of the 3rd century. And linguistic analysis does not offer a solid basis to affirm that they are substantially older than the sectarian Qumran literature.

Faculteit Letteren   Antoon SCHOORS
Blijde-Inkomststraat 21
B-3000 Leuven

---

121. L.H. SCHIFFMAN, *4QMysteries*[b], p. 205.
122. A. LANGE, *In Diskussion mit dem Tempel*, p. 130: "Späte Vokabeln und Konstruktionen wie das persische Lehnwort רז (älteste Belege im Hebräischen sind Sir 8,18; 12,11), das aramäische Lehnwort כשר (die ältesten Belege der Wurzel im Hebräischen sind Est 8,5; Koh 2,21; 5,10; 11,6; Sir 13,4), das Part. Hi. der Wurzel בין (die ältesten Belege im Hebräischen sind 1 Chr 15,22; 2 Chr 34,12; Dan 8,23; Sir 10,1; 38,4; 42,21; 4Q381 45$_1$) und im temporalen Sinn gebrauchtes עם mit Infinitiv (עם התהלכו 4Q417 3 I$_{12}$; die ältesten Belege im Hebräischen sind Esr 1,11; Sir 38,23; 40,14) zeigen, daß MLM nicht viel früher als vor dem Ende des 3. Jh. v.Chr. verfaßt worden sein kann".

II
CONTRIBUTIONS TO SPECIFIC TEXTS

TOWARDS A RECONSTRUCTION OF THE BEGINNING OF 4QINSTRUCTION

(4Q416 FRAGMENT 1 AND PARALLELS)

OVERLAPS BETWEEN 4QINSTRUCTION MANUSCRIPTS

In a concise and lucid article Annette Steudel described several stages and procedures in the work on the fragments found in the Judaean Desert[1]. Her article focusses on two main aspects of the physical work on the fragments, namely the assembling of the many fragments into manuscripts, and the material reconstruction of these manuscripts. The assembling of the fragments was largely done in the 1950s and the 1960s, whereas the material reconstruction of manuscripts remains to a large extent an unfinished task.

Steudel is primarily concerned with the material reconstruction of manuscripts, not with the textual reconstruction of compositions. Therefore she does not discuss in detail the important role which textual overlaps between fragments can have in reconstructions. First, textual overlaps provide the evidence that different manuscripts are copies of the same composition, or, at least, represent versions of the same composition. Thus, Strugnell already observed in 1955 that 4Q423 was a copy of the work represented by 1Q26, and that 4Q415, 4Q416, 4Q417 and 4Q418 were copies of one sapiential composition[2]. Even in 1955 Strugnell considered the possibility that all these six manuscripts belonged to one work, but it was only in the 1990s that the textual overlaps between 4Q418 and 4Q423 were identified. Likewise, textual overlaps between 4Q418a and 4Q418 provided the evidence that 4Q418a was another copy of 4QInstruction. Second, textual overlaps may help one to arrange the fragments of individual manuscripts. For example, the textual overlaps with 4Q416 2 enabled Strugnell to arrange 4Q418 fragments 7-10. Similarly, my identification of more 4Q418 fragments belonging to the same section (4Q418 64+199+66) gives some clues per-

---

* This paper is a product of a project on 4QInstruction for which I was granted a postdoctoral fellowship by the KNAW, the Royal Netherlands Academy of Arts and Sciences.
1. STEUDEL, *Assembling*.
2. STRUGNELL, *Travail d'édition*, p. 64.

taining to the height of the columns of 4Q418[3]. Third, textual overlaps often add to our knowledge of the text. Words preserved in one fragment may supplement the text of the parallel fragment.

In the official *DJD* editions, as well as in many other publications on the Dead Sea Fragments, the terms 'overlap' and 'parallel' are not always distinguished clearly. To my knowledge, no attempt has been made to define the differences between 'overlap' and 'parallel'. Therefore I suggest the following distinctions. Two or more fragments of different manuscripts overlap if the graphical correspondences between the texts of the fragments allow for the possibility that they preserve part of the same section of a composition. Two or more fragments of different manuscripts are parallel if they attest the same section of a composition. Hence, whereas 'overlap' refers to a preserved graphical agreement between fragments, 'parallel' expresses the conviction that a preserved or reconstructed textual correspondence between fragments should be attributed to the fact that the fragments preserve a corresponding text belonging to different copies of the same work.

In many cases, overlap and parallel coincide to such an extent that the distinction is merely academic. Yet, one should take notice of cases where an 'overlap' need not imply a 'parallel', or when fragments are 'parallels' without overlapping. A few examples taken from 4QInstruction fragments may illustrate this. The conglomerate of fragments numbered 4Q418 43 overlaps with 4Q417 1 i (formerly numbered 2 i) to such an extent that it is clear that the fragments are parallels. The small fragment 4Q418 44 reading]ובסוד[in line 1, and]ל[in line 2 also graphically overlaps with 4Q417 1 i, but the overlap is so limited that we can not be certain that the fragments are parallels (it is likely that they are parallels because 4Q418 44 has the same material appearance as 4Q418 43, and the graphical sequence ובסוד is only preserved in 4Q417 1 i). The question whether overlaps really indicate parallels surfaces when the overlaps are minimal. Thus, the last line of 4Q415 2 i reads ḿ[והתחדש, whereas the top line of 4Q418 236 can also be read]והתחדש[ḿ. The only overlap between these fragments is therefore והתחדש, whereas the preceding letter in both texts may be a final *mem*. The *hitpaʻel* of √חדש is used very rarely in the Dead Sea Fragments, but it is, of course, possible that והתחדש was used more than once in 4QInstruction. In such cases one needs to take other evidence or clues into account. An example of a parallel without real overlap is found in the parallel between 4Q416 1 and 4Q418 1. 4Q418 1 preserves some forty-five letters, but only one or two letters overlap with 4Q416 1. In this case, the parallel is

---

3. TIGCHELAAR, הבא ביחד.

plausible in view of the clauses which result from the combining of the text of the two fragments.

The manuscripts of 4QInstruction are desperately in need of different methods which may further the reconstruction of the composition. The fragments attest at least eight fragmentary copies of the composition, but apart from the long section covered by 4Q416 2, 4Q417 2 (formerly numbered 4Q417 1), and the parallel fragments of 4Q418 and 4Q418a, we are at a loss where to place the numerous medium-sized and small fragments of the manuscripts. Elgvin has attempted to situate the largest fragments in the scrolls[4], but his material reconstruction differs at essential points from that of Steudel and Lucassen[5]. I have focussed, on the other hand, on the possibility of reconstructing the text by identifying more joins and overlaps. These different approaches are not competitive (though they might result in contradictory conclusions), but complementary. Results from one approach may further the investigation using the other method, and vice versa. In the case of the 4QInstruction manuscripts we are still very much at the beginning of the process of reconstructing the manuscripts and the composition.

At the Tübingen Forschungsseminar, I presented a few joins and overlaps, mainly with regard to 4Q418 fragments. One of those joins has been published in a separate article[6], and most of the other suggestions are referred to in some manner in the *DJD* edition[7] and included by me in the Dead Sea Scrolls Study Edition[8]. Therefore, this article will present new suggestions on reconstructing one part of the composition, namely the beginning of 4Q416, on the basis of overlapping fragments. These new suggestions have in part, but not completely correctly, already been included in the revised edition of the Study Edition[9], and will also be presented in my forthcoming book on 4QInstruction. In this article, however, I wish to discuss the evidence in more detail, presenting all considerations *in extenso* to the reader. The reason is that proposals with regard to the reconstruction of texts are often based on cumulative evidence, and the failure to present all one's thoughts may lead to a rash dismissal of a proposal because the evidence would not be sufficient[10].

4. ELGVIN, *Reconstruction*; *Analysis*, pp. 11-35.
5. Cf. STRUGNELL, HARRINGTON & ELGVIN, *Qumran Cave 4. XXIV*, p. 19.
6. TIGCHELAAR, הבא ביחד.
7. STRUGNELL, HARRINGTON & ELGVIN, *Qumran Cave 4. XXIV*.
8. GARCÍA MARTÍNEZ & TIGCHELAAR, *Study Edition*.
9. GARCÍA MARTÍNEZ & TIGCHELAAR, *Study Edition* Revised.
10. Cf. the discussion between LYONS, *4Q285 and 11Q14* and TIGCHELAAR, *Few Data*.

Ideally, the reader who wants to follow the arguments step by step should consult the photographs of the discussed fragments. My observations on the fragments are based on an intensive examination of the reproductions of the photographs in the Facsimile[11], the Microfiche[12], and the CD-ROM edition[13], as well as upon a thorough examination of the fragments and the PAM photographs in the Rockefeller Museum. An indispensable help was a draft of the editors' *DJD* edition which enabled me to compare their transcriptions of the text and descriptions of the fragments, with the fragments themselves.

4Q416 1 AND OVERLAPPING 4Q418 FRAGMENTS

Strugnell's Identifications in the 1950s

4Q416 frag. 1 was assembled in the 1950s. It consists of two large pieces (lines 1-10; lines 9-18) and one small piece (lines 13-15). The two large pieces are first joined in PAM 41.783 (August 1955), and the small piece is added to the fragment in PAM 42.556 (May 1958). The join of these pieces is certain, and the fragment may be transcribed as follows:

4Q416 1

כֹּל רוֹחֹ]	1
ולתכן חפצוֹ]	2
מועד במועד וֹ]	3
לפי צבאם למ°°]	4
וממלכה למֹד]	5
לפי מחסור צבאם]	6
וצבא השמים הכֹין עֹ]	7
למופתיהמה ואתות מו[ן	8
זה לזה וכל פקודתמה יֹ[ ]סֹפרו[ן	9
בֹּשֹמים ישפוט על עבודת רשעה וכל בני אמתוֹ יֹרצוֹ לֹ]	10
קצה ויפחדו ויריֹעו כל אשר התגללו בה כי שמים יֹראֹוֹ[ן	11
[י]מֹים ותהמות פחדו ויתערערו כל רוח בשר ובני השמיֹ[ם	12
[מש]פטה וכל עולה תתם עוד וֹשלם קץ האמֹ[ת	13
בכל קצי עד כי אל אמת הוא ומקדם שנֹי]	14
להכֹין צדק בין טוב לֹרֹעֹ לֹ]]רֹ כל משפֹּ[ט	15
[י]צר בשר הוֹאה ומבינוֹ]	16
בֹראתוֹ לֹיֹ הֹ°]	17
[ ]וֹדֹ[°]	18

---

11. EISENMAN & ROBINSON, *Facsimile Edition*.
12. TOV, *Microfiche*.
13. LIM, *CD-ROM*.

This transcription differs in a few details from the editors' transcription in the *DJD* volume, namely in line 4 ‏למ°[‎, in line 10 בֹּשָׁמַיִם, line 13 ‏[מש]פטה, and line 17 בֹּרֹאתִיה‎. The *DJD* transcription is superior to Strugnell's preliminary transcription, which served as the basis for the text recorded in the Preliminary Concordance[14], which in turn was taken over by Wacholder and Abegg[15]. A translation will be given below, but here we may observe that the preserved text of this fragment is not addressed to a second person, but gives a third person description throughout. The contents are not paraenetic, but cosmological and eschatological.

The most remarkable feature of the fragment is its very wide right margin of *ca.* 3 cm. According to the editors there is some stitching at the right edge of the fragment, and a small piece of a preceding sheet, presumably a *page de garde* or handling sheet. In fact, I was not able to discern the stitching in the Museum, but that may be due to the present mounting of the fragment. The protective netting which is now placed on top of the fragment may have obscured any traces of stitching or of holes for the stitching. Such wide margins are quite uncommon within a scroll, and the editors therefore believe that the width of the margin indicates that it belonged to the first sheet of the manuscript. Thus, the eschatological contents, dealing with the Last Judgment, would have served as an introduction to the composition, and the fragment would stem from the first column of the scroll.

The fragment preserves remnants of eighteen lines, whereas the columns 4Q416 2 ii-iii consist of twenty-one lines. Elgvin compares the column height of frag. 1 and frag. 2 iii, and thinks it is probable that the column to which frag. 1 belonged had only nineteen lines[16]. However, Elgvin's calculation, based upon the height of fragments 1 and 2, does not seem to take account of the fact that frag. 2 suffered more from shrinkage than frag. 1. It is therefore possible that the column of frag. 1 had twenty or even twenty-one lines. It is not very likely that the manuscript began with the words of line 1 (that is, if one should read כֹּלֹ רֹוחֹ), and therefore one may assume that one to three lines are missing before the first preserved line of 4Q416 1.

The Preliminary Concordance and the placement of the fragments in PAM 43.484 show that Strugnell had observed in the 1950s that at least three 4Q418 fragments overlapped with the text of 4Q416 1. These three fragments do not physically join, but are given one number, 4Q418 2. In

---

14. RICHTER, *Preliminary Concordance*.
15. WACHOLDER & ABEGG, *Preliminary Edition 2*.
16. ELGVIN, *Analysis*, p. 15.

the *DJD* edition these fragments are numbered 4Q418 2, 2a and 2b. In spite of the relatively large number of variant readings (listed further below), the overlap between 4Q418 frag. 2 and 4Q416 1 is beyond doubt, as can be seen from the transcription of frag. 2. The corresponding text of 4Q416 1,9-16 is underlined.

4Q418 2 (2, 2a, 2b)

[ו֯ זה ל֯]זה וכול פקודתמה ו֯ ספרו	1
ב[שמים] ישפו֯[ט על] עבודת רש[ע]ה וכול] בני אמתו י֯רצו֯ ל	2
קצה]ו֯י֯ופחדו [וי]ר֯ע֯ו כול אשר הת֯]גללו בה כיא שמים יראו	3
ימים]ותהום פחדו ויתר֯[כול רוח בשר ובני השמים	4
משפ[טֹ֯הֹ֯ וכול עולה תתם עד י֯שלם]קץ האמת	5
[בֹ֯כוֹל קצי עד כיא אל אמת הוא] ומקדם שני֯	6
]ל להבין צדיק בין טוב לרעֹ֯] ל ר כול משפט	7
כי]א יצר בשר הואה ומבינ֯י֯°[ ]	8
]ל[ ]ל[	9

On the left of 4Q418 2 lines 7 and 8 Strugnell placed 4Q418 3 in PAM 43.484. This fragment preserves the left margin, as well as ש̇פט[in line 1, and מ[in line 2. The placement indicates that Strugnell thought it possible that ש̇פט[corresponded to 4Q416 1,15 כל משפ]ט.

The placement and numbering of 4Q418 1 show that Strugnell also considered the possibility that this fragment had a text parallel to 4Q416 1. This possibility is indicated in the Preliminary Concordance, in the transcription of 4Q418 1,3, where the Preliminary Concordance records מחסור צבא[ם ומשפט כולם. It is clear that the unique phrase מחסור צבאם is derived from 4Q416 1,6. On the other hand, the Preliminary Concordance does not supply readings in the other entries. The *DJD* edition combines the texts of 4Q416 1 and 4Q418 1 as follows.

4Q418 1

לפי צבאם למ[שֹ֯וֹר במשורה ול°[	1
לממלכה וממלכה למד֯ינה] ומדינה לאיש ואי֯ש֯]	2
לפי מחסור צבא[ם֯ ומשפט כולם לו֯]	3
] vacat [	4
[ומאורות]]ל[	5

The *waw* before למ[שֹ֯וֹר in *DJD* is probably a mere typo. In the comments on 4Q416 1,7 the editors discuss the problems with regard to the *vacat* in line 4 and the placement of the words of 4Q416 1,7-8 in the lines of 4Q418 1,4-5. Their suggestions are not completely clear to me, but the following solution is possible.

לפי צבאם למ]שׁוֹר במשורה ול[°	1
לממלכה וממלכה למדינה] ומדינה לאיש ואִישׁ]	2
לפי מחסור צבא]ֹם ומשפט כולם לו[ן	3
[vacat [וצבא השמים הכוֹן ע	4
[ומאורות] [לֹ[מופתיהמה ואתות מו	5

Apart from the *mem* in line 3, and perhaps the *lamed* in line 5, the fragments do not graphically overlap (the *sin* in line 1 corresponds to a tiny trace in 4Q416). Rather, the fragments are regarded as parallels in view of the possibility that they preserve parts of the same section of a composition. 4Q418 1 supplements 4Q416 1 in such a manner that the combined texts result in convincing continuous clauses. From a textual point of view the join of the text of the two fragments is suggested by the phrases in 4Q416 1,5 [וממלכה למדֹ and 4Q418 1,2 [ואִישׁ ומדינה לאיש [. In addition, מאורות fits rather well in a section dealing with the צבא השמים. Apart from these textual joins, the placement of 4Q418 1 in the proximity of 4Q418 2 is suggested by the physical characteristics of the fragments. Though 4Q418 1 is darker than 4Q418 2, the fragments are very much alike, and quite different from the other 4Q418 fragments. One may also note that both in 4Q418 1, and in 4Q418 2, the lengths of the lines are more or less the same as those of 4Q416. In sum, the suggestion that 4Q416 1 and 4Q418 1 are parallel texts is not based on graphical overlaps, but on textual and physical grounds.

In conclusion, according to Strugnell's work in the 1950s, 4Q416 1 overlapped with 4Q418 2, 2a and 2b, and possibly with 4Q418 3, whereas he considered the possibility that 4Q416 1 and 4Q418 1 were parallels. Also, the fact that 4Q416 frag. 1 was given the first number in the manuscript, indicates that he thought it likely that this fragment belonged to the beginning of the manuscript.

Elgvin's Suggestions in the 1990s

At the beginning of the 1990s, Torleif Elgvin, a student of Emanuel Tov, began working on the Cave 4 sapiential texts. In his first presentation on these texts, he argued that 4Q418 213 overlapped not only with 4Q416 1 but also with 4Q418 2: "The letters שלם of the word ישלם of the text of 4Q416 1 13 appear in two different fragments of 4Q418 – frgs. 2 and 213. Both fragments definitely preserve the text known from 416 1. This overlap therefore demonstrates without any doubt that 418 preserves remnants of two copies of Sap. Work. A"[17]. In later publications[18] he

---

17. ELGVIN, *Admonition Texts*, p. 180.
18. ELGVIN, *Reconstruction*.

developed this thesis, and in his dissertation[19] he proposes the following views.

First, the fragments which were catalogued at the beginning of the nineties as 4Q418 consist of remnants of two copies of 4QInstruction. The first copy, which Elgvin called 4Q418a, consists of most of the 4Q418 fragments. The second copy, which he called 4Q418b, consists of the fragments found in PAM 43.687, as well as 4Q418 1, 2, 4, and 286.

Second, the text of 4Q416 1 is paralleled by fragments of 4Q418a and 4Q418b. Some of the 4Q418a fragments overlap with 4Q418b fragments, which proves beyond doubt that we are indeed dealing with two separate manuscripts. The following 4Q418a fragments overlap, according to Elgvin, with 4Q416 1: 4Q418 73, 201, 212 and 213. In addition the text of 4Q416 1 is paralleled by the following 4Q418b fragments: 4Q418 1, 2, 286.

Third, 4Q416 1 is, in spite of its wide margin, not the first column of the manuscript. This thesis is mainly based on the purported parallel of 4Q418 201,1-2 with 4Q416 1,2-3. Since 4Q418 201 preserves the top margin, the preceding lines of 4Q416 should have corresponded to 4Q418 fragments of a preceding column. Therefore, at least one column preceded 4Q416 1, but the stitching in 4Q416 1 indicates that at least one sheet preceded this fragment.

A few elements of Elgvin's proposals are to the point, but on the whole his suggestions are untenable. Elgvin does not transcribe the 4Q418 fragments, nor does he reconstruct the 4Q418 lines. Instead, the text of those fragments is included in his reconstruction of 4Q416 1. In order to discuss his proposals, I present part of his reconstruction of 4Q416 1[20] (the line numbering is according to the *DJD* edition).

4Q416 1,1-3 according to Elgvin (4Q418 73 dotted underline; 4Q418 210 underline)

1   כֹּל רֹוחֹ[ן] בשר
2   ולתכן חפצוֹ [עַל כַל עַולה ואשר? לַ]נהיה הודיע אל נח קץ בקץ?]
3   מועד במועד וֹ[יסגר בעד כול בני עולה ויפקוד כל בשר?]

4Q416 1,11-14 according to Elgvin (4Q418 213 dotted underline; 4Q418 212 underline)

11   קצה ויפחדו ויריעו כל אשר התגללו בֹהֹ כי שמים יֹרֹ[י]עֹוֹן תרעש ממלכת רשעה?]
12   מים ותהמות פחדו ויתערערו כל רוח בשר ובני השמי[ם יגילו ביום]

19. ELGVIN, *Analysis*.
20. ELGVIN, *Analysis*, pp. 97-98, 238.

13 [מֹשׁ]פָּטָה וכל עולה תתם עד יֻשׁלַם_קֵץ הָאֱמֹ]ת   וישלוט[?]
14 בכֹל קצי עַד כי אל אמת הוא ומקדם שני[ו

The four fragments of which the text is indicated by underlining in these transcriptions belong to Elgvin's 4Q418a. The underlining shows that 4Q418 73, 212, and 213 suppose a line that is just as long or slightly longer than the lines in 4Q416 1, whereas, according to Elgvin's reconstruction, the lines in 4Q418 201 would be much shorter than those in 4Q416 1.

This strange divergence of line lengths indicates that there is a problem, but Elgvin's interpretation of the first line of 4Q418 201 is also questionable. He translates הודיע אל נח[by "he made known to Noah". However, neither Noah nor the flood are mentioned anywhere in the remainder of 4QInstruction, and Noah's name is spelled נוח in the Qumran orthography. A more likely reading would be נח]לת. Moreover, the preposition אל is not used with הודיע except for Isa 38,19 אב לבנים יודיע אל־אמתך, where אל introduces the thing which is made known ל 'to' someone. Isa 38,19 witnesses the normal use of הודיע with ל to indicate the persons being taught. Hence, it is much more likely that אל is not the preposition, but the subject of הודיע, that is 'God'. In sum, Elgvin's placement and interpretation of 4Q418 201 in the text of 4Q416 1 are without any solid basis. This also implies that Elgvin's main argument to dismiss the probability that 4Q416 1 stems from the first column of the manuscript is not valid.

Elgvin's claim that 4Q418 73 and 4Q416 1,1-2 overlap is not impossible. However, the only overlapping phrase, כול רוח (the reading is quite uncertain in 4Q416 1,1), is used several times in the preserved fragments of 4QInstruction (4Q416 1,1. 12; 4Q418 59,2; 73,1; 76,1; 81,1-2; 286,1), and the plausibility of the identification depends on whether the phrase ולתכן חפצו על כול ע[makes sense in the section. It should be noted that the meaning of תכן חפץ is unclear (but see below), and that תכן is usually not used with על (only in the phrase ותכן על סלע מבניתי in 1QHª XV,11-12 = Sukenik VII,8-9).

The identification of the overlaps between 4Q418 213 and 212 on the one hand, and 4Q416 1 on the other is at first sight much more promising. According to Elgvin, five out of six lines of these two fragments partially overlap with 4Q416 1. However, here again, Elgvin does not reconstruct the 4Q418 lines. A full reconstruction of these lines would have shown that if לֹם[corresponds to ושלם in 4Q416 1,13, the lines would be of rather irregular length. Moreover, the traces after לֹם[do not easily correspond to the words following ושלם in 4Q416 (further on in the line is a *lamed*, barely recognizable in the photographs, but clear in the fragment). Another issue with which Elgvin does not deal adequately, is the width of the lacuna between 4Q418 213 and 4Q418 212. Apart from the fact that one should probably read with the editors יראֹוּ[in stead of יר[י]עֹוּ[, and that the reconstruction מֹמֹּלֹכת רשעה is not the only possibility, one should take account of the width of the gaps between 4Q418 213 and 212. This can be demonstrated by reconstructing 4Q418 213 and 212 with Elgvin's proposal to read a verbal form, e.g. יגילו, between בני שמים and ביום משפטה.

4Q418 213 + 212 (text 4Q416 1 underlined)

1 [בה כי ש[מ]ים יראֹוּ[   ]תרעש ממֹּלֹ]
2 ב[שר ובני שמים] יגילו ב[י]וֹם משפטה]
3 [לֹםֹ[ ]°לֹ°[   ]בכו]לֹ[קצי]עד]

A typewritten transcription can not reproduce the irregular spacing of the manuscript, but it is clear that in line 1 some letters, e.g. וגם, could have stood between יראֹוּ[and תרעש[. Elgvin's reconstructed יגילו in line 2 demands little space, and a longer word like ישמחו would allow for a longer word in the gap in line 1. Also, the space between the fragments in line 3 is much smaller than indicated in Elgvin's transcription of 4Q416. The latter problem is solved if one assumes that לֹםֹ[does not correspond to ישלם. These inaccuracies on Elgvin's part do not, however, imply that his identification of the overlaps is wrong, merely that his reconstructions are not completely correct.

In sum, Elgvin's identification of 4Q418 213 and 212 with 4Q416 1 is plausible in view of the extensive overlap. The graphical overlap between 4Q418 73 and 4Q416 1 need not per se imply that the fragments are parallels. The placement of the text of 4Q418 201 in this section lacks all grounds.

With regard to the other manuscript which he identified, namely 4Q418b, Elgvin identifies three fragments as overlapping with 4Q416 1, namely 4Q418 1, 2, and 286. The first two overlaps were already identified by Strugnell. 4Q418 286 has the following text:

1 [כֹול רוח]
2 [°ח°]
3 [מֹועד וֹ]
4 [°°ד]

The fragment is no more on the Museum Plate, and the reading must therefore be based on the photographs. The last letter of line 2 may be read as *pe*; the last letter of line 3 is read by Elgvin as *bet* (thus also the Preliminary Concordance, whereas the editors now read *waw*); line 4 may be read]בֹּעֵד[(Preliminary Concordance:]° בֹּעֵד[). If one reads in line 2 ולתכן[חֹפֹּ]צו (but the traces of the first letter do not look like final *nun* at all), then all letters of the first three lines overlap with 4Q416 1,1-3. The remnants of line 4 should correspond to some text of 4Q416 1,4, but the combined text of 4Q416 1 and 4Q418* 1, לפי צבאם למֹ]שׁוֹר במשורה ול°, does not agree with 4Q418 286,4. Therefore Elgvin places]בֹּעֵד[in 4Q416 1,3, resulting in the following reading of 4Q416 1,1-4:

<u>כֹּלֹ רֹוֹחֹ]ן</u>   1
ולתכן <u>חפצו</u>]   2
<u>מועד במועד ו</u>]יסגר <u>בעד</u>   3

This is only possible if 4Q418 286 had a large space of almost one line between במועד and ויסגר, but if 4Q286 line 3 suggests]מֹועד וֹ[rather than]בֹ מועד[, there would have been a large space between ויסגר and בעד. In sum, the occurrence of the words כול רוח and מועד in 4Q416 1,1-3 and 4Q418 286,1-3, as well as the possibility to read]חֹפֹּ in 4Q418 286,3, suggest that the fragments overlap, but the problems of placing the letters of 4Q286 4 in the text of 4Q416 1 should be considered as a serious difficulty.

The reader who has examined the proposals, now also understands why Elgvin placed the text of 4Q418 201 in the section of 4Q416 1. The identification of the overlap between 4Q418 286 and 4Q416 1 presented the additional word בֹּעֵד, which was the link with 4Q418 201,2 בעד.

The DJD Edition

Elgvin proposed a distinction between two manuscripts, one consisting of most 4Q418 fragments, and another consisting of the fragments in PAM 43.687 as well as 4Q418 1, 2, 4, and 286. Strugnell had already separated the PAM 43.687 fragments from 4Q418 in the 1950s. Those fragments are now treated as a separate manuscript 4Q418a, distinct from 4Q418, in the *DJD* edition. The editors do not, however, agree with Elgvin that 4Q418 1, 2, and 286 belong to 4Q418a. In a codicological excursus[21] they point out that Strugnell originally had overlooked the palaeographical differences between 4Q418 1, 2 and the other 4Q418 fragments. Nonetheless, in spite of the different hands, they maintain that 4Q418 1-2 belong to the 4Q418 manuscript. Since the fragments belong to the beginning of the manuscript, and there are no

---

21. STRUGNELL, HARRINGTON & ELGVIN, *Qumran Cave 4*. XXIV, pp. 226-227.

other 4Q418 fragments overlapping with 4Q416 1, they launch the hypothesis that 4Q418 1-2 belonged to a repair sheet of 4Q418.

Apparently, Elgvin's identification of 4Q418 213 as overlapping with 4Q416 1 was convincing to the editors. Therefore they added 4Q418 213 to 4Q418 2, resulting in the following reading of 4Q418 2,3-5:

3   קצה [ויֹפחדו [וי]רֹעוּ כול אשר התֹ[גללו] בה כי שמים ירא]°[
4   ימים]ותהום פחדו ויתרֹ[כול רוח ב]שר ובני השמי[ם]
5   [יגילו ביום השפ]טֹהֹ וכול עולה תתם עד ישלם [קץ האמת] °° לֹם °°° לֹ[

This *DJD* transcription is not completely consistent and correct. In 4Q416 1,11 the editors read]יראוֹ, but in 4Q418 2,3 they transcribe [°]ירא. In 4Q418 2,4 they mistakenly print [ם]השמי as in 4Q416 1,12, whereas 4Q418 213 (=2c) reads שמים without article. The transcription of 4Q418 213,3 in line 5 is not correct. One should read]לֹ° [ ]° לֹם[. The other traces which the editors transcribe are shadows in the photographs of abraded edges of the fragment.

The *DJD* transcription does not take account of the spaces between 4Q418 2 and 4Q418 213. The space which is needed in 4Q418 2,3 for the letters תגללו is just large enough to accommodate [כול רוח ב] in line 4. There is not enough space for the remainder of the word beginning with]ויתרֹ.

The editors explicitly reject Elgvin's identification of 4Q418 201, but do not discuss Elgvin's proposals with regard to 4Q418 73 and 212. The lack of any discussion about the possibility of an overlap between 4Q416 1 and 4Q418 212 is somewhat surprising, since, according to the editors, "[o]n material grounds, frgs. 211–214 may be placed in close proximity each to another".

One gets the impression that the editors were not in favour of separating 4Q418 1-2 from 4Q418, and therefore launched the hypothesis of a repair sheet. Textually, but not materially, they could fit in 4Q418 213 which does not overlap with 4Q418 2. 4Q418 212, on the other hand, overlaps with 4Q418 2, and for that reason the editors may have chosen not to discuss the possible overlap of this fragment at all.

Reconsidering the Codicological Evidence

Both the editors and Elgvin agree that 4Q418 1 and 2 are different from the other 4Q418 fragments. One's first impression may be that the hands are similar, but 4Q418 1-2 have traits which are not attested in the other fragments. For example, the descenders of *qop* and final *nun* are more curved than in the 4Q418 counterparts. The ruling lines in 4Q418 1 and 2 are quite distinct, whereas the fragments of 4Q418 have faint dry lines.

The skin of 4Q418 1 and 2 is thicker than that of the other 4Q418 fragments, and the colour of the skin is much darker than in most other 4Q418 fragments. In other words, 4Q418 1-2 differ in many respects from the other 4Q418 fragments.

Elgvin assumed that 4Q418 1-2 belonged to the same manuscript as the fragments in PAM 43.687 (4Q418a in *DJD*). However, the hands are not the same, and the skin is very different. Whereas 4Q418 1-2 are thick, the 4Q418a fragments are thin and brittle. Only 4Q418a 24 and 25 are thicker (according to the editors; the fragments are missing from the Museum Plate), but the hand of those two fragments is different from the other 4Q418a fragments, and the identification of 4Q418a 24 and 25 as 4Q418a fragments should be rejected. In short, the only physical features common to 4Q418 1-2 and 4Q418a are the dark colour of the fragments and the presence of distinct dry lines.

As mentioned above, the editors suggest that 4Q418 1-2 belonged to a repair sheet of 4Q418. This is a creative but questionable hypothesis. How can one determine that fragments belong to a repair sheet? And, even if fragments may have belonged to a repair sheet, how can we know to which manuscript this repair sheet was added? Why should 4Q418 1-2 have belonged to a repair sheet of 4Q418, and not, e.g., of 4Q417 or 4Q423? The editors' main argument seems to be that there are no other 4Q418 fragments which convincingly can be attributed to the beginning of the composition. Is this the case?

The editors' implausible distant join between 4Q418 2 and 4Q418 213 (= 2c) already indicates that 4Q418 213 may be just one of those 4Q418 fragments which does belong to the beginning of the composition. Apart from the fact that the gaps between 4Q418 2 and 4Q418 213 can not be filled up in a regular manner, one should also observe that in all respects 4Q418 213 is different from 4Q418 1 and 2. Its skin and hand are like that of the other 4Q418 fragments, and not like 4Q418 1-2. Also, it has no distinct ruling lines, in contrast to 4Q418 1 and 2. Thus, whereas 4Q418 1 and 2 differ from the other fragments of 4Q418 in all respects, 4Q418 213 is similar to the 4Q418 fragments, and different from 4Q418 1-2. In my opinion, the conclusion is inevitable: 4Q418 213 does not belong to the so-called repair sheet of 4Q418 1-2, but is a 4Q418 fragment corresponding to 4Q416 1.

Could there have been a doublet in 4Q418? 11Q19 (11QT[a]) shows that the text of a repair sheet may overlap with the text of the main manuscript. The bottom part of the last column of the repair sheet (11Q19 V,6-11) overlaps with part of the next column (11Q19 VI,2-8). Apparently, the repair sheet in 11Q19 allowed for more text than the original damaged sheet. The scribe who copied the beginning of 11Q19 completed the copying up to the end of the sheet, rather than leaving the bottom part of the last column of the sheet empty. The situation in 4Q418 is not comparable to the one in 11Q19, though. If the editors are correct in arguing that 4Q416 1 belonged to the first column of the manuscript (and I think they are), then 4Q418 213 should also have belonged to the first column of 4Q418, that is, to the sheet which, according to the editors, would have been damaged. Alternatively, one may refer to the doublet in 1QM, between 1QM XII,7-16 and XIX,1-8. Regardless of the explanation of this doublure in 1QM, it can not be excluded that any manuscript contained a similar kind of doublure. But then, such an hypothesis should only be considered if other explanations fail.

In other words, the editors' suggestion that 4Q418 1-2 belonged to a repair sheet of 4Q418 is highly speculative, but without any real evidence. Moreover, the overlap between 4Q418 213 and 4Q416 1 indicates that there were 4Q418 fragments which belonged to the same section.

Neither the editors, nor Elgvin, call attention to the fact that 4Q418 2a, that is the small fragment reading in line 1]לֹ זה ‪î‬[, and in line 2]שמים[, is completely different from 4Q418 1, 2, and 2b, and similar to the other 4Q418 fragments. 4Q418 1, 2, and 2b are dark and have ruling lines, whereas 4Q418 2a has no clear ruling lines and has a lighter colour, like the 4Q418 fragments. In short, 4Q418 213 and 2a overlap with 4Q416 1, but so do 4Q418 1, 2, and 2b. These fragments are clearly different, and can not be attributed to the same manuscript. Since it is highly unlikely that 4Q418 1, 2, 2b belonged to a repair sheet, and since Elgvin's thesis that 4Q418 1, 2 belong to 4Q418a should also be dismissed, one can only draw the conclusion that 4Q418 1, 2, and 2b must be separated from 4Q418 and be regarded as the remnants of a separate manuscript. In the remainder of this article I will refer to that manuscript as 4Q418*.

Schematically, one may present the different views as follows:

Fragments	*DJD*	Elgvin	Tigchelaar
4Q418 5ff.	4Q418	4Q418a	4Q418
4Q418 2c (=213)	repair sheet		
4Q418 2a	of 4Q418	4Q418b	
4Q418 1, 2, 2b			4Q418*
4Q418a	4Q418a		4Q418a

Does 4Q418* only consist of 4Q418 1, 2, and 2b? 4Q418 3 has more or less the same colour as 4Q418 1 and 2, and it also has clear ruling lines like these fragments (the ruling lines are thicker, though). Therefore, one may identify this fragment as a 4Q418*, and not as a 4Q418 fragment. 4Q418 4 is darker than 4Q418 1, 2, 2b and 3, and much darker than the other 4Q418 fragments. Therefore, its identification as a 4Q418 fragment is unlikely. But are there good reasons to regard it as a 4Q418* fragment? The darkness of the skin of 4Q418 5 is intermediate, lighter than 4Q418*, and corresponding to the colour of some of the brittle parts of the fragments of 4Q418. In short, 4Q418* consists of 4Q418 1, 2, 2b, and 3, and possibly of 4Q418 4.

What is the use of establishing whether the fragments belong to one, two, or three manuscripts? According to the editors "the choice will be of purely codicological interest – our knowledge of the *text or texts* edited as 4Q418 will remain unchanged"[22]. This is not true, as can be demonstrated by Elgvin's identification of 4Q418 212 as overlapping with 4Q416 1. The reassignment of 4Q418* 1, 2, 2b to a different manuscript, makes it possible to look for other possible overlaps between 4Q418 fragments on the one hand, and 4Q416 1 and 4Q418* on the other hand. Such partial overlaps could yield additional text not supplied by 4Q416 and 4Q418*.

4Q418 Fragments Overlapping with 4Q416 1, 9-18

Elgvin correctly observed that 4Q418 1 and 2 (but not 2a!) do not belong to 4Q418. Above I discussed his identifications of overlaps of 4Q418 fragments with 4Q416 1. I concluded that his suggestion that 4Q418 213 and 212 overlapped with 4Q416 1 was plausible. Also, I referred to the fact that the editors stated that on material grounds, 4Q418 211–214 may be placed in close proximity each to another.

To what extent is material similarity of skin and colour of help in determining whether fragments should be placed close to one another? Strugnell records that the large fragments of 4Q418 were "grouped by surface, colour, etc., each surrounded by the smaller fragments that most closely resemble them". On the other hand, he warns that this "tentative ordering of the fragments, [is] not offered with any confidence; after all, patches of the skin or surface of 1QIsa[a] from the beginning of that scroll can look very close in appearance to others from its middle or end, and the same may be true of the larger pieces of 4Q416 and 4Q418. This ordering on grounds of appearance alone should then be combined with

---

22. *Qumran Cave 4*. XXIV, p. 227.

the suggestions of the morpho-phthiseo-critical analyses of Stegemann and others, and with yet others that come from lexical study; and even then the real work of material reconstruction will have only just begun"[23]. In short, fragments of similar material appearance may, but do not of necessity, stem from the same section of a scroll.

The physical appearance of fragments is, on the one hand, related to the appearance of the sheet they came from and, on the other hand, a result of the circumstances they have been exposed to. Thus, fragments which form a perfect fit, may still have a different appearance, because of differences in, e.g., light or humidity. This means that even if fragments are presently materially different, this does not exclude the possibility that they stem from the same section. On the other hand, it is more likely that fragments which have a similar or identical material appearance originate from the same sheet. Physical appearance is therefore a supportive, not a conclusive, piece of evidence.

Departing from Elgvin's view that 4Q418 213 and 212 overlap with 4Q416 1, one may examine other fragments of a similar physical appearance, first of all those fragments which are placed close to 4Q418 212 and 213 on the Museum Plates. Here I present a list of such fragments which theoretically may overlap with 4Q416 1. The lines are partially restored according to the possible overlap.

4Q418 208 (cf. 4Q416 1,11-13?)

כו[ל אש]ר התגללו	1
וי[רֹעוֹ [כול רוח בשר	2
ה[אֹמת]	3

The overlap of this fragment with 4Q416 1,11-13 is somewhat dubious. The first problem is found in line 2. The editors read] דֹעוֹ[. The sharply angled stroke of the first letter is indeed more typical of *dalet* than of *resh*, but the differences are not clear-cut, and several examples of *resh* with sharply angled strokes are found in this hand. More problematic is the fact that] וי[רֹעו would give a third variant to 4Q416 1,12 ויתערערו and 4Q418* 2,4]ויתרֹ. The meaning of ויתערערו, "and they will be laid bare", or "and they will be demolished", in relation to כול רוח בשר is not clear, and the meaning of the broken word in 4Q418* 2 could well have resembled that of ויריעו, "and they will cry out". In that case one may reconstruct in 4Q418* 2,4 ויתרֹ[ועעו. In 4Q418 208,2 this reconstruction is not possible, but one may consider וי[רֹעו, a variant of ויריעו (cf. 4Q416 1,11 ויריעו and the parallel וי[רֹעו] in 4Q418* 2,3; Isa 15,4

---

23. *Qumran Cave 4*. XXIV, p. 212.

MT יְרִיעוּ; 1QIs[a] יר׳עו). The variant reading of 4Q418 208 may have been influenced by the preceding phrase, one line earlier, ויפחדו וייר(י)עו. A third problem concerns the first letter of line 3. Strugnell's preliminary reading אמֿת[in line 3, is now dismissed by the editors. Indeed, *alep* is a difficult reading, but perhaps not impossible.

4Q418 209 (cf. 4Q416 1,9-10)

1	וכול פקודתמה י]שֿלֿיֿמוֿן[ויספרו
2	על עבו]דֿת רש[עה וכול בני

The overlap consists of the letters]דֿת רש[, a combination which is found in the Qumran texts only in the phrases עבודת רשעה and עדת רשעה. An alternative reading]דֿת רש[would allow for להכרת רשעים/ל. In 4QInstruction עבודת רשעה is found in 4Q416 1 and 4Q418 121. The first letter of line 1 may be read in several ways, but the reading י]שֿלֿיֿמוֿ fits nicely in the lacuna of 4Q416 1,9. Cf. 1 Enoch 5,3 for 'complete their tasks', and 1QS X,6-7, בהשלם חוק תכונם. The remaining space in 4Q416 1,9 allows for one or two letters before]סֿפרו[.

4Q418 212 (cf. 4Q416 1,11-14)

1	תרעש ממֿקֿ]ומה[
2	ב]יֿום משפטה[וכול עולה
3	בכו]לֿ[קצי]עד[כי אל אמת

Elgvin suggested in line 1 תרעש ממל]כת רשעה, but, as the editors point out, the last trace of line 1 may belong either to *lamed* or *qop*. In the latter case the text may "form an allusion to, or quotation of, Isa 13,13 ותרעש הארץ ממקומה". The words of line 1 should be reconstructed in between the "fear of the *heavens*" and the "terror of the *seas* and the *depths*". Therefore, a reference to the "shaking of the *earth*" would fit better than the "shaking of the kingdom of wickedness".

4Q418 213 (cf. 4Q416 1,11-13)

1	]בה כי ש]מ[ים יֿראֿו[
2	ב]שר ובני שמים[
3	]לֿםֿ°[ ]לֿ°[

4Q418 217 (cf. 4Q416 1,16-17?)

1	י]צר [בשר הזֿאה
2	בראתיֿוֿ]כֿ[יא

The overlap is minimal, and the main reason for placing the fragment close to the other fragments is its physical similarity.

4Q418 218 (cf. 4Q416 1,10?)

1   [ישפ֯ו֯ט על עבודת רשעה]

The overlap is minimal, and the main reason for placing the fragment close to the other fragments is its physical similarity.

4Q418 224 (cf. 4Q416 1,17?)

1   ברא[ת֯י֯ו כי֯א֯]
2   [כ֯ו֯ל֯]°[

Once again, the overlap is minimal, and the main reason for placing the fragment close to the other fragments is its appearance on the same Museum Plate.

For the sake of completeness I add a transcription of frag. 2a:

4Q418 2a (cf. 4Q416 1,9-10)

1   [ו֯ זה ל֯]זה וכול פקודתמה
2   ב[שמים] ישפוט על עבודת רשעה

Some of these fragments are very small, the overlap being therefore very limited. Yet, their physical similarity may be taken as an indication that they could all have stemmed from the same section of the scroll. It should also be observed that a reconstruction of the lines of these fragments of 4Q418 shows that all these fragments, if they indeed belong to the section, are not haphazardly distributed, but may belong to three vertical strokes. Thus, frag. 2a should be placed to the right of frag. 218 and above 208. It is even possible that these fragments physically join. Likewise, frag. 209 should be placed immediately above frag. 213. Frag. 217 may, according to the reconstruction, be placed immediately above frag. 234, these fragments sharing parts of the same letter (*kap*). In other words, with regard to most individual fragments, the grounds for identification are meagre, but the case becomes more convincing when one considers the cumulative evidence.

A complete reconstruction of the lines is difficult because of the possibility of variant readings (note the variants between 4Q416 1 and 4Q418* 2), and the different sizes of spacing in the fragments (compare, e.g., 4Q418 213 lines 1 and 2). Nevertheless, one may hesitantly reconstruct the conglomerate of the fragments transcribed above as follows.

RECONSTRUCTION OF THE BEGINNING OF 4QINSTRUCTION 117

4Q418 2a, 209, 218, 208, 2c (=213), 212, 217, 224

1 [ ]ו זה ל[זה וכול פקודתמה י]שׁ̇לׄיׄמוֹ] ויספרו
2 [ ]ב[שמים ישפ̇וֹ]ט על עבו[דת רש]עה וכול בני אמתו ירצו ל[קצה
3 [ויפחדו וירעו כו]ל אש[ר התגללו]בה כי ש[מ]ים ירֹאֹוּ [תרעש ממֹק̇]ומה ימים
4 [ותהום פחדו וי]רֹעו [כול רוח ב]שר ובני שמים] ב[יום משפטה] וכול עולה תתם]
5 [עד ישלם קץ ה]אֹמת] [לׄםׄ[ ]ׄ ל̇] בכו]לׄ] קצי [עד] כי אל אמת]
6 [הוא ומקדם שני עולם   להכון צדק בין טוב לרע ל ר כול משפט [
7 [ ]י[צר]בשר הואה ומביניׄ°
8 [ ]ברא[תֹיֹ כיֹאׄ] הׄ°
9 [ ]וֹדׄ °   [כוֹלׄ]

Perhaps not all of these fragments should be placed in the conglomerate. I think it is very probable that 4Q418 2a, 209, 212, and 213 overlap with 4Q416 1 and should be joined together in one conglomerate of fragments. The placement of 4Q418 217, 218 is quite plausible, that of 4Q418 224 possible, and that of 4Q418 208 possible but also problematic. 4Q418 73, which according to Elgvin overlaps with 4Q416 1,1-2, presents in line 1 the letters [כול רוח ב] which would fit textually in line 4 of the conglomerate, between frags. 208 and 213. Yet, materially the fragment does not fit, or only with the greatest difficulty.

This conglomerate of small overlapping 4Q418 fragments does not add very much to the text already known from 4Q416 1 and 4Q418 1, 2, 2b. One may take notice of the following additional text and variants.

Line 1. The reading]שׁ̇לׄיׄמוֹ[of 4Q418 209 is uncertain, but this reading and its placement supplies most of the letters missing in 4Q416 1,9: זה לזה וכול פקודתמה י]שלימו וי[ספרון].

Line 3. 4Q418 212,1 supplies the letters]תרעש ממֹק̇[. The reading וגם (ו)ארץ] תרעש ממֹק[ומה or]תרעש ממֹק̇[ומה ארץ based on Isa 13,13 gives the nice sequence heaven – earth – seas and the deep.

Line 4. 4Q418 208,2 gives the variant וי]רֹעו[, for which see the discussion above.

Line 4. 4Q418 212,2, reading]יום משפטה[, supplies some missing letters of 4Q416 1, which only has the letters]פטה[in line 13, restored by the editors to [הש]פטה.

Line 5. 4Q418 208,3 has the reading]אׄמת[, corresponding to 4Q416 1,13 האמ]ת. This parallel would exclude the alternative reading of האבׄ]דון in 4Q416 1.

Line 5. 4Q418 213, 3]לׄ° [ ]°לׄםׄ[. The reconstruction shows that לׄם[does not belong to ישלם. Instead, the line gives a few letters not preserved in 4Q416 and 4Q418*. Should one read עו]לׄם?

Line 9. 4Q418 224,2 gives the additional letters]כוֹלׄ °[.

Of course, it is possible that more of the fragments on this Museum Plate preserve text which should be placed in, or close to, the section of 4Q416 1. For example, 4Q418 214 which is physically similar to 4Q418 212 and 213, may be placed some lines lower at the bottom of the 4Q418 column. Also, physically similar fragments need not belong to the same column. A fragment belonging to the left part of a column may appear similar to one from the next column.

Apart from 4Q418* 1, all the other discussed fragments overlap with the bottom part of 4Q416 1, namely with lines 9-18. These lines can now be reconstructed as follows:

4Q416 1,9-18

9   זה לזה וכל פקודתמה י[שלימו וי]ספרו[ן]
10   בֹּשָׁמים ישפוט על עבודת רשעה וכל בני אמתו ירצוֹ לֹ]
11   קצה ויפחדו ויראֹעו כל אשר התגללו בה כי שמים יראֹוֹ]   תרעש ממקומה   [
12   [י]מים ותהמות פחדו ויתערערו כל רוח בשר ובני השמיֹ[ם יגילו ביום]
13   [מש]פטה וכל עולה תתם עוד ושלם קץ האמֹ[ת   לֹמֹ°°לֹ   [
14   בכל קצי עד כי אל אמת הוא ומקדם שני]   לֹ]
15   להכֹון צדק בין טוב לרֹעֹ לֹ]   רֹ] כל משפֹ[ט   [א]
16   [י]צר בשר הוֹאה ומבינֹיֹ°]   [ל ל
17   בראתיוֹ כֹי הֹ]
18   [   ]°דֹ[כוֹלֹי°

The main problem resides in the reconstruction of the end of line 11. In the conglomerate of 4Q418 fragments one may reconstruct, e.g., וגם [תרעש ממקֹ[ומה ארץ, which would result in a line of the same length as the other lines. However, the same reconstruction in 4Q416 1,11 gives a line which is much longer than line 12. How can one explain this discrepancy between 4Q416 and 4Q418? One may dismiss the identification of the overlap between 4Q418 212 and 4Q416 1, even though other considerations suggest the overlap. Alternatively, one may assume an irregularity in 4Q416 1, e.g., that one of the words was omitted, and perhaps subsequently added supralinearly. Or, otherwise, the text of 4Q416 might have contained a variant. For example, 4Q416 1,11 may have omitted the word ממקומה. After all, the expression תרעש הארץ(ו) is quite common in the Hebrew Bible, with or without a qualifier like ממקומה or מקצפו. Of course, the supposition of an irregularity or variant in a reconstruction is an admission of weakness. On the other hand, the few lines of 4Q416 1,11-14 display many variants *vis-à-vis* 4Q418* 2, and the assumption of yet another variant may therefore not be too far-fetched. One might, in that case, reconstruct 4Q416 1,11-12 as follows:

RECONSTRUCTION OF THE BEGINNING OF 4QINSTRUCTION

11 קצה ויפחדו וירוֹעו כל אשר התגללו בה כי שמים ירֹאוּן] וגם תרעש ארץ[
12 [יֹ]מֹים ותהמות פחדו ויתערערו כל רוח בשר ובני השמיֹם יגילו ביום[

The length of these lines corresponds exactly to the length of the lines in 4Q416 2 iii.

In Search for 4Q418 Fragments Belonging to the Beginning of the Work

A search for overlaps with the first part of 4Q416 1 is more difficult. Even with the additional words of 4Q418* 1, only a small part of the section remains, and the chances of overlaps are therefore rather small.

4Q416 1,1-8 + 4Q418* 1

1 כֹּלֹ רֹוֹחֹ[
2 ולתכן חפצוֹ]
3 מועד במועד וֹ[
4 לפי צבאם לֹמֹ[שׁוֹר במשורה ולֹ°
5 וממלכה למדֹ[ינה ומדינה לאיש ואיש
6 לפי מחסור צבאם [ומשפט כולם לֹוֹ
7 וצבא השמים הכֹיןֹ עֹ]   ומאורות[
8 למופתיהמה ואתות מו]

Different approaches are possible. Are there 4Q418 fragments which are physically similar to those already identified as overlaps of 4Q416 1? Is it feasible on textual grounds that they should be placed in the lacunae of 4Q416 1? Or, are there other fragments which overlap with the combined text of 4Q416 1 and 4Q418* 1, and might contextually belong to that section?

Both the editors and Elgvin point out that 4Q418 211 is physically similar to 4Q418 212 and 213, but Elgvin acknowledges that he did not succeed in combining it with the text of 4Q416 1,1-16[24]. The fragment should be transcribed as follows:

4Q418 211

1 [°°] [הֹמה]
2 [ובצאתם]
3 [מֹ בכול עֹוֹבֹוֹרֹתמה הלוֹ]א
4 [יֹד עולה כיא יבוֹא סוף]
5 [מֹתֹ]

Line 4 seems to have an eschatological content, and the few words in lines 2-3 may perhaps be related to heavenly phenomena. Line 2

---

24. ELGVIN, *Analysis*, p. 238.

] ובצאתם[may refer to the rising of luminaries, and the rare word עוֹבוֹרֹתמה in line 3 can mean (cf. the editors' discussion) 'their produce/ grain', 'their pregnancy', but also 'their intercalation'. Nonetheless, it is not at all clear to me where one could place the text of this fragment in the section. This also goes for the other 4Q418 fragments which are more or less similar to 4Q418 212 and 213.

Another fragment, which does not have the same material appearance, provides, however, a promising overlap with 4Q416 1. The editors read in 4Q418 229,]כֹּבֹו אוֹ תֹ°[, and note that the last word can also be read]ולת°. In fact, the latter reading is to be preferred. There is no left leg of a *he*, and the traces above the ceiling line fit with *lamed*, not with *he*. The lacuna between או and]ולת° is much larger than a normal word-dividing space, and, e.g., אוֹ[ר], easily fits, whereas even אוֹ[ט] is possible (the edges around the hole are abraded). A possible reconstruction would be כו]כֹבֹי אוֹ[ר], as in Ps 148,3 (cf. also Sir 50,6). Little remains of the last letter of the line, namely a descender and a small part of the head. The letter may, e.g., be *kap*, in which case the last word may be read ולתכֹ[ן. Words beginning with ולת are quite rare, and the possible reading ולתכֹ[ן called 4Q416 1,2 to mind. The whole fragment can be read as follows:

כו]כֹבֹי אוֹ[ר] ולתֹכֹ[ן	1
ירוֹצוֹ מעת עֹ] [	2
להדמות בכו]	3
ת	
]°[ ]°°[	4

The last trace of line 2 may also belong to *shin*, *ayin* or *sade*. Perhaps one might combine the words of this fragment with those of 4Q416 1 + 4Q418* 1.

4Q416 1 (4Q418 229 underlined)

כֹל רֹוֹחֹ]	1
ולתכן חפצוֹ [ירוצו מעת עולם] כוכבי אור]	2
מועד במועד וֹ] להדמות בכו [	3
לפי צבאם למֹ]שוֹר במשורה ולֹ° ת למלכה]	4
וממלכה למדֹ]ינה ומדינה לאיש ואיש	5

The overlap is restricted to part of one word, and therefore the textual join is speculative. Nonetheless, 'shining stars' may fit in a section which deals with the luminaries, and the partly reconstructed phrase "since the time of eternity they run, season upon season, and" may not be impossible. For the 'running' of luminaries, cf. perhaps 1 Enoch 75,8.

For the idea of eternal pursuit of the courses of the luminaries, cf. Ps. Sol. 18,12-14 and 1 Enoch 69,20-21. In another context, one might instead suggest מעת עֶ[רב לעת בוקר. It is more difficult to explain the third line, and to connect the words to 4Q416 1,4 לפי צבאם. The editors discuss the possible meanings of להדמות. Since this line may still be connected to the luminaries, one should perhaps reconstruct a negation before להדמות[, e.g., ואין]להדמות, "without coming to a stand-still", or לוא ...[להדמות. This would be a slight variation from the more common statement in literature of the period that the luminaries do not alter or change their courses.

Is it possible to relate]לפי צבאם למֹ[שׁוֹר במשורה[of 4Q416 1,4 to]להדמות בכו[, and to restore the lacuna between the phrases? The editors discuss the words למֹ[שׁוֹר במשורה, and tentatively derive משורה from the roots שרה or שרר, 'rule'. This meaning may be attested in Isa 9,5 where the Masoretic text reads המשרה, and 1QIsa[a] המשורה, and משור would be an Aramaising infinitive (cf. Qimron §330.1.b). Therefore they translate: "according to their host to r[ule by dominion". This explanation is attractive since it seems to fit the context. The notion that the luminaries 'rule' is quite common, though usually expressed by המשיל and ממשלת, and in Aramaic by שלט. I do not want to rule out this suggestion, but one should also consider two other possibilities which are not mentioned by the editors. First, משורה is mentioned a few times as a measure of liquids in the Hebrew Bible. In Ezek 4,11 and 16 one finds מים במשורה and לחם במשקל, in Lev 19,35 three types of measure are mentioned, במדה ובמשקל ובמשורה, and 1 Chr 23,29 joins משורה and מדה. In view of the frequent use of משקל and מדה in 4QInstruction, משורה may have here a similar general meaning (whereas it is used as a measure of liquid in 4Q299 6 i 5 ובמשורה ישקו). Yet, this does not explain the word למשור, assuming that 4Q416 למֹ[שׁ] and 4Q418*]שור[should be joined. Secondly, משורה may perhaps be a variant spelling of מסורה, with interchange of *samek* and *sin*. The word מסורה is attested in 1QS X,4, and in Aramaic in 4Q204 (4QEn[c]) 1 i 19 (cf. 1 Enoch 2,1). Milik suggests in both texts the meaning "'station', or more accurately, 'relative position of a star in relation to others'"[25]. Even though it is not clear from which root מסורה stems (סור[26] or אסר[27]?), משור could also be an infinitive, the phrase משור במשורה perhaps meaning something like "to make an orbit", or "to keep station". The broken word of 4Q418 229,3 בכו[ן is, of course, easily restored to ל[בכו, and one can imagine that the text said something like

---

25. MILIK, *Aramaic Fragments*, p. 187.
26. KNIBB, *Book of Enoch* 2, p. 61.
27. BLACK, *Book of Enoch*, p. 109.

"and in all their paths they go according to their host, to rule by dominion (or: to keep station)". However, a reconstruction like בכו]ל דרכיהם בכו]ל מסלותם ידרוכו] לפי צבאם or ילכו] לפי צבאם, would demand quite some space in between the preserved clauses, resulting in lines of inequal length in 4Q418. Instead of בכו]ל דרכיהם ילכו, one can also read בכו]ל עת ילכו, "continually they go", or even בכו]שר ילכו, "properly they go". The latter corresponds in meaning to 1 Enoch 2,1.

How plausible is the identification of 4Q418 229 as a parallel to 4Q416 1 and 4Q418* 1? The fragments overlap with regard to ולתכֿ, and it is possible to construct a composite text which makes sense. On the other hand, the lines of 4Q418 would be slightly shorter than those of 4Q416 1, whereas the 4Q418 fragments overlapping with 4Q416 9ff indicate that there the lines of 4Q418 would be slightly longer. This difference does not support the identification, but the divergence is not that large, and could be explained by small changes within a column with regard to spacing and size of letters. I did not pay special attention to the physical characteristics of 4Q418 229, and Strugnell's observations on frag. 229 are contradictory. Thus he states that "[o]n material grounds frgs. 229, 230, and 238 should be placed close to each other. Furthermore, they are perhaps to be associated with frgs. 147–165". On the other hand, he remarks that "[f]rgs. 198–202 (and perhaps frgs. 228 and 229) resemble each other in quality of skin, in size of writing, and in approximate height of the uninscribed margin above the ruled column". Then again, "Frgs. 234 and 235, if rightly assigned to 4Q418, would have stood close together and close to frg. 229". These different observations show the difficulties in describing the 4Q418 fragments. This also goes, e.g., for 4Q418 199, which, Strugnell claims, is similar to frags. 198 and 200-201, but completely different from 4Q418 64 and 66 with which it forms a perfect join. In point of fact, the upper part of frag. 199 is different from the lower part, the top being light and similar to frags. 64 and 66, the bottom darker and stained. In short, Strugnell's observations about the material appearance of 4Q418 229 do not of necessity invalidate the identification.

Tentatively, one might pursue the possibility that, as Strugnell suggests, 4Q418 238 should be placed close to 4Q418 229 on material grounds. The fragment can be transcribed as follows:

4Q418 238

[מֹשכיל וֹא]	1
]אׄ וֹ²מעשה[	2
התבו]נֹן בנהיי עׄ]ולם	3

RECONSTRUCTION OF THE BEGINNING OF 4QINSTRUCTION 123

4 [נצֹ֯חׄ֯יׄ]
5 [יום]
6 [לׄ]

At first sight little connects the fragment to 4Q416 1. However, one may speculate on the possibility that the description of the luminaries was preceded by a call to consider or to contemplate, as in 1 Enoch 2-5. The Aramaic terms used in these chapters, חזו or לכו (חזו)א, and אתבוננא, correspond to the imperatives הבט and התבונן which are used throughout 4QInstruction. The עׄ]ולם נהיי (or supply עׄ]ולמים or עׄ]ד) may be a reference to celestial beings, though it is not certain whether the participle refers to the future. As such, it may perhaps be parallel to 4Q416 1,1 כֹל רׄוׄחׄ[or include the luminaries. The words נצח and יום might fit somewhere in the lacunae of 4Q416 1,1-2 or 1-3, but any textual reconstruction based upon these words would be entirely speculative. If the fragment did indeed belong to the section, it would preserve the very beginning of the composition, and line 1 might be the first line of the column. In that case מׄשכיל[might be part of an address to a בן משכיל (cf. 4Q417 1 i 25), or a reference to the "instructor". However, since the fragment does not overlap with 4Q416 1, and does not provide any plausible textual joins, this identification is no more than a possibility.

The incorporation of all the preceding suggestions in the text of 4Q416 1 results in the following text and translation.

1 כֹל רׄוׄחׄ[כוכבי אור[
2 ולתכן חפצֹיׄ]   ירוצו מעת עולם[
3 מועד במועד וֹ[ואין להדמות בכושר ילכו[
4 לפי צבאם למׄ[שור במשורה ולׄי°   ת   למלכה[
5 וממלכה למדֹ[ינה ומדינה לאיש ואיש
6 לפי מחסור צבאם [ומשפט כולם לוֹ
7 וצבא השמים הכֹין עׄלׄ[ומאורות[
8 למופתיהמה ואתות מו[עדיהמה
9 [זה לזה וכל פקודתמה זֹ[שלימו ו]ספרו[
10 בֹשמים ישפוט על עבודת רשעה וכל בני אמתוֹ ירצוֹ לׄ[ו
11 קצה ויפחדו וירוֹעו כל אשר התגללו בה כי שמים יראוֹן] וגם תרעש ארץ[
12 י]מׄים ותהמות פחדו ויתערערו כל רוח בשר ובני השמיׄ[ם יגילו ביום[
13 [מש]פטה וכל עולה תתם עוד וֹשלם קץ האמ[ת   לׄםׄ°°°לׄ [
14 בכל קצי עד כי אל אמת הוא ומקדם שנׄי[עולם   ל[
15 להכֹין צדק בין טוב לרֹעֹ לׄ[ ]רׄ כל משפׄ[ט   [א
16 [י]ׄצר בשר הואה ומבינוׄ[°   [ל ל [
17 בֹראתיוֹ כֹי הׄ[]°
18 [°וׄד[ ]   כוׄלׄ[°

Variants

4Q416		4Q418*		4Q418	
1,11	וירי̇עו	2,3	וי̇ר̇ע̇ו		
1,11 (?)	[וגם תרעש ארץ]			212,1 (?)	וגם תרעש ממק̇[ומה ארץ]
1,12	ותהמות	2,4	ותהום		
1,12	ויתערערו	2,4	ויתר̇]	208,2	וי̇]ר̇ע̇ו (?)
1,12	השמ̇י̇]ם			213,2	שמים]
1,13	עוד י̇שלם	2,5	עד י̇שלם		
1,15	להכ̇ן צדק	2,7	להבין צדיק		

Translation

1. every spirit [stars of light,]
2. and to mete out the tasks of [they run from eternal time,]
3. season upon season, and [without standing still. Properly they go,]
4. according to their host, to ru[le by dominion, and to   for kingdom]
5. and kingdom, for pr[ovince and province, for each and every man,
6. according to the poverty of their host. [And the regulation of them all belongs to him
7. And the host of heavens he has established ov[er   and luminaries]
8. for their portents, and the signs of [their] se[asons
9. one after another. And all their assignments [they] shall [complete, and they shall] count (?) [
10. in heaven He shall pronounce judgment upon the work of wickedness, and all His faithful children shall be favourably accepted by [Him
11. its end. And they shall be in terror. And all who defiled themselves in it, shall cry out. For the heavens shall fear, and the earth too shall be shaken (from its place)]
12. The [s]eas and the depths shall be in terror, and every spirit of flesh will cry out. But the sons of heaven [shall rejoice in the day of]
13. its [judg]ment. And all iniquity shall come to an end, while the period of truth will be completed [
14. in all periods of eternity. For He is a God of truth, and from before the years of [eternity
15. So that the righteous may distinguish between good and evil, so that [ ] every regula[tion

16. [incl]ination of the flesh is he/it. And from understanding (?) [
17. His creatures, for [
18. [ ] [

Comments

In the translation above some of the variant readings are preferred above the readings of the text of 4Q416. Since there is no need to repeat the comments of the editors, the following comments only serve as additional remarks.

Ll. 1-2. The words of the composite text [ולתכן חפצ̇י [כו]כבי או[ר] may belong to two parallel clauses, e.g., "to establish the circuits of the sta]rs of lig[ht], and to mete out the tasks of [the luminaries of …]". The editors dismiss the reading חפצי, because a first person suffix would not fit in the text. Yet, חפצי may also be the plural noun in the construct state, not meaning "pleasures", but "tasks", as in, e.g., 1QS III,17 and 1QH^a IX,15 (Sukenik I,13). In the latter text חפצי[ה]ם is parallel to משאם and עבודתם.

L. 3 מועד במועד. The phrase should be compared to the common expression שנה בשנה.

L. 6 ומשפט כולם. It is likely that משפט here, and possibly also in line 15, is not "judgment", but "ordinance", "law", or the like, as, e.g., in 1QS III,17 משפטי כול and probably 1QH^a IX,11 (Sukenik I,9) ומשפט לכול מעשיהם.

L. 9 זה לזה. The phrase need not be preceded by a verb of speech (the editors suggest יגידו), but may express the idea that the periods succeed one after another, as in 1QS X,4.

L. 14 ומקדם שנ[י] עולם. Cf. the editors' comments to 4Q416 1,14 and 4Q418 69 ii 12. Apparently שני עולם is used as an alternative for the simple עולם. For מקדם עולם, cf. CD II,7 (not XI,7).

Conclusions

To what extent do the identifications of overlaps as presented above contribute to the reconstruction of 4QInstruction?

I have argued in the discussion of the codicological issues that 4Q418 1 and 2 belong neither to 4Q418 nor to 4Q418a. The editors' hypothesis that these fragments were part of a repair sheet is unfounded, and should be dismissed in favour of the assumption that these fragments are remnants of a separate manuscript (4Q418*). This implies that the preliminary suggestions on 4Q418 by Steudel and Lucassen, as presented in the *DJD* volume, are untenable.

The identification of nine 4Q418 fragments overlapping with 4Q416 1 has the merit of slightly reducing the large number of small isolated 4Q418 fragments. At first sight the overlapping 4Q418 fragments add little to the text of 4Q416 and 4Q418*. Yet, these few additional words give a better understanding of parts of the section.

According to the editors the first part of 4Q416 1 speaks about "God's orderly rule over the cosmos – the heavenly hosts and the luminaries". Indeed, the preserved text of 4Q416 1 and 4Q418* 1 only allows for such a general description. The additional words of 4Q418 229 and 209, however, show that these verses contain the well-known motif of the orderly courses of the luminaries in accordance with their tasks. This understanding suggests that 4Q416 1,2 should not be read ולתכן חפצו, "and to order His (?) good pleasure", but ולתכן חפצי, "and to mete out the tasks of". Likewise, וכל פקודתמה in 4Q416 1,9 is not "and all their visitation (?)", but "and all their assignments", to be supplemented with ישלימו, "they shall complete", which is provided by 4Q418 209,1. In view of this context one should probably understand משפט in line 6 as "regulation", not as "judgment". The section may indeed describe God's orderly rule over the cosmos, but the specific intent is that the luminaries comply with God's decrees.

The section on the luminaries thus serves as an introduction to the main part of 4QInstruction, in which men and women are admonished to comply to their determined tasks. The phrase that God has allotted the inheritance (נחלה) of every living being (4Q418 81,20; 4Q416 3,2) seems to express the idea that God has determined everyone's position in life. On the other hand, the section on judgment (4Q416 1,10-14) which immediately follows the section on the luminaries, possibly refers to the consequences of obedience or disobedience to God's decrees. Unfortunately, the words which could have expressed the connection between the two sections have been lost in the manuscripts.

Apart from the identified overlaps of 4Q418 fragments with 4Q416 1, other 4Q418 fragments might also belong to the column, and it is not impossible that some might preserve parts of the opening lines of the composition. Thus, one may tentatively consider the possibility that 4Q418 238 belonged to the beginning of the column. This would imply that the third-person description of 4Q416 1 and parallels was embedded in a second person address, which admonished the addressee to contemplate.

Qumran Instituut   Eibert J.C. TIGCHELAAR
Nieuwe Kijk in 't Jatstraat 104
9712 SL Groningen
The Netherlands

DER WEISHEITSTEXT 4Q185
EINE NEUE EDITION[1]

In DJD V hat J.M. Allegro[2] als 4Q*185* einen bisher unbekannten hebräischen Text veröffentlicht, von dem er ohne nähere Inhalts- und Gattungsangabe die Photographien (Plates XXIX-XXX), eine Transkription des hebräischen Textes, die Übersetzung und einige wenige Anmerkungen gegeben hat.

J. Strugnell[3] hat sich in einer umfangreichen Rezension nicht damit begnügt, in die üblichen Klagen über die unzureichende Qualität der Edition von DJD V einzustimmen, sondern hat Lesungen und Verständnis auch dieses Textes entscheidend verbessert. Neben der Edition werden die Vorschläge von J. Strugnell daher durchgehend berücksichtigt[4].

J. Strugnell hat auch erste Hinweise zum Charakter des Textes und zur Gattungsfrage gegeben[5]: »selon toute probabilité l'ouvrage est sapientiel dans sa langue et dans ses thèmes, et [...] il appartient au genre 'instruction', ou peut-être 'testament', d'un sage (ou d'un personnage historique) addressé à 'mes fils' ou 'mon peuple'«. Damit ist der Grundcharakter des Textes durchaus richtig getroffen, doch scheinen aufgrund einiger verbesserter Lesungen genauere Aussagen möglich zu sein; dieser Beitrag beschränkt sich jedoch auf eine Neuedition und Übersetzung.

Die folgenden Anmerkungen zur Einordnung der Fragmente sowie die hier gegebenen Transkriptionen stehen selbstverständlich unter dem

---

1. Teile der Einleitung und des Textes in: LICHTENBERGER, *Mahnrede*. Der Beitrag geht auf Arbeiten zurück, die ich 1973-1977 in der Marburger Qumranforschungsstelle unter der Leitung von H. Stegemann durchführen konnte. Ihm sei noch einmal herzlich gedankt. Für die Herstellung der Druckvorlage danke ich Stefan Krauter, für die Durchsicht Dr. Armin Lange.
2. ALLEGRO, *Qumran Cave 4*. I, pp. 85-87, Plates XXIX-XXX.
3. STRUGNELL, *Notes en marge*; zu 4Q*185*, pp. 169-273.
4. Die Übersetzungen von GARCÍA MARTÍNEZ, *Dead Sea Scrolls Translated*, pp. 380-382; vgl. auch ID. – TIGCHELAAR, *Study Edition*, Bd. 1, pp. 378-381; MAIER, *Texte*, Bd. 2, pp. 132-135; VERMES, *Dead Sea Scrolls 4th edition*, pp. 275-276 und HARRINGTON, *Wisdom Texts from Qumran*, pp. 35-39, fußen auf Strugnells Verbesserungen. Bei Harrington finden sich auch Erläuterungen zur Gattung und zum Aufbau. TOBIN, *4Q185*, WHITE CRAWFORD, *Lady Wisdom* und VERSEPUT, *4Q185* gehören zu den wenigen, die dem Text Aufmerksamkeit geschenkt haben. Für den Hinweis auf die beiden Letztgenannten und hilfreiche Gespräche danke ich Prof. Dr. John Kampen. Vgl. weiter HARRINGTON, *Wisdom Texts*, pp. 976-980.
5. STRUGNELL, *Notes en marge*, p. 269.

Vorbehalt einer Kontrolle an den Originalen. Einige neu vorgeschlagene Lesungen wurden durch bessere Photographien möglich[6]; doch trotzdem bleiben sowohl verschiedene Lesungen von J.M. Allegro und J. Strugnell fraglich, wie auch eigene Vorschläge teilweise ungesichert, da nicht immer zu entscheiden ist, ob es sich bei den einzelnen fraglichen Stellen um Schriftreste, Tintenkleckse oder Flecken auf dem Leder bzw. um Lederbeschädigungen handelt[7].

Die Edition bietet den Text auf drei Kolumnen als die Fragmente 1-2; diese drei Kolumnen erweisen sich freilich aufgrund der auf den Photographien erkennbaren Risse als aus wesentlich mehr Fragmenten zusammengesetzt. Vier weitere Fragmente wurden vom Editor nicht eingeordnet (Fragm. 3-6).

Problematisch erscheint die Anfügung der Z. 1-3 in Kol. III schon wegen des größeren Abstands des Schriftbeginns vom Nahtrand gegenüber den Zeilen 7-13; aber auch die Zusammengehörigkeit von Z. 1-2 und Z. 3 ist wegen des nicht übereinstimmenden rechten Schreibrandes in Frage zu stellen. Daher empfiehlt es sich, die Z. 1-2 als Fragment 7, die Z. 3 als Fragment 8 hier auszugliedern. Die Einfügung des Fragments 3 innerhalb von Kol. III durch Strugnell, *Notes en marge*, p. 272 ist wahrscheinlich, der genaue Ort hingegen nicht völlig gewiß (s. unten die Anmerkung zu 1-2 III 7).

Die Einordnung des Fragments Planche I h bei Strugnell, *Notes en marge*, p. 257 in Kol. III ist nicht zu sichern: Der Abstand des Beginns der letzten Zeile des Fragments h zum Rand ist größer, als daß bei einer Anfügung an den Lederrest in Kol. III der Zeilenbeginn mit den übrigen Zeilenanfängen in einer Linie läge; zudem stimmen die Bruchränder nicht überein. – In Anbetracht der wenigen erhaltenen Buchstaben auf Fragment h sind definitive Aussagen über die Zugehörigkeit zu 4Q*185* kaum möglich, sie ist eher fraglich (s. besonders ב und ק); von einer Einordnung und Berücksichtigung wird daher hier abgesehen.

Auf der Photographie ist nicht eindeutig zu erkennen, ob auf Fragment 1 ganz rechts unten noch ein ל der Zeile 15 einer Kol. I vorhergehenden Kolumne zu lesen ist; träfe dies zu, wären – abgesehen davon, daß die Fragmente aus weiteren Kolumnen stammen können – Reste von sicher insgesamt vier Kolumnen erhalten. In jedem Fall aber läßt der Nahtrand rechts auf vorhergehende Kolumnen schließen, wobei nicht sicher ist, ob sie in denselben Textzusammenhang gehören.

---

6. PAM 41307; 41585; 43439; 43514.
7. STRUGNELL, *Notes en marges*, p. 269: »Les difficultés de lecture proviennent du fait que le manuscrit porte beaucoup de taches d'encre accidentelles, qui ne sont pas de lettres, tandis que sa surface est détériorée en un certain nombre d'endroits«.

Die Edition gibt keine Datierung der Handschrift aufgrund paläographischer Bestimmungen. Strugnell, *Notes en marge*, ordnet sie unter Verweis auf ה, כ, מ und ק der späthasmonäischen Zeit zu (p. 269).

Der Text selbst ist mit Sicherheit älter und reicht seiner Entstehung nach wahrscheinlich in vorqumranische Zeit. Folgende Gründe sind dafür namhaft zu machen:

1. Im Verhältnis zu den sog. typischen Qumranschriften findet sich ein z. T. auffälliger Gebrauch der Defektivschreibung[8]. Das läßt auf eine Vorlage schließen, die wenig intensiv von der Pleneschreibung Gebrauch machte.
2. Der Text bietet eine Anzahl von Wörtern, die zum ersten Mal in dem durch die Qumrantexte verfügbaren Schrifttum auftauchen[9].
3. Der Text läßt typische qumranische Theologumena vermissen, sondern lehnt sich stark an weisheitliche Formen und Gedanken an[10].
4. Ein besonders wichtiges Argument für eine frühe Entstehung des Textes ist die freie, d. h. außerhalb eines Bibelzitates vorkommende Verwendung von יהוה (1-2 II 3) und אלהים (1-2 I 14; häufig in Kol. III belegt oder zu ergänzen). H. Stegemann[11] hat nachgewiesen, daß ein derartiger Gebrauch ins dritte bzw. gegebenenfalls in den Anfang des zweiten vorchristlichen Jahrhunderts verweist, es sich jedenfalls für die mit Sicherheit in der Qumrangemeinde entstandenen Texte nicht nachweisen läßt[12].

Die genannten Argumente können für eine vorqumranische Entstehung des Textes sprechen. Die Existenz innerhalb der Qumranfunde belegt den Gebrauch in der Qumrangemeinde; die späthasmonäische Handschrift bezeugt vielleicht, daß er in der Qumrangemeinde kopiert wurde[13].

Gattungsmäßig läßt sich der Text im weiteren Sinne zur Gruppe weisheitlicher Mahnreden stellen[14]. Wir finden aber innerhalb dieser Rahmengattung verschiedene Gattungselemente, die dem Text in ihrer Folge eine starke Bewegtheit geben, z. B. Belehrung mit Lehreröffnungsanruf (1-2 I 7-9), Elemente der Vergänglichkeitsklage (1-2 I 9-13), Erinnerung an Geschichte (1-2 I 14-15)[15], Imperativreihen (1-2 I 13-II 2; 1-2

---

8. Z. B. 1-2 I 9 רוחתיו; s. auch 1-2 II 14 אבתיו; dazu auch STRUGNELL, *Notes en marge*, p. 269. Vgl. auch den Beitrag von A. SCHOORS im vorliegenden Band.
9. 1-2 I 10 חציר; Verbum חקר in 1-2 II 1; Substantive דש in 1-2 II 12; dazu das problematische עגו in 1-2 I 11.
10. S. dazu die Anmerkungen zur Übersetzung, wichtigster Referenztext ist jetzt 4QInstruction[b].
11. STEGEMANN, ΚΥΡΙΟΣ, pp. 256f.; 178f.
12. Vgl. dazu auch den Beitrag von J. STRUGNELL im vorliegenden Band.
13. Zu den die Handschrift 4Q185 und den von ihr bezeugten Text betreffenden Einleitungsfragen vgl. auch den Beitrag von A. LANGE im vorliegenden Band.
14. Vgl. aber den Beitrag von J. STRUGNELL im vorliegenden Band.
15. Vgl. dazu auch den Beitrag von G.J. BROOKE im vorliegenden Band.

II 3-4), Einrede von Frevlern (1-2 II 9-11), Makarismen (1-2 II 8-9; 1-2 II 13-15)[16].

In den Anmerkungen soll im weiteren Verlauf das Verhältnis zum Alten Testament und zu den Qumrantexten aufgezeigt werden. Zuvor wird eine Transkription des hebräischen Textes mit Diskussion und Begründungen für Lesungen und Ergänzungen vorgelegt. Dabei wurden wahrscheinliche Ergänzungen in den Text aufgenommen, weniger sichere sind in den Anmerkungen zum hebräischen Text aufgeführt.

HEBRÄISCHER TEXT

1-2 I

1 [...] ○ ○ [
2 [....]
3 [...].כֹ̇י ○.[○
4 [...].טָהור וקדושׁ̇[. ○
5 [...] כנק]מתו וכחמתו [. ○
6 [...] ש[ל]ו[ש] ועד עשר פעמים [. ....]
7 [... .]. ואין כח לעמוד לפניה ואין מקוה
8 לוֹעם] אף אלהינו] ומי יכלכל לעמוד לפני מלאכיו כי באש
9 להבה ישפט] ועמ]וֹ רוחתיו ואתם בני אדם א[ין כח]כי הנֹה
10 כחציר יצמח ופאֹרתֹו יפרח כציץ חסדו נשב]ה בו[רוחו
11 ויבש עגזו וציצו תשא רוח עד אֹיֹקום לעמֹ]דו מל]בֹד
12 [וֹ]יֹבקשוהוֹ ולא ימצאהו ואֹי̇ן מקוה vacat ולא ימצא כי רוח
13 והוא כצל ימיוֹ עֹל האֹר]ץ[ועתה שמעו נא עמי והשכילו
14 לי פתאיִם יֹתומו מן [ג]בורת אלהינו וזכרו נפלאים עשה
15 במצרים ומופתיוֹ בֹ]ארץ חם[ויֹעדץ לבבכֹם מפני פחדו

1-2 II

1 ועשו רצונו .[...........] נ]פשכם כחסדיו הטבים חקרו לכם דרך
2 לחיים ומסלהֹ[. ....] ○ שארית לבניכם אחריכם ולמה תתנו
3 [לבב]כֹם לשחת[........] מ[שפט שמעוני בני ואל תמרו דברי יהוה
4 [וֹ]אל תֹצעדו]דרך אשר צוה לי[עֹקב ונתיבה חקק לישחק הלוא טב יום
5 אחד [תער]וֹךְ בעשרֹ [. ......] ○ יֹרֹאֹתו ולא לעתת מפחד ומפח יקוש
6 [...]○[. ....].○ ○ ולהא]מן[מן מלאכיו כי אין חשך
7 וֹאפֹלה ○.[............].○○ הוא ○.[.....]ב[י]נ]תֹו ודעתו ואתמה
8 מה תֹת[בון]ננו .... מ]לפניו תצא דעה לכל עם אשרי אדם נתנה לו
9 בן אד]ם .... יוד[עֹים וֹאל יתהלל]ו[ן רֹשעים לאֹמור לא נֹתנה

---

16. Vgl. dazu auch den Beitrag von H.-J. FABRY im vorliegenden Band. Außerdem in Kürze vom Verf. *4Q525 im Rahmen der Seligpreisungen des Frühjudentums*; *Makarisms in Matthew 5:13ff in their Jewish Context*.

DER WEISHEITSTEXT 4Q185 – EINE NEUE EDITION

10 לי ולֹא̇ אדרשנה אלהים נתנה לישראל וכֹובד ט̇וב זבדה וֹכֹל עמו גאל
11 והרג שׂ∘∘∘∘.[. . . . . . .]אבׄ. . . .[.יאמר המתכבד בה ישֹאנה יֹרוׄשה
12 ומצאה לֹו כי רׄבׄה יבוֹלה ועמה̇ ארך יֹמים ודשן עֹצם ושמחת לבב עשׄר וכבוׄד̇
13 וחסדיו לֹעׄמיה וישׂוֹעוֹתׄיׄו לוׄכֹל בניה אשרי אדם יעשנה ולא יגׄוֹעׄל עלׄה . .]∘
14 מרמה לא יבקשנה וֹבׄחלקות לֹא יׄחזׄיקנה כן תתן לאבתיו כן ירשנהֹ̇ ויעשׄנה̇
15 בכל עז כחו ובכל מאׄ]דו לאין חסׄר ויורישנה לצאצאיו ודעתו לעׄמיה לׄרוב

1-2 III

1 . . . .
2 . . . .
3 . . . .
4 . . . .
5 . . . .
6 . . . .
7 . . . .] הנוׄתׄן . . . . אלׄ]הׄ]ים כוׄנן [. . . . . .]
8 . . . .]∘∘ אלׄ]הים יבחן כל מזׄמׄ]וׄת לבב
9 והוׄאׄ . . . . אלהים עשה דברי ברי]ת ו [. . . . . . .]
10 ולׄא עׄ]שה אלׄ]הים מש]פט במסורתׄ [ויד]ע [. . . . .]
11 הלֹא אֹלהיׄ]ם עשה לבותׄ וידׄ]ע מזמותיהם אלהים יביט
12 אלֹ כל חדרי בטן ויחפש כליתוׄן אלׄ]הׄ]ים עשה
13 לשון וידע דברה אלהים עשה ידים [וידע פעלתיהן
14 [. . . . .] אם ט̇וב ואם רעׄ [. . . . .]
15 [. . . . .] במחשׄ]בות [. . . . .]

Fragmente

4 I

1 [∘ לעוֹלם
2 שׄ]פׄטי ∘∘ ויׄשבוֹן]
3 . . . קודש[

4 II

1 ו∘∘∘[
2 ונדריבה ∘∘[

5

1 ו∘]
2 מופׄ]ט
3 הדרׄ]

6

1 [∘∘∘]
2 והריׄאׄתי א∘[
3 בנׄיׄ]

7

1   א].[ה כי טו[ן
2   וממאורות ו ו[○ ○
3   [..]○ ○[

8

1   ום[○

ANMERKUNGEN ZUM HEBRÄISCHEN TEXT

1-2 I

Zeile 1: Zeilenende: Es ist fraglich, ob es sich um einen Schriftrest handelt; wenn ja, dann ○ ה[.
Zeile 3: Allegro, *Qumran Cave 4*. I,]כֿוֹ○[auch]כֿוֹ○[möglich; es ist nicht sicher, ob der dunkle Punkt links unten neben י bzw. ו ein Buchstabenrest ist und ob er zu einem neuen Wort gehört – weswegen dann ein Wortzwischenraum anzunehmen wäre – oder ob er Teil des Wortes ist, zu dessen Bestandteilen auch כֿי bzw. כֿוֹ gehören.
Zeilenende: Buchstabenrest?
Zeile 4: Zeilenende: Buchstabenrest?
Zeile 5: Möglicherweise zu ergänzen כנק[מֹתו; Allegro, *Qumran Cave 4*. I, p. 85; Strugnell, *Notes en marge*, p. 269 מתו.
Mit Strugnell, *Notes en marge*, p. 269 וכחמתו]; die Klammer ist gegenüber Strugnell, *Notes en marge*, um einen Wortzwischenraum nach links zu rücken. Zur Verschiebung des oberen Fragments nach links richtig Strugnell, *Notes en marge*, p. 269.
Zeilenende: Buchstabenrest?
Zeile 6: Lies möglicherweise ש[ל]ו[ש; der Punkt unter dem מ in Z. 5 kann – sofern er Schriftrest ist – nur zu einem ל in Z. 6 gehören. Allegro, *Qumran Cave 4*. I, p. 85 [ש.
Der senkrechte kurze Strich vor פֿעמים könnte – falls Schriftrest – Teil eines ל sein. Dann müßte man mit Strugnell, *Notes en marge*, p. 269 dessen Tilgung annehmen.
Zeile 7: Zeilenende: Wahrscheinlich folgt auf מקוה – so auch Allegro, *Qumran Cave 4*. I, p. 85; Strugnell, *Notes en marge*, p. 272 – kein weiteres Wort.
Zeile 8: Die Lesung Strugnell, *Notes en marge*, p. 269 לזעם] erscheint gut möglich, vgl. Nah 1,6; als Ergänzung könnte [אלהינו אף לזעֹם] sachgemäß sein, vgl. Thr 2,6. Strugnell, *Notes en marge*, p. 272: »the indignation of her wrath«; neben לזעם] wäre wohl auch לזעֹף] אף [אלהינו, vgl. Jes 30,30, möglich.

Zeilenende: Mit Strugnell, *Notes en marge*, p. 269 gegen Allegro, *Qumran Cave 4*. I, p. 85 ist באש zu lesen.

Zeile 9: Allegro, *Qumran Cave 4*. I, p. 85 י[ו]שפטו; Strugnell, *Notes en marge*, p. 272: »will *they judge* the ... of His spirits«; beide nehmen als Subjekt die מלאכים von Z. 8 an; trifft das zu, würde zu dem Schrifttrest nach der Lücke die Ergänzung ישפט[וה]ו passen. Bei Gott als Subjekt sollte man lesen ישפט ועמ[ו] רוחתיו, weniger wahrscheinlich ישפט לפנ[י]ך oder [ביד]י oder [בתו]ך.

Zeilenende: Da mit größter Sicherheit]כי הנה (so auch Allegro, *Qumran Cave 4*. I, p. 85; Strugnell, *Notes en marge*, p. 272) zu lesen und als Neueinsatz aufzufassen ist, ist eine Lesung wie אדם אי זה דר[כו wenig wahrscheinlich. Wie in 1-2 II 3 ist בני Anrede (Plural plus Suffix der 1. Person Singular), ist also nicht wie Allegro, *Qumran Cave 4*. I, p. 86; Skehan (nach Strugnell, *Notes en marge*, pp. 269.272) Nomen regens zu אדם. Daher ist es auch weniger wahrscheinlich, daß ein Weheruf fortsetzte (Skehan nach Strugnell, *Notes en marge*, pp. 269.272 [א]וי לכם), sondern eine Aussage über die Nichtigkeit des Menschen, die Thema der folgenden Zeilen ist, ist zu erwarten; so könnte z. B. ergänzt werden: אדם א[פס הוא, oder אדם א[ין הוא besser vielleicht אדם א[ין כח הוא.

Zeile 10: Drittes Wort: Allegro, *Qumran Cave 4*. I, p. 85; Strugnell, *Notes en marge*, p. 272 מארצו ist paläographisch nicht sicher und vom Sinn her (es wird vom Menschen gesprochen!) nicht passend. Besser wäre evtl. באמצו, doch sprechen auch dagegen paläographische Gründe: Vor dem von Allegro, *Qumran Cave 4*. I, und Strugnell, *Notes en marge*, gelesenen ersten Buchstaben (מ) gibt es einen Schrifttrest, der nur zu י, ו, ז passen kann; der vermeintliche erste Buchstabe ist weiter weder מ noch ב, sondern wahrscheinlich פ. Das folgende א ist sicher. Der Buchstabe danach ist wahrscheinlich ר. Was von Allegro, *Qumran Cave 4*. I, und Strugnell, *Notes en marge*, als צ gelesen wird, ist besser der linke Teil eines ת, dessen rechter Abstrich verloren ist; letzter Buchstabe ist ein sicheres ו. Daher ist mit großer Sicherheit zu lesen: וּפֹאַרְתּוֹ.

Gegen Allegro, *Qumran Cave 4*. I, p. 85; Strugnell, *Notes en marge*, p. 272 ופרח ist יפרח zu lesen; ופארתו erfordert gleichfalls eine andere Sticheneinteilung als Allegro, *Qumran Cave 4*. I, und Strugnell, *Notes en marge*; s. Übersetzung.

Zeilenende: Mit der Übersetzung von Strugnell, *Notes en marge*, p. 272 ist in Ergänzung von Allegro, *Qumran Cave 4*. I, p. 85 und Strugnell, *Notes en marge*, p. 269 רוחו נשב[ה בו] (trotz der Bedenken Strugnell, *Notes en marge*, p. 269) zu lesen; vgl. Jes 40,7.

Zeile 11: Wie Strugnell, *Notes en marge*, p. 269 erkennt, sind die Schriftspuren eindeutig עֻזּוֹ; auf den Photographien ist freilich nicht erkennbar, daß ע getilgt worden sein soll, so daß גזו zu lesen wäre. Da eine sinnvolle Lösung von עגו möglich erscheint (s. Übersetzung), sollte man auch auf die von Skehan (nach Strugnell, *Notes en marge*, p. 270) vorgeschlagene Metathese zu גזעו verzichten.

Die Bedeutung von אִי'קוֹם (Negation אי verbunden mit Nomen יקום) wird von Allegro, *Qumran Cave 4. I* (p. 87: אייקום »non existence«; p. 86: »oblivion«) richtig erfaßt und ist grammatikalisch möglich (s. die Komposita von אי mit einem Nomen in dem Eigennamen איכבוד [1 Sam 4,21] und einem Adjektiv אי נקי [Hi 22,30], vgl. Gesenius-Kautzsch, Hebräische Grammatik, ND 1962, §152q; häufiger sind analoge Bildungen mit לא, s. Gesenius-Kautzsch, Grammatik, §152a, Anm. 2) und gibt guten Sinn (s. auch Strugnell, *Notes en marge*, p. 270), so daß die Emendation Skehans (אין <מ>קום) nicht erforderlich ist (mündliche Mitteilung Skehans an Strugnell; vgl. Strugnell, *Notes en marge*, p. 270). אִי'קוֹם ist paläographisch dem Vorschlag אנ'קום (Strugnell, *Notes en marge*, p. 270) vorzuziehen. Fraglich bleibt freilich die Lesung des folgenden. Sicher sind ל und wohl auch ע, danach sind im Prinzip ב, מ, vielleicht auch כ, נ, פ, צ möglich, so daß alle Ergänzungen hypothetisch bleiben. Die Vorschläge von Strugnell, *Notes en marge*, p. 272 »*so that it passes away like a name that perishes*«, was hebr. לעבו]ר כשם או[בד entsprechen würde (p. 270 nur או[בד . . . לעבו]ר כ. bzw. anstelle לעמו]ר steht לעמו]ד), und Skehan (nach Strugnell, *Notes en marge*, p. 270) וציצו תשא רוח עד אין <מ>קום לעמוד כי יאבד »*and the wind carries off its blossom leaving him no place to stand; for he perishes*«, sind sachgemäß, wenn auch nicht sicher. Ein ähnlicher Gedanke könnte auch ausgedrückt werden durch die Ergänzung לעבו]ר הוא ולא[בד »er muß verschwinden und vergehen«. Es wäre aber auch möglich, daß noch eine Aussage über die Schönheit der Blume gemacht worden war; mit den Schriftspuren würde dann diese Ergänzung *übereinstimmen*: לעבו]דת חֶ[מֹד »das anmutige Geschöpf«, d.h. im Zusammenhang: »bis zum Nichtsein gelangt das anmutige Geschöpf«, d.h. daß es überhaupt nicht mehr da ist. Vielleicht darf auch wegen des folgenden Satzes diese Ergänzung vorgeschlagen werden: עד אִי'קוֹם לעמֹ]דו מל[בד, wörtl. »für [seine Stä]tte (gibt es) nu[r noch] Nichtsein«.

Zeile 12: Die Lesungen Allegro, *Qumran Cave 4. I*, p. 85 מֹרוח »from the wind« (p. 86) und Skehan (nach Strugnell, *Notes en marge*, p. 270) מרוח (»and finds no place of rest / none to give him rest«, Strugnell, *Notes en marge*, p. 272 Anm. 21) sind paläographisch nicht

möglich wegen eines Wortzwischenraumes vor רוח. Die Schriftspuren legen nahe, mit Strugnell, *Notes en marge*, p. 270 כי רוח zu lesen, doch ist es fraglich, ob seine Übersetzung (»*for it is but breath*«, p. 272) sachgemäß ist, zumal wenige Worte vorher רוח der göttliche Feuerhauch ist und dagegen רוח hier als vergänglicher Hauch zu verstehen wäre. Eine sachgemäße Lösung erhält man, wenn man כי im Sinne von כי אם versteht (כי anstelle כי אם s. Gesenius-Kautzsch, Grammatik §163a; A. Kropat, *Syntax*, p. 31) und daher übersetzt: »und es wird nichts mehr gefunden außer dem Wind«.
Nach רוח Spatium von 5 Buchstabeneinheiten (BE).
Nicht sicher entscheidbar, ob יִבְקְשׁוּהוּ (Allegro, *Qumran Cave 4*. I, p. 85; Strugnell, *Notes en marge*, p. 272) oder וִֹיבְקְשׁוּהוּ zu lesen ist. Das vermeintliche ו könnte aber lediglich eine Lederschwärzung sein.
Zeile 13: Mit Strugnell, *Notes en marge*, pp. 270.272 erscheint (gegen Allegro, *Qumran Cave 4*. I, p. 85 [ר]על האו ˚ ˚ ˚ י כצל (והוא) כצל ימוֹֹ עַל הֹאָֹר[ץ] als sachlich zutreffend (zur Wendung vgl. 1 Chr 29,15; Hi 8,9). Paläographisch bestehen freilich Bedenken: In ימוֹ ist sicher lediglich ימ; danach Schriftreste von mindestens zwei Buchstaben. Liest man ימוֹֹ, ist der Wortabstand zum nächsten Wort sehr groß, jedoch möglich. Das Wort danach ist nach den Schriftspuren eher כֹול. Im Hinblick auf die gute Belegbarkeit der Wendung und der ganzen Vorstellung bleiben wir beim Vorschlag Strugnells.
Zeile 14: Wie Strugnell, *Notes en marge*, p. 270 richtig bemerkt, sind פתאום und פתאים gleichfalls möglich; der große Kopf des י spricht eher für פתאים. Allerdings bleibt das Problem der Abgrenzung, das sich mit dem der Lesung des folgenden Wortes berührt: Allegro, *Qumran Cave 4*. I, תמו˚ (p. 86: »*be destroyed*«); Strugnell, *Notes en marge*, p. 270 möchte das in Rede stehende Wort zu der Reihe von Imperativen rechnen (זכרו, השכילו, שמעו) und entsprechend den Schriftresten והכֹמו lesen; dies müßte aber in וחכמו korrigiert werden (»*and draw Wisdom*«, p. 273).
Zu lesen ist dagegen offensichtlich וֹתֹוֹמו als Warnung (s. das folgende) mit פתאים zu verbinden: פתאים יתומו מן [ג]בורת אלהיו.
Gegen Allegro, *Qumran Cave 4*. I, p. 85 [ח]ברות mit Strugnell, *Notes en marge*, p. 270 [ג]ברות zu lesen.
Gegen Allegro, *Qumran Cave 4*. I, p. 85; Strugnell, *Notes en marge*, pp. 270.273 אלהים ist אלהיוֹ zu lesen.
Mit Allegro, *Qumran Cave 4*. I, p. 85 ist gegen Strugnell, *Notes en marge*, p. 270 nicht נפלאות, sondern נִפְלָאָֹיֹם zu lesen. Auffällig ist der Wechsel von נפלאים und der suffigierten Form ומופתיו. S. aber den ähnlichen Wechsel Ps 105,27 ומפתים – אתותיו.

Zeile 15: Die Ergänzung von Strugnell, *Notes en marge*, p. 270 ב[ארץ
חם] ist sowohl vom vorhandenen Raum als auch sachlich zutreffend
(Ps 105,27; 106,27); möglich wäre natürlich auch ב[שדה צען], vgl. Ps
78,43. Immerhin erwägenswert erscheint eine Ergänzung nach Ps
105,5; 1 Chr 16,12 ומופתיו ו[משפטי פיו]. Das Doppelglied ist abhängig
von וזכרו נפלאים עשה במצרים : וזכרו ומופתיו ב[ארץ חם]. Vgl. dazu Ps
105,5; 1 Chr 16,12; אשר kann nach נפלאים ausfallen.

1-2 II

Zeile 1: Mit Strugnell, *Notes en marge*, p. 270 ועשו רצ[ונו]; Allegro,
Qumran Cave 4. I, p. 85 hat lediglich ועשו ר[. Für die Ergänzung der
Lücke wäre es von Bedeutung zu wissen, ob נ[פשכם Subjekt oder Objekt ist, ob z. B. zu ergänzen ist תנו נ[פשכם . . .] (vgl. Esr 10,11) oder
ותתענג נ[פשכם כחסדיו הטבים (vgl. Jes 55,2). Vorhergegangen sein kann
ein weiterer Imperativ mit Nomen (z. B. והשלימו חפצו) oder eine
präpositionale Bestimmung zu עשו רצונו wie z. B. בכל לבבכם.
Zeile 2: Allegro, *Qumran Cave 4*. I, מסלה; lies mit Strugnell, *Notes en
marge*, ומסלה] und ergänze weiter ל[ארך ימים].
Allegro, *Qumran Cave 4*. I, p. 85 liest]לשארית und übersetzt entsprechend, p. 86 »for a remnant« deutet also den Schriftrest vor ש als
Unterteil eines ל. Strugnell, *Notes en marge*, ist vorsichtiger und
liest, wie aus seiner Übersetzung »a remnant etc.« zu schließen, offensichtlich nur שארית[. Betrachtet man das Unterteil verschiedener ל,
so stellt man fest, daß es im allgemeinen tiefer liegt als im vorliegenden Fall. ל ist also zwar möglich, aber keineswegs zwingend; erwägenswert sind ו oder ה. Im Falle von לשארית könnte man ergänzen:
ומסלה] לארך ימים לשים לכם] לשארית שים לשארית vgl. Mi 4,7. Ist
ושארית zu lesen, ergänze z. B. ומסלה] לארך ימים לשים שם ושארית. Zu
שם ושארית vgl. 2 Sam 14,7.
Zeile 3: Zeilenbeginn: Allegro, *Qumran Cave 4*. I, p. 85 כם; Strugnell,
Notes en marge, p. 270 [נפש]כם; eher ist zu erwarten נפשותי]כם, doch
das ist zu lang, daher besser לבב]כם].
Allegro, *Qumran Cave 4*. I, p. 85]לשא; Strugnell, *Notes en marge*,
p. 270 לשוא (p. 273: »*vanity*«); paläographisch ist auch möglich
לשח]ת. Die Fortsetzung entweder entsprechend Strugnell, *Notes en
marge*, p. 273, »and your ... to ... of judgement« oder z. B.: ומזמתכם
תמאס צדק ומ[שפט.
Zeilenmitte: Mit Strugnell, *Notes en marge*, ist sicher zu lesen שמעוני,
gegen Allegro, *Qumran Cave 4*. I, p. 85 שמעתי.
Mit Strugnell, *Notes en marge*, p. 270 sicher ואל gegen Allegro,
Qumran Cave 4. I, p. 85 יצל »*let him deliver*« (p. 86).

Zeile 4: Mit Strugnell, *Notes en marge*, p. 271 [ו]אֹל gegen Allegro, *Qumran Cave 4*. I, p. 85 אל.
Ergänze in der Lücke z. B. [ו]אֹל תצעדו [דרך אשר יצוה לי]עֹקב; Strugnell, *Notes en marge*, p. 273 »[n]or walk in [… but in the way He laid down for Ja]cob«. Allegro, *Qumran Cave 4*. I, p. 87 (Anmerkung) erwägt, ob auch תצערו »do not treat as insignificant« zu lesen ist, doch handelt es sich um ein sicheres ד, nicht ר.
Zeilenmitte: Gegen Allegro, *Qumran Cave 4*. I, p. 85 חתימה »formula« lies mit Strugnell, *Notes en marge*, p. 271 ונתיבה.
Zeilenende: In טוב ist ו supralinear nachgetragen.
Unter dem offensichtlichen Einfluß von Ps 84,11 lesen Allegro, *Qumran Cave 4*. I, p. 85 מעשרֹ]ה ₀₀₀[ ] הלוא טֹב יום אחד »Is not one day [...] better than ten[...« und Strugnell, *Notes en marge*, p. 273 »Is not one day in His *house* better [...]«, dem die Ergänzung בבי]תֹוֹ nach אחד zugrundeliegen würde. Mit Recht verweist Strugnell, *Notes en marge*, p. 272 darauf, daß מעשר]ה nicht möglich ist, da der erste Buchstabe ein deutliches ב ist. Darum erwägt er, בעשו]ת zu lesen. Doch auch diese Lösung kann nicht voll befriedigen. Löst man sich von der genannten Psalmstelle, so erscheint eine andere Interpretation als vertretbar: עשר muß nicht Zahlwort sein, sondern kann als Nomen »Reichtum« aufgefaßt werden, das ja im Wortfeld weisheitlicher Texte häufig ist. Die Schriftspuren vor בעשר[ermöglichen die Ergänzung תערֹ]וֹךְ. Man erhält die Lesung: הלוא טום יום אחד[תער]וֹךְ בעשר] וכבוד. »Reicht sie nicht täglich (יום אחד = jeder Tag, Gesenius-Buhl, s. v. אחד, S. 23,4) Gutes dar an Reichtum und Ehre...«; עשר speziell von der Weisheit s. 4*Q185* 1-2 II 12 (?); Prov 3,16; 8,18; s. weiter zur Wendung Prov 22,4; 1 Chr 29,28; 2 Chr 17,5; 18,1; 32,27. Vielleicht auch statt וכבוד zu ergänzen דעתו, vgl. Röm 11,33.
Zeile 5: Nach der Lücke: יֹרֹאתו ₀[ist sicher; ergänze evtl.: להתהלך [בֹּיֹרֹאתו. לעתת ist trotz der Schwierigkeit des Verständnisses paläographisch völlig sicher; es müßte als nicht gerechtfertigter Ausweg erscheinen, wollte man לעונת lesen (ו und נ oben verbunden wie ähnlich in שמעוני Z. 3). Zur Ableitung s. Anm. zur Übersetzung.
Zeile 6: Zeilenbeginn: Ergänze vielleicht [ומפ]חֹת entsprechend den Reihungen Jes 24,17; Jer 48,43; CD 4,14. Wahrscheinlich folgt ein Versglied, das ebenfalls davon spricht, daß keine Gefahr oder Bedrohung für den besteht, der den gebotenen Weg befolgt.
Nach der Lücke: Allegro, *Qumran Cave 4*. I, p. 85 [₀₀הֹ₀₀ולֹ]; Strugnell, *Notes en marge*, p. 271 להבדיל oder להשמר. Jedoch scheint der Buchstabe nach ה ein א zu sein, so daß sich die Lesung anbietet ולהא[מן] מן מלאכיו »und sicher zu sein vor seinen Engeln«; s. dazu unten die Anmerkungen zur Übersetzung.

Zeilenende: Es ist nicht eindeutig wahrnehmbar, ob in חשך supralinear ו nachgetragen wurde.

Zeile 7: Zeilenbeginn: Der Vorschlag von Strugnell, *Notes en marge*, p. 271 וְאָפְלָה ist paläographisch und inhaltlich zu bestätigen. Offen bleibt, auf wen zu beziehen ist (auf Gott, die Weisheit / das Gesetz, die Engel?).

Nach der Lücke: הוא ist sicher lesbar; die Schriftspuren davor und danach lassen sich nicht mit Sicherheit identifizieren. Allegro, *Qumran Cave 4*. I, p. 85]∘∘הֹ הוא ∘∘[; Strugnell, *Notes en marge*, keine Lesung bzw. Übersetzung.

Unbefriedigend Allegro, *Qumran Cave 4*. I, p. 85 [ ]ויעי ידעתי; besser Strugnell, *Notes en marge*, p. 271 ר[צֹונו ודעתו, möglich auch ב[ינ]תֹו ודעתו.

Zeile 8: Zeilenbeginn: Allegro, *Qumran Cave 4*. I, p. 85 ת∘[ ]∘∘[; Strugnell, *Notes en marge*, p. 271 תת[בו]נֹנֹו paläographisch vertretbar. Nach der Lücke: Lies מ[לפניו (Allegro, *Qumran Cave 4*. I, p. 85 [לפניו); Strugnell, *Notes en marge*, p. 271 »for] from His presence ...« setzt wohl auch מ[לפניו voraus.

Allegro, *Qumran Cave 4*. I, רעֹה (»evil«, p. 87), so auch Strugnell, *Notes en marge*, p. 273; die von Strugnell, *Notes en marge*, p. 271 erwogene Lesung דעה erfordert nicht unbedingt eine Textkorrektur; vgl. das ד in ודשן (Z. 12).

Zeile 9: Zeilenbeginn: Lies sicher בן אדֹ[ם gegen Allegro, *Qumran Cave 4*. I, p. 86]∘מֹ א und Strugnell, *Notes en marge*, p. 271 כן; ergänze z. B. בֹנֹ אדֹ[ם חזקה לו להתחשב עם יוד[עֹים.

Nach der Lücke: Allegro, *Qumran Cave 4*. I, p. 86 דֹ∘ [; Strugnell, *Notes en marge*, p. 271 paläographisch besser ר[עים, doch könnte dieser Stichos inhaltlich noch den Makarismus fortsetzen, so daß sich die Ergänzung יוד[עֹים nahelegen würde.

Mit Allegro, *Qumran Cave 4*. I, p. 86 und Strugnell, *Notes en marge*, p. 271 וֹאֹל יתהֹלֹלֹ[ון; zum Verständnis s. die Übersetzung.

Zeilenende: Gegen Allegro, *Qumran Cave 4*. I, p. 86 יֹמֹנֹה ist Strugnell, *Notes en marge*, p. 271 נתנה zu folgen.

Zeile 10: Zeilenbeginn: Den Grundgedanken der Rede des Frevlers hat Strugnell, *Notes en marge*, p. 273 erkannt: »'She hath not been given to me, nor [hath She been measured out to me', For God gives Her] to Israel, and with *the measure of goodness* He measures Her out...«, doch sind einzelne Änderungen an den Lesungen und Ergänzungen erforderlich: Die ablehnende Haltung des Frevlers könnte sich fortsetzen in der Aussage ולא] אדרשנה (vgl. in 4QInstruction[b] 2 III 12f. den dort freilich anders begründeten Einwand: אביון אתה אל תאמֹר רש אני ול[וא] אדרוש דעת, Fragm. 2, Z. 9f). Dann ist fortzufahren entsprechend

Strugnell, *Notes en marge*: »Gott hat sie (allein) Israel gegeben (אלהים נתנה [לישראל)«. Doch sollte dies noch – gegen Strugnell, *Notes en marge* – zum Widerspruch des Frevlers gehören. Die Lesung von Allegro, *Qumran Cave 4*. I וּמֹֽמֹּֽד]ֹת טֹ[ב ימדה, der sich Strugnell, *Notes en marge*, p. 273 in seiner Übersetzung weitgehend anschließt, ist fraglich im Hinblick auf das vermeintliche zweite מ in וּמֹֽמֹּֽד]ֹת, bei dem es sich vielmehr um ein sicheres ב handelt. Das gleiche gilt für das angebliche ימדה, in dem ebenfalls das מ durch ב zu ersetzen ist. Die übrigen Buchstaben sind weiter in der von uns angegebenen Weise zu lesen: In dem von uns gebotenen וכֹובד ist neben dem ב der Rest eines ו erhalten. Der Grundstrich gehört zu dem כ; zu זבד טוב s. Gen 30,20.

Zeile 11: Zeilenbeginn: Strugnell, *Notes en marge*, p. 271 [וֹהרג שנאוֹ] ח[כֹמֹ]תוֹ ist paläographisch kaum möglich; lies vielleicht וֹהרג שמֹי בֹּמצֹ]רים, ein Gedanke, der mit dem Gericht an den Ägyptern (evtl. 1-2 I 6.14f) korrespondieren würde. Im folgenden läßt sich lediglich [אבֹּ (so Allegro, *Qumran Cave 4*. I, p. 86) lesen, dem mit einzelnen Schriftspuren kein zusammenhängender Sinn abzugewinnen ist.

Nach der Lücke: Die Lesung nach יאמר ist in der Tat »désespérée« (Strugnell, *Notes en marge*, p. 271). Besser als die paläographisch und morphologisch schwierige Form המתשבח von Strugnell, *Notes en marge*, p. 271 und das keinen Sinn ergebende המתמֹ ॰ ॰ ॰ von Allegro, *Qumran Cave 4*. I, p. 86 paßt zu den Schriftspuren המתכֹּבֹּדֹ. Das folgende ist wohl zu lesen בֹֹה ישֹאנה יוֹר[ֹשה, entsprechend Allegro, *Qumran Cave 4*. I, p. 86 בה ישאנה [שה gegen Strugnell, *Notes en marge*, p. 271 ככה מצאנה.

Zeile 12: Zeilenbeginn: Allegro, *Qumran Cave 4*. I, p. 86 יֹ॰[ ]॰ בֹה ומצאה יֹבֹילֹה; Strugnell, *Notes en marge*, p. 271 ומצאה וחזק בה ונחלה (p. 273: »and hold fast to Her and get Her as an inheritance«) ist paläographisch nicht zweifelsfrei: בה ist sicher zu lesen, freilich könnte es auch Teil eines Wortes sein; nach מצאה steht sehr wahrscheinlich לו. Das letzte Wort ist nicht sicher ונחלה, eher יבֹולֹה. Daher wird vorgeschlagen zu lesen: ומצאה לו [כי] רֹבֹה יבֹולֹה »sie reicht für ihn aus, fürwahr, reich ist sie in bezug auf ihren Ertrag« (מצאל = ausreichen, s. Num 11,22; Ri 21,14); möglich wäre auch die Übersetzung »und er soll sie finden«, vgl. Prov 3,13. Lesung und Übersetzung von Allegro, *Qumran Cave 4*. I, בה יכילה »*By her he will sustain her*« geben wenig Sinn.

Zeilenmitte: Hier ist Strugnells Vorschlag sachgemäß (*Notes en marge*, p. 271): ועמה] ארך י[מים ודשן עֹצֹם (gegen Allegro, *Qumran Cave 4*. I, p. 86 ורשף עינֹיֹם).

Zeilenende: Ergänze עשֹר וכבוֹ[ד, von der Weisheit Prov 3,16; 8,18.

Zeile 13: Allegro, *Qumran Cave 4*. I, p. 86 עלמיה »her youth«, so auch Strugnell, *Notes en marge*, p. 273, ist hier unpassend. Vielmehr ist der Gedanke zu erwarten, daß »seine« (scil. Gottes) Gnadengaben an die gegeben werden, die die Weisheit annehmen.

Lies und ergänze entsprechend der vorangehenden Anmerkung hier וישועת]יו לכל בניה oder auch nur וישועת]יו לבניה.

Zeilenende: Die Lesungen und Übersetzungen von Allegro, *Qumran Cave 4*. I, und Strugnell, *Notes en marge*, können hier nicht voll befriedigen: Allegro, *Qumran Cave 4*. I, p. 86 ולא יאל על]ו [ ] (p. 87: »and is not willing«); Strugnell, *Notes en marge*, p. 271 (»hypothétiquement«) ולא דגל עליה («and does not play tricks against Her; nor with a spirit of deceit...«, p. 273). Das Wort nach ולא ist möglicherweise (ע in Falte verschwunden?); danach könnte man gut ergänzen על]ילותי]ה, besser jedoch על]ת [. . .]₀. Z. 14 מרמה ist als adverbieller Akkusativ (vgl. Gesenius-Kautzsch, Grammatik §188q) asyndetischer Beginn eines neuen Stichos. Zum Joch der Weisheit, vgl. Sir 6,30; 51,26; s. auch Matth 11,29. Falls entgegen dem soeben Gesagten mit Strugnell, *Notes en marge*, p. 273 וברו]ח מרמה zu ergänzen wäre, sollte stärker ובפ]י מרמה in Erwägung gezogen werden (vgl. Ps 109,2; Jes 53,9; weiter Pss 17,1; 36,4; 52,6).

Zeile 14: Zeilenmitte: ובחלקות לא יחזיקנה ist Allegro, *Qumran Cave 4*. I, und Strugnell, *Notes en marge*, zu folgen.

Lies וישש]נה oder besser וישמר]נה. Strugnell, *Notes en marge*, p. 271 (»peut-être«) וחזק] בה ist vielleicht weniger wahrscheinlich wegen des Vorkommens von חזק wenige Wörter zuvor.

Zeile 15: Sicher mit Strugnell, *Notes en marge*, p. 271 ובכל] מא]דו. Vielleicht besser als Allegro, *Qumran Cave 4*. I, p. 86; Strugnell, *Notes en marge*, p. 271 חקר zu lesen לאץ חסר.

Wohl kein Neueinsatz, sondern ein paralleles Glied zu ויורישנה לצאצאיו, so daß zu lesen und zu ergänzen ist ודעתו לע]מ]יה ל[רוב. Nach dem in der Einleitung Gesagten ist Kol III Z. 1 gegen Allegro, *Qumran Cave 4*. I, nicht – auch Strugnell, *Notes en marge*, folgt Allegro, *Qumran Cave 4*. I – Fortsetzung von 1-2 II 15; daher sind Lesungen, die von einem Zusammenhang ausgehen oder einen solchen konstruieren, nicht möglich. Dennoch kann natürlich mit ודעתו ein neuer Satz beginnen, doch ist ein paralleles Glied zu ויורישנה לצאצאיו wahrscheinlicher.

1-2 III

Die Kolumnenbreite von Kol. III läßt sich mit einiger Wahrscheinlichkeit mit Hilfe der Zeilen 11 und 12 berechnen: In Zeile 11 ist nach ויד]ע ein Objekt mit Suffix, das sich auf לבות bezieht, zu ergänzen. Der Beginn in Zeile 12 erfordert, daß אלהים als Subjekt plus ein Verbum in Zeile 11 standen. Ähnliches gilt auch für den Übergang von Z. 12 zu 13: Auch hier muß angesichts der aus Z. 13 hervorgehenden Kürze der Glieder lediglich am Ende von Z. 12 אלהים עשה (oder evtl. ein anderes Verbum) gestanden haben. Wir kommen also auf eine Kolumnenbreite von 36 (Z. 12) bis 43 (Z. 11) BE.

Zeile 7: Zeilenbeginn: Allegro, *Qumran Cave 4*. I, p. 86]ה₀₀; lies möglicherweise הנו̇תן; es ist nicht sicher, ob ה dabei Artikel oder Fragepartikel ist. Die Einordnung von Fragment 3 der Edition in den Rahmen dieser Kolumne (so Strugnell, *Notes en marge*, p. 272) ist sehr wahrscheinlich, wenn auch der genaue Ort unsicher ist. Die Bruchränder sind nicht so eindeutig, als daß ein Zusammenhang im Bereich der Z. 10 zwischen Kol. III und Z. 4 von Fragment 3 zwingend wäre; auch spricht die Schwierigkeit des sich in Z. 10 ergebenden Satzes eher gegen einen Zusammenhang an eben dieser Stelle. Wegen der u. E. sicheren Zugehörigkeit zu Kol. III belassen wir das Fragment jedoch an der von Strugnell, *Notes en marge*, vorgeschlagenen Stelle.
Nach der Lücke: Ergänze die Schriftreste evtl. zu אל[ה̇י̇]ם כו̇נ̇ן.

Zeile 8: Zeilenbeginn: Reste von zwei oder drei Buchstaben; nicht sicher identifizierbar.
Zeilenende: Lies und ergänze מז̇מ̇]ות לבב; Allegro, *Qumran Cave 4*. I, p. 87]₀₀; Strugnell, *Notes en marge*, p. 272 מז̇מ̇ות.

Zeile 9: Zeilenbeginn: Lies mit Allegro, *Qumran Cave 4*. I, p. 86 und Strugnell, *Notes en marge*, p. 273]והוא.
Zeilenmitte: Es ist nicht sicher, ob vor עשה ein Schriftrest ist (so Allegro, *Qumran Cave 4*. I, p. 87), weswegen dann ועשה (Strugnell, *Notes en marge*, p. 273 offensichtlich ו]עשה) oder weniger wahrscheinlich יעשה zu lesen wäre; handelt es sich nicht um einen Schriftrest, könnte man אלהים [עשה ergänzen (s. Z. 13).
Zeilenende: Lies mit Allegro, *Qumran Cave 4*. I, p. 87; Strugnell, *Notes en marge*, p. 273 דברי ברי]ת.

Zeile 10: Zeilenbeginn: ולא (Allegro, *Qumran Cave 4*. I, p. 86 ו̇א̇ל; Strugnell, *Notes en marge*, p. 272 ולוא) scheint sicher zu sein. Wenn Fragment 3 richtig eingeordnet ist, kann man den Anfang kaum anders lesen als Strugnell, *Notes en marge*, p. 272: ע̇ש̇ה א[להים מש]פט.
Zeilenmitte: Dieses Wort fordert eine Lesung nach dem Vorschlag von Allegro, *Qumran Cave 4*. I, p. 87 במסורת gegen Strugnell, *Notes en marge*, p. 272 במסורד̇ים »upon *those that turn away*« (p. 273). Um Sinn zu ergeben, müßte ולא an einen vorhergehenden Fragesatz anknüpfen (vgl. Gesenius-Kautzsch, Grammatik §150a) »und hat nicht Gott das Recht zur Verpflichtung gemacht?«.

Zeile 11: Zeilenbeginn: Lies mit Strugnell, *Notes en marge*, p. 273 הלא
א[להי]ם; Allegro, *Qumran Cave 4*. I, p. 86 ‎[ ]ֹ ֹ ֹ הלֹ ם.
Zeilenmitte: Lies gegen Allegro, *Qumran Cave 4*. I, p. 86; Strugnell, *Notes en marge*, p. 273 לביתוֹ ein sicheres לבות.
Entsprechend Z. 13 וידע legt sich die Ergänzung nahe וידֹ[ע, ergänze vielleicht weiter מזמותיהם.
Lücke: Der Beginn von Z. 13 אל כל חדרי בטן erfordert am Ende von Z. 11 die Ergänzung אלהים יביט; da in Z. 13 die Frageform aufgegeben ist, ist es nicht sicher, ob vor אלהים יביט ein Fragepronomen הלא zu stehen hat.
Zeile 12: Zeilenmitte: Allegro, *Qumran Cave 4*. I, p. 86 כלותוֹ[; Strugnell, *Notes en marge*, כליתי, lies כליתו (Defektivschreibung für כליותיו?).
Der Beginn von Z. 13 erfordert wieder die Ergänzung am Ende von Z. 12 אלהים עשה. Es scheint, als würde das Schaffen Gottes in diesem Abschnitt immer mit עשה bezeichnet, so daß es bei den Ergänzungen nicht angezeigt ist, ein anderes Verbum zu wählen. Ähnliches gilt für den jeweiligen Nachsatz, der Z. 11 und 13 mit וידע fortgeführt wird.
Zeile 13: Lücke: Sind die Erwägungen in der vorangehenden Anmerkung richtig, ist zu vermuten, daß nach אלהים עשה ידים mit וידע פעלותיהן fortzufahren ist; sollte man וידע durch ein anderes Verbum ersetzen, würde sich והכן nahelegen.
Zeile 14: Es ist sehr fraglich, ob am rechten Kolumnenrand das Fragment h von Strugnell, *Notes en marge*, p. 257 (Planche I) einzuordnen ist, da die Bruchränder dies nicht zwingend ergeben und auch kein zusammenhängender Text entsteht; darum wird hier auf eine Einordnung verzichtet.
Lies mit Strugnell, *Notes en marge*, p. 272 אם[טוב ואם רע]; Allegro, *Qumran Cave 4*. I, p. 86 [טוב ואם רֹ]ֹ.
Zeile 15: Lies mit Allegro, *Qumran Cave 4*. I, p. 86; Strugnell, *Notes en marge*, p. 273 ב]מחש[בות.

Fragmente

4 I

Zeile 1: So Allegro, *Qumran Cave 4*. I, p. 87, jedoch nicht sicher לעד?
Zeile 2: Allegro, *Qumran Cave 4*. I, p. 87 [ֹוטֹ ֹ ֹ וישֹ ֹ].

4 II

Zeile 1: Allegro, *Qumran Cave 4*. I, p. 87 ולֹעֹמֹיֹ, sehr unsicher.
Zeile 2: Allegro, *Qumran Cave 4*. I, p. 87 ונדיבה וֹ].

5

Zeile 2: Allegro, *Qumran Cave 4*. I, p. 87]מיפ.
Zeile 3: Allegro, *Qumran Cave 4*. I, p. 87]∘הדׄ.

6

Zeile 1: Allegro, *Qumran Cave 4*. I, p. 87]∘מׄ∘[.
Zeile 2: Allegro, *Qumran Cave 4*. I, p. 87]∘אתי∘∘וה.
Zeile 3: Allegro, *Qumran Cave 4*. I, p. 87]∘∘ב[.

7

Zeile 1: Allegro, *Qumran Cave 4*. I, p. 87 אלׄיה.
Allegro, *Qumran Cave 4*. I, p. 86]פׄניׄ; Strugnell, *Notes en marge*, p. 272 möglicherweise richtiger טונ[ב.
Zeile 2: So mit Allegro, *Qumran Cave 4*. I, p. 86 eher als mit Strugnell, *Notes en marge*, p. 272 ממגרות.

8

Zeile 1: Allegro, *Qumran Cave 4*. I, p. 86]∘מו.

ÜBERSETZUNG

1-2 I

Für die Z. 1-6 ist keine stichische Gliederung möglich; ab Z. 7 wird für den gesamten Text eine stichische Anordnung versucht unter genauer Berücksichtigung der Lücken; dabei entsprechen ab Zeile 8 zwei Punkte im deutschen Text einer Buchstabeneinheit des hebräischen Textes.

(1-2) [...]
(3) [...] denn(?) [...]
(4) [...] rein und heilig [...]
(5) [...] entsprechend seiner Rache und entsprechend seines Zorns [...
(6) [...] drei und bis zu zehnmal [...]
[... (7)
und er (bzw. man) hat keine Kraft, vor ihr zu bestehen,
und keine Hoffnung (8) angesichts des zornigen [Grimms unseres Gottes].
Und wer hielte es aus, vor seinen Engeln zu (be)stehen,
denn mit (9) loderndem Feuer richtet er [und bei] ihm sind seine Geister.
Aber ihr, meine Söhne,
der Mensch i[st kraftlos]!
Denn siehe, (10) wie Gras sproßt er
und seine Schönheit blüht wie eine Blume;
(doch) seine Anmut, weh[t] sein (scil. Gottes) Wind [darüber],

(11) dann vertrocknet sein Wurzelstock
und seine Blüte nimmt der Wind weg,
so daß [an seiner Ste]lle [gar] nichts mehr ist
(12) und es ist nichts mehr da außer (dem) Wind. *vacat*
Man sucht ihn,
aber man findet ihn nicht
und er hat keine Hoffnung
(13) und seine Tage sind wie ein Schatten auf der Er[de].
Und nun hört, mein Volk,
und gewinnt Einsicht von (14) mir!
Toren kommen um vor der [M]acht unseres Gottes!
So gedenkt der Wundertaten, die er (15) in Ägypten getan hat,
und seiner Zeichen im [Lande Ham],
so daß euer Herz aus Furcht vor ihm erschrecke!

1-2 II

(1) Und tut seinen Wil[len ...]
(und) eure See[le ...] entsprechend seinen guten Gnadengaben.
Sucht für euch den Weg (2) zum Leben
und den Pfad [...]
[...] zu einem Rest [...]
für eure Kinder nach euch.
Und warum gebt ihr (3) euer [Herz] dem Verder[ben] hin
[...R]echt
Hört auf mich, meine Söhne,
und seid nicht widerspenstig gegen die Worte Jahwes
(4) [und] übertretet nicht [den Weg, den er Jak]ob [gebot],
und den Pfad, den er Isaak wies.
Re[icht] sie nicht (5) täglich Gutes dar
an Reichtum [...]
[...] in der Furcht vor ihm,
und nicht (vom Wege) abgedrängt zu werden durch Schrecken und der Falle des Vogelstellers
(6) [...]
[...]
Und sic[her] zu sein vor seinen Engeln
denn es gibt keine Finsternis (7) und Dunke[lheit ...]
[...]
[...] er [...] seine Erkenntnis und sein Wissen.
Aber ihr,
(8) warum ach[te]t ihr auf [...]

[von] ihm her kommt Erkenntnis zu jedem Volk.
Glückselig der Mann, dem sie gegeben ist,
(9) der Mens[ch] [...]
[... Wiss]enden.
Und nicht sollen sich die Frevler töricht verha[lten] und sagen:
(10) »Mir wurde sie nicht gegeben
und nicht [will ich nach ihr fragen].
[Gott hat sie] Israel [gegeben]
und als ein gu[tes] Geschenk hat er sie geschenkt
und sein ganzes Volk hat er erlöst,
(11) aber er hat getötet [...]
[...]«
Der sich ihrer rühmt soll sagen:
»Er soll sie nehmen als Bes[it]z
(12) und sie reicht aus für ihn.
[Fürwahr], sie ist reich in bezug auf ihren Ertrag«!
Und bei ihr sind
[langes L]eben
und Üppigkeit der Kraft
und Freude des Herzens,
Reich[tum und Eh]re,
(13) und seine Gnadengaben sind für ihre Völker
und [seine] Rettungstaten für [a]l[l ihre Kinder].
Glückselig der Mann, der sie tut
und ihr Joch nicht verach[tet ...]
(14) (der sie) trügerisch nicht sucht
und mit Täuschungen sie nicht festhält.
Wie sie seinen Vätern gegeben wurde,
so nimmt er sie in Besitz,
[und er soll] sie [tun] (15) mit aller Kraft seiner Stärke
und mit seinem ganzen Ver[mö]gen,
unaufhörlich.
Und er soll sie seinen Nachkommen vererben.
Und die Erkenntnis von ihm [ihren] Völkern [in] Menge.

1-2 III

(7) Wer hat gege[ben ...]
[G]o[tt] hat fest[gesetzt ... (8) ...]
[...
[Go]tt prüft alle Gedan[ken des Herzens]
(9) Und er [...]

[Gott] hat die Worte des Bund[es] gemacht
[und er ...]
(19) Ha[t(?)] Go]tt nicht das Re[cht] als Richtschnur gemacht
[und er kennt ...]
(11) Hat G[ott] nicht die Herzen gemacht
und er wei[ß ihre Gedanken?]
[Gott sieht] (12) in alle Kammern des Innersten
und er prüft ihre Nieren
[G]o[tt] [hat] die (13) Zunge [gemacht]
und er kennt ihr Wort.
Gott hat die Hände gemacht.
[und er kennt ihre Taten]
[(14) ...] [es sei] gut oder böse[
[(15) ...] im Planen [...]

Anmerkungen zur Übersetzung

1-2 I

Zeile 4: rein und heilig] טהור וקדש wird auf Gott zu beziehen sein, wie das Suffix der beiden nächsten erhaltenen Wörter.

Zeile 5: Zorn] Vgl. Ez 25,14.

Zeile 6: zehnmal] Der Bezug ist nicht ganz klar: zehn könnte als runde Zahl für eine große Häufigkeit stehen, vgl. Gen 31,7; 1 Sam 1,8; Hi 19,3; Bar 4,28. Möglich wäre auch eine Anspielung an Num 14,22 (zehnmaliges Versuchen trotz der Wunder Jahwes bei der Wüstenwanderung), weniger wahrscheinlich ein Bezug auf die Zehn Gebote. Am sichersten ist die Deutung auf die zehn ägyptischen Plagen, die in Z. 14 und 15 erneut aufgegriffen werden.

Zeile 7: Kraft] Wendung wörtlich Dan 11,15; Esr 10,13.

ihr] Das Suffix der 3. Pers. fem. Sing. könnte sich auf נקמה bzw. חמה (Z. 5) beziehen. Ob ein Zusammenhang mit den entsprechenden Suffixen von Kol. II (dort wohl das Gesetz bzw. die mit ihm identifizierte Weisheit, vgl. Dtn 4,6, s. auch Strugnell, *Notes en marge*, p. 269) anzunehmen ist, kann von dieser einzelnen Stelle nicht sicher entschieden werden. Jedoch gibt es auch in Kol. II den wiederholten Wechsel von Suffixen der 3. Pers. fem. Sing. mit denen der 3. Pers. masc. Sing. (von Gott).

Hoffnung] Strugnell, *Notes en marge*, p. 269 versteht מקוה verbal und übersetzt (p. 272): »and none to support« (ואין מקוה), doch legen die Wendungen יש מקוה (Esr 10,2; 1QH 3,20; 6,6; 9,14; f 1,7) und אין מקוה (1 Chr 29,15) ein substantivisches Verständnis nahe.

Zeile 8: zornigen] Vgl. Nah 1,6.
aus] Aufnahme von Mal 3,2f.
Engeln] Auch hier ist wohl ein Bezug zu den ägyptischen Plagen, vgl. besonders Ps 78,49.
Zeile 9: Feuer] Vgl. Jes 66,14-16.
Söhne] Zur Form des Lehreröffnungsanrufs vgl. TSim 4,7 καὶ ὑμεῖς τέκνα μου; die Anrede »meine Söhne« nochmals 1-2 II 3.
kraftlos] Vgl. z. B. Ps 62,10.
Zeile 10: Gras] Zu Wortfeld und Kontext s. Jes 40,6-8; Pss 90,5-6; 103,15.16; Jes 51,12.
Schönheit] פארה ist bibl.-hebr. nicht im Sinne von »Schmuck, Zierde« belegt; es handelt sich um eine qatal-Bildung (fem.) von פאר II.
Anmut] Zur Konstruktion s. Gesenius-Kautzsch, Grammatik §143a.
darüber] (Anm. 16) s. Jes 40,7.
Zeile 11: vertrocknet] Jes 40,7.
Wurzelstock] Das Arabische bietet für עגז tatsächlich eine sinnvolle Ableitung: *aʿǧāz* »Hinterteil, Hinterer«; s. die kuriose, von Strugnell, *Notes en marge*, p. 270 mitgeteilte Bedeutung von *iʿajazat^{un}*; *a. annahal* sind jedoch die Stümpfe der Palmbäume (H. Wehr, *Arabisches Wörterbuch*, p. 533b). Es ist sehr wohl möglich, daß mit עגז der untere Teil der Pflanze gemeint ist. Das Nebeneinander von Vertrocknen des Stumpfes und dem Hinweggenommenwerden der Blüte durch den Wind betont die Totalität des Vergehens (s. auch עד אי֯קו֯ם).
weg] Zu Kontext und Terminologie s. Jes 40,24.
ist] S. o. Anmerkung zu 1-2 I 11.
Zeile 12: Wind] S. o. Anmerkung zu 1-2 I 12.
findet ihn nicht] Zum Suchen-Nichtfinden vgl. Ez 26,21; Ps 37,36.
Hoffnung] 1 Chr 29,15.
Zeile 13: Erde] Vgl. zum Topos 1 Chr 29,15; Hi 8,9; weiter Ps 144,4; Qoh 6,12; 8,13; auch Pss 102,12; 109,23.
Volk] Zur Eingangsformel vgl. Pss 78,1; 81,9; 81,14.
Zeile 14: kommen um] Zur Abgrenzung und Lesung s. o. Anmerkungen zu 1-2 I 14.
vor der Macht unseres Gottes] Eigentlich wäre Assimilation zu erwarten, s. aber auch 1-2 II 6.
Zeile 15: getan hat] Vgl. Ez 3,20; Ri 6,13; Mi 7,15; Pss 105,5.13f; 106,7; Neh 9,17.
Ham] Pss 106,21; 105,27.
erschrecke] Die Taten Jahwes in Ägypten als Warnung; vgl. bes. SapSal 16,6.

1-2 II

Zeile 1: Willen] Vgl. Esr 10,11.

Gnadengaben] Diese stichische Aufteilung setzt die Ergänzung ועשו רצ[ונו בכל לבבכם ותתענג נ]פשכם voraus: »Und tut seinen Willen von ganzem Herzen, so daß eure Seele sich ergötze entsprechend seinen guten Gnadengaben«. Zur Verbindung von חסד und טוב vgl. Pss 69,17; 109,21; auch Ps 63,4.

Zeile 2: Leben] Vgl. Prov 6,13; Jer 21,8; Mt 7,14; Apg 1,28; Hebr 10,20; der Verweis von Allegro, *Qumran Cave 4*. I, p. 87 auf 1QH 15,22 ist unzutreffend.

Pfad] Diese stichische Gliederung setzt die Ergänzung ומסלה] לארך ימים voraus (»Und den Pfad zum langen Leben, um euch zu einem Rest zu machen für eure Kinder etc.«) bzw. [ומסלה] לארך ימים לשם שם ושארית (»Und den Pfad zum langen Leben, um einen Namen und einen Rest zu erhalten für eure Kinder etc.«).

nach euch] Vgl. Dtn 29,11; wörtlich Lev 25,46; 1 Chr 28,8.

warum] ולמה vielleicht eher als Frage (so Allegro, *Qumran Cave 4*. I, p. 86; Strugnell, *Notes en marge*, p. 273) als im Sinne von »damit nicht«.

Zeile 3: Herz] נתן לב ל vgl. 1 Chr 20,19.

hin] Diese Gliederung setzt die Ergänzung voraus: ומזמתכם תמאם צדק ומ[שפט (»und euer Denken verachtet Gerechtigkeit und Recht«).

Söhne] Vgl. zur Wendung TRub 2,1; von Allegro, *Qumran Cave 4*. I nicht als Lehreröffnungsruf erkannt.

widerspenstig] Vgl. Pss 107,11; 105,28.

Jahwes] Zum freien Gebrauch des Gottesnamens s. o. p. 129.

Zeile 4: gebot] Vgl. 1QS 1,13; 3,11: Parallel »Wege« – »Pfade« von Gottes Gebot Bar 4,13.

Isaak] Zur Form ישחק statt יצחק s. Jer 33,26; Am 9,16; Ps 105,9; 4Q*180* 1,5; 4Q*181* 2,1.

Zeile 5: täglich] Zu Lesung und Übersetzung s. o. Anmerkung zu 1-2 II 4.

Reichtum] Diese Stichenanordnung setzt folgende Ergänzung voraus: בעשר] דעתו להתהלך [ביראתו (»am Reichtum [seiner Erkenntnis, zu wandeln] in der Furcht vor ihm«).

abgedrängt] לעתת ist paläographisch sicher. Allegro, *Qumran Cave 4*. I, p. 86 faßt לעתת als Plural von עת plus ל (vgl. Pss 9,10; 10,1 לעתות), »for periods«. Strugnell, *Notes en marge*, vermutet ein unbekanntes Verbum im Infinitiv und fragt nach einem Zusammenhang mit arab. ʿatta »affliger«. Am nächstliegenden ist jedoch die Annahme einer Polelform von עות II (»beugen, krümmen«) im Passiv (vgl. von רום die Form רומם, Gesenius-Kautzsch, Grammatik §72m). Zur Defektivschreibung s. die Beispiele der Defektivschreibung in diesem Text: 1-2 I 9; 1-2 II 14; 1-2 III 12. Wahrscheinlich liegt die Vorstellung von der Gefährdung des Weges dahinter (vgl. Ps 146,9, עות im Piel!). Zur Gefahr auf dem Weg durch פח, פחד und יקוש s. Prov 3,23-26; Hi 22,10; Jes 24,18; Jer 48,44; Hos 9,8; Am 3,5; Pss 91,3; 119,110; 140,6; 141,9f; 142,4; Jer 18,22; Prov 22,5.

Schrecken] Vgl. Jes 24,17; Jer 48,43; CD 4,15.

Vogelstellers] Vgl. Hos 9,8; Ps 91,3; 4QTest 24.

Zeile 6: Vielleicht ist entsprechend der Anmerkung zum hebr. Text וֹמפּ[חֹ]וֹת zu lesen. Es folgen wahrscheinlicher zwei sehr kurze Glieder (jeweils ca. 14 BE), als ein sehr langes (28 BE).

Engeln] Dieser Gedanke kontrastiert mit der Straffunktion der Engel in 1-2 I 8f. Wer sich dem Gesetz/der Weisheit unterwirft und ihre Gaben annimmt, steht nicht unter ihrer Bedrohung (vgl. Ex 12,23; Ps 78,49-53). Hi 4,18 könnte andererseits nahelegen zu übersetzen: »und zuverlässiger zu sein als seine Engel«, doch erscheint dies weniger wahrscheinlich.

Zeile 7: Dunkelheit] Vgl. חשך אפלה Ex 10,22; וחשך ואפלה Jo 2,2; Zeph 1,5; s. auch ähnlich Hi 34,22 אין חשך ואין צלמות.

Bis דעתו sind zwei Stichen ausgefallen.

Zeile 8: ihr] Es folgt ein Objekt und ein Stichos, der möglicherweise eine Rede einleitet. Wer das Subjekt ist, ist nicht sicher zu entscheiden. So könnte ein Frommer sagen: »Von ihm her ergeht Erkenntnis (דעה) auf jedes Volk«, womit die Allgemeinheit der Weisheit für alle Völker zum Ausdruck gebracht würde, der sich auch die Heiden öffnen sollen; zur Universalität der Weisheit vgl. Prov 8,1ff; Sir 24,6. – Ist רעה statt דעה zu lesen, könnte man darin den Einwand eines Heiden sehen, der in Gott eine Bedrohung sieht.

Glückselig] In Z. 8 und 13 finden sich zwei Makarismen, die in Beziehung zueinander stehen: Z. 8 glückselig, dem sie gegeben ist; Z. 13 glückselig, der sie tut. Zu Makarismusreihungen s. K. Koch, *Formgeschichte*, pp. 7-9; M. Sæbø, אשרי; H. Cazelles, אשרי; C. Westermann, *Gebrauch von* אשרי.

Zeile 9: Mensch] Dieser Sticheneinteilung liegt folgende Ergänzung zugrunde: בן אד[ם חזקה לו להתחשב עם יוד]עים (»der Mens[ch, der sie für sich ergreift, um gerechnet zu werden zu den Wisse]nden«).

sagen] Vgl. Ps 10,3f; SapSal 2,1ff.

Zeile 10: Gott hat sie Israel gegeben] Israel als Empfänger der Weisheit (bzw. des mit ihr identifizierten Gesetzes) Dtn 4,6; Sir 24,7-12; Bar 3,37.

geschenkt] Vgl. Gen 30,20.

Zeile 11: getötet] Es muß ein Objekt folgen und ein neuer Halbvers.
  Besitz] Zu den Gütern, die die Weisheit gewährt, s. z. B. Prov 3,16f; 8,14ff.32ff.
Zeile 12: Leben] Vgl. Prov 3,16.
  Kraft] Prov 15,30.
  Freude des Herzens] Vgl. Jer 15,16; Ct 3,11; Qoh 5,19; Jes 30,29; Sir 30,22; 34,28; Ez 36,5; Ps 4,8.
  Ehre] Prov 3,16; 8,18.
Zeile 13: Völker] Hier wird deutlich die Universalität der Weisheit ausgesprochen: Sie ist nicht allein Israel gegeben, sondern für alle Völker.
  Rettungstaten] Zur Parallelität von ישוע und חסד vgl. Ps 13,6.
  Joch] Vgl. Sir 6,30; 51,17.26; Mt 11,29.
Zeile 14: trügerisch] Zur Asyndesis s. Gesenius-Kautzsch, Grammatik §120h.

1-2 III

Zeile 9: Worte des Bundes] דברי ברית vgl. Dtn 28,69.
Zeile 10: Richtschnur] Vgl. Ez 20,37.
Zeile 12: Innerstes] Vgl. Prov 18,8; 20,30; 26,22; 20,27.
  Nieren] Vgl. Jer 11,20; 17,10; Ps 7,10.
Zeile 13: Wort] Vgl. 1QH 1,27, vgl. dazu R. Bergmeier / H. Pabst, *Lied*.

Institut für antikes Judentum und　　　　Hermann LICHTENBERGER
hellenistische Religionsgeschichte
Liebermeisterstraße 12
72076 Tübingen
Deutschland

III
THE WISDOM TEXTS FROM QUMRAN AND THE ANCIENT NEAR EAST

TUN-ERGEHENS-ZUSAMMENHANG, KLAGEERHÖRUNG UND THEODIZEE IM BIBLISCHEN HIOBBUCH UND IN SEINEN BABYLONISCHEN PARALLELEN

Das folgende Referat wird in der Hoffnung vorgelegt, daß für das Verständnis von Weisheitstexten aus Qumran, auch wenn diese nicht ausdrücklich thematisiert werden, das biblische Buch Hiob mit seinen babylonischen Paralleltexten[1] ein heuristisch bedeutsames Analogon bietet. Dafür empfiehlt sich das biblische Hiobbuch schon dadurch, daß es den Kanon weisheitlicher Gattungen vom *māšāl* über die 'weisheitliche Lehrerzählung'[2] zum Streitgespräch durchläuft. Dem Streitgespräch sind, was den Anteil Hiobs betrifft, Elemente aus den Klage- und Bittpsalmen des Einzelnen inkorporiert; dabei wird die Anklage Gottes zeitweise dominant. In den abschließenden Gottesreden tritt dann das Motiv der Bestreitung zwar zurück; es ist in deren Rahmenstücken aber immer noch vorhanden.

In den meisten babylonischen 'Hiobtexten', etwa in der bekannten Monologdichtung *Ludlul bēl nēmeqi* »Preisen will ich den Herrn der Weisheit (Marduk)«[3], überwiegt das Klage-Erhörungs-Paradigma[4]; sie entsprechen dem poetischen Corpus des Hiobbuches, Kap. 3-31*; 38,1-42,6*, allerdings ohne den Dialogpart der Freunde. Dagegen folgt die »Babylonische Theodizee«[5] ganz dem Modell des Streitgesprächs; hier fehlt eine von der Gottheit gefügte Schicksalswende: der Gesprächspartner des Duldenden muß so etwas wie eine Problemlösung aus sich selbst produzieren[6].

1. DER *MĀŠĀL* ALS »WEISHEITLICHER KUNSTSPRUCH«

Die 'Weisheit' nimmt beim Einzelspruch ihren Ausgang. Eine Ereignisfolge von hohem Spannungsgehalt kommt, wie Hiob 1,13-22 paradigmatisch zeigt, in einem poetisch geformten, hier doppel-

---

1. Editionen und Literatur bei VF., *Hiobproblem*, pp. 49-69.180-183 mit Anmerkungen pp. 145-147.197f.
2. Cf. VF., *Lehrerzählung*, passim.
3. Deutsche Übersetzung W. VON SODEN, *Leidender Gerechter*, cf. GEORGE & AL-RAWI, *Sippar Library*, pp. 187-201.
4. Cf. zum Terminus GESE, *Lehre und Wirklichkeit*, pp. 63-69.
5. Deutsche Übersetzung VON SODEN, *Babylonische Theodizee*
6. Ein Vergleich von *Ludlul bēl nēmeqi* mit der »Babylonischen Theodizee« findet sich bei VF., *Parallelen*, passim.

ten *māšāl* des Betroffenen, sozusagen gelegentlich, zu Abschluß und Klärung[7]:

> Nackt bin ich aus dem Schoß meiner Mutter gekommen,
> und nackt werde ich dahin zurückkehren.
> JHWH hat gegeben, JHWH hat genommen;
> der Name JHWHs sei gelobt (1,21).

Im Grunde sagt der Spruch nur etwas zu der Situation, aus der er sich ergibt; er verkündet keine darüber hinausgehende Wahrheit. Das wird noch deutlicher an der nachfolgenden Situation von 2,9f., in der sich der eigentliche *māšāl*, nämlich

> Auch das Gute nehmen wir von Gott -
> sollten wir das Schlechte nicht (hin-)nehmen? (2,10aβ),

erst durch eine Anrede Hiobs an seine Frau, V.10aα, in die Ereignisfolge einfügt.

Selbstverständlich aber ist eine Überzeugung nötig, die die Situation gemeinsam mit anderen, ähnlichen oder vergleichbaren Situationen umgreift, damit es zum klärenden Abschluß einer Ereignisfolge in ihr kommen kann. Hiob 1,21 setzt voraus, daß der Mensch zwischen Geburt und Tod keinen Anspruch an JHWH hat; was immer ihm widerfährt, kann nur ein – freilich auch resigniertes – Gotteslob motivieren. 2,10 hat wie 1,21 eine hinnehmende religiöse Haltung zur Voraussetzung. Letztlich kann jede Ordnungsvorgabe zur Bildung eines *māšāl* die Handhabe geben: in den beiden genannten *mᵉšālîm* ist es anders als in der Hiobrahmenerzählung, der sie angehören, nicht der von Gott garantierte Tun-Ergehens-Zusammenhang; auch Ordnungsvorgaben, die nicht ausdrücklich religiös begründet sind, können Einzelerfahrungen in sinngebende Kontexte einzuordnen gestatten.

In jedem Fall verhalten sich die meisten *mᵉšālîm*, wie ihre indikativische Sprachform zeigt, gegenüber der Ereignisfolge, die sie hervorruft, reaktiv. Dennoch zeigt schon die Wiederverwendung eines *māšāl* in einer neuen, meist ähnlichen Situation, indem sie seine Überlieferung begründet, daß das einmal Ausgesprochene eine erste Allgemeingültigkeit gewinnt. Durch immer wiederholten Gebrauch, durch Sammlung und Verschriftung, werden die *mᵉšālîm* schließlich zum Regulativ eines handelnden Zugriffs auf die Wirklichkeit: sie übernehmen, wie aber auch schon Hiob 2,10 als Einzelspruch zeigt, imperativische Implikationen; im Proverbienbuch und anderen Spruchsammlungen sind eigentliche Mahnsprüche dennoch relativ selten.

Ein Großteil der Überzeugungskraft von *mᵉšālîm* liegt, da sie eine Kunstgattung darstellen, in der dichterischen Kraft ihrer sprachlichen

---

7. Cf. zum folgenden die ähnlichen Ausführungen von JOLLES, *Formen*, pp. 150-170.

Gestaltung: die Form steht für eine gleichsam feiernde Haltung gegenüber der Wirklichkeit; die in einer Einzelerfahrung entdeckte oder wiedergefundene, weil vorausgesetzte Ordnung der Welt hat etwas Numinoses, das nicht so sehr zu analytischer Beobachtung als vielmehr zu religiöser Verehrung den Anlaß gibt. Zugleich mag auch ein Bildungsanspruch der Träger weisheitlicher Spruchdichtungen, dessen Humanismus nicht nur einer religiösen Fundierung bedarf, das ästhetische Medium als Spiegel seines aristokratischen Anspruchs gebraucht haben. Im Gegensatz zu den volkstümlichen Sprichwörtern, die auch $m^e\check{s}\bar{a}l\hat{\imath}m$ heißen[8], kann man die in Spr 10-29(-31) gesammelten Sentenzen und Hiob 1,21; 2,10 als 'weisheitliche Kunstsprüche' bezeichnen[9].

Daß die Sprüche in Spr 10-29(-31) – etwa mit C. Westermann[10] und F. Golka[11] – näher an die volkstümlichen Sprichwörter zu rücken wären, widerraten nicht nur die strenge poetische Form und der 'gehobene' Wortschatz, sondern auch Inhalte wie Tischsitte (23,1-3), Karriereverhalten (18,12; 22,4; 29,23), Gelassenheit (14,29f.; 17,27f.) u.ä., die auf die 'Abgehobenheit' eines institutionellen Trägers der betreffenden Sprachkunst schließen lassen. So läßt sich die Urban- und Dorfkultur Kanaans im Ausstrahlungsraum der altorientalischen Hochkulturen, in der sich das geistige Leben Israels abspielt, auch nicht mit der Ewe-Kultur Westafrikas und anderer afrikanischer Völker vergleichen, bei denen Westermann und Golka nach Parallelen suchen. Vielmehr müßte meines Erachtens die hellenische Gnomik des 7./6. Jh.s vor Chr., deren Hervorbringungen wir verstreut in der frühgriechischen Lyrik, bei Pindar, bei den Vorsokratikern, aber auch geschlossen bei eigentlichen »Gnomikern« wie Solon, Phokylides und Theognis finden, zum Vergleich herangezogen werden[12]: schon die geographische Nähe, aber auch die

---

8. So in erzählenden Kontexten Ri 8,21; 1 Sam 16,7; 1 Kön 20,11, dazu wie in Hiob 1f. aus spannungsvollen Situationen Jer 23,28b = Ez 18,2; Ez 16,44; in 1 Sam 10,12 = 19,24 bezeichnet $m\bar{a}\check{s}\bar{a}l$ im spannungsvollen Erzählkontext die »Redensart«. Der Begriff hat ein weites Bedeutungsspektrum: die $m^e\check{s}\bar{a}l\hat{\imath}m$, die offenbar schon in früher Zeit im 'Volksmund' lebten, haben mit denen von Spr 10-29(-31) im Grunde nur 'den Namen gemein'; das in das Proverbienbuch eingegangene 'Volksgut' wurde entsprechend umgeformt, wie schon EISSFELDT (*Maschal*, p. 47) betonte.

9. Cf. zur Semantik von $m\bar{a}\check{s}\bar{a}l$ KLEIN, *Kohelet*, pp. 16-39, zum weisheitlichen Kunstspruch im Alten Testament pp. 40-62.

10. *Weisheit*, passim, cf. DERS., *Wurzeln*, dazu: DERS., *Forschungsgeschichte*, wo auf ähnliche Thesen anderer wie R.B.Y. SCOTT, J.M. THOMPSON, C.R. FONTAINE, F.W. GOLKA (Anm. 11), G. VANONI hingewiesen wird.

11. *Weisheitsschule*, passim; DERS., *Ursprung*, passim; DERS., *Flecken,* passim; DERS., *Spots*, passim.

12. Cf. zur Gnomik allgemein ZELLER, *Philosophie*, pp. 155-158; DERS., *Gnome*, passim (Lit.), zur Gnomik bei Pindar cf. SCHADEWALDT, *Lyrik*, p. 227; LESKY, *Geschichte*, p. 234; DIHLE, *Literaturgeschichte*, pp. 85.90, und BREMER, *Pindar*, pp. 364f.402.

kulturmorphologische Ähnlichkeit ist hier größer. Vor allem: von einer volkstümlichen Spruchweisheit ist der Weg zu den weisheitlichen Lehrgedichten in Spr 1-9, den Weisheitspsalmen und Jesus Sirach sowie zur weisheitlichen Auseinandersetzungsliteratur wie Hiob und Kohelet viel schwerer zu finden. Schließlich lassen sich auch für den akkadischen Bereich, wie schon W.G. Lambert[13] gezeigt hat, »popular sayings« von »proverbs« unterscheiden: »popular sayings« sind einsprachig akkadisch; unter »proverbs« transkribiert, übersetzt und kommentiert Lambert sumerisch-akkadische Bilinguen, meist aus der Bibliothek Assurbanipals, Kunstspruchsammlungen, die sich zweifelsfrei einem schulischen Überlieferungswillen verdanken; unter seinen »Babylonian proverbs« findet sich unter anderem eine kurze akkadisch-hethitische Bilingue aus Boghazköj.

2. DIE HIOBRAHMENERZÄHLUNG

Auch eine Erzählung hat es zunächst wie der *māšāl* mit einer einmaligen Ereignisfolge zu tun. Ihr Anspruch, Gehör zu finden, begründet sich aber auch hier durch die paradigmatische Funktion des Erzählten: der Handlungsablauf muß durch die gestalterische Kraft des Erzählens dem Hörer oder Leser eine Handhabe zur Bewältigung analoger Abläufe und Situationen bieten, wenn die Erzählung Interesse finden soll; der betreffende Bedarf ist insofern derselbe, der auch die Wiederverwendung, Überlieferung, Sammlung und Verschriftung von *mᵉšālîm* steuert. Durch ihre regulative Funktion entsteht ein Gegenmodell zu inakzeptablen Zufällen: jede künstlerisch gelungene Erzählung verleiht dem Erzählten eine Art Notwendigkeit, die den Bedeutungs- und Sinnbedarf ihres Adressaten befriedigt.

Der paradigmatische Charakter des Einmaligen tritt bei narrativen Gattungen von lehrhafter Funktion in den Vordergrund. Bei der Hiobrahmenerzählung als 'weisheitlicher Lehrerzählung', die darin den Legenden und ein wenig den Märchen ähnlich ist[14], äußert sich die dichterische Gestaltungskraft in einer geradezu symmetrischen Aufbaustruktur[15], die freilich auf Kosten der sprachlichen Detaillierung wirksam zu werden scheint. Darin steht die Hiobrahmenerzählung zusammen mit der Josephsgeschichte (Gen 37; 39-50), den Geschichten von Daniel als weisem

---

13. LAMBERT, *Literature*, pp. 213-221 gegenüber pp. 222-282.
14. Cf. zur Legende JOLLES, *Formen*, pp. 23-61, zum Märchen pp. 218-246; zur wunschbestimmten Moral des Märchens pp. 238-246.
15. Cf. dazu VF. *Lehrerzählung*, passim; DERS., *Hiobrahmenerzählung*, passim, bes. pp. 24-28.

Mantiker (Dan 2; 3,31-4,34; 5)[16], den Büchern Esther und Tobit sowie den Aḥiqar-Erzählungen und der Abraham-Sara-Erzählung in 1QGenAp 19,10-20,32[17]: sie alle gehören mit ihren märchenhaften oder legendären Konnotationen ebenfalls der Gattung 'weisheitliche Lehrerzählung' an und dienen so dem erzählerisch-fiktiven Erweis eines Tun-Ergehens-Zusammenhangs, der sich dank göttlicher Providenz zwar langsam, aber am Ende nur um so gründlicher durchsetzt. – Allerdings zeigen die Satansszenen in Hiob 1,6-12; 2,1-7 bereits »den Verlust der Eindeutigkeit dessen, was zwischen Gott und den Menschen gilt«[18]; zwar nicht ausdrücklich Gottes Gerechtigkeit, die eine Wette auf Kosten des Menschen für immerhin akzeptabel hält, wohl aber der Eigennutz hinter weisheitlicher Frömmigkeit, die Gott nicht »umsonst fürchtet« (1,9), begründet eine Kritik am weisheitlichen Zugriff auf die Wirklichkeit.

Dennoch scheint es der volkstümlichen Erzählung zunächst gelungen zu sein, (1.) mittels eines sie verkörpernden Handlungsträgers die weisheitliche Tugend eines Festhaltens an religiöser »Integrität« (*tummā* Hiob 2,3.9) und einer Glück wie Unglück hinnehmenden Daseinshaltung (2,10) zu imitabler Darstellung zu bringen und (2.) die Wirklichkeit nach Maßgabe eines Ordnungspostulats zu interpretieren, aufgrund dessen die dargestellte Tugend als sinnvoll und lohnend erscheint; wo aber die Bestätigung der weisheitlichen Tugend durch die Wirklichkeit einmal (noch) ausbleibt, überbrückt (3.) eine selbstvergessene Geduld die Zeitspanne, bis sich so etwas wie eine Wahrheit der Wirklichkeit[19] realisiert. – Ein Antiheld wie Hiobs Frau bestätigt die zu Hiobs Frömmigkeit oppositiven Untugenden[20].

Der kritische Leser freilich durchschaut den moralistischen Bestätigungsmechanismus, der diesen und ähnlichen Geschichten zugrunde liegt; ihn irritiert insbesondere das realitätsvergessene Zurechterzählen

---

16. Cf. VF., *Märchen*, passim.
17. Cf. LANGE, *Wisdom Didactive Narrative*, passim.
18. SPIECKERMANN, *Satanisierung*, pp. 435.
19. Auch in bezug auf dieses Problem berührt sich die alttestamentliche Weisheit mit einer Fragestellung der mittelalterlichen Philosophie bis einschließlich zur vorkantischen Aufklärung; cf. dazu PIEPER, *Wahrheit*, passim. Seit I. KANT sind wir jedoch geneigt, 'Wahrheit' nicht in den Dingen, sondern allein in den Urteilen über sie zu finden oder auch zu vermissen, und zwar eher auf der syntaktischen als auf der semantischen Ebene. Allerdings entsteht sofort das Folgeproblem, ob es eine Wahrheit des Denkens gebe, auf der die Wahrheit aller Urteile beruht: das Denken empfängt seine Nötigung aus dem jederzeit von uns geforderten handelnden Umgang mit der Wirklichkeit und könnte wie dieser Elemente einer Fehlanpassung an unsere Umwelt enthalten; der Mensch ist auch das Sorgenkind der Wirklichkeit.
20. Auf der Ebene nicht des Umgangs mit der Wirklichkeit, sondern seiner weisheitlichen Steuerung durch einen Gottesumgang hat mit seiner Frage in 1,9 auch der Satan eine Antiheldenrolle. Cf. Anm. 40.

des Seienden zu einer Scheinwelt, in der sich am Ende alles nach den Wünschen des Menschen zu richten hat. Die allgemein in den weisheitlichen Überzeugungen und speziell in der Ideologie der 'weisheitlichen Lehrerzählung' umgesetzte Strategie der emotionalen und scheinrationalen Assimilation einer Wirklichkeit, in der man gut überleben will, ist allzu offensichtlich. Entsprechend kann die kritische Frage des Satans nach dem Eigennutz weisheitlicher Frömmigkeit (1,9) nur in seinem Sinne beantwortet werden; denn daß die Tugend des Helden schließlich eine triumphale Bestätigung finden muß (42,10.12-17[21]), zeigt umgekehrt, wie schnell die weisheitliche Religion zusammenbrechen würde, wenn die von ihr behauptete sittliche Weltordnung sich nicht endgültig bewährte. – Die Erzählung gesteht den Wirklichkeitsverlust, mit dem sie die Befriedigung eines religiösen Harmoniebedürfnisses erkauft, beiläufig selber ein: zwar steht vor dem Höhepunkt der sogenannten 'Prüfungen' Hiobs noch nicht fest, ob Hiob Gott »umsonst« fürchtet; wohl aber muß Gott eingestehen, daß er Hiob, vom Satan dazu aufgereizt, »umsonst verderbt« hat (2,3). Da Gott am Ende Genugtuung schenkt, richtet sich die hier aufscheinende Frage allerdings nicht schon als Theodizeeproblem an Gott selbst, sondern allenfalls an den Weltumgang des Erzählers und der von ihm vertretenen Religion: muß sie nicht notwendig Gott ins Unrecht setzen, weil sie mit der Welt nicht zurechtkommt? Stellt die weisheitliche Ordnungsideologie nicht ein Signifikatensystem ohne Referenzbezug dar, ein Syndrom von Bedeutungsträgern, das nicht authentisch über sich hinauszuweisen vermag? Handelt es sich nicht gar um eine realitätsunabhängige 'autonome' Sinngebung, die nur als reines Sprachgeschehen ihre Geltung hat? Weil aber Signifikate ohne Referenzbezug leer sind, bleibt letztlich ein bloßes Spiel von Signifikanten ohne Signifikat zurück.

In der jüdischen, christlichen und islamischen Wirkungsgeschichte[22] hat allein der Stoff der Hiobrahmenerzählung, der in späteren Texten der Haggada und des ḥadīṯ vielleicht in älterer Form vorliegt, ein Echo gehabt. Im »Lob der Väter der Vorzeit« preist Sir 49,9 Hiob als den, »der alles in Gerechtigkeit ausrichtete«[23]. Jak 5,11 hebt hervor, daß der Herr aus »innigem Erbarmen« und »Mitleid« auf Hiobs geduldiges Ausharren ein gutes Ende folgen ließ; ähnlich stellt der Qurʾān in Sure 21,83f; 38,41-44 Hiob als vorbildlichen Muslim dar. Eine oberflächliche

---

21. Die in 42,11 erzählte Handlung gehört ursprünglich in den Kontext des Leidens Hiobs; cf. VF., *Hiob*, pp. 23-26.
22. Cf. VF., *Hiob*, passim; *Hiobproblem*, pp. 23-37.
23. Cf. zu Ergänzung und Übersetzung des hebräischen Textes im Gegensatz zu 𝔊 SAUER, *Sirach*, p. 629.

Vereindeutigung der Wirklichkeit findet in drei Weltreligionen ein verdächtig einmütiges Gehör; der anklagende Rebell des Corpus des Hiobbuches dagegen bleibt nahezu unberücksichtigt.

Ein Beispiel dafür, wie Ordnungsvorgaben durch weisheitliche Erzählungen vorausgesetzt und bestätigt werden, ist auch die akkadische Humoreske vom »Arme(n) Mann von Nippur« aus dem 8. Jh. vor Chr.[24], die zur Hiobrahmenerzählung und deren Gattungsverwandten eine Kontrastparallele darstellt. Hier und dort soll durch den erzählten Handlungsablauf der Gegensatz zwischen dem inneren Wert des Helden und seinem äußeren Ergehen ausgeglichen werden: in der Erzählung vom »Armen Mann« wird, dem Plot der Hiobgeschichte nicht unähnlich, ein beklagenswertes Unrecht, wie es die Armut und daraus folgende Erniedrigungen des Handlungsträgers durch Reiche und Mächtige darstellen, am Ende mit märchenhafter Eindeutigkeit aufgehoben; ein egalitäres Rechtsempfinden auf Seiten des Adressaten findet so eine zugleich rationale wie emotionale Genugtuung. Ein Kontrast zur Hiobrahmenerzählung liegt insofern vor, als der innere Wert des »Armen Mannes« nicht in weisheitlich frommer Rechtschaffenheit, sondern in seiner von List nicht freien, bauernschlauen Überlegenheit über die Wechselfälle des Lebens besteht; mit den humoristischen verbinden sich dabei auch sozialkritische, im besonderen obrigkeitskritische Züge[25]. Hier und dort wiederum bildet die einfache Konfiguration von Helden und Antihelden das dramaturgische Gerüst für eine Reihe von schlichten wertrelevanten Oppositionen, die den moralisch-ästhetischen Reiz dieser Geschichten ausmachen; wer sich mit Hiob oder dem »Armen Mann« identifiziert, mag in solchen wunschbestimmten Problemlösungsmustern seinen Trost finden, was im Falle des »Armen Mannes« oder auch der biblischen Daniellegenden[26] zugleich für die eigene soziale Dürftigkeit entschädigt. – Um das Harmoniebedürfnis ihrer Adressaten zu befriedigen, bedarf die Erzählung vom »Armen Mann« aber weder der Vorsehung noch eines Gottes: die prinzipiell geordnete Wirklichkeit schafft selbst den gerechten Ausgleich[27], der die Schadenfreude des kleinen Mannes weckt; allenfalls erscheint ein dem Alltag entrückter König (Z. 71) dabei wie der Pharao der Josephsgeschichte in einer Adjuvantenrolle.

24. Einschlägige Literatur und deutsche Übersetzung: VON SODEN, *Leidender Gerechter*, pp. 174-180; cf. zur Exegese VF., *Hiobrahmenerzählung*, dort weitere Literatur p. 22[14].
25. So spielt ein Bürgermeister (ḫazanu) die Rolle eines Antihelden, dessen ungerechtes Verhalten dreimal durch die Rache des Helden gestraft wird: die schnöde Abweisung des Armen vor allem steht einem Vertreter der Obrigkeit schlecht an; cf. VF., *Hiobrahmenerzählung*, p. 31 mit Anm. 37 und 32.
26. Cf. meine in Anm. 16 zitierte Arbeit.
27. Cf. zur Selbstwirksamkeit dieses Ausgleichs KOCH, *Vergeltungsdogma*, passim.

3. Der Hiobdialog und die Gottesrede(n)

Den Dichter des Corpus des Hiobbuches (Kap. 3-31*; 38,1-42,6*[28]) ließ die Rahmenerzählung unbefriedigt. Sein Problem war nicht der verborgene Eigennutz weisheitlicher Frömmigkeit, sondern die ebenfalls schon in den Satansszenen angezeigte Uneindeutigkeit des Gott-Mensch-Verhältnisses, wenn Gott Hiob nämlich »umsonst verderbt« (2,3). So wird, wenn man den Maßstab des Tun-Ergehens-Zusammenhangs unvoreingenommen an den Umgang Gottes mit den Menschen legt, das Theodizeeproblem dringend: Hiob trägt es gegenüber Gott mit der abgewandelten Topik der Klage- und Bittpsalmen des einzelnen, insbesondere in Form der Anklage Gottes aus[29], die zu der hinnehmenden Haltung von 2,10 im Gegensatz steht. Gegenüber den drei Freunden, die die weisheitliche Vergeltungsdoktrin zunächst in freundlichem Werbeverhalten[30], dann aber in zugespitzter Feindseligkeit vertreten[31], spricht er seine Zweifel an einer sittlichen Weltordnung in Form weisheitlicher Streitreden aus.

a. Die Anklage Gottes ist für den Hiob des Dialogs (Kap. 3-31*) wie für dessen Dichter die beinahe einzige Weise des Festhaltens an Gott, die ihm in seinem Leiden und angesichts der Sinnwidrigkeit menschlichen Daseins als möglich erscheint. Aufgegeben wird die Gottesbeziehung umgekehrt nicht in einzelnen blasphemischen Ausuferungen dieser Anklage[32], sondern allenfalls in der Verfluchung des eigenen Geburtstages (3,2-10), wenn die Flucht in die Beziehungslosigkeit noch das Totenreich als ein Idyll erscheinen läßt (Vv. 11-19); ihre Entsprechung

---

28. Mit Sicherheit sekundär sind innerhalb Kap. 3-31*; 38,1-42,6* meines Erachtens nur das Gedicht Kap. 28 und die Schilderungen von Behemot und Livjatan 40,15-41,26. Zweifelhaft erscheinen mir 9,5-10 (G. Fohrer) oder doch zumindest Vv. 8-10 (G. Hölscher) sowie 39,13-18 (cf. Anm. 63). Zur Zweizahl der Gottesreden cf. Anm. 41.

29. 7,12ff.; 9,27ff.; 10,3ff.; 13,24ff.; 14,1ff.; 30,20ff. – Zur Funktion der Anklage Gottes im Psalter und im Zusammenhang des Theodizeeproblems cf. vf., *Gottesfrage*, passim.

30. Der Aufforderung an Hiob, sich an Gott zu wenden (5,8 im Munde des Eliphas), die geradezu mit einer Heilsankündigung verbunden werden kann (8,5-7 im Munde Bildads), folgt Hiob mit denjenigen Elementen seiner Rede, die der Gattung 'Klage- und Bittpsalm des einzelnen' entsprechen, also auch mit der Anklage Gottes, was den Freunden allerdings verborgen zu bleiben scheint.

31. Zur Dramatik des Streits Hiobs mit seinen Freunden cf. Westermann, *Aufbau*, pp. 40-51.

32. So etwa, wenn Hiob in 16,9 den Terminus für den menschlichen Feind des Betenden, nämlich ṣār, auf Gott bezieht; cf. 6,4; 7,20b; 10,3b.16 u.ö. Dagegen ist mit dem rāšā´, in dessen Hand nach 9,24 'äräṣ »das Land / die Erde« gegeben ist, nicht Gott, sondern die persische (oder hellenistische) Fremdherrschaft gemeint, wie die ähnliche Wendung in 15,19 zeigt; zu Keel, *Entgegnung*, pp. 126.157.159.

im Buch Kohelet (4,2f.) ist denn auch kaum mit dessen mühsam festgehaltenem Schöpferglauben zu vereinbaren[33]. Daß die Anklage Gottes im Munde Hiobs zwar nicht in Liturgie und Gebetspraxis der christlichen Kirchen, wohl aber in nachchristlich-säkularistischer Literatur, etwa bei Bertolt Brecht und Albert Camus, mannigfach nachwirkt, darf nicht verwundern: Atheisten mögen 'Gott' ad hoc entwerfen, um für ihre Klage über verzweiflungsvolle Weltzustände eine Adresse zu finden[34]; wenn M. Nilsson mit der Definition von Religion als »Protest des Menschen gegen die Bedeutungslosigkeit der Ereignisse«[35] recht hat, bleibt einer nachtheistischen Religiosität kaum ein anderer Ausweg. Jedenfalls eröffnet die Anklage Gottes und die psalmistische Klage, auf der sie als ihrem konventionelleren Hintergrund beruht, eine letzte Möglichkeit, auch dann noch an der Kommunikation mit Gott festzuhalten, wenn eine – weisheitliche oder wie immer begründete – Daseinszustimmung nicht mehr erschwinglich scheint. Wenn also Religion nicht an Daseinszustimmung als an ihre Voraussetzung gebunden ist, zeigt der Extremfall der Anklage Gottes, daß die psalmistische Gebetsreligion eine Sinngebung an das Sinnlose, wenn sie nicht anders erreichbar ist, durch Herausforderung an die sinnspendende Instanz zu erzwingen sucht: um eine gegenständliche Rettung geht es Hiob im Laufe des Dialogs immer weniger[36]; es ist der Glaube an Ordnung und Sinn der gottgelenkten Wirklichkeit, den er sich selbst in seinen blasphemischen Ausfällen, aber auch in seiner Hoffnung auf einen »Anwalt«[37] und in seinen Selbstrechtfertigungsversuchen[38] zu erhalten sucht.

Zu dem weisheitlichen Streit Hiobs mit seinen Freunden um die Realität eines Tun-Ergehens-Zusammenhangs steht dabei seine Klage insofern in Beziehung, als auch Hiob vom Postulat eines Tun-Ergehens-Zusammenhangs ausgeht: sein Vorwurf an Gott hat ja zum Inhalt, daß Gott diesen Zusammenhang nicht mehr garantiert; entsprechend kann das Theodizeeproblem, das im Dialog mit Gott zur Anklage führt, im

---

33. Cf. VF., *Plausibilitätsverlust*.
34. Cf. VF., *Altes und Neues*, passim.
35. *Religion*, pp. 391-464.
36. Die wenigen Bitten Hiobs richten sich im Laufe des Dialogs immer ausschließlicher auf das negative Anliegen, daß Gott von seinen Vernichtungsschlägen ablassen möge, damit Hiob aufatmen und zu seiner Verteidigung reden kann (9,34f.; 13,21-23, cf. 23,3-12; 31,35-37). Dazu will er Gott als seinem Ankläger in Person begegnen (13.3.14f.; 14,13-17; 23,3-7). Den ersten Teil des Dialogs durchzieht in Anknüpfung an Kap. 3 sein Wunsch zu sterben (6,8-10; 7,15.21; 10,1a.18-20). Cf. WESTERMANN, *Aufbau*, pp. 81-84.
37. 16,18; 17,3; 19,23f.; 31,35. Zu Gott als *gôʾēl* im Sinne von »Anwalt« cf. Jer 50,34; Ps 119,54; Spr 23,11. Die Analogie der »Babylonischen Theodizee« Zz. 295-297 (s.u. sub 4c) gestattet aber auch, an einen menschlichen Fürsprecher o.ä. vor Gott zu denken.
38. 6,28-30; 9,21; 10,7; 13,18f.; 23,7.10-12; 27,2-6; 31.

Gespräch mit den Freunden diskursiv, im Streitgespräch, ausgetragen werden. Schließt Hiob von seinem Schicksal auf ein Versagen Gottes, so schließen die Freunde von Hiobs Schicksal auf seine Schuld, mag diese ihm selbst auch unbewußt geblieben sein (22,4ff.); ja, nach 11,6bff.; 15,16 liefert gerade die Anklage Gottes den Freunden gegen Hiob den gewünschten Beweis dafür, daß Gott gegen ihn recht habe. Wie so oft im Bemühen um das Theodizeeproblem wird Gott auf Kosten des Menschen entlastet. – Wen wundert es, wenn Hiob mit ironisch-parodistischer Umkehrung des Tun-Ergehens-Zusammenhangs in 21,8-13.16 nachgerade das Glück der Frevler preist?

Die Position der Freunde ist in all dem durch die Selbstrückbezüglichkeit eines auch von der Geschichte und ihrer Erfahrung unabhängigen homöostatischen Systems bestimmt: selbstregulative Rückkopplungszusammenhänge schaffen die Möglichkeit der Verdinglichung religiöser Erfahrungen zu einer Doktrin, die sich gegen die Wirklichkeit immunisiert; so bewegen sich die Urteile der Freunde auf dem Gegenpol der offenen Erfahrungsbewältigung in einem jeweilig-gelegentlichen *māšāl*, der erst im Wiedergebrauch, sekundär mithin, eine Verallgemeinerung gestattet.

b. An den Hiobdialog schließt sich das Erscheinen und Reden Gottes als der in den Widersprüchen der Wirklichkeit sinngebenden Instanz (Kap. 38,1ff.)[39] an. In beidem geschieht zugleich Gottes Zuwendung an Hiob und offenbar auch dessen Heilung, von der nachher nicht mehr erzählt wird[40]. Für ein weisheitliches Problem wird somit eine nichtweisheitliche Lösung angeboten. Zugleich aber weisen die Rahmenverse der Gottesrede(n)[41] Hiobs Anklage mit dem Hinweis auf die Beschränktheit menschlichen Daseins zurück; die Demütigung weisheitlichen Erkenntnisstolzes, die darin für Hiob liegt, bewegt sich auf der Ebene eines Arguments Zophars in 11,7-11[42] (cf. auch 15,7-13). Unklar bleibt, ob die

---

39. Cf. zum folgenden VF., *Antwort*, passim.

40. Die Verbindung von Gotteserscheinung und Heilung scheint auch in der arabischen Hiobüberlieferung vorausgesetzt; cf. VF., *Hiob*, pp. 35f. – Im Blick auf das Fehlen des Heilungsmotivs in 42,10ff. die Satansszenen 1,6-12; 2,1-7 zu streichen, deren zweite die Krankheit Hiobs motiviert, empfiehlt sich umgekehrt nicht: auf diese Weise würde auch die Formulierung des Problems der Rahmenerzählung, nämlich 1,9, getilgt.

41. 38,2f.; 40,2; 40,7-9.14. Die sich auch in der doppelten Rahmung bekundende Doppelung der Gottesreden zu eliminieren, sehe ich keinen zwingenden Grund; ein Gleichgewicht zwischen beiden Gottesreden ergibt sich freilich erst nach der Einfügung von 40,15-41,26.

42. Das Gotteslob im Munde Zophars ist weniger als Einfügung verdächtig denn dasjenige im Munde Hiobs 9,(5-)8-10; cf. das aretalogische Lob im Munde des Eliphas 5,9-14. Die beiden Motive des Gotteslobs in 11,7-11, nämlich das Lob des Herrn der Natur

der Anklage Gottes als Maßstab zugrunde liegende Vergeltungsdoktrin bei solcher Erkenntniskritik schon jetzt mitgemeint ist; eine ausdrückliche Zurückweisung der Freunde, die diese Doktrin vertreten, erfolgt jedenfalls erst in dem Prosastück 42,7-9[43]. – Das Corpus der Gottesreden ist sodann ein Selbsthymnus Gottes als des Weltschöpfers, wobei die Realität, an der Hiob leidet, mythisch überhöht ist: dazu wird eine vorfindliche Sachwelt animatisiert[44], das Bedrohliche unterdimensioniert[45], der in ihr wirksam werdende Segen Gottes dagegen überdimensioniert[46]; die weit auseinanderstrebenden Tierschilderungen schließlich versuchen, die der Realität innewohnenden Sinnwidersprüche paradigmatisch zumindest in sinnvollere Widersprüche umzusetzen[47]. Hiob reagiert entsprechend nicht nur in reuevoller Vernunftbescheidung, sondern auch in verhaltener Dankbarkeit (42,1-6). – Religion als Protest gegen die Bedeutungslosigkeit des Seienden zeigt nun eine Sinngebung an das Sinnlose in positiver Weise. Gegenüber der sogenannten Realität verhält sie sich autonom: tatsächlich nehmen ja schon unsere Sinne nur wahr, was wir zum Überleben in der Wirklichkeit brauchen; entsprechend interessengelenkt ist, auch außerhalb des Religiösen, die Organisation der Sinnesdaten durch die Vernunft, die die Wirklichkeit nochmals unseren Bedürfnissen anpaßt. Was die Wirklichkeit als solche ist, wissen wir ohnehin nicht. J.W. von Goethe sah darum auch die Funktion der Kunst gegenüber J.P. Eckermann darin, »gleich den Griechen ... dasjenige wirklich zu machen, was in natürlichen Erscheinungen nur Intention geblieben ist«[48] Religion dürfte diese Funktion früher und gründlicher

(Vv.7-10) und das der (Individual-)Geschichte, das sich auf Hiob beziehen läßt (11), entsprechen den tragenden Motiven der beiden Gottesreden. Als entscheidende Differenz bleibt: die Rede von Gott in 11,7-11 enthält nicht die Zuwendung Gottes in dessen Selbstverherrlichung von 38,1ff.; in 11,5 wünscht Zophar, daß Gott *gegen* Hiob »reden« und »seine Lippen auftun« werde.

43. Möglicherweise bezieht sich der auffällig harte Tadel in 42,7-9 auf eine frühere Versucherrolle der Freunde, die jetzt an die Frau übergegangen ist, cf. VF., *Hiob*, pp. 9-16.

44. So etwa, wenn das Meer in 38,8-11 wie ein Wickelkind vorgestellt wird. In Vv. 12-17 scheint die Morgenröte – offenbar in Nachfolge der kanaanäischen Gottheit *Šḥr* – personhaft vorgestellt; cf. 3,9; 41,10, ferner Jes 14,12. Vv.16-30 enthalten Elemente einer mythischen Topographie mit archaisierender Kosmosbeseelung in Vv. 28f. Vv. 31-38 entfalten eine mythische Himmelskunde, die die Realität mit Imaginärem überlagert und ihr dadurch Vertrautheit und Heimatlichkeit verleiht. Zu den Bildern der Gottesrede als »alte(r) Naturpoesie der Erde«, in der »alles... personificirt« wird, cf. HERDER, *Geist*, pp. 213ff., bes. pp. 228f.

45. Auch hierzu wäre auf die Vorstellung des Meeres als Wickelkind 38,8-11 zu verweisen.

46. 38,26f. – Zu den Angaben in Anm. 44-46 cf. die Einzelbeobachtungen bei VF., *Antwort*, pp. 212-217.

47. Cf. VF., *Antwort*, pp. 218f.

48. *Eintragung*.

wahrgenommen haben: die Kunst übernimmt sie in dem Maße, wie Religion kraftloser wird; die künstlerischen Elemente der Gottesreden dienen auch darum der Lösung eines religiösen Problems.

Mit der Hiobrahmenerzählung bildet das poetische Corpus des Buches insofern eine von dessen Dichter konzipierte Einheit, als beide Teile von einer Not- und Klagesituation zu einer Erhörung und Wiederherstellung des Protagonisten führen; Kap. 3-31*; 38,1-42,6* als Klage-Erhörungs-Paradigma fügt sich so in die Hiobrahmenerzählung; entsprechend konnte deren Schluß (42,10ff.), obwohl der Hiobdialog zur Doktrin der Rahmenerzählung in Spannung steht, in das Ganze des biblischen Buches aufgenommen werden.

4. Die babylonischen Hiobdichtungen

Was im Hiobbuch zu einer komplexen Ganzheit zusammenwächst, das Klage-Erhörungs-Paradigma auf der einen und die weisheitliche Auseinandersetzung um das Theodizeeproblem auf der anderen Seite, verteilt sich in der babylonischen Hiobliteratur auf zwei Texttypen.

a. Die Texte des ersten Typs, dem fast alle Parallelen angehören, darunter *Ludlul bēl nēmeqi* aus dem 12. Jh. vor Chr.[49], sind Klage-Erhörungs-Paradigmen in monologischer Form; die Problemerörterung im Streitgespräch ist in ihnen ohne Entsprechung, obwohl sich der Leidende in II 33-47 kognitive Trostgründe vorhält. – Zwar hat keine dieser Dichtungen einen Prosarahmen wie das biblische Hiobbuch oder auch der aramäische Aḥiqar. Gleichwohl aber verbinden sie die weisheitlich-lehrhafte Darstellung einer Ereignisfolge, an deren ersehntem Ende sich der Tun-Ergehens-Zusammenhang in glücklicher Weise verwirklicht, mit der Dramatik eines Durchgangs des Leidenden von der Klage zum Dank für Erhörung; zumindest mit der letzteren ist auch Ps 22 in der jetzt vorliegenden Gestalt zu vergleichen[50]. Der Spannung, die zwischen der Hiobrahmenerzählung und dem poetischen Corpus besteht, ist in den babylonischen Parallelen nichts an die Seite zu stellen. Die Welt ist im Sinne eines weisheitlich-religiösen Ordnungspostulats in der Zeit der babylonischen Texte noch besser in Ordnung als in der der relativ späten biblischen Dichtung: wenn schon nicht die Wirklichkeit selbst, so doch die in ihr agierenden Götter vermö-

---

49. Cf. zur Datierung VON SODEN, *Leidender Gerechter*, p. 112.

50. Ursprünglich endete der Psalm, wie noch *ᶜanîtānî* in V. 22bβ anzudeuten scheint, mit der Bitte um Rettung in Vv. 21f. Auch das kurze Lobgelübde V. 23 könnte allenfalls noch zum ursprünglichen Psalm gehören. In V. 24 spätestens beginnt die mutmaßliche Ergänzung; cf. Anm. 57.

gen schlußendlich dessen Anspruch auf den Erweis von Gerechtigkeit in den individuellen Schicksalen zu befriedigen; immerhin bleibt in den Klagepartien die Anklage der Gottheit, hier vor allem als Vorwurf an den persönlichen Schutzgott und die Schutzgöttin (*ilī* / *ištarī*) sowie die Schutzgenien *šēd dumqi* und *lamassu*, nicht aus, da sie zum Repertoire religiöser Leidbewältigung gehört[51].

Ludlul bēl nēmeqi kann an manchen Stellen aber auch zur Einzelerklärung des biblischen Hiobbuches und der Klage- und Bittpsalmen des einzelnen dienlich sein. Den Anlaß zu den Klage-Erhörungs-Paradigmen gibt wohl ursprünglich der dankbare Rückblick auf die Gott bzw. Götter umgreifende Ordnung der Wirklichkeit: das durch Not, Gebet und göttliche Hilfe umrissene Geschehen ist befriedigend zu dem Zustand zurückgekehrt, wie er vor der Not bestand: entsprechend beginnen die babylonischen 'Handerhebungs'-Gebete[52], *Ludlul bēl nēmeqi*[53] und Ps 22[54] mit einem hymnischen Aufgesang an den Gott, der geholfen hat; insbesondere in der punischen Religion bezeichnen Opfer, Stele und Votivinschrift das glückliche Ende des betreffenden Geschehenszusammenhangs[55]. – Anders als in allen vergleichbaren biblischen Texten fehlt in *Ludlul bēl nēmeqi* die Bitte: sie ist den Herausforderungen der Götter in der Klage impliziert; so folgt die Erzählung der Schicksalswende in III 9 ganz unvermittelt auf diese. – Während im biblischen Hiobbuch das Erscheinen Gottes die Schicksalswende herbeiführt, geschieht sie in III 9-47 durch die Traumerscheinung von vier priesterlichen oder göttlichen Gestalten, die sich als Gesandte anderer priesterlicher oder göttlicher Gestalten legitimieren (Z. 15.18.25f.42)[56]. – Am Ende werden »alle Münder« der Babylonier (IV 99f.) Marduks Großtaten verherrlichen; die »[Um]-wölkten, so viele es gibt«, sollen ihn preisen (112)[57].

---

51. Zur Identität von *šēd dumqi* und *lamassu* cf. VON SODEN, *Schutzgenien*, passim, zu ihrem Verhältnis zum persönlichen Schutzgott p. 151.
52. Cf. MORAN, *Notes*, passim; dazu LEE, *Gattungsvergleich*, speziell zu den hymnischen Einleitungen pp. 28ff.108ff.
53. I 1-36 zeigt den üblichen hymnischen Prädikationsstil: Marduk wird hier als Gott gepriesen, der im Schicksal der Menschen und überhaupt Wandlungen hervorruft, was sich in der im folgenden dargestellten Klageerhörung aufs neue bewährt hat.
54. V(v). 4(-6) einer »ersten Redaktion« zuzuschreiben, besteht darum kein Anlaß; zu HOSSFELD, in: HOSSFELD/ZENGER, *Psalmen*, pp. 145.149. Ein ähnliches Hymnenelement findet sich in Ps 80,2, einem Klage- und Bittpsalm des Volkes. – Cf. zur Beziehung von *Ludlul* und Ps 22 LEE, *Gattungsvergleich*, pp. 175-185.
55. Cf. VF., *Weihinschriften*, passim.
56. Auch darin mag man eine Analogie zur Verbindung von Gotteserscheinung und Heilung sehen, wie wir sie in der arabischen Hiobüberlieferung (Anm. 40) finden; cf. VF., *Hiob*, pp. 36f.
57. Die universale Ausweitung des vom Betenden initiierten Gotteslobs hat in der mutmaßlichen Ergänzung zu Ps 22, nämlich Vv. (23-)24-32, eine Parallele: nicht nur

b. Einem zweiten Typ babylonischer Paralleltexte zum biblischen Hiobbuch gehört fast nur die schlecht erhaltene »Babylonische Theodizee« an, die W. von Soden in die Zeit zwischen 800 und 750 vor Chr.[58] datierte. In ihr wird das Theodizeeproblem im weisheitlichen Streitgespräch eines Leidenden mit dessen Freund (Singular!)[59] erörtert – außerhalb der Kommunikation mit der Gottheit; Entsprechungen zu den 'Handerhebungs'-Gebeten oder den Klage- und Bittpsalmen des einzelnen fehlen mithin. Der Diskurs nähert sich der theologischen Geistesbeschäftigung, zu der er eine ans Manieristische grenzende Verfeinerung seiner archaisierenden Sprache aufbietet[60], wie sie selbst Hiob 3,1-42,6* nicht in gleichem Maße kennt: nicht die Hinwendung zur Gottheit, das Nachdenken über sie motiviert den Text; was im biblischen Dialog zwischen Hiob und seinen Freunden neben der klagenden Anrede an Gott einherläuft, hat sich von dieser getrennt. Das Postulat einer sittlichen Weltordnung im Sinne der weisheitlichen Religion ist fraglich geworden; in dieser Fraglichkeit wird es erörtert; lediglich die letzten drei Zeilen, 295-297, richten einen Wunsch, nicht eine Bitte an den persönlichen Schutzgott[61], die Schutzgöttin ($^{d}iš\text{-}tar$) und eigenartiger Weise an den König[62]. Die Klage über das Ausbleiben einer retributiven Gerechtigkeit des Gottes (Zz. 70-75.251) und die resultierende Not des Leidenden (48-55.243-253.265-275) gegenüber dem Glück des Frevlers (50-53.70f.) geschieht also nicht, um auf den Gott einzuwirken; selbst die Drohung,

---

Israel (24) und »alle Enden der Erde« (28), auch die Toten (30) und die kommenden Geschlechter (31) werden einbezogen. Das widerrät, in 28-32 eine abermalige, endzeitbezogene Ergänzung von 24-27 zu vermuten (so HOSSFELD, *Psalmen*, pp. 144f.151): es handelt sich in 24-27 und 28-32 um denselben Enthusiasmus, der auch in *Ludlul* alle vorstellbaren Dimensionen sprengt.

58. V. SODEN, *Babylonische Theodizee*, p.143; LAMBERT, *Literature*, p. 67, dachte an eine Entstehung um 1000 vor Chr.

59. Das schlecht erhaltene mittelassyrische Fragment KAR 340 = VAT 9943, pl. 25 (Transkription und englische Übersetzung bei LAMBERT, *Literature*, pp. 90f.) gehört offenbar zu einem der »Babylonischen Theodizee« ähnlichen Dialog mit *einem* Gefährten bzw. Freund (*ib-ri... tap-pe-e* Z. 4); auf die dialogische Struktur des Textes weist auch die viermal wiederholte abwehrende Wendung: *at-ta la-a tu-kal-lam-an-ni (tu-ka-la-ma-an-ni) a-ja-ši* »wirst du mich nicht (eines anderen) belehren« (11.13.15.17). Daß der Leidende im Buch Hiob drei Dialogpartner hat, ist offenbar eine Innovation.

60. Zu den literarischen Finessen des Textes cf. auch VON SODEN, *Babylonische Theodizee*, p. 143.

61. Der Plural in *liš-ku-nu ilū* Z. 295 ist mit dem Singular *li-ir-šá-a diš-tar* Z. 296 nicht kongruent. Der Singular *id-da-[an-]ni*, dem im Keilschriftkommentar *id-dan-ni* entspricht (LAMBERT, *Literature*, p. 88), ist dagegen richtig und weist auf ein Subjekt *ilu* »der (persönliche Schutz-)Gott« hin; cf. VON SODEN, *Babylonische Theodizee*, p. 157 mit n. zu Z. 295.

62. VON SODEN, *Babylonische Theodizee*, p. 146, schien vorauszusetzen, daß sich der Dulder am Ende einem Schiedsspruch des Königs unterwirft; als »Verehrer von Gott und König« (*ka-ri-bu ša i-li ú šar-ri*) stellt sich auch der Dichter in dem Akrostichon vor, das den Text gliedert. Leider ist die Verbalwendung in Z. 297 nur durch Ergänzung zu gewinnen.

fortan jede religiöse Observanz zu beenden (135), soll allein den Freund beeindrucken, an den sich auch alle werbenden (1ff.23f.45f. u.ö.) und gelegentlich ironisch übertreibenden (67f.) Anreden ebenso wie die wenigen Bitten (25f.265f.287f.) richten.

Der Freund sucht schon zu Anfang das Schicksal des Leidenden dem allgemeinen Menschenlos, besonders der Sterblichkeit, zu subsumieren (16f.). Daß der Mensch das Sinnen und Planen des Gottes nicht begreifen kann, sagt der Freund in Zz. 255f.264, wozu er in 257-263 Sinnwidrigkeiten benennt, die an Ähnliches in Hiob 39,13-18[63] und bei den Paradoxographen seit dem Hellenismus[64] erinnern. Auch an Vorwürfen läßt er es nicht fehlen. Am Ende bietet er eine kognitive Lösung an, die freilich die Götter, welche die Menschheit schufen, – in einer Art Flucht nach vorn und mit einem Einschlag von Sozialkritik[65] – nur auf sublimere Weise belastet:

> Sie haben geschenkt der Menschheit die mehrdeutige Rede;
> mit Lügen und Unwahrheit beschenkten sie sie für immer.
> Volltönend äußern sie, was für den Reichen gut ist:
> »er ist ein König, ein reicher Besitz steht ihm zur Verfügung«.
> Wie einen Dieb behandeln sie schlecht den schwächlichen Menschen;
> mit Niedertracht beschenken sie ihn, stellen ihm mit Mord nach.
> Bösartig packen sie ihm jegliches Übel auf, weil er der Führung (?) ermangelt;
> in Kraftlosigkeit lassen sie ihn vergehen, löschen ihn aus wie glühende Asche (Zz. 279-286)[66].

Ist die Mehrdeutigkeit, die Unwahrhaftigkeit menschlicher Rede für Mängel der *Erkenntnis* einer sittlichen Weltordnung ursächlich, von der die Ordnung selbst unberührt bleibt? Aber warum sollten als Paradigmata solcher Mängel gerade eine verbale Bevorzugung des Reichen und eine unmittelbare Benachteiligung des Armen genannt werden? Stehen also Mehrdeutigkeit und Unwahrhaftigkeit menschlicher Rede für die

---

63. Cf. zu Übersetzung, Intention und Echtheit von Hiob 39,13-18 VF., *Straußenperikope*, passim.
64. Am Anfang dieser Literatur stehen Bolos, Kallimachos, Antigonos von Karystos, Philostephanos, Nymphodoros und andere. Vor allem sucht Plutarch immer wieder nachzuweisen, daß Paradoxa nur scheinbar widersinnig sind, tatsächlich aber dem tiefer Blickenden ihren Sinn enthüllen; cf. OPPERMANN, *Paradoxa*, p. 500. Die im »Physiologos« (2. Jh. n.Chr.) gesammelten Paradoxa aus dem Tier- und Pflanzenreich haben weithin die Naturkunde des Mittelalters beherrscht. Im 2./3. Jh. nach Chr. ragt Claudius Ailianus mit 17 Büchern Περὶ ζῴων ἰδιότητος hervor, die im stoischen Geist, dazu auf unterhaltsame Weise die verborgene Weisheit der Natur aufzuweisen versuchen. Zur paradoxographischen Literatur allgemein cf. noch LESKY, *Geschichte*, p. 953.
65. Sehr stark wird dieses Motiv von BUCCELLATI, *Teodicea*, zu Zz. 276ff. betont.
66. Übersetzung nach VON SODEN, *Babylonische Theodizee*, p. 157.

Mängel der sittlichen Weltordnung selbst, mit der man sich, da Götter sie verursacht haben, eben abfinden muß? Oder soll wie in Hiob 4,17-21; 15,14-16; 25,4-6 nur bewiesen werden, daß, wenn jedermann böse ist, es ein Leiden von Unschuldigen, die sich beklagen könnten, nicht gibt? Jedenfalls wird die Gottheit hier nicht wie bei den Freunden Hiobs auf Kosten des Menschen entlastet.

Entsprechend dem rein diskursiven Charakter der Dichtung richten sich die Dankbarkeit (287) wie das abschließende Hilfegesuchen des Leidenden (288) an den Freund, den er mit ähnlichen Demutsgebärden wie der Fromme seinen Gott zur Hilfe zu motivieren sucht. Der »Helfer«, den er sich danach von Göttern und dem Könige wünscht (295-297), ist wohl mit dem Freund, dessen Hilfe in den unmittelbar vorangehenden Zeilen (288.290) erwartet wird, vergleichbar[67], vielleicht aber auch zu dem »Zeugen« (*'ēd // šāhēd*) von Hiob 16,19 oder dem »Anwalt« (*gō'ēl*) von 19,25 in Analogie zu bringen.

c. Wir sahen, daß in den babylonischen Texten vom Typ des *Ludlul bēl nēmeqi* die für die weisheitliche Lehrerzählung charakteristische Ereignisfolge mit derjenigen des Klage-Erhörungs-Paradigmas, wie es sich außer in *einem* Strang des Hiob-Corpus in Ps 22 darstellt, im großen und ganzen übereinkommt. Dieser Befund hat meines Erachtens seine letzte Ursache in einem humanethologischen Tatbestand: die Abfolge der Handlungsschritte scheint hier wie dort in einem präverbalen, biologischen Programm vorgegeben; sie wurzelt in Handlungssequenzen von der Art, wie sie E.S. Gerstenberger[68] in seiner Analyse von Klage- und Bittpsalmen sowie der babylonischen 'Handerhebungs'-Gebete für den zwischenmenschlichen Bereich und stammesgeschichtlich vorgeprägte Verhaltensmuster, damit aber auch für deren außerhumane Präfigurationen dargestellt hat.

Schon der Tun-Ergehens-Zusammenhang ist eine symbolische Tauschzeremonie, bei der zwischen Mensch und Wirklichkeit, Mensch und Gott eine 'soziale' Interaktion stattfindet, die den menschlichen Tugenderweis wie einen Guthabentransfer handhabt, der der Sicherung gleichsam eines Zukunftskapitals dienen soll[69]. Zwischen dem Menschen und der Gottheit, die die Wirklichkeit an den Menschen vermittelt,

---

67. Insbesondere ist das Objekt *re-ṣa* »einen Helfer« in Z. 295 durch die Wendung *re-ṣa u tuk-la-tum* »einen Helfer und Unterstützung« in Z. 290 vorbereitet.

68. *Mensch*, passim.

69. Cf. hierzu und zum folgenden BURKERT, *Kulte*, pp. 158-188. – Daß man sich durch Güterverzicht »einen Schatz im Himmel« erwirkt, sagt ausdrücklich Mk 10,21 parr. in der Perikope vom reichen Jüngling.

findet ein Kreislauf des Gebens und Nehmens, aber auch des Versagens und der Genugtuung statt[70]; so werden Gott, Welt und Mensch im Gleichgewicht gehalten. Wie moralisches Verhalten in der Gesellschaft gerade bei Inkaufnahme von Nachteilen durch eine symbolische Transaktion einen Prestigegewinn schafft, der für später um so größere Vorteile in Aussicht stellt, so bietet ein soziomorphes Wirklichkeitsverständnis[71] imaginäre Motive an, den entsprechenden symbolischen Zinskapitalismus auch auf den zeitabschreitenden Umgang mit Gott zu übertragen, einem Gott, den man etwa mit Opfern (Hiob 1,5), Anbetung (1,20f.) und Schuldvermeidung (1,22; 2,10b) für spätere Benefizien (42,10ff.) gewinnt. – Was aber geschieht, wenn sich die Gott wie ein Kredit angebotene Guttat (Spr 19,17) einmal nicht innerhalb zumutbarer Zeit auszahlt? Klage und Bitte machen dann zunächst von dem Wissen Gebrauch, daß man Gott bzw. den Göttern nichts »geben«, sondern sie allenfalls umgekehrt durch die Demonstration von Bedürftigkeit beeindrucken kann: gerade sie ist eine Weise, Gott über sich zu »erhöhen«; die 'soziale' Disproportion zwingt ihn geradezu, sich herabzuneigen und durch Hilfe ein Gleichgewicht wie zwischen verhandlungsfähigen Partnern zu schaffen. Wird allerdings zwischen einer gütelosen Größe Gottes und einer unerfüllten Bedürftigkeit des Menschen ein zu großer Kontrast wahrgenommen, so vermag der Vorwurf an Gott die gottmenschliche Kommunikation in eine Nullpunktsituation zu führen, um sie am Ende auf einer sublimeren Ebene neu zu begründen.

Die »Babylonische Theodizee« dagegen wahrt gegenüber den egoistischen Interessen hinter menschlichem Gottesumgang eher die Distanz der Reflexion; nicht umsonst ist sie der jüngste unter den hier einschlägigen Texten. Die Elemente der 'Handerhebungs'-Gebete, des Klage-Erhörungs-Paradigmas werden aus dem weisheitlichen Diskurs wieder ausgeschieden; eine Vergleichbarkeit mit den alttestamentlichen Klage- und Bittpsalmen des einzelnen entfällt mithin. – Am ehesten in der »Babylonischen Theodizee« also geschieht ein erster tastender Schritt vom Mythos zum Logos, von der Gottes*beziehung* zu einer zwar kritischen, aber noch unbeholfen stammelnden Gottes*spekulation*[72].

---

70. Ein entsprechender Kreislauf findet nach dem bekannten Satz des Anaximander zwischen den Dingen überhaupt statt: »Woraus ... die Dinge ihre Entstehung haben, dahinein findet auch ihr Untergang statt gemäß der Schuldigkeit; denn sie leisten einander Sühne (δίκην) und Buße für ihre Ungerechtigkeit gemäß der Verordnung der Zeit«; cf. meinen in Anm. 33 genannten Artikel und BURKERT, *Kulte*, pp. 163.188, hier mit noch anderen hellenischen Beispielen.
71. Cf. zum Begriff TOPITSCH, *Ursprung*, passim.
72. VON SODEN, *Babylonische Theodizee*, p. 145 fand »etwas wie eine Absage an den Glauben am Schluß«, was den Tatbestand wohl ein wenig übertreibt; allerdings ist unbe-

d. Aber ist eine solche Proto-Metaphysik allein wegen ihres eher 'theoretischen' Charakters gegen die Steuerung religiösen Verhaltens, Sprechens und Denkens durch Lebensinteressen[73] schon besser versichert? 'Wirklichkeit' ist nicht einmal in einer Metatheorie, wie sie hier abschließend vorgetragen wird, mehr als ein Konstrukt unserer Sinnesorgane und unseres Verstandes, das historisch durch unsere Erziehung, vor allem aber genetisch und stammesgeschichtlich durch unsere Biologie bestimmt ist. Selbst wenn wir das Denken denken, konstruieren wir es[74] – wenn auch vielleicht nicht nach Maßgabe unserer vordergründigsten Gefühls- und Verstandesinteressen, so doch immer noch nach Maßgabe einer Intuition von Humanität, die axiomatisch bleibt. Weil wir den Zirkel von Wahrnehmung einerseits und funktioneller Interpretation des Wahrzunehmenden im humanen Lebensinteresse andererseits niemals verlassen können, ist ein entsprechendes Maß an erkenntnistheoretischer Skepsis unvermeidlich[75]. Aber auch ein skeptisches Urteil über alle

---

streitbar, daß dem in *Ludlul bēl nēmeqi* »so lebendigen Marduk-Glauben hier ein müde gewordener Glaube gegenübersteht, dem eine in die Zukunft weisende Kraft abhanden gekommen ist« (p. 146).

73. Für diese Steuerung etwa ist es eine humanbiologische Voraussetzung, daß wir Geschehnisse und Dinge um so eher als 'real' ansehen, als sie leichter in einen bereits vorhandenen Kontext passen und so einer latent vorhandenen Bedeutung zugeordnet werden können, die einen handelnden, also auch erwartungsvollen Umgang mit ihnen sowie zwischenmenschliche Verständigung darüber ermöglicht; cf. STADLER/KRUSE, *Wirklichkeitskriterien*, passim. Wir machen uns freilich meist nicht klar, daß es daher immer nur selektive Wahrnehmungen unserer Welt sind, die wir nach Bedeutungen absuchen, um ihnen einen 'Welt'-Sinn zu entnehmen.

74. Dies gilt insbesondere auch von der mathematischen Logik. Dazu SCHRÖDINGER: »Wie in aller Welt wollen wir entscheiden, ob ein allgemeiner Zug unserer Erfahrung eher durch die Beschaffenheit unseres Geistes bedingt ist als durch eine Eigenschaft, die allen diesen objektiv existierenden Dingen in gleicher Weise eigentümlich ist?« (*Naturwissenschaft*, p. 176). Nur wenn wir diese Frage offenlassen, sind wir in der Lage, Wirklichkeit und Bewußtsein von ihr gleichzeitig zu erfassen und nicht etwa umgekehrt das 'Vorhanden-Sein' entweder ('idealistisch') der Welt oder ('realistisch') des Ich in deren Normativität für das Erkennen zu leugnen; im etymologischen Sinne ist aber auch die ontisch-noëtische Wechselwirkung von Welt und Ich 'vor Handen' d.h. für eine über sich selbst aufgeklärte Skepsis auf ein Ich bezogen, das sie zu denken sucht.

75. Im Grunde meinte dies schon LORENZ (*Rückseite*, pp. 15ff.), wenn er seine erkenntnistheoretische Haltung als »hypothetischen Realismus« bezeichnete: »Die Organisation der Sinnesorgane und der Nerven, die es Lebewesen möglich macht, sich in der Welt zurechtzufinden, ... ist ... zwar für das Individuum insofern 'apriorisch', als sie vor jeder Erfahrung da ist ... und da sein muß, damit Erfahrung möglich werde. Ihre Funktion ist aber historisch (scil. naturgeschichtlich [H.-P. Müller]) bedingt und nicht notwendig, es kann auch andere Lösungen geben« (p. 20). Der Schluß vom Überleben einer Gattung auf die Realadäquanz ihrer Wirklichkeitswahrnahme ist schon logisch unzulässig: da unsere Wirklichkeitswahrnahme vom Überlebensinteresse bestimmt ist, gewinnt sie ihre Überzeugungskraft aus ihrer Übereinstimmung mit dem Überlebensinteresse, nicht aus derjenigen mit der Realität; die Tatsache eines menschlichen Selektionserfolges ist auch insofern kein erkenntnistheoretisches Argument, als die Umwelt, in der Selektion erfolgt,

unsere Urteile, ein Metaurteil, geschieht noch im Horizont humanen Lebensinteresses sowie der entsprechenden kollektiv festgelegten Konstanz unseres Wahrnehmens und Denkens[76]; es befindet sich immer noch in einem selbstrückbezüglichen Zirkel, der sich weiter ins Unendliche projiziert[77]: das Metaurteil, daß alle Urteile einem Lebensinteresse dienen, ist wahrscheinlich nur auf sublimere Weise interessegelenkt[78]; weder der Urteilende noch der Träger eines Metaurteils genießt oder erleidet je einen Lebensdispens.

Rockbusch 36   Hans-Peter MÜLLER
48163 Münster
Deutschland

---

nur negativ »für Aussterben, nicht aber (scil. positiv) für Überleben verantwortlich gemacht werden« kann (cf. VON GLASERSFELD, *Konstruktivismus*, passim, bes. p. 22).

76. Unberührt bleibt hier das erkenntnistheoretische Problem, das mit der jeweiligen sprachlichen Verfaßtheit unseres Denkens gegeben ist. Wie wir nur solche Eindrücke wahrnehmen können, die sich physiologisch in uns fortpflanzen, so können wir auch nur solche Erkenntnisse haben, die den je konventionellen sprachlichen Mitteln, den semantischen und syntaktischen Medien unseres Denkens, entsprechen. Die Grammatik ist eine Zwischenwelt von Wirklichkeit und kollektivem Geist, dem das Individuum wenig entgegenzusetzen hat, weil die Struktur der Grammatik letztlich evolutiv programmiert ist. Die jeweilige grammatische Struktur einer Sprache oder Sprachengruppe ist darüber hinaus kontingent: hätte DESCARTES *cogito ergo sum* zur Basis seines (und unseres) Denkens gemacht, wenn er in einer Ergativsprache zu denken gelernt hätte, die bei fientisch-transitiven Verben den betreffenden Satz statt vom Subjekt vom Objekt her konstruiert?

77. Auch die Einsicht, daß der Zirkel von Erkenntnis und Lebensinteresse nicht verlassen werden kann, führt als solche nicht aus ihm heraus. Sie ist eine negative Metaerkenntnis, aus der sich keine positive Aussage gewinnen läßt – weder auf der Objektebene (cf. Anm. 75), noch auf der Metaebene, in keinem Fall aber auf der Ebene des Unbedingten, genauer: der Negation jeder Bedingtheit, der ein entsprechendes Metaurteil über die Bedingtheit aller Erkenntnis durch Lebensinteressen angehören müßte. Wir können uns von keiner Mensch-Umwelt-Beziehung und von keinem Denken über die Mensch-Umwelt-Beziehung eine Vorstellung bilden, für die die Dialektik von Erkenntnis und Interesse nicht bereits bestände; ein Sinn, der jedem Zweck vorausliegt und darum nicht durch einen Zweck bedingt wäre, kann sich nicht ergeben (zu LÜKE, *Erkenntnistheorie*, pp. 149-165).

78. Der Verdacht, daß etwa auch die Evolutionäre Erkenntnistheorie, mag sie im Gegensatz zum idealistischen Transzendentalismus auch empirisch motiviert sein, eine Projektion unseres Geistes ist, der sich lebensoptimistisch ihm selbst gemäße 'Vorteile' – etwa im Erkenntniskalkül – sichert, läßt sich nicht grundsätzlich widerlegen; die Evolutionäre Erkenntnistheorie ist insofern selbst ein Teil des Phänomens, das sie erklärt.

DIE WEISHEIT DES ACHIKAR
UND DER *MUSAR LAMMEBIN* IM VERGLEICH

I. Die Weisheit des Achikar

1. Fund und Inhalt

Bei den Ausgrabungen auf der Nil-Insel Elephantine machten die deutschen Ausgräber unter Leitung von O. Rubensohn im Jahre 1906 bedeutsame Papyrus-Funde[1], die 1911 von E. Sachau publiziert wurden[2]. Bei diesen Papyri fanden sich 11 Blätter mit 14 teilweise nur fragmentarisch erhaltenen Kolumnen, die die Erzählung vom weisen Achikar und eine Anzahl von etwas über 100 Weisheitssprüchen enthielten[3].

Die Erzählung vom weisen Achikar spielt am Hofe der neuassyrischen Könige Sanherib (705-681 v. Chr.) und seines Nachfolgers Asarhaddon (681-669 v. Chr.). Achikar war Schreiber, Ratgeber und Siegelbewahrer des Sanherib. Als er im Alter fortschritt und seine Aufgaben immer weniger wahrnehmen konnte, adoptierte er, da er selbst keine eigenen Kinder hatte, seinen Neffen und unterwies ihn in der Weisheit, worunter die Grundlagen der Berufsausübung im Sinne der praktischen Weisheit zu verstehen sind. In der Folgezeit trat der Neffe an die Stelle seines Onkels. Dieser erhoffte sich Wohlergehen für die Zeit seines Ruhestandes durch den Einfluß seines Neffen, mußte aber entdecken, dass sein Neffe ein Komplott gegen ihn geschmiedet hatte mit dem Ziel, seinen Onkel zu vernichten. Der Offizier, Nabusumiskun, der Achikar aufspüren und umbringen sollte, kannte Achikar allerdings, da ihm Achikar vor einigen Jahren das Leben gerettet hatte. Achikar bat um sein Leben, erhielt auch sein Leben geschenkt, und man ermordete an seiner Statt einen Sklaven. Achikar wurde eine zeitlang versteckt, und dem König Asarhaddon wurde der Vollzug des Mordes überbracht. An dieser Stelle bricht der aramäische Roman ab. Es folgen dann die Weisheitssprüche, die allerdings zum Teil sehr fragmentarisch sind, wodurch ihr

---

* Ich danke Herrn Dr. A. Lange für wichtige Hinweise zu den Qumran-Texten.
1. Vgl. Honrath - Rubensohn - Zucker, *Bericht*.
2. Vgl. Sachau, *Papyrus*.
3. Vgl. die Editionen des Achikarromans und der Sprüche durch Sachau, *Papyrus*, pp. 147-182 mit Tafeln 40-50; Cowley, *Aramaic Papyri*, pp. 204-248; Porten -Yardeni, *Textbook*, pp. 22-57 und der Sprüche durch Kottsieper, *Sprache*, pp. 9-14. Neuere Übersetzungen finden sich u.a. bei Grelot, *Documents*, pp. 427-452; Lindenberger, *Proverbs*; Id., *Ahiqar*; Kottsieper, *Sprache*, pp. 15-24; Id., *Geschichte*, pp. 324-347.

Verständnis enorm erschwert ist. Die hier referierte Abfolge der Papyri entspricht der von E. Sachau initiierten Anordnung, der die vier Papyri mit der Erzählung über das Schicksal des Achikar den übrigen sieben Papyri mit den Weisheitssprüchen vorangestellt hat, da für ihn innerhalb der Papyri keine Abfolge erkennbar war[4]. Dieser von E. Sachau eingeführten Anordnung des Stoffes folgten einige spätere Ausgaben und Übersetzungen[5]. Demgegenüber plädieren andere Autoren für eine Integration der Sprüche in die Achikarerzählung, die sich somit als Rahmen um die Sprüche legt[6].

2. Literarische Aspekte: Herkunft, Genese und Datierung der Weisheitssprüche

Im folgenden will ich mich wegen des später folgenden Vergleiches mit dem musar lammebin ausschließlich auf die Spruchweisheit des Achikarromans[7] konzentrieren. Das Abfassungsdatum der Achikarpapyri aus Elephantine liegt im 5. Jh. v. Chr. Bereits E. Sachau stellte für die materiale Basis der Achikarpapyri fest, dass es sich bei ihnen um Palimpseste handele, die ursprünglich mit Verzeichnissen oder Rechnungen beschriftet waren und die dann sekundär (um 407 v. Chr.) mit dem Achikarroman und den Weisheitssprüchen von einer Hand beschrieben wurden[8]. Allerdings sind weder der Achikarroman noch die Weisheitssprüche in der Kolonie von Elephantine entstanden. Dies wird durch die Tatsache unterstrichen, dass schon recht früh in der Forschung gesehen wurde, dass die Sprüche des Achikarpapyrus einen älteren Sprachstil als die Rahmenerzählung aufweisen. Diese Rahmenerzählung kann man aufgrund des Reichsaramäischen dem 6. Jh. v. Chr. zuschreiben. Insofern wurde recht bald klar, dass Sprüche und Roman sekundär zusammengesetzt sind. Oder anders gesagt: Es gibt eine ältere aramäische Spruchsammlung, vor die bzw. um die herum der Achikarroman als situative Verortung, um die Sprüche in die Ausbildung des

---

4. Vgl. SACHAU, *Papyrus*, p. 147 und im Tafelband die Tafeln 40-43 mit der Achikarerzählung und die Tafeln 44-50 mit den Sprüchen.
5. Vgl. etwa COWLEY, *Aramaic Papyri*, pp. 204-248; LINDENBERGER, *Ahiqar*, pp. 494-507; PORTEN - YARDENI, *Textbook*, pp. 24-53.
6. Vgl. etwa GRELOT, *Documents*, pp. 432-451; KOTTSIEPER, *Geschichte*, pp. 324-347.
7. Die Zitation der Achikarsprüche erfolgt nach der Zählung von COWLEY. Zu den Problemen der von KOTTSIEPER vorgeschlagenen Zählung vgl. RÖMHELD, *Weisheitslehre*, pp. 113-114 Anm. 1.
8. Vgl. dazu SACHAU, *Papyrus*, pp. 148-149.181-182.

Neffen einzubringen, angeordnet wurde. Dieser Sachverhalt gibt noch einmal mehr die Berechtigung, die Sprüche für sich zu betrachten. Es wurde allerdings auch die Ansicht geäußert, daß einige Sprüche auf die Rahmenerzählung hingeordnet und insofern als redaktionell einzustufen sind[9].

Datierung und Herkunft der Sprüche werden allerdings in der Forschung kontrovers beurteilt. Zunächst ist zu sehen, dass, obwohl das Manuskript in Ägypten gefunden wurde, weder sprachliche noch inhaltliche Indizien dafür vorliegen, dass wir es hier mit einem ägyptischen Text oder einem von Ägypten beeinflußten Text in aramäischer Sprachgestalt zu tun haben. Man geht eher davon aus, dass der Dialekt der Sprüche den ältesten Zeugnissen des Reichsaramäischen bzw. der jüngeren Phase des Altaramäischen benachbart ist. Insofern kommt J.M. Lindenberger bei seiner Bearbeitung der Sprüche auf ein Datum am Anfang des 7. Jh. v. Chr. Er ist der Meinung, dass die Sprüche oder eine frühere Sammlung dieser Sprüche in Nordsyrien entstanden, wo sich während der ersten Hälfte des 1. Jt. v. Chr. mehrere aramäischsprachige Königreiche in ihrer Blütezeit befanden. Desweiteren verweist er zugunsten des nordsyrischen Urprungs auf eine Anzahl von Gottheiten, deren Namen zum Teil auch in den Königsinschriften Nordsyriens auftreten[10]. Aus philologischen Gründen klassifiziert J. Tropper die Sprache der Sprüche als »Frühreichsaramäisch« zusammen mit den Barrakib-Inschriften von Zincirli und den Nerab-Stelen. Damit sind wir auch wieder in Nordsyrien[11].

Hiervon unterscheidet sich der Ansatz von I. Kottsieper. Er datiert die Spruchsammlung in die letzten Jahrzehnte des 8. bzw. in den Beginn des 7. Jh. v. Chr., somit in eine Zeit, in der die südsyrischen Aramäergebiete noch nicht in assyrische Provinzen verwandelt worden waren. Was die Herkunft der Sprüche angeht, so denkt Kottsieper aufgrund einer Analyse des Dialektes der Sprüche an den südsyrisch-libanesischen Raum, da diese ihmzufolge einen starken kanaanäischen Einschlag aufweisen. »Somit können sie als ein Zeugnis der Weisheitstraditionen angesehen werden, wie sie im ersten Viertel des 1. Jt. v. Chr. bei den

---

9. Vgl. dazu RÖMHELD, *Weisheitslehre*, pp. 113-115; KOTTSIEPER, *Geschichte*, pp. 321-322.
10. Vgl. LINDENBERGER, *Proverbs*, pp. 19-20; ID., *Ahiqar*, p. 482.
11. Vgl. TROPPER, *Inschriften*, pp. 297-300.

südsyrischen Aramäern und damit in direkter Nachbarschaft zu Israel gepflegt wurden«[12]. Hinsichtlich der Datierung der Achikarsprüche führt J.C. Greenfield Argumente sprachlicher und stilistischer Art für eine Ansetzung in der Zeit Asarhaddons (681 - 669 v. Chr.) an[13]. Hiermit ist auf anderem Wege eine Übereinstimmung mit dem von Kottsieper vorgebrachten Datierungsansatz erzielt.

Auch wenn bezüglich der vorgebrachten Datierungs- und Verortungsvorschläge sicherlich noch nicht das letzte Wort in der Forschung gesprochen ist – hier können vor allen Dingen weitere Funde aramäischer Texte aus Syrien deutlichere Kriterien an die Hand geben –, so ist doch mittlerweile ersichtlich, dass wir es bei den Sprüchen mit einem Produkt aus dem Raum Syrien zu tun haben. Deshalb ist als weiteres nach der Wirkungsgeschichte der Spruchweisheit vor allem auf die Literatur Palästinas im Alten Testament und in Qumran zu fragen.

3. Wirkungsgeschichte

Grundsätzlich läßt sich festhalten, dass kaum ein Literaturwerk der semitischen Antike so bekannt war wie der Roman des weisen Achikar. Es finden sich spätere Übersetzungen und Rezensionen dieses Romans in christlicher Zeit u.a. in Syrisch, Arabisch, Armenisch und Altslavisch, dazu Fragmente in Äthiopisch und später dann noch Übersetzungen in das Georgische, Alttürkische, Rumänische, Russische, Serbische und Neusyrische. Eine griechische Version, die allerdings verloren gegangen ist, muß ebenfalls existiert haben[14]. Der Einfluß des Achikar auf den griechischen Aesop-Roman des 1. Jh. n. Chr.[15], die griechischen Achikar-Notizen[16] und eine Mosaikdarstellung des Achikar aus Trier, das sog. Philosophenmosaik oder auch Mosaik des Monnus, aus dem 3. Jh. n. Chr. seien in diesem Zusammenhang ebenfalls erwähnt[17]. Das geographische Zentrum, von dem aus der Achikarroman nach Süden, Norden und Westen verbreitet wurde, ist Syrien.

Unter diesem Abschnitt ist vorrangig auf das Tobitbuch einzugehen, da der Autor des Tobitbuches die Geschichte des Achikar und einiges

---

12. KOTTSIEPER, *Geschichte*, p. 321; vgl. ID., *Sprache*, pp. 241-246; ID., *Weisheit*, pp. 130-138.
13. Vgl. GREENFIELD, *Wisdom*, pp. 48-50.
14. Vgl. zu den Übersetzungen CONYBEARE - HARRIS - LEWIS, *Story*; NAU, *Histoire*; KÜCHLER, *Weisheitstraditionen*, pp. 319-363; FALES, *Riflessioni*, pp. 51-58.
15. Vgl. dazu KÜCHLER, *Weisheitstraditionen*, pp. 338-344.
16. Vgl. dazu KÜCHLER, *Weisheitstraditionen*, pp. 344-347.
17. Vgl. dazu KÜCHLER, *Weisheitstraditionen*, pp. 352-355; METZLER, *Ahiqar*.

aus der Spruchweisheit des Achikarromans gut kannte[18]. So wird Tobit als der Onkel des Achikar dargestellt (Tob 1,21-22). Achikar unterstützt Tobit während seiner Krankheit (Tob 2,10) und nach Tob 11,19 freuen sich Achikar und sein Neffe Nadab über die Rückkehr des Tobit und die Heilung seines Vaters Tobias. In Tob 14,10 wird dann das, was Nadab seinem Onkel Achikar angetan hat, vom sterbenden Tobit dem Tobias erzählt. Einer der Sprüche der Achikarweisheit findet sich ebenfalls im Tobitbuch, wenn auch in einer etwas entstellten Form (Tob 4,17).

Hinsichtlich weiterer alttestamentlicher Bücher und ihrer Beziehung zur Spruchweisheit des Achikar ist die Weisheitsliteratur zu nennen. Aus diesem Bereich haben sich mannigfache Beziehungen in formaler, philologischer und inhaltlicher Hinsicht ergeben, auf die hier nur summarisch verwiesen werden kann[19].

II. QUMRAN

Fragmente des Achikarromans bzw. der Achikarweisheit wurden in Qumran nicht gefunden. Auch hinsichtlich eines Vergleiches des in Qumran gefundenen Weisheitstextes *musar lammebin* mit dem Achikarroman muß festgehalten werden, dass sich ein direkter Einfluß der Achikarweisheit auf den *musar lammebin* nicht nachweisen läßt. Dem widerspricht nicht, dass sich zwei inhaltliche Parallelen zwischen den Weisheitssprüchen des Achikar und dem *musar lammebin* finden. So besagen Spruch 43 aus dem Achikar und 4Q417 1 I$_{21f.}$ übereinstimmend, aber in anderer Formulierung, dass man sich keine Ruhe gönnen soll, bevor eine Schuld zurückgezahlt sei. Dazu paßt eine weitere Übereinstimmung beider Textcorpora, derzufolge man keinen Streit mit einem Höhergestellten anfangen soll (Achikarspruch 142; 4Q417 1 I$_{1-5}$). Auch hier wird dasselbe Anliegen in unterschiedlicher Formulierung vorgebracht. Beide Übereinstimmungen können als weisheitliches Allgemeingut angesehen werden, eine literarische Abhängigkeit läßt sich in keinem von beiden Fällen nachweisen[20]. Angesichts dieser Lage muß der Vergleich zwischen der Achikarweisheit und dem *musar lammebin* nach bestimmten Gesichtspunkten vor sich gehen, anhand derer es

---

18. Vgl. zu Achikar im Tobitbuch NAU, *Histoire*, pp. 49-59; RUPPERT, *Funktion*; KÜCHLER, *Weisheitstraditionen*, pp. 364-379; LINDENBERGER, *Ahiqar*, pp. 488-490; DESELAERS, *Buch Tobit*, pp. 424-450; GREENFIELD, *Ahiqar*.
19. Vgl. dazu im einzelnen KÜCHLER, *Weisheitstraditionen*, pp. 380-385; LINDENBERGER, *Ahiqar*, pp. 486-490; KOTTSIEPER, *Weisheit*, pp. 138-158.
20. Vgl. zu diesen Parallelen auch ELGVIN, *Reconstruction*, p. 560 mit Anm. 6.

gelingen kann, zwei unterschiedliche und literarisch voneinander unabhängige Weisheitscorpora in einen Vergleich zueinander zu setzen.

III. ZUM VERGLEICH ZWISCHEN ACHIKARWEISHEIT UND DEM *MUSAR LAMMEBIN*

Der unter dem Titel *musar lammebin*[21] bekannte Text 4QSapA setzt sich aus mindestens sieben Handschriften aus den Höhlen 1 und 4 in Qumran zusammen. Im einzelnen handelt es sich um 1Q26, 4Q415, 4Q416, 4Q417, 4Q418, 4Q418a und 4Q423[22], deren Schrift als frühherodianisch (30-1 v. Chr.) einzustufen ist, bzw. im Falle von 4Q423 als spätherodianisch (1-50 n. Chr.) qualifiziert wird, so dass die Handschriften in das Ende des 1. Jh. v. Chr. oder in die erste Hälfte des 1. Jh. n. Chr. einzuordnen sind[23].

Ein Vergleich der Sprüche des Achikarbuches mit dem *musar lammebin* läßt sich anhand von vier großen Themenkomplexen beider Textcorpora durchführen. Dabei sind der formale Aufbau und die Themen, die Adressaten und der Sitz im Leben der Texte, die Lebenswelten und die Götterwelten der jeweiligen Textcorpora zu besprechen.

1. Formaler Aufbau und Themen

Die Weisheit des Achikar stellt sich auf den ersten Blick als eine Sammlung von Sprüchen dar, der Ordnung und Komposition abzugehen scheinen. Durch deren nachträgliche Eingliederung in bzw. an den Achikarroman entsteht der Eindruck einer geschlossenen Lehrrede, die allerdings nicht vorliegt; vielmehr ist von einer sekundären Sammlung von Einzelsprüchen auszugehen.

Diese Einzelsprüche begegnen in formal sehr unterschiedlicher Gestalt. B. Porten hat 17 »structures and themes« herausgehoben: Deity and man (wisdom; determinism; retribution), animal proverbs, household (number of sons; discipline of son; pride in parents; family treachery; discipline of slave; acquisition of slave), obedience to king, verbal discretion,

---

21. Vgl. zu diesem und weiteren Titeln des Werkes LANGE, *In Diskussion mit dem Tempel*, p. 127 Anm. 49.
22. Vgl. zu Editionen und Übersetzungen WACHOLDER - ABEGG, *Preliminary Edition* 2, pp. 44-123; MAIER, *Texte*, pp. 426-485; HARRINGTON, *Wisdom Texts from Qumran*, pp. 42-59; STRUGNELL - HARRINGTON - ELGVIN, *Qumran Cave 4. XXIV*.
23. Vgl. zu den Einleitungsfragen LANGE, *Weisheit und Prädestination*, pp. 46-50; ID., *In Diskussion mit dem Tempel*, pp. 127-131; ELGVIN, *Reconstruction*; HARRINGTON, *Wisdom Texts from Qumran*, pp. 40-41; STRUGNELL - HARRINGTON - ELGVIN, *Qumran Cave 4. XXIV*, pp. 1-40.41-43.73-80.143-150.211-224.475-478.501.505-507.

anthropological observations, golden mean, poverty and wealth, truth and falsehood, ingratitude, borrowing, caution, opposition to wicked, plant proverb, diligence, acceptance of lot, serving a master[24].

Hinsichtlich der Erforschung der Kompositionsstruktur der Sprüche steht die Arbeit noch recht am Anfang. Wurden bislang mehrfach die mangelnden Ordnungsstrukturen hervorgehoben, so hat sich zuletzt A. Scherer paradigmatisch um die Erforschung der Kompositionsstrukturen von Sprüchen 126-141, die den ökonomischen Bereich zum Thema haben, bemüht und hier Strukturen aufweisen können[25]. Die Rahmung des *musar lammebin* ist völlig anders als die Rahmung der Weisheitssprüche im Achikarroman. Fragment 1 von 4Q416 bietet den Rahmen des Weisheitswerks. Dieser Rahmen hat als Thema die Kosmologie und Eschatologie und er handelt vor allem vom Gericht zwischen den Guten und den Bösen. Somit sind die folgenden Weisheitssprüche Anleitungen für ein Leben gemäß der gottgewollten Ordnung, um dem endzeitlichen Gericht über die Frevler nicht zu verfallen[26]. A. Lange hat für *musar lammebin* herausgestellt: »Es finden sich Paränesen, Lehrgedichte und hymnisches Material. Die Grundorientierung des Textes ist ethisch-epistemologischer Natur. Über weite Strecken dominieren Imperative und Jussive den Text, letztere gern mit '*l* negiert. Man darf wohl von einer ethischen Grundausrichtung von 4QSapA ausgehen«[27]. Geht man die Weisheitssprüche des *musar lammebin* im Vergleich zu den Weisheitssprüchen des Achikarromans durch, so entfällt der Bereich von Fabeln und Zahlensprüchen; wir haben vielmehr Sentenzen und Mahnsprüche.

Als ein wichtiges Leitwort durchzieht der *rz nhyh* (»das Geheimnis des Werdens«) den Text. Hierunter läßt sich ein außerbiblisches Lehrkompendium verstehen, für welches unterschiedliche Qumranschriften in Frage kommen könnten[28].

Hinsichtlich des Gesamtaufbaus des *musar lammebin* hat D.J. Harrington festgestellt: »This Qumran sapiential work is a wisdom instruction expressed in small units and put together without much apparent

---

24. PORTEN - YARDENI, *Textbook*, p. XVI; vgl. zur Einführung in die Themen und die Stilmittel der Achikarsprüche noch MCKANE, *Proverbs*, pp. 156-182 und WATSON, *Ahiqar Sayings*.
25. Vgl. SCHERER, *Vielfalt*.
26. Vgl. HARRINGTON, *Wisdom Texts from Qumran*, p. 41.
27. LANGE, *Weisheit und Prädestination*, p. 48.
28. Vgl. die Belege für *rz nhyh* in Qumran bei HARRINGTON, *Raz Nihyeh*, pp. 551-552 und zur inhaltlichen Bestimmung des *rz nhyh* die Überlegungen bei HARRINGTON, *Raz Nihyeh*, pp. 550-551.552-553; ID., *Wisdom Texts from Qumran*, p. 49; ELGVIN, *Mystery to Come*, pp. 131-139.

concern for logical or thematic progression. In form and content it is similar to Sirach, parts of Proverbs (especially 22,17-24,22), late Egyptian wisdom writings, Jesus' instructions in the Synoptic Gospels, and the letter of James. In the instructional setting the senior sage gives advice to a novice sage. In some places the senior sage's appeal is to pragmatism or to reward and punishment at the judgment, while in other places there are deductions from and symbolic uses of Scripture«[29].

2. Adressaten und Sitz im Leben der Texte

In den Achikarsprüchen wird als Adressat »mein Sohn« genannt. Hiermit ist die Form der klassischen Weisheitsanrede gewählt. Wir haben also keine Gemeinschaft und keinen bestimmten Titel vor uns. Durch die sekundäre Einfügung der Sprüche an bzw. in den Achikarroman entsteht der Eindruck einer geschlossenen Lehrrede. Aber dies wird den ursprünglich unabhängig vom Achikarroman entstandenen und überlieferten Sprüchen nicht gerecht.

Es wäre verfehlt, auf dieser Basis von der Sohnesanrede bzw. einer Lehrrede auf die Institution der Schule, die der Achikarweisheit zugrundeliegen solle, zurückzuschließen, da deren Existenz im Syrien des 8. vorchristlichen Jahrhunderts doch stark bezweifelt werden muß[30]. Es dürfte vielmehr das Ausbildungswesen in der Hand der Väter bzw. Verwandten, die ihre Nachfolger in bestimmte Positionen einweisen wollten, gelegen haben. Dafür liefert die Rahmenerzählung des Achikarromans den besten Beleg. Der Vorteil dieses Systems für die einmal zu einem Amt gekommene Familie liegt auf der Hand: »By limiting the teaching of state affairs to his sons, the state scribe reinforced the family position at Court and prevented the rise of potential rivals to his descendants«[31]. In welcher Weise die Unterweisung des Nadin durch Achikar vonstatten ging, läßt der Achikarroman nicht erkennen. Jedoch kann man J.C. Greenfield zustimmen, wenn er vermutet: »It may be assumed that the then prevalent method of copying 'wisdom texts' and learning them by rote is meant, and the sayings in the 'Words of Ahiqar' are thought to have been used for Nadin's education«[32].

---

29. HARRINGTON, *Wisdom Texts from Qumran*, p. 40.
30. Vgl. LIPINSKI, *Scribes*, pp. 161-164; KOTTSIEPER, *Weisheit*, pp. 155-158.
31. LIPINSKI, *Scribes*, p. 164.
32. GREENFIELD, *Wisdom*, p. 45.

Es ist interessant, daß die Tiersprüche z.T. nur Naturbeobachtungen auflisten, z.T. aber hieraus auch Vergleiche mit dem menschlichen Verhalten ziehen. Damit erfolgt eine Ethisierung der Naturbeobachtungen. Aus einer Erkenntnis wird eine Regel für die Anwendung gezogen. Dies deutet auf Ausbildungs- oder Erziehungszwecke hin[33]. Der Sitz im Leben der Achikarsprüche ist allerdings nicht einfach mit einer berufsbezogenen Ausbildung gegeben. Es liegt hier ein Standesethos vor, mit dem allgemein auf das Leben im Beruf und in der Öffentlichkeit vorbereitet wird. Dieser Sitz im Leben gilt auch für die alttestamentlichen Mahnsprüche, mit denen der Achikarroman in dieser Hinsicht vieles gemeinsam hat. Somit geben uns die Achikarsprüche einen Einblick in das Standesethos und seine Vermittlung im Syrien des ausgehenden 8. oder beginnenden 7. Jh. v. Chr.[34].

Desweiteren fällt in den Achikarsprüchen die geringe soziale Differenzierung auf: »Hier liegen Armut und Reichtum, Knechtschaft und Herrsein nahe beieinander und können jedem einzelnen begegnen. Entsprechend werden Hinweise darauf gegeben, wie man sich als Armer und Diener, als Reicher und Herr zu verhalten hat. Die Not des Fremden steht genauso im Blick wie das Verhalten gegenüber dem König. Auch die Abhängigkeit vom guten Ruf, der durch die Familie geschädigt werden kann, spielt eine Rolle«[35]. Dies verweist auf die Situation in der Hauptstadt eines aramäischen Kleinkönigtums.

Als Adressat des *musar lammebin* hat man angesprochen: »The one being instructed engages in business, has dealings with all kinds of people, and may marry a wife and have children«[36]. Hiermit scheint also kein besonderer Berufsstand wie in der Achikarweisheit angesprochen zu sein. Dieser erste Eindruck täuscht jedoch. Es gibt hinsichtlich des Adressatenkreises eine interessante Übereinstimmung zwischen den Achikarsprüchen und dem *musar lammebin*. Diese besteht darin, dass sich die Achikarsprüche an einen künftigen Beamten oder Höfling wenden, der *musar lammebin* an einen *mebin*, d.h. an einen Schüler.

Hatte A. Lange noch hervorgehoben: »*mbyn* bezeichnet somit in 4QSap A eine institutionalisierte Lehrer- bzw. Ratgeberpersönlichkeit, die über die Fähigkeit verfügt, offenbartes Wissen zu verstehen und zu

---

33. Vgl. KOTTSIEPER, *Weisheit*, p. 143; vgl. zu den Tierparabeln und -fabeln der Achikarsprüche noch die interessanten Beobachtungen bei OETTINGER, *Weisheitssprüche*.
34. Vgl. zum Standesethos RICHTER, *Recht*.
35. KOTTSIEPER, *Weisheit*, p. 138.
36. HARRINGTON, *Wisdom Texts from Qumran*, p. 41.

lehren«[37], so wird jetzt der *mebin* als Schüler bzw. Student verstanden, wohingegen der Lehrer ein (in den Texten mit diesem Titel nicht genannter) *maśkil* wäre[38]. Der musar lammebin läßt also ein Schüler-Lehrer-Verhältnis erkennen, worin er mit der Weisheit des Achikar überein stimmt.

Der Sitz im Leben des *musar lammebin* wird desweiteren deutlich durch die kosmologische und die eschatologische Rede, die dieses Werk einleitet (4Q416 1)[39]. Diese sollte den Horizont für die folgenden Weisheitstexte abstecken, da diese konzipiert sind »to help the one who is being instructed both to align himself with the correct order of the cosmos ... and to prepare for the divine judgment where the righteous will be vindicated and wickedness will be destroyed forever«[40].

In der Entstehungszeit dieses Werkes (Ende des 3. oder Beginn des 2. Jh. v. Chr.) kann man wohl von einer Lesekultur in Jerusalem ausgehen. Auch die Tatsache, dass Fragmente von sieben Manuskripten des *musar lammebin* in Qumran vorliegen, deutet in diese Richtung. Was die Relevanz des *musar lammebin* angeht, so wurde zuletzt herausgestellt: »The abundance of copies of this work at Qumran suggests that the work, whatever its origins, was treated as important, authoritative, perhaps even 'canonical', among the Qumran community – at least if 'canonical' is taken as meaning 'used frequently and with authority'. It is only at Qumran that we know it to have been transmitted«[41]. Somit dürfte der Leserkreis des *musar lammebin* größer sein als der ursprüngliche Leserkreis der Weisheit des Achikar im ausgehenden 8. oder im beginnenden 7. Jh. v. Chr. Allerdings nimmt die Leserrezeption des Achikarromans später enorm zu.

3. Die Lebenswelt

In den Sprüchen des Achikar ist für die Bestimmung der Lebenswelt die häufige Nennung des Königs und der Reichen signifikant. Es geht also um die Unterweisung eines jungen Mannes bzw. Schülers zum rechten Verhalten angesichts dieser Höhergestellten. Hierzu paßt auch die situative Einfügung an bzw. in die Rahmenerzählung des Achikarromans sehr gut.

---

37. LANGE, *Weisheit und Prädestination*, pp. 56f.
38. Vgl. STRUGNELL - HARRINGTON - ELGVIN, *Qumran Cave 4*. XXIV, p. 3.
39. Der noch in der Diskussion befindlichen Frage, ob 4Q416 1 eine sekundäre Einleitung darstellt, soll hier nicht vorgegriffen werden.
40. HARRINGTON, *Wisdom Texts from Qumran*, p. 41.
41. STRUGNELL - HARRINGTON - ELGVIN, *Qumran Cave 4*. XXIV, p. 2.

Die Lebenswelt der Achikarweisheit ist somit die des syrisch-aramäischen Königtums, welches kundige Beamte zu seiner Verwaltung benötigt, die sich über die rein technische Ausbildung (Lesen, Schreiben, Verwaltung) hinaus ihrer Stellung gemäß am Hof und in der Gesellschaft bewegen sollen.

Der *musar lammebin* kennt hingegen diese Welt nicht. König, Höflinge und Verwaltung spielen keine Rolle. Es wurde vorher bei der Nennung des Adressatenkreises schon darauf verwiesen, daß derjenige, der vom *musar lammebin* instruiert wird, sich in Geschäften engagiert, mit allen Arten von Menschen zu tun hat, heiraten und Kinder haben kann. Waren in der Achikarweisheit die Reichen genannt, so geht es im *musar lammebin* eher um Armut, bei der man fast den Eindruck hat, sie werde idealisiert.

Es ist aber auch zu sehen, dass der *musar lammebin* nicht die für den *yahad* charakteristischen Strukturen der qumranessenischen Texte aufweist. Insofern ist von A. Lange der *musar lammebin* am Jerusalemer Tempel verortet worden, da er ein für Weisheitstexte ungewöhnlich starkes kultisches Interesse aufweist[42].

Neben der Relevanz des Kultes ist der ökonomische Aspekt der im *musar lammebin* aufgezeigten Lebenswelt nicht zu vernachlässigen. Es ist häufig von Armut, Darlehen, Depositenrecht und Bescheidenheit die Rede (4Q416 2 I-IV; 4Q417 1 I). Ob dies die Hauptthemen des *musar lammebin* sind, oder diese zufällig für uns aufgrund des fragmentarischen Fundzustandes der Texte im Zentrum der Texte stehen, muß offen bleiben[43]. Es dürfte sich allerdings bei der Nennung der Armut kaum um eine spirituelle Armut handeln, auch wenn eine Tendenz dazu in den Texten unverkennbar ist[44].

Ein weiterer Aspekt der Lebenswelt im *musar lammebin* ist durch die Nennung von Eltern, Ehen, Frauen und Kindern gegeben (4Q416 2 III$_{15}$-IV$_{13}$). Die Perspektive hierbei ist die des Mannes, der ja der Adressat der Lehren ist. Dazu kommt, dass von einem Manne auch derartige Lehren ausgehen. Die Eltern sind zu ehren, da sie dem Sohn das Ohr geöffnet haben für das Geheimnis, welches kommen soll. Die Frau untersteht dem Mann in puncto Gelübde und sie darf ihn vom Studium nicht abhalten. Die Kinder sind streng zu erziehen. Ein wichtiger, gerade angeklungener Aspekt der Lebenswelt des *musar lammebin* ist

---

42. Vgl. LANGE, *Weisheit und Prädestination*, pp. 48-49; ID., *In Diskussion mit dem Tempel*, pp. 130-131.
43. Vgl. HARRINGTON, *Wisdom Texts from Qumran*, p. 46.
44. Vgl. HARRINGTON, *Wisdom Texts from Qumran*, pp. 46-47.

gegeben mit dem Studium. Armut oder Frauen sollen vom Studium nicht abhalten; Studieninhalt ist das »Geheimnis des Werdens«, d.h. ein außerbiblisches Lehrkompendium.

Eher ungewöhnlich für ein Weisheitswerk ist die direkte Anrede an die Frau (4Q415 2 II$_{1-9}$). Die Frau wird hierin aufgefordert, ihren Schwiegervater (?) wie ihren Vater zu ehren, bei ihrem Mann zu bleiben und der Ehe treu zu sein und das Lob aller Männer zu erzielen[45].

4. Die Götterwelt

In den Sprüchen des Achikar tritt, wie bei einem Textcorpus der aramäischen Königszeit nicht anders zu erwarten, ein polytheistisches Göttersystem auf. So ist ganz selbstverständlich davon die Rede, dass Böses von den Göttern nicht ausgeht (135), dass jemand bei den Göttern verflucht ist (160), die Götter Menschen und Völker verwerfen (162), die Götter ihre Weisheit kundgetan haben (94) und diese bei den Göttern geehrt ist (95). Die Götter unterstützen einen Klagenden, wenn er bei ihnen beliebt ist (115). Oder die Götter richten das Böse der Menschen (124), und wenn die Augen der Götter über den Menschen sind, so werden diese leben (124).

Interessant ist der Spruch 126: Hier haben wir das Wort 'lh im Plural, aber das Verb im Singular. Liegt damit ein Irrtum des Schreibers im Hinblick auf den Numerus des Verbs vor[46], so dass auch hier das polytheistische Referenzsystem nicht verlassen wäre, oder ist hier tatsächlich die Rede von einem persönlichen Gott, da 'lhy' analog zum hebräischen Plural 'aelohim dem Sinne nach als Singular zu verstehen ist[47]?

Hinsichtlich der einzelnen Götter treten nach der Übersetzung und Interpretation Lindenbergers, die weitgehend in der Forschung rezipiert wurde, El, Baʿalšamin und Šamaš auf. Allerdings wurden hieran auch Zweifel laut: So ist fraglich geworden, ob 'l als Gottesname 'El' oder als Gottesbezeichnung 'Gott' zu interpretieren sei[49]. Auch die Deutung von šmin und bʿl qdšn auf Baʿalšamin hin stellt sich anders dar, wenn

---

45. Vgl. HARRINGTON, *Wisdom Texts from Qumran*, p. 57; STRUGNELL - HARRINGTON - ELGVIN, *Qumran Cave 4. XXIV*, p. 48.
46. Vgl. LINDENBERGER, *Proverbs*, p. 118.
47. Vgl. KOTTSIEPER, *Geschichte*, p. 328 Anm. 1a und zuletzt ID., *El - ein aramäischer Gott*, p. 88.
48. Vgl. LINDENBERGER, *Gods*; ID., *Ahiqar*, pp. 484-486 und zu El und Šamaš in den Sprüchen bes. KOTTSIEPER, *El - ferner oder naher Gott?*, pp. 28-37.
49. Vgl. dazu GREENFIELD, *Wisdom*, pp. 50-51; MAIER - TROPPER, *El*, pp. 77-78.79-80 und dazu KOTTSIEPER, *El - ein aramäischer Gott*, pp. 87-89.

man *bš[mi]n* lokal als »in den H[imme]l ...« versteht[50]. So bleibt als sicher zu interpretierender Gottesname nur Šamaš übrig, der überhaupt die bedeutendste Stellung unter den Gottheiten in den Achikarsprüchen einnimmt. Dessen Position als Gott der Gerechtigkeit paßt zur ethischen Ausrichtung der Weisheitssprüche.

Demgegenüber ist die Götterwelt des *musar lammebin* die der jüdischen Religion des 2. Jh. v. Chr. So läßt 4Q416 1 erkennen, dass von Gott im Singular die Rede ist und dass zusätzlich eine Heerschar/Söhne des Himmels existieren. Dieser Sachverhalt korrespondiert dem Pantheon der nachexilischen Zeit in Judäa, wie es von L. K. Handy herausgearbeitet wurde. Dieses umfaßt nur noch zwei Schichten: Den höchsten Gott und eine Fülle von Botengestalten, die auch als himmlischer Thronrat verstanden werden können. Der Bereich der höheren wirkmächtigen Gottheiten und der Handwerkergötter ist im Unterschied zu den spätbronzezeitlichen und z.T. auch eisenzeitlichen Panthea Syrien-Palästinas ausgefallen[51]. Ein Hinweis auf einen himmlischen Thronrat kann auch in der Qualifikation Gottes als »der Gott der Furchtbaren« = Engel gesehen werden (4Q417 1 I).

In den folgenden Sprüchen ist immer die Rede von nur einem göttlichen Handlungsträger. Dieser wird wie in Fragment 1 als *'l* "Gott" benannt; das Tetragramm tritt im *musar lammebin* überhaupt nicht auf.

Die Funktion Gottes ist vor allem die des Richters, der die Frevler vernichtet und die Gerechten errettet. Gott erhebt den Armen und versetzt ihn in ein himmlisches Erbe.

Desweiteren wird Gott bezeichnet als *'l hadea^{c}ot* »ein Gott des Wissens/der Erkenntnis« (4Q417 1 I). Dieses auch in der LXX-Vorlage von 1 Sam 2,3 und mehrfach in Qumrantexten belegte Epitheton, welches eine Bezeichnung des die Ordnung von Sein und Geschichte festlegenden Schöpfergottes darstellt[53], paßt gut zu der Relevanz des Studiums, welches ja mehrfach in diesen Weisheitstexten hervorgehoben wird.

Bei der Nennung der Kinder des Seth (4Q417 2 I$_{15}$) hat man einen Bezug auf die Sethiten in Num 24,17 erwogen[54]. Mittlerweile ist dies,

---

50. Vgl. KOTTSIEPER, *Sprache*, p. 20; PORTEN - YARDENI, *Textbook*, p. 37.
51. Vgl. dazu HANDY, *Dissenting Deities*; ID., *Host of Heaven*.
52. Vgl. HARRINGTON, *Wisdom Texts from Qumran*, p. 54; STRUGNELL - HARRINGTON - ELGVIN, *Qumran Cave 4. XXIV*, p. 156.
53. Vgl. dazu und zu den Nachweisen der Qumranbelege LANGE, *Weisheit und Prädestination*, pp. 62.150-151; STRUGNELL - HARRINGTON - ELGVIN, *Qumran Cave 4. XXIV*, p. 158.
54. So HARRINGTON, *Wisdom Texts from Qumran*, p. 55.

aber auch der Bezug zu Gen 4,25f., wo Seth als Sohn Kains und Vater des Enosch vorgestellt wird, als unwahrscheinlich hingestellt worden[55]. Insofern scheint es gerechtfertigt, von einer anderen Basis auszugehen. Es ist an eine Rezeption des ägyptischen Gottes Seth (= Baal) zu denken, der in diesem Text als Widersacher Gottes und Verursacher allen Übels aufgefaßt wird[56].

V. SCHLUSS

Bei den Weisheitssprüchen des Achikarromans und dem *musar lammebin* handelt es sich um zwei von einander unabhängige Weisheitswerke. Der Aspekt der literarischen Unabhängigkeit von einander wird verstärkt durch die unterschiedliche geographische und zeitliche Ansetzung, die für die Achikarsprüche auf das Syrien des ausgehenden 8. bzw. beginnenden 7. Jh. v. Chr. und den *musar lammebin* auf das Jerusalem des endenden 3. oder beginnenden 2. Jh. v. Chr. verweisen. Diese Werke geben dementsprechend auch Einblick in unterschiedliche ethische und theologische Vorstellungsbereiche. Gerade im gegenseitigen Vergleich lassen sich die Charakteristika eines jeden dieser beiden Werke gut herausarbeiten. Dabei ist ein Befund auffällig. Die Weisheit des Achikar und der *musar lammebin* partizipieren zwar an gemeinsamen weisheitlichen Traditionen, aber die Achikarweisheit, die sonst im antiken Judentum rezipiert wurde, fand in den *musar lammebin* keinen Eingang.

Eberhard-Karls-Universität Tübingen Herbert NIEHR
Theologicum
Liebermeisterstr. 12
D-72076 Tübingen
Deutschland

---

55. Vgl. STRUGNELL - HARRINGTON - ELGVIN, *Qumran Cave* 4. XXIV, p. 163.
56. Vgl. grundsätzlich zu Seth und seinen alttestamentlichen Bezügen VAN DER TOORN, *Seth*.

IV

THE WISDOM TEXTS FROM QUMRAN AND THE HEBREW BIBLE

DIE SELIGPREISUNGEN IN DER BIBEL UND IN QUMRAN

Die Bergpredigt beim Evangelisten Matthäus wird eingeleitet durch die Seligpreisungen (Mt 5,3-12), unübersehbare rhetorische Signale am Beginn des ersten Redekomplexes bei diesem Evangelisten. Kompositorisch stehen sie in mehrfacher Hinsicht in Beziehung zu anderen Texten: einmal zum unmittelbar folgenden Text des Vaterunsers, dann zur Bergpredigt insgesamt, dann zum Abschluß des letzten Redekomplexes dieses Evangeliums, der durch Weherufe abgeschlossen wird, und schließlich zum Text des gesamten Evangeliums.

Völlig anders stellt sich die kompositionelle Einbindung im Evangelium des Lukas (Lk 6,20b-23) dar. Hier liegt eine auch im Wortlaut von der matthäischen Fassung abweichende insgesamt weitaus kleinere Reihe von Makarismen vor, die nun am Eingang der Feldrede in unmittelbarem Kontrast zu den folgenden Weherufen stehen, offensichtlich also nicht Bestandteil eines großen Kompositionsbogens zu sein scheinen.

Die den beiden Evangelisten gemeinsamen vier Seligpreisungen gehen über die Logienquelle Q in die Zeit vor den Evangelisten zurück. Für die ersten drei Makarismen gegenüber den Armen, Hungernden und Weinenden wird ein Ursprung in der jesuanischen Predigt selbst, für den vierten Makarismus gegenüber den Geschmähten und Verleumdeten (»um meinetwillen«/»wegen des Menschensohnes«) ein Ursprung in der nachösterlichen Gemeinde angenommen. Während in der Makarismenforschung meistens der matthäischen Fassung ein traditions- und redaktionsgeschichtliches prius eingeräumt wird, sieht man zunehmend auch in der lukanischen Fassung den ursprünglicheren Zustand bewahrt[1]. Als Alttestamentler bleibe ich bei diesen oberflächlichen Beobachtungen stehen und gebe gerne den Stab weiter an kompetente Neutestamentler.

Im Alten Testament scheint die Sachlage sich grundsätzlich von den Beobachtungen im Neuen Testament zu unterscheiden, da hier die Makarismen in der Regel nur als Solitäre begegnen und deswegen kompositorisch nicht so wuchtig wirken.

---

1. Vgl. H. MERKLEIN, *Jesu Botschaft*, pp. 45-51; DERS., *Jesusgeschichte*, pp. 79-82.

Die Literatur zu den Seligpreisungen ist kaum noch zu übersehen[2]. So ist sicher das meiste bereits längst geschrieben. Und trotzdem erscheint es mir sinnvoll, die Diskussion wieder aufzugreifen, weil die zwar schon seit längerem bekannte Makarismenreihe aus Qumran (4Q525)[3] inzwischen endlich in der offiziellen Edition vorliegt und zudem in mehreren bedeutenden Untersuchungen von E. Puech gewürdigt worden ist.

I. ALLGEMEINE BEOBACHTUNGEN

Die Seligpreisung oder Makarismus (von griech. μακάριος, hebr. אשרי, 'ašrê) als Gattung begegnet einerseits in kultischen Kontexten (Ägypten[4], Griechenland, Altes Testament) als Gratulationsformel, die den glücklich preist, der sein Leben in Einklang mit der göttlichen Weisung und/oder den Regeln der Weisheit gestaltet, dann auch als Begrüßungsformel (z.B. in Griechenland; im AT vgl. 1 Kön 10,8), als ein »Gruß in Form der Aussage«[5]. Kann die Seligpreisung in der griechischen Literatur auch an Götter[6] gerichtet sein, so ist im AT diese grundsätzlich nur auf Menschen bezogen. Ist eine solche an Gott gerichtet, so wird sie nicht mit אשרי, sondern mit בָּרוּךְ formuliert[7]. Dies weist auf die Notwendigkeit hin, formal die Seligpreisung von der Segnung zu unterscheiden[8]. Die griechische Literatur kennt die Seligpreisung auch im Rahmen der liturgischen Initiation (Demeter-Hymnus; eleusische Mysterien[9]). In Erinnerung daran wurden den gestorbenen Mysten »orphische Goldplättchen« mit den Makarismen ihrer Initiation mit ins Grab gegeben. Auch die Makarismen in Qumran zeigen eine Nähe zu den Introitus-Ritualen der Gemeinde.

In der alttestamentlichen Literatur sind die Seligpreisungen relativ häufig vertreten (ca. 50 Belege)[10], das Neue Testament kennt 41 Belege[11]. Die Schriftrollen von Qumran kennen die Seligpreisungen

---

2. Dazu vgl. etwa die Lexikonartikel HAUCK & BERTRAM, μακάριος; CAZELLES, אשרי; R.F. COLLINS, Beatitudes; J. SCHMID, Seligpreisung; STRECKER, μακάριος sowie etwa die ausgedehnten Literaturangaben in den Kommentaren, hier besonders U. LUZ, Matthäus, pp. 198-218.
3. H.-J. FABRY, Makarismus, pp. 362-371.
4. J. ASSMANN, Loyalismus, pp. 29ff.; vgl. auch J. DUPONT, Béatitudes, pp. 185-222.
5. I. BROER, Seligpreisungen.
6. Homer, Odyssee 5,7.
7. Vgl. Gen 9,26; 24,27; Ex 18,10.
8. Dazu vgl. C.H. DODD, Beatitudes, pp. 1-10; K. KOCH, Formgeschichte, pp. 21-23.
9. H.D. BETZ, Makarismen, pp. 25ff.
10. H. CAZELLES, אשרי, pp. 481-485.
11. Mt 13mal, Lk 15mal, Joh 2mal, Röm 3mal, Jak 1mal, Offb 7mal; vgl. J.A. FITZMYER, Collection, pp. 509f.

ebenfalls, sogar auch die Reihenbildung, wie sie dann besonders im NT bei Mt und Lk zu beobachten ist.

Als nachalttestamentliche Sonderform begegnet der »satirische Makarismus«: »Selig sind die Sünder; sie haben ihr ganzes Leben lang Gutes gesehen. Nun sind sie (auch) in Glück und Reichtum gestorben« (äthHen 103,5f.).

Die Seligpreisung ist Ausdruck der praktischen Lebenserfahrung[12] und hat ihren Ursprung in der Weisheitsliteratur[13] als »geprägte Sonderform der weisheitlichen Konditionalsätze«[14], in der auf der Basis des Tun-Ergehens-Zusammenhanges Wege zu einem gelingenden Leben genannt werden (vgl. Spr 3,19-23) und ein heilvolles Lebensmodell als »soteriologische Ganzheit«[15] entworfen wird. Als solche ist die Seligpreisung auch als »Makarismus des Weisen«[16] in der griechischen. Literatur verbreitet, der in der Regel konventionelle Werte auf den Kopf stellt (»Anti-Makarismus«[17]). Dies schließlich ist ein Charakteristikum der apokalyptischen Seligpreisung, die unter Einbeziehung des Eschatons die Umwertung der Werte konsequent durchführt. Auf diese Weise konnte die Seligpreisung zu einer apokalyptischen Gattung modifiziert und dabei zu einer fundamentalen theologischen Definition des Gerechten schlechthin werden, die die Werte der menschlichen Gesellschaft in die Krise führt.

Richtete sich die Seligpreisung in Psalmen und Weisheitsliteratur auf ein innerweltliches Wohlergehen (Sir 25,8) und auf das Verhältnis des Menschen zu Gott (Ps 33,12), so zielte sie in der Apokalyptik auf das zum gegenwärtigen Leben gegensätzliche Ergehen in der Zukunft.

II. Formale Beobachtungen

Formal zeigt die Seligpreisung wenig Beweglichkeit. In der einfachsten Form nennt sie in der partizipialen oder nominalen Bezeichnung den/die Gepriesenen als Aussage über (3.sg./pl., so traditionell und bei Mt) oder als Anrede/Zuspruch an jemanden (2.sg./pl., so bei Lk); durch *waw* angeschlossen oder in einem ὅτι-Satz (*kî*) kann dann eine knappe, in der apokryphen Literatur (äthHen 58,2; 99,10; slawHen 42,11) z.T. umfangreiche Begründung beigefügt werden, wobei diese aus der weisheitlichen Erfahrung oder als Verheißung aus der Zukunft genommen

---

12. HAUCK & BERTRAM, μακάριος, pp. 365-373.
13. U. LUCK, *Matthäus*, pp. 55f.
14. Vgl. I. BROER, *Seligpreisungen* und v.a. C. KÄHLER, *Makarismen*.
15. K. BERGER, *Formgeschichte*, pp. 188ff.
16. B. GLADIGOW, *Makarismus*, pp. 404-433.
17. BETZ, *Makarismen*.

werden kann. Auch aus der unterschiedlichen Häufigkeit beider Formen z.B. im AT läßt sich nicht zwingend eine Diachronie herleiten.

Formale Erweiterungen liegen vor in der näheren Charakterisierung der als »selig« Gepriesenen durch einen Relativsatz (Mt 11,6; Lk 7,23; 11,27f.; 23,29), dann in einer zusätzlichen Begründung, die syndetisch (Mt 13,16f.; Lk 10,23f.) oder asyndetisch angeschlossen werden kann (Mt 24,46f.; Lk 12,37.43).

Ursprünglich begegnen die Seligpreisungen einzeln (z.B. Ps 1,1), dann auch paarweise (Pss 84,4f.; 119,1f.; 128,1f.; Sir 14,1f.), als Trias (Sir 25,8f.; Lk 6,20f.), in Siebener- (slawHen 52) und schließlich in einer Doppelvierer-Reihe, die redaktionell zur Neunerreihe erweitert wurde (4Q525 [nach der Rekonstruktion von Puëch]; Mt 5,3-12). In Sir 14,20-15,1 liegt eine Neuner-Reihe, in Sir 25,7-11 sogar eine Zehner-Reihe vor. Solche Reihen von Seligpreisungen können kontrastierend mit Reihen von Weherufen zusammengestellt werden (Lk 6,24-26; äthHen 99,10ff.; slawHen 52,1f. syrBar 10,6f.), eine Kombination, die offensichtlich auf eine ältere Tradition zurückgeht[18].

Die Gattung der Seligpreisungen wird gedeutet als weisheitliche Paränese, als parakletischer Zuspruch der Rechtfertigung (bes. in protestantischen Kommentaren), als ethische Ermahnung (Gegenstück zum Dekalog; bes. Kirchenväter und katholische Kommentare) und als Lebensordnung für die Gemeinde unter dem Aspekt des Bundes. In der Reihenbildung werden die Seligpreisungen zu einem Güter- und Wertekatalog der sie tradierenden Gesellschaft. Als sicher darf gelten, daß die Seligpreisung als »paradoxer kerygmatischer Makarismus«[19] primär eine Zuspruchsfunktion, erst sekundär eine paränetische Abzweckung erhalten hat. Dies gilt besonders für die Seligpreisungen in apokalyptischen Kontexten.

Der Sitz im Leben der Seligpreisungen im AT wird häufig im Kult gesehen: als liturgischer Zuruf[20], Segenswunsch (Cazelles) oder als weisheitliches Erkenntnis-Angebot paränetisches »Mittelglied zwischen Aussagewort und Mahnwort« (Zimmerli); die Seligpreisung im NT hat man in der Paränese[21] oder in der Taufliturgie[22] ansiedeln wollen. Einerseits ist für das AT jedoch der weisheitliche Hintergrund nicht zu übersehen (vgl. z.B. Hiob 5,17; Kähler), andererseits hat – so Gnilka – die

---

18. I. BROER; *Seligpreisungen*, pp. 37f.
19. N. WALTER, *Bearbeitung*, p. 253.
20. E. LIPINSKI, *Macarismes*, pp. 325-330.
21. KÄHLER, *Makarismen*.
22. G. BRAUMANN, *Problem,* pp. 253-260.

Seligpreisung ihren Ort im Evangelium, da sie ein festes Traditionsstück des frühchristlichen Bekenntnisses für den um seines christlichen Bekenntnisses willen Leidenden ist.

III. Altes Testament

Im AT begegnen ca. 50 Seligpreisungen (davon drei in 2. sg.[23], eine in 2. pl. [Jes 32,20]) zuerst wohl in der Weisheitsliteratur, dann relativ spät vornehmlich in Psalmeneröffnungen (Pss 1,1f.; 32,1; 41,2; 106,3; 112,1; 119,1f.), signifikant als Formelement in der Inklusion der Psaltereröffnung (Pss 1,1; 2,12), in den Abschlüssen einiger Psalmenbücher (Pss 41,1.14; 89,16.53 in Korrespondenz zur *barûk*-Formel der Gottespreisung), in der Rahmung der Hallel-Psalmen (Pss 112,1; 119,1) und im makrotextuellen Brückenschlag von der Tora zum Psalmenbuch (Dtn 33,29 und Pss 1,1; 146,5) und zum prophetischen Kanon (Jos 1,8; Mal 3,12). Sie begegnet nicht in der gesetzlichen Literatur und nur einmal in narrativem Kontext (1 Kön 10,8; 2 Chr 9,7). Sie gilt dem, der sich sozial verhält (Spr 14,21; Ps 41,1), ein gutes Familienleben pflegt (Spr 25,7f.; Pss 127f.; 144), die Gemeinschaft mit Gott sucht (Jes 30,18; Ps 2,12) und seine Weisung achtet (Spr 29,18; Jes 56,2; Pss 112,1; 128,1). Sind sie hier »Bestätigung geglückten, weltzugewandten, lebensbejahenden Daseins« (Fischer) und die dahinter stehende Realität göttlicher Lohn für menschliche Mühen (Ps 144,15) oder gar sein unbedingtes Geschenk (Dtn 33,29; Pss 65,1-5; 84,5.6.13; 89,16), so wird in der spätisraelitischen Literatur – in apokalyptischen Kontexten – mit der Seligpreisung und ihrer paradoxen Formulierung eine Zukunft angesagt, die sich radikal von der Gegenwart unterscheiden wird.

In Sir 14,20-15,1 liegt ein ausgedehnter Makarismus vor, der – obwohl nur durch eine einleitende μακάριος-Formel eröffnet – insgesamt 9 Doppel-Makarismen enthält und damit unmittelbar mit 4Q525 vergleichbar ist[24]. Eine weitere Makarismenreihe zeigt Sir 25,7-11, wo um zwei mit μακάριος eingeleiteten Seligpreisungen insgesamt zehn Makarismen angeordnet sind, die zudem durch einen gestaffelten Zahlenspruch als dekalogische Größe verstanden werden wollen. Inhaltlich zeigt diese Reihe eine große Nähe zu Ps 15,1ff.: Selig gepriesen wird der, der seine ganze Aufmerksamkeit der Weisheit widmet.

---

23. Dtn 33,29; Ps 128,2; Koh 10,17.
24. E. Puech, *Béatitudes*, pp. 353-368.

IV. ZWISCHENTESTAMENTLICHE LITERATUR UND QUMRAN

Um den Übergang von weisheitlichen Makarismen alttestamentlicher Prägung hin zu den eschatologisch-apokalyptischen Makarismen des Neuen Testamentes zu überbrücken, wird auf die Makarismen in der zwischentestamentlichen Zeit verwiesen. Selig gepriesen werden der Gerechte (äthHen 58,5; vgl. 81,4; 82,4) und derjenige, der die Weisheit annimmt (99,10), die Gottesfürchtigen und Gesetzestreuen (slawHen 42,79), denen ein Leben ohne Ende in Aussicht gestellt wird.

In Qumran begegnet אשרי als Einleitung einer Seligpreisung außerordentlich selten, insofern sich nur an drei (vier?) Stellen Makarismen aufweisen lassen:

- In 4Q163 (pJes^c)[25] liegt ein Zitat aus Jes 30,18 vor.
- In 4Q185 (Sapiential Work)[26] handelt es sich um eine sehr fragmentarisch erhaltene weisheitliche Mahnrede[27], die – in späthasmonäischer Zeit geschrieben[28] – Elemente aus Jes 40,6-8 und aus dem Spr-Buch aufgenommen hat, dem anthologischen Stil des Sirach sehr nahe steht und deshalb der frühjüdischen Weisheitsliteratur (Ende 3. Jh. v.Chr.) entstammen könnte[29]. Die beiden Makarismen (Fragm. 1-2, Z. 8 und 13) haben wegen ihrer Parallelität zu Aufmerksamkeitsrufen, Geboten und Verboten und wegen ihrer Kontrastellung zu Wehe-Rufen ohne Zweifel den paränetischen Charakter der praktischen Weisheit: Selig gepriesen wird derjenige, dem »sie« (Weisheit und/oder Tora) gegeben ist (Z. 8) und der, der »sie« tut (Z. 13; vgl. Spr 3,13).
- In 4Q525 (Béat) 2 ii 1-4[30] liegt eine Makarismen-Reihe vor, die unmittelbar nach der Makkabäerzeit[31] in zeitlicher und theologiegeschichtlicher Nähe zu Sirach (14,20-27+15,1f.; 25,7-10) abgefaßt wurde. Sie besteht aus mindestens vier Seligpreisungen, die jeweils aufgrund ihres antagonistischen Charakters als Doppelmakarismen (»Selig, der ... und der nicht ...«) verstanden werden können. Sie sind jeweils durch ein *vacat* im Text abgegrenzt. Am Beginn des Textes läßt sich ohne Mühe und überzeugend ein fünfter Makarismus rekonstruieren. Diese rekonstruierte Fünferreihe wird durch ein weiteres *vacat* vom Posttext abge-

---

25. J.M. ALLEGRO, *Qumrân Cave 4*. I, p. 22.
26. J.M. ALLEGRO, *Qumrân Cave 4*. I, pp. 85-87.
27. H. LICHTENBERGER, *Weisheitliche Mahnrede*, pp. 151-162.
28. Vgl. D.J. HARRINGTON, *Wisdom Texts*, pp. 35-39.
29. T.H. TOBIN, *4Q185*, pp. 145-152.
30. E. PUECH, *Qumrân grotte 4*. XVIII, pp. 115-178.
31. Die von G.J. BROOKE, *Matthew's Beatitudes*, pp. 35-41, bes. p. 35 genannte Zeitstellung 50 v. Chr. – 50 n. Chr. berücksichtigt nur die paläographischen Vorgaben.

trennt, obwohl dieser – im Blick auf Mt 5,11f. – als eine vergleichbare formal überbordende Ausweitung des letzten Makarismus angesehen werden kann. Puëch geht nicht weiter auf den antigonischen Charakter der einzelnen Seligpreisungen ein (wodurch de facto bereits eine Zehnerreihe erreicht wird), meint jedoch, noch weitere vier Makarismen im verlorenen Prätext rekonstruieren zu müssen, um so eine der Bergpredigt ähnliche (Neuner-)Reihe zu erreichen.

In formaler Analogie zu den Seligpreisungen der Bergpredigt und in inhaltlicher Aufnahme von Pss 1,1; 15,2f. u.a. werden konkrete Lebensregeln aufgestellt: selig gepriesen wird der, der der wahren Weisheit anhängt, an »ihren« Gesetzen festhält, »ihr« zujubelt und zustrebt. Die schwebende Ambivalenz des femininen Suffixes wird erst im abschließenden, die formale Stereotypie auflösenden Makarismus aufgelöst: »Selig der Mensch, der die Weisheit erreicht und wandelt in der Tora des Äljon« (Z. 3f.). Wie in 4Q185 werden auch hier Weisheit und Tora in eins gesetzt, wodurch im letzten Makarismus eine umfangreiche Lebensbeschreibung des Gerechten gelingt. Obwohl ich heftige Bedenken[32] gegenüber der von Puech vorgeschlagenen Rekonstruktion der Makarismen-Reihe anmelden möchte, dürfte seine Auffassung zutreffen, daß die bekannten Makarismen-Reihen gemeinsame formale Kriterien aufweisen, zugleich auch inhaltlich die Kombination von weisheitlichen und eschatologischen Elementen gemeinsam haben[33]. Die ausufernde Ausdehnung des letzten Makarismus (Z. 3-7), die an die formsprengenden Elemente mit Chorschluß-Charakter in der abschließenden Seligpreisung der Bergpredigt (Mt 5,11f.) erinnert und damit sich als ein festes Formelement einer Makarismen-Reihe ausweist, könnte der Analyse von 1QH VI,2f. neue Impulse geben.

- Die in 1QH VI,2f.[34] von E. Puech vorgeschlagene Rekonstruktion[35] ist inzwischen in der Forschung weitgehend akzeptiert worden[36]. Danach

---

32. Von den von Puech rekonstruierten vier ersten Makarismen ist schlichtweg keine einzige Spur im Text vorhanden. Das Argument, daß der obere Teil der Kolumnen abgebrochen ist, rechtfertigt selbstverständlich die Annahme, daß dort einmal ein Text gestanden hat, mehr aber auch nicht. Geht man schließlich von der Beobachtung aus, daß in den erhaltenen Makarismen (der erste ist allerdings überzeugend rekonstruierbar) jeweils Positiv- und Negativqualifikationen parallel genannt sind (»Doppel-Makarismen«), dann kommt schon eine Zehnerreihe zustande, die eine Rekonstruktion weiterer fünf Makarismen aus dem Nichts unseriös macht.
33. E. PUECH, *4Q525,* pp. 80-106.
34. Neue Zählung; nach der alten Zählung 1QH XIV,2f.
35. E. PUECH, *Un hymne essénien,* pp. 59-88: Puech zählt den Beleg als 1QH VI,13f. (p. 66).
36. Vgl. z.B. G.J. BROOKE, *Matthew's Beatitudes,* pp. 35-41; J.A. FITZMYER, *Collection,* p. 511; F. GARCÍA MARTÍNEZ & E.J.C. TIGCHELAAR, *Study Edition I,* p. 153.

läßt sich hier eine Seligpreisung erschließen, die »die Männer der Wahrheit und die Erwählten der Gerechtigkeit, die nach Wissen und Einsicht streben ..., die die Vergebung lieben, die Armen des Geistes und die Gereinigten ..., die sich zusammennehmen bis zur Zeit deines Gerichtes und die auf deine Rettung warten«, selig preist und damit weitgehend der abschließenden Seligpreisung in 4Q525 entspricht. Inhaltlich werden wieder die für die essenisch-sadoqidische Frömmigkeit charakteristischen Themen (Weisheit suchen, Streben nach Reinheit, Selbstkontrolle, Armenfrömmigkeit u.a.) angesprochen. Besondere Aufmerksamkeit verdient die in der Forschung bereits vor den Qumranfunden schon immer intensiv beachtete Bezeichnung πτωχοὶ τῷ πνεύματι (Mt 5,3), die zwar in der äquivalenten Wendung »Arme des Geistes« (ענוי רוח)[37] bisher in Qumran nachgewiesen werden konnte[38], nun aber auch gleich zweimal im Kontext von Seligpreisungen vorliegt. So kann sie nun einerseits mit der Wendung »Demut seiner Seele« (ענות נפשו) von 4Q525 2 ii 6 zusammengesehen werden und von hierher vielleicht eine intensivere Erklärung finden, andererseits aber ist ihre kontextuelle Einbindung in 1QH VI für die weitere Klärung des Beleges in der Bergpredigt hilfreich. Formal zeigt diese Seligpreisung eine Mischung aus praktisch-weisheitlichen und eschatologisch-apokalyptischen Elementen. Die kontextuelle Einbindung zwischen einem *maśkîl*-Hymnus und einem »soteriologischen Bekenntnis« läßt vermuten, daß diese Seligpreisung pastoral abgezweckt ist und die Situation der bedrängten Gemeinde vor Augen hat.

Brooke betont zu Recht, daß die qumranischen Makarismen mehr oder weniger deutlich mit Initiationsriten verbunden sind, also im Kontext der Neuaufnahmen von Eintrittswilligen stehen und hier die Funktion des ermunternden Zuspruches haben. Auch von hierher ließe sich eine interessante Perspektive für die kontextuelle Deutung der Makarismen in der Bergpredigt gewinnen.

V. NEUES TESTAMENT

Im NT nehmen die Synoptiker die formale Funktion der Seligpreisungen auf, wenn sie sie an den Anfang der Bergpredigt/Feldrede (Mt 5,3-12; Lk 6,20-22) setzen und damit diese eindrucksvoll als Tora des neuen Gottesvolkes (vgl. Mt 5,17) qualifizieren. »Makarismen mit der inneren Motivation des Habens und Seins sind zu unterscheiden von solchen mit der inneren Motivation des Tuns. Erstere, in der Regel uneschatologisch,

---

37. Vgl. z.B. D. FLUSSER, *Blessed*, pp. 1-13.
38. Vgl. 1QM XIV,7 par. 4Q491, Fragm. 8-10 i 5; 1QS IV,3.

sind für die Weisheitsliteratur üblich, zweitere finden sich in der späteren Prophetie und richten den Blick auf die Zukunft, in der der ob seines Tuns glücklich Gepriesene seinen Lohn erhält (vgl. Jes 30,18ff.; 56,2), wobei dann in der Tat eschatologische Konnotationen angesprochen sein können«[39]. Die Seligpreisungen bilden entsprechend bevollmächtigte Ansage[40] und Zuspruch des Gottesreiches und die Proklamation des eschatologischen Heils[41], ursprünglich als unbedingter Heilszuspruch an die fundamental Bedürftigen (Mt 5,3.4.6 par. Lk 6,20.21: Arme, Hungernde, Traurige), dann paränetisch auch an die ethisch Qualifizierten (Mt 5,5.7-10: Barmherzige, Sanftmütige, Friedensstifter etc.) und schließlich an die verfolgte Gemeinde (Mt 5,11f.) gerichtet. Die vielfach geäußerte traditionsgeschichtliche Rückführung der Seligpreisungen auf Jes 61,1ff. wird gegenwärtig kritisch diskutiert. Die Anordnung der Seligpreisungen in einer Makarismen-Reihe hat im hebräischen AT keine Vorlage, findet aber in Sir 14,20-15,1f.; 25,8-9 und Qumran eindeutige Vorläufer.

In **redaktionsgeschichtlicher** Sicht gehören die Seligpreisungen weitgehend bereits zur Logienquelle Q (durch π-Alliteration gekennzeichnet[42]), die jedoch den Evangelisten Matthäus (als Q^M) und Lukas (als Q^L) in divergierender Form vorgelegen haben könnte[43]. Es zeichnet sich ein vorsichtiger Konsens darüber ab, daß eine ursprüngliche Makarismen-Trias aus Q unter Aufnahme einer zweiten Trias (ebenfalls aus Q [?]) plus V. 5 in der matthäischen Tradition zur Siebenerreihe mit dem Ziel der Ethisierung der Seligpreisungen[44] ausgestaltet worden ist. In einer weiteren Redaktion habe der Evangelist selbst sie auf neun Makarismen ausgeweitet und durch das Lohn-Motiv (V. 12) mit dem »Vaterunser«-Gebet (Mt 6,5) verbunden[45], um auf diese Weise zu betonen, daß das Gebet zum gelingenden Leben gehöre. Als Einleitung zum ersten Redekomplex stehen sie zugleich in Korrespondenz zum Abschluß des letzten Redekomplexes in Mt 25,31-46, wo von den Verfluchten die Rede ist, die das jesuanische Liebesgebot nicht akzeptiert haben. Lukas habe nur den Grundbestand von Q (allerdings in einer variierenden

---

39. H.-J. FABRY, *Makarismus*, p. 364.
40. T.Y. MULLINS, *Ascription*, pp. 194-205.
41. H. MERKLEIN, *Jesusgeschichte*, p. 80.
42. C. MICHAELIS, *π-Alliteration*, pp. 148-161.
43. Dazu bes. R.A. GUELICH, *Beatitudes*, pp. 419f.; I. BROER, *Seligpreisungen* und H. FRANKEMÖLLE, *Makarismen*, pp. 52-75.
44. Diese Ethisierung geschah bereits in der vormatthäischen Tradition, so GUELICH, *Beatitudes*, p. 432.
45. R.A. GUELICH, *Beatitudes*, p. 432.

Form) beibehalten. Der Anredecharakter der lukanischen Seligpreisungen besagt weder etwas über ein formgeschichtliches prius[46], noch ist er zwingend als lukanische Redaktion auszumachen, da bereits das Alte Testament selbst einige Seligpreisungen in der 2. sg./pl. kenne und Ähnliches auch in äthHen 56,21 vorliege[47]. Dagegen hält Merklein, daß Lukas die vier Seligpreisungen aus der Logienquelle genommen habe, sie konsequent in die Anredeform umformuliert habe, um aus der ursprünglichen Proklamation konsequent eine Zusage mit Anspruchscharakter zu machen. Der gleiche Anspruch stehe hinter der lukanischen Kombination der Seligpreisungen mit den unmittelbar folgenden Weherufen: »Volk und Jünger sind vor Jesus versammelt. Beiden Gruppen gilt die Feldrede. Mit dem Adressaten 'Volk' ist die Hoffnung verbunden, daß möglichst viele zu Jüngern werden. Auf die Jünger aber sind die Augen Jesu gerichtet, erwartungsvoll, herausfordernd: Sie sollen ihr Jünger-Sein nun existentiell einholen – nach den Maßstäben der Feldrede. Zwischen Seligpreisungen und Weherufen verläuft die Grenze, die über die tatsächliche Jüngerschaft entscheidet«[48].

Für Puech und Brooke liegt in 4Q525 ein wichtiges Dokument vor, das eine neue Annäherung an die **traditionsgeschichtlichen** Fragen im Zusammenhang mit den Seligpreisungen der Bergpredigt erlaubt. Ohne Zweifel bilden die antigonisch gestalteten »Doppel-Makarismen« und der ausgedehnte summarische Abschlußmakarismus in 4Q525 ausgezeichnete Vorlagen für Mt 5,4-12. Sieht Puech in der matthäischen Makarismen-Reihe eine bis ins Letzte ausgefeilte und nach festen Regeln ausgearbeitete Komposition, die in der semitischen Umwelt ihre klare Pendants habe[49], so gilt es umgekehrt für Brooke jedoch als erwiesen, daß aufgrund der Stichometrie sich eine Verbindung von 4Q525 mit den Makarismen in der lukanischen Feldrede nahelege, so daß Lukas dem semitischen Original näher stehe[50]. Die Summe der Beobachtungen mag zeigen, daß eine breitere jüdische Makarismen-Vorlage existierte, als sie jetzt noch aufgrund der Quellen sichtbar ist. An die in der jüdischen Tradition allenthalben sichtbare Personifikation der Weisheit hat Mt in seiner Makarismen-Reihe angeknüpft, wenn er in der abschließenden Seligpreisung durch das ἕνεκεν ἐμοῦ »um meinetwillen« den Sprecher der Bergpredigt mit der Weisheit identifiziert.

---

46. In dieser Hinsicht ist E. Puech zu einer klaren Entscheidung gekommen, da er die lukanische Fassung als »secondary and later one« herausstellt; vgl. E. PUECH, *Beatitudes*, p. 362.
47. Vgl. E. SCHWEIZER, *Formgeschichtliches*, pp. 123f.
48. H. MERKLEIN, *Jesusgeschichte*, p. 81.
49. E. PUECH, *Beatitudes*, p. 362.
50. G.J. BROOKE, *Matthew's Beatitudes*, p. 37.

Hinter den Seligpreisungen steht die weisheitliche Welterfahrung, daß eine fundamentale Bedürftigkeit aufgrund der durch Sünde gestörten Schöpfungsordnung ein gelingendes Leben der Betroffenen nicht mehr zuläßt. Deshalb wird ihnen in der Seligpreisung genau dieses Gelingen parakletisch zugesprochen. Da die Seligpreisungen formal und inhaltlich so deutliche Bezüge zu anderen geschlossenen Textkorpora (1 Petr 1,6; 4,13f.; Jak 1,2.12; BarApk 48,48-50; 52,5-7; 54,16-18) zeigen, die man als »gemeinsame spätjüdisch-urchristliche Tradition über die Freude angesichts des Leidens«[51] und der Verfolgung bezeichnen könnte, wird man die neutestamentlichen Seligpreisungen als »apokalyptischen Zuspruch« der Gottesherrschaft zu interpretieren haben an den, der die »bessere Gerechtigkeit« lebt (Mt 5,20); bei Lk werden die Seligpreisungen durch die Konfrontation mit den Weherufen als »Entscheidungsrufe« (Luck) gedeutet. Als Reihe bilden sie besonders bei Mt ein Korpus, das in seiner Funktion mit den Tugendtafeln des AT (vgl. Pss 15; 24,3-6) zu vergleichen ist und die Einlaßbedingungen für den Zugang zur Gottesherrschaft nennt.

»Unbeschadet förmlicher Verschiedenheiten zwischen den Makarismen des AT und des NT entspricht die atl. Seligpreisung im Gehalt weitgehend der des NT: Sie ist Verkündigung der durch Gnade geschaffenen, durch Gnade aufrechterhaltenen, durch Gnade dem eschatologischen Ziel entgegengeführten Relation zwischen Gott und Mensch im Lebensbund der Gnade«[52].

Zu weiteren Makarismen in der frühnachchristlichen Tradition vgl. das Thomas-Evangelium 54; 69,1f.; 68 sowie rabbinische und samaritanische Belege bei Billerbeck I 189.

VI. Abschliessende Gedanken

Ausgehend von der weisheitlichen Bestätigung des gelingenden Lebens über die dieses Gelingen zusprechenden und bestätigenden Begrüßungsformulierungen gewinnt die Seligpreisung in der Kombination zur Makarismenreihe die Valenz eines Wertekataloges. Da die Seligpreisungen aber immer schon Zuspruch gelingenden Lebens sind, sind sie zugleich auch moralischer Appell, den Weg dieses gelingenden Lebens auch aktiv zu gehen. Der Wertekatalog ändert sich damit zum Tugendkatalog.

---

51. G. EICHHOLZ, *Auslegung*, p. 51.
52. W. KÄSER, *Beobachtungen*, pp. 249f.

Bereits in der frühjüdischen Tradition wird die Seligpreisung als einzelne oder auch als Reihe in den eschatologischen Kontext gestellt, fungiert nun als Proklamation des eschatologischen Heils, der »endgültigen, nie mehr zurücknehmbaren Erwählung Israels bzw. des eschatologischen Gottesvolkes, dem das künftige Heil verheißen und in Sündenvergebung und Erwählung jetzt schon zugeteilt wird«[53]. Zeigte das Frühjudentum – vor allem in der qumranessenischen Ausprägung – noch in aller Deutlichkeit, daß der Charakter der Seligpreisung aus dem Angebot nahtlos hinüberreicht in den Anspruch, nämlich sich ganz der Weisheit und der Tora zu verschreiben, so zeigen die Makarismen in Bergpredigt und Feldrede – zumindest im jesuanischen Grundbestand – hier einen fundamentalen Unterschied. Kombiniert Matthäus über die Urfassung hinaus in der Letztfassung Zuspruch und Anspruch der Seligpreisungen und stellt in einem gewaltigen Kompositionsbogen nahezu sein ganzes Evangelium in diesen Anspruch hinein, so wird bei Lukas deutlich, daß die Seligpreisung auch den Menschen in die Entscheidung rufen will, das aber in einer völlig anderen Weise: nun nämlich das Angebot Gottes, der des Menschen Leben gelingen lassen will, anzunehmen.

Turmfalkenweg 15   Heinz-Josef FABRY
53127 Bonn
Deutschland

---

53. H. MERKLEIN, *Jesusgeschichte*, pp. 80f.

BIBLICAL INTERPRETATION IN THE WISDOM TEXTS FROM QUMRAN

I. INTRODUCTION

The availability since 1991 of all the scrolls found in the eleven caves at or near Qumran has radically changed our understanding of the contents and significance of the Qumran library. Before 1991 the focus of attention was largely on the so-called sectarian compositions and on the so-called biblical manuscripts (as far as they were known)[1]. This was so much the case that, for example, when Y. Yadin published his edition of the Temple Scroll, he had no hesitation in assigning it directly to the community under the editorship of the Teacher of Righteousness himself[2]. Whilst the general availability of texts since 1991 has shed much further light on the sectarian compositions and on the transmission of the text of most of the biblical books in the three centuries before the fall of the temple in 70 CE, it is in the whole area of non-biblical, non-sectarian texts that our knowledge of the significance of the scrolls found at Qumran has been changed most radically. Amongst these changes are to be found our perceptions of the wisdom traditions passed on in the late second temple period[3].

Ever since 1991 the major issues of debate have concerned the halakha of the sect (spurred on by the publication of MMT), the history of the community (provoked by the 4Q copies of the Rule of the Community), and the parabiblical material (now largely available in four volumes in the Discoveries in the Judaean Desert series). Concern with the wisdom texts has lagged behind, though it is now rapidly on the increase as the overall bibliography in this volume indicates clearly, and it will continue to develop now that both the sapiential volumes in the Discoveries in the Judaean Desert series are published[4].

---

1. "So-called" in the first case because it is still far from clear what sociological terms are suitable for describing the community that lived at Qumran and the wider movement of which it was a part; and in the second case because the term Bible sets up a somewhat anachronistic category for the scriptures held to be authoritative by various groups of Jews in the late second temple period.

2. See Y. YADIN, *Megillat Ha-Miqdash*, pp. 302-303.

3. The wisdom texts from Qumran have been most suitably integrated into the overall picture of such traditions in the late second temple period by J.J. COLLINS, *Jewish Wisdom*.

4. T. ELGVIN et al., *Qumran Cave 4*. XV; J. STRUGNELL, D. HARRINGTON, T. ELGVIN, *Qumran Cave 4*. XXIV.

The purpose of this study is to offer a preliminary taxonomy of some of the uses of scripture in some of the compositions that are generally assigned to the generic category of wisdom literature. In fact, as is well known, pericopae of many different genres fall within this broad descriptive band. This study has no particular view on where the limits of the category should be drawn; there is more than enough material which can be widely accepted to fall within the category to enable us to make progress in investigating the use of authoritative scriptures in these traditions.

II. PRELIMINARY OBSERVATIONS

Several preliminary observations need to be made to set the parameters of the more detailed discussion which will follow.

Though the so-called *Instruction* (*Mûsār leMēvîn*) survives in several manuscripts and is capable of extensive reconstruction, it remains true that from the Qumran caves there is no single manuscript of a wisdom composition which survives in its entirety or nearly so. It is possible to argue that the beginning of *Instruction* (*Mûsār leMēvîn*) is extant in part in 4Q416 1 and that 4Q298, if classified as a wisdom text, is also preserved from the beginning. However, for the most part the wisdom texts are extant only in a fragmentary form with no largely complete exemplars such as can be found in the more complete manuscripts from caves 1 and 11.

This observation is significant because it means that there is little or no basis for any overall comparison between the wisdom compositions found at Qumran and those compositions which were subsequently collected together for inclusion within the collection of Writings (Kethubim) later to be found in the Bible itself. There are no titles, no attributions of authorship, no colophons defining purpose and intention. So for example, as far as we can tell, there is little reference in the non-scriptural wisdom collections found in the Qumran caves to the archetypal authorship of Solomon; in fact Solomon figures barely at all in the whole extant corpus from Qumran. A tantalizing exception may be the *Ways of Righteousness* (4Q420-421) which T. Elgvin has suggested is constructed partially in imitation of Proverbs, with an admonitory and discursive opening section (matching Proverbs 1-9) and then concrete advice (matching Proverbs 10-31), but not enough text survives for the comparison to be assessed in any detail[5].

---

5. See ELGVIN, *4QWays of Righteousness*, p. 189.

Because in general the wisdom material from the Qumran caves is so fragmentary, it is difficult to discern any overall pattern in the manuscript remains which might provide some clue as to the function of the wisdom compositions. Some of the texts might have been produced for didactic purposes in a particular setting, some of them might have been portable handbooks. Some might have used earlier wisdom books to suggest that their continuation with earlier traditions was the basis for the authority of their own teachings. It is difficult to discern whether these compositions should be set in temple, court, school or home. As a result of this uncertainty, it is consequently also unclear quite how scriptural texts may have influenced some of the contents of these wisdom compositions. If they had had a place in the temple, then the cultic use of certain texts such as the Psalms in some form might have influenced their formation and phraseology; if they had had a setting elsewhere, then the scriptural texts associated with that setting might have been a formative influence on the compositions themselves.

Despite these matters of overall uncertainty which surround the wisdom compositions found in the Qumran caves, certain overall features are worth considering. To begin with, apart from the *Targum of Job*, which in any case assumes a Hebrew base text, most of the compositions which can be broadly assigned to the category of wisdom are written in Hebrew. Here is a first indication that the materials as a subgroup of the Qumran library are in some measure presented as in imitation of scriptural models. Unlike some of the narrative interpretations or speculative views of eschatological matters, the wisdom materials reflect explicitly the practice in the library of presenting halakhic materials and rule books exclusively in Hebrew. If the wisdom compositions found at Qumran were reflections of popular folklore, then one might expect more material in vernacular Aramaic. But amongst the texts which may be broadly categorized as wisdom the few exceptions to the Hebrew-only rule are to be found amongst the so-called testaments which are connected directly with the Patriarchs and in the Enoch compositions which are on the generic borderline between wisdom and apocalyptic[6]. No post-Mosaic figure offers instruction in Aramaic[7].

---

6. A helpful comment on the place of the Enoch materials in understanding the wisdom traditions found at Qumran can be found in HARRINGTON, *Wisdom Texts from Qumran*, pp. 10-12; more detail can be found in T. ELGVIN's study *Mystery to Come*, in which Elgvin concludes that "*4QInstruction* represents a bridge between the apocalyptic *Enoch* literature and the clearly defined sectarian community" (p. 150).

7. Important remarks on the Hebrew and Aramaic of the scrolls are made by D. DIMANT, *Qumran Manuscripts*, pp. 34-35.

A further overall point can be made. It should be noted that no wisdom materials primarily associated with the Jewish dispersion have been found amongst the collection at Qumran. The collection is broadly on a different trajectory from that to be identified in the range of compositions associated with Egyptian Judaism: there is no Wisdom of Solomon, 3 Maccabees or 4 Maccabees. There is thus a modern predisposition in reading the wisdom compositions found at Qumran to read them in light of scriptural antecedents, since there seems to be little that matches explicitly the philosophical and ethical concerns of the broader hellenistic world view which we know was available even in Palestine from the fourth century BCE or even earlier. Apart from the later biblical books themselves, the copies of Ben Sira found at Qumran are as close as the wisdom literature from the Qumran caves comes to the cosmopolitan traditions of even the immediate environment.

It is unclear precisely when the major part of the Kethubim came together as an authoritative collection. In some instances, it is possible to suppose that the wisdom compositions found at Qumran are contemporary with some of those compositions which later came to be part of the authoritative collection of Jewish scriptures. In other words, in some instances we cannot be precisely clear how later "biblical" wisdom books circulated authoritatively in the middle of the second temple period. It may even be possible to argue that some items in the wisdom corpus from Qumran reflect the authoritative base texts from which some matters in the biblical wisdom books were themselves later exegeted. Thus one should not necessarily assume the priority of the biblical wisdom collection and the secondary character of the non-scriptural materials found at Qumran.

This last point can be illustrated with reference to *Instruction* (*Mûsār lᵉMēvîn*). It is intriguing to note that in a certain respect this resembles a rewritten form of the Book of Proverbs, not in close detail in every pericope as is the case in the *Reworked Pentateuch* manuscripts in relation to the Torah, but in assembling sets of pericopae on various disparate themes concerning everyday behaviour. G. Vermes has identified the composition as "unquestionably sectarian"[8], Elgvin as a close predecessor of the Essene community or from the first formative phase of the sectarian movement[9], but A. Lange has placed the composition more subtly in the pre-Essene (pre-community) mould[10]. J. Strugnell and

---

8. G. VERMES, *Complete Dead Sea Scrolls in English*, p. 402.
9. T. ELGVIN, *4QWays of Righteousness*, p. 173.
10. A. LANGE, *Weisheit und Prädestination*, pp. 47-49; *Wisdom and Predestination*, p. 341, n. 2.

D. Harrington, the editors of the principal edition of the manuscripts of *Instruction* (*Mûsār l^eMēvîn*), see it as a missing link between Proverbs and Ben Sira, in its origins independent of the Qumran sectarian writings. The fact that there are more copies of this work preserved and in a better state than there are of any of the so-called biblical wisdom books, suggests that for the Qumran community, even though the composition was not sectarian in origin, it was as important as any wisdom composition which was more widely accepted, at least later on, as far as we can tell. Strugnell and Harrington reckon that it had almost attained canonical status at Qumran[11].

Some wisdom compositions are probably sectarian in the strict sense, or at least to be considered as edited by sectarian redactors (4QWays of Righteousness)[12], but most are not[13]. Some compositions are composite and so may have largely non-sectarian contents which in their final form are capable of being read from the sectarian viewpoint because of the final resting place of the tradition within a sectarian context. In those non-scriptural wisdom composiitons which are closest to the sectarian outlook we might expect to find a predominance of references and allusions to the books of Genesis, Deuteronomy, Isaiah and the Psalms, which can be seen to have formed a kind of "canon within the canon" for the community[14].

III. BIBLICAL WISDOM BOOKS

A brief list of the manuscripts of the biblical wisdom books is as follows: 4Q102 and 4Q103 are Hebrew fragments of the Book of Proverbs written out in verse form (as was Masada Ben Sira); 4Q109 and 4Q110 are fragmentary copies of Qohelet; 2Q15, 4Q99, 4Q100, and 4Q101 (in palaeo-Hebrew) are fragmentary copies of Job. In addition 2Q18 seems to be part of Ben Sira and Sirach 51 is represented in an alternative form in 11Q5 (11QPs^a)[15]. The Song of Songs is also represented in four manuscripts, though it is doubtful that we should designate this a wisdom book; two of its three cave 4 exemplars seem to be excerpted texts, but

---

11. J. STRUGNELL, D. HARRINGTON and T. ELGVIN *Qumran Cave 4*. XXIV, pp. 30-31.
12. See ELGVIN, *4QWays of Righteousness*, p. 173.
13. I do not consider that 4Q525 is a sectarian composition, despite the work of J.C.R. DE ROO, *Qumran Sectarian Document*.
14. As I have argued in *"The Canon Within the Canon"*.
15. For brief helpful comments on the significance of these manuscripts, see HARRINGTON, *Wisdom Texts from Qumran*, pp. 15-18.

no satisfactory explanation has yet been provided for how the selection of passages, which is different in the two copies, was made[16].

In the context of this study it is important to ask whether any of the variants discernible in the biblical manuscripts might be described as inner-biblical exegesis. Because they were first made known by J. Muilenburg in 1954[17], the significant non-orthographic variants in 4QQoh[a] were incorporated by F. Horst in the edition that is now reproduced in BHS. Qoh 5,14 begins with *ky'* in 4QQoh[a] rather than *k'šr* as in the MT; this stylistic difference makes for no change in meaning since the clause it introduces is given as the reason for what is stated in the preceding clause: wealth can be lost in a bad venture so that there is nothing to support the children who are entirely dependent upon their parents. Or again, in 4QQoh[a] Qoh 5,15 (Heb) the sentence opens with *gm* rather than the *wgm* of the MT; this may be a minor stylistic improvement so as to make Qoh 3,15 match 3,16 which opens with *gm*. These variations mean little exegetically. Similar examples can be found in Qoh 6,6 (*w'lw* MT; *w'm l'* 4QQoh[a]; MT simply has the contracted form); Qoh 6,8 (*ky' mh* MT; *kmh* 4QQoh[a]; virtually no difference in meaning), Qoh 7,5 (*g'rt* MT; *g'rwt* 4QQoh[a]; singular for plural). Perhaps the most interesting variant is at Qoh 7,19 where the MT reads *hḥkmh t'wz lḥkm*, "wisdom strengthens the wise", whereas 4QQoh[a] in agreement with the LXX reads *hḥkmh t'zr lḥkm*, "wisdom aids (or assists) the wise". Has the *resh* been added or omitted? This is almost certainly to be described as scribal error rather than the deliberate exegetical adjustment of the text for the clarification of the plain sense. The variants in the manuscripts of Job and Proverbs are of a similar sort; none are readily identifiable as exegetically changing the meaning of the text; they are minor stylistic alterations.

The difficulties of reading and understanding the Book of Job are legion for both the modern and the ancient reader. The *Targum of Job* from Qumran furnishes us with an overt attempt at exegetical clarification through translational paraphrase. For example in the rendering of Job 38,3-13 in 11QtgJob 30,1-10 Job 38,3-13 is adjusted in minor ways as Harrington for one has observed[18]. These adjustments effect the mythological imagery of the Hebrew original and its rhetorical structure. In the first place, whereas the Hebrew talks of the morning stars

---

16. For details on the textual affiliation of these scriptural wisdom manuscripts and for further bibliography, see E. Tov, *Significance,* pp. 306-307.

17. J. MUILENBURG, *Qoheleth Scroll.*

18. HARRINGTON, *Wisdom Texts from Qumran,* pp. 18-22.

"singing", the targum states that they "shone" reducing an anthropomorphism to a statement of what stars do every night. Or again, whereas the Hebrew Job 38,7 refers to the "sons of God" crying out, the targum renders this as "angels of God", perhaps in an attempt to protect the uniqueness and transcendence of God[19]. Secondly, whereas the Hebrew Job has God ask questions in the third person, in the targum the questions are all put to Job directly in the second person. The result is a consistent rhetorical pattern which runs through from Job 38,4 to Job 38,12. Unless we suppose that the translator was working from an alternative form of Hebrew Job, this change suggests literary sensitivity on the part of the targumist.

In 11QtgJob 38,7-8 there is a classic example of exegetical clarification in the targumist's translation. The Hebrew has posed a longstanding difficulty: what did Job's friends give him? Each presented him with *qśyṭh* and a ring of gold. *Qśyṭh* is commonly related to the cognate Arabic root *qśṭ* from which the noun "scales" is derived; hence perhaps the term in Job is to be understood as "something weighed". The targumist offers a clear rendering of the term: for him it means "ewe lamb". Whether this is correct or not is beside the point; the targumist has given a clear rendering of a rare word. This kind of exegetical clarification is common not only in the targumim but also in the rewritten Bible texts. This is a particular example of the improvement of the plain meaning of the text, simple-sense exegesis.

IV. Particular Uses of Scripture

Beyond the presentation and re-presentation of scriptural wisdom materials in the scriptural manuscripts found at Qumran, there are many different ways in which authoritative scriptural traditions are used in the wisdom compositions found in the Qumran caves. In this section of this essay, several of these will be briefly outlined in relation to various genres: wisdom as poetry, as halakhah, as parenesis, as narrative exegesis, and as akin to pesher. In this way it is hoped that the variety of the ways in which scriptural traditions can be used will become readily apparent.

A. Wisdom as Biblical Poetry.

The major formal characteristic of much wisdom instruction is its quasi-poetical presentation. The arrangement of some of the biblical

---

19. See further W. H. BROWNLEE, *Cosmic Role of Angels*.

wisdom materials in poetic half-lines, even on the Qumran manuscripts[20], shows us that the scribes were thoroughly aware of the poetic character of the wisdom materials[21]. Pithy maxims are presented in poetic parellelisms; groups of wisdom instructions are ordered climactically. The overall character of much wisdom material is atomistic. There is little that can be assigned to an overall grand narrative or a systematic ethic. The primary use of scripture in many wisdom compositions is the allusory anthologisation of traditions. The wisdom authors may not always be aware of their sources, but they pluck the best flowers from a number of sources and put them together in a new arrangement which has a fresh attractiveness for the reader or hearer. Again, the reader or hearer is not required to be able to identify the sources of all the phrases in earlier traditions, but the more educated will be able to discern something of what is taking place. Beyond the wisdom materials, the many new hymnic compositions at Qumran function in a very similar way as new poetic compositions are formed from old favourites.

Since all the principal editions of the wisdom compositions found at Qumran list scriptural references where similar phraseology is to be found, reference to one small set of examples will suffice to illustrate this allusory use of scripture. In his discussion of Qohelet and the wisdom circles of the Jerusalem temple, A. Lange has observed how various parts of Qohelet are alluded to, notably in the Qumran Book of Mysteries. Although he refers to the phraseology of Qohelet which is reused in the Book of Mysteries as part of a citation, in fact the Qohelet passages are not repeated verbatim. There are minor adjustments as the language of the scriptural source is reworked into the new composition in an appropriate way. Lange points to the use of Qoh 6,8.11 in 1Q27 1 ii 3 and Qoh 5,5 in 1Q27 6, lines 2-3[22].

B. *Wisdom as Halakhah*

Since much of the wisdom tradition is instruction for how one should lead one's life, it is not surprising that some scriptural interpretation in the wisdom texts can be understood as halakhic exegesis. This takes essentially two forms.

---

20. And in the copy of Ben Sira from Masada, now reproduced in *Masada VI*, pp. 152-225.

21. The presence of vacats in the wisdom compositions may serve a similar literary function, not only breaking up large units of text, but highlighting smaller elements. These smaller elements are indicated by vacats notably in the presentation of the macarisms in 4Q525.

22. A. LANGE, *In Diskussion mit dem Tempel*, pp. 125-126.

In the first place halakhic exegesis is offered through the broad imitation of the content of scriptural models in the wisdom books themselves. Here it is a matter of seeking wisdom and walking in her ways, as is paramount in the macarisms of 4Q525[23]. The halakhah is based in practical advice for everyday living which is the application of various of the principles underlying the Torah, rather than the application of individual rulings (*mishpatim*) or statutes (*ḥuqim*).

In the second place, some parts of the wisdom compositions found in the caves at Qumran seem to imply halakhic exegesis of a more specific kind. In this category are those instructions which appear to take a ruling from the Torah and interpret it in some way. Here are three examples.

(a) Honouring one's wife. In a recent study J. Strugnell has argued that the instruction in 4Q416 2 ii 21 is a matter of legal interpretation[24]. The passage at the very bottom of a column in a broken context, reads *wgm 'l tql kly [ḥ]yqkh*, "And also do not curse the vessel of your bosom" (i.e. "your wife"). By juxtaposing this with Deut 27,16, *'rwr mqlh 'byw w'mw*, "cursed is the one who despises his father or his mother", Strugnell has proposed that the passage is intended to extend the positive command of the Decalogue, "honour your father and mother". This commandment is expounded in 4Q416 2 iii 16-19 and in Sir 3,7, but only in relation to father and mother. Strugnell proposes that the exegetical strategy in 4Q416 2 ii 21 involves the extension of the commandment to include one's wife. Since most legal interpretation of this kind depends upon the suitable juxtaposition of two passages to create a new ruling, it is necessary to ask where the second passage is. The phrase *'št ḥyqw*, "wife of his bosom", occurs in Deut 13,7 and 28,54. In the former one's wife is one of a number of relations (mother and father are not included in the list) who might lead one into idolatry; in the latter the desperate disobedient man denies food to his brother, his wife and his children. The significant person in both these lists who is not a blood relation is the wife. Since Deut 27,15, immediately before 27,16, concerns the idolator, it may act as a tertium quid for the extension of the honour commandment to include the wife.

---

23. See the studies by G. J. Brooke, *Matthew's Beatitudes*, and E. Puech, *Un Hymne essénien*, and also the principal edition of 4Q525 by him in *Qumrân grotte 4. XVIII*.

24. J. Strugnell, *Wives and Marriage*; see also the version of the same argument in the principal edition of 4Q416 by J. Strugnell and D. J. Harrington in *Qumran Cave 4. XXIV*, pp. 108-109.

(b) Mixtures. In 4Q418 103 ii 7-9 we read: "Lest it form something of mixed kinds like a mule, And (lest) thou become as one who we[ars *sha'aṭnez*], made of wool and flax, And (lest) thy toil be like (that of) one who plo[ughs] with ox and a[s]s [to]geth[er], And (lest) moreover thy crops b[e for thee like] (those of) one who sows diverse kinds, and of one who takes the seed and the full *growth* and the yi[eld of] the [vineyard *together*], to be set apa[rt (for the sanctuary)"[25]. The text speaks against mixtures of all kinds. In the Torah laws against mixtures are to be found in Lev 19,19: "You shall not let your animals breed with a different kind; you shall not sow your field with two kinds of seed; nor shall you put on a garment made of two different materials". In Deut 22,9 legislation is similar: "You shall not sow your vineyard with a second kind of seed, or the whole yield will have to be forfeited, both the crop that you have sown and the yield of the vineyard itself". In 4Q418 the juxtaposition of the two biblical verses is clear: on the one hand, for example, the references to mixed animal breeding and mixed clothing derive from Lev 19,19, whereas the allusion to the yield of the crop derives from Deut 22,9. From the same verse "vineyard" is suitably restored in 4Q418 103 ii 9.

In MMT B 75-79 the combined law on mixtures is offered as the halakhic justification for legislation against mixed marriages either between priests and non-priests or between Israelites and non-Israelites[26]. It is likely that the combination of two passages of law as is implied in 4Q418 was also used as the legal justification for some other kind of mixture not specified in scripture itself. Sadly the context of 4Q418 is rather broken at this point, but the general theme of the fragmentary remains concerns wealth and prosperity. A partially extant phrase which follows this ruling on mixtures reads: *hwnkh 'm bśrkh*, "your wealth with your relations"[27]. Perhaps there was advice against mixing your wealth with that of your relations. Here there is a real possibility that the juxtaposition of the scriptural laws on mixtures provides the standard justification for extending the law to include other matters involving "mixing" which have to do with sex and money.

---

25. Trans. by J. STRUGNELL and D. J. HARRINGTON in *Qumran Cave 4*. XXIV, pp. 330-333.

26. E. QIMRON and J. STRUGNELL, *Qumran Cave 4*. V, pp. 171-175. QIMRON prefers to understand that the prohibition is against priests and non-priests, whereas J. BAUMGARTEN prefers to understand it as against marriage of any Israelite with a non-Israelite.

27. In the principal edition of the manuscript STRUGNELL and HARRINGTON translate the phrase as "thy wealth together with thy *cattle*" (*Qumran Cave 4*. XXIV, p. 331) and comment (p. 334) that "the remaining text seems unrelated to the theme of *kl'ym*, unless as an extension of the notion of mixing together things set apart for God".

(c) Vows. A third example of halakhic exegesis within a wisdom text can be seen in 4Q416 2 iv 6-9: "Over her spirit he has set you in authority so that she should walk in your good pleasure, and let her not make numerous vows and votive offerings; turn her spirit to your good pleasure. And every oath binding on her, to vow a vow, annul it according to a (mere) utterance of your mouth; and at your good pleasure restrain her from performing [...]"[28]. In general the biblical basis for this advice to the husband with regard to the behaviour of his wife is to be found in Num 30,6-15, an extensive passage on how a wife's vows can be annulled by her husband, but only if he discovers them swiftly and revokes them explicitly. A similar instruction about annulling the wife's vows occurs in CD 16,10-12.

What kind of halakhic procedure is being followed in these passages? It seems that an extended law of Numbers is reduced in both 4Q416 and CD. Whereas Numbers allows some of the wife's vows to stand or suggests that if there is a delay between the husband's discovery of the vow and his annulling of it that he should bear the consequences, in both subsequent passages, the law is simplified and made more severe, by suggesting that all vows made by a wife should be annulled and directly. This is a process of simplification and clarification which restricts the rights of the wife but reduces the likelihood of misunderstanding.

C. Wisdom as Parenesis

One of the major features of much parenetic or exhortatory material in Jewish tradition is its use of past historical circumstances which are recorded in scripture. These references are usually made in one of two ways. Firstly, past historical events can function as the markers which give the reader a sense of identity. A major example of this phenomenon is in 4Q185 1-2 i 13-15, which is an exhortation to seek wisdom. The hearer is encouraged by just such historical recollection: "And now, please, hear me, my people! Pay attention to me, simpletons! Draw wisdom from the [p]ower of our God, remember the miracles he performed in Egypt, his portents in [the land of Ham]. And may your heart tremble because his terror ..."[29]. Here the recollection of the actions of God in Egypt provides the reader with a sense of identity and through that a

---

28. Trans. D. HARRINGTON, *Wisdom Texts from Qumran*, p. 44.
29. Trans. F. GARCÍA MARTÍNEZ and E. J. C. TIGCHELAAR, *Study Edition* I, p. 379.

means of motivating certain kinds of behaviour[30]. Sound exhortation preaches not just what people should do, but offers some reason as to why they should do it. In other words, it covers both practice and motivation. The biblical language, such as "seed of Abraham" (4Q302 1 i 7), found in the Admonitory Parable (4Q302) serves a similar function. B. Nitzan associates the historical opening section of what survives in this very fragmentary piece with the admonitions of 4Q381 and the Damascus Document[31].

Secondly, past historical events can be used as primary examples to encourage a particular way of behaviour in the hearer or reader. Such examples can be either positive or negative. Again in 4Q185 (1-2 ii 4) appeal is made to "[the way which he commanded to J]acob and the path which he decreed to Isaac"[32]. Of interest here is the combination of Jacob and Isaac in parallelism. The text is fragmentary but it is clear that it did not continue with Abraham. Why should Jacob and Isaac be held up as exemplary in some fashion? What was it about these two figures which suggested they were suitable models for those who seek wisdom? The priority given to Jacob may be suggestive, since he was both persistent with the man with whom he wrestled but was also charged with building an altar at Bethel and in effect establishing the priesthood[33]. 4Q413, a "Composition concerning Divine Providence", exhorts "the reader to consider carefully the events of the past, which demonstrate that whoever follows God has been rewarded, while whoever did not has failed to survive"[34]. No specific events are mentioned in the four lines of the single fragment that survives, but the overall function of what survives of 4Q413, like several other wisdom compositions referred to in this study, is exhortatory.

D. Wisdom as Narrative Exegesis

Apart from the parenetic or exhortative use of historical events and the narratives which convey them, scriptural narrative is assumed and interpreted in another significant way in the wisdom materials found at

---

30. For further detail concerning the biblical allusions in this passage, see H. LICHTENBERGER, *Weisheitliche Mahnrede*, p. 156, esp. n. 29; LICHTENBERGER also compares this part of the exhortation with Wis 16,6.
31. B. NITZAN, *4Q302/302a*, pp. 153, 167; and the principal edition by her in T. ELGVIN et al. *Qumran Cave 4*. XV, pp. 129-131.
32. Trans. F. GARCÍA MARTÍNEZ and E. J. C. TIGCHELAAR, *Study Edition* I, p. 379.
33. As the Book of Jubilees makes out.
34. E. QIMRON, *4QComposition Concerning Divine Providence*, p. 169.

Qumran. This use of scripture is not explicit, but depends upon the hearer's or reader's assumed ability to locate the resonances of the instruction as based in the authoritative traditions known elsewhere.

A prime example of this is to be found in the way there is a significant number of passages in the wisdom materials from Qumran which echo the narrative of Genesis 2-3. For example, in 4Q416 2 iii 20-iv 5 there are several allusions to the narrative and marriage practice enshrined in Genesis 2-3 reflected in the advice to the young husband: "Walk together with the helpmeet of your flesh [...] iv 1 his father and his mother [...] 2 you He has set in authority over her, [...] her father 3 He has not set in authority over her; from her mother He has separated her, and toward you shall be [her desire, and she will become] 4 for you one flesh. Your daughter to another He will separate, and your sons [...] 5 And you will be made into a unity with the wife of your bosom for she is the flesh of your nakedness"[35]. The echoes of Genesis 2,24 ("therefore a man leaves his father and mother and clings to his wife, and they shall become one flesh") and 3,16 ("Your desire shall be for your husband, and he shall rule over you") are readily apparent. Furthermore there is a larger issue which might be very good advice for all married couples: the advice in general is for the couple, with authority given to the man, to be like Adam and Eve, put together by God himself, not put together by anybody else.

Familiarity with biblical narrative also provides us with a reason for supporting those who would argue that in 4Q417 2 i 16 Enosh should be understood as a reference to the biblical figure Enosh and not as a general reference to mankind[36]. The preceding context justifies such a view since there is mention of the sons of Seth: "For engraved is that which is ordained by God against all the iniquities of the children of Seth. And written in His presence is a book of memorial of those who keep His word. And that is the vision of meditating (or, Hagu) on a book of memorial. And He gave it as an inheritance to Enosh together with a spiritual people"[37]. Enosh was son of Seth. At one stroke the wisdom writer incorporates both an item which has an eschatological or prophetic ring to it[38], as well as an allusion to the significance of Enosh as the father of some specialist spiritual knowledge (prayer)[39].

---

35. Trans. D. J. HARRINGTON, *Wisdom Texts from Qumran*, p. 44.
36. For looking to Genesis to explain Enosh see the detailed arguments of A. LANGE, *Weisheit und Prädestination*, pp. 87-88.
37. Trans. D. J. HARRINGTON, *Wisdom Texts from Qumran*, p. 53; slightly adapted, since HARRINGTON allows more for the ambiguity: "to humankind (or, Enosh)".
38. Cf. Num 24,17; 1QM 11,6; CD 7,21; 4QTestimonia.
39. See the detailed study on Enosh by S. FRAADE, *Enosh and His Generation*.

The "Book of Memorial" found in this passage in 4Q417 is another allusion to a scriptural narrative which the reader or hearer would probably be able to identify easily. In Malachi 3,16-18 (as well as some other scriptural passages) reference is made to the book of remembrance in an eschatological context. The book contains the names of those who "revered the Lord and thought on his name". The passage is known to have been significant for the Qumran community and the movement of which it was a part[40]. The scriptural allusion serves to distinguish between two kinds of people and takes the wisdom instruction from being general and universalistic to being particularly for an elect group. In this way the scriptural passage serves both as a source for the vocabulary and theme of the new wisdom instruction and is also interpreted by it.

E. Wisdom as Pesher

It is clear that there is no explicit quotation of scripture in the wisdom compositions found in the Qumran caves which then is given interpretation by pesher. However, it is possible to view something in the wisdom texts found at Qumran as reflecting a similar point of view concerning the insight of the instructor. In 1QpHab it is made clear that in the view of the author God has made known to the Teacher of Righteousness "all the mysteries of his servants the prophets"[41]. The teacher as interpreter knows what the prophets themselves did not know. Their prophecies need unlocking through divine assistance verifiable through exegetical procedure; their prophecies are *razim*, "mysteries", like dreams or visions which are not properly understood until interpreted by a seer or wise man, like Daniel.

The distinctive phrase *rz nhyh* which occurs in both 4QInstruction and extensively in the fragmentary remains of the *Mysteries* composition suggests something similar. Just as the prophecies of old are viewed in reality as something more complex than their authors understood, so there is an additional source of practical advice and its justification in the *raz nihyeh*. It is almost certain that the phrase does not refer to anything scriptural and so in one sense it falls beyond the scope of the use of scriptural traditions which is the concern of this presentation. However, the presence of the *rz nhyh* in the wisdom compositions suggests an attitude to wisdom traditions which is similar to the attitude to the Torah which is found in later strictly sectarian compositions: there is tradition which is available to everybody, the *nigleh*, and there are things

---

40. Cf. 4Q253a (= pMalachi); CD 20,17-21.
41. 1QpHab 2,8-9; 7,4-5.

known only to the initiated, the *nistarot*. Thus in relation to the Law, the literary prophets (including the Psalms) and the wisdom traditions there is special knowledge. The *raz nihyeh* is special knowledge but it is probably not entirely divorced from the tradition. As D. J. Harrington has pointed out in 4Q418 184,2 the phrase occurs in association with *byd mwšh*, suggesting a direct connection with traditions passed on by Moses including the Torah itself[42].

V. WISDOM TENDENCIES

The purpose of this section of the study is not to outline a general theory concerning the content of the collection of wisdom compositions from Qumran but to ask a more specific set of questions concerning what the use of the scriptural traditions in the wisdom texts may indicate about certain tendencies in the material.

A. *The Universal and the Particular*

Whereas a general trajectory in some wisdom literature which became biblical and also in its non-biblical non-Israelite counterparts tends to highlight matters which expound universal characteristic human behaviour and attitudes, it is important to ask whether such universal concerns, some of which can indeed be found in authoritative scriptural antecedents, are also found in the wisdom materials discovered in the Qumran caves.

It seems appropriate to give a mixed answer to this question. On the one hand, some matters are addressed in very universalistic tones. Advice on marriage, for example, is based in matters of universal appeal discernible in Genesis 2-3. The basis of the wisdom presented in *Mysteries* lies in the created order[43]. The three so-called Meditations on Creation (4Q303-305) fall in the same category: in the few surviving fragments there is much language from Genesis 2 together with some hints of Job[44]. Likewise 4Q411, the so-called *Sapiential Hymn*, seems to be a poetic rewriting of parts of Genesis 1 and 2. On the other hand, some compositions also reflect a more particularist approach. This can be observed in the appeal to historical examples which are exclusively Israelite, in the reference to particular scriptural laws, some of which

---

42. D. J. HARRINGTON, *Raz Nihyeh*, p. 552.
43. Cf. 4Q299 5.
44. E.g., *nplwt 'l* (Job 37,14; 4Q303 3).

have been discussed above, in the appearance of the elect, and in the eschatological character of some elements in the wisdom compositions found at Qumran, not least in the Mysteries. It is difficult to discern whether the *raz nihyeh* belongs to the universalist or to the particularist outlook of the traditors of these compositions. It is clear that scriptural antecedents give permission for both universalist and particularist developments in the wisdom traditions in the non-scriptural wisdom compositions found at Qumran.

B. The Special and the Ordinary

Overall the biblical wisdom books do not contain any esoteric advice. The Book of Proverbs in particular contains some insights which can be described as distinctively Israelite, such as the description of Wisdom herself, but the advice given is with reference to everyday affairs, the ordinary.

The Qumran wisdom traditions continue this approach in many respects. *Instruction* (*Mûsār leMēvîn*) is principally constituted of such ordinary advice concerning family and business affairs, relationships with friends and the establishment of self-esteem. It is such general concerns which have made some rightly reticent to suggest that it is strictly a sectarian composition; in general it follows the trajectory of the scriptural wisdom books which are concerned with ordinary everyday matters. Yet, in addition to such everyday concerns, there is a tendency in several of the wisdom compositions found at Qumran to suggest that there is special knowledge available to the elect which will in the end separate them and their behaviour from the supporters of Belial. This esoteric knowledge confirms the notion that some of the wisdom materials in the compositions found at Qumran reflect the apocalyptic traditions of the Enoch writings more than the traditions of the wisdom schools which are more readily visible in the wisdom books which later became biblical. This is implied in the *Mysteries* text in the way in which it is the unlawful behaviour of the nations which is the sign that the eschatological vindication of the righteous is near. More especially it is the character of 4Q298, the instruction for all the sons of dawn. Here there are some traces of scriptural phraseology, not just from wisdom books but also from the prophets, but such phrasing does not control the discourse in any way. The edition of 4Q298 by S. Pfann and M. Kister is revealing for how little recourse is made to scriptural antecedents for the better understanding of the partially extant phrases of the manuscript[45].

---

45. S. J. PFANN and M. KISTER, *4Q298*.

In some compositions the two aspects of the ordinary and the special are woven together. Thus, for example, in the very composite work, *The Ways of Righteousness* (4Q420-421) which is extant in two copies, some material is squarely in imitation of biblical proverbial maxims whilst other sections are clearly to do with the practices of those who are sectarian initiates (4Q421 1a i). In all these wisdom compositions found at Qumran there is more going on than the straightforward development of scriptural ideas.

C. *The Rich and the Poor*

We have earlier noted that in more than one wisdom composition found at Qumran there is a standard view on reward and punishment. The righteous are rewarded and the wicked punished; such, it is claimed, is self-evident from scriptural examples. This scriptural trajectory in wisdom is taken up eschatologically in some of the compositions found at Qumran: the reward for righteous behaviour and faithfulness will come in the future end-time.

The viewpoint that the righteous are rewarded in this life is challenged within the biblical wisdom traditions for being too simplistic. The eschatological reworking of the traditions concerning reward may account for why a text such as *Instruction* (*Mûsār l^eMēvîn*) should have several pericopae addressed directly to the poor[46]. The advice is offered to them in particular. Beyond recognizing that the term 'ebyon became a quasi-technical designation for the community at Qumran or the wider movement of which it was a part, it is important to ask to what set of biblical traditions interest in the poor directs the modern reader. What tradition is developed here? Put another way, the majority scriptural view that good behaviour leads to long life, children and especially wealth does not pervade all the wisdom compositions found at Qumran, not even all the non-sectarian ones. There is thus an element in some of the wisdom compositions found at Qumran which openly subverts models of reward found in scriptural antecedents.

D. *The Righteous Sufferer*

Above all it is the Book of Job which addresses the problem of the righteous person who suffers. Together with a range of compositions, such as the Hodayot, several of the wisdom texts found at Qumran seem to take up the same theme. Two passages can be mentioned in particular.

---

46. As D. J. HARRINGTON has noted: *Wisdom Texts from Qumran*, pp. 45-46.

Firstly, in 4Q541 there seems to be the portrayal of one or more future priests, perhaps concluding with an eschatological figure who is put to death but through whose death there is much rejoicing[47]. These priests are wise instructors; of the one described in the extensive fragment 9 we learn that he has wisdom and will make expiation for all the sons of his generation and he will be sent to all the sons of his people. But he will be reviled and persecuted. In several places the language of the servant songs of Isaiah is used to highlight the role of the priest figure. For example in the very small fragment 6, line 3, it seems that there is a Hebraism: in this Aramaic text the word *mk'wbykh* is borrowed from Isa 53,3-4, "a man of sorrows/burdens" (*mk'bwt*), "he has carried our burdens" (*mkw'bynw*)[48]. In some other places there may be similar echoes of Isaiah. It seems as if one of the aspects of the portrayal of these wise priests who endure suffering and persecution is modelled on the suffering servant. Here there is a transforming adaptation of a representative penitent into the classic figure of some wisdom literature, the righteous sufferer who in the end is vindicated. The transformation is thoroughgoing as the line of figures are clearly priestly, an aspect not discernible in the scriptural antecedents.

Secondly, in 4Q525, the so-called *Beatitudes* text, the principal fragment contains a set of beatitudes the last one of which is directed at the man who has attained wisdom:

> Blessed is the man who has attained wisdom and walks in the law of the Most High. He directs his heart towards her ways, and restrains himself by her corrections, and always takes delight in her chastisements. He does not forsake her when he sees distress, nor abandon her in time of strain. He will not forget her [on the day of] fear, and will not despise [her] when his soul is afflicted. For always he will meditate on her, and in his distress he will consider [her].

The opening phrasing of this closing beatitude has echoes of Psalm 1,1-2 and Psalm 119,1. In both those Psalms there is the use of *hlk* with *twrt 'dny* (*yhwh*). In 4Q525, as often in the scrolls from Qumran, the tetragrammaton is replaced with an alternative form of address[49]. The remaining language in this passage of 4Q525 has some echoes in the

---

47. A preliminary edition of the text is available in E. PUECH, *Apocryphe de Lévi*, pp. 449-489; now labelled 4QApocryphe de Lévi[b]? ar: see E. PUECH, *Qumran grotte 4. XXII*, pp. 225-226. The overlap between the genres of testamentary and sapiential literature justify use of this text in this context.

48. On this aspect of the composition see G. J. BROOKE, *4QTestament of Levi[d](?)*.

49. One might consider this a matter of preserving the sanctity of the divine name, a tendency already visible in Neh 10,30 which speaks of walking in the *twrt 'lhm*, "the Law of God".

Hodayot. Overall in terms of persecution there is no development directly from a scriptural model, such as Job. Rather the sufferings are more akin to those who experience eschatological anguish and affliction according to Daniel 12, a chapter which itself concludes with a macarism.

E. Personified Wisdom

Last but not least, mention should briefly be made of the personified wisdom motif. The portrayals of Wisdom in Proverbs 1-9 and Job 28 are assumed and built on in various ways in several of the wisdom texts found at Qumran. These developments are all non-sectarian, either as elements within non-sectarian compositions[50] or as parts of non-sectarian sections in evidently composite works such as 4Q421 *Ways of Righteousness*. One should resist such descriptions as T. Elgvin's labelling of Wisdom as a "hypostatic concept"[51], but acknowledge that the texts from Qumran show the richness of the traditions which increasingly come to associate wisdom personified with the Law as in the approximately contemporary Ben Sira 24.

VI. CONCLUSIONS

In conclusion, the use of earlier scriptural traditions in the wisdom texts found at Qumran is very diverse. In some instances there is extensive dependence on the presentation of wisdom instructions, as on Proverbs 22,17-24,22 in *Instruction (Mûsār l ͤMēvîn)*. In other places little or no dependence can be discerned beyond the occasional scriptural phrase which is worked into a new expression.

Most of the use of scripture in the Qumran wisdom texts is a matter of allusion; sometimes that may be best understood by paying attention to the original context, sometimes not. As to the rest, some exegesis can be broadly termed halakhic, the juxtaposition of two or more passages to make new rules; some is exhortatory, recalling past scriptural events to provide motivation and example; some is narrative, in which scriptural stories are assumed for providing the ethos of a particular ethical stance; some is clearly directed to assert that scripture alone is not sufficient for those who would lead a wise life.

50. 4Q185; 4Q525 2 ii 2-9; 4,6-13; 11QPs^a 154,5-15; Sir 51.
51. T. ELGVIN, *Ways of Righteousness*, p. 190.

In the wisdom compositions, such as *The Ways of Righteousness* which reflect aspects of sectarian idiom, and in some measure also in their immediate predecessors in the Qumran library, the scriptural wisdom traditions are made eschatological: here is the stress on what is particular in the texts, the justification for the suffering of the righteous in the community, the attention paid to the poor. Throughout, however, there remains a concern with the overall scripturally endorsed order of the cosmos as set up by the God of knowledge. It is that order to which individuals are summoned, in which they are encouraged to live out their righteous lives, and in whose restoration they will ultimately participate.

Dept. of Religions and Theology George J. BROOKE
University of Manchester
Oxford Road
Manchester, M13 9PL
England

V
THE WISDOM TEXTS FROM QUMRAN AND ANCIENT JUDAISM

ENOCH AND THE BEGINNINGS OF JEWISH INTEREST IN NATURAL SCIENCE

THE JEWS AND NATURAL SCIENCE

In his 1995 monograph *Jewish Thought and Scientific Discovery in Early Modern Europe* David Ruderman discusses the question of Jewish attitudes towards and involvement in science[1]. There is, as has long been noted, an intriguing problem here. Jews in modern times have made a massive contribution to the advancement of the natural sciences, a contribution out of all proportion to their numbers. How is this striking fact to be explained? Are Jews genetically predisposed to be good at science, as some have seriously but implausibly argued. Or does the explanation lie in cultural factors, such as the nature of traditional Jewish education or traditional Jewish love of learning? Or are social forces at work – the desire to escape from exclusion and gain acceptance and influence in the host society which has come to accord great prestige to scientific knowledge? Ruderman problematizes the question by showing that Jewish involvement in science did not begin with emancipation in the nineteenth or early twentieth centuries but can be traced back to the early modern period. In the sixteenth and seventeenth centuries Jews were already studying science, especially medicine, and their numbers were sufficiently large as to have had an impact on Jewish religious thought[2]. As a preface to his study of the early modern period, Ruderman briefly surveys Jewish attitudes towards nature in the Middle Ages but makes no serious attempt to investigate Jewish engagement with science any earlier in Jewish history.

In the present paper I shall attempt, somewhat speculatively, to carry the story further back. I realise that in doing so I run considerable risks. The enterprise may seem grossly anachronistic, and I may project modern debates and modern ideas on to earlier and very different societies.

---

* The present paper benefited not only from the comments of the members of the Tübingen Seminar on the Wisdom texts from Qumran, but from criticisms offered by colleagues at Yale (Dale Martin, Harry Attridge and Abe Malherbe), when a version of it was given there.

1. RUDERMAN, *Jewish Thought*.
2. A case in point is the sixteenth century Italian scholar Ovadiah Sforno whose philosophical and medical training are very evident in his Bible commentaries.

Science today and the society in which it functions look nothing like science or society in the Middle Ages or in antiquity. I am prepared to run that risk. As an historian I am still wedded to the construction of grand narratives. I also hold that analogy is one of the historian's fundamental tools: the past, if it is understandable at all, is accessible only through analogy, through a risky but inevitable process of "translation" into narratives that make sense in terms of our own experience of the world. And, I would suggest, it is no less meaningful to talk about Jewish science, or the lack of it, in antiquity than it is to talk about Greek or Babylonian science, both of which have been the subject of extensive investigation[3].

Before we go any further we need a working definition of "science". For our present purposes it is vitally important to avoid one that is too theoretical or exclusive. Since the collapse of Newtonian physics, the supreme exemplar for two centuries of a scientific view of the universe, the nature and definition of science have become philosophically problematic. I am not interested here in this philosophical debate[4]. I am writing as an historian, and as an historian it seems to me obvious that science is a social construct which changes over time. History is littered with sciences – alchemy is a case in point – which have become discredited, and which today are excluded from the scientific curriculum. In the past, however, these subjects were most assuredly regarded as sciences. Though not "true" in the sense that contemporary science is "true", they are "science-like": they display the assumptions and the articulation of scientific disciplines and in some cases can be shown by historians to have contributed directly to the rise of modern science. For our present purposes we can identify 'science' wherever we find a strong interest in understanding how the physical world works, provided three simple conditions are fulfilled: (1) There is an explicit or implicit assumption that nature is regular and is governed by immutable laws which are accessible to the human mind. (2) An attempt is made to produce a rational model of the physical world which reduces the bewildering complexities of natural phenomena to a small number of underlying primary elements, or to the operation of a small number of fundamental laws. (3) Explicitly or implicitly, a significant element of direct observation of the physical world is involved.

In attempting to trace the earlier history of science two points should be borne in mind. First, experiment plays a major role in modern science. Hypotheses are formulated and experiments devised to test them. In early science, however, experimentation of this type seems to

---

3. See, for example, LLOYD, *Science*.
4. It is clearly summarized in FISCH, *Rational Rabbis*, pp. 1-39.

have been rare. It would be a mistake, however, to suppose that if such experimentation is absent, then science is absent. Such an argument has been used in the past to deny that the Greeks possessed any science in any serious sense of that term. Though planned experimentation in the modern sense was comparatively rare, science in antiquity was, to varying degrees, empirically based (one thinks of how the Babylonians' painstaking observations over many centuries of the motions of the heavenly bodies formed the bedrock of early astronomy). And, indeed, I doubt that we can meaningfully talk of science unless there is an element of direct observation of nature. Any proposed scientific model should be, however inadequately or obliquely, either inferred from observation of natural phenomena, or verified by such observation. Second, it may be difficult to distinguish sharply in pre-modern times between science on the one hand and technology and magic on the other. Craftsmen and magicians are, like scientists (at least applied scientists), concerned with exploiting the forces of nature. Technology in the past, as today, has been a great promoter of scientific discovery, but there is surely a distinction to be drawn between the craftsman and the scientist: both may be interested in knowing how things work, but it is the scientist who tries to explain why they work as they do, who formulates theories of nature. The scientist and the magician can be distinguished in a similar way. Magic may seem at times to be predicated on rational assumptions about the mechanistic workings of nature, which the magician can influence by employing the right verbal formula or *materia magica*, but magical texts do not make these assumptions explicit or create a model of nature to make their magical praxis intelligible. The prescriptions of a magician to cure an ailment, even when they contain proposals which are sensible and which may prove efficacious, are an intellectual world away from the rational medicine of a Galen. The scientist, the craftsman and the magician are distinguishable, and were distinguished even in antiquity, though one may merge imperceptibly into the other[5].

SCIENCE AND THE TALMUDIC MIND

Jewish involvement in science is not hard to document in the Middle Ages and even in Gaonic times, when Jews engaged seriously with

---

5. In other words I am using 'science' in broadly the sense in which it is used by standard historians of science such as SARTON, *Introduction*, THORNDIKE, *History*, and NEEDHAM, *Science*. If their enterprise is valid, then, *si parva licet componere magnis*, so is mine.

Islamic philosophy[6]. But can we find evidence for scientific interest among Jews in the preceding Talmudic age? Jacob Neusner has argued that not only is science absent from classic Rabbinic Judaism but more fundamentally the logic of Rabbinic discourse, as exemplified in the Mishnah, the foundation document of Rabbinism, is incompatible with scientific modes of thinking and discovery[7]. The implication seems to be that Rabbinical Jews, by their very mental formation, were inhibited from doing science. Menachem Fisch has responded to Neusner's claim by arguing that, on the contrary, the rationality that lies behind the modern scientific enterprise is highly congruent with the rationality of Talmudic discourse[8]. The argument is interesting, but far too essentialist for my purposes[9]. If we descend from this highly abstract, theoretical plane, and look pragmatically at historical realities, we find that there is, in fact, considerable evidence for interest in the workings of nature in Rabbinic literature and Rabbinic society, and, indeed, at a theological level statements occur in the classic Rabbinic sources which can be taken as encouraging and legitimating such an interest. Certain factors may, indeed, have inhibited serious Rabbinic involvement in science. Cosmology (*Maʿaseh Bereʾshit*) was famously declared to be an esoteric subject, which could not be expounded before two people (that is to say

---

6. One thinks of Levi ben Gerson with his Jacob's Staff, his modified astrolabe and his criticisms of the Ptolemaic model of planetary motion, or of Abraham ibn Ezra with his interests in mathematics and astrology. For an excellent overview of Jewish science in the Middle Ages see LANGERMANN, *Science*. Further, SINGER, *Science* with the postscript by GOLDSTEIN, *Astronomy*. Further bibliography may be gleaned from RUDERMAN, *Jewish Thought*, pp. 375-82.

7. NEUSNER first published his views in the pamphlet *Science in Judaism* and then in a modified form as *Science in the Mind of Judaism*. It is hard to see how the position adopted there squares with his later book *Philosophy* in which he argues that "the method and the message of the Mishnah fall into the classification of philosophical methods and messages of the Greco-Roman philosophical tradition. The method is like that of Aristotle; the message, congruent with that of Neo-Platonism" (p. xi). But if the rationality of the Mishnah is congruent with the rationality of philosophy but not congruent with the rationality of science, it seems to follow that the rationality of philosophy is not congruent with the rationality of science. This is surely a paradoxical conclusion, questionable both in terms of history (which has never sharply differentiated between philosophy and science) and in terms of logic. See further his *Jerusalem and Athens*. FISCH also notes this problem with Neusner's position (*Rational Rabbis*, p. 197).

8. FISCH, *Rational Rabbis*.

9. I find myself very much in agreement with RUDERMAN's comment: "Although there are some truth and considerable insight in their [NEUSNER's and FISCH's] positions, neither offers, to my mind, an adequate historical explanation of the dynamic and complex interactions between science and Judaism. Such theoretical-typological discussions tend to reduce reality to a single categorization or abstract definition, flattening the differences of specific times and places into homogeneous, immutable and predictable entities called science and Judaism" (*Jewish Thought*, p. 4).

it could only be studied and taught one-to-one)[10]. If this injunction was followed to the letter it would certainly have hampered interest in one fundamental scientific discipline, since it is hard to see how science could have flourished in the rabbinical schools without a free exchange of ideas. There was also the so-called ban on the study of 'Greek wisdom' (*hokhmat yevanit*), which, whatever this term embraced, would surely have included Greek science[11]. Since the dominant science of the Rabbis' day was Greek, to cut oneself off from Greek science was to condemn oneself to a scientific backwater.

However, we do not know to what extent, if at all, these injunctions were observed. And, despite them, knowledge of contemporary science can be found scattered throughout the *Talmud* and related literature. Given that the *Talmud* is essentially a book of law, the quantity of this material is actually rather impressive. Take one example, about which I have written at length elsewhere – Rabbinic knowledge of dream interpretation[12]. *Bavli Berakhot* 55a-57b contains within it a substantial dreambook comparable in many ways to the *Oneirocritica* of Artemidorus Daldianus. Dream interpretation was a science in antiquity, with an extensive literature going back to Babylonia. In the case of its most sophisticated practitioners it was empirically based: Artemidorus spent a lifetime travelling around talking to professional dream interpreters and collecting data from them, which they had accumulated from contacts with their clients. Ancient dream interpretation, as Freud saw, anticipated modern psychology in much the same way as alchemy anticipated modern chemistry. The Rabbinic dreambook is not, as one might have expected, based upon the Bible, in which dream messages and dream interpretation play a significant role. It is firmly grounded in contemporary science.

And what are we to make of the *Sefer Yetzirah*? This remarkable and enigmatic little book, which may have been composed in Palestine as early as the third or fourth century CE is essentially a scientific treatise[13]. It was, of course, to become one of the foundation documents, along with

10. *Mishnah Hagigah* 2,1.
11. *Mishnah Sotah* 9,14; *Tosefta ʿAvodah Zarah* 1,20; *Bavli Menahot* 99b; *Bavli Bava Qamma* 83a. See further my essay *Problematic Categories*.
12. *Talmudic Dreambook*.
13. See DAN, *Three Phases*. The contrast between *Sefer Yetzirah* and another early Jewish cosmological work, the *Seder Rabba di-Bere'shit*, helps to point up just how "scientific" *Sefer Yetzirah* is. *Seder Rabba di-Bere'shit* offers a model of the cosmos, arranged in concentric circles, but it is essentially a symbolic model and apparently arbitrary – symmetry for theological rather than cosmological reasons; it shows no relation to the world as we experience it, or to the science of the day. In no way could *Seder Rabba di-Bere'shit* be treated as scientific.

the Hekhalot literature, of the Jewish mystical canon, but its mystical interpretation probably does not predate the late twelfth century[14]. Certainly Saadya in his influential commentary on it treats it as a straight-forward treatise on cosmology[15]. *Sefer Yetzirah* proposes essentially an atomic model of the cosmos, in which all the diverse entities of the phenomenal world are seen as different combinations of twenty-two primary elements, symbolized by the twenty-two letters of the Hebrew alphabet. The work is implicitly based on Genesis 1, in that it develops the basic assertion of Genesis that the world was created by the speech of God. God, of course, speaks Hebrew: therefore, it follows that the structure of Hebrew holds the key to the structure of the cosmos. The relationship is symbolic and metaphorical: just as the vast universe of Hebrew discourse is produced by endless combinations of the twenty-two letters of the Hebrew alphabet, so the cosmos can be seen as the product of infinitely varying combinations of twenty-two basic elements. The author of the *Sefer Yetzirah* confirms this model by finding the number twenty-two (in patterns of twelve, seven and three, corresponding to the structure of the Hebrew alphabet) running through the three domains of the cosmos – space, time and the human body. *Sefer Yetzirah* may take Genesis 1 as its starting point but what strikes the reader most forcibly about it is its independence of the Bible. It also illustrates well how thin was the partition between science and magic in antiquity. It is obvious from a close reading that *Sefer Yetzirah* is advocating more than a passive knowledge of the physical world. If one understands how God created the world, then one may be able to control nature and even create new beings. Later Jewish magic seized on this aspect of the *Sefer Yetzirah* and believed that it held the secret of how to make a homunculus, or *golem*. This may sound like hocus pocus, but it is not too far removed from the modern scientific belief that if one knows nature's laws, then one may be able to control nature and even replicate its processes in the laboratory.

We do not know who wrote *Sefer Yetzirah*, or what his relationship was towards the Rabbinic establishment of his day. There may be an allusion to the work in the *Talmud Bavli*[16]. Even if there is not,

---

14. Among the earliest to give it a mystical interpretation was the 'Unique Cherub' Circle of the Rhineland: see DAN, *Unique Cherub*.

15. All the major early commentaries on the *Sefer Yetzirah* treat it as a scientific work: see JOSPE, *Sefer Yetzira*.

16. *Bavli Sanhedrin* 67b: "Abaye said: The laws of sorcery are like the laws of Sabbath: certain actions are punished by stoning, certain actions are exempt but forbidden, and certain actions are entirely permitted. He who does a deed is stoned; he who holds the eyes is exempt, yet it is forbidden. What is entirely permitted? Such as the action of

circumstantial evidence suggests that whoever wrote the *Sefer Yetzirah* belonged to what may broadly be termed Rabbinic society. The fact that he wrote in elegant Rabbinic Hebrew points in this direction: it is hard to envisage an audience for such a treatise in third or fourth-century Palestine outside Yeshivah-trained scholars. It should also be borne in mind that *Sefer Yetzirah* was transmitted to posterity through Rabbinic channels. It seems legitimate, therefore, to take it as evidence for scientific speculation within Rabbinic culture in the Talmudic period.

There is other concrete evidence of scientific interest among Jews in late antiquity. As Raphael Patai has shown Jews were involved in alchemy, possibly from its earliest phases[17]. And they were seriously interested in medicine already in Talmudic times: this is demonstrated by the *Talmud* itself (Julius Preuss collected and analysed the Talmudic material nearly a hundred years ago[18]), and by *Sefer ha-Refu'ot* attributed to Asaf ha-Rofe, which Elinor Lieber has expended much effort in elucidating for us[19]. Whatever the deep 'logics' of the *Talmud* may be, it is simply not true as a matter of historical fact to say that Jews – even Rabbinic Jews – were totally uninterested in the natural sciences in late antiquity.

I alluded earlier to the idea that the Rabbinic worldview was not necessarily hostile to the study of nature. This comes out in a striking manner in the pericope which opens *Midrash Bere'shit Rabba*[20]. This

Rav Hanina and Rav Oshaia, who spent every Sabbath eve studying the Laws of Creation (*hilkhot yetzirah*), by means of which they created a third-grown calf and ate it".
17. PATAI, *Alchemists*.
18. *Medizin*.
19. See, for example, her excellent survey *Asaf's Book*.
20. *Bere'shit Rabba* 1,1: "*In the beginning God created* (Gen 1,1). R. Hoshaʿyah commenced [his exposition thus]: *Then I was by Him, as a nursling* (amon); *and I was daily all delight* (Prov 8,30). Amon means tutor; *amon* means covered; *amon* means hidden; and some say, *amon* means great. Amon means tutor, as you read, *As an omen (nursing-father) carries the sucking child* (Num 11,12). Amon means covered, as in the verse, Ha'emunim (*they that were clad* – i.e. covered) *in scarlet* (Lam 4,5). Amon means hidden, as in the verse, *And he concealed* (omen) *Hadassah* (Est 2,7). Amon means great, as in the verse, *Are you better than No-amon* (Nah. 3,8)? which is rendered, Are you better than Alexandria the Great, which is situated among the rivers? Another interpretation: *amon* means a workman (*uman*). The Torah declares: 'I was the working tool of the Holy One, blessed be he'. In human practice, when a mortal king builds a palace, he builds it not with his own skill but with the skill of an architect. The architect, however, does not build it out of his head, but employs plans and diagrams to know how to arrange the chambers and the wicket doors. Thus God consulted the Torah and created the world, while the Torah declares, *In the beginning God created* (Gen 1,1), *Beginning* here referring to the Torah, as in the verse, *The Lord made me as the beginning of his way* (Prov 8,22)". The *darshan* has correctly identified the basic assertion of Proverbs 8, namely that *Hokhmah* is the underlying, rational order of the universe. He simply assumes that Torah and *Hokhmah* must be identical. See further below.

pericope is attributed to Rabbi Hosha⁽yah of Caesarea Maritima, who was a contemporary of Origen and may have met and debated with the Christian sage. According to Hosha⁽yah the Torah is the blueprint of creation: 'God looked into the Torah and created the world'. Torah is the underlying principle, the *Hokhmah*, of nature. Expressed here is a deep sense that Torah and nature are congruent. But from this it is easy to argue that the study of the one is as legitimate as the study of the other, and, to pick up Fisch's point, that the study of both should be governed by the same rational procedures. Study of nature cannot on this view be inhibited by any fear of a conflict between 'revelation' and 'science', since both are *a priori* based upon the same laws. It is interesting to see how this insight works itself out later in *Midrash Rabba*. When questions arise about the workings of nature, the Rabbis sometimes find the answers in Torah, and sometimes in direct observation of nature itself[21]. Logically it is all one to them. From a modern scientific point of view this position is naive and untenable. No modern scientist would accept a revealed text as evidence for how nature works: the only valid data for understanding nature are derived from nature itself. But at least this pericope implies that nature functions according to immutable laws that are knowable, and it hints at the idea that the study of nature is as desirable as the study of Torah. The Rabbis' position may not be all that far from that of the devout scientist who believed that when discovering nature's laws he was "thinking God's thoughts after him".

ENOCH AS THE PATRON OF SECOND TEMPLE JEWISH SCIENCE

Is it possible to push the story back further still and to find an interest in nature among Jews in the Second Temple period? This brings us to Qumran. In the library of the Qumran sect, both in the sectarian texts and in writings such as the Books of Enoch and Jubilees, which the sect held in high esteem, we find a wealth of interest in the workings of nature and in modelling the cosmos. Different branches of science are represented: cosmology and cosmography, astrology and astronomy (the two disciplines were not clearly distinguished in antiquity), meteorology, calendrical science and physiognomy. The presence of physiognomy comes as something of a surprise, but it should be remembered that physiognomy was a science in antiquity, every bit as much as dream interpretation. It had a well-established technical literature going back to

---

21. See, for example, *Bere'shit Rabba* 4,4 and 6,8.

Babylonia, and in various guises (e.g. phrenology) it remained a 'science' down to the nineteenth century[22]. Like dream interpretation, the more sophisticated forms of physiognomy appear to have been based on observation of the relationship of character to physical type, and it too anticipated certain aspects of modern science, particularly in the field of psychology.

The calendar in *1 Enoch* 72 provides an instructive example of this Second Temple Jewish science[23]. It fits admirably the pragmatic definition of science which I proposed earlier. It clearly attempts to uncover the laws of nature (in this case those governing the sun's motion through the heavens during a solar year), and it provides a rather sophisticated model which integrates in a reasonably satisfactory way a number of precise observations of natural phenomena (see Figure 1). The model is based on the fundamental observation that the sun rises and sets during the year at different points on the eastern and western horizons. From the standpoint of an observer in the northern hemisphere the southernmost point is marked by the winter solstice and the northernmost by the summer solstice. The sun reaches the mid-point between these two extremes at the spring and the autumn equinoxes. The length of daylight and darkness varies according to the position at which the sun rises and sets. The further south the shorter the daylight. The minimum period of light occurs at the winter solstice, the maximum at the summer solstice. The proportions of daylight to darkness are measured on a 18 point scale (implying an eighteen hour day), so that at the equinoxes the ratios are 9:9 and at the solstices 12:6. The eastern and western horizons between the solstice points are divided equally into six matching gates. The sun rises and sets twice in each of these gates as it moves northwards and southwards along the horizons, thus giving twelve months. This division is clearly based not on the movement of the sun but on the movement of the moon, and is dictated by an attempt to fit twelve lunations into the solar year. The author seems to be aware that this cannot be done, so he varies the length of his months. Normal months are thirty days in length, but the months in which the solstices and equinoxes occur are each given an added day. The result is a solar year of 364 days.

All this may seem rather primitive and obvious, but we should not underestimate how revolutionary both in content and in method such a text must have seemed when it first appeared in Israel. 1 Enoch 72 belongs to the *Book of the Heavenly Luminaries*, the earliest section of

---

22. See further my essay *Physiognomy*.
23. See the fundamental discussion by NEUGEBAUER, *Appendix A*.

1 Enoch, and is probably to be dated to the late Persian period (around 400 BCE). No earlier text remotely similar to this in its attitude towards nature has survived in the literature of ancient Israel. And we are reasonably sure as to the origins of its doctrine: it is to be found not in earlier Jewish sources but in Babylonian astronomy. It marks the introduction of alien wisdom to Israel.

The Enochic literature contains the highest surviving concentrations of Jewish science from the Second Temple period and much of this science is linked directly or indirectly with the name of the predeluvian patriarch. Enoch is depicted as a great sage, as the fount of all scientific wisdom. Enoch received this wisdom by divine revelation: it was disclosed to him by angels or in visions. There are parallels in Egyptian, Babylonian and other early scientific traditions for presenting science in the form of revelation from the gods, and it is tempting, at first sight, to suppose that in the *Books of Enoch* this is no more than a literary convention. But there may be more to it than meets the eye. At some point in the evolution of the Enochic literature an author or redactor *must* have known that the knowledge which he was presenting was *not* disclosed by angels but had come from contemporary, non-Jewish sources. Much of it, as we have already noted, appears to have been borrowed from Babylonian science some time in the Persian period. The author or authors, however, did not choose to present their information as simply borrowed from contemporary science. The cosmology of *1 Enoch* is in many ways no more crude than the cosmologies of Anaximander or of the other pre-Socratic philosophers, yet *they* do not seem to have resorted to claims of divine revelation. One might equally contrast the attitude of the author of Genesis 1. His account of creation in its present redactional setting within the Pentateuch is implicitly claimed to be divine revelation, but, taken on its own, it makes no such claim. The author tells his tale simply and directly, and does not inform us how he knew such things. Why, then, do the authors of the Enochic literature wrap their doctrine up so comprehensively in the mantle of divine revelations and visions?

I think the answer must, in part, lie in the fact that they were consciously attempting to domesticate within Jewish tradition a body of alien wisdom. They were, at least at the outset, fully aware of the newness of their doctrine – that they were propagating ideas never before heard in Israel. It was for this reason that they insisted so emphatically that in fact they were disclosing old wisdom that was already alluded to in the venerable traditions of Israel. The choice of Enoch as the patron on whom to pin this new teaching is interesting. The brief references to

Enoch in Genesis 5 are highly suggestive and hint at a fuller story. It has long been suspected that in the form of the Pentateuch which we now have Enochic material has been edited out. Given that the P-strand of the Pentateuch to which Genesis 5,21-24 belongs is post-exilic, some have suggested that the Enochic literature may actually contain some of these excluded traditions. However, as I understand it, the dynamics of the relationship between the Enochic literature and Genesis 5 are quite different. I have argued elsewhere[24] that the relationship is essentially midrashic. That is to say, the authors of the Enochic literature are exploiting a narrative lacuna in an authoritative text as a way of legitimating new teaching. This implies a certain distance – a discontinuity – between the legitimating text and the doctrine being legitimated. Whatever Genesis 5,21-24 alludes to, it was not Enochic science.

But why precisely Enoch? Why not, for example, Adam? If antiquity was a virtue then surely the progenitor of humankind would have been an obvious choice. Adam is certainly used to validate doctrine in later pseudepigrapha. There is probably an element of opportunism in the choice of Enoch. Midrashists cannot pick and choose: they have to seize on lacunae wherever they happen to occur. But within the grand narrative of Biblical history Enoch suited well the purposes of the Enochic circles. He lay far back in time, before the Flood destroyed human life and disrupted human knowledge[25]. *And* he was older and more venerable than Moses. I have suggested elsewhere that there is something anti-Mosaic in the Enochic literature[26]. It cannot be accidental that it ignores Moses, and attributes its teaching to someone else. The earliest layers of the Enochic tradition must virtually coincide with the so-called reforms of Ezra. Whatever we may think about the historicity of the Books of Ezra and Nehemiah, they do seem to point to a successful attempt in the Persian period, possibly with Persian royal support, to reconstitute Jewish society in Judah on the basis of the Torah of Moses. That the earliest Enochic writings ignore these developments can hardly be accidental. And there is merit in the suggestion that when the Enochic writings came to be canonised into a Pentateuch, the intent was not simply to imitate the Mosaic Pentateuch, but to challenge it.

Later tradition constantly senses a rivalry between Enoch and Moses. A number of the Enochic traditions were later transferred to Moses in a

---

24. *Second God*.
25. It is also possible that he is being tacitly equated with some Mesopotamian culture-bringer, such as Enmeduranki.
26. *Second God*, pp. 117-110.

way that suggests that later writers were uneasy with the powers and authority being granted to Enoch and felt that they should be claimed for Moses. The well-known ambivalence of Rabbinic literature towards Enoch is, I would suggest, motivated by a sense that he is a rival to Moses[27]. There is no way in which one religious system can accommodate two such figures of authority. The circles which stand behind the *Books of Enoch* were, I would argue, proposing an Enochic paradigm for Judaism in opposition to the emerging Mosaic paradigm – a paradigm based primarily on science as opposed to one based primarily on law. They were innovators: they had taken on board some of the scientific thought of their day and had used it aggressively to promote a new Jewish worldview.

This analysis of the Enochic literature begins to suggest something of the profile of the shadowy group or groups that stand behind these texts. They were, in a sense, modernists. That is to say, they were intellectuals who had access to foreign ideas and were open to the scientific thought of their day. And they were prepared to integrate these novel ideas into a new form of Judaism. But the picture would be incomplete if we failed to spot a deep ambivalence in the Enochic literature towards new knowledge. This comes out in a startling contradiction that lies at the heart of the texts as we now have them. There are two great bodies of knowledge referred to in this literature. On the one hand there is the knowledge of nature conveyed by Enoch: this is good. On the other hand there is the body of knowledge conveyed by the Watchers: this is bad. It led directly to the corruption of human society, and to the catastrophe of the Flood. There is no suggestion that the knowledge brought by the Watchers was false knowledge. It was heavenly in origin and mediated by angels, just like Enoch's knowledge. The Watchers were as much culture-bringers as was Enoch. But the knowledge they brought, like the knowledge of Prometheus, was knowledge which Heaven did not want to be disclosed to humankind.

This is intriguing. How can we separate between these two types of knowledge? This brings us to another central theme of the Enochic literature – divine judgement. Side by side with the modernist science of the Enochic literature is a powerful strand of moralizing, conservative ethics. The scientific vision of the cosmos is constantly exploited to ram home the message of divine punishment for sin, and sin is defined not primarily in terms of breaches of the Sinai-covenant (as we would

---

27. See especially *Bere'shit Rabba* 25,1.

expect in a Moses-orientated worldview), but in terms of life-style, such as the use of cosmetics and jewellery. The vision of the world projected by the Enochic literature is paradoxically *both* modernist *and* reactionary. The circles which produced it saw a strong analogy between the state of society in their own times and the condition of the world before the Flood. There was the same radical corruption. The sins of the Watchers were being repeated in their day, and just as God had responded in the past to such radical evil with overwhelming punishment from which only a righteous remnant escaped, so he was about to do the same again. The world stood once more under the threat of imminent catastrophe. Just as Enoch, the preacher of righteousness, had warned the wicked in his day, so the Enochic circles were warning the wicked in their day and telling them to flee from the wrath to come.

It is noteworthy that the knowledge brought by the Watchers is strongly technological in character: 'magical medicine, incantations, the cutting of roots, and plants... the making of swords and knives, and shields and breastplates... bracelets, decorations, shadowing of the eye with antimony, ornamentation, the beautifying of the eyelids, all kinds of precious stones, and all colouring tinctures and alchemy'[28]. For all its modernism 1 Enoch has a whiff of technophobia about it: it is suspicious of technological change. I suspect that this stratum of the literature relates to a period of growing prosperity and materialism, allied to rapid technological development. The situation was not congenial to the conservative mentality of the group. I do not know whether there is anything in the archaeological or the historical record which would enable us to pin-point this time more exactly. I doubt that there is. It is all a matter of subjective perception, which may not correlate all that obviously with historical reality as we can now perceive it. But that the author or authors of these traditions were opposed to social and technological changes taking place in their society is hardly in doubt.

I have already noted that two major images of Enoch dominate the surviving Second Temple period literature – Enoch the Sage who reveals the secrets of nature, and Enoch the Preacher of Righteousness who rebukes the sins of his generation and warns of divine judgement. Corresponding to these two images are the two major themes of *1 Enoch* –

---

28. *1 Enoch* 7,1 + 8,1. I quote here the translation by ISAAC, *1 Enoch*, p. 16. Isaac's rendering "alchemy" is speculative and based on his Ms A (Kebran 9/II). The Ethiopic literally means 'transmutation of the world'. It should be noted that the third/fourth century CE alchemical writer Zosimus attributes the introduction of alchemy to the Watchers, and that Enoch came to be closely linked with alchemy through his identification with Hermes Trismegistus. See PATAI, *Jewish Alchemists*, pp. 16 and 33.

'science' and 'ethics', descriptions of the cosmos and divine judgement. The two images and the two themes are tightly intertwined in *1 Enoch*. Part of the cosmography is devoted to describing the places of punishment of the Watchers and those who follow their evil ways. A close analysis of the literary traditions leaves me in little doubt that Enoch the Sage and the Culture-bringer is earlier than Enoch the Preacher of Righteousness. Enoch was first exploited in order to validate and domesticate a body of foreign scientific knowledge. Only later – perhaps some one hundred and fifty years later – was this same Enoch the Sage transformed, for reasons which are not entirely clear, into Enoch the Preacher of Righteousness, and the Enochic traditions spun to present a sombre message of impending divine judgement. The same analysis suggests that the Watchers have also undergone a transformation. It is probable that originally they were good – heavenly messengers who descended to earth to bring mankind divine knowledge and to promote the advancement of human culture. When those cultural advances, again for reasons that are no longer apparent, came to be regarded as negative the Watchers were transformed into fallen angels, who had brought forbidden knowledge to mankind and corrupted them, and they were linked with the Sons of God in Genesis 6 who entered into illicit union with the daughters of men[29].

SCIENCE IN THE ACHAEMENID EMPIRE

Can we sketch in any more detail the profile of the group or groups that produced the Enochic literature, and relate them more precisely to their times? Most would agree that *1 Enoch* has strong links with the ancient Jewish wisdom tradition. Within that tradition two contrasting views of physical world can be found in the Persian period[30]. First there is the attitude expressed in the speeches of Yahweh at the end of the Book of Job (chapters 38-41). There Yahweh confronts Job with a catalogue of the wonders of nature. No explanation is offered as to how nature works, only a lyrical description of its mysteries. Indeed the speeches are predicated on the assumption that the ways of God in the physical world are unfathomable to the human mind; the appropriate response to them is one of humility and praise, not study and explanation: 'The Lord answered Job out of the whirlwind, and said, Who is

---

29. *Jubilees* 4,15 hints at this more positive evaluation of the Watchers.
30. In general see GESE, *Wisdom Literature*.

this that darkens counsel without knowledge? Gird up now your loins like a man; for I will demand of you, and declare you unto me. Where were you when I laid the foundations of the earth? Declare if you have understanding. Who determined the measures thereof, if you know? Or who stretched the line upon it? Whereupon were the foundations thereof fastened? Or who laid the cornerstone thereof?' (Job 38,1-6)[31]. The author of these lines would surely have regarded it as futile, if not impious, to attempt to discover and to explain how nature works. The dating of the Book of Job is notoriously uncertain, but these speeches probably come from roughly the same time as the Enochic Book of the Heavenly Luminaries. The widely accepted fifth-century dating for Job would suit my present argument very well.

The second attitude towards nature is implicit in a text also dating from around the same period – Proverbs 8. There wisdom is personified as the master craftsman who assisted God in the creation of the world. The world is based on wisdom; *hokhmah*, to use the terminology of Heraclitus, a Greek near-contemporary of the author of Proverbs 8, is the Logos of nature[32] – an equation which Philo was later perceptively to develop[33]. But it is this very same wisdom which is said to reside with men, and which they are called upon to embrace and to make their own: "When God marked out the foundations of the earth, then I [Wisdom] was by him, as a master craftsman (אמון); and I was daily his delight, rejoicing always before him; rejoicing in his habitable earth; and my delight was with the sons of men. Now, therefore, my sons, hearken unto

---

31. Qohelet 3,11 is sometimes cited as evidence of scepticism towards man's ability to understand the physical world: את הכל עשה יפה בעתו גם את העלם נתן בלבם מבלי אשר לא ימצא האדם את המעשה אשר עשה האלהים מראש ועד סוף, but the text is a well-known crux. The NRSV probably correctly conveys the sense: "He has made everything suitable for its time; moreover he has put a sense of past and future into their minds, yet they cannot find out what God has done from the beginning to the end".

32. See, e.g., DIELS-KRANZ[11] Frgs 1, 2, 50 and 114, with the commentary of KIRK, *Heraclitus*, pp. 32-71: Frg. 1: "Of the Logos, which is as I describe, it men always prove to be uncomprehending, both before they have heard it and once they have heard it. For although all things happen according to this Logos, they [men] are like people of no experience, even when they experience such words and deeds as I explain, when I distinguish each thing according to its constitution and declare how it is; but the rest of men fail to notice what they do after they wake up, just as they forget what they do when asleep". Frg. 2: "But although the Logos is common the many live as though they had a private understanding". Frg. 50: "Listening not to me but to the Logos it is wise to agree [ὁμολογεῖν] that all things are one". Frg. 114: "Those who speak with sense must rely on what is common to all, as a city must rely on its law, and with much greater reliance: for all laws of men are nourished by one law, the divine law; for it has as much power as it wishes and is sufficient for all and is still left over" (translations by KIRK).

33. Philo's Logos is indebted not only to the Platonic Logos but to the ancient Hebrew concept of Wisdom.

me: for blessed are those who keep my ways. Hear instruction, and be wise" (Proverbs 8,29-33). It would not be hard to deduce from this passage, though the text does not explicitly do so, that it is perfectly possible, legitimate, and, indeed, desirable to study the wisdom that fashioned the world.

The circles that inaugurated the Enoch tradition took the Proverbs 8 line. They were as impressed as the author of Job by the wonders of nature, but they saw this as no bar to studying or to explaining how nature worked. They had, as Isaac Newton would have appreciated, the attitude of the true scientist: awe before nature, but at the same time an irresistible urge to probe its mysteries, and when the mystery is explained, the awe is not dispelled but only deepened. The circles that stand behind *1 Enoch* seem to have emerged in Israel in the later Persian period. Their science, as we have already noted, appears to have been drawn largely from Babylonian sources. This is hardly surprising. Babylonia dominated early science, particularly the exact sciences[34], and Babylonian scientific ideas were certainly transmitted westwards to the Greeks, and, as *1 Enoch* and related texts make clear, to the Jews.

This westward transmission of Babylonian ideas would have been facilitated by the political and cultural conditions that prevailed under the Persian Empire. It is surely highly significant that the language of the Enochic traditions is Aramaic. This fact is usually not paid the attention it deserves. In the fifth or early fourth century BCE in Judah it was probably something of an innovation to write a work such as the *Book of the Heavenly Luminaries* in Aramaic. Aramaic was, indeed, spoken by many in post-exilic Judah (though not precisely the Aramaic of *1 Enoch*, which is in a high, literary register), but Hebrew was by no means dead, and it remained unquestionably the language of literature. The reason for the Aramaic is quite simple: Aramaic was the *lingua franca* of the Persian Empire for administrative and diplomatic purposes; and it probably functioned as the language of international culture as well. It was in Aramaic that the Enochic circles received the Babylonian scientific traditions; it was in Aramaic that they preserved them. The ideas were new in Israel and Hebrew as yet lacked a technical, scientific vocabulary in which to express them. An analogous situation arose in the early Middle Ages, when Jews began to write in Arabic, not so much because it was the vernacular, but because it was the language of high culture and science, and Hebrew had yet to develop a scientific vocabulary. But the Arabic scientific literature which the Jews

---

34. See NEUGEBAUER, *Sciences*.

read, was not, at least initially, transmitting *Arabic* ideas, but rather *Greek* ideas in Arabic dress.

The Enochic circles were obviously well educated: they had mastered literary Aramaic and they had access to foreign literature. Most likely, therefore, they belonged to the scribal and priestly classes in Jerusalem. They seem to have retained some sort of existence over a considerable period of time, and to have continued to work on and develop the Enochic traditions. That development, as we have noted earlier, was increasingly in a moralising direction. The science was put directly to the service of religion, to support a message of impending divine judgement. The Enochic literature was, as we know, taken up by the Qumran community, for reasons which are not immediately apparent. The Qumran community had its own sectarian view of the world, focused sharply on a model of time which portrayed nature as moving purposefully towards a climactic final conflict between the cosmic principles of light and darkness (a notion very probably indebted to Persian thought). The message of impending catastrophic judgement in the Enochic literature was doubtless congenial to them in a general way, but there is little sign of the detailed Enochic cosmographies playing a central role in sectarian thinking.

The standard explanation of Qumranian interest in Enoch is that the Qumranians, in opposition to the Jerusalem priesthood, had adopted the Enochic solar calendar, and needed both the Enochic science and the authority of the Enochic literature to sustain its position. However, this view is not without problems. It is likely that the Enochic 364-day solar calendar did, originally, represent an attempt to reform the Jewish calendar, in accordance with the best science of the day. It is possible that the new calendar was presented as a way of living more in accord with the laws of nature and of God. But, of course, the calendar does not work, and it would not have taken long for people using it to notice that it does not work: without correction it should have been obvious within thirty years that it was badly out of synch with nature. And in a community that may have lasted almost two hundred years, the discrepancy would have become glaring and disastrous. The calendar may have been retained as an ideal model of time – a kind of model not unknown to modern science. It may have come to represent how time ideally should run, and perhaps would run in the future, when the natural order was no longer disturbed by evil. It is, of course, possible that as a community of scholars, the Qumranians valued the Enochic texts for their own sake as learned, and, indeed, edifying literature, without being too deeply influenced by them. But the simplest explanation is surely that Enoch features at Qumran because the circles who founded Qumran were linked in some way to the circles that studied the Enochic tradition. Enoch was part of their intellectual baggage. The Jerusalem Temple in the Second Temple period was probably a locus not just of ritual, but of a vigorous intellectual life, and may have housed a school or schools. This should, in principle, cause no surprise: great temples had from hoary antiquity been centres of learning in the Near East. Qumran was founded by renegade Jerusalem priests. The founders of Qumran were associated with the school, or the circle, in the Jerusalem Temple which had preserved and studied the Enochic literature, and they brought copies of the texts with them from there to Qumran.

Be this as it may, if my analysis is even half correct, then it points to a rather interesting conclusion. Sometime in the late Persian period, say around 450-400 BCE, under the influence of Persian and, ultimately, of Babylonian ideas, Jews for the first time became interested in producing scientific models of the workings of the natural world. Though to some extent anticipated by the simplified, largely demythologized account of the origin of the world in Genesis 1 and by the assertion that behind the natural order lies a *hokhmah* accessible to the human mind in Proverbs 8, the approach to nature displayed in the Enochic *Book of the Heavenly Luminaries* is unprecedented in Jewish literature. It seems to mark a turning-point in Jewish intellectual history – the emergence, for the first time, of what might properly be called a scientific attitude.

One might compare the analogous intellectual revolution which had taken place about a hundred years earlier in the Greek world, under the influence, possibly, of similar intellectual stimuli. I refer to the rise of the Ionian school of Greek philosophy and science. The Ionians too produced new, rational models of the cosmos – models little more sophisticated than those of the Jewish Enochic circles, but which in the *Heilsgeschichte* of western civilization are traditionally seen as the beginnings of Greek, and indeed of European, science. In both cases – the Jewish and the Greek – the new models of the universe marked a qualitative break from pre-existing mythical and epic pictures of the world. In the case of the Greeks those earlier pictures were to be found in Homer and in Hesiod; in the case of the Jews they were enshrined primarily in the opening chapters of Genesis. In both cases some reference was made in the new models to the old mythical ideas. This is certainly the case in *1 Enoch* which, at least in its present form, bears a loosely exegetical relationship to Genesis 1, but there seem to have been allusions to the traditional cosmogonies in the Ionian cosmologies as well.

The question of eastern influences on the Ionians is controversial, but in the wake of the 'orientalizing revolution'[35] it is now widely acknowledged that external ideas played a significant role in the development of Ionian thought[36]. The source or sources of those ideas is not entirely clear. The Greeks themselves looked to Egypt, but modern scholarship points more emphatically to Babylonia and Persia. The Ionians are unlikely to have known much about Persian ideas before 540 when the Persians reached the Aegean coast. Only in the time of Heraclitus do we find more or less convincing evidence of distinctively Iranian influences on Greek thought[37]. However, the rather sharp distinctions often drawn between Babylonian, Persian, Egyptian and Canaanite thought may be misleading. The picture that is now emerging is of an increasingly internationalized culture in the Near East in the sixth and fifth centuries BCE, with a remarkably free interchange of ideas among the educated elites. This may have come about in part through migration of individuals (Martin West assigns a major role to wandering Magi[38]), but politics,

---

35. See BURKERT, *Orientalizing Revolution*.

36. For an overview of the question see HUSSEY, *Presocratics*, pp. 1-31. Though his account is generally balanced, HUSSEY still wants to reserve something unique for the Ionians. He maintains that "the core of the Milesian revolution, namely the development of a reformed theology based on general principles, and the correlative vision of a universe governed by universal law, cannot be paralleled, as yet, from anywhere outside Ionia' (p. 29)". But if the argument of the present paper is correct then a group of Jews seem to have reached more or less the same position at more or less the same time as the Ionians. HUSSEY notes the attitude towards nature in Job and shrewdly compares it with Pindar, but he misses the significance of Proverbs 8, or even of the heavily demythologized account of the origins of the world in Genesis 1, which, as we noted earlier, in itself makes no claim to prophetic revelation. HUSSEY's grasp of ancient Jewish sources is notably uninformed. He also tends to tie the Milesian revolution too tightly to the political conditions of the city-state. This seems to imply that science and philosophy can only flourish under "democracy". The Milesian philosophers were almost certainly from a rather different social background from that of the members of our Enochic circles in Jerusalem. The former seem to have been men of affairs, with no obvious religious role, whereas the latter were probably priests. But it would be wrong to deduce from this that these two groups would automatically have held fundamentally different views of the world, and that the priests could not have been rational or scientific. Nevertheless HUSSEY's willingness seriously to entertain the possibility of eastern influences on the Ionians marks a seismic shift from the older histories of the Presocratics such as KIRK & RAVEN, *Presocratic Philosophers* and GUTHRIE, *Greek Philosophy*.

37. See WEST, *Greek Philosophy*, pp. 111-202.

38. *Greek Philosophy*, chap. 7, "The Gift of the Magi". There are persistent rumours in the Greek doxographical tradition that some of the Ionian thinkers were actually themselves of "oriental" stock, but it is hard to know what credence to give to these traditions. WEST provides a wealth of oriental parallels to the Presocratics, some more convincing than others, which build cumulatively into a conclusive case. However, his historical explanation of these parallels leaves something to be desired. He is a Pan-Iranist, who paints a rather romantic picture of Magi scattering from Persia eastwards into India, where they lay the foundations of Indian philosophy and westwards into Asia Minor where they

and concomitant linguistic and commercial factors, were probably more decisive. In the sixth century the Babylonians dominated the Near East politically: that doubtless fostered trade and gave the whole region a *lingua franca*, Babylonian. When the Persians succeeded the Babylonians as the political masters, Aramaic replaced Babylonian as the *lingua franca*. This almost certainly did not mean the end of Babylonian cultural influence, since Babylonian ideas were probably carried over into Aramaic. Local intellectual elites were able to buy into this international culture by learning Babylonian and Aramaic. Greeks would have had a flying start in the case of Aramaic, given that it was written in basically the same alphabet as they had adapted for their own language.

What I am suggesting, then, is that we can identify at least two groups within this international culture, one in Miletus in western Anatolia and one in Jerusalem in Judah, which, independently of each other but influenced by the free circulation of ideas through the Levant and the Near East, developed a view of nature which within their own societies was radically new and which can for the first time be meaningfully labelled as 'scientific'. This interest in nature, inaugurated among Jews in the Persian period, continued in fits and starts down to the Middle Ages. In the Middle Ages and early modern times, as Ruderman has shown, it gathered pace. In the nineteenth century, as a result of political emancipation, many Jews again rediscovered the natural world. The result, in the twentieth century has been some of the greatest achievements of scientific thought. From Enoch to Einstein is a long and tortuous road. At times the traces are scuffed and the track almost disappears. But it looks like a road which the historian of Judaism could and should map along the whole of its length[39].

Department of Religions & Theology　　　Philip S. ALEXANDER
University of Manchester
Manchester M13 9PL
England

---

profoundly shape Greek thought. And like most writers on these subjects he ignores the linguistic question: through the medium of which language did these ideas spread?

39. Whether or not it is meaningful to talk about *Jewish* science cannot be discussed here. For the historian of Judaism the important point is the extent to which religious ideas and scientific ideas interacted in Judaism. See further PATAI, *Alchemists*, pp. 517-18.

ENOCH AND THE BEGINNINGS OF JEWISH INTEREST IN NATURAL SCIENCE   243

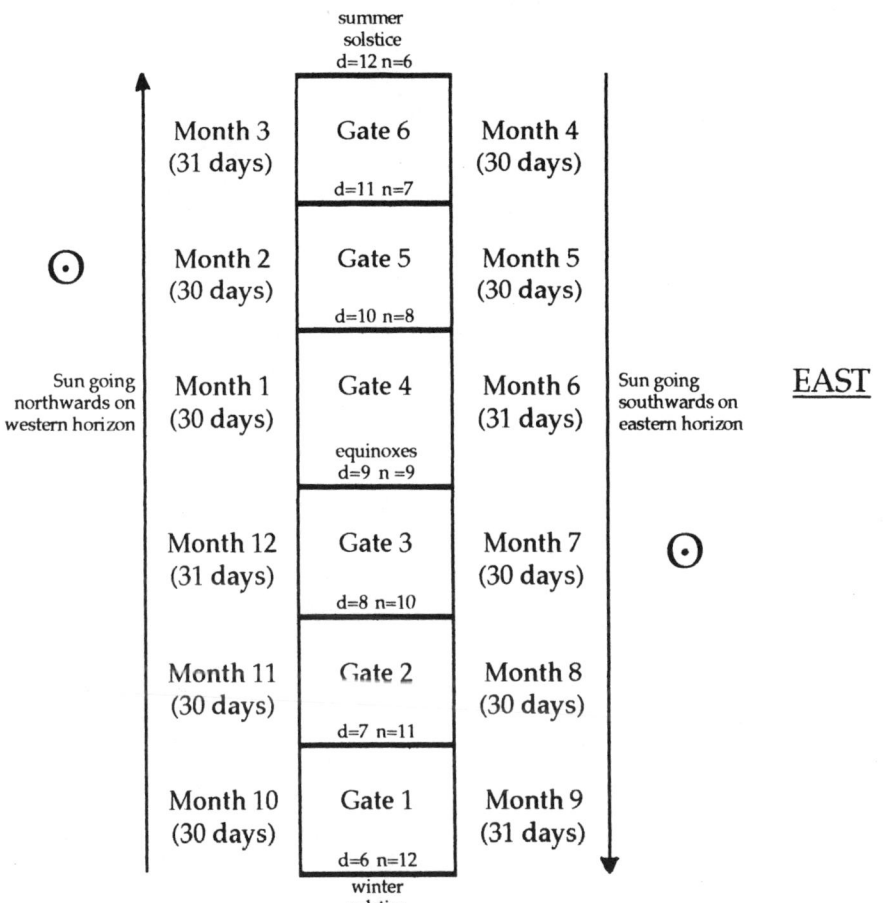

d = day   n = night

Months 1-3 = FIRST SEASON   Months 4-6 = SECOND SEASON

Months 7-9 = THIRD SEASON   Months 10-12 = FOURTH SEASON

4QINSTRUCTION AND THE POSSIBLE INFLUENCE
OF EARLY ENOCHIC TRADITIONS
AN EVALUATION

The purpose of this article is briefly to evaluate claims regarding the relationship between one of the major 'sapiential' documents that has recently come to light, namely 4Q*Instruction*, and the Enochic traditions preserved in *1 Enoch*. The fragmentary remains of 4Q*Instruction*, which has also been known under the designations *Sapiential Work A* and 4Q*Musar Lemevin*, have only recently been published in the DJD series (vol. XXXIV) in editions, respectively, by John Strugnell and Daniel Harrington (4Q415-417, 418a-b) and Torleif Elgvin (4Q423)[1]. Nevertheless, 4Q*Instruction* was already subjected to considerable scholarly attention[2] since the Hebrew texts from Cave 4 were made available in 1992 through Benjamin Z. Wacholder and Martin B. Abegg's preliminary text edition based on the early concordance of editors[3] and could be checked against photographs published, initially in 1991, by Robert Eisenman and James Robinson in their *Facsimile Edition*[4] and, more officially in 1993, by Emanuel Tov in collaboration with Stephen J. Pfann in *The Dead Sea Scrolls on Microfiche*[5]. Without question, these materials have provided a basis for augmenting our understanding of wisdom tradition and the tradents thereof during the second century BCE. Among other things, they have generated interest due to their special blend of ideas associated with "wisdom" tradition, on the one hand, with those informed by an apocalyptic worldview, on the other[6].

It is not surprising, therefore, that the content of the 4Q*Instruction* fragments has been compared with other roughly contemporary Jewish compositions which likewise combine sapiential with apocalyptic tradi-

---

1. *Qumran Cave 4*. XXIV.
2. So, in particular, the introductory discussions and analyses by Armin LANGE, *Weisheit und Prädestination*, pp. 45-92; Daniel R. HARRINGTON, *Wisdom at Qumran* and *Wisdom Texts from Qumran*, pp. 40-59. Of particular interest here are, further, the following articles by Torleif ELGVIN: *Admonition Texts*; *Reconstruction*; *Wisdom, Revelation, and Eschatology*; *Early Essene Eschatology*; *Mystery to Come*; and *Wisdom and Apocalypticism*.
3. *Preliminary Edition 2*, pp. 44-154 and 166-73.
4. *Facsimile Edition*.
5. *Microfiche Edition*.
6. So, e.g., Daniel R. HARRINGTON, *Approaches* and John J. COLLINS, *Jewish Wisdom*, pp. 226-9.

tions, such as the book of Daniel, *1 Enoch* (especially the *Book of Watchers*, the *Book of Dreams*, and the "Apocalypse of Weeks" within the so-called *Epistle of Enoch*), the *Damascus Document*, the *Community Rule* (so 1Q*Serek ha-Yahad* III,13-IV,26), and the *Hodayoth*. On the basis of such a comparison, Elgvin has reached two main conclusions about the tradition-historical context of 4Q*Instruction*. Firstly, terminological affinities have led him to maintain that 4Q*Instruction*, which does not contain any specifically "sectarian" language, influenced the language used by the Qumran covenanters in their own compositions such as *inter alia* 1QH^a XVIII, 29-30 (see 4Q418 55,10) and *The Book of Mysteries* (1Q27; 4Q299/300/301)[7]. Secondly, Elgvin argues that the similarities between 4Q*Instruction* and the Enochic traditions in the *Book of Watchers*, *Book of Dreams*, and "Apocalypse of Weeks" – not as numerous as the similarities with the Qumranic compositions – suggest "some kind of dependence between these writings"[8]. The nature of this dependence is for him one in which each of the Enochic works in question has influenced the writer(s) of 4Q*Instruction*. Elgvin's conclusions are certainly possible, but to what extent do they stand up to closer scrutiny? In particular, does the evidence provide enough of a warrant to take the dependence of 4Q*Instruction* on the early Enoch traditions for granted[9]?

The claim that different works of *1 Enoch* may be assigned a tradition-historical priority over 4Q*Instruction* seems predicated on further views not articulated as clearly by Elgvin, namely, that (a) each aspect of the influence is of a literary nature; (b) the similarities between these traditions are better explained in terms of dependence rather than on the basis of common source; and, correspondingly, that (c) each of the Enochic works must have been written before 4Q*Instruction* was composed. Herewith, a detailed discussion of the alleged areas of Enochic influence will help determine the degree to which Elgvin's hypothesis may be confirmed, refuted, or modified.

---

7. See ELGVIN, for example, in *Reconstruction*, p. 561 and *Mystery to Come*, p. 116. There is nothing, however, which specifically identifies *The Book of Mysteries* as one of the "sectarian" documents.

8. *Reconstruction*, p. 561.

9. This is the force of Elgvin's reasoning in *Mystery to Come*, p. 146: "Since 4Q*Instruction* draws upon the Enoch tradition, …". His view of this literary dependence seems less the product of analysis than a point of departure indebted to the views of George W.E. NICKELSBURG and John J. COLLINS who have argued that the origins of the Qumran community are to be found in pre-Essene circles which *inter alia* produced the *Epistle of Enoch*; cf. especially *ibid.*, p. 117 and n. 12.

(A) *Inheriting the Earth* (*1 En* 5,7 and 4Q418 81,14). According to the *Book of Watchers* (hereafter *BW*), which dates to at least the 3rd century BCE[10], it is "the righteous" (5,6) who are expected to "inherit the earth" (Cod.Pan. to 5,7 κληρονομήσουσιν τὴν γῆν[11]). What is the identity of "the righteous"? Firstly, they are contrasted with "the sinners" and "impious ones" whose lot is to be cursed (5,5.6.7). Secondly, they are also described as the "chosen" or "elect ones" (5,8-οἱ ἐκλεκτοί); indeed, according to the Greek text of Codex Panopolitanus, omitted in Ethiopic recensions[12], it is "the elect" who "will inherit the earth". There is no indication that the author(s) used any of these designations as technical terms to refer to a specific group or community[13]. Rather, the horizon is a future (though imminent) eschatological judgement and blessing: sinners will be cursed and die on account of divine wrath (cf. 5,9), while the righteous are to be given "light and joy and peace" (5,7) and "will fill out the number of the days of their life" (5,9). One may surmise that the author(s) believed that the community to which (t)he(y) belonged formed the basis of those who would receive these blessings, but there is no language here which claims that these blessings have been realised. The giving of "wisdom" (Cod.Pan. σοφία) in 5,8 is eschatological, that is, only then will "the chosen" no longer commit wrong "whether through wickedness[14] or through haughtiness".

The text in 4Q418 81,14 is more difficult to interpret because its connection to the immediate and overall context remains unclear. The line reads, [בשפ‏ל כי ארץ נוחלי כול יתהלכו .. תבו]ל ה..] ("... wor[ld].. will walk all who inherit the land, for in..["). The text strikes a promisorial tone. However, unlike the passage in *BW*, the emphasis falls on movement, perhaps of an unrestricted kind, while the inheritance of the land is itself

---

10. This date relates to chapters 1-36 of *BW* as a whole, whatever the antiquity of the sources incorporated into chapters 6-19. This depends in part on the palaeographical analysis of the earliest manuscript, 4Q201 (=4Q*Enoch*ª), to the first half of the 2nd century BCE as well as on indications therein that the copyist was working from a *Vorlage*; cf. J. T. MILIK, *Aramaic Fragments*, pp. 25-28 and 141.

11. The Greek tradition agrees here with the Ethiopic versions. Unfortunately, there is no corresponding text extant among the Dead Sea Aramaic fragments.

12. Codex Panopolitanus reads as follows: "Then there will be given (τότε δοθήσεται) to the elect ones light and joy, *and they will inherit the earth*". The omission of this sentence in the Ethiopic recensions is likely due to a translation or copying error committed on the Greek (less likely, Ethiopic) level of transmission (see the following τότε δοθήσεται).

13. The "distant generation" in *1 En* 1,2, on behalf of whom the visions are ultimately given to 'Enoch', is identified as "the elect" (1,3).

14. The Cod.Pan. ἀλήθειαν is probably a corruption from ἀδικίαν (from which the Ethiopic translations are more likely to have derived).

assumed. It is difficult to determine more precisely to whom the expression "all who inherit" refers. For clues one may first look to the closest possible antecedent in line 12: "everyone who is called by his name (is/will be) holy[..." a phrase which takes up the foregoing mention of "a fountain for all the holy ones" in the same line[15]. In line 11 the text exhorts the addressee, who is privileged to receive understanding, to "honour his holy ones" (cf. also line 1), which seems to be a precondition for receiving his inheritance from God (i.e. "before you take your inheritance from his hand ..."). It is likely, therefore, that the one addressed is included among those who inherit the earth in line 14. Elgvin distinguishes between those who will be called "holy" at the end of line 12 and those "holy ones" just referred to in lines 11-12; he argues that the former denote human members of the community (as in 4Q417 2 i 19) while the latter signify the angels[16]. This distinction allows Elgvin to assume that the co-inheritors of the addressee would, in contrast to the angels, be the community of human saints. The description of the sage's privileged position in the earlier part of 4Q418 81,1-3 would seem to support this view: after all, the sage is distinguished "from every spirit of flesh" and in this capacity he has been given "an inheritance among the sons of Adam" who have been given (as an inheritance) authority over the things God has created. And so, it might seem from this that those inheriting the earth in line 14 consist of those "sons of Adam" who, in analogy to the addressee (line 4), will have consecrated themselves for God's purposes[17] and who have been given a special responsibility as stewards of God's creation (Gen 1,26-28; Ps 8,6-8).

The main issue is, however, the degree to which angels who are blessed and honoured (lines 1, 11) might also be referred to by the expression "those who inherit the earth". Here one may note that in line 4 the sage brings honour to God by consecrating himself. He is able to do this because of his privileged position described in two parallel phrases in lines 4-5: "he has placed you as a holy of holies [for the whole]world, and among all[the e]l[im he has cast your lot". It is possible that, by extension, both the immediate addressee *and* a human community, who are "heirs of the earth", share this position among the angels. Although the language of 'blessing' and 'honouring' in the sense

---

15. On the reading "fountain", see the discussion below and n. 27.
16. ELGVIN, *Mystery to Come*, p. 120 and n. 17.
17. While a special position of the sage or teacher addressed cannot be denied, one cannot lose sight of the fact that in some sense he is also understood as representative of others.

of venerative respect[18] is here being restricted to angelic beings[19], there are no clearcut consequences drawn for cosmology: when it comes to the position of the sage, the "earthly" and "heavenly" spheres are not separated. Indeed, in 4Q*Instruction* the angels themselves can be said to "inherit", whether it be "eternal property" in 4Q418 55,12[20] or "eternal life" in 4Q418 69 ii 13. If, then, the expression "heirs of the earth" in 4Q418 81,14 designates the sage and a (righteous) human community, this inheritance may be understood against the wider context of angelology; their privilege is regarded as a kind of *participation* in the privileges accorded to angels, a feature which will later be more consistently worked out among the writings composed by the Qumran community[21].

These observations show how the notion of inheriting the earth in 4Q418 goes beyond that envisioned by *1 Enoch* 5,7, in which an analogy between the righteous human community and angels does not occur. If there is a direct relationship between these traditions, therefore, it is easier to explain the expression in 4Q*Instruction* on the basis of *BW* than vice versa. However, other than the fact that among Jewish traditions before the Common Era inheriting the earth is extant in these two texts alone[22], it remains difficult to show precisely how the text in *BW* lies directly behind an appropriation of it in 4Q418. Nevertheless, if the Enochic tradition has been formative for the language of 4Q418 81,14 at all, then its sense has been significantly altered. Whereas inheriting the earth is strictly eschatological in *BW*, 4Q*Instruction* leaves the impression that, by virtue of participation in the angelic privileges, the sage and perhaps even the community to which he belonged already anticipate this position in the present.

(B) *The Plant Metaphor* (*1 En* 10,3.16; 84,6; 93,5.10 and 4Q418 81,13; 4Q423 1-2 i 7). Unlike the motif just discussed, the "plant" or "planting" motif used as a metaphor is more widespread; it is not only attested in the Enochic literature and 4Q*Instruction*, but also among the Qumran documents (1QS VIII,5; XI,8; 1QH XIV,15; XVI,6) as well as

18. The honour accorded to human beings by 'the angels of holiness' in 4Q418 55,10 is of a different kind, referring to the ranking of humans in relation to one another according to their insight (the same phrase recurs in 1QH X,27-28).

19. Concerning the motif of directing venerative language towards angels among the *Shirot 'Olat ha-Shabbat* (4Q400 2,1-9; 4Q403 1 i 31-33) and the *milḥamah* benedictions in 11Q14, see Loren T. STUCKENBRUCK, *Angel Veneration*, pp. 150-64.

20. While the context does distinguish the angels of holiness from humanity, the latter can be characterised as 'those who inherit truth' (4Q418 55,6).

21. See n. 19 above.

22. The language next occurs in a Christian context during the late first century, i.e. in Mt 5,4.

already in the biblical tradition (esp. Isa 60,21; 61,3)[23]. Patrick A. Tiller has offered a thorough analysis of the metaphor in each of these texts. In so doing, his approach has been comparative and, unlike Elgvin, he has not ventured any claim about the tradition-historical relationship between the occurrence of the metaphor in 4QInstruction and its usage in 1 Enoch. The focus here will be to examine whether, as Elgvin suggests, the occurrence of the phrase 'eter[nal] planting' in 4QInstruction (so for example מטעת עו[נ]לם in 4Q418 81,13; another passage in 4Q423 1-2 i 7 simply reads במטעת) may be traced to the influence of Enochic tradition. In the present discussion, the texts from 4QInstruction shall be reviewed before the passages from the books in 1 Enoch are considered.

The expression במטעת in 4Q423 – it may be translated either 'through the planting/plantation of' or 'by the plant of' – is the only word preserved on the bottom line 7 from fragments 1-2. It would seem difficult, therefore, to say much about the particular meaning of the word in the text. However, the preceding lines of the text contain strong allusions to agricultural conditions based on the Eden narrative in Genesis (esp. Gen 2,9 [line 1]; 2,15 [line 2]; 3,18 [line 3]; 3,14 [line 4]; 3,16 [line 5]). Of particular interest may be line 2, in which the third person of Genesis 2,15 has been readapted in the second person: "and he has caused you to rule over it to till it and to keep it" (ובו המשילכה לעבדו ולשמרו). If the second person singular refers to the addressee, then the agricultural terminology from Genesis 2-3 is being reused for purposes of exhortation. It is not impossible, then, that the words "tree", "garden" (line 1), "thorns and thistles" (line 3) and even "plant(ing)" (line 7) are being applied metaphorically. In that case the one addressed is reminded of his responsibility to nurture those assigned to his care, whether it be a community at large in need of guidance and direction or a specific community for which he acts as a leader. Aside from a possible metaphorical use, there is not sufficient context, however, to allow for any of these meanings to be discerned with precision.

More can be observed with respect to the occurrence of מטעת עו[נ]לם in 4Q418 81,13, which is located in the same passage discussed in section A above. The "eter[nal] planting/plant/plantation" is open to several interpretations. The expression could refer to (1) the present or (2) future insight and understanding given to the "holy" community (cf. lines 2-3,14,20); (3) the present or (4) future community of "holy" ones (cf. line 12); or to (5) the community of angels (cf. 1-2,11-12). Though it

---

23. Cf. further Jub 1,16; 16,26; 21,24, and 36,6 in which the expression 'righteous plant' denotes both the historical and future, eschatological Israel in a restored state.

remains impossible to specify just what the "eternal plant(ing)" signifies, some observations from the context in relation to the possible interpretations listed may suggest a way forward. The notion of insight or wisdom, of course, plays a major role throughout the document, and in the present fragment (line 9) the addressee is told he has been given שכל along with dominion over 'his treasure' (ובאוצרו המשילכה) and "an ephah of truth" (ואיפת אמת). In this sense, he can be addressed as "you who understands" (אתה מבין, line 15; see also 4Q417 2 i 14,18; בן משכיל 4Q417 2 i 25). However, the extent of his wisdom remains incomplete, and he is reminded that further understanding will come to him as he continues to seek it[24]. Along these lines elsewhere in 4QInstruction, although 'the mystery of existence' has been revealed to the addressee (4Q416 2 iii 17-18) and there are "those who understand the mystery of existence" (4Q418 123 ii 4), the addressee is nevertheless repeatedly encouraged to investigate (הבט-4Q416 2 iii 14), observe (הגה-4Q416 2 i 5; 4Q417 2 i 2, 18), and meditate on it (הגה-4Q418 43-45 i 4), and to understand "your mysteries" (4Q417 2 i 25). The provisional, incomplete nature of this wisdom, which includes the knowledge of God's engraved design for all creation and for the periods of history (4Q418 123 ii 2-8), makes it seem unlikely that it would have been described as an "eternal plant(ation)", unless the term עולם is to be understood in an inceptive sense (i.e. a plantation which leads or grows to eternity). In the absence of any immediate indicators within the context, the expression thus probably has neither the instruction by the author(s) nor the understanding given to the addressee in view.

Elgvin interprets "eternal plant" as the "remnant community". They consist of those "holy" elect ones among humanity who are "called by his name" and to whom God has already opened "a fountain of insight" (4Q418 81,11)[25]. This community is, in Elgvin's view, not one that assumes "a clearly-defined role in history"; rather, the plant metaphor seems to provide a fitting image for a community which is regarded as "the nucleus of the future-restored Israel", much as in Isaiah 60,21; 61,3; and Ezekiel 31[26]. Although none of the 4QInstruction fragments use remnant language, the notion that מטעה represents a community of some kind does find support in the context of 4Q418 81. If the reading "fountain" in line 12 is to be accepted[27] – that is, "open a fountain (for)

---

24. So as may be inferred from line 17: 'you will understand (התבונן) exceedingly, and from everyone who instructs you (ומיד כול משלצלכה) continue to take[...]'.
25. ELGVIN, *Mystery to Come*, p. 125.
26. *Ibid.* and ELGVIN, *Reconstruction*, pp. 561-2.
27. That is, reading פתח [ב]קור (see the same expression on line 1, also in the context of blessing 'the holy ones') instead of פתח [ב]שיר, as e.g. Florentino GARCÍA MARTÍNEZ

all holy ones" – then it is possible to interpret the term in relation to the plant(ing) metaphor in line 13[28]. If the fountain is intended for "all the holy ones", then it is quite plausible that the watering metaphor may be extended to the community itself with the designation "eternal plantation". In this way, the fountain (perhaps wisdom given to the teacher addressed) is that which feeds or waters the eternal plantation (that is, the community of "holy ones").

Less clear, however, is what sort of community may be referred to. While Elgvin assumes this is a human community, Tiller is correct in noting the close alignment in lines 11-12 between the angelic "holy ones" whom the addressee is told to honour (line 11; cf. also line 1) and those "holy" ones who will be called by his name (line 12b), the latter no doubt referring to the human community[29]. It is between these references that the expression "open a fountain (for?) holy ones" occurs. While the text in line 12 certainly comprehends an elect human community, it would be misleading to suppose that the angelic are therefore not included. The phrase is ambiguous: the fountain is either *for* (implied) the holy ones or *of* the holy ones. The latter rendering would signify that the chosen community is being allowed to receive or participate in that which belongs to the angels. Indeed, in 4Q418 55, the vigilant "angels of holiness" (line 8 – מלאכי קודש) who pursue "after all the roots of understanding" (line 9) are contrasted with a lazy and sedentary humankind (line 11)[30]. It is these angels or "sons of heaven" who will (in the future) become heirs of an "eternal holding" (4Q418 55,12 - אחזת עולם) and inherit "eternal life" (4Q418 69 ii 12-13 – חיים עולם). Significantly, this contrast does not function so much to differentiate between the human and angelic spheres as to hold out the activities of the angels as exemplary[31]. In fragment 81 the watering from the fountain may thus signify the participation of the community in the activities which characterise God's holy ones in heaven. In turn, it would not be misleading to suggest that for the author(s) of 4QInstruction the "eternal plant(ing)" is, in principle, the elect community *insofar as it participates in the angelic community* in anticipation of

---

and Eibert TIGCHELAAR, *Study Edition* II, p. 872. The ligature atop the left vertical stroke of a letter following the lacunae is more consistent with a ק than with ש; *contra* STRUGNELL, HARRINGTON, & ELGVIN, *Qumran Cave 4*. XXIV, p. 308, the lacunae on line 12 and the variegated shape of the tail of ק in the manuscript make it possible to restore מ[קור.

28. This association between 'plant(ing)' and 'fountain' is proposed by TILLER, *Eternal Planting*, p. 326.

29. TILLER, *Eternal Planting*, p. 326.

30. A similar contrast is in 4Q418 69 ii 10-15.

31. The implication of 4Q418 69 ii 12-14 is that since the angels do not slacken in their pursuit of insight and knowledge, neither should the human elect.

eternal life. The association of the metaphor with the angelic "holy ones" and "sons of heaven", though in relation to a more clearly identifiable group in the present, is picked up again in the Qumran *Community Rule* (1QS XI,7-9) and *Hodayoth* (1QH XIV,12b-16a)[32].

No association between the chosen righteous and angels is, by contrast to 4Q*Instruction*, suggested in the mention of "the plant of truth" in the *Book of Watchers* (*1 En.* 10,15-16). In this passage, which preserves divine instructions to the angel Michael concerning the eschatological judgement, the destruction of the souls of the Watchers and their offspring along with the eradication of injustice and evil deeds from the earth are to be accompanied by the appearance of a "plant of truth/righteousness" (cf. נ]עבת קוטמא, 4QEnoch[c] 1 v 4); in a parallel phrase, this time is characterised as one when "deeds of truth/righteousness will be planted forever"[33]. The plant here most likely refers to the *human* community of those who survive the judgement into the future eschatological age of blessing, peace, and unhindered productivity. This interpretation is supported by verse 17, in which the Aramaic text of 4QEnoch[c] 1 v 5 uses the word קש[יטין (= Eth. and Cod.Pan.: οἱ δίκαιοι) to denote "the righteous ones", who "*will escape*" (4QEnoch[c] 1 v 5: יפלטון) and "live until they beget thousands" (so the preferable text as represented by Cod.Pan. and Eth. ms. EMML 2080; Aramaic not extant). Verses 15-16, then, are oriented around the eschatological future (i.e. the real future from the perspective of the author), much like the passage in *1 Enoch* 5 discussed above. However, as the analysis of Devorah Dimant has shown, an early editor at verse 3 of chapter 10 developed this tradition by strengthening the analogy between the eschatological era and the biblical flood and assigning the plant metaphor to a context of promises made to Noah[34]. The angel Sariel is told to instruct Noah that "*he will escape* [the coming deluge] *forever, and from him will be planted a plant, and it will stand all the generations of eternity*"[35]. The text looks

---

32. See the discussions of these texts in TILLER, *Eternal Planting*, pp. 328-31.
33. Much as the Ethiopic versions, Cod.Pan. renders the expressions, respectively, with τὸ φύτον τῆς δικαιοσύνης καὶ τῆς ἀληθείας and <τὰ ἔργα τῆς δικαιοσύνης καὶ τῆς ἀληθείας> εἰς τοὺς αἰῶνας (restoring an omission through homoioteleuton in the manuscript; cf. Matthew BLACK, *Apocalypsis*, p. 26). Since elsewhere in Cod.Pan. only δικαιο- root words correspond to passages in which the Aramaic קשט root words occur (10,17-18; 13,10; 14,1; 22,14; 32,3), it is likely that the more wooden lexical corresponding term ἀλήθεια was later added to produce a hendiadys.
34. DIMANT, *Fallen Angels*, pp. 109-112.
35. This text, not attested in the shorter Ethiopic versions, is preserved by Greek Syncellus. Although the text is poorly preserved among the Aramaic Enoch fragments, it is nevertheless consistent with it, if Milik's restorations of 4QEnoch[a] are correct; MILIK, *Aramaic Fragments*, pp. 161-2 and TILLER, *Eternal Planting*, p. 317.

forward to a plant, a righteous community, which will arise from Noah's progeny[36]. Unlike verse 16, the text of 10,3 refers to a group within the present age, perhaps one which is thought to have begun with Abraham (though he is nowhere mentioned in the *Book of Watchers*) and which already exists in the real author's or editor's day as a historical fulfillment of the promise to Noah. Whether this community is regarded as ethnic Israel as a whole or a narrower group is not clear, and there is insufficient specificity to suggest that already something like a righteous remnant is in view. In either case, it is a historical group. The editor of verse 3 applied the plant metaphor to emphasise that *this community*, however defined, is the nucleus of the one which will survive into the eschatological age in verses 16-17. The thrust of verses 3 and 16 together is thus closer than verse 16 (if taken by itself) to 4Q*Instruction*'s interest in an existing community, called 'chosen ones of truth' and "sons of his truth" (4Q418 69 ii 10; 4Q416 1,10), who will be found "favourable" when God "will wield judgement against the work of wickedness" (4Q416 1,10). However, the scope of the community in 4Q*Instruction* seems to be narrower, if "plant(ing)" there is strictly equivalent to a particular group within historical Israel[37].

The texts in *1 Enoch* 10,3.16 have been discussed in some detail because they lie in the background to the additional occurrences of the plant metaphor in the *Book of Dreams* (*1 En.* 84,6) and the *Apocalypse of Weeks* (*1 En.* 93,5.10). *1 Enoch* 84,6 occurs at the end of a petitionary prayer by Noah (vv. 1-6) that God would grant him offspring to survive the flood, while destroying those who have incurred divine anger. Noah asks that his offspring, called "the flesh of righteousness and uprightness", be established "as a plant of the eternal seed". The plant refers to Noah's progeny, but the stress may fall on the expression with the *nomen rectum* (Eth.: *zar' la'alam*). Unlike *1 Enoch* 10,3, the plant seems to *contain* an eternal seed and without being directly identified with it. In other words, if the author had a righteous community in

---

36. I am not convinced that the text refers to the existence of a righteous community 'from the time of Noah on' (so TILLER, *Eternal Planting*, p. 317) since here it is Noah, and not the 'plant', who survives the flood.

37. I accept that none of the technical language occurs in the sapiential document which would relate it to the community at Qumran. However, since the expression 'chosen ones of truth' in 4Q418 69 ii 10 does not occur anywhere in the Hebrew Bible and may well be translated '*truly* chosen ones' (so STRUGNELL, HARRINGTON & ELGVIN, *Qumran Cave 4*. XXIV, p. 283), it seems that the author(s) had a specific readership, however defined, in view.

mind at all, it is here represented by the seed within the plant rather than by the plant itself[38]. Hence there is no attempt to identify the plant as such with any particular group, whether it be historical or eschatological. Rather, what in *1 Enoch* 10,3 is represented by the plant metaphor has in 84,6 been identified with the eternal seed within the plant.

The metaphorical usage of "plant(ing)" in the *Apocalypse of Weeks* is more directly influenced by the *Book of Watchers*. The apocalypse opens in *1 Enoch* 93,2 with a summary of what it is essentially about: "concerning the sons of righteousness", "the chosen ones of the world", and "the plant of truth/righteousness"[39]. It is likely, therefore, that these three groups are not simply to be equated[40]. In the third week (93,5), "plant" (Eth. *takla*) occurs twice. At the end of this period, "a man shall be chosen as the plant of righteous judgement, and after him there shall come forth a plant of righteousness for ever". The term does not in either case refer to Noah, whose appearance in history has been assigned to the second week (v. 4 – "a man will be saved"). Since the fourth week refers to the Sinai event, there is little question that in verse 5 Abraham corresponds to the first "plant" while the eternal "righteous plant" represents Abraham's offspring. Here two differences from the usage of "plant" in *1 Enoch* 10,3 may be observed: (1) the metaphor is given two referents, whereas in 10,3 only the progeny of Noah is essentially in view; and (2) the metaphor is applied to the story of Abraham, not to that of Noah. It remains unclear from 93,5 whether the second "plant", which comes after Abraham, refers to a particular individual (such as Isaac or even Jacob[41]); to a corporate, ethnic Israel which shall last eternally through a righteous remnant; or even to a righteous remnant which only consists of the chosen ones. Adjudicating between these interpretive possibilities hinges on how the "plant" is related to the expression "forever". The word itself makes it difficult to restrict the meaning to a historical personage in the biblical history. If it is not meant to describe the "plant" as a whole, then it is unlikely that it alludes

---

38. It seems, therefore, that attempts to harmonise this text with the remaining occurrences of "plant(ing)" in *1 Enoch* are to quick to equate "plant" with "eternal seed"; so, e.g., STRUGNELL, HARRINGTON & ELGVIN, *Qumran Cave 4*. XXIV, p. 322.

39. I assume from 4QEnoch\ :sup:`g` 1 iv 12-13, which corresponds to 93,10, that the Aramaic קשׁט lies ultimately behind the Ethiopic term *sedeq* (neither Aramaic nor Greek evidence exists for this verse); cf. n. 30 above. The Ethiopic version followed by Michael A. KNIBB (*Book of Enoch 2*, p. 223) probably goes back to a hendiadys: "righteousness and uprightness".

40. As reasoned correctly by TILLER, *Eternal Planting*, p. 319.

41. See concerning the difficulties in the text and its interpretation Ephraim ISAAC, *1 Enoch*, p. 74 and n. 1; Matthew BLACK, *Book of Enoch*, p. 372; and TILLER, *Eternal Planting*, p. 321 and n. 22.

to the entire ethnic Israel, both the good and bad, but rather to a remnant therein. If, however, what is eternal describes the "plant of righteousness" itself, then the "plant" refers to a group, a "true Israel", which provides a continuous link between biblical and eschatological history.

The meaning of the second "plant" in 93,5 must take into account the seventh week given in 93,10, which is largely preserved in the Aramaic of 4QEnoch^g 1 iv 12-13. Herewith is a translation based on this text, with restorations, in turn, derived (so also Milik), from the Ethiopic: "And with its end] there shall be chosen e[lect one]s (י[תבחדון ב]חיד[ין) as witnesses of righteousness (לשהדי קשט) from the eternal plant of righteousness (נ]עבת [קשט על[מ]א), to whom shall be given sevenf[old] teaching concerning wisdom and knowledge". The "eternal plant of righteousness" is distinguished from the elect ones who are expected to be selected from it; if this plant is the same as the one which followed Abraham in the third week (v. 5), then the "plant" itself refers to Israel as a larger unit, while the chosen are those with whom the author of the apocalypse identifies, that is, the righteous community of his day. The *Apocalypse of Weeks*, then, speaks of "plant" as a broad community which, in turn, serves as the salvation historical context within which the righteous will be identified. The influence of the *Book of Watchers*, if 10,3 and 10,16 are taken together, is clear: there is in history a "plant", an "open" community, within which the eschatological, elect community will take shape.

As in the case of *1 Enoch* 10,3.16 and 84,6, therefore, the "plant" metaphor in the apocalypse does not carry the restricted sense of "community of chosen ones", much in contrast with 4Q*Instruction*[42]. Again in view of Elgvin's thesis, one would have to reason that if the latter has been influenced by the Enochic tradition at all, it is necessary to explain how the "plant" metaphor has been transformed into a designation for a community which could already be addressed as "chosen ones of truth"[43]. Rather than analysing the Enoch traditions and 4Q*Instruction* in

---

42. The similarity between *1 Enoch* and 4Q*Instruction* seems to be overstated by ELGVIN (*Mystery to Come*, p. 121), when he maintains that, "Similar to the Enochic books, 4Q*Instruction* does not ascribe to the remnant community a clearly-defined role in history as do later sectarian writings, although the designation 'eternal planting' indicates that the community is the nucleus of the future-restored Israel". Cf. further *ibid.*, p. 116: "Both works... use the phrase 'eternal planting' for the elect community (*1 En.* 10.16; 84.6; 93.5, 10; 4Q418 81.13; 4Q423 1-2.7)". Although ELGVIN's view is articulated with more nuance in his most recently published discussion (*Wisdom and Apocalypticism*, pp. 242-3), his view of 4Q*Instruction*'s indebtedness to *Book of Watchers* and the *Apocalypse of Weeks* is retained. The essential difference between these traditions, however, is that the "plant" metaphor seems to refer to a narrower community in Israel in the sapiential document, whereas it denotes a much broader unit in the Enochic tradition.

43. See n. 37 above.

terms of linear influence in one direction, another possibility presents itself: both traditions emerge as attempts during the 3rd and 2nd centuries BCE to come to terms with alternative interpretive possibilities with respect to metaphorical usage of "plant(ing)" in Isaiah 5,7; 60,21; and 61,3[44]. Whereas the Enoch texts seem to derive conceptually from Isaiah 5,7, in which God's "pleasant planting" is broadly identified as "the men of Judah", the sapiential work's narrowed usage is more in line with the passages from deutero-Isaiah[45]. Both, however, have introduced something new, namely, the explicit notion that the plant(ing) itself is somehow eternal[46]. This shared feature does not have to be regarded as evidence of influence of the Enochic upon the other tradition, but may simply be explained against the apocalyptic backdrop that informed respective attempts to come to terms with a satisfactory interpretation of Isaiah 60. The *Apocalypse of Weeks*, like 4Q*Instruction*, may have been composed within a community whose adherents understood themselves as a chosen group living penultimate to the eschatological transformation of the cosmos, but the "plant(ing)" imagery is used in a very different way.

(C) *Walking in Eternal Light* (*1 En.* 92,4; 4Q418 69 ii 14). The common phrase "they shall walk in eternal light" is added to the other similarities by Elgvin to create the impression of dependence between the Enochic writings and 4Q*Instruction*. In fact, Elgvin is convinced in this case that "[t]he discourse in 4Q418 69 draws directly upon the *Epistle of Enoch*" (i.e. *1 En.* 91-105), thus providing some evidence for the dates of composition for both documents[47].

While the phrase does in fact occur in both documents, it should be remembered that it is only extant in Ethiopic in *1 Enoch* 92,4, while preserved in Hebrew in 4Q418 69 ii 14. The text of the latter runs as follows: הלוא באור עולם יתהל[כו ("Do [they] not wal[k] in eternal light?").

---

44. See the review of these texts in TILLER, *Eternal Planting*, pp. 314-5. The possibility of the early Enochic writings and the sapiential document drawing on common biblical or exegetical traditions is not considered by ELGVIN (cf. e.g. *Mystery to Come*, p. 116).

45. The direction taken by 4Q*Instruction* no doubt paved the way for the even narrower application of the metaphor in relation to the Qumran community; cf. 1QH XIV,15; XVI,6; 1QS VIII,5-6; and XI,8.

46. Isa 60,21 announces that "all the righteous will inherit the land forever (לעולם)", but does not specify that the "shoot of his plant" is eternal as such.

47. That is, if the pre-Essene 4Q418 69 is influenced by the *Epistle of Enoch*, then it must have been composed sometime between 160 and 130 BCE, pushing the date of the *Epistle* back to the first half of the century; ELGVIN, *Mystery to Come*, p. 117. While I find the date assigned by Elgvin to the *Epistle* to be wholly plausible, I am not convinced that a tradition-historical relationship with 4Q*Instruction* ought to be used as part of the argument.

Despite the shared concept, the context differs sharply in both works. In 4Q418 69 the phrase occurs in the context of an address to the 'chosen ones of truth' (line 10), who are exhorted not to slacken in their pursuit of insight and knowledge (lines 11-12). They are challenged through a comparison with the behaviour of "the sons of heaven" (lines 12-13) – these are the angels – who, by contrast, would not admit to tiring in "the works of truth" (lines 13-14). The author then asks a rhetorical question about walking in eternal light, holding up the privileged existence of angels, who will inherit eternal life (line 13), before his readers. The phrase denotes an activity of angelic beings which the author can assume his readers take for granted. Implicit is the expectation that if the chosen ones do not tire in performing deeds of truth, they too shall "walk in eternal light". The text does not specify whether this can already be realised by the elect in the present or may be anticipated in the future age. As has been noted above, 4QInstruction has a strong emphasis on the participation of the righteous community in the activities and privileges of the angels.

Before any comparison is offered between 4QInstruction and the Enoch tradition, it should be recognised that the interpretation of the latter is anything but straightforward. The text of 1 Enoch 92,4 and its interpretation are complicated for two main reasons. Firstly, in the absence of both the Greek and Aramaic evidence for this text, the precise parallel between 4QInstruction and 1 Enoch 92,4 depends to some degree on how one resolves a text-critical problem arising among the Ethiopic versions. It is not immediately clear which readings of the Ethiopic manuscripts are to be preferred. Whereas, similar to 4QInstruction, the manuscript from Tanasee (Kebran 9/II) followed by E. Isaac[48] reads the plural, most of the manuscripts attest the singular, as followed by Michael A. Knibb and Siegbert Uhlig: "*he* shall walk in eternal light"[49]. If the subject is singular, then it may either refer to a specific figure (i.e. to a particular righteous one) or be a collective singular that denotes those who are righteous in general[50]. The second problem is closely related to the first, the identity of "the righteous one". The passage at 92,3 introduces "a righteous one" who "shall awaken from sleep"; this term continues

---

48. See in CHARLESWORTH, *Pseudepigrapha I*, p. 74. The plural reading is further supported by British Library Orient No. 485 and the Appendix to Berlin Orient Petermann II. See UHLIG, *Henochbuch*, p. 710 n. 4 c; KNIBB, *Book of Enoch 1*, p. 348.

49. KNIBB, *Book of Enoch 1*, p. 222.

50. The renderings of ISAAC and KNIBB correspond, respectively, to their translations (and, hence, implicit interpretations) of 'righteous one' in 91,10-11. BLACK (*Book of Enoch*, pp. 282 and 284) and UHLIG (*Henochbuch*, p. 710 and n. 4 b) prefer the collective singular interpretation.

to act as the referent throughout verses 3 and 4. The question is how the Ethiopic traditions may have understood the figure(s) in relation to the notion of walking in eternal light: (a) In the case of the plural reading, it is the activity of the righteous one which makes it possible for *others* to walk in eternal light. The way is thus opened up for a messianic interpretation (so Isaac). The image of being awakened from sleep in 92,3 could then refer to an initial or final appearance of the figure, perhaps in terms of his resurrection. (b) The singular reading could likewise be interpreted in relation to a special eschatological figure; the righteous one, in addition to being given power[51], would then be the same one who "shall walk in eternal light". (c) In the case of a collective singular, the righteous one denotes the righteous community who survive into the eschatological age. In this case, the image of being awakened from sleep in 92,3 would likely refer to the general resurrection of the righteous. Walking "in eternal light" in 92,4b could then be read in contrast with what immediately follows in 92,5a, according to which the destruction of sin shall occur "in darkness". Because sin will have altogether perished and vanished in the eschatological age, the righteous community will be able to live without any worry that sinning is close at hand.

None of the possible interpretations of *1 Enoch* 92,4 presents itself with the kind of tradition that would readily have given rise to 4Q418 69 ii 14. Although the *Epistle of Enoch* does elsewhere co-ordinate the righteous ones with the activity of angels in heaven (104,4; cf. 104,2), there is no reference in 92,2-5 to angels playing any particular role in the events described. It is far easier to suppose that the common phraseology and general framework of the *Epistle* and 4Q*Instruction* are to be explained by a common tradition or by (less likely) a common social milieu, rather than pressing their shared expressions into the alternatives of influence of one tradition upon the other. Even more precarious is the notion that precisely this similarity can be used to date the Enochic *Epistle* and the sapiential work in relation to one another.

(D) *The "mystery of existence"* (4Q*Instruction*) and *"sevenfold instruction"* to the eschatological community (*1 En* 93,10). In conjunction with his view that "[t]he *Epistle of Enoch* is a main source for the

---

51. At least this much can be attributed to the figure. Unfortunately, ISAAC, despite acknowledging some of the variants among the manuscripts, offers a thoroughly messianic translation of 92,2-5. And so, he adopts the reading in 92,4 that has the figure 'judging' (with Tanasee 9; Abbadie collection no. 35; and EMML 82), whereas otherwise the verb is 'to be' (KNIBB and UHLIG translate 'live').

compiler of *4QInstruction*"⁵², Elgvin identifies the phrase רז נהיה ("mystery of existence") which occurs throughout the sapiential document, with the "sevenfold wisdom and learning" in *1 Enoch* 93,10 (so 4QEnoch^g 1 iv 13) to be granted to the elect at the dawn of the eschatological age. It is not explicitly said that the "mystery of existence" is written. However, it can be the object of study (e.g. 4Q416 2 iii 14; 4Q417 2 i 6; etc.). Moreover, closely linked with this "mystery of existence" in 4Q*Instruction* is a "book of meditation" (cf. 4Q417 2 i 13-18 // 4Q418 43-45 i 10-14), also called a "book of remembrance", which God "has not yet given to the spirit of flesh". This book seems to be contrasted with "a statute engraved by God for all the iniquity of the sons of perdition" (perhaps the Torah already revealed at Sinai; 4Q417 2 i 17). It is a heavenly book, "written before him [God] for those who keep his word" (4Q417 2 i 16-17)⁵³. If this book is related at all to the "mystery of existence", an identification that is not explicitly made, then 4Q*Instruction* may have in view the full disclosure of the ethical and cosmological order that God has determined for all creation, the basis upon which the author's teaching is already founded. Such a notion of a heavenly book designed exclusively for the discerning righteous and which is distinguished from the Torah revealed at Sinai comes close indeed to the "wisdom and learning" to be given the elect in *1 Enoch* 93,10, while accessibility to wisdom is possible in the meantime when the righteous investigate, contemplate, and meditate on the "mystery of existence".

Elsewhere, in the *Epistle of Enoch*, the patriarch claims to have read "the tablets of heaven", first in the summary introduction to the Apocalypse of Weeks (93,2) and, secondly, in advance of assuring the righteous of their rewards and sinners of their punishment (103,2). These tablets are to be distinguished from the instruction designated for the chosen in 93,10. Their content, which concerns the ultimate fate of the righteous and the wicked, is being already made partially available through the *Epistle* itself, while the "sevenfold instruction", hidden from humanity in this age, is reserved *in toto* for the elect. Unlike the 'mystery of existence' in the sapiential document, there is no sense in the *Epistle* that the eschatological teaching in 93,10 is already being disseminated, unless it corresponds directly to the tablets seen by the patriarch. Thus there is no specific correlation between the sevenfold instruction in

52. ELGVIN, *Mystery to Come*, p. 138.
53. ELGVIN, *Mystery to Come*, pp. 141-3. Although there is considerable room for dispute concerning the terms הגי ("Hagy" or "meditation") and שית (a proper name [Seth?] or "perdition"), the contrast between a fully disclosed law and one that will only be revealed to the righteous elect ("those who keep his word") seems sufficiently clear.

1 Enoch 93,10 and the רז נהיה since the former does not actually come to the righteous in this age while the latter is already part of the sapiential instruction itself. It may therefore be misleading for Elgvin to have suggested a simple identification of the "mystery of existence" with the consistently eschatological instruction of the Seventh Week. Nevertheless, the sapiential work and *Epistle of Enoch* make room for motifs, respectively, which contain a notion of wisdom remaining hidden until the end (the "book of meditation") and being passed on in this age by Enoch to his progeny (the "tablets").

Conclusion. The present review of evidence adduced by Elgvin in favour of a literary relationship of dependence between *1 Enoch* and 4Q*Instruction* confirms significant parallels that demonstrate the usefulness of comparison between the two traditions. It is not impossible that the Enochic traditions have exerted an influence on ideas found in the sapiential document. At the same time, however, the specific claim that 4Q*Instruction* drew directly on the Enochic tradition in formulating its distinct ideas is difficult to substantiate. In particular, it is not clear that the differences can be adequately explained by mutation of a borrowed idea. Moreover, the possibility that these traditions were both shaped by a common tradition-historical milieu has not been given sufficient consideration. Given the differences between the Enochic complex of traditions and those preserved through 4Q*Instruction*, it seems unlikely that both derive from a sociologically continuous group which expressed itself in various or evolving ways. More plausible is the possibility that, in addition to the Book of Daniel, we have to do with a growing body of sources extant from the 2nd century BCE whose ideas were able to cross-fertilise as their distinct forms of apocalyptic wisdom took shape.

Department of Theology
University of Durham
Durham DH1 3RS
UK

Loren T. STUCKENBRUCK

TWO EARLY JEWISH APPROACHES TO WISDOM
SIRACH AND QUMRAN SAPIENTIAL WORK A

The *Book of Sirach* is the most extensive witness that we have for early Jewish wisdom[1]. The Hebrew original was composed at Jerusalem in the early second century B.C. (ca. 180) by "Jesus son of Eleazar son of Sirach" (50,27). It was translated into Greek by the author's grandson in Egypt about 117 B.C. In its traditional form it consists of fifty-one chapters – a very large book and so a treasure of information about wisdom teachings in second-century Judaism.

The Qumran text known as Sapiential Work A (known alternatively as 4QInstruction or *Mûsār lĕMēbîn = MLM*) is also a large wisdom text[2]. It appears in fragmentary form in six (or more) Hebrew manuscripts (1Q26, 4Q415, 416, 417, 418, 423). The manuscripts are Herodian in their script, and the fact that six copies of the work were found in the Qumran library indicates that it was regarded as important there. Although it shares some vocabulary and concepts with such "sectarian" works as the *Rule of the Community* and *Hodayot*, it contains none of their distinctively sectarian elements and organizational figures. The original setting and date of the work are hard to determine. But its emphasis on financial dealings and family life preclude an origin in the "monastic" setting envisioned at Qumran by many. An origin in the second century B.C. (or even earlier) – roughly contemporary with *Sirach* – seems likely. Whether it was directly associated with the Jewish movement of which the Qumran group was a part, or was simply regarded as "good reading" at Qumran, is not clear. It is a large book – not as large as Sirach but still very large in comparison with other early Jewish wisdom texts found at Qumran[3] or known from other sources.

---

1. A retouched version of *Approaches*, presented here by permission of Sheffield Academic Press. For recent research on Sirach, see D.J. HARRINGTON, *Sirach Research* and A.A. DiLELLA, *Ben Sira*.
2. The Qumran Cave 1 manuscript (1Q26) appeared in D. BARTHÉLEMY & J.T. MILIK, *Qumran Cave 1*, pp. 100-102. The Cave 4 manuscripts appeared recently in STRUGNELL, HARRINGTON & ELGVIN, *Qumran Cave 4. XXIV*. Translations of large parts of the work are presented in F. GARCÍA MARTÍNEZ, *Dead Sea Scrolls Translated*, pp. 383-383; and M. WISE, M.G. ABEGG, and E. COOK, *Dead Sea Scrolls*, pp. 378-390. For general treatments, see T. ELGVIN, *Admonition Texts*; D.J. HARRINGTON, *Wisdom at Qumran*; and L.H. SCHIFFMAN, *Reclaiming the Dead Sea Scrolls*, pp. 203-206.
3. See D.J. HARRINGTON, *Reasons*; and *Wisdom Texts from Qumran*.

I want to compare and contrast these two early Jewish wisdom books. The text of *Sirach* will generally be cited according to the New Revised Standard Version. The text of *Sapiential Work A* is based on the version that John Strugnell and I have developed in connection with our edition in the Discoveries in the Judaean Desert series.

The comparison of the two works is meant to be systematic. It first deals with matters of literary genre – both the large genre of the work as a whole, and the smaller literary forms that make up the whole. Next it considers the traditions used in the texts – the commonplace wisdom traditions and topics as well as biblical (especially the Torah) and other materials. Then it takes up the world views of the two books – their approaches to creation, dualism, the divine mysteries, and eschatology. Finally it discusses the life-setting and community that are implied by each text in an effort to be precise about their social location.

Throughout the comparison, particular attention will be given to the relation between wisdom and apocalyptic – its relative absence in *Sirach*, and its impressive presence in *Sapiential Work A* from Qumran. Here I use the term "apocalyptic" simply to describe ideas and images associated with the eschaton, not to refer to the literary genre of apocalypse or to characterize apocalyptic thought as an extreme form of eschatology.

Genre

Both *Sirach* and *Sapiential Work A* are best described as wisdom instructions. Both presuppose a setting in which a senior sage addresses someone in search or in need of instruction ("my son" in *Sirach*, "you who understand" or "O understanding son" in *Sapiential Work A*). The senior sage imparts instructions in the form of short packets or paragraphs on various topics. Whatever "proverbs" (far more in Sirach than in *Sapiential Work A*) and other wisdom forms are used, are generally integrated into the larger instructional format. In both texts the instructions are usually formulated with the aid of parallelism – either synonymous or antithetical (though the fragmentary state of *Sapiential Work A* sometimes destroys the parallels and makes any restoration a guess).

Wisdom books generally do not follow tight outlines. Rather, most of them give the impression of being collections or anthologies. This is the case with both *Sirach* and *Sapiential Work A*.

The most obvious structural features in Ben Sira's wisdom instruction are the hymn about the glory of God made manifest in creation

(42,15–43,33) and the poetic retelling of the exploits of Israel's heroes (44–50). For the earlier parts of the book, many commentators point to the series of wisdom poems (1,1-10; 4,11-19; 6,18-37; 14,20–15,10; 24,1-33; 38,24–39,11) as being structurally significant and giving the instructions on various topics an orderly framework. There are blocks of teachings about sin in chapters 16–23 and about speech in chapters 18 – 20. But beyond these obvious structural features it is hard to see how the small pieces fit together on anything more than an anthological basis.

Sirach contains treatments of some topics discussed in the best preserved parts of *Sapiential Work A*: money matters (3,30–4,10; 29,1-20; 29,21-28), social relations (7,18-36; 8,1-19; 11,29–12,18; 33,20-33), women (9,1-9; 23,22-26; 25,13–26,27; 36,26-31; 42,9-14), and family relations (3,1-16; 7,23-25; 16,1-4; 30,1-13; 41,5-10; 42,9-14). Other topics that are prominent in *Sirach* – fear of the Lord, friendship, table manners, sickness, sin, speech, death, and wisdom as an explicit topic – are absent from the extant fragments of *Sapiential Work A*. Of course, there is no way to know whether those topics appeared in parts of the text that have been lost.

All of the manuscripts of *Sapiential Work A* are fragmentary. And there are few cases of running text that allow us to see what the sequence of thought was. Indeed, in 4Q418 alone there are about three-hundred fragments, many of them the size of a postage stamp. But there are overlaps among the manuscripts that can help in reconstructing fairly full sections of wisdom instruction at some points (especially 4Q416 2 and 4Q417 1-2 and their parallels).

Since it has a large right-hand margin, 4Q416 1 may mark the beginning of *Sapiential Work A*. If that is so, the part of the text in this fragment would serve to place the sapiential instructions that follow in a cosmic and eschatological framework. Several other large fragments in 4Q418 (55, 69, 81, 126, 127) also refer to creation and judgment as the framework for righteous action in the present.

The best preserved sections of *Sapiential Work A* (4Q416 2 and 417 1-2, and the overlapping material) are wisdom instructions with second-person masculine singular imperatives ("do this") and admonitions in the negative ("you shall not") – as in most of *Sirach*. There are calls to the hearer ("you who understand") and frequent reminders about the listener's poverty ("you are poor"). Whether the reference is to economic or spiritual poverty (or both) is not clear. The main topics of these instructions are money and other possessions, social relations, and family matters. There are frequent exhortations to meditate on the "mystery that is to be/come," which is apparently the key to understanding creation, ethics, and eschatology. There are also references to heavenly tablets and books associated with the eschatological judgment (see 4Q417 1 i 15-17).

Torleif Elgvin has proposed a reconstruction of *Sapiential Work A* that offers a comprehensive outline for most of the work[4]. Using the methods developed by Hartmut Stegemann for reconstructing texts from scattered fragments, Elgvin developed the outline for a book that in 4Q416 consisted of twenty-three columns. The early columns (III-VI) corresponded to the topics treated in 4Q416 2/4Q417 2 and parallel fragments: financial matters and business dealings, social relations, and family matters. Then there was an eschatological discourse (cols. VII-VIII = largely 4Q416 1 and 3) followed by reflections on God's "mystery" and by instructions to walk in righteousness and to praise God (cols. X-XI = largely 4Q417 1). Other parts dealt with the lot of the elect (col. XV = 4Q418 81), rewards and punishments (XX, XXIII = 4Q418 55), the conditions of the farmer (XXII = 4Q423 1 and 2), and a final warning about the coming judgment (XXIII = 4Q418 127).

The most common small literary form is the wisdom instruction. In other words, the large wisdom instruction is made up of smaller wisdom instructions. There are frequent direct addresses, imperatives and prohibitions, and reasons for following the advice. The material is usually gathered in short units or paragraphs on the various topics – as in *Sirach*.

There is nothing in *Sapiential Work A* like the historical survey in *Sirach* 44–50. Neither are there numerical sayings (see *Sir* 23,16-17; 25,1-2, 7-11; etc.), acrostics (*Sir* 51,13-30), or beatitudes (*Sir* 25,8-9). The almost complete absence of beatitudes in *Sapiential Work A* is striking in light of their presence in other Qumran wisdom texts (see 4Q185, 4Q510). Even more striking is the almost complete absence of true proverbs. Whereas some sections of *Sirach* are collections of proverbs, *Sapiential Work A* is relentless in its commitment to give instructions along with the reasons for following the advice.

Sapiential Work A shares with *Sirach* the common sapiential vocabulary, i.e. the many different terms for wisdom and knowledge, and for the act of knowing or understanding. Its best preserved parts are noteworthy for their many words for "poverty" and "poor." Whether poverty was a major theme in the work or is prominent due to the accident of preservation, is hard to determine as is the precise sense of the terms (economic, spiritual, etc.).

---

4. T. ELGVIN, *Reconstruction*.

The most important term in *Sapiential Work A* is *rāz nihyeh* ("the mystery that is to be/come"). It occurs about thirty times. The parallel expressions suggest that it refers to knowledge of righteousness and iniquity in the future and in the present. The most peculiar term is the noun '*wt*, which occurs about fifteen times and whose etymology and meaning remain obscure. There are also some verbal links to the *Rule of Community, Hodayot,* and *Damascus Document*.

Traditions

By their very nature wisdom books are traditional. They try to distill the practical experience and insights of human beings through the ages on various issues. And so the search for parallels is practically endless. Paying loans back, avoiding business dealings with strangers, honoring one's parents, and relating to one's wife in proper fashion are not new or original topics, however much we may need to be reminded of them. And so it is not surprising that *Sirach* and *Sapiential Work A* share familiar sapiential traditions on various topics. Four examples – concerning loans, surety, parents, and wives – will illustrate the common wisdom traditions and in some cases their distinctive approaches to them.

With regard to financial matters *Ben Sira* stresses the need to pay back loans: "Pay back your neighbor when a loan falls due" (29,2). Likewise, *Sapiential Work A* counsels vigilance in paying back loans: "If men's money you borrow for your poverty, do not let there be repose for you day or night, nor rest for your soul until you have restored to your creditor your debt in full" (4Q417 2 i 21-23).

Ben Sira regards standing surety for one's neighbor as the duty of a "good person" (29,14). But he warns about the danger involved in doing so: "Do not go surety beyond your means; think any pledge a debt you must pay" (29,14). He recognizes that sinful people can manipulate the system (see 29,16-20), and observes that a person's life may be at stake: "Forget not the kindness of your backer, for he offers his very life for you" (29,15). In *Sapiential Work A* there is a similar insistence on the seriousness of standing surety: "On account of your friends you have given away all your life for its price. Hasten and give what is his (the creditor's) and take back your purse" (4Q416 2 ii 5-6). Another text underlines the life-and-death character of such transactions: "Do not sell your self for money...do not sell your glory for any price nor give your inheritance in exchange for surety for a sum of money" (4Q416 2 ii 17-18). In the context of how one should handle a deposit entrusted by a stranger, the addressee is warned: "Do not let your 'spirit' be taken as a pledge for it" (4Q416 2 iii 6-7).

Family relations is a common wisdom topic. There are some good parallels between what *Ben Sira* says about honoring one's parents (3,1-16) and the advice given in *Sapiential Work A*. Just as *Ben Sira* says that "whoever honors his father will live a long life" (3,6), so the Qumran text urges the addressee to honor his parents "for the sake of your life and the length of your days" (4Q416 2 iii 19). *Ben Sira* says that "his father's glory is a person's own glory" (3,11), and the Qumran text advises: "Honor them for the sake of your own honor" (4Q416 2 iii18).

There are, however, some unusual emphases in the generally conventional materials relating to parents in *Sapiential Work A*. First there is the connection made with the addressee's poverty: "Honor your father in your poverty and your mother in your low estate" (4Q416 2 iii 15-16). Then there is a daring comparison: "For as God (reading *'l* with 4Q418 rather than *'b*) is to a man, so is his mother" (16). Finally there is the suggestion that parents deserve respect and honor because of their role in instructing their son in what is truly important: "they have uncovered your ear to the mystery that is to be/come" (18). This text presupposes a "family" rather than "monastic" setting and links standard biblical/sapiential teaching to what is the central (and distinctive) concept of the whole work: "the mystery that is to be/come."

A fourth topic shared by *Sirach* and *Sapiential Work A* concerns women in general and wives in particular. *Ben Sira*'s views on this issue are well known: "With a dragon or a lion I would rather dwell than live with an evil woman" (25,16); "In a woman was sin's beginning; on her account we all die" (25,24); and "Better a man's wickedness than a woman's goodness" (42,14).

Sapiential Work A assumes that the one being instructed will marry a wife (see 4Q416 2 iii 19–iv 11)[5]. But he is warned against being distracted "from the mystery that is to be/come" (iii 20-21). The sage is here especially concerned to reinforce the husband's authority over his wife. He gives particular attention to the husband's power to annul his wife's vows and votive offerings: "Every oath binding on her, to vow a vow, annul it according to the mere utterance of your mouth and at your good pleasure restrain her from performing her vow" (iv 8-9). On these matters the Qumran text lacks the obsessive (even misogynist) tone of Ben Sira. But it does insist on the patriarchal/hierarchical relationship between husband and wife.

---

5. J. STRUGNELL, *Wives and Marriage*.

Another text in *Sapiential Work A* (4Q415 2 ii 1-9) appears to give advice directly to the wife of the one being instructed in most of the work. The advice is quite conventional, in keeping with the patriarchal assumptions of the work. She is told to honor her father-in-law as her own father, to cling to her husband's bosom, not to neglect her "holy covenant" (the marriage bond), and to be a subject of "praise on the mouth of all men". Though the advice is conventional, the fact that a woman is directly addressed is unusual in Jewish wisdom literature.

Besides treating common wisdom topics, *Sirach* and *Sapiential Work A* both use traditions from the Torah as part of their wisdom instructions. For example, *Ben Sira*'s advice about parents and children takes as its starting point the Decalogue's precept to "honor your father and your mother" (Exod 20,12; Deut 5,16). And his teachings there expand upon the biblical promise "that your days may be long and that it may go well for you" (Deut 5,16). The same passages seem to be in the background of *Sapiential Work A*'s treatment of the topic, as the discussion above indicates.

In Sapiential Work A there are other appeals to Torah traditions. For example, the section on relations with one's wife (4Q416 2 iii 19 – iv 6) takes as its main texts Gen 2,24 ("therefore a man leaves his father and mother and clings to his wife, and they become one flesh") and 3,16 ("your desire shall be for your husband, and he shall rule over you"). The instruction about annulling the wife's vows and votive offerings (4Q416 2 iv 6-13) is based on Num 30,6-15. And one of the "agricultural" texts (4Q418 103) invokes the biblical law of "mixed things" (see Lev 19,19; Deut 22,9-11) in the course of its advice.

Thus both *Sirach* and *Sapiential Work A* weave Torah instructions into their sapiential instructions. Though these traditions presumably carry a certain authority, in neither work is this made explicit by the use of introductory formulas (as in Matthew's Gospel) or even an acknowledgement that a Torah text is being quoted. The Torah traditions are simply part of the advice.

Given the fragmentary character of *Sapiential Work A*, it is difficult to say what traditions were not in it. But on the basis of what we do have, we can say that *Sapiential Work A* lacks any personification of Wisdom and any extended meditation on wisdom (unless "the mystery that is to be/come" plays an analogous role). There is no interest in Israel's history (cf. *Sirach* 44–49) or the Jerusalem temple and its priesthood (cf. *Sirach* 50).

Ben Sira's lack of interest in apocalyptic traditions is well known. Although there is no explicit denial of life after death, neither is there much affirmation of it (see 38,21-23). The most important form of immortality is the good "name" – the reputation and memory that one leaves behind (41,1-4). The closest thing to an apocalyptic scenario comes in the prayer for God's people in 36,1-22: "Hasten the day, and remember the appointed time" (36,10). But even here *Ben Sira*'s focus seems to be on some event in the near future (the overthrow of Antiochus III or Seleucus IV?).

What most sets *Sapiential Work A* apart from *Sirach* is its lively interest in apocalyptic[6]. Although there are no periodizations of history, calendar reckonings, or cosmological maps as in some other apocalyptic texts, the future judgment overseen by God and his angels provides the horizon against which the instructor gives advice. Throughout the work there are appeals to study or meditate on "the mystery that is to be/come," and to live one's life in accord with it. Whereas *Ben Sira* shows no interest in angels, *Sapiential Work A* imagines a correspondence between the angels' existence in the heavenly court and the life of the wise/righteous on earth. These topics will be treated in more detail in the following section.

WORLD VIEW

Ben Sira treats creation in three long poems (16,24–18,14; 39,12-35; 42,15–43,33). They serve as a theological underpinning or framework for his many short wisdom instructions. Much in these creation poems simply echoes earlier biblical material. There is great emphasis on the order of creation and the divine wisdom made manifest in it, the central place of humankind within creation, the gift of the Law as the divinely revealed guide for human action, and the call to those who have strayed to repent and return to God.

Though biblical and traditional in his statements about creation, *Ben Sira* makes his own distinctive theological contribution (perhaps in response to Qohelet[7]) with his treatment of theodicy in the context of creation. There he articulates what has come to be known as the doctrine of "the pairs". The teaching is summarized in *Sir* 33,15: "See now all the works of the Most High: they come in pairs, the one the opposite of the other." It is also expressed in 42,24: "All of them come in twos, one corresponding to the other; yet none of them has He made in vain".

---

6. T. ELGVIN, *Early Essene Eschatology*.
7. A. LANGE, *In Diskussion mit dem Tempel*.

Both texts attribute absolute sovereignty to God the creator. But they account for the duality in human history and experience by appealing to the order of creation. This is a modified dualism (as at Qumran), but without any appeal to a subordinate evil power like the Angel of Darkness (as in 1QS iii-iv).

For *Ben Sira*, God's creations are objectively good but can result in punishment for the wicked: "For the good all these are good, but for the wicked they turn out evil" (39,27). This is, of course, a neat but simplistic solution to the question of theodicy. It leaves out the reality of innocent suffering and suggests that those who suffer natural calamities and the ravages of war must be among the wicked: "Fire and hail, famine, disease: these too were created for punishment. Ravenous beasts, scorpions, vipers, and the avenging sword to exterminate the wicked: All these were created to meet a need and are kept in his storehouse for the proper time" (39,29-30).

Ben Sira's approach to creation is basically biblical and traditional. His innovative approach to theodicy is neat but somewhat timid. He acknowledges the existence of a certain duality in creation without developing it in much detail and declares that natural catastrophes are primarily intended to punish the wicked.

The appeal to creation as a theological basis for wisdom instruction is also prominent in *Sapiential Work A*. But whereas *Ben Sira* seems intent on describing and glorifying God's creation, the Qumran wisdom text is less speculative and more interested in the moral consequences of creation and divine election. God has separated the wise from the "spirit of flesh". Therefore, "you, separate yourself from everything that He (God) hates and guard yourself from everything that His soul detests" (4Q418 81 ii). The addressee is urged repeatedly to recall his "inheritance" and his "portion" and his "glory" that God has granted him. As in *Sirach* there are two kinds of people corresponding to a certain modified dualism within creation. *Sapiential Work A*, however, puts more emphasis on God's activity in choosing the righteous and on the responsibility that the righteous have in acting in a manner appropriate to their "lot" or "inheritance".

God's sovereignty in creating and preserving the universe is affirmed in 4Q418 126, 1-10: "Nothing will cease from all their host.... He numbers all, and they did not come to be without His good pleasure." It also stresses the discriminating judgment (election) of God that has already separated the good and the wicked, and looks forward to the future judgment that will bring vengeance on the "masters of iniquity" and vindication for the "poor ones".

The coming divine judgment on human actions is frequently proposed in *Sapiential Work A* as a motive for good action in the present: "Study (or, inherit) your reward, remembering the requital, for it comes" (4Q417 1 i 14). Then using the motif of the heavenly tablets or books and the language of Exod 32,16, the instructor warns: "Engraved is the ordinance, and ordained is all the punishment". The heavenly tablet or book (see *Jub* 30,20-22; 1 *Enoch* 47,3; 108,3) apparently contains a list of evil deeds and their punishments[8].

In 4Q418 69 the "foolish ones" are warned that "to the everlasting pit shall your return be ... its dark places shall cry out ... those who investigate the truth shall be roused up for your judgment" (6-7). The destiny of the foolish is annihilation: "Then will all the foolish in mind be destroyed" (8).

In 4Q418 126 ii the righteous are promised that "upon the power of God and the greatness of His glory together with His goodness and His great mercy shall they meditate, and upon His faithfulness shall they reflect always. Continually shall they praise His name" (9-11). The righteous will enjoy an angelic existence. To exhort the righteous not to grow weary in seeking wisdom, the sage uses the example of the "sons of heaven, whose lot is eternal life" (4Q418 69,12-13). Indeed, the righteous already participate in the glorious existence of the angels: "among all the godly ones He has cast your lot, and has magnified your glory greatly" (4Q418 81, 4-5).

God's plan is called the *rāz nihyeh* ("the mystery that is to be/come")[9]. The many references to this term assume that the speaker and the one being instructed know to what it refers, though we as outsiders are never given a definition. There is no reason to identify it with the Torah. It could be a book (like the "Book of Meditation") or an epitome of basic teachings (as in 1QS iii-iv). Or it could be an oral or (lost) written esoteric teaching. From its various uses and their contexts, it clearly concerns creation, behavior in the present, and the coming judgment. The translation "mystery of being" seems too metaphysical and static. The expression functions in an elusive and encompassing way – something like the "kingdom of God" in the Synoptic Gospels.

What "the mystery that is to be/come" is can best be approached by referring to some words and phrases that accompany it. Most of the verbs are second-person singular imperatives and occur in the context of the instructor's advice to "test", "study", "meditate", "understand", and "look at, gaze". The nominal phrases parallel to it include "all the

---

8. A. LANGE, *Weisheit und Prädestination*; and ID., *Wisdom and Predestination*.
9. D.J. HARRINGTON, *Rāz Nihyeh*.

ways of truth and all the roots of iniquity" (4Q416 2 iii 14); "the birth-time of salvation, and ... who is to inherit glory and iniquity" (4Q417 2 i 10-11); "the inheritance of everything that lives" (4Q418 2 i 18); "the generations of man" (4Q418 77, 2); and "the weight of the times and the measure" (4Q418 77, 4). These parallels suggest that the "mystery" concerns creation, ethics, and eschatology.

Those who apply themselves to the mystery can expect rewards in the present: "Then you shall know to discern between good and evil" (4Q417 1 i 7); and "You shall know what is allotted to it, and in righteousness shall you walk" (4Q417 1 iii 9). Such promises underscore the ethical dimension of the mystery.

Whatever the "mystery" was, the ways in which the speaker refers to it suggest that it provides a revelation to those who study it. And the content with its cosmological, ethical, and eschatological aspects indicates that the mystery has been revealed (directly by God or through angels?) and that the instructor is intent on emphasizing the duty of those who would be wise and righteous to apply themselves to it.

There is surely an esoteric dimension to the *rāz nihyeh* in *Sapiential Work A*. This stands in contrast to *Ben Sira*'s method of deriving wisdom instruction principally from practical human experience (the usual source of sapiential teachings), creation, and the Torah and Israel's history.

The world view of *Sapiential Work A* seems midway between *Ben Sira*'s timid doctrine of the pairs and the fully fleshed out dualistic schema of 1QS iii-iv with its Angels of Darkness and Light. The Qumran text assumes a God more active and involved in creation and human affairs than *Sirach* does. Its emphasis is on the election that God has imposed on creation and on the moral consequences of being the object of God's grace or good pleasure.

COMMUNITY

The setting for both *Sirach* and *Sapiential Work A* is instructional. In each book a senior sage imparts advice to younger men and uses direct address, generally in the masculine singular.

If the autobiographical wisdom poem in *Sir* 51,13-30 came from *Ben Sira* (and there is some dispute about this), then we know that he ran a wisdom school ("the house of instruction", 51,23) and promised great results to those who came to study with him ("you will acquire silver and gold", 51,28). A fuller prospectus for *Ben Sira*'s school appears in the section on the activity of the scribe (38,34b–39,11). His students will learn not only traditional wisdom but also "the law of the Lord's covenant" (39,8). This education will prepare them not simply for the "scribal" life of copying documents or teaching young people but for political leadership and for advising kings and princes (see 38,32b-33). Moreover, *Ben Sira* was well disposed toward the priesthood and worship at the Jerusalem temple. His survey of Israel's history climaxes with a beautiful description of a temple service at which Simeon the high priest presides (see 50,1-21). Some have even suggested that *Ben Sira*'s school was officially linked with the Jerusalem temple.

Sapiential Work A does not contain any autobiographical notices as *Sirach* does throughout (see Sir 24,30-34; 33,16-19; 34,9-13; 39,12-13; 50,27; 51,13-30). Whatever can be said about its life setting must be deduced from the text itself. The form and content of the instructions suggest a "school" setting (as in *Sirach*), though precisely how the school is to be imagined (a tutorial?) is not clear. The instructor uses the address "son" and appears to be superior in wisdom and in age.

The one being addressed may simply be anyone in search of wisdom. But more likely he is in the process of being integrated into the life and teachings of a Jewish movement (which at some point was related directly or indirectly to the Qumran people). In one passage (4Q417 1 i 1-17) there may possibly be hints that he is being groomed to exercise leadership. There he is told that applying himself to "the mystery that is to be/come" will equip him with the requisite knowledge about the cosmos, behavior, and rendering judgments in the present. Perhaps *Sapiential Work A* was intended as a handbook for training leaders within a Jewish movement.

The person being instructed in *Sapiential Work A* was not a "monk". Much of the advice concerns financial matters. He is presumed to be involved in loans and standing surety for others. He has business and social dealings with various kinds of people in society. He continues his relationship with his parents. He is expected to marry and to exercise proper authority over his wife.

The fact that at least six copies of the work were found at Qumran indicates its importance there. It may have simply been popular there (as *1 Enoch* was) but not directly related to the Qumran group – a wisdom book that was part of a Jewish library in the first century. Or *Sapiential Work A* could have been composed for the non-"monastic" branch of the Qumran or Essene movement. Or the work may have been associated with the foundational, pre-Qumranic phase of the Jewish (Essene, Sadducean?) movement in the second century B.C. or even earlier. The latter two settings would explain both the "secular" dimension of many teachings and the links to the "sectarian" works found at Qumran.

Whichever of these three life-settings is chosen, *Sapiential Work A* was roughly contemporary with *Sirach*, providing evidence for a major crossroads in Jewish intellectual and religious history. Both works join wisdom and Torah traditions. Whereas *Sirach* represents the fusion of wisdom/Torah and priestly/temple traditions, *Sapiential Work A* uses wisdom/Torah traditions alongside or in the framework of a dualistic and eschatologically oriented theology.

This comparison of *Sirach* and *Sapiential Work A* with reference to genre, traditions, world view, and community reveals two of the options current in early Jewish wisdom literature. While *Ben Sira* was not interested in (or perhaps opposed to) apocalyptic, the author of *Sapiential Work A* was keenly interested in fitting together wisdom and apocalyptic[10].

Weston Jesuit School of Theology   Daniel J. HARRINGTON
3 Phillips Place
Cambridge MA 02138
USA

---

10. T. ELGVIN, *Wisdom, Revelation, and Eschatology.*

THE QUMRAN SAPIENTIAL TEXTS
AND THE RULE BOOKS

I. INTRODUCTION

I think it will be useful to preface my observations with a few sentences on where I stand on the question of communities behind the scrolls as well as key texts such as the Damascus Document, the Community Rule and the Rule of the Congregation. I share the conviction of those scholars who have argued that the Qumran texts reflect the life and thought of more than one community and find it useful to think of these in terms of a parent movement and an off-shoot community. I further hold that both groups have left behind communal legislation, that is rules dealing with matters of community organization and authority. Thus, in my view, the bulk of the communal legislation in the Laws of the Damascus Document and the communal legislation preserved in 1QSa refer to the parent group whereas most of the Community Rule describes the *yaḥad*, an off-shoot of the parent group. However, the situation is more complex and it is, in fact, impossible to allocate each document *in toto* to a particular background. Very frequently the *yaḥad* or the S-tradents have left their mark on the final form of documents that contain a great deal of pre-Qumranic material[1]. Conversely, although the bulk of the Community Rule contains material that describes the organization of the *yaḥad* it also contains remnants of communal rules that go back to its parent group. An important example of the latter kind are the rules on entering the community by swearing an oath in 1QS 5,7-9 which envisage a much simpler procedure than that found in 1QS 6,13-23. Moreover, this simpler procedure of admission mirrors the practice described in the Damascus Document in CD 15,5-10[2]. I have further ar-

---

* I gratefully acknowledge the financial contributions of the Deutsche Forschungsgemeinschaft and the Graduiertenkolleg of the University of Tübingen towards the cost of my visit to Tübingen to deliver this paper. I would further like to thank our hosts Prof. Lichtenberger and Dr. Lange for their generous hospitality during my stay. Finally, I should like to thank the participants at the Oberseminar in Tübingen as well as a research seminar at the University of Maryland for their comments.

1. Cf. HEMPEL, *Nucleus of 1QSa*, where I argue for the presence of a number of redactional passages in 1QSa such as 1QSa 1,1-3. See further my identification of a Serekh-redaction in the Laws of the Damascus Document, cf. HEMPEL, *Laws of the Damascus Document*.

2. For a fuller discussion see HEMPEL, *Community Structures*, esp. pp. 70-73.

gued elsewhere, that aside from the communal legislation the Laws of the Damascus Document contain a stratum of halakhic traditions that do not reflect any organized community and go back to priestly circles in the Second Temple Period[3].

The specific question I would like to address in this paper is the relationship of the Qumran wisdom texts to the Rule Books. I will begin by raising a number of questions we need to ask in order to clarify the topic at hand. It is much more difficult to find answers to most of the questions at this point. The Qumran wisdom material has only relatively recently begun to arouse intense scholarly interest, and the coming years might see more and more of these questions answered. However, in view of the fragmentary state of preservation of many of the texts a good number of questions will, I fear, remain unanswered.

When dealing with the Rule Books I will pay particular attention to those parts of these works that deal with communal legislation, or the rules proper contained within them. I set this emphasis because those sections take us closest to the communities reflected in the texts. As far as the sapiential texts are concerned I will pay particular attention to those texts that have recently been published.

II. The Questions

A question that is frequently being raised is: are the Qumran wisdom texts sectarian? Thus, Collins identifies the following as "one of the most persistent problems in the study of the sapiential materials in the Dead Sea Scrolls",

> Should they be regarded as products of the community, or communities, responsible for hiding them in the caves, or should they be viewed as part of the general heritage of Judaism around the turn of the era?[4]

I would prefer to reformulate the question and ask: are there any sectarian elements in the wisdom texts? Or, do they display any signs of redactional activity? That is, are there any indications that the Qumran tradents of these texts have left their mark on the material? One of the characteristics of the Qumran wisdom texts that unites them as a category is, of course, their wisdom component. That is, they display

---

3. HEMPEL, *Laws of the Damascus Document*.
4. COLLINS, *Jewish Wisdom*, p. 113. On this question see further DIMANT, *Qumran Manuscripts*; HARRINGTON, *Wisdom Texts from Qumran*, pp. 75-80; LIPSCOMB & SANDERS, *Wisdom at Qumran*, pp. 277-278; STEGEMANN, *Library of Qumran*, p. 100; and VAN DER WOUDE, *Wisdom at Qumran*, esp. pp. 254-255.

sapiential terminology, forms and concerns. A great deal of the material that displays these characteristics does not seem to display sectarian features. It may be helpful, therefore, to allow for the possibility that what is presented by Collins as alternatives, sectarian or inherited traditions, may well both be present in this material alongside one another. And a scenario along such lines has been proposed by Elgvin with reference to 4QWays of Righteousness[5]. In the context of this debate Harrington has drawn attention to the presence of copies of both Sapiential Work A and Mysteries in Cave 1, the cave from which many of the key sectarian texts were recovered[6]. This is noteworthy but I am not sure it is a decisive consideration as the presence of a clearly pre-Qumranic work like the Genesis Apocryphon in Cave 1 may illustrate[7]. So much on formulating the bigger questions.

III. Three Qumran Sapiential Works

In what follows I will consider three of the Qumran sapiential texts (Mysteries, Sapiential Work A and Ways of Righteousness) and the question of their provenance.

1. The Book of Mysteries

This work is preserved in a number of fragmentary copies, and I will here consider only the question of whether it displays any signs of a Qumranic redaction. Collins has recently drawn attention to 4Q299 8,6 and argued on the basis of the statement "with great insight he opened our ears" (ברוב שכל גלה אוזננו),

> "The appeal to special revelation suggests strongly that the Book of Mysteries originated in a sectarian milieu[8]."

The statement in question seems to me rather general, and I would be reluctant to build a case for sectarian provenance on this rather slender

---

5. ELGVIN argues that 4Q420-421 comprise early sapiential traditions alongside later sectarian editing, cf. ELGVIN, *Ways of Righteousness*, p. 202.
6. See HARRINGTON, *Wisdom Texts from Qumran*, p. 75.
7. For a different assessment of the Genesis Apocryphon see REEVES, *Noah*. REEVES argues that the Genesis Apocryphon may be a sectarian work based on a halakhic parallel between 1QapGen 10,15 and Jubilees and the Temple Scroll. Since I would consider neither of the two latter works as of sectarian origin I am not convinced by his case. Note, however, REEVES' cautious final sentence where he argues "that *Genesis Apocryphon* was a sectarian *or proto-sectarian* (emphasis mine) product" (p. 418).
8. COLLINS, *Jewish Wisdom*, p. 128.

piece of evidence. 4Q299 8,6 seems to refer to the divine origin of enlightenment that is revealed to those who devote themselves to the study of wisdom, a notion that is not uncommon in the wisdom tradition and not exclusively sectarian[9]. A statement referring to special revelation is clearly sectarian only if the revelation is linked to a particular group as is the case, for instance, in the famous Well Midrash in the Admonition of the Damascus Document in CD 3,12ff. By contrast, the national terms of reference employed in 4Q299 6 ii 8; 10; 60,4 suggest a non-sectarian provenance for this work as has been convincingly argued by Lange[10]. More particularly Lange has proposed, on the basis of a considerable number of cultic references present in the work, that Mysteries emerged from priestly circles[11]. The all-Israel perspective of Mysteries is particularly pronounced in 4Q299 10. It is interesting to note the use of the term 'judges' (שופטים) in lines 5 and 7 of this fragment in a clearly non-community specific manner. The context in which the judges operate in this fragment seems to be Israel and the nations, cf. the references to "all the nations" (כול גואים) and "Israel" (ישרא[ל]) in line 3. In the Laws of the Damascus Document and 1QSa, by contrast, the biblical terminology "judges" is applied to refer to a group within the community, cf. CD 15,4; 16,19 par. 4QD^e 6 iv 13; CD 9,10; 10,1.4-7a; 14,13; 1QSa 1,15.24.29.

Ambiguous is the partially preserved reference to "those who have turned from transgression" (שבי פש[ע) in 4Q299 71,1. This expression is applied to the particular circumstances of a movement in the Damascus Document in CD 2,5 par. 4QD^a 2 ii 5; CD 20,17 and occurs further also in 1QS 10,20 par. 4QS^f IV,10. Since the expression is scripturally based (cf. Isa 59,20) there is no need to assume it has a sectarian connotation in Mysteries[12]. The expression "all the fathers of the congregation" (כול אבות העדה) in 4Q299 76,3 is similarly based on scripture (cf. Num 31,26) but also occurs in a community specific sense in 1QSa and perhaps also in

9. Cf. also the reference to a sealed vision in terms reminiscent of Daniel in 4Q299 3 c par. 4Q300 1 a ii -b, cf. SCHIFFMAN, *Mysteries*, pp. 43-44, 102-103 and COLLINS, *Jewish Wisdom*, p. 128.

10. See LANGE, *Physiognomie oder Gotteslob*, pp. 284-286.

11. LANGE, *Physiognomie oder Gotteslob*, p. 286 where he concludes, "Myst. wurde somit in weisheitlichen Kreisen verfaßt, deren kultisches Interesse auf eine Nähe zum Tempel deutet". He further argues that Mysteries goes back to "einer am Tempel beheimateten weisheitlichen Gruppe" (p. 287).

12. Cf. SCHIFFMAN, *Mysteries*, p. 83. See also ALEXANDER & VERMES, *Qumran Cave 4. XIX*, p. 165 ad 4Q260 IV,10. ALEXANDER & VERMES conclude, "In Qumran Hebrew שבי פשע is virtually a title of the Community" (p. 265). For a similar view see DIMANT, *Qumran Manuscripts*, p. 41 n. 45. However, since שבי פשע is a scripturally derived expression I would be inclined to allow for the possibility of different shades of meaning in different Qumran contexts.

the War Scroll[13]. Finally, the occurrence of the expression "time of wickedness" (קץ רשעה) in 4Q301 3a-b, 8 has lead Schiffman to observe, "This usage certainly places the document as a 'sectarian' work"[14]. It seems equally likely to me that we have here a redactional phrase that was appended at the end of a hymnic section. The four lines of text that precede the line in question contain poetic material in praise of God that displays no signs of sectarian provenance. This is followed in line 8 by a partially preserved reference to the time of wickedness which follows on somewhat uneasily from the preceding hymn of praise. In sum, the bulk of Mysteries seems to contain traditional sapiential material interspersed with a small number of ambiguous terms attested both in the Bible and sectarian contexts and one apparently sectarian turn of phrase.

2. *Sapiential Work A*

Vermes has argued that Sapiential Work A is "unquestionably sectarian and displays a terminology akin to the Community Rule, the Damascus Document and the Thanksgiving Hymns"[15]. Lange, Tiller and Strugnell, by contrast, have argued that it is a pre-Qumranic composition that does not presuppose a particular community setting[16]. Harrington has formulated his position on 4QSapiential Work A along the following lines,

> Some of the language in the more theological parts of the work can be found in the so-called sectarian writings from Qumran (Community Rule, Thanksgiving Hymns, Damascus Document, etc.). But the work presupposes a secular or non- "monastic" setting[17].

Elsewhere he seems to single out Sapiential Work A and Mysteries as shedding some light on a broad Second Temple movement and tentatively associates them with the movement described in the Damascus Document[18]. Against an association with the communal situation re-

---

13. Cf. SCHIFFMAN, *Mysteries*, p. 86.
14. *Mysteries*, p. 119.
15. VERMES, *Complete Dead Sea Scrolls in English*, p. 402.
16. See LANGE, *Weisheit und Prädestination*, pp. 45-92 where his treatment of 4QSapiential Work A is presented under the heading "nichtessenische und protoessenische Texte"; TILLER, *Eternal Planting*, pp. 324-325; STRUGNELL, *Wives and Marriage*, p. 546 where he notes, "*4Q415ff.* has nothing characteristically sectarian in it, in matter or language"; and STRUGNELL, *Sapiential Work*.
17. HARRINGTON, *Wisdom Texts from Qumran*, pp. 40-41. See also HARRINGTON, *Approaches*, pp. 25, 36-37.
18. HARRINGTON, *Reasons*, p. 253 where he observes, "To assume that the Qumran wisdom texts are merely 'library books' seems unlikely. Rather, at least some of them such as Sapiential Work A and the Book of Mysteries (both in Cave 1-1Q26 and 1Q27) probably represented the distinctive intellectual and religious heritage of a larger move-

flected in the Laws of the Damascus Document speaks the absence of the institutions and officials such as the camp (מחנה) and the overseer (מבקר) in 4QSapiential Work A. The similarities between both works are confined to rather general features such a married life-style and the private ownership of property. It is often noted by scholars that a work like Sapiential Work A deals with traditional wisdom themes such as advising caution in financial matters and marital advice and thus clearly presupposes family life and private property. It is not impossible to explain this, as Harrington seems to favour, as indicating the provenance of these instructions from a community that lived an integrated life in society at large. A much simpler explanation, however, is to suppose that the material is traditional wisdom which originated from a non-community specific background and reflects wisdom traditions that were cherished in society at large. To introduce an intermediary entity of a movement that very much resembled society at large behind such instructions should only be done on the basis of positive evidence. In the absence of positive evidence the former kind of reasoning resembles the argument that if we were to be presented with the photograph of a polar bear to say that it is in fact not a polar bear but a person dressed up in a very convincing polar bear outfit. This is a provocative way of putting it but I hope it clarifies my point. Harrington's singling out above of "the more theological parts of the work" is interesting and might well hold the key to these questions. It seems conceivable to me that Sapiential Work A is a composite work and that large parts of it comprise a collection of traditional sapiential material whereas other portions may have originated with a particular strand in Second Temple Judaism, though not the *yaḥad*, but perhaps its forerunners[19]. In light of its fragmentary character it may not be possible to unravel the literary growth of Sapiential Work A with confidence. We can, however, endorse Harrington's basic distinction between the pragmatic instruction material and the more abstract or theological elements. As has been noted by Harrington and others this mixture of pragmatical guidelines interspersed with theological passages is known also from Ben Sira[20]. Elgvin has highlighted the potential significance of distinguishing various lay-

---

ment within Second Temple Judaism". See further HARRINGTON, *Wisdom at Qumran*, pp. 151-152.

19. Cf. STRUGNELL, HARRINGTON & ELGVIN, *Qumran Cave 4*. XXIV, p. 12 for a similar assessment. See also p. 36 in this volume for a slightly different view.

20. HARRINGTON, *Wisdom Texts from Qumran*, p. 40. See also COLLINS, *Jewish Wisdom*, p. 118. On Ben Sira and Sapiential Work A see further AITKEN, *Apocalyptic* and HARRINGTON, *Approaches*.

ers in Sapiential Work A along similar lines[21]. In 4Q416 2 iii we seem to have one of the, in Harrington's terms, "more theological passages" alongside practical instructions[22]. It is noteworthy that the theological admonitions are here linked to the more worldly instructions in two cases. Thus, as has been noted by Strugnell & Harrington, the instructions to honour father and mother and relations between husband and wife are intrinsically linked with the instruction to devote oneself to the study of the mystery to be. This has been clearly spelt out by Strugnell & Harrington,

> This Qumran text is furthermore distinctive in that it links family obligations and interactions to the "mystery that is to come" – the maven should honour his parents because they uncovered his ear to "the mystery that is to come" (4**Q416** 2 iii 18), and, while "keeping company with" his wife, he should take care not to be distracted from "the mystery that is to come" (4**Q416** 2 iii 20-21)[23].

This close link between practical instruction and the theological concerns of this text is intriguing and may indicate that both aspects of the text cannot be neatly separated across the board. It may be that the redactor responsible for combining the theological parts of the work with the practical sapiential advice was responsible for the intertwining of both in these two cases. In any case, the two passages that establish a close connection between practical advice and theological reflection seem to me an important crux in the evaluation of this text.

3. 4QWays of Righteousness

This text has recently been published by Elgvin who describes it as a composite wisdom text that contains sectarian organization and halakhic material alongside traditional wisdom elements[24]. In an article that has recently appeared in *Revue de Qumran* Eibert Tigchelaar convincingly shows, however, that 4Q420-421 is best understood as a Rule rather than a sapiential text[25]. Tigchelaar offers improved readings and restorations

---

21. ELGVIN, *Reconstruction*, pp. 560-562. See also ELGVIN, *Mystery to Come*, esp. p. 115 n. 10 where he comments, "The discourses have more 'sectarian terminology' than the sections with wisdom sayings. The wisdom sayings might reflect an older tradition, to which a writer close to the early Essene community added discourses of his own".
22. Cf. HARRINGTON, *Wisdom Texts from Qumran*, p. 45.
23. STRUGNELL, HARRINGTON & ELGVIN, *Qumran Cave 4. XXIV*, p. 35. See further HARRINGTON, *Approaches*, p. 30.
24. Cf. ELGVIN, *4QWays of Righteousness*, p. 173. See further ELGVIN, *Wisdom in the Yaḥad*.
25. TIGCHELAAR, *Sabbath Halakha*. I would like to thank the author for making his article available to me before its publication.

of a number of fragments and notes textual overlap with the work Halakhah B (4Q264a) to be published by J. M. Baumgarten. 4QWays of Righteousness is fascinating because of the way in which it combines sapiential elements, communal organization and halakhic material. However, in the light of Tigchelaar's work it is now clear that the full text of this composition will only be available after Baumgarten's edition of 4QHalakhah B has appeared[25a].

IV. WISDOM ELEMENTS IN THE RULE BOOKS

The question of whether there are any wisdom elements in the Rule Books is much easier to answer than the reverse which has been my concern thus far. Wisdom elements in the Rule Books are clearly present, and this has frequently been emphasized by scholars[26]. I will deal with this aspect of the debate by focusing on three specific issues that shed light on the relationship of the Rule Books to the Qumran sapiential texts: the mystery to be, the Book/Vision of Hagi, and the maskil.

1. Raz Nihyeh

Of all the passages in the Rule Books that display wisdom features one is particularly noteworthy, and that is the occurrence of the expression רז נהיה "the mystery to be" in the Community Rule in 1QS 11,3-4. It is of particular interest because this expression is characteristic of a number of sapiential works from Qumran such as Sapiential Work A and Mysteries, and its meaning in the sapiential corpus has been the subject of considerable scholarly debate[27]. One could argue that the presence of this expression which is so characteristic of key Qumran sapiential texts in the community text *par excellence* indicates a close connection between works like Mysteries and Sapiential Work A and the *yaḥad*. However, things are more complex than that. The expression רז נהיה occurs in the context of the hymn that makes up the final portion of 1QS, and this hymn is missing in one of the Cave 4 manuscripts of

---

25a. For the edition see now J.M. BAUMGARTEN, *Qumran Cave 4. XXV*, pp. 53-56. Cf. also STRUGNELL in the present volume p. 45.

26. Thus, VAN DER WOUDE aptly notes, "wisdom terminology also abounds in non-sapiential writings found among the Dead Sea Scrolls"; *Wisdom at Qumran*, p. 256. Cf. also VAN LEEUWEN, *Scribal Wisdom* and LANGE, *Weisheit und Prädestination*.

27. See, for instance, COLLINS, *Jewish Wisdom*, p. 123; ELGVIN, *Mystery to Come*, pp. 131-139; HARRINGTON, *Wisdom Texts from Qumran*, p. 78; HARRINGTON, *RĀZ NIHYEH*; HARRINGTON, *Approaches*, pp. 34-35; LANGE, *Weisheit und Prädestination*, pp. 45ff.; SCHIFFMAN, *Mysteries*, p. 31; SCHIFFMAN, *Reclaiming the Dead Sea Scrolls*, p. 206.

the Community Rule. Thus, 4QS^e has the calendric text Otot after the section on the maskil in 1QS 9,26 in place of the short calendric section and the final hymn found in 1QS[28]. In any case, it seems likely that the hymn originally existed independently before its incorporation into some versions of the Community Rule[29]. Thus, the presence of the expression רז נהיה in 1QS 11 whilst significant does not provide a decisive clue to the relationship between the Rule Books and the Qumran wisdom works. Its presence in the final hymn of 1QS can be reconciled with the view that the mystery is a pre-sectarian concept.

2. *The Book of Hagi*

Another major link between the Rule Books and Sapiential Work A is the occurrence in both of the term Hagi (הגי). In this case we are on firmer ground in the sense that the Book of Hagi (ספר ההגי) is referred to in contexts in the Rule Books that are clearly describing matters of communal organization rather than blocks of material that may have been combined with communal legislation at a secondary stage such as 1QS's final hymn. In other words, in the Laws of the Damascus Document and in 1QSa the Book of Hagi is firmly rooted in the structure of a community (cf. CD 10,6 par. 4QD^a 8 iii 5 and 4QD^e 6 iv 17; CD 13,2; 14,8 par. 4QD^b 9 v 12 and 1QSa 1,7). The community behind the communal legislation in both the Laws of the Damascus Document and 1QSa is, as I have argued elsewhere, best identified with the parent group of the *yaḥad*[30]. The passages in question specify that both ordinary community members and leading figures are to be familiar with the contents of the Book of Hagi. It is interesting that the expression 'the Book of Hagi' occurs in the communal legislation of the parent movement and is entirely absent from the Community Rule. This absence from the Community Rule is particularly striking in the case of 1QS 6,3-4 (par. 4QS^d II,7-8; 4QS^g 2a-c, 2-3; 4QS^i 1,4-5) where virtually the same statement occurs as in CD 13,2 though significantly without the reference to the Book of Hagi. Thus, CD 13,2 reads,

ובמקום עשרה אל ימש איש כהן מבונן בספר ההגי על פיהו ישקו כולם

And in a place of ten there shall not be lacking a priest who is learned in the Book of Hagi. All of them shall obey him.

---

28. Cf. ALEXANDER & VERMES, *Qumran Cave 4. XIX*, pp. 129-152; GLESSMER, *Sabbatstruktur*; METSO, *Primary Results*; and METSO, *Textual Development*, pp. 48-54.
29. Cf. ALEXANDER & VERMES, *Qumran Cave 4. XIX*, p. 152 and METSO, *Textual Development*, p. 144.
30. See HEMPEL, *Nucleus of 1QSa* and HEMPEL, *Laws of the Damascus Document*, esp. pp. 149-151.

1QS 6,3-4 par., on the other hand, lacks the reference to the Book of Hagi and reads,

ובכול מקום אשר יהיה שם עשרה אנשים מעצת היחד אל ימש מאתם איש כוהן

"And in any place where there are ten men from the council of the community there shall not be lacking among them a priest"

The only other occurrence of the term Hagi usually rendered "meditation" occurs in Sapiential Work A where we find a reference to 'the vision of Hagi' (חזון ההגי) in 4Q417 2 i 15-16, cf. also 4Q417 2 i 17[31]. Apart from being struck by the significance of this overlap between the Laws of the Damascus Document, 1QSa and Sapiential Work A it is exceedingly difficult to be sure what this book/vision contained because the references in the Damascus Document and 1QSa tell us nothing about its contents and the reference to it in Sapiential Work A is both fragmentary and difficult. Lange has argued, taking up an earlier suggestion by L. Ginzberg, that the term should be rendered "Buch bzw. Vision der Erklärung" and that its contents were of a halakhic nature[32]. This seems plausible with reference to the Damascus Document and 1QSa. I am not convinced, on the other hand, that the character of the vision in Sapiential Work A is best perceived as halakhic. In 4QSapiential Work A 2 the vision of Hagi is identified with the Book of Remembrance. Thus, if the vision were understood in halakhic terms the same would apply to the Book of Remembrance. It seems more likely to me, however, that the Book of Remembrance is referring to a heavenly record of human conduct, cf. Mal 3,16-18[33].

3. The Maskil[34]

The participle maskil is clearly a sapiential term which is further associated with duties of a sapiential nature in some of the Rule Books. The form also occurs in some of the Qumran sapiential texts. Moreover the term maskil has a pervasive presence in the scrolls also outside of the Rule Books and the sapiential texts. Thus, it occurs frequently in the li-

---

31. Cf. HARRINGTON, *Reasons*, p. 253; HARRINGTON, *Wisdom Texts from Qumran*, pp. 55-56; and WACHOLDER & ABEGG, *Preliminary Edition* 3, p. xiii. See also COLLINS, *Likeness of the Holy Ones*.

32. Cf. LANGE, *Weisheit und Prädestination*, pp. 84-85. See also GINZBERG, *Jewish Sect*, pp. 49-51. Further, LICHTENBERGER, *Menschenbild*, pp. 27-28 where he remarks with reference to the Book of Hagi in CD and 1QSa, "es ist wohl ein Gesetzeswerk".

33. See the contribution by G.J. BROOKE in this volume. Further, COLLINS, *Likeness of the Holy Ones*, p. 609 n. 2; and ELGVIN, *Mystery to Come*, pp. 139-147.

34. See KAMPEN, *Diverse Aspects*, pp. 238-239; LANGE, *Weisheit und Prädestination*, pp. 144-164; KOSMALA, *Maskil*; NEWSOM, *Sage*.

turgical corpus of the scrolls such as the Songs of the Sabbath Sacrifice, the Rule of Blessings, and the Songs of the Maskil[35]. On this occasion I will pay particular attention to the material that refers to the maskil as the instructor or those passages that describe the role of the maskil as part of a social group. As we will see maskil occurs in the latter sense frequently in the Rule Books but much more rarely so in the wisdom texts. The term is absent from what remains of Mysteries. In what follows I will limit myself to the following texts: Sapiential Work A, 4QWays of Righteousness, the Damascus Document, the Community Rule, and 4Q298 Address of the Maskil to the Sons of Dawn.

3.1. Maskil in Sapiential Work A

According to the *Concordance* published as Fascicle 4 of the Preliminary Edition of the Dead Sea Scrolls by Wacholder and Abegg the participle maskil occurs once in 4Q417 (2 i 25) and three times in 4Q418 (21,2; 81,17; 238,1)[36]. In two instances in 4Q418 (21,2 and 238,1) the relevant fragments are so small and the context is so fragmentary that it is impossible to make much of them. Maier translates the former with "verständig"[37] and represents the latter as "Maskîl"[38], a differentiation that appears to be fairly arbitrary given the limited evidence. In the two remaining passages that preserve a sufficient amount of text to permit a relatively informed judgment the term does not appear to refer to a particular office. Thus, in 4Q417 2 i 25 it occurs in a formally coherent unit that comprises participles (frequently "understanding one" בן מבין or מבין, and in this case בן משכיל "wise one") followed by an imperative and an object to which a second person singular suffix may be appended (cf. 4Q417 2 i 13-14 and the present passage 2 i 25 whereas a similar construction without the suffix occurs in 2 i 18). That is, *maskil* seems to be used synonymously with *mebin* in this case. Similarly in 4Q418 81,17 the construction "all your wise teachers" (כול משכילכה) indicates that the reference is not to an office held by an individual. In sum, there is no clear-cut case in Sapiential Work A where the participle refers to a particular office.

3.2. Maskil in 4QWays of Righteousness

In 4Q421 the term maskil occurs twice. Scholars are in disagreement on how to understand the participle, and the context of both occurrences

---

35. Cf. NEWSOM, *Sage*, who is able to show that some of the issues raised in the liturgical material overlap with the topics of instruction entrusted to the maskil elsewhere.
36. WACHOLDER & ABEGG, *Concordance*, p. 251.
37. MAIER, *Texte*, p. 451.
38. MAIER, *Texte*, p. 481.

is fragmentary³⁹. In the first case it occurs alongside another participle נבון "discerning" and seems to have the meaning "wise one" (4Q421 1a ii-b, 10). The second occurrence in 4Q421 1a ii-b, 12 may refer to the office of the maskil in connection with reproof although it is difficult to be sure. It is noteworthy that the topic of rebuke is dealt with in the Community Rule (1QS 5,24-6,1 par.), the Damascus Document (CD 9,2-8.16-20 par.) and 4Q477, but in none of these passages is the maskil involved in the process.

3.3. Maskil in the Damascus Document

Baumgarten has tentatively proposed restoring a reference to the maskil as part of the title of the work in 4QDᵃ⁴⁰. No strong case can be built on such an entirely hypothetical restoration. In fact, the complete lack of references to this figure in the Admonition might even speak against it. We will see below, however, that 4Q298 may provide some support for Baumgarten's proposal. CD 12,20b-22a par. 4QDᵃ 9 ii 7-8 announces rules for the wise leader with the words,

ואלה החקים למשׂכיל להתהלך בם עם כל חי למשפט עת ועת

And these are the statutes by which the maskil shall deal with all the living according to the rule appropriate for every time.

This announcement is almost identical to the heading that introduces the section on the maskil in 1QS 9,12 par. 4QSᵉ III, 6-8⁴¹ which reads,

אלה החוקים למשׂכיל להתהלך בם עם כול חי לתכון עת ועת למשקל איש ואיש ...

These are the statutes by which the maskil shall deal with all the living according to the rule appropriate for every time and according to the weight of each man....

Unlike 1QS where this heading introduces a section of rules describing the role of the maskil no such rules follow in the Laws of the Damascus Document. As far as the Damascus Document is concerned I have argued elsewhere that this heading forms part of remnants of traditions dealing with the maskil that have been overshadowed by the figure

---

39. Cf. ELGVIN, *Wisdom in the Yaḥad*, p. 215; KAMPEN, *Diverse Aspects*, p. 233 and n. 99; MAIER, *Texte*, p. 489; TIGCHELAAR, *Sabbath Halakha*, p. 370; WISE, ABEGG, & COOK, *Dead Sea Scrolls*, p. 390.

40. Cf. BAUMGARTEN, *Qumran Cave 4. XIII*, pp. 31-32. Similar restorations that include a reference to the maskil in the opening lines of a work have been proposed also for the War Scroll and the Community Rule, cf., for instance, VAN DER PLOEG, *Guerre*, pp. 54-55 and CARMIGNAC, *Première ligne*.

41. Immediately preceding this heading the sizeable block of material attested in 1QS 8,15-9,11 is lacking from 4QSᵉ, cf. ALEXANDER & VERMES, *Qumran Cave 4. XIX*, p. 148; METSO, *Primary Results*.

of the overseer (מבקר) in the Laws in their present form[42]. The tradition complex dealing with the maskil in the Damascus Document is made up of the present heading and CD 13,22 par. where we have the fragmentary remains of a concluding statement, "[And] these are the ordi[nan]ces for the wise leader" ([אלה המש[פט]ים למשכיל). I have further assigned CD 13,7c-8 and CD 13,14-15a to this complex of traditions[43].

3.4. Maskil in the Community Rule

The term maskil occurs in a number of places in the Community Rule and, as is the case in the Damascus Document, chiefly in headings. Carmignac followed by others suggested reconstructing למשכיל in 1QS 1,1 as part of the title of the Community Rule[44]. The introduction to the teaching on the two spirits makes reference to the maskil in 1QS 3,13. Furthermore, 4QS[b] IX,1 par. 4QS[d] I,1 begin the section parallel to 1QS 5,1 with the words מדרש למשכיל which are significantly absent in the parallel text of 1QS 5[45]. Finally, 1QS 9 comprises two further headings that refer to the maskil in 1QS 9,12 par. 4QS[e] III,6-7 and 1QS 9,21 par. [4QS[b] XVIII,4-5, largely reconstructed]; 4QS[d] VIII,5-6; 4QS[e] IV,2-3.

Of all these passages 1QS 9,12-26 par. is the most instructive in informing us about the role of the maskil, and in what follows I shall focus on this material. By delineating this section on the maskil to run until 1QS 9,26 I follow Knibb[46]. It seems clear that after the lacuna in 1QS 9,26 we have the beginning of a new section that eventually leads to the hymn in 1QS 10,9ff. The only other passage that seemingly goes into detail about the content of the maskil's teaching is the Instruction on the Two Spirits in 1QS 3,13-4,26 par. This part of 1QS is absent from 4QS[d] and 4QS[e], and I am convinced by the arguments of those who have pro-

---

42. Cf. HEMPEL, *Laws of the Damascus Document*, pp. 105-106, 118-121, 123-125, 150, 189.

43. A further possible reference to the maskil is partially preserved in 4QD[a] 5 i 17. This passage uniquely combines terminology characteristic of the Admonition and the Laws and probably belongs to a bridging passage that links both parts of the work, cf. further HEMPEL, *Laws of the Damascus Document*, pp. 171-174.

44. Cf. CARMIGNAC, *Première ligne*; DUPONT-SOMMER, *Essene Writings*, p. 72 n. 3. More recently a reconstruction along these lines has been accepted by METSO, *Textual Development*, pp. 111-112 and with reference to 4QS[c] by ALEXANDER & VERMES, *Qumran Cave 4. XIX*, p. 70, see also p. 32.

45. See ALEXANDER & VERMES, *Qumran Cave 4. XIX*, p. 96; HEMPEL, *Comments*; METSO, *Textual Development*, pp. 135-136; VERMES, *Preliminary Remarks*. On the differences between 1QS 5 and 4QS see also ALEXANDER, *Redaction-History*; BOCKMUEHL, *Redaction and Ideology*; VERMES, *Leadership*.

46. Cf. KNIBB, *Qumran Community*, pp. 141-144. This delineation has also been adopted by METSO, *Textual Development*, pp. 118-119. For the view that the section on the maskil runs until 1QS 10,5 see NEWSOM, *Sage*, p. 374. See further ALEXANDER, *Redaction-History*, pp. 441-442.

posed that it constitutes an originally independent section that was secondarily associated with the Community Rule and the maskil[47].

Let me return, therefore, to 1QS 9,12-26. Whereas several passages are associated with the maskil in the title or heading, this passage is followed by a series of statements that are specifically describing his role[48]. Wernberg-Møller has suggested, by contrast, that in 1QS 9,12ff.

> ...the ensuing injunctions are most naturally taken as applying to the community as a whole, and not only to the teacher of the society.[49]

Hence he translates maskil as "wise man"[50]. Admittedly, some of the statements in 1QS 9,12ff. are ambiguous. In the majority of cases it seems quite clear, however, that the injunctions refer to a leader. Note, for example, the frequent third person plural suffixes ("them") which express the interaction between the individual figure of the maskil who is entrusted with guiding, instructing or weighing those in his charge. What is more, community members are unambiguously referred to in this section with a range of terms other than maskil such as "sons of Zadok / righteousness" (בני הצדוק/הצדק)[51], "chosen of the time" (בחירי העת), or "those who choose / the chosen of the way" (בוחרי / בחירי דרך)[52].

It seems likely to me that 1QS 9,12-26 comprises pre-sectarian traditions associated with the maskil. Remnants of this complex of traditions are also found in the Laws of the Damascus Document, as I suggested above. The community situation that emerges from 1QS 9,12-26 resembles neither the bulk of the Community Rule nor the Laws of the Damascus Document precisely. Metso seems right when she notes that "... the passages addressed to the *maskil* in IX,12-26 can easily be interpreted as referring to an already existing communal life"[53]. However,

---

47. Cf. J. FREY, *Dualistic Thought*, pp. 289-307; LANGE, *Weisheit und Prädestination*, pp. 127-128; METSO, *Textual Development*, pp. 139-140; STEGEMANN, *Textbestand und Grundgedanken*; and STEGEMANN, *Library of Qumran*, p. 110.
48. Cf. METSO, *Textual Development*, p. 145.
49. P. WERNBERG-MØLLER, *Manual of Discipline*, p. 66.
50. Cf. e.g. *Manual of Discipline*, p. 35. So also ELGVIN, *Wisdom in the Yaḥad*, p. 215.
51. 1QS 9,14 reads "the sons of Zadok" (בני הצדוק) whereas 4QS^e III,10 has "the sons of righteousness" (בני הצדק). Even prior to the availability of the variant in 4QS^e a number of scholars had proposed emending 1QS's text to read "the sons of righteousness". For a recent discussion of this passage which argues against emending the text of 1QS see KUGLER, *Note*.
52. Whereas 1QS 9,17-18 reads "those who choose the way" (בוחרי דרך), 4QS^d VIII, 2 and probably also 4QS^e III,16 read "the chosen of the way (בחירי דרך), cf. ALEXANDER & VERMES, *Qumran Cave 4. XIX*, p. 118.
53. *Textual Development*, p. 144.

the terms used to refer to this group are distinctive from the terminology of "*yaḥad*" (יחד) and "rabbim" (רבים) that were to become the standard self-designations in the Community Rule in its final form. Nor do we find any "camp" (מחנה) or "congregation" (עדה) terminology familiar from the communal legislation in the Damascus Document. The one occurrence of *yaḥad* in 1QS 9,18-19 seems disruptive and is likely to be secondary. Thus, right in the middle of a statement outlining the maskil's role of guiding and instructing "those who choose / the chosen of the way" (1QS 9,16b-19a par. 4QS^d VIII,2 and 4QS^e III,16) 1QS 9,18-19 appends "among the men of the *yaḥad*" (בתוך אנשי היחד). The text as it stands implies a sub-group of "those who choose / the chosen of the way" among the larger entity of the men of the *yaḥad*. It seems likely that the self-designation "those who choose / the chosen of the way" which, particularly on the reading attested in 4QS$^{d \text{ and } e}$, mirrors the earlier expression "chosen of the time" (1QS 9,14) is original and that the terminology "men of the *yaḥad*" (אנשי היחד) was inserted at a later time. We have positive manuscript evidence that this kind of editorial process did occur in 1QS 9,5-6 where the expression "men of the *yaḥad*" occurs but is absent from the parallel in 4QS^d VII,6[54].

The evidence of 4QS^e can easily be reconciled with the suggestion that the long section on the duties of the wise leader originated independently. The text of 4QS^e III,6 moves directly from the equivalent of 1QS 8,15 to the equivalent of 1QS 9,12[55]. Thus, the text of 4QS^e resumes with the heading announcing the duties of the wise leader in 1QS 9,12 which might suggest that the latter material circulated as an independent unit before being incorporated into the S tradition.

As has often been noted 1QS 9,15-16 seems to allot a role to the maskil in the admission process of new members[56]. However, in the detailed legislation on the admission into the *yaḥad* in 1QS 6,13ff. it is the paqid who is in charge of the process and in CD 15 it is the mebaqqer. It seems that the legislation and procedure underwent development in the course of time, and that some elements of the maskil tradition became subsumed in the duties of other functionaries. The maskil's role appears to build on his particular gifts of insight that allow him to judge the spiritual makeup of individuals rather than focusing on administrative

---

54. Cf. ALEXANDER & VERMES, *Qumran Cave 4. XIX*, pp. 113-114; METSO, *Textual Development*, pp. 44-45. See also ALEXANDER, *Redaction-History*, p. 441 n. 7.
55. Cf. ALEXANDER & VERMES, *Qumran Cave 4. XIX*, p. 148; METSO, *Primary Results*.
56. Cf., for instance, NEWSOM, *Sage*, p. 376.

duties⁵⁷. It is for this reason that in my view the maskil and the mebaqqer have distinct roles and should not be identified⁵⁸.

The evidence on the maskil in the Community Rule seems to point in two directions. On the one hand, maskil traditions appear to comprise traditional material that pre-dates the *yaḥad* as in 1QS 9. On the other hand, references to this individual are found at key junctures in 1QS in its final form which goes back to the time of the *yaḥad*. Matters are further complicated by the evidence of the heading in 1QS 5,1 where the maskil is absent over against the parallels in 4QS$^{b \text{ and } d}$ (4QS^b IX,1 and 4QS^d I,1). A comparable conclusion has been reached by Metso who detects early and late maskil material in the Community Rule. She seems to me on the right track when she advocates maskil material as part of an early source as well as references to this figure that were introduced at a later stage "for editorial purposes"⁵⁹. More detailed work may need to be done to isolate the early traditions associated with the maskil in the Community Rule outside of 1QS 9,12-26. Metso suggests 4QS^d I,1ff par. 4QS^b IX,1ff, and I would want to argue for an incorporation of the remnants of a maskil tradition in the Damascus Document into the larger picture⁶⁰.

3.5. Maskil in 4Q298 Address of the Maskil to the Sons of Dawn

Finally the figure of the maskil occurs in the title of the recently published text 4Q298⁶¹. The editors argue that the work comprises an address by the maskil to novices in the process of joining the community and describe the function and content of the work as follows,

> Since this composition seems to be an introductory address, it is probable that he [the maskil] is speaking to novices and that the term "Sons of

---

57. Cf. NEWSOM, *Sage*, p. 382 where she observes with reference to the maskil, "he also had insight into character, into the "spirits" of individuals, a knowledge he used very directly to form the membership of the sect". See further ALEXANDER, *Physiognomy*, esp. p. 391, who suggests that the maskil might have employed physiognomy in order to assess the merits of community members.

58. For the view that the maskil and the mebaqqer are titles referring to one and the same official see KNIBB, *Qumran Community*, p. 121; NEWSOM, *Sage*, p. 375; and VERMES, *Complete Dead Sea Scrolls in English*, p. 29. For a different view see HEMPEL, *Community Structures*, pp. 81-82.

59. METSO, *Textual Development*, p. 145.

60. Cf. METSO, *Textual Development*, p. 145 where she notes, "It may be asked whether the sections addressed to the *maskil* in 4QS^b 5,1 ff./4QS^d 1 I,1ff. (par. 1QS V,1ff.) and in 1QS IX,12-16 originate from a common source, from some kind of handbook addressed to the leader of the Essene communities". Note that METSO's numeration of the columns of the 4QS manuscripts predates the system eventually adopted in DJD 26. The latter is used in this paper. See further METSO, *Textual Development*, p. 139 n. 106. For my views on the place of the maskil in the Damascus Document see section 3.3 and n. 42 above.

61. See PFANN & KISTER, *4Q298*.

Dawn" implies that these individuals are "dawning" out of the darkness and into the light, and are thus on the verge of becoming "Sons of Light"[62].

The editors further propose connecting this text with the admission process as described in 1QS 6,13ff. Their basic contention has been accepted by Collins[63], Kampen[64], and considered plausible by Harrington[65]. Despite such wide-ranging support in favour of the editors' reconstruction of the document's function the evidence on which this hypothesis is based is very slender indeed. The main arguments brought forward are the text's introductory character and the assumption that the term "sons of dawn" designates novices. Let me deal with each one in turn. Firstly, the character of the document as an introductory address is nowhere substantiated by the editors, and I am not sure what they mean by it. I suspect what is meant is that the text was material taught to novices which presupposes rather than establishes the argument they are trying to make. We are left with the term "sons of dawn" (בני שחר) as the only and vital clue, and there is no indication anywhere in the scrolls that this term designates novices. In particular the texts describing the admission process in some detail in both the Damascus Document and the Community Rule never use the term. In fact, they do not use light and darkness imagery either. Moreover, where the imagery of light and darkness does occur it is assumed that individuals are born with a particular portion of light and darkness, and the notion that one's light-darkness ratio can be improved through teaching and instruction is nowhere expressed[66]. It seems much more likely to me that the term "sons of dawn" is no more than a synonym for "sons of light"[67]. At the very most the interpretation put forward by the editors is one of many possibilities, and it is certainly not warranted to read the entire text from the outset with this very thinly supported hypothesis in mind[68].

Also rather far-fetched is the tentatively proposed idea that the partially preserved expression "[those who pur]sue righteousness" (ורוד[פי

---

62. PFANN & KISTER, *4Q298*, p. 17. See also KISTER, *4Q298*, p. 238; PFANN, *4Q298*, p. 225.
63. COLLINS, *Jewish Wisdom*, p. 128.
64. KAMPEN, *Diverse Aspects*, p. 233.
65. HARRINGTON, *Review of Qumran Cave 4. XV*, esp. p. 357 and HARRINGTON, *Wisdom Texts from Qumran*, p. 65.
66. Cf., for instance, STEGEMANN, *Textbestand und Grundgedanken*, pp. 117-121.
67. The self-designation "sons of dawn" also occurs in CD 13,14-15 following the reading of S. SCHECHTER and J.M. BAUMGARTEN, cf. SCHECHTER, *Documents*, p. 13 and BAUMGARTEN, *Ban on Commerce*. The collaborative DJD edition of 4Q298 is contradictory with regard to the reading of CD 13,14-15, cf. PFANN & KISTER, *4Q298*, p. 16 n. 28 with p. 21.
68. A commendably cautious note has entered the edition of 4Q298 at one point but that is the exception, cf. PFANN & KISTER, *4Q298*, p. 21 where the hypothesis that the expression "sons of dawn" refers to catechumens is specified as "tentative".

צדק]) in 4Q298 1-2 i 2, which is based on Isa 51,1 as noted in the commentary, might refer to "catechumens"[69]. Here the editors propose the idea of a progression from pursuers of righteousness to those who know righteousness. It is again preferable to think of both terms as synonyms[70].

Of great interest are the close terminological parallels between the Community Rule and 4Q298 in what the editors label a "list of Essene virtues"[71]. There is, however, no indication in these virtues to suggest that they originated with the Essenes or the Qumran sect. By contrast, the editors themselves quite correctly note a dependence on biblical precedents, especially Micah 6,8 and Zeph 2,3. The parallels with Micah extend beyond terminology to overlaps in sequence.

As far as the use of the term maskil in 4Q298 is concerned the editors' interpretation of the participle as referring to the office of the wise leader seems convincing to me. The designation "sons of dawn" does seem to refer to a particular group placed under his guidance. It seems appropriate, therefore, to add this fascinating new text to the growing body of maskil traditions in the scrolls. Finally, in support of his proposed restoration of a reference to the maskil in 4QD^a 1 Baumgarten refers to the occurrence of the term maskil in the title of 4Q298[72]. One may add to this that the formal similarity between the body of 4Q298 and the early portions of the Admonition of the Damascus Document, such as the calls to hearken for instance (cf. 4Q298 3-4 ii 3-4 and 4QD^a 1 a-b 5; CD 1,1; 2,2.14)[73], may provide some additional support for Baumgarten's restoration.

V. CONCLUSION

To conclude, it emerges from the discussion offered above that the relationship between the Qumran sapiential texts and the Rule Books is a complex one, and the topic is sure to arouse a great deal of further discussion. I was only able to scratch the surface on this occasion. The

---

69. PFANN & KISTER, *4Q298*, p. 22.
70. Cf. 4Q299 8,7 for the comparable term "those who pursue knowledge" (רודפי דעת), cf. SCHIFFMAN, *Mysteries*, p. 50. See also 4Q424 3,2, cf. BRIN, *Wisdom Issues*, p. 298 where he lists the expression "those who pursue knowledge" as a standard wisdom expression. See further BRIN, *4Q424 Fragment 3*, p. 277.
71. Cf. PFANN & KISTER, *4Q298*, p. 16.
72. Cf. BAUMGARTEN, *Qumran Cave 4. XIII*, p. 32.
73. A further call to hearken occurs in 4QD^e 2 ii 19. On this passage see HEMPEL, *Laws of the Damascus Document*, pp. 163-170 and HEMPEL, *Damascus Document and 4QMMT*.

most interesting and fascinating result of the above discussion, to my mind, is the presence of a number of overlapping terms and ideas between the material that describes organizational matters in the Rules and the sapiential texts as was the case particularly with the Book/Vision of Hagi. As far as the maskil is concerned we noted the presence of a sizeable tradition complex in the Laws of the Damascus Document, the Community Rule and 4Q298. More texts could be added to these that fall outside the scope of this paper. His role seems to have become merged with later traditions in the course of the literary growth of the Laws of the Damascus Document and the Community Rule. In the Qumran sapiential texts the participle maskil occurs, but in the bulk of the wisdom corpus it proved difficult to establish clear-cut cases where it refers to a particular office with the notable exception of 4Q298.

Meyerhoff Center for Jewish Studies   Charlotte HEMPEL
University of Maryland
College Park, Maryland
USA

FRÜHJÜDISCHE WEISHEITSTRADITIONEN
IM SLAVISCHEN HENOCHBUCH
UND IN QUMRAN

Seit das slavische Henochbuch im Jahre 1896 aus seinem langen Dornröschenschlaf auferweckt wurde, scheint es heute nach gut 100 Jahren wieder in einen erneuten Halbschlummer gesunken zu sein. Vielleicht war der Kuß nicht kräftig genug – vielleicht ist auch die Hecke zu dornig geblieben. Jedenfalls taucht es im wachen Bewußtsein vieler Untersuchungen, die Geschichte und Literatur des frühen Judentums zum Inhalt haben, nur als ein schemenhaftes, fremdes Wesen auf – wenn überhaupt. Gerade in der Qumranforschung macht sich dieser Sachverhalt schmerzlich bemerkbar. Durch den Fund der aramäischen Fragmente aus Höhle 4 ist die Henochtradition zwar auf ganz neue Weise in die Diskussion geraten. Ihre genauere Kenntnis hat sich längst auch als unverzichtbar für nahezu jeden Themenkreis erwiesen, der in den Schriften vom Toten Meer begegnet. Aber dennoch bricht alle Beschäftigung mit der Henochtradition dann abrupt nach ihrem Niederschlag in der griechischen und äthiopischen Übersetzung ab. Daß die Rolle Henochs als einer der wichtigsten Offenbarungsträger und Weisheitslehrer im frühen Judentum indessen auch in der alexandrinischen Diaspora nachweisbar ist und dort in Gestalt des slHen zu eigenständiger Blüte gelangte, wird weithin ignoriert. Sicher wirkt hier in der Qumranforschung noch immer das Verdikt J.T. Miliks nach, der das Buch als ein Produkt des byzantinischen Mönchtums betrachtete[1] – obgleich seine Argumente längst widerlegt und als Ergebnis irrtümlicher Lektüre erkannt sind[2]. Denn es ist schon erstaunlich, wenn selbst J.C. VanderKam in seinem jüngsten kenntnis- und materialreichen Buch den Urvater Henoch zwar als »man for *all generations*« präsentiert, dennoch aber jene Generationen im 1.Jh.n. Chr., die Henoch in die Welt einer hellenistischen Metropole versetzten,

---

1. MILIK, *Aramaic Fragments,* pp. 107-124.
2. MILIKs Argument mit dem (rekonstruierten!) Terminus συρμαιογραφεῖν in 22,11 als eines Neologismus aus dem 9. Jh. läßt sich aus textkritischen und traditionsgeschichtlichen Gründen nicht halten; seine Behauptung einer Widerspiegelung der im Umkreis des Studiosklosters praktizierten Sukzessions- und Investiturpraxis hat am Text des slHen nicht den geringsten Anhalt. Vgl. ausführlich BÖTTRICH, *Weltweisheit,* pp. 39-40, 46-47, 128-129.

nur am Rande erwähnt[3]. G. Boccaccini konstruiert sogar eine eigenständige Gruppierung im frühen Judentum, die er als »Enochic Judaism« von den Qumran-Essenern absetzt – dem wichtigsten und einflußreichsten Protagonisten der Henochtradition außerhalb Palästinas aber gesteht er dabei nicht mehr Raum zu, als gerade zwei knappe Absätze bieten[4]. Selbst die intensive Debatte um den 364-Tage-Kalender hat zwar über äthHen 72-82, die Qumrantexte und Jub hinaus selbst die entlegensten Spuren dieses »verdrängten« Kalenderkonzeptes aufgespürt, seine massive Bezeugung und gleichzeitig wichtigste Nachwirkung im slHen bislang aber selbst komplett verdrängt[5].

Die folgenden Ausführungen haben deshalb die Absicht, das slHen da in den Blick zu rücken, wo die Texte aus Qumran im weiteren Kontext frühjüdischer Theologie diskutiert werden. Für die Frage weisheitlichen Denkens braucht die Relevanz des slHen dabei kaum eigens betont zu werden. Denn konsequenter als die vorausliegende Henochtradition hat gerade der Autor des slHen die Gestalt des Patriarchen auf den Charakter des exemplarischen Weisheitslehrers festgeschrieben. Bevor jedoch die Eigenheiten weisheitlichen Denkens im slHen dargestellt und in Beziehung zu den Weisheitstraditionen aus Qumran gesetzt werden können, müssen zunächst noch einmal die wichtigsten Einleitungsfragen kurz in Erinnerung gerufen werden.

---

3. VANDERKAM, *Enoch*, pp. 158-161. Dieses »curious book« sei lediglich »a convenient end point for the study of such material in Jewish (?) texts outside the Rabbinic corpus.« (158). Das Fragezeichen hinter »Jewish« ist indessen völlig unbegründet – ebenso wie die Aussage, daß es für eine Datierung »no strong clues« gebe (siehe unten). Selbst für einen »Endpunkt« sollte man dann letztlich mehr Aufmerksamkeit erwarten – um so mehr, wenn man das slHen sachgemäßer als einen erneuten »Höhepunkt« betrachtet.

4. BOCCACCINI, *Beyond the Essene Hypothesis*. Warum die Geschichte dieses »Enochic Judaism« nicht mit der Geschichte der mündlichen und schriftlichen Henochtradition verbunden sein sollte, leuchtet in keiner Weise ein – zumal, da das slHen doch wohl etwas mehr bietet als nur »the mere reference to the figure of Enoch« (13). Auch der »Wechsel des Protagonisten« am Schluß des Buches (von Henoch zu Melchisedek) verbleibt im Rahmen der Tradition. Eine solche methodische Vorentscheidung scheint doch eher aus der Scheu vor einem als schwierig empfundenen Text geboren zu sein.

5. Vgl. ALBANI, *Verdrängtes Konzept*. Der detaillierte Überblick von 46 Seiten erwähnt das slHen mit keinem Wort, obgleich gerade der Umstand, daß hier der 364-Tage-Kalender unverstanden, aber unbeirrt als offenbarte Weisheit präsentiert wird, das fraglos bedeutendste Beispiel für Verbreitung und Faszination des Konzeptes im 1.Jh. liefert. Hier mögen die Korruptionen des Konzeptes im slHen durch spätere Bearbeitungen verwirrend gewirkt haben – für die Grundschicht indessen ist der 364-Tage-Kalender eindeutig nachweisbar und bestimmt eine ganze Reihe wichtiger Textpassagen. Im nachgeholten Gespräch mit M. Albani ist inzwischen der Plan einer gemeinsamen Aufarbeitung der astronomisch-kalendarischen Aussagen des slHen ins Auge gefaßt. Inzwischen vgl. die entscheidenden Sachverhalte bei BÖTTRICH, *Weltweisheit* pp. 48-52 p. 114-115; *JSHRZ* V/7 zu slHen 11-17.

I. Einleitungsfragen zum slHen

Immer wieder begegnet man auch in der jüngsten Literatur dem Urteil, daß über die Einleitungsfragen zum slHen nichts Genaueres gesagt werden könne[6] – was dann wiederum dazu führt, seinen Text weithin auszublenden. Für ein solches Urteil gibt es jedoch keinen Grund. Seit durch F. I. Andersen 1977[7] alle jene Fragen wieder neu aufgeworfen worden sind, die mit der Ausgabe von A. Vaillant 1952[8] geklärt schienen, ist die Diskussion um das slHen ein gutes Stück weiter gekommen. Zeit, Ort, benutzte Traditionen, religionsgeschichtliches Milieu und theologisches Profil lassen sich inzwischen sehr eindeutig bestimmen[9].

Die wichtigste Frage gilt der Datierung. Als erledigt kann man jene Argumente einer Spätdatierung betrachten, die sich auf kalendarische Indizien stützten oder die Bogomilen im 12. Jh. als Urheber in Vorschlag brachten[10] – was hier an Beobachtungen formuliert wurde, gehört in den Bereich späterer Überlieferungsgeschichte. Ebenso entbehrt Miliks fatale Datierung ins 9. Jh. jeden Anhaltes am Text. Angesichts des Stoffes, der sein Grundgerüst aus der vorausliegenden, durch den Überlieferungszu-

---

6. Vgl. z.B. Oegema, *Hoffnung und Gericht*, p. 285: »Über den Sitz im Leben (ägyptisches Judentum laut Charles oder byzantinisches Mönchtum laut Milik?) sowie über das Verhältnis des Hen(slav) zu anderen (biblischen oder apokryphen) Büchern ist nichts mit Sicherheit zu sagen.« – bereits die Alternativen, vor allem aber dieses kurze und pauschale Statement bleiben entschieden hinter dem Stand der ansonsten auch von Oegema notierten neueren Forschung zurück.

7. Charlesworth, *Pseudepigrapha Seminars*. Das Referat Andersens entwarf damals in Auseinandersetzung mit Vaillant die Linien einer neuen Interpretation, die in der Übersetzung für die OTPs 1983 dann umgesetzt sind. Dieser Umstand ist in der Folge sehr viel weniger wahrgenommen worden als die vorsichtigen Formulierungen Andersens in der Einleitung zu seiner Übersetzung, die seither immer wieder isoliert und in einem verallgemeinernden Sinne zitiert werden.

8. Vaillant, *Le livre*, erstellte eine kritische Edition der kürzeren Fassung, die dank der bequemen franz. Parallelübersetzung zur meistbenutzten Textgrundlage wurde. Kritik meldete sich allein gegen Vaillants Datierung und Einschätzung des slHen als eines christlichen Textes, ohne daß solche Kritik jedoch umfassend begründet worden wäre. Man bezog sich auf den Text Vaillants (samt der darin enthaltenen Vorentscheidungen), hielt sich aber bei den Einleitungsfragen zurück.

9. Vgl. Böttrich, *Weltweisheit*; dazu Böttrich, *JSHRZ* V/7 – der Band bietet den Text in neuer Übersetzung, versehen mit ausführlichen Anmerkungen. Die wichtigsten slav. Texte sind zugänglich bei Sokolov, *Slavjanskaja Kniga Enocha*; diese Sammlung von Hss. und Studien wurde 1910 postum veröffentlicht; die wichtigste Hs. (R) läßt sich durch eine latein. Begleitübersetzung bei *Sokolov* relativ leicht erschließen. Verwirrung herrscht angesichts der Kapitel- und Verszählung: Vaillant hatte die von Sokolov eingeführte Teilung in 24 Kapitel übernommen, während ein Großteil der Übersetzungen jener Gliederung der Erstausgabe von Charles 1896 folgte, die ihrerseits auf der Gliederung der Hs. P aufbaut. Dieses System mit 73 Kapiteln hat Andersen modifiziert (ihm folgt auch JSHRZ V/7) – es stellt den sinnvollsten Kompromiß dar.

10. Vgl. Böttrich, *Weltweisheit*, pp. 28-31; *JSHRZ* V/7, pp. 803-804.

sammenhang des äthHen bekannten, Henochtradition bezieht, konzentriert sich die Frage deshalb auf eine Datierung des slHen vor oder nach dem Jahre 70. Dabei lassen sich nun gerade im slHen so viele Indizien für die Existenz des Tempels und den fraglosen Vollzug des Kultes finden[11], daß eine Entstehung vor 70 nicht nur als denkbar, sondern als relativ sicher angenommen werden kann. Bereits die zahlreichen Opferbestimmungen, die mit dem Tieropfer und den Verpflichtungen zur Wallfahrt[12] das zentrale Heiligtum voraussetzen, sprechen hier eine deutliche Sprache. Vor allem aber zeigt die urzeitliche Etablierung des Opferkultes an dem Ort Achuzan / Jerusalem, daß der Jerusalemer Tempel als ein seit Urzeiten ausgewiesener und durch ununterbrochene Tradition legitimierter Ort dargestellt werden soll – zur eigenen Selbstvergewisserung ebenso wie zum Zwecke seiner Erklärung gegenüber einer andersgläubigen Umwelt. Das stärkste Argument aber ergibt sich aus der internen Kalenderrechnung des Buches[13]. Gezielt und offensichtlich wohlüberlegt fällt jenes urzeitliche »Kultgründungsfest« in slHen 68/69 auf das Sommersolstitium am 17. Tammuz[14]: Dabei erstrahlt das Angesicht des Methusalem beim Antritt seines priesterlichen Amtes »wie die Sonne, die in der Mitte des Tages aufgeht« (69,10). Unter dem Datum des 17. Tammuz aber hat das rabbinische Judentum später der Zerstörung des Tempels unter Titus gedacht[15]. Auch wenn man hier eine zeitliche Differenz veranschlagen muß – schon unmittelbar nach der Katastrophe des Jahres 70 dürfte es undenkbar gewesen sein, ganz unbedarft gerade diesen Termin zu wählen, ohne daß dabei Trauer oder Hoffnung in irgendeiner Weise mitschwingen würden. Ein solches Indiz gestattet deshalb eine sichere Entscheidung, die weit zuverlässiger ist als so manche vage Beobachtung zur Datierung anderer frühjüdischer Schriften. Der Bezug auf die vorausliegende Henochtradition, der sich an einigen Stellen sogar mit wörtlichen Entsprechungen in den griechischen Fragmenten präzise belegen

---

11. Von Opfern ist nicht erst im dritten Teil die Rede – schon in der Abschiedsrede am Beginn der Himmelsreise in 2,2 werden sie angemahnt und bilden ebenso in Mahnreden und Testament einen festen Bestandteil der Paränese. Die Terminologie ist vielfältig und zielt entweder auf Tieropfer (Schaf, Rind, Jungstier, Taube) oder allgemein auf die Darbringung von »Gaben«. Opferpraxis kommt unbetont, aber allgegenwärtig zur Sprache. Weder wird hier Vergangenes konserviert noch idealisiert – alle Aussagen atmen gegenwärtige Alltäglichkeit.

12. Nur so lassen sich z.B. 61,4-5 und 62,2-3 verstehen, die vor einem Bruch von Gelübden im Blick auf die Darbringung von Gaben warnen.

13. Vgl. dazu vor allem die Rekonstruktion von GOUDOEVER, *Calendars*.

14. Das wird durch 48,2 bestätigt. Die Beschreibung der Investitur spielt offensichtlich auf das Datum an.

15. Vgl. vor allem jTaan 68c; bTaan 26b. Später ist damit dann auch die Erinnerung an die Zerstörung Jerusalems durch die Babylonier verbunden worden.

läßt, spricht insgesamt für eine Entstehung des slHen nach der Zeitenwende. Das slHen ist also mit großer Sicherheit als eine Schrift aus dem 1. Jh.n.Chr., noch vor der Tempelzerstörung im Jahre 70, zu betrachten.

Auch die Lokalisierung kann sich auf eine Reihe plausibler Anhaltspunkte stützen. Unübersehbar prägt die Situation der Diaspora das ganze Buch. Es ist in einer universalistischen Perspektive geschrieben, der national-messianische Züge völlig fremd sind und die den jüdischen Glauben mit Vorstellungen der griechisch-hellenistischen Philosophie zu vermitteln sucht. Sprache, Metaphorik und Wissensspektrum setzen ein weltoffenes, städtisches Zentrum voraus, in dem jüdische und hellenistische Bildung einander begegnen. Allein das spricht bereits für Alexandrien. Vorstellungen speziell der ägyptischen Mythologie und Religiosität kommen hinzu. Anklänge an Philo finden sich zahlreich[16]. Der Stellenwert der Wallfahrt und Details zu in Ägypten nachweisbaren Schlachtungsbräuchen[17] flankieren diese Beobachtungen. So kann das alexandrinische Judentum mit hoher Wahrscheinlichkeit als Herkunftsort des slHen angesehen werden.

Die Abhängigkeit des slHen von der älteren Henochtradition fällt schon bei flüchtiger Lektüre auf[18]. Sie ist indessen kein später und ferner Nachhall alter, längst schon konservierter Überlieferungen. Das slHen steht vielmehr mitten drin in dem kreativen und produktiven Prozeß jener lebendigen, theologisch äußerst fruchtbaren Auseinandersetzung mit der Gestalt des Urvaters Henoch. Es fällt noch in die Hochblüte dieser Tradition hinein und nimmt an ihrer Ausgestaltung maßgeblich teil. Eindeutig greifbar wird der Bezug im Blick auf das angelologische Buch (äthHen 1-36), das astronomische Buch (äthHen 72-82) sowie die Mahnreden Henochs (äthHen 91-105). Hier reicht das Spektrum von allgemeinen Parallelen über konkrete Anspielungen bis hin zu wörtlichen Übereinstimmungen. Von besonderer Bedeutung ist die Beobachtung, daß die Verwandlung Henochs in einen der »Herrlichen des Herrn« slHen 22 deutlich die Einsetzung Henochs zum Menschensohn äthHen 71 aufnimmt. Überhaupt müssen äthHen 70-71, die als Anhang zu den Bilderreden gelten, dem Autor bekannt gewesen sein. Auch der immer wieder als merkwürdig betrachtete Wechsel des Protagonisten von Henoch auf Melchisedek in slHen 71-72 findet eine Erklärung in der

---

16. Zu nennen wären etwa die Sonnentiere Phönix und Chalkedrios (12,1); der Sonnenhymnus (15,2); die Gestalt des Adoil (25,1); das Gericht auf der Seelenwaage (52,15) u.a.m.; zu Philo läßt sich eine durchgängige Nähe beobachten.

17. Vgl. z.B. 59,3. Diese Anordnungen sind eher auf eine in Ägypten verbreitete Praxis als auf die Eigenheit einer häretischen Gruppe (so S. PINES) zurückzuführen.

18. Vgl. genauere Nachweise in BÖTTRICH, *JSHRZ* V/7, pp. 807-808.

Aufnahme von Noah-Traditionen, wie sie ja längst mit der Henochtradition verbunden waren. Eindeutig läßt sich auch der Einfluß des Sirachbuches nachweisen. Die vielen Anklänge an Motive und Themen anderer frühjüdischer Schriften bleiben für eine Feststellung direkter literarischer Beziehungen zu allgemein, machen jedoch die Einbettung des slHen in die Literatur des hellenistischen Judentums auf eindrückliche Weise sichtbar. Die Behauptung eines genuin christlichen Textes steht hier nicht nur einer erdrückenden Übermacht traditioneller jüdischer Theologumena gegenüber – ihr fehlt zudem jeder auch nur einigermaßen plausible positive Anhalt am Text.

Eine religionsgeschichtliche Einordnung des slHen fällt somit nicht schwer. Die Schrift gehört in das hellenistische Diasporajudentum Alexandriens, das sich gegenüber einer religiös vielfältigen, synkretistischen Umwelt behaupten muß. Es speist sich dabei aus apokalyptischen Traditionen, rückt sie jedoch in den Horizont eines weltoffenen, kosmopolitischen Denkens. Selbstvergewisserung hinsichtlich des überkommenen Glaubensgutes und dessen werbende Vermittlung in die hellenistische Welt hinein erscheinen dabei als die vordringlichen Interessen, die den Trägerkreis dieser Schrift bestimmen. Es versteht sich von selbst, daß die vorgegebenen Überlieferungen dabei umgeschmolzen bzw. neu ausgeprägt werden müssen. Aus den zeitlich-horizontalen Erwartungen der Henochapokalyptik ist ein konsequent vertikales, räumlich-jenseitiges Weltbild entstanden. Die weisheitlichen Züge der Tradition sind ganz in den Vordergrund gerückt. Alles zielt darauf ab, Henoch durch die Offenbarungen seiner Himmelsreise zum urzeitlichen Lehrer der Menschheit zu qualifizieren. Auch der letzte Teil, der um die Gestalten Methusalem, Nir und Melchisedek kreist, folgt diesem Ziel: Er stellt den Beginn der Menschheitsgeschichte dar, die von Befolgung oder Abweisung der Lehren Henochs bestimmt wird. In dieser menschheitlichen Perspektive finden dann auch einige in der Umwelt des Trägerkreises anerkannte Lehren der griechisch-hellenistischen Philosophie ihren selbstverständlichen Platz. Was sich da an kosmologischen oder anthropologischen Grundeinsichten findet, kann ebenfalls nur in der offenbarten Weisheit Gottes verankert sein. Um einer solchen Synthese willen nimmt der Autor dann auch manche Spannungen und Ungereimtheiten in Kauf. Aber trotz aller Öffnung verbleibt er dennoch streng auf dem Boden des jüdischen Grundbekenntnisses – wie ein roter Faden durchzieht die Betonung der Einzigkeit Gottes das ganze Buch. Der Apokalyptik wird man das slHen somit nur bedingt zurechnen können[19]. Durchaus nicht zufällig kommt

---

19. Zur Problematik vgl. COLLINS, *Genre Apocalypse*; BÖTTRICH, *Weltweisheit*, pp. 209-211.

das Buch dann gerade in der frühen jüdischen Mystik noch einmal zu Ehren. Hier sind die weisheitlich-spekulativen Traditionen alexandrinischer Prägung offenbar in einer Weise präsent gewesen, die den Merkaba-Mystikern einen leichten Zugang boten[20]. Auf jeden Fall zeigt das slHen entgegen manchen gewichtigen Teilen seines Stoffes eine größere Nähe zu jüdisch-hellenistischen Weisheitstraditionen, die im Umfeld etwa eines Philo ihren eigenständigen Platz behaupten können.

So bleibt nur noch das theologische Profil des Buches zu skizzieren. Von dem kompilatorischen Textcharakter des sogen. äthHen hebt sich die konzeptionelle Geschlossenheit des slHen bereits deutlich ab. Der Aufbau läßt eine überlegte Gestaltung des Stoffes erkennen, deren Intention in der aufeinander abgestimmten und miteinander vielfach verquickten Abfolge dreier großer Themenkomplexe sichtbar wird. Grundlegend wird im ersten Teil (1-38) die Qualifizierung Henochs als eines weisheitlichen Offenbarungsträgers vorgestellt: in Gestalt seiner Himmelsreise, der Einsicht in die himmlischen Bücher und einer großen Gottesrede, wobei Henoch selbst schon vollgültige Aufnahme in den Kreis des himmlischen Hofstaates findet. Im zweiten Teil (39-67) kommt nun die aus solcher Weisheit gespeiste Ethik zur Sprache – vorgetragen in Gestalt testamentarischer Mahnreden an einen zunehmend größer werdenden Hörerkreis. Der dritte Teil (68-73) schließlich schildert die Folgen solcher Belehrung nun durch die Begründung eines priesterlichen Dienstes in der Nachfolge Henochs und bringt damit in Gestalt des zentralen Opferkultes jüdische Identität und praktizierte Frömmigkeit zur Darstellung. Daß auch dieser letzte Teil einen integralen Bestandteil des ganzen Buches darstellt, belegt nicht nur die handschriftliche Überlieferung; auch inhaltlich würde dem Buch eine wichtige Dimension fehlen, wenn der Text mit der endgültigen Entrückung Henochs endete[21]. Der urzeitliche Rahmen umspannt nun einmal die Zeit von der Weltschöpfung bis zur Flut, und die Tatsache, daß die Belehrungen Henochs nur von einem Teil der urzeitlichen Menschheit realisiert werden und das Flutgericht nicht verhindern können, verlangt eine Erklärung. Weisheit, Ethik und Kult sind also die Themenfelder,

---

20. Anspielungen auf das slHen im sogen. hebrHen sind m.E. eindeutig erkennbar; zur Rezeption der Henochtradition in einem offensichtlich zweisprachigen Milieu jüd. Theologie in Nordafrika (ca. 2.-6. Jh.) vgl. noch BÖTTRICH, *Beobachtungen*.

21. Seit CHARLES in seiner Editio princeps jenen Teil mit der Melchisedekgeschichte in einen Anhang verbannt hatte, ist eine besondere Zurückhaltung gegenüber dem inzwischen als Kap. 69-73 gezählten Abschnitt bestehen geblieben. CHARLES besaß damals nur einen ungenügenden Einblick in die handschriftliche Überlieferung; die ursprüngliche Zugehörigkeit zum Text läßt sich mittlerweile zweifelsfrei nachweisen – vgl. BÖTTRICH, *JSHRZ* V/7, p. 806.

auf denen der Trägerkreis des slHen einen Konsens, einen modus vivendi oder zumindest Anerkennung gegenüber seiner Umwelt sucht, was der Autor des Buches wiederum auf stimmige Weise mit Hilfe der Henochtradition gestaltet hat. Dem Synkretismus seiner Umwelt liefert er sich dabei nicht aus, auch wenn er ihm mitunter sehr nahe kommt. Aber er will vom Standpunkt seines Gottesbekenntnisses aus das Gemeinsame formulieren, das alle Menschen als Geschöpfe Gottes verbindet und als allgemeingültige Weisheit allen Menschen zugänglich ist. Sein theologisches Anliegen zielt damit auf Vermittlung – nach innen ebenso wie nach außen. Dafür gab es schon bald nach 70 in dem sich neu formierenden Judentum keinen Raum mehr. So kann es auch kaum verwundern, daß sich nun ausschließlich die christliche Theologie, von einigen jüdisch-mystischen Zirkeln abgesehen, des Buches annahm[22]. Hier mußte die universale, menschheitliche Perspektive des slHen auf ein neues, interessiertes Publikum stoßen.

Im Verlaufe einer komplizierten Überlieferungsgeschichte ist das slHen um einige jüdisch-mystische, frühchristliche und byzantinisch-chronographische Zusätze erweitert worden, die sich indessen relativ gut vom zugrundeliegenden Text unterscheiden lassen[23]. Als ein viel schwerwiegenderes Hemmnis für die Benutzung des Textes hat sich seine Existenz in wenigstens zwei unterschiedlich langen Rezensionen erwiesen[24]. Nach der Erprobung verschiedener Hypothesen kann heute die längere Textfassung wieder als die ursprünglichere gelten. Außer Beobachtungen an den Kontextmanuskripten der einzelnen Handschriften sprechen vor allem literarkritische Beobachtungen dafür, daß die kürzere Fassung als Ergebnis redaktioneller Arbeit im Bereich der slavischen Überlieferung zu betrachten ist. Mit dem Text der längeren Fassung, reduziert um die (wenigen) als Interpolationen erkennbaren Stücke, liegt somit eine ausreichend sichere Basis für das Studium des slHen vor.

Nach dieser kurzen Bestandsaufnahme der jüngsten Forschungsergebnisse dürfte es nicht mehr fraglich sein, daß dem slHen im Konzert frühjüdischer Theologie eine wichtige Stimme zukommt. Sowohl in bezug auf die Henochtradition als auch im Blick auf weisheitliche Spekulationen insgesamt bietet es eine besonders interessante, weil in einem vergleichbaren Zeitraum ganz eigenständig ausgeprägte Variante. So besteht die berechtigte Hoffnung, daß im Lichte der weisheitlichen Spekulationen des slHen auch das Profil der Weisheitstexte aus Qumran schärfer hervortritt – und umgekehrt.

22. S. oben Anm. 20.
23. Vgl. BÖTTRICH, *Weltweisheit*, pp. 109-130; *JSHRZ* V/7, pp. 802-805.
24. Vgl. BÖTTRICH, *JSHRZ* V/7, pp. 788-795.

II. WELTWEISHEIT ALS OFFENBARUNGSWISSEN

1. Weisheitliche Strukturen

Der weisheitliche Charakter des slHen tritt bereits in formaler Hinsicht deutlich zutage. Wenn nach dem Urteil P. von der Osten-Sackens die Apokalyptik als »spätes und eigenartiges Kind der Prophetie«, das sich »obschon bereits in jungen Jahren nicht ohne Gelehrsamkeit, erst mit zunehmendem Alter der Weisheit geöffnet hat«, zu betrachten ist[25], dann trifft dies auf das Verhältnis von apokalyptischen und weisheitlichen Zügen im slHen in besonderem Maße zu. Die ältere, apokalyptisch geprägte Henochtradition gibt mit Himmelsreise, Überlieferung vom Engelfall und letztlicher Entrückung Henochs auch den Grundriß der Komposition vor. Ausgeführt wird der Plan dann aber im slHen als dem wichtigsten Zeugnis einer fortgeschrittenen Entwicklung der Henochtradition so, daß weisheitliches Denken endgültig als die dominierende Größe erscheint.

1a. Henochs Testament

Formaler und theologischer Mittelpunkt ist der zweite Teil des Buches, der in 40-67 Mahnreden Henochs an seine Söhne enthält. Nach einem ersten Reisebericht (40,1-42,5) und ersten daraus abgeleiteten Mahnungen (42,6-54,1) folgt der Text in 55,1-67,3 dann ganz klar der Gattung frühjüdischer Testamentenliteratur[26]. Ein Anfangsrahmen (55,1-57,2) erklärt die Situation des nahen Abschiedes und bestimmt den Adressatenkreis, dem das Vermächtnis des Patriarchen dann in zwei längeren Redeeinheiten (58,1-63,4 / 65,1-66,8) vorgetragen wird[27]. Sorgfältig setzt der Autor dabei seine theologischen Akzente: In der ersten Rede leitet Henoch alle Ermahnungen aus den Gegebenheiten der göttlichen Weltschöpfung ab, während er in der zweiten Rede dann stärker den Ausblick auf das künftige Gericht hin öffnet und so zum Schlußrahmen (67,1-3) der endgültigen Entrückung überleitet.

Aber schon die Himmelsreise des ersten Teiles (1-38) enthält eine Reihe von Texteinheiten, die sich weisheitlichen Gattungen zuordnen lassen: In 1,1-10 z.B. hält Henoch eine erste Abschiedsrede vor den versammelten Söhnen; die Erkundungen während seines Aufstieges durch

---

25. VON DER OSTEN-SACKEN, *Apokalyptik*, p. 63. Zur Diskussion vgl. MICHEL, *Weisheit und Apokalyptik*.
26. Vgl. grundlegend VON NORDHEIM, *Lehre*.
27. Der Adressatenkreis weitet sich allmählich aus: Methusalem versammelt in 38,3 zunächst die »Söhne« bzw. die »Hausgenossen« des Patriarchen, ab 57,1 kommen »die Ältesten des Volkes« hinzu, ab 64,1 wird »das ganze Volk« mit einbezogen.

die sieben Himmel werden immer wieder in listenartigen Aufzählungen festgehalten[28]. Tugend- und Lasterkataloge[29] oder das wohlbekannte Zwei-Wege-Schema[30] bündeln die Einsichten, die aus der Konfrontation mit den gefallenen Wächtern resultieren. Nicht anders steht es im dritten Teil (68-73), der außer der zentralen Geburtsgeschichte des Melchisedek die Priester Methusalem und Nir als paradigmatische Fromme präsentiert, die aus der Weisheit Henochs gespeist die urzeitliche Menschheit führen.

1b. Rezeption von Gen 1-3

Die theologische Position des slHen zeigt sich besonders anschaulich da, wo die Thematik von Erschaffung und Sündenfall des Menschen aufgenommen wird. Sie hat ihren Ort in der großen Gottesrede (24-35) und stellt im Rahmen des Sechstagewerkes eine der markantesten Ausgestaltungen gegenüber der biblischen Tradition dar (30,8-32,2). In Henochs Reisebericht sowie in der ersten Rede des Testamentes kommen das Schicksal der Voreltern (41,1; 42,5) und die Herrschaft Adams über die Tiere (58,1-3) noch einmal unter paränetischen Interessen zur Sprache. Diese Gestalt der Rezeption von Gen 1-3 ist von einer Prägnanz, wie sie in der frühjüdischen Literatur ihresgleichen sucht – auch wenn dies in den einschlägigen Arbeiten bislang kaum wahrgenommen wird[31].

Schlüsselcharakter besitzt der Abschnitt 30,8-14, der von der Erschaffung Adams aus sieben Bestandteilen der Natur sowie von der Bildung seines Namens als eines Akronyms aus den griechischen Bezeichnungen der vier Himmelsrichtungen handelt[32]. Deutlicher noch als in anderen Zusammenhängen wird hier das Anliegen des Autors spürbar, die biblische Glaubenstradition mit dem Wissen seiner hellenistischen Umwelt zu verbinden. Besonders in der Vorstellung vom Menschen als einem

---

28. 13,3-4 (Sonnentore); 16,2 (Mondtore); 23,1-2 (Offenbarungsgegenstände); 30,3 (Planetenliste); 30,8 (Elemente für Adams Erschaffung); 30,9 (Eigenschaften Adams).
29. Tugendkataloge: 9,1; 43,2-3; 66,6; Lasterkataloge: 10,4-6; Tugend- / Peristasenkatalog 66,6.
30. 30,15: die dem Adam vorgelegten Wege heißen »Licht und Finsternis«; 42,10 spricht vom »zeitlichen Weg dieser nichtigen Welt« und dem »rechten Weg, der in jenen endlosen Äon führt«. Dem Schema korrespondiert die Entgegensetzung von »gut / böse« (30,15); »Gute / Böse« (61,2); guten und bösen Orten (8-10; 61,2); »Gerechten / Ungerechten« (46,3).
31. Als Beispiel kann die Arbeit von LEVISON, *Portraits*, gelten, der das slHen unter Berufung auf F.I. ANDERSEN bewußt ausläßt. Dabei werden – wie so oft – die zurückhaltenden, vorsichtigen Äußerungen ANDERSENs (z.B. »in every respect... an enigma«) verallgemeinernd zum entscheidenden Charakteristikum gemacht. Auch der Aufsatz von HAYWARD, der 1992 in JSJ erschien und die Arbeit von LEVISON fortführen will, erkennt eine Lücke lediglich hinsichtlich der Adamfigur im Liber Antiquitatum Biblicarum.
32. Vgl. zu dieser Passage ausführlich BÖTTRICH, *Mikrokosmos*.

Mikrokosmos schlägt sich das Erbe einer langen philosophischen Tradition, in der auch Philo steht, spürbar nieder. Stoisches Gedankengut findet sich darin ebenso wie Elemente, die im Schrifttum der hippokratischen Schule begegnen. Eine solche interpretierende Nacherzählung der biblischen Überlieferung läßt ihre leitenden Motive deutlich erkennen: Der Mensch erscheint als Teil der Welt, eingefügt in eine umfassende Ordnung, ausgerüstet mit der Weisheit Gottes und eingesetzt zum »König der Erde«. Aus dieser Ordnung, die von ihrem Schöpfer her lebt, resultiert seine Verantwortung. Im Rahmen dieser Ordnung wiederum realisiert sich sein Menschsein, weswegen er der Erkenntnis in die Zusammenhänge des Weltganzen bedarf – einer Erkenntnis, an der grundsätzlich die gesamte Menschheit teilhaben kann.

Dieses stark weisheitlich geprägte Programm ließe sich im Einzelnen an der gesamten Aufnahme der biblischen Urgeschichte im slHen nachweisen. Bemerkenswert ist in diesem Zusammenhang noch, was bereits vor dem Angriff des Satans gegen Adam berichtet wird: Gott habe dem Adam seinen Willen gegeben und ihm die Wege von Licht und Finsternis vorgelegt, er aber habe sein Wesen nicht erkannt und sei somit aus Unwissenheit der Versündigung erlegen (30,15-16). Deshalb gilt dann auch in 31,7 Gottes Fluch der Unwissenheit des Menschen. Das sind klare Akzente. Unverkennbar tritt in einer solchen Darstellung die paränetische Absicht des Autors hervor.

Es bleibt noch zu erwähnen, daß auch die Erzählung von der wunderbaren Geburt Melchisedeks (71-72) dieser Tendenz folgt. Die Tradition atl. Geburtsgeschichten wird hier mit Elementen aus äthHen 106 (Geburt des Noah) verbunden und in den zeitlichen Rahmen der Generationen vor der Flut eingefügt[33]. Unmittelbar nach der Geburt aber erfolgt eine endgültige Entrückung Melchisedeks »in das Paradies Eden«. Die Melchisedekerzählung des slHen liefert damit nicht die Geschichte des Priesterkönigs aus Gen 14, sondern stellt die Erschaffung eines Urbildes für das irdische Priestertum dar, das nach dem kurzen Intermezzo einer wunderbaren Geburt ausschließlich als jenseitiger Garant jeder priesterlichen Ordnung auf Erden fungiert[34]. Auch hier beherrscht das Interesse an weisheitlichen Ordnungsstrukturen den überlieferten Erzählstoff.

---

33. Die Erzählung bietet eines der interessantesten Beispiele solcher Geburtsgeschichten überhaupt und tritt mit ihrer Voraussetzung einer übernatürlichen Zeugung den seltenen Aussagen Philos in Cher 40-48 zur Seite. Für das Studium der Geburtsgeschichten bei Mt und Lk gewinnt sie größte Bedeutung – auch wenn man sie bislang noch immer in der Diskussion übersieht.

34. Vgl. ausführlich BÖTTRICH, *Weltweisheit*, pp. 204-209.

1c. Himmlische Buchführung

Das Motiv himmlischer Bücher oder Tafeln ist sowohl im alten Orient als auch in der hellenistischen Welt weit verbreitet gewesen. Auch die entsprechenden Aussagen in AT und NT sind vor diesem Hintergrund zu verstehen. Umso wichtiger sind die Belege, die nun in Qumran greifbar geworden sind und das bislang bekannte Bild vertieft haben[35].

Versucht man, diese himmlischen Bücher nach funktionalen Gesichtspunkten zu unterscheiden, dann lassen sich vor allem drei Kategorien erkennen: Die erste könnte man mit der Bezeichnung »deterministische Bücher« versehen, da sich in ihnen nicht allein die Ordnung der Welt oder der Ablauf der Geschichte, sondern auch das Leben eines jeden Menschen im voraus fixiert findet. Eine zweite Kategorie umfaßt »dokumentarische Bücher«, wozu die Bücher der Werke, das Buch des Lebens oder die Protokolle des künftigen Gerichtes zu rechnen wären. Eine dritte Kategorie stellen schließlich solche Bücher dar, in denen direkte Anweisungen für das Leben der Frommen enthalten sind und die man vielleicht als »gesetzliche Bücher« bezeichnen müßte. Vielfältig sind auch die Vorstellungen über den Ursprung dieser himmlischen Bücher bzw. über die Verantwortlichkeit, in der sie sich befinden[36].

Ein herausragender Zug der Henochtradition besteht nun darin, den Urvater in eine enge Beziehung zu jener himmlischen Buchführung zu setzen. In der Welt Gottes wird ihm zunächst Einsicht in verschiedene Arten himmlischer Bücher gewährt[37], als deren Autoren Engel, namentlich Uriel und Michael, erscheinen. Er selbst aber erhält den Vorzug, an dieser Buchführung beteiligt zu werden. Als »Schreiber der Gerechtigkeit«[38] übermittelt er eine im Auftrag der gefallenen Wächter angefertigte Bittschrift, nimmt gemeinsam mit Uriel die Aufzeichnung der astronomisch kalendarischen Ordnung in Angriff – vor allem aber prägt er sich den Inhalt der himmlischen Tafeln ein, der dann in den späteren Lehrvorträgen bzw. deren Nachschrift wiederkehrt und so Eingang in die heiligen Schriften der Henochtradition findet[39].

Diese Rolle Henochs, die in der älteren Tradition zwar sehr klar, jedoch noch wenig strukturiert begegnet, wird im slHen aufgenommen und zu einem Grundpfeiler der gesamten Konzeption ausgebaut. Sowohl

---

35. Vgl. den gediegenen Exkurs bei LANGE, *Weisheit und Prädestination*, pp. 69-79, der sich vor allem durch die Aufarbeitung der Qumran-Belege auszeichnet. Hier hätten die Aussagen im slHen einen weiteren, wichtigen Bezugspunkt darstellen können.
36. Vgl. insgesamt BÖTTRICH, *Weltweisheit*, pp. 157-161 und 172-175.
37. Das betrifft z.B. die »Tafeln des Himmels«, das Buch der Werke, Protokolle über Verfehlungen, »das heilige Buch«, das Buch des Lebens oder Namenslisten der Gerechten.
38. Vgl. zum Titel äthHen 12,4; 15,1.
39. Vgl. besonders äthHen 81,1-2; 93,2; 103,2; 106,19; 107,1.

die Gestalt der himmlischen Buchführung als auch die Rolle Henochs verändern sich dabei auf charakteristische Weise. Zunächst findet man das himmlische »Scriptorium« im sechsten Himmel lokalisiert (19,1-6), wo die sieben Erzengel mit dem Studium und der Verwaltung des gesamten Kosmos beschäftigt sind. Zu ihren Aufgaben gehört es u.a. auch, »Taten und Leben« aller Menschen aufzuschreiben. Dies geschieht ganz offensichtlich unter dem Vorsitz des Vrevoil / Uriel, der den anderen gegenüber »schneller an Weisheit« ist und seinerseits nun »alle Werke des Herrn« niederschreibt[40]. Er ist es auch, der die himmlischen Schatzkammern verwaltet, in denen ein Korpus besonderer, durch kostbare Wohlgerüche ausgezeichneter Bücher ihren Platz hat[41]. Nachdem Henoch selbst in einen der »Herrlichen des Herrn« transfiguriert ist[42], wird er durch Gottes Spruch dem Vrevoil zugesellt, der die Bücher aus den Schatzkammern herbeibringt und Henoch in ihren Inhalt einführt. Von Vrevoil mit einem »Schreibrohr der Schnellschreibung« ausgerüstet, setzt er sich nieder und fertigt nach Diktat eine Kopie dieser Bücher an. Damit ist seine Aufgabe aber noch nicht erschöpft. Über das direkte Kopieren der himmlischen Bücher hinaus rückt Henoch auch in die kreative Position des Protokollanten für die Werke der Menschen ein und avanciert schließlich zum Buchführer des künftigen Gerichtes[43]. Es scheint, als ob er darin seine Vorgänger im Erzengelrang endgültig ablöste oder ihnen doch zumindest übergeordnet würde. Die gesamte himmlische Buchführung gelangt damit nicht nur zur Kenntnis Henochs – sie gerät auch vollständig in seine Hand. Ein größeres Maß an weisheitlicher Legitimation läßt sich kaum denken.

40. Bereits in äthHen 33,3-4 hat Uriel Schreiberfunktion, die sich auf seine Domäne – die astronomisch kalendarische Ordnung – bezieht; bezeichnenderweise schreibt er diese Dinge gezielt für Henoch auf. Neu ist im slHen eine solche Führungsposition unter den himmlischen Schreibern, ebenso die zentrale Verwaltung der himmlischen Buchführung.

41. An dieser Stelle (22,11) machte Milik bekanntlich seine These von den »schnell = in Minuskeln geschriebenen Büchern« fest und leitete daraus die Spätdatierung des gesamten Textes ab. Der Text vermag die Bürde eines solchen Argumentes nicht zu tragen – besonders angesichts der großen textlichen Unsicherheiten zur Stelle. Aus dem Gesamtduktus ergibt sich lediglich die ausgezeichnete Geltung der Bücher; Schnellschreibung hingegen ist nur für die Kopiertätigkeit Henochs erforderlich.

42. 22,8-10 beschreibt den Vorgang durch Salbung und Einkleidung – »und ich war wie einer von seinen Herrlichen, und es gab keinen wahrnehmbaren Unterschied.« In 37,1-2 erfolgt vor der befristeten Rückkehr auf die Erde lediglich eine »Abkühlung« durch einen eisigen Engel, um die Erscheinung Henochs unter den Menschen erträglich zu machen. Zu seinem neuen Status gehört es hinzu, kein Verlangen mehr nach Speise oder »irdischer Süßigkeit« zu empfinden (56,1-2).

43. Vgl. 40,13; 43,1; 50,1; 52,15; 53,2-3; 64,5; 65,5; 66,8; 68,2. Im Gegensatz zu äthHen 13,4-6 und 14,4-7 verfaßt er jedoch keine Bittschrift für die gefallenen Wächter, wenngleich auch das slHen in diesem Zusammenhang die Frage der Fürbitte reflektiert (7,4-5; 18,7).

Besondere Aufmerksamkeit verdient dabei der Inhalt der himmlischen Bücher, und zwar jener, die Henoch nach Diktat kopiert. Ausdrücklich und mehrfach heißt es, daß sie die Ordnung des Kosmos enthalten[44]. Angefangen von botanischen Details bis hin zur Bewegung der Gestirne bieten sie in enzyklopädischer Fülle alles, was Gottes Schöpfung beinhaltet. Daß darin auch der Plan der Geschichte enthalten sei, läßt sich kaum ausschließen, wird jedoch nicht eigens erwähnt. Zeitabläufe und geschichtliche Ereignisse sind für den Autor des slHen Themen, die bestenfalls ganz am Rande, und auch dann nur verhalten, anklingen[45]. Alles ist auf den Bau des Kosmos, seinen Ursprung in Gottes Schöpfung sowie seinen Bestand durch die himmlische Verwaltung abgestellt. Dezidiert kann man die aus den Schatzkammern geholten Bücher deshalb als »Bücher der göttlichen Weltordnung« bezeichnen. Ihre Kopien ergeben am Ende eine Zahl von 366 Büchern, was ihren Inhalt noch einmal symbolisch zum Ausdruck bringt. So wie die Lebensjahre Henochs einen Bezug auf das Sonnenjahr verraten, spiegelt auch die Zahl der Bücher erschöpfende Vollständigkeit wider, wobei man evtl. an 365 plus 1 (nämlich das slHen selbst als eine Art Wegweiser für das »Korpus«) denken kann.

Diese Bücher sind es, die Henoch nun zum Zwecke der Bekanntgabe unter den Menschen seiner Generation abschreibt. Fraglos handelt es sich dabei um den interessantesten Punkt. Zwar weiß auch die ältere Henochtradition davon, daß sich die Henochschriften aus den Vorträgen des Patriarchen speisen, die wiederum auf der Einsicht in die Tafeln des Himmels beruhen. Den Gedanken eines direkten Transfers aber entwickelt erst das slHen. Im Himmel geschrieben und durch göttlichen Auftrag auf Erden verbreitet – so werden die himmlischen Bücher der Weltordnung Gottes zum unüberbietbaren Garanten jener heiligen Schriften, die unter den Tradenten der Henochtradition in Geltung stehen. Und wenn die in einem »Henochpentateuch« (die These Miliks vorausgesetzt) zusammengefaßten Bücher der älteren Tradition durch ihre Zahl einen Bezug auf Israel beabsichtigt haben sollten, so könnte

---

44. So vor allem die Liste in 23,1-2; deren Zusammenfassung 23,3; die summarische Aussage 54,1.

45. Geschichtliche Abläufe deuten sich erst im dritten Teil an – kommen aber angesichts der nahen Flut nicht über zwei Generationen (Methusalem – Nir) hinaus. Von einer zeitlichen Gliederung des »irdischen Äons« ist in 65,2.34 zu lesen – aber sie dient weniger einer Periodisierung der Geschichte als vielmehr der besseren Erkennbarkeit des menschlichen Lebens (»damit er sein Leben zähle... und seine Sünden bedenke«) und wird somit der Paränese dienstbar gemacht. Allein 33,1-2 läßt den Gedanken von sieben Weltwochen anklingen – jedoch wiederum nur deshalb, um die Auflösung der Zeit in der achten Weltwoche einzuführen.

man in den 365/366 Büchern des slHen einen Anspruch auf universale Geltung der Offenbarungen Henochs vermuten. Zugleich wird damit eine kaum noch überschaubare Fülle von Schriften suggeriert, die allein schon durch ihre Menge Geheimhaltung verhindert – und wohl auch verhindern soll.

Einen ausschließlich deterministischen Charakter kann man diesen Büchern somit nicht mehr zuschreiben. Sie dienen dazu, Anleitung für ein gerechtes Leben zu geben. Insgesamt taucht der Gedanke der Prädestination in der himmlischen Buchführung des slHen nur noch am Rande auf[46]. Daß er dem Autor jedoch nicht fremd ist, zeigt sich in einem anderen Zusammenhang: an der Art seines Umganges mit dem Tierkreis und der Legitimierung von Brontologien als eines Ausdruckes göttlicher Weisheit[47].

1d. Makarismen als favorisierte Form der Paränese

Eine wichtige, bislang noch kaum gewürdigte Bedeutung kommt den Makarismen im slHen zu. Die weisheitliche Prägung dieser Gattung paränetischer Rede ist längst erkannt. Besonders in den Texten aus Qumran haben Makarismen in letzter Zeit verstärkt Aufmerksamkeit gefunden.

Fragt man nach der Verbreitung von Makarismen in der frühjüdischen Literatur[48], dann zeigt sich ein überraschender Befund: Statistisch gesehen übertrifft das slHen mit 22 Makarismen alle übrigen Schriften deutlich. Selbst eine Weisheitsschrift wie das Sirachbuch kommt auf gerade einmal 11 Belege; im gesamten AT lassen sich ca. 45 Belege feststellen. Man kann den Makarismus damit als eine für das slHen besonders charakteristische Form weisheitlicher Paränese betrachten.

Alle Makarismen bleiben auf den Teil der Mahnreden konzentriert, wobei jedoch eine größere Formenvielfalt ins Auge fällt. 42,6-14 bietet eine Aufreihung von neun Gliedern; in 52,1-14 findet sich eine alternierende Reihe von sieben Gliedern, in der Seligpreisung und Fluch auch inhaltlich aufeinander bezogen werden. Die Apodosis wird sowohl in der Form »μακάριος ὁ ἄνθρωπος« als auch in der Form »μακάριος / ἐπικατάρατος ὅς« gebraucht. Die Protasis erscheint als einfache oder mehrgliedrige Aussage, der in einigen Fällen ein zusätzlicher Kausal- oder Finalsatz angefügt ist, wodurch dann die endzeitlichen Konsequenzen gegenwärtigen Verhaltens noch einmal nachdrücklich unterstrichen werden.

---

46. 23,4 soll Henoch u.a. »alle Seelen der Menschen, soviel auch [noch] nicht geboren sind, und ihre Orte...« aufschreiben; in 53,2-3 kommt Henoch auf genau diesen Punkt seiner Niederschrift noch einmal zurück.
47. Vgl. 23,1; 30,6; 40,9; insgesamt BÖTTRICH, *Astrologie*.
48. Vgl. die grundlegende Arbeit von KÄHLER, *Makarismen*.

Inhaltlich dominieren in der Protasis Aussagen, die auf ein sozialgerechtes Verhalten zielen – besonders in der Aufreihung 42,6-14: mehrfach kommt die Ausführung eines gerechten Gerichtes zur Sprache, die Hilfe für die Bedürftigen, dann aber auch ganz einfache Maximen wie Wahrheit, Liebe, Barmherzigkeit oder Sanftmut. In der alternierenden Reihe 52,1-14 geht es zentral darum, Gott und seine Werke zu preisen, die Fundamente der Väter zu bewahren oder Frieden und Liebe zu üben, wobei dann als Kehrseite solchen Verhaltens die Verachtung des Nächsten als ein letztlich gegen Gott gerichtetes Vergehen bewertet wird[49]. Selig können ganz unmittelbar auch jene gepriesen werden, die »in die guten Häuser eingehen« oder die dem großen Gericht entrinnen werden. Beachtung verdient schließlich der Makarismus in 42,14 mit seiner Betonung rationaler Fähigkeiten: »Selig sind, welche jedes von Gott gemachte Werk des Herrn begreifen und es preisen«. Im Zusammenhang der Sündenfallgeschichte war bereits die Unwissenheit Adams hinsichtlich seiner Befähigung zum Guten wie zum Bösen als der entscheidende Auslöser benannt worden – »deshalb ist Unwissenheit das Übel der Versündigung« (30,16).

Insgesamt bieten die Makarismen des slHen einen wichtigen Ansatzpunkt, um das Verständnis des Autors von Sünde und Gericht zu erfassen. Ein Verhalten, das der Schöpfungsordnung Gottes entspricht und das im konkreten Fall vorzugsweise an Beispielen sozialer Gerechtigkeit entfaltet wird, vermag vor dem großen Gericht zu bewahren. Hier haben die erzählerischen Passagen der Himmelsreise bereits die Heils- und Unheilsorte vor Augen geführt. Die Mahnreden Henochs nehmen die Thematik auf und betonen unter wiederholtem Bezug auf das Bild von der Waage[50] die Unbestechlichkeit der alternativen Entscheidung. Daß dabei die Möglichkeit der Fürbitte abgelehnt wird[51], gehört zu den besonderen Zügen des slHen. Wer um die Ordnungen Gottes weiß, dem wird keine spätere Entschuldigung mehr zugestanden.

2. Henoch als exemplarischer Weiser

Weisheit erscheint im slHen vor allem als eine Eigenschaft Gottes bzw. der Wesen in Gottes Welt[52]. Ob die Sophia dabei auch unter dem

---

49. Noch deutlicher, wenngleich nicht in Gestalt eines Makarismus, findet sich dieser Gedanke in 44,2-3.
50. Damit endet die alternierende Reihe in 52,1-14.15; vgl. bereits 44,5.
51. Im Blick auf die gefallenen Wächter (7,4-5; 18,7), im Blick auf die Menschen (53,1-4; 62,2); die Erwartung wird formuliert in 64,5.
52. Textlich unsicher bleibt das Proömium 1a,3; eindeutig sind 30,12; 33,3; 48,4; nach 30,10 spricht Gott einen »weisen Spruch«; Weisheit wird in 22,10 Vrevoil und den Engeln zuerkannt.

Begriff einer »Hypostase« erfaßt werden kann, läßt sich nicht eindeutig entscheiden[53]. Auf jeden Fall tritt sie grundlegend im Zusammenhang des Schöpfungswerkes hervor und ist in der planvollen Verwaltung des Kosmos am Werk.

Noch vor seiner Himmelsreise kann auch Henoch schon als ein »weiser Mann« charakterisiert werden, wenngleich diese Aussage im Proömium textlichen Unsicherheiten unterliegt. Solche Weisheit verbleibt indessen im Bereich von Lebenserfahrung und praktischer Klugheit, wie das die Hinzufügung des Epithetons »τεχνίτης« verdeutlicht[54]. Entscheidendes Gewicht hat erst die Schilderung der Art und Weise, wie Henoch im Verlauf seiner Himmelsreise Weisheit erwirbt. Sie wird als eine Einweihung in die Geheimnisse Gottes geschildert, die verschiedene Stufen zunehmender Qualifizierung durchläuft. Grundlegend gilt: Der Impuls geht dabei von der Initiative Gottes aus – die Weisheit ist offenbarte Weisheit[55]. Auf göttlichen Befehl erscheinen zwei Engel, die Henoch durch die sieben Himmel führen; auf göttlichen Befehl hin wird Henoch durch Vrevoil mit dem Inhalt der himmlischen Bücher bekannt gemacht; Gott selbst schließlich würdigt Henoch des Platzes zu seiner Linken und führt ihn in einer langen Rede in die Geheimnisse des Schöpfungswerkes ein. Zwar gleicht die Himmelsreise gelegentlich einer naturwissenschaftlichen Expedition – Henoch mißt, prüft, notiert und fragt. Doch Aufschluß erhält er erst durch die Auskünfte seiner Reisebegleiter, die zugleich als Deuteengel fungieren. Immerhin kann er in dieser ersten Phase noch von eigenen Erfahrungen ausgehen. Mit der Einsicht in die himmlischen Bücher jedoch führt ihn Vrevoil dann in den Wissensstand der Erzengel ein. Durch die Gottesrede schließlich gelangt Henoch zu einem auch die Erzengel überragenden Wissen[56]. Es leuchtet ein, daß er für diese letzten beiden Qualifikationsetappen eigens in einen der »Herrlichen des Herrn« verwandelt werden muß, wodurch unterstrichen wird: Dieses Wissen gehört allein der Welt Gottes an.

Während Henoch im ersten Teil Weisheit erwirbt, übermittelt er im zweiten Teil diese Weisheit an seine Söhne bzw. an die gesamte urzeitliche Menschheit. Das geschieht ausdrücklich im Auftrag Gottes – und es geschieht auf eine doppelte Weise. Zum einen unterrichtet Henoch die

---

53. Am ehesten kommen in Betracht 30,8 (die Weisheit schafft den Menschen) und 33,4 (»meine Weisheit ist meine Beraterin«); offen bleiben 30,12; 33,3; 48,4.
54. Ähnlich rechnet auch 43,2 zu den Unterschieden, die zwischen Menschen bestehen, »Weisheit des Herzens«. Die umfassendste Materialsammlung zu den Traditionen über Eigenschaften und Funktionen Henochs bietet BERGER, *Henoch*.
55. Zur Vielfalt der Zugangswege vgl. insgesamt KÜCHLER, *Weisheitstraditionen*.
56. Das wird ausdrücklich vermerkt in 24,3; 40,3.

Menschen seiner Generation durch Lehrvorträge, zum anderen hinterläßt er ihnen seine 366 Bücher zur Verbreitung und Weitergabe an die folgenden Generationen. Was an Wissen für ein gerechtes Leben in Übereinstimmung mit Gottes Schöpfungsordnung vonnöten ist, wird somit grundlegend in den urzeitlichen Lehren Henochs – seien sie mündlicher oder schriftlicher Art – verankert. Henoch ist damit als maßgeblicher und exemplarischer Weiser beschrieben. Denn seine Söhne folgen nun im dritten Teil den Lehren ihres Vaters, die sie zu treuen Händen übernehmen und weitergeben.

Die Rolle des Weisheitslehrers wird schließlich mit der des himmlischen Schreibers verbunden. Hier zieht die Gestalt Henochs im slHen Traditionen an sich, die in der hellenistischen Religiosität mit verschiedenen Schreibergottheiten verbunden waren. Die Zuverlässigkeit des Kopisten der himmlischen Bücher setzt sich dabei in der Unbestechlichkeit des künftigen Protokollanten bei dem »großen Gericht« fort.

3. Eigenheiten der Weisheit im slHen

Weisheit steht im slHen in einem unauflösbaren Zusammenhang mit der Schöpfungsordnung Gottes. Durch Gottes Weisheit ist die Schöpfung in das Dasein getreten. Durch Gottes Weisheit wird ihr Bestand garantiert. Und nur durch die Offenbarung göttlicher Weisheit kann der Mensch Einblick in die Schöpfungsordnung Gottes erhalten und sein Leben entsprechend führen. Es scheint, als ob ein eigenständiger Zugang zu solcher Weisheit verneint werden sollte.

Dieser Eindruck gewinnt an Gewicht, wenn man den Geheimnischarakter der Weisheit im slHen erkennt[57]. Daß Henoch solcher hohen Offenbarungen gewürdigt wird, zeichnet ihn weit vor den übrigen Menschen aus. Seine Weisheitslehren wiederum gelten zuerst denen, die ihrer würdig sind[58]. Hier läßt sich jedoch eine merkwürdige Spannung beobachten: Einerseits sollen die Bücher Henochs umfassend bekannt gemacht werden[59], andererseits liest man von verschiedenen Maßnahmen, die ihrem Schutz dienen[60]. Im letzten Teil, der auf den abschließenden Flutbericht zuläuft, wird die weitgehende Ablehnung der Lehren

---

57. Den Begriff (»meine [Gottes] Geheimnisse«) gebraucht nur 24,3; textlich unsicher ist 36,3. Der Sache nach aber ist der Geheimnischarakter der göttlichen Weisheit an der Art ihrer Offenbarung deutlich genug ablesbar.

58. Das trifft zuerst die Sippe; die Bücher sollen nach der Flut dann »treuen und mir wohlgefälligen Männern« gezeigt werden (35,2).

59. Vgl. 3,8-9; 35,3; 36,1; 47,1-2; 48,6-7; 54,1; 68,2.

60. 33,3 (der Erzengel Michael als Vermittler); 33,11-12 (Ariuch und Pariuch als Wächter der Bücher).

Henochs[61] dann erzählerisch durch die Bedrohung des Melchisedekknaben in Szene gesetzt. Die Anweisungen zum Umgang mit den Büchern schwanken zwischen Offenheit und Abgrenzung. Grundsätzlich aber stehen sie allen Menschen offen.

Ganz anders stellt sich die Situation dar, wenn man die Inhalte der offenbarten Weisheit betrachtet. Schöpfung und Fall sowie die Verfehlung der Engel betreffen zunächst Themen, die einer konkreten Übermittlung bedürfen und nur dem jüdischen Frommen schon vertraut sind. Die astronomischen Einsichten Henochs, die in der Schilderung des vierten Himmels breiten Raum einnehmen, erschließen sich dagegen auch bis zu einem gewissen Grade der allgemeinen Beobachtung. Das wird daran deutlich, daß der Autor des slHen über die Tradition von äth-Hen 72-82 hinaus mit weiteren Kenntnissen hantiert, die dem Bereich der griechisch-hellenistischen Astronomie entstammen[62]. Er trägt keinerlei Bedenken, sogar den Tierkreis als eine Schöpfung Gottes darzustellen und Henoch als Verfasser von Brontologien einzuführen[63]. Ein solches Verfahren läßt sich auch in anderen Zusammenhängen feststellen. Vor der Schilderung des Sechstagewerkes greift er kosmogonische Vorstellungen aus der ägyptischen Mythologie auf[64]; die Erschaffung des Menschen verbindet er mit der Mikrokosmosidee und der stoischen Lehre von den Seelenteilen[65]; durch die Unterscheidung von Aër und Äther oder Sichtbarem und Unsichtbarem greift er eine philosophische Terminologie auf, die in der hellenistischen Welt weit verbreitet war[66]. Die Reihe ließe sich fortsetzen. Wenn der Kenntnisstand hellenistischer Wissenschaft auf diese exemplarische Weise in der offenbarten Weisheit Gottes verankert wird, dann ist das als ein Signal zu verstehen: Die besten Einsichten, mit denen die Gebildeten in der Umwelt des slHen leben, stehen zu der Weisheit Gottes nicht in Widerspruch. Vielmehr noch – sie haben in dieser Weisheit längst schon (unbewußt) ihren wahren Ursprung. Ein wenig mag darin auch die Vorstellung von Israel als

---

61. Bereits 48,7-9 verhandeln Annahme und Ablehnung der Bücher Henochs – und die daraus resultierenden Folgen.

62. So z.B. die Stadien / Tierkreiszeichen 13,2; der gekrönte Helios 14,2; der 28jährige Zyklus 15,4 (unsicher, weil seine Kenntnis erst später nachweisbar ist); der Metonische Zyklus 16,8; die kristallenen Planetensphären 18,1 / 48,1; die Planetenreihe 30,3; die 182 Parallelkreise nach Geminos 48,1.

63. Vgl. ausführlich BÖTTRICH, *Astrologie*.

64. 24,3-28,4. Die Schöpfung beginnt damit, daß die beiden Äonen (der zeitliche und der zeitlose) »hervorgerufen« werden, die aus sich heraus dann die sichtbare Welt ins Dasein entlassen.

65. Vgl. 30,8-14; die Lehre von den Seelenteilen klingt an in 30,9.

66. Zu Äther und Aër vgl. 3,2; Sichtbares / Unsichtbares begegnet z.B. in 24,2.4; 25,1; 48,4.5; 65,1.

der Mutter der Weisheit oder der Überlegenheit jüdischer Weiser im Wettstreit mit ihren nichtjüdischen Kollegen anklingen. Der Ton liegt jedoch darauf, daß die dem Henoch offenbarte Weisheit der Menschheit als Ganzer von Urzeiten her schon anvertraut ist. Deutlicher als um Wettbewerb geht es um die Suche nach Konsens. Und solcher Konsens ist möglich, weil die urzeitliche Weisheit Henochs offensichtlich auch in der hellenistischen Welt ihre Spuren hinterlassen hat. Zumindest sollen die Leser des slHen aufgrund ihrer Lektüre zu dieser Erkenntnis geführt werden.

Es fällt auf, daß die Thora in den Büchern Henochs nur andeutungsweise sichtbar wird[67]. Anders als z.B. im Jub, wo die himmlischen Tafeln eine ganze Reihe wohlbekannter halachischer Themen enthalten, kommen in den himmlischen Büchern des slHen gesetzliche Bestimmungen so gut wie gar nicht vor[68]. Auch in den zahlreichen Makarismen sucht man einen Bezug auf die Thora vergebens. Indessen zeigt eine Untersuchung der ethischen Mahnungen, daß deren Themenkreise weitgehend mit den Themen der später unter der Bezeichnung »noachidische Gebote« verhandelten Forderungen übereinstimmen[69]. Hier tritt noch einmal jene universale Perspektive hervor, die dem gesamten slHen zu eigen ist. Nicht nur um der Vermeidung von Anachronismen willen sind alle Bezüge auf die Thoraweisheit vermieden. Die Präsentation des offenbarten Wissens in Gestalt einer Weltweisheit entspricht vielmehr dem Grundanliegen des slHen überhaupt.

Auf diese Akzentsetzung läßt sich auch der Sachverhalt zurückführen, daß geschichtliche Ereignisse im slHen überhaupt keine Rolle spielen. Erst im dritten Teil werden mit der Schilderung vom Beginn einer priesterlichen Sukzession Ansätze geschichtlichen Denkens erkennbar. Sie gelangen jedoch kaum zur Entfaltung und erhalten in der jeder Zeitfolge merkwürdig enthobenen Geburtsgeschichte Melchisedeks sofort wieder ein Gegengewicht. Alles Denken ist im slHen auf den Bestand der Welt ausgerichtet, in dem der große Äon den gegenwärtigen Äon dieser Weltzeit bereits umfaßt. Gerade diese besondere Form des Äonendualismus zeigt, wie konsequent alle zeitlichen Erwartungen in ein räumlich vertikales Schema transformiert worden sind[70].

---

67. Gelegentlich wird von »Gesetzlosigkeit« oder von »gesetzlos handeln« gesprochen, »Gebote« oder »Belehrungen« werden genannt; vgl. BÖTTRICH, *Weltweisheit*, pp. 178-180. Damit haben sich dann aber alle Anspielungen auch schon erschöpft.

68. Konkrete Weisungen Henochs (basierend auf den Büchern) lassen durchaus Gebote der Thora erkennen, etwa die Aufforderung zum Schutz von Witwe, Waise und Fremdling (42,9 u.ö.). Direkte Bezüge hat der Autor indessen sorgsam vermieden.

69. Vgl. BÖTTRICH, *Weltweisheit*, pp. 184-189.

70. Vgl. BÖTTRICH, *Weltweisheit*, pp. 164-169.

Der weisheitliche Charakter des slHen gewinnt sein Profil also vor dem Hintergrund eines Ordnungsdenkens, das in der älteren Henochtradition schon bereit lag, nun aber in konsequenterer Weise durchgeführt und auf die Situation der Existenz in einer andersgläubigen Umwelt zugeschnitten ist. Einsicht in die Ordnung der Welt, die als Schöpfung des einen Gottes auch Nichtjuden als nachvollziehbar erscheint, wird die Grundlage für ein gerechtes Leben und werbende Offenheit gegenüber allen Menschen.

III. WEISHEIT IM SLHEN UND IN QUMRAN

In diesem letzten Abschnitt kann es nicht darum gehen, einen vollständigen Vergleich aller relevanten Termini, Vorstellungen oder konkreten Aussagen vorzunehmen. Die wichtigsten Bezugsfelder sind ohnehin schon zur Sprache gekommen. Sie sollen im folgenden nur noch einmal anhand einiger ausgewählter Beispiele und im Gegenüber zu drei begrenzten Textkomplexen konkretisiert werden.

1. 4QSapiential Work A (4Q417)

An Umfang und Bedeutung kommt dem als *Sapiential Work* A bezeichneten Text unter den neuen Weisheitstexten aus Qumran sicher die größte Bedeutung zu[71]. Soviel sich erkennen läßt, liegt sein Schwerpunkt bei Mahnungen, die auf der Einsicht in das »Geheimnis des Werdens / רז נהיה« beruhen. An diesem Terminus, der für den gesamten Text zentrale Bedeutung besitzt, wird erkennbar: Es gibt eine Zeit und Raum umfassende Ordnung, die Ursprung und Bestand der Welt ebenso wie Ursprung und Geschichte der Menschheit enthält. Sie kann Gegenstand forschender Betrachtung und Inhalt göttlicher Offenbarung sein. In jedem Falle aber hat ihre Erkenntnis unmittelbare ethische Relevanz. »רז נהיה bezeichnet somit ein Phänomen, das ethische, historische, nomistische, eschatologische und urzeitliche Komponenten in sich vereinigt. Es handelt sich um eine Welt- bzw. Schöpfungsordnung, die ethische und historische Komponenten enthält und sich dereinst im Eschaton erfüllt«[72].

---

71. Text bei STRUGNELL, HARRINGTON & ELGVIN, *Qumran Cave 4*. XXIV; MAIER, *Texte* II, pp. 430-485; dazu LANGE, *Weisheit und Prädestination*, pp. 45-92.
72. LANGE, *Weisheit und Prädestination*, p. 60.

Es liegt nahe, daß dieses Phänomen auch mit Hilfe des Schöpfungsthemas erläutert wird. Am Beispiel der Erschaffung der Frau erweist sich das ordnende Schöpfungshandeln Gottes als ein Vermischen und Unterscheiden. Namentlich die Unterschiede, auf denen die Schöpfungsordnung aufbaut, erlangen für den Weisen erkenntnisleitenden Charakter. Aus der Wahrnehmung von Unterschieden vermag er zur Einsicht in die grundlegenden Gegensätze zu gelangen und seine Entscheidung für Licht, Wahrheit oder Gerechtigkeit zu treffen.

Von Gewicht ist vor allem die Frage, wie das »Geheimnis des Werdens« ergründet werden kann. Die gelegentlichen Imperative »erforsche das Geheimnis...« führen hier leicht in die Irre. Denn grundsätzlich erschließt sich das »Geheimnis des Werdens« nur durch göttliche Offenbarung. Eine entscheidende Rolle spielt dabei das »Buch der Erinnerung«, von dem Enosch einst in einer »Vision der Erklärung« Kenntnis erhalten und diese durch Überlieferung den folgenden Generationen übermittelt hat. In dem »Buch der Erinnerung« aber, das als wichtigster Teil der himmlischen Buchführung betrachtet werden muß, ist die gesamte Schöpfungs- oder Weltordnung einschließlich der Thora, also das »Geheimnis des Werdens« in seiner Fülle, schriftlich niedergelegt. Solche Offenbarung wird nur einem kleinen Kreis zuteil, der darin Kenntnis von jener Urordnung der Welt besitzt und sein Leben entsprechend einrichtet.

Die Analogien zu der grundlegenden Vorstellung einer göttlichen Weltordnung im slHen springen sofort ins Auge. Das Thema der Schöpfung hat entscheidendes Gewicht. Dem biblischen Sechstagewerk wird sogar noch eine Weltentstehungstheorie vorausgeschickt, die das planmäßige Handeln Gottes in der gleichzeitigen Heraufführung zweier Äonen veranschaulicht. Das Schöpfungshandeln erscheint als ein unterscheidendes und abteilendes – wobei dann auch im slHen die Unterschiede erkenntnisleitenden Charakter gewinnen[73]. Den spannendsten Vergleichspunkt aber bietet sicher das Motiv der Bücher, in denen Henoch die göttliche Weltordnung erkennt, kopiert und auf Erden überträgt. Auch hier beruht die Einsicht allein auf der offenbarenden Initiative Gottes. Auch sie werden zur Grundlage ethischer Unterweisung. Anders als in *Sapiential Work* A fehlt ihnen indessen jeder Bezug zur Thora, und auch ein exklusiver Charakter ist ihnen fremd. Im slHen drängt sich eher der Eindruck auf, daß die Bücher entgegen ihrer ursprünglichen Bestimmung nur auf einen kleinen Kreis beschränkt

---

73. Vgl. slHen 43,1-3 – vor dem Hintergrund von Sir 33,7-15.

geblieben seien, was ihrem grundlegend universalen Charakter jedoch widerspricht. Die Einsicht in eine weisheitliche Urordnung zielt hier weniger auf Gruppenidentität als auf Verständigung. Für solche Akzentverschiebungen sind ohne Frage die spätere Zeit und die Situation einer weltoffenen hellenistischen Metropole wie Alexandrien verantwortlich zu machen.

2. *Book of Mysteries (1Q27)*

Weitaus schwieriger als in *Sapiential Work A* sind Inhalt und Intention jenes als *Book of Mysteries* bezeichneten Textes zu bestimmen[74]. Eine sachliche Nähe ergibt sich jedoch vor allem aus dem Terminus vom »Geheimnis des Werdens«, der auch hier eine zentrale Rolle spielt. Der besondere Akzent dieses Textes liegt auf der Ankündigung des Gerichtes. Die Frevler, die das »Geheimnis des Werdens« nicht erkannt haben, werden gemäß jener Urordnung der Welt letztlich vernichtet werden. Sie erscheinen zudem als solche, die die »wunderbaren Geheimnisse [zu Unrecht] festhalten«, was wohl auf die illegitime Wissensvermittlung durch gefallene Engel und deren verhängnisvolle Weitergabe anzuspielen scheint. Darin läßt sich, wenn man diesen Hintergrund voraussetzt, Polemik gegen magische oder astrologisch-mantische Weisheitslehren vernehmen[75].

Die Gerichtsthematik spielt auch im slHen eine wichtige Rolle. Daß sie zuerst am Beispiel der gefallenen Engel eingeführt wird, resultiert aus dem Bezug auf die ältere Henochtradition. Eigenartigerweise begegnet Henoch den Gefolgsleuten und ihren Anführern jedoch an unterschiedlichen Straforten in der himmlischen Welt, die sich auch durch unterschiedliche Strafmaße unterscheiden[76]. Noch auffälliger aber ist der Umstand, daß die Schuld der Wächter (»Grigori«) allein durch den Tatbestand des Abfalles vom Herrn sowie der Vermischung mit den Menschentöchtern bezeichnet wird. Ein »Verrat« himmlischer Geheimnisse oder die Übermittlung besonderer Fertigkeiten wie in der vorausliegenden Tradition kommt gar nicht vor. Ihre Schuld besteht allein darin, daß sie gegen die von Gott geschaffene Ordnung verstoßen haben, so wie

---

74. Text bei SCHIFFMAN, *Mysteries*; MAIER, *Texte* II, pp. 252-270; dazu LANGE, *Weisheit und Prädestination*, pp. 93-120.

75. So LANGE, *Weisheit und Prädestination*, besonders pp. 109-119.

76. Die Gefolgsleute sind im zweiten Himmel inhaftiert und werden gequält (7,1-5); die Anführer sind im fünften Himmel untergebracht und leiden lediglich unter ihrem Ausschluß vom himmlischen Gottesdienst (18,1-9).

das die Frevler unter den Menschen auch, wenngleich in einem anderen Rahmen, tun. Die Unterdrückung eines solchen Hauptzuges der Überlieferung vom Engelfall kann nur bewußt geschehen sein. Der Autor des slHen vermeidet es offensichtlich, polemische Töne gegen magische oder mantische Weisheit in seiner Umwelt verlauten zu lassen. Er versucht sie statt dessen zu integrieren, rechnet den Tierkreis unter Gottes Schöpfungswerke oder macht Henoch zum Verfasser von Brontologien. Erneut zeigt sich, wie das zugrundeliegende Konzept in einer anderen Zeit und Umwelt Modifikationen erfährt.

3. Beatitudes (4Q525)

Dieses interessante Textstück wird seiner eingeführten Bezeichnung nur teilweise gerecht[77]. Makarismen begegnen sogleich zu Beginn, werden dann aber über den längsten Teil durch weisheitliche Ermahnungen fortgesetzt. Bedeutsam erscheint die einleitende Bemerkung, daß die Weisheit von Gott stamme sowie der Umstand, daß Weisheit im wesentlichen als Thoraweisheit beschrieben wird. Sachlich konzentrieren sich Makarismen und Ermahnungen auf Themen wie Reinheit des Herzens oder Wahrheit der Rede, auf die Entscheidung für den rechten Weg oder Demut und Redlichkeit.

Ein Vergleich mit dem slHen bietet hier nur wenig Anhaltspunkte. Wenn jedoch in der Forschung bislang die Nähe dieses Textes vor allem zu Sir oder Mt gesucht worden ist[78], dann stellt sich sehr wohl die Frage, ob nicht das slHen als profiliertester Vertreter von Makarismen im frühen Judentum als ein viel näherliegender Vergleichstext herangezogen werden sollte. Dabei sind natürlich auch die Differenzen unübersehbar: Im slHen fehlt jeder Bezug zur Thora, während man die starke Konzentration auf Themen der Sozialethik wiederum in 4Q525 vermißt. Was sonst an Motiven anklingt, gehört eher zu dem breiten Spektrum weisheitlicher Ermahnung, an dem beide Vergleichstexte auf jeweils eigene Weise teilhaben. Herz, Zunge und Lippe sind dabei die Stichwörter, die noch die größte Aufmerksamkeit verdienen. Beide Texte zeigen, wie eine gemeinsame Tradition weisheitlicher Ermahnung in unterschiedlichen Kontexten adaptiert werden konnte.

---

77. Text bei PUECH, *Qumran grotte 4*. XVIII; MAIER, *Texte* II, pp. 698-698.
78. So z.B. PUECH, *Un hymne essénien*.

Schluss

Insgesamt läßt sich festhalten: Das slHen vermag für die Kenntnis weisheitlichen Denkens im Judentum der hellenistisch-römischen Zeit wichtige Aufschlüsse zu liefern. Es sollte aus der Diskussion um die Qumrantexte und deren frühjüdisches Umfeld nicht länger ausgeblendet werden.

Juliusstraße 5
04315 Leipzig
Deutschland

Christfried Böttrich

THE ODES OF SOLOMON
AND THE JEWISH WISDOM TEXTS

INTRODUCTION

My assigned task in this international seminar on Qumran and Wisdom is to seek to discern how and in what ways, if at all, the *Odes of Solomon* are related to the Jewish Wisdom texts. This is a wise assignment, since the thought of the *Odes* is close to many of the Qumran ideas and the Odist may have once been an Essene, as J. Carmignac and I have tried to reveal[1].

At the outset, it is necessary to clarify the key terms. The *Odes* were claimed to be docetic and heretical by P. Battifol[2]; yet, we must avoid the terms "heretical" and "orthodoxy". They are certainly anachronistic for the time the *Odes* were composed. We have also learned not to talk about Palestinian versus Hellenistic Judaism, as if the Hellenistic World had not penetrated deep into ancient Palestine. C. H. Dodd's response to A. Schweitzer's thorough-going eschatology led him initially to talk about the oxymoron "realized" eschatology. Such is obviously logically impossible, hence we should speak only about futuristic and **realizing** eschatology. Both the former and the latter types of Endtime speculation are found in Second Temple Judaism and within so-called Early Christianity, including the sayings of Jesus.

We have learned that pre-70 Judaism was neither monolithic nor orthodox. This former reconstruction was caused by misusing Rabbinic sources as if they were eyewitness accounts of events when the Temple cult was in full force. We have learned to talk not about "Ancient Judaism" but about "Early Judaism" which parallels Early Christianity. We have also learned to think about the varieties of Judaism before 70 CE without suggesting our reader imagine only chaos and disunity. Study of the Pentateuch, worship, shared creeds (esp. the Shema), and the allegiance to one God tended to unite Galileans, Qumranites, Samaritans, and Judeans[3].

---

1. See esp. CARMIGNAC, *L'auteur des Odes*. CHARLESWORTH, *Odes*.
2. BATTIFOL, *Odes*, pp. 94ff.
3. For my recent reflections, see the introduction to CHARLESWORTH, *Pseudepigrapha*.

Most importantly, we have learned about another false dichotomy. In the first century CE, and up until the defeat of Bar Kokhba in 136 CE[4], it is frequently impossible to distinguish Jewish from so-called Christian phenomena. Jesus and Paul were certainly Jews. Despite the efforts of many New Testament specialists during this century both should be understood first and foremost in terms of Judaism. The fascination of scholars in the Religionsgeschichtliche Schule who interpreted Paul primarily, or only, in terms of the mystery religions is over, and I think we can report that the narrow perspective of this Schule ist tot.

Dead Sea Scrolls experts have proved, on the one hand, that this ancient Jewish library represents the ideas of Jews living in many parts of ancient Palestine, and, on the other hand, that Jesus'[5] and Paul's roots are firmly planted in Jewish soil. J. D. G. Dunn, for example, answers decisively and persuasively the question of the source of Paul's "works of the law" and the reason he was in a polemical posture against an interpretation of Torah; it is represented by 4QMMT from Qumran[6]. That is to say, Paul was not a non-Jewish thinker dead set against Judaism; he was proud to be a Jew and argued vehemently against what he deemed to be a perversion of Judaism. Thus, to divide first-century phenomena into "Jewish" and "Christian" writings is to succumb to a false, misleading, and anachronistic distinction. This perspective reveals that the inability of scholars for almost a century to decide if the *Odes* are Jewish or Christian results sometimes from assuming a false dichotomy.

The perception of the varieties of Judaism before 70 CE helps us understand why A. Harnack could not grasp the type of Judaism represented by the *Odes*, and so felt forced to inaugurate the idea that the *Odes* are an early Jewish hymnbook that was redacted by a "Christian"[7]. Today, we know that Harnack's conception of Judaism before 70 CE was wrong. That is, one cannot so neatly separate "Jewish" ideas from "Christian" concepts. The latter is primarily the former. In light of our new understanding of the vast varieties of thought within Early Judaism and our perception of the Jewish character of the original decades of so-called Christianity, Harnack's observations regarding the Jewish origin of the *Odes* make good sense. Yet, there is no need to doubt the unity of the *Odes* (as he later admitted).

---

4. An inscription found at Beth Shean indicates that Bar Kokhba was still active in the early months of 136.
    5. See the authoritative discussions in CHARLESWORTH (ed.), *Jesus*.
    6. See DUNN, *Paul and the Dead Sea Scrolls*.
    7. See HARNACK and FLEMMING, *Psalmbuch*.

DEFINITIONS

What do we mean by the *Odes of Solomon?* They are forty-two Odes known from early lists of pseudepigraphical works, and quoted by Lactantius and the author of the *Pistis Sophia*. The collection, except for Odes 1 and 2, was discovered by J. R. Harris in 1909. The author of the *Odes* most likely attributed these hymnic compositions to Solomon, because of the biblical record that he composed hundreds of psalms and hymns and was God's "beloved" – a *terminus technicus* that appears frequently in the *Odes*, sometimes as a circumlocution for the author. The document was obviously not composed in one year but over a period of decades; the latest possible date for the final collection is 135 CE. The original language is possibly Greek, but most likely a form of early Aramaic-Syriac. Specialists, like H. Gunkel, who judged the *Odes* are to be considered "gnostic," stressed that it was a form of early Gnosticism or gnosis. I have tried to show that in terms of gnosis the *Odes* are closest to the *Hymn of the Pearl* and the *Gospel of Truth*, and these texts clearly antedate 125 CE. Research since Gunkel has pointed out a strong and deep relation with the documents composed at Qumran. I have come to conclude that the Odist had been an Essene, but probably not a Qumranite as J. Carmignac argued.

The links between the *Odes* and the Gospel of John are manifest and permeating. How do we explain this established and acknowledged relationship? The best solution is to imagine that the Odist may have become a member of the Johannine circle or School, since, as experts have demonstrated, it is as unlikely that the Odist knew the Gospel of John as it is that the Fourth Evangelist utilized the *Odes*. R. Bultmann's argument that the *Odes* represent the type of thought behind the Fourth Gospel needs to be reexamined and recast in terms of our better understanding of the Jewish roots of Christianity and the origins of Gnosticism[8].

In understanding the *Odes* it is essential to recognize that the author claimed that he was a priest (20,1), and that as the ploughman moves ahead by spreading the earth, and the helmsman advances by spreading the seas, so the Odist moves towards God by composing Odes. Note his own words:

> As the occupation of the ploughman is the ploughshare,
> And the occupation of the helmsmen is the steering of the ship,
> So also my occupation is the psalm of the Lord by his hymns (16,1).

---

8. For bibliography and discussions of these scholarly debates, see CHARLESWORTH, *Critical Reflections*.

The Odist is clearly gifted; as I said well over thirty years ago, he deserves to be called the poet laureate in the early generations of Jesus' followers. Note, for example, this beautifully crafted thought:

> As the **wind** moves through the harp
> And the strings begin *speaking*,
>
> So the **Spirit** of the Lord is *speaking* through my members,
> And I am *speaking* through his love (Ode 6,1-2)[9].

This poem is appealing in translation; it is much more impressive in the original Syriac. There is paronomasia, alliteration, and echo repetition in the utilization of the Stichwort "wind" or "Spirit," the repetition of the verb "to speak," and the preposition "through". The Odist also has endeavored to bring out the poetic dimension of his work and to enunciate the continuous action of speaking by three times choosing a different form of the participle of this verb. The Odist may well have developed this appealing simile by observing a powerful wind moving the strings of a harp. Perhaps he did observe this phenomenon, since he claims to possess a harp on which he creates music and sings to the Lord (Ode 26,3).

What did Jews mean when they talked about "Wisdom"? One way of answering that question would be to come up with a modern construct. The better approach would be to listen to an early Jew defining Wisdom. A good definition of Wisdom is provided by the author of *4 Maccabees*. About the same time as the *Odes* were composed this Jew, heavily influenced by Greek and Jewish traditions, wrote the following:

> Wisdom (*Sophia*), I submit, is knowledge of things divine and human, and of their causes. And this wisdom, I assume, is the culture we acquire from the Law, through which we learn the things of God reverently and the things of men to our worldly advantage (4 Macc 1,16-17)[10].

Recent research on Jewish Wisdom has convinced me of the following:
1) No synthesis is possible. In fact, it is unwise to omit outstanding aspects of Wisdom which would be eliminated by any synthesis. Wisdom is about life experiences; and –if anything– life defies any coherent synthesis.

---

9. I have used bold script, italics, and underlining to clarify the way the Odist has constructed this Ode by repeating, in different ways, the ideas that unite the thought and the poetry. For the sake of the present study I have translated the verses differently than in my edition of the *Odes*.

10. All quotations from the OTP are taken from CHARLESWORTH (ed.), *Pseudepigrapha I and II*. The translation is by H. ANDERSON, *4 Maccabees*. The quotation from 4 Macc is important in discerning that early Jewish gnosis is similar to, yet dissimilar from, early Gnosticism. Especially, note how gnosis is derivative from Torah (*tou nomou*).

2) Characteristic of Wisdom Literature are sayings in the indicative mood which are often exhortatory. These are usually based on experience. Admonitions based on experience appear in a positive and negative form.
3) Jewish Wisdom is not to be defined and categorized as revelatory discourse. It is literature based on practical experience, and does not necessarily involve the norms, traditions, or claims associated with the religion of Israel or Judaism.
4) Wisdom develops within Judaism until she is clearly personified as Lady Wisdom, especially in Sirach 24, Baruch 3-4, and the Wisdom of Solomon 7-9. As such she is identified with Torah. I am convinced that we should not be satisfied only with the concept of personification. Wisdom, like the highest of the archangels, is reputed by Jews, especially in the first century BCE and following, to act like a being separate and hypostatic[11].
5) Wisdom does not command but persuades, especially in Proverbs. She brings into human society the divine voice. Wisdom is sometimes depicted as the one who is sent by God to humans (Sir 24).
6) Eventually many Jews thought that Wisdom existed before creation. She was in the beginning with God. Therefore, in some ways Wisdom was involved in the act of creating before time. She is sometimes declared to be the one who created all things.
7) The main Qumran compositions, namely the *Rule of the Community* and the *Hodayot*, contain Wisdom traditions[12]. All of the Wisdom books found in the Hebrew Bible have been found in the Qumran caves. A vast amount of new, previously unknown, Wisdom books and traditions have been found in the Qumran caves and have been recently published[13]. I am not persuaded that a convincing case can be made between which of these texts were composed at Qumran or which were penned elsewhere; hence, I shall treat them as texts known at Qumran and perhaps elsewhere also in Early Judaism.

A scholar working on the *Odes* once told me one could ignore almost everything written on this early document, because virtually all scholars have been wrong. The judgment of this person's peers was that he had

---

11. Here I differ with my esteemed colleague R. Murphy. I am not convinced that Second Temple Judaism stressed always and everywhere a thought that can be labeled "monotheistic". Also, there are developments of Wisdom beyond those of a personified Wisdom in Proverbs; but these bring us into the centuries that follow the Old Testament. See MURPHY, *Tree of Life*, p. 133.

12. See the similar thoughts by HARRINGTON, *Wisdom Texts from Qumran*.

13. See CHARLESWORTH *et al.* (eds.), *Dead Sea Scrolls*, esp. vol. 4A; and esp. ELGVIN, M. KISTER, *et al.*, *Qumran Cave 4. XV*.

been wrong. Thus, it is imperative to study the erudite and informative publications on the *Odes* by such leading lights as Harnack, Gunkel, Bultmann, Harris and Mingana, Batiffol, Carmignac, Testuz, Bacon, and Chadwick. One should not expect to understand the *Odes* in one week or one month. One must read them and re-read them, preferably in Syriac, before one should venture any opinion about them. E. A. Abbott, who had mastered early Christian literature, devoted ten days to studying the *Odes* after their *editio princeps* by J. Rendell Harris in 1909. Notice his words in *Light on the Gospel from an Ancient Poet*:

> The ten days led me to three conclusions, 1st, that Dr. Harris was probably right in assigning to the hymns (in their original language) a very early date indeed, possibly even before 100 A.D.; 2nd, that there was much, very much, well worth understanding in them; 3rd, that what I understood about them on the tenth day – in comparison with what I ought to understand – was practically nothing at all[14].

Unfortunately, too many critics have not spent enough time with the *Odes* and have thus understood practically nothing about them.

Methodology

How do we begin so that we do not dictate conclusions but stay close to our search for fresh answers? Our question must be focused. Our present question is "How are the *Odes* related, if at all, to Jewish Wisdom texts?" I presently do not know, and I will endeavor to keep this question in central focus.

The question is refined, appropriate, and timely since a great deal of the Qumran Wisdom texts have just been published or become the subject of special concern; for example, the entire fascicle of *Dead Sea Discoveries* 4.3 (1997) is devoted to "Wisdom at Qumran." It is also a question that has been neglected. Most of the work on the links between the *Odes* and scripture has been devoted to the New Testament alone and geared to discerning either whether they are a "Christian" composition or whether the Odist knew one or more of the documents later collected into the New Testament.

At the outset, we all know that a hymnbook does not quote other texts. It will at best only allude to them. From the method called Intertextuality we have learned that a later text, especially in the biblical stream of tradition, typically quotes or echoes an earlier text. That is,

---

14. ABBOTT, *Light*, p. viii. Also, see ABBOTT, *Early Christian Poetry*.

later texts contain "intertexts" from pre-texts and these earlier texts help shape the formation of the subsequent text. Thus, for example, the author(s) of the *Rule of the Community* not only quotes Isa 40,3, to prepare במדבר a Way for Yahweh, he also provides an echo of the key word in the pretext Isaiah. That is, the Qumranites have heard the Voice and went למדבר. Echoing in the attentive ear is the Stichwort מדבר. This example clarifies both what is a quotation and what is an echo of a pretext now seen as an intertext within a later Jewish text. With this hymnbook called the *Odes of Solomon* we may search only for semi-quotations and echoes of pretexts.

Other methodologies are also important and imperative for us to use. Thus, it is certain that the author of the *Odes* is directly dependent on the Davidic Psalter. Unlike the *Hodayot*, the *Odes* follow the neat presentation of thought according to *parallelismus membrorum*. Also, inherited from the Psalms and from other portions of scripture is the use of paronomasia, rhythm, assonance, and repetition. Indeed, it is clear that the *Odes*, written by a genius who has mastered the art of poetry, witness to the main feature of Semitic poetry: repetition.

Finally, we must allow for what I have termed **the prism effect**. That is, formerly parallel lines will be shifted when we move from texts that contain the Jewish expectation of the coming of the Messiah to texts which preserve the first Jewish celebrations over the appearance of Jesus whom some Jews hailed as the Messiah. Hence, while the Qumranites looked for "the coming of the prophet and the Messiahs of Aaron and Israel" (1QS 9,11)[15], the Odist rejoices in the coming of the Messiah. Note his words:

> The dove fluttered over the head of our Lord Messiah,
> Because he was her head. (Ode 24,1)

> For I believed in the Lord's Messiah,
> And considered that he is the Lord. (Ode 29,6)

> We live in the Lord by his grace,
> And life we receive by his Messiah.

> For a great day has shined upon us,
> And wonderful is he who has given us of his glory. (Ode 41,3-4)

When one has memorized the Psalter, as scholars have demonstrated the Odist had, it becomes apparent how he has recast phrases from it, always thinking about his faith in Jesus as the Messiah promised to

---

15. For the text and translation see E. QIMRON and CHARLESWORTH, in CHARLESWORTH et al. (eds.), *Dead Sea Scrolls* 1, pp. 40-41.

God's chosen and covenanted people. Thus, the well known phrase in Psalm 84,10, "For a day in your courts is better than a thousand elsewhere," appears in Ode 4,5 as "For one hour of your faith/ Is more excellent than all days and years"[16]. Thinking about the early followers of Jesus, who clearly stressed the supreme importance of Love, we can imagine many of them moving from a celebration of Torah as Law to an elevation of Torah as Love. If so, we will readily understand the echo, and probable semi-quotation, of Psalm 1,2 in Ode 41.

Psalm 1,2 stands out in the Psalter not only because of its initial place but also its sublime thought. It salutes the righteous one of whom the Psalmist writes, "And in the Law of the Lord he meditates day and night" (Ps 1,2). This verse appears in the Odes as the following semi-quotation:

> And let our faces shine in his light,
> And let our hearts meditate in his love,
> By night and by day. (Ode 41,6)

This alteration of traditions by the affirmation that Jesus is the One-who-was-to-come is the prism effect. If we seek to discern the Wisdom traditions in the *Odes* we must allow for the occasional deflection and alteration caused by the Odist's belief that Jesus is the long awaited Messiah (cf. e.g. Ode 24).

Thesis

There is no thesis to this exploration. I seek rather to ask, if the *Odes* have been influenced by Jewish Wisdom, and if so, to what extent. That is, are the *Odes* to be understood, not only as a document in the flow of the Psalter and of the Jewish apocalyptic works, but also within the stream of Jewish Wisdom? This question is motivated both by the international recognition that the *Odes* are to be understood within Judaism and by my discovery, preparing the initial stages of this lecture, that they often contain sayings, ideas, and linguistic features apparently inherited from or shaped by Jewish Wisdom. The proper method then is to focus on the *Odes*, to concentrate on passages that indicate some influence from Jewish Wisdom, and then to seek to discern antecedents. The apparent circularity is demanded by any careful and thorough research, since one cannot begin such an investigation ignorant of Jewish Wisdom

---

16. All Hebrew is from the BHS. All translations of the Bible are from the NRSV, unless otherwise noted. All Syriac and translations of the *Odes* are from CHARLESWORTH (ed.), *Pseudepigrapha* or from CHARLESWORTH, *The Odes of Solomon*.

or the *Odes*. Thus, the search will benefit from over thirty years of similar explorations. Yet, at the outset, I must confess keen interest in the ways the questions before us will be answered. What will we learn?

Preliminary Observations

I have found sayings and ideas, as well as linguistic features that seem to be shaped by or inherited from Jewish Wisdom. I shall organize my search under these two categories: sayings and ideas, and then linguistic features.

Sayings and Ideas. The Odist claims that "the Spirit of the Lord ... teaches the sons of men to know his [the Lord's] ways" (Ode 3,10). This teaching appears to derive from Jewish Wisdom traditions. Also from Jewish Wisdom is the following assertion:

> The Father of knowledge
> Is the Word of knowledge.
>
> He who created wisdom (*ḥkmt'*)
> is wiser (*ḥkym hw*) than his works. (Ode 7,7-8)

This teaching is reminiscent of the *Rule of the Community*, especially the instruction by the משכיל that the Sons of Light are to know that "from the God of knowledge comes all that is and will be" (1QS III,15). That is, under the influence of Jesus' use of Abba the Odist may have shifted "God of knowledge" to "Father of knowledge." Both the author of this section of 1QS and the Odist use similar terms to depict the Creator. The Odist wishes to stress the absolute superiority of the Creator. The Odist also wants to stress that the heart of the Most High "is superior to **all wisdom**" (Ode 28,20). Should we suggest, that the Odist is more interested in stressing monotheism than some of his Jewish contemporaries? What else could be the meaning of introducing into a hymnbook the claim that the Creator is "wiser than his works," and that the Most High is "superior to all wisdom"? The Odist seems to be reacting against some Jewish teaching. Why?

The Odist also states that "those who had not the truth with them" are those "lacking in **wisdom**" (Ode 24,10-11). They are those "who exalted themselves" (Ode 24,11), which is reminiscent of those who were the enemies of the Qumranites and the Righteous Teacher (cf. the *Hodayot* and the *Pesharim*).

Reminiscent of the teachings in Jewish Wisdom are numerous questions, statements, and exhortations in the *Odes*. Only select examples must now suffice for our present purposes. The Odist asks the following question that is shaped by Wisdom traditions:

> Who is able to distinguish love,
> Except him who is loved? (Ode 3,4)

This perception evolves out of one's own experience; and that is one of the dimensions of Jewish Wisdom Literature (ἀνθρωπίνων πραγμάτων [4 Macc 1,16]). The following statement by the Odist also evolves from one's own experience:

> There is no hard way where there is a simple heart,
> Nor barrier for upright thoughts,
>
> Nor whirlwind in the depth of the enlightened thought.
>
> Where one is surrounded on every side (by) pleasing country,
> There is nothing divided in him. (Ode 34,1-3)

The following exhortation in the *Odes* is shaped by Wisdom traditions:

> Be **wise**[17] and understanding and vigilant. (Ode 3,11)

These are remarkable elements from admonitions in Jewish Wisdom, since they appear in a hymnbook and sometimes interrupt the flow of thought. Some seem to be a characteristic *non sequitur*. For example, note the context of the question about the ability to distinguish love:

> For I should not have known how to love the Lord,
> If he had not continuously loved me.
>
> Who is able to distinguish love,
> Except him who is loved?
>
> I love the Beloved and I myself love him,
> And where his rest is, there also am I. (Ode 3,3-5)

In between two parallel stichoi about loving the Lord –the Beloved– the Odist inserts a Wisdom statement about the ability to distinguish love. The attractiveness of his composition may miss readers until they perceive how deeply Jewish is the Odist. Within Early Judaism by the first century CE Wisdom, apocalypticism, and many other elements swirled together and often shaped a new composition. It becomes clear that we should continue our search for Wisdom elements and traditions within the *Odes*; it promises to be rewarding.

---

17. The Syriac root is the same as "Wisdom".

Linguistic Features. The *Odes*, like some of the great Jewish apocalypses, notably *1 Enoch*, *4 Ezra*, *2 Baruch*, *2 Enoch*, and the *Apocalypse of Abraham*, indicate how Wisdom traditions join with apocalypticism to form a literary masterpiece. The work the Odist produces, however, is not an apocalypse. It is a hymnbook. A case study representative of this genre in the *Odes* is Ode 38. It concerns the Odist's ascent into the chariot of Truth, which is personified, even perhaps hypostatized.

Ascent with the Truth

Notice how the personification, and even hypostatization, of Wisdom seems to help shape the presentation of "Truth," who – not which – is able to lead the Odist and to walk with him. A similar ability is attributed in Judaism to "the Word"[18]. Note the following selections from Ode 38:

How Truth Became a Haven of Salvation

> I went up into the light of Truth as into a chariot,
> And the Truth led me and caused me to come.

> And caused me to pass over chasms and gulfs,
> And saved me from cliffs and valleys.

> And became for me a haven of salvation,
> And set me on the place of immortal life. (Ode 38,1-3)

Going with the Truth

> And he went with me and caused me to rest and did not allow me to err;
> Because he was and is the Truth.

> And there was no danger for me because I constantly walked with him;
> And I did not err in anything because I obeyed him.

> For Error fled from him,
> And never met him. (Ode 38,4-6)

Truth's Wisdom Apocalypse

> But Truth was proceeding on the upright way,
> And whatever I did not understand he exhibited to me:

> All the drugs of error,
> And pains of death that are considered sweetness.

---

18. See CHARLESWORTH, *Christology*.

> And the corrupting of the Corruptor,
> I saw when the Bride who was corrupting was adorned,
> And the Bridegroom who corrupts and is corrupted.
>
> And I asked the Truth, 'Who are these?'
> And he said to me: 'This is the Deceiver and the Error.'
>
> And they imitate the Beloved and his Bride,
> And they cause the world to err and corrupt it.
>
> And they invite many to the wedding feast,
> And allow them to vomit up their **wisdom** and their knowledge,
> And make them senseless,
>
> Then they abandon them;
> And so they stumble about like mad and corrupted men.
>
> Since there is no understanding in them,
> Neither do they seek it. (Ode 38,7-15)

The Odist's Declaration of Being Planted

> But I have been made **wise** so as not to fall into the hands of the Deceivers,
> And I myself rejoiced because the Truth had gone with me.
>
> For I was established and lived and was redeemed,
> And my foundations were laid on account of the Lord's hand;
> Because he has planted me.
>
> For he set the root,
> And watered it and endowed it and blessed it,
> And its fruits will be forever.
>
> It penetrated deeply and sprang up and spread out,
> And it was full and was enlarged.
>
> And the Lord alone was glorified,
> In his planting and in his cultivation;
>
> In his care and in the blessing of his lips,
> In the beautiful planting of his right hand;
>
> And in the attainment of his planting,
> And in the understanding of his mind.

Doxology

> Hallelujah. (Ode 38,16-22)

This is a complex and beautiful Ode. It would take an entire book to capture all its traditions and subtleties. The chariot vision reminds us of the advances made in grasping the origins of hekaloth mysticism, which probably first appears in the *Angelic Liturgy* (Songs of the Sabbath Sacrifice)[19].

---

19. NEWSOM & CHARLESWORTH with H.W.L. RIETZ & B.A. STRAWN, *Angelic Liturgy*.

Looking down from his ascent, as it were in a chariot with the Truth, the Odist sees the world marred by a deep *cosmic* dualism[20]. These verses remind us of the dualism that so profoundly shaped all Qumran theology and also paradigmatically defined the Fourth Gospel[21]. The vision of the world below is reminiscent of *1 Enoch* and strikingly similar to the *Apocalypse of Abraham* 9-29. Perhaps the most impressive conceptual link is between Ode 38 and the *Testament of Abraham* 10-14 [Recension A; cf. 8-12 in Recension B], in which Michael takes Abraham on a chariot above the world and he sees primarily the dualism of two ways. Sinless Abraham is especially disturbed by the sins being committed on the earth.

Since our present search is to seek new insights regarding the Wisdom traditions in the *Odes* we are led to stress the contrast brought out by the Odist. It is between those who "vomit up their **wisdom**" and the Odist who has "been made **wise**" so that he will not fall "into the hands of the Deceivers"; that is, into the hands of the Corruptor who is also the Bridegroom who corrupts. Thinking about the Odist's depiction of those who are without wisdom and knowledge, I am immediately reminded of the misfortunes caused by the evil woman in the Qumranic *Dame Folly and Lady Wisdom* (formerly *The Wiles of the Wicked Woman*). In this text Dame Folly leads people astray by uttering evil nonsense.

The key question Ode 38 raises, as we think about the possible Wisdom traditions behind and within it, is 'Why has the Odist chosen "Truth"'? Is Truth a substitute for Wisdom? The answer seems to be "yes". What other Jews attributed to Wisdom the Odist attributed to Truth. Why has the Odist made such a shift?

In Ode 24 the Odist tends to equate truth with wisdom. This Ode in lines 10-11, like Ode 38, is an element from Jewish Wisdom embedded in the *Odes*. The Odist equates "those who had not the truth with them" with those who "were lacking in wisdom." As some Jews would speak about Wisdom, so the Odist praises God because "truth flows from my mouth" (12,2). The Odist may have even thought about his compositions as "the odes of your truth" (14,7); that is, the odes of the Lord's truth (14,6).

These observations do not answer the question why the Odist chose Truth over Wisdom. There is no obvious answer. Is it because of some unattractive uses of Wisdom by other Jews? Is it the result of his acceptance of Jesus' message and decision to believe the early kerygma? The

---

20. See also Ode 17:5, "And the thought of truth led me, / And I went after it and wandered not."

21. D. Dimant argues that dualism shaped Qumran theology. See DIMANT, *Dualism*. J. Ashton has rightly claimed that the Fourth Evangelist had dualism in his bones. See ASHTON, *Fourth Gospel*, p. 237.

Odist speaks about God, the Lord, Christ, and the Holy Spirit, but it is not evident he is thinking about one of these as the Truth. Has the Odist avoided Wisdom and chosen Truth because in his community Christ was equated with Wisdom and he, perhaps agreeing with that concept, chose to speak about Truth? Or, is it because he was disturbed by the dichotomy of ignorance and knowledge in the world and thought Truth was better suited for expressing this concept than Wisdom?

These are questions aroused by thinking about the Odes and Jewish Wisdom, but they cannot be answered within the present confines. We must focus our attention on two interrelated questions: How are the *Odes* influenced by the Wisdom tradition in the well-known biblical and apocryphal Wisdom books, and how are they influenced by or similar to the recently published Wisdom books and traditions preserved in the documents found in the Qumran caves?

FIRST QUESTION: *Have the Odes been influenced by the previously known Wisdom Literature, like Proverbs, Job, Ecclesiastes, Sirach, the Wisdom of Solomon, 3 and 4 Maccabees, and Pseudo-Phocylides?*

All of these are well known to scholars and antedate 136 CE. It is clear that the Odist's preoccupation with the way or "the Way" is influenced by Jewish Wisdom (Ode 11,1-3). The concept of the way is multifaceted and has not been shaped by the so-called Christian focus. The way may denote the way to the new Jerusalem, the far-off city, the Rule (or Kingdom) of God (Ode 18,3), or the way to Paradise (Odes 11 [entire] and 20,7). Abbott was certainly correct to emphasize that for the Odist the way is the Lord's (Ode 17,3); that is, it is the way of Jesus Christ[22]. The way is thus a person, as in the Fourth Gospel (Jn 14,6). Perhaps this Odist's conception derives from the Jewish understanding of Wisdom as the way.

As in Jewish Wisdom so in the *Odes* a perfect woman is depicted calling all humanity. This influence on the Odist is most evident in Ode 33, which U. Wilckens argued is situated between Jewish and gnostic Wisdom teachings[23]. After describing the call of the Corruptor, the Evil One, the Odist describes the appeal of "the perfect Virgin," which surely is shaped by the portrayal of Wisdom in Proverbs and subsequent Wisdom texts.

---

22. ABBOTT, *Light*, p. 151.
23. U. WILCKENS, *Weisheit und Torheit*, pp. 135-59.

Note in particular Ode 33,5-13,

> However, the perfect Virgin stood,
> Who was preaching and summoning and saying:
>
> "O you sons of men, return,
> And you their daughters, come.
>
> And leave the ways of that Corruptor,
> And approach me.
>
> And I will enter into you,
> And bring you forth from destruction,
> And make you wise in the ways of truth.
>
> Be not corrupted
> Nor perish.
>
> Obey me and be saved,
> For I am proclaiming unto you the grace of God.
>
> And through me you will be saved and become blessed.
> I am your judge;
>
> And they who have put me on shall not be falsely accused,
> But they shall possess incorruption in the new world.
>
> My elect ones have walked with me,
> And my ways I will make known to them who seek me;
> And I will promise them my name".

Virtually every stichos in Ode 33 is indebted to Jewish Wisdom. A striking parallel is found in Proverbs 8[24]. In Ode 33,1 the Virgin calls. In Proverbs 8,1, Wisdom calls. In Ode 33,5 and in Proverbs 8,2 she stands. In the Odes the Virgin calls out to all so that they will be saved from the Corruptor, but in Proverbs 8 Wisdom calls to all so that they will choose wisdom as the most precious possession. The Jewishness of the *Odes* again becomes apparent when the Odist has the Virgin state that "through me you will be saved" (Ode 33,11). That statement seems surprising in light of the kerygma found in the New Testament writings; in these works it is Jesus or Christ who is portrayed as the one who saves. He is also categorized as the judge, but in Ode 33,11 the Virgin states that "I am our judge." What is the meaning of these surprising observations? This is not the place to follow up such intriguing questions. We must remain focused on Wisdom traditions.

---

24. At the beginning of this century C. Bruston perceived that there is "clairement allusion à la description de la sagesse dans le livre des Proverbes (ch. 8)"; BRUSTON, *Cantiques*, p. 27. This is one of the very few published comments about the general relation between the *Odes* and Wisdom traditions. Of course, there are comments about the relation of the *Odes* to other wisdom books, esp. the Wisdom of Solomon.

What does the Virgin symbolize for the Odist? The answers have been ingenious. H. Leclercq thought that she represented "la communauté de Jésus"[25]. C. Bruston claimed that she denoted "la parole de Jésus-Christ"[26]. J. H. Bernard opined that she symbolized the church[27]. While each of these is conceivable, it is much more likely that the Virgin appears as Wisdom in Ode 33,5-13. J. R. Harris and A. Mingana stated it precisely: "That the perfect Virgin is Wisdom (or Christ speaking as Sophia) may be seen by comparing the language with Proverbs i.20, 21, or Proverbs viii.1sqq"[28]. They claimed that the "key to the Ode lies in the Proverbs of Solomon, and especially in the eighth chapter"[29].

Their advice should be seriously considered. In Ode 33,3 the Corruptor, who did not appear as the Evil One, stands and calls from "the peak of a summit." This concept seems shaped by the thoughts of the author of Proverbs who depicts Wisdom calling from "the heights" (Prov 8,2). In the Ode the Virgin calls to "the sons of men," and in Proverbs 8,4 Wisdom calls to "the sons of men"[30]. In the Ode the Virgin promises those who heed her that they will "become blessed" (Ode 33,11). In Proverbs, Wisdom promises those who keep her ways will be blessed (8,32.33). The Odist may have memorized Proverbs 8 since he apparently was influenced by it in other places. For example, his repetitive reference to love, and being loved (e.g. Ode 3)[31], may have been shaped, *inter alia*, by Proverbs 8,17, "I love those who love me". Finally, Ode 7,8, "He who created wisdom", may be an echo of Proverbs 8,22 in which Wisdom states that the Lord "created me" (*qnny* [cf. Gen 14,19.22]; LXX: *ektise me*).

Unlike Proverbs, Job and Ecclesiastes have left virtually no discernible influence on the Odist. Any conclusions that the author of the *Odes* chose Proverbs because it was composed by Solomon, to whom the Odist most likely attributed his composition[32], seem to fade with the recognition that there is little evidence that he used the Wisdom of Solomon. It is only vaguely possible that the Odist composed Ode 23,1-3 with the Wisdom of Solomon in mind. The Odist states that joy, grace,

---

25. CABROL & LECLERCQ, *Dictionnaire* 12/2.
26. BRUSTON, *Cantiques, ad loc.*
27. BERNARD, *Odes, ad loc.*
28. HARRIS & MINGANA, *The Odes of Solomon*, vol. 2, p. 375.
29. HARRIS & MINGANA, *The Odes of Solomon*, vol. 2, p. 376.
30. Unfortunately, the NRSV is often not helpful in critical research; the Hebrew is translated (to avoid so-called sexist language) "O people".
31. Also, see Jn 14,21; 15,16, and 1John 4,10.
32. See CHARLESWORTH, *Fourteen Literary Collections*, esp. pp. 194-95.

and love are for the holy ones and the elect ones. The author of the Wisdom of Solomon wrote that "grace and mercy are upon his holy ones, and he (the Lord) watches over his elect" (Wis 3,9), and again that "God's grace and mercy are with his elect, and that he watches over his holy ones" (Wis 4,15). It is obvious that the Odist may have known and been influenced by these passages in the Wisdom of Solomon, but they only preserve concepts well known to early Jews. We know this now, thanks to the documents found in the Qumran caves; hence, it is unwise to conclude with Harris and Mingana that "Ode xxiii.1-3 ... is based directly upon some sentences in the Wisdom of Solomon iii.9 and iv.15"[33].

Sirach, however, seems to have been a favorite of the Odist. Harris and Mingana were convinced that "the 12th Ode is a Wisdom composition, showing striking parallelism with the *Praises of Wisdom* in Sirach xxiv"[34].

Let us now examine this undeveloped claim. Is it possible, probable, or certain that the Odist knew and developed some thoughts and expressions from Sirach 24?

At the outset, it would be understandable for the Odist to be fond of Sirach 24. In contrast to the apocalypses that portray Wisdom finding no place on earth and returning to heaven (e.g. 1 En 42,1-3), Sirach asserts that Wisdom found a "dwelling in Jacob" (Sir 24,8) and a "resting place" in Jerusalem (Sir 24,11). This is surely the position of the optimistic Odist who is characterized by rejoicing. In harmony with Sirach, the Odist emphasizes that "the dwelling place of the Word is man" (Ode 12,12).

It seems that in Ode 12 the Odist speaks as Wisdom. The claim that "like flowing waters, truth flows from my mouth" (Ode 12,2) sounds like an echo of Sirach 24,25-27.30 which state that Wisdom "overflows" like the Pishon, "runs over" like the Euphrates, and "pours forth instruction like the Nile". The Odist's "the narrators of his glory" (Ode 12,4) may be an echo of Sirach's claim that Wisdom "tells of her glory" (24,2). The Odist's statement that "he is the light and dawning of thought" (Ode 12,7) may be an echo of Sirach's assertion that he "will again make instruction shine forth like the dawn" (Sir 24,32). The rare expression "the mouth of the Most High" appears in both Ode 12,11 and Sirach 24,3; and it is conceivably a semi-quotation or a portion of a pretext (Sirach) in an intertext (Ode 12,11).

It is apparent also that Sirach has left echoes in other Odes. The statement in Ode 7,8 and Proverbs 8,22 is also found in Sirach 24,9. In this

---

33. HARRIS & MINGANA, *The Odes of Solomon*, vol. 2, p. 116.
34. HARRIS & MINGANA, *The Odes of Solomon*, vol. 2, p. 116.

verse Wisdom states that the Most High "created me" before the ages, and in the beginning. The Odist claims that "the Most High" "gave me immortal rest" (Ode 11,12) and that he "became like the land that blossoms and rejoices in its fruit" (Ode 11,12). The Odist affirms that he is planted (Ode 38,17) like the trees in Paradise (Ode 11,18). This verse sounds like an echo of Wisdom's statement that "the Most High" (Sirach 24,3) "gave me rest " (Sirach 24,11) and that she then grew like "a cedar in Lebanon, and like a cypress on the heights of Hermon" (Sirach 24,13). The Odist shifts from Sirach's "Zion" and "Jerusalem" to "your land", and "your Paradise". Is it not probable that the shift is caused because the Odist composed this Ode after the destruction of Jerusalem in 70 CE?

The Odist contends that the water that flows from the "living fountain of the Lord" (Ode 30,1) is for all the thirsty, and "much sweeter is its water than honey,/ And the honeycomb of bees is not to be compared with it" (Ode 30,4). This sounds like an echo from Sirach 24 in which Wisdom claims that "those who drink of me will thirst for more" (Sir 24,21), and "the memory of me is sweeter than honey, and the possession of me sweeter than the honeycomb" (Sir 24,20). This appears to be a strong echo of Sirach in the *Odes*. If so, we have made an amazing discovery that helps confirm that the Odist knew Sirach. As far as I now know, this echo has not been heard by other scholars.

I have found another passage in the *Odes* that may be seen as an echo from Sirach. In Ode 16 we find the following:

> And he fixed the creation and set it up,
> Then he rested from his works.
>
> And created things run according to their courses,
> And work their works,
> For they can neither cease nor fail.
>
> And the hosts are subject to his Word. (Ode 16,12-14)

The same celebration of the Lord's creating act, and with the same expressions – such as "his works", "cease not", and "his Word" – are found in Sirach and may derive from this Wisdom text. Note Sirach 16,26-28[35],

> When the Lord created his works from the beginning,
> And, in making them, determined their boundaries,
>
> He arranged his works in an eternal order, ...

---

35. Translation and arrangement is mine.

> And <u>they do not cease</u> from <u>their works.</u>
>
> They do not crowd one another,
> And they <u>never disobey his word</u>.

Numerous words found in Sirach reappear in Ode 16 and usually with the same context – the Lord's first act of creating (underlined words draw attention to words and concepts shared by Ode 16 with Sirach 16)[36]. Similar ideas are found in *1 Enoch* 2,1 and 5,2, *Psalms of Solomon* 18,12-14, and *2 Baruch* 48,9, but only with Sirach is Ode 16 so close. The words found in both Sirach and Ode 16 look like echoes from Sirach that had been memorized by the Odist.

Additional examples of echoes of Sirach in the *Odes* could be given[37], but these must suffice for now. There is no reason to doubt that the Odist probably had portions of Sirach memorized.

There is no convincing evidence that the Odist knew or was influenced by *3 Maccabees*, *4 Maccabees*, or *Pseudo-Phocylides*. That is because they are probably too late for him to have known them or been influenced by them; also they do not reflect Judean thought as does Sirach. It seems clear that the *Odes* were not composed in Egypt but somewhere in ancient Palestine or southwestern Syria.

We have discovered that the *Odes* are not influenced by Job and Ecclesiastes, and probably not from the Wisdom of Solomon. They are influenced in significant ways by Proverbs and Sirach. We have seen that the Odist appears to have memorized portions of Proverbs and Sirach. He does not merely quote from them.

That is significant. One can quote from a document without understanding it. But echoes from memory, which is what we have found, indicate that Jewish Wisdom is part of the being of the Odist. That means that the *Odes* took shape within the stream of Jewish Wisdom Literature. We now turn to the second question.

SECOND QUESTION: *Have the Odes been influenced by the recently published Wisdom Literature; that is, the wisdom documents found only in the Qumran Caves?*

Again, I must be selective and focus on only the most important or exciting possibilities.

---

36. It seems to be mere coincidence that both poetic compositions were numbered 16, but this entire question needs to be explored.
37. See CHARLESWORTH, *The Odes of Solomon*, pp. 55, 72, 73, 114, 80, and 86.

The first pertains to the sapiential poem called the *Hymn to the Creator* (11Q5)[38]. This hymn is so strikingly similar to the *Odes* that it elicits the following question: "Did the Odist know it?". That possibility will be hard to demonstrate, and we are merely seeking to discern how and in what ways, if at all, the *Odes* are influenced by or indebted to Jewish Wisdom Literature. We shall thus begin with this focused question: Are the *Odes* influenced by the Jewish type of thought found in the *Hymn to the Creator*? To answer this question we must alter our approach, and begin by examining the full composition:

> Great and holy (is) Yahweh,
> The holiest of the Holy Ones from generation to generation.
>
> Splendor precedes him,
> And following him (is) the rush of many waters.
>
> Mercy and truth surround his presence;
> Truth and justice, and righteousness (are) the foundation of his throne.
>
> Separating light from deep darkness,
> He established the dawn by the knowledge of his heart.
>
> When all his angels had witnessed it they sang aloud;
> For he showed them what they had not known:
>
> crowning the hills with fruits,
> good for every living being.
>
> Blessed be he who makes the earth by his power,
> Establishing the world by his wisdom.
>
> In his discernment he stretched out the heavens,
> And brought forth [wind] from [his] st[orehouses].
>
> He made [lightning for the rai]n,
> And caused mist[s] to rise [from] the end of [the earth][39]. (11Q5 XXVI,9-15)

As in the *Odes* the poetry can be arranged into bicolons which are often constructed according to *parallelismus membrorum*.

The sapiential thought of the *Hymn to the Creator* courses through the *Odes* which are full of creation motifs. Note, for example, the following observations that point out that this *Hymn* and the *Odes* are flowing within the same Jewish Wisdom tradition. That the Lord (Yahweh) is the

---

38. As D.J. Harrington states, the *Hymn to the Creator* "is sapiential in the sense that it celebrates God's wisdom and understanding made manifest in creation." HARRINGTON, *Wisdom Texts from Qumran*, p. 25.

39. For the text and translation see SANDERS with CHARLESWORTH and RIETZ, *Hymn to the Creator*. I have changed "in his wisdom" to "by his wisdom" and arranged the sapiential poem as poetry.

"holiest of the Holy Ones" (11Q5 XXVI,9) is parallel to the Odist's depiction of "the Lord's high place" in heaven (Ode 36,1-2) and the claim *ex ore Christi* that "I was the most glorified among the glorious ones,/ And the greatest of the great ones" (Ode 36,4). The idea of creation, obviously derived from Genesis 1, is similarly expressed in this *Hymn* and the *Odes*.

The author of the Qumran text wrote, "Separating light from darkness, he established the dawn by the knowledge of his heart" (11Q5 XXVI,11-12). This expression and thought is similar to the Odist's concept that "the worlds were made ... by the thought of his heart" (Ode 16,19). Also, the author of the *Hymn* mentions how God separated "light from darkness"; this is in line with the Odist's frequent dualistic use of light and darkness in the *Odes*; for example, "For he made the sun for the day so that it will be light;/ But night brings darkness over the face of the earth"[40]. Thinking of God's creating act, the author of the *Hymn* wrote that the Lord in "his discernment ... stretched out the heavens" (11Q5 XXVI,14); the Odist, also thinking about creation, wrote "He [the Lord] expanded the heaven,/ And fixed the stars" (Ode 16,11). After the first day of creation the Lord showed the angels "crowning hills with fruits, good food for every living being" (11Q5 XXVI,13); this concept is similar to the description of Paradise in the *Odes*: "And there is nothing in it that is barren,/ But everything is filled with fruit" (Ode 11,23). The issue is not that the Odist knew the *Hymn to the Creator* (which is conceivable), but that he lived within the world of thought represented by the *Hymn*.

As we turn to more of the Qumran Wisdom Literature published recently, we need to observe two factors. First, over 90% of Israelite and Jewish Wisdom traditions are not characterized by Israelite or Jewish concepts or unique perspectives, like the Covenant, the Law, the Land, the elect people, and the Sabbath. Jewish Wisdom traditions are harmonious with the world of Wisdom known from Assyria, Babylon, Persia, Egypt, Greece, Rome, and elsewhere. Wisdom is the collection of humanity's observations of what distinguishes a wise person from a person lacking in wisdom. There is nothing peculiarly Jewish in that sentiment. Second, most of what is newly published is paralleled by earlier phrases and concepts in Proverbs, Ecclesiastes, Sirach, and the Wisdom of Solomon. One dimension of these Qumran texts does stand out in the stream of Israelite

---

40. A similar thought is found in the *Book of Mysteries* lines 3-4 in which wickedness is contrasted with righteousness and darkness with light. The context is also Endtime speculation.

and Jewish Wisdom literature. For the first time Wisdom is presented within a mixture of Endtime speculation (eschatology) and apocalypticism.

The *Odes* represent this same unique mixture. Virtually every line in these texts and the *Odes* is an example of this fact. They provide a glimpse into the world of early Jewish thought in which ancient paradigms and genres have flowed into one another. Moreover, in the *Odes*, as in the Qumran Wisdom texts, there is the same emphasis on mystery, wisdom, and in a realizing context with the Endtime in view. In addition to the many examples already reviewed with other concerns before us, here are some additional examples.

In *Words to the Sons of Dawn* (4Q298), which would appear too fragmentary and generic to offer any fruitful parallels to the *Odes*, we find a mixture of Wisdom and Endtime speculation in a paraenetic context:

> and you who love kindness, and humility; and a[dd kn]owledge of the appointed [t]imes, whose interpre[ta]tion [I will recou]nt, in order that you may give heed to the **end** of the ages and that you may look upon for[m]er things in order to **know**" (Frg. 3-4 ii, lines 7-10)[41].

Note that the same genre, with Wisdom mixed with eschatology and paraenesis is found in Ode 7:

> For towards **knowledge** he has set his way,
> He has widened it and lengthened it and brought it to complete perfection.
>
> And he set over it the traces of his light,
> And it proceeded from the beginning until the **end** ...
>
> And hatred shall be removed from the earth,
> And with jealousy it shall be drowned. ...
>
> Confess his power
> And declare his grace. (Ode 7,13-14.20.26)

In the full sense of the term "eschatology" appears in the *Odes* almost always as an expression of joy in light of a realized messianism (cf. Ode 41,3-4).

Also in *Words to the Sons of Dawn* (4Q298) we find emphases typical of the *Odes*. Note how similar is the opening to this Qumran fragment and the beginning of Ode 9:

> Lend your e[ar to me, a]ll men of understanding;
> [And you who pur]sue righteousness, do understa[n]d my words; ...
> (4Q298 Frgs. 1-2 i lines 1-2)

---

41. For text and translation see M. KISTER and S.J. PFANN, in ELGVIN *et al.* (eds.), *Qumran Cave 4*. XV, pp. 25-27.

Here is the opening of the Ode:

> Open your ears,
> And I will speak to you.
>
> Give me yourself,
> So that I may also give you myself. (Ode 9,1)

In the *Odes* we find the same stress on hearing in the exhortative form "give ear," so typical of *Words to the Sons of the Dawn* (cf. also Frgs. 3-4 ii line 4). The declarative is also found in the *Odes*:

> Ears I have acquired,
> And I have heard his truth. (Ode 15,4)

In *Mysteries* (4Q299-301) we hear repeatedly about "the mystery of that which was coming into being (רז נהיה)" and "the sign to you that it is taking place" so that "wickedness is removed from before righteousness, as darkness is removed from before light. (Then) as smoke wholly ceases and is no more, so shall wickedness cease forever."[42] In the same Wisdom genre is Ode 29, "And the Lord overthrew my enemy by his Word,/ And he became like the dust which a breeze carries off" (Ode 29,10). Also reminiscent of *Mysteries* is Ode 18:

> And ignorance appeared like dust,
> And like the foam of the sea.
>
> And vain people thought that it was great,
> And they became like its type and were impoverished.
>
> But the wise understood and contemplated,
> And were not polluted by their thoughts. ... (Ode 18,11-13)

Obviously, no scholar needs to be told that in the *Odes* we are confronted with a more realizing eschatology. As I pointed out years ago, Ode 8 is similar to *Mysteries*[43]. Note this passage which is constructed *ex ore Christi*:

> Hear the word of truth,
> And receive the knowledge of the Most High.
>
> Your flesh may not understand that which I am about to say to you.
> Nor your garment that which I am about to show to you.

---

42. For text and translation see L.H. SCHIFFMAN, in ELGVIN *et al.* (eds.), *Qumran Cave 4.* XV, pp. 35-36, 105. For his poetic rendering, see p. 38. For 1Q27, see D. BARTHÉLEMY and J.T. MILIK, *Qumran Cave 1*, p. 103.
43. CHARLESWORTH, *The Odes of Solomon*, p. 43. Ode 8 is also close to 1QH 19.10 [= 11.10 in Sukenik's numbering].

> Keep my **mystery**, you who are kept by it;
> Keep my faith, you who are kept by it.
>
> And understand my knowledge, you who know me in truth;
> ... (Ode 8,8-11)

Given the new christological context, it is surprising how close this Ode is to *Mysteries*. Also strikingly similar to *Mysteries* and representing the paraenetic nature of the Wisdom genre is the following passage in Ode 18:

> Let not light be conquered by darkness,
> Nor let truth flee from falsehood. (Ode 18,6)

As in *Mysteries* so here in the *Odes* we discover the same dualistic thought expressed in terms of light, which is truth, and darkness, which is falsehood. This is close to *Mysteries* in which light is righteousness and darkness is wickedness. As we have already seen in discussing Ode 33 and 38, in the *Odes* truth is associated with righteousness and falsehood with wickedness.

We turn now to the most extensive Qumran Wisdom text, the so-called *Sapiential Work A* or *Instruction* (1Q26, 4Q415-418, 4Q423)[44]. It was popular at Qumran since six manuscripts have been recovered from the Qumran caves. Each is in an early or late formal Herodian script. It cannot be designed for the celibate and monastic priests living at Qumran, because of its concern for commerce; but it could be a non-Qumran Essene document, like the *Damascus Document*. Harrington points out that this work of wisdom instruction is similar to Proverbs, Sirach, "late Egyptian wisdom writings, Jesus' instructions in the Synoptic Gospels, and the letter of James"[45]. Neither he nor another scholar has thought about comparing *Sapiential Work A* (or *Instruction*) with the *Odes*. As will become clear this is a fruitful inquiry.

Again it is best to start with the Qumran text and then search the *Odes* for possible similarities and parallels. This is essential, as we have already seen, because the traditions flow chronologically from Qumran towards the *Odes* and perhaps into them.

In *Sapiential Work A* we find a wisdom exhortation: "Do not sell yourself for money. ... And not for any price do you sell your glory, ..." (4Q416 2 ii 17-18). At a time when Jews did purchase other humans, even fellow Jews, as slaves this is a wise saying. It is paralleled in the

---

44. As HARRINGTON states, "The most extensive wisdom writing in the Qumran library is a wisdom instruction sometimes designated as Sapiential Work A." HARRINGTON, *Wisdom Texts from Qumran*, p. 40. For the translation cited herein see pp. 42-59.
45. HARRINGTON, *Wisdom Texts from Qumran*, p. 40.

Odes in a saying that is also a wisdom paraenesis: "You should not purchase a stranger because he is like yourself ..." (Ode 20,6).

In *Sapiential Work A* we find frequently a reference to the coming "mystery". The following wisdom exhortation, within an Endtime speculation, is typical of early Jewish Wisdom; and it is in a poetic style similar to the synonymous *parallelismus membrorum* of the *Odes*[46]:

> Study the mystery that is to be,
> And understand all the ways of truth,
> And all the roots of iniquity you shall contemplate.
>
> And then you will know what is bitter for a man
> And what is sweet for a fellow. (4Q416 2 iii 14-15)

This excerpt from *Sapiential Work A* looks like one of the *Odes*. There are parallels to it in most of the *Odes*. The following example must suffice:

> Keep my mystery, you who are kept by it; ...
> And understand my knowledge, you who know me in truth; ... (Ode 8,10-11)

Like *Sapiential Work A* this Ode is a Wisdom paraenesis and it is in an eschatological context; note a preceding verse: "And peace was prepared for you,/ Before what may be your war" (Ode 8,7). Reminiscent of the portion of *Sapiential Work A* just quoted, especially the final stichoi, is Ode 18:

> And ignorance appeared like dust,
> And like the foam of the sea.
>
> And vain people thought that it was great,
> And they became like its type and were impoverished.
>
> But the wise understood and contemplated,
> And were not polluted by their thoughts; .... (Ode 18,11-13)

This section of the *Odes* is an aspect of Jewish Wisdom, and like *Sapiential Work A* it urges contemplation, while saluting the wise and defaming the vain who are like sea foam. It is even conceivable that we have an echo of this text or this tradition in the *Odes*. Again, like an Ode is 4Q417 2 i 6-9:

> By day and by night meditate on the mystery that is to be,
> And study it always[47].
> And then you will know truth and iniquity; ...

---

46. I have presented HARRINGTON's translation with stichoi.
47. Again, I have set HARRINGTON's translation to verse.

> For the God of knowledge is the foundation of truth,
> And by the mystery that is to be He has laid out its foundation,
> And its deeds He has prepared with [...] wisdom,
> And with all cunning He has fashioned it.

Again, this excerpt from this Qumran text looks like an Ode. In Ode 11 we find a statement similar to the final section quoted from *Sapiential Work A*:

> From the beginning until the end
> I received his knowledge.
>
> And I was established upon the rock of truth,
> Where he had set me. (Ode 11,4-5; cf. Ode 22,12)

When we turn to so-called 4Q*Sapiential Work C* (4Q424) we find linguistic features characteristic of the *Odes*. For example, note this use of sapiential simile in poetic form from so-called *Sapiential Work C* (4Q424) Frag. 3,4-5:

> Like one who winnows in a [weak] wind that cannot purify,
> So is one who speaks to an ear that does not hear,
> And pronounces their vow to one slumbering in a spirit of [...].

This same genre appears in Ode 42:

> Like the arm of the bridegroom over the bride,
> So is my yoke over those who know me. (Ode 42,8)

The realizing eschatology within a Wisdom context is impressive and links this Ode with early Jewish Wisdom traditions.

Another interesting Qumran text is *Beatitudes* (4Q525) which clearly contains Wisdom traditions. The following thought and genre is very close to the *Odes*:

> [Happy is the one who speaks truth] with a pure heart
> And does not slander with his tongue.
>
> Happy are they who cling to her statutes
> And do not cling to the ways of iniquity. (4Q525 2 ii 1-2)[48]

Formerly, the following section of the *Odes* led scholars to think about the Beatitudes attributed to Jesus. Now, it is certain that prior to Jesus, Beatitudes existed in Jewish Wisdom traditions. Note the use of the formula "Happy is" or "Blessed are" in the *Odes* (6,13; 11,18; 12,13; 30,7):

---

48. Translated by HARRINGTON in *Wisdom Texts from Qumran*, p. 66.

> Blessed are they who by means of him have perceived everything,
> And have known the Lord in his truth. (Ode 12,13)

It is obvious that the Qumran Wisdom texts significantly help us understand the *Odes* and place them within Early Judaism. Some portions of the *Odes*, as we have seen, are deeply indebted to Jewish Wisdom traditions.

Conclusion

We began by asking one focused question: How are the *Odes* influenced by the Jewish Wisdom traditions, if at all? We have learned a surprising amount.

First, we observed how important is the method of exegesis called intertextuality. Second, we have recognized that the best way to learn about the ways an ode or hymn, even a hymnbook, is shaped by earlier traditions in the full range of biblical writings is to seek to discern a semi-quotation or echo in an intertext from a pretext. Third, we perceived that like the early Jewish Wisdom texts, the *Odes* demonstrate how in Second Temple Judaism Wisdom, apocalypticism, and eschatology are intertwined. Fourth, by studying the Jewish Wisdom traditions that may have helped shape the *Odes* we obtained a clearer perception of the meditative and contemplative elements in the *Odes*. Fifth, this study helps isolate the importance of the paraenetic traditions in the *Odes*. Sixth, it is now certain that the *Odes* are not only shaped by Jewish Wisdom but that this hymnbook took shape within the evolution of Jewish Wisdom Literature. We may conclude, therefore: "Die Oden Salomos kommen aus der Entwicklungsgeschichte der jüdischen Weisheitsliteratur".

Princeton Theological Seminary James H. Charlesworth
CN 821 Princeton NJ 08542-0803
USA

»SIE WIRD DIR NICHT IHRE KRAFT GEBEN«
ADAM, KAIN UND DER ACKERBAU IN
4Q423 2₃ UND APC MOS 24

1. EINLEITUNG

Das zweite Fragment des unpublizierten Weisheitstextes 4Q423 Sapiential Work V[1] (im folgenden 4Q423 2) ist auf Gen 2-3 bezogen, in welcher Form dieser Bezug stattfindet, kann hier nicht geklärt werden; der Erhaltungszustand des Textes läßt vielleicht auch kein abschließendes Urteil zu. Es kann hier genauso wenig erörtert werden, welche Funktion dem Text, von dem Fragment 2 Zeugnis ablegt, und der heute großenteils in den Bereich der unsichtbaren Wirklichkeit übergegangen ist, einmal im Rahmen des weisheitlichen Werkes als Ganzen zukam. Hier soll lediglich die dritte Zeile dieses Fragments (4Q 423 2₃) eingehender untersucht und mit einer außerqumranischen Parallele (Apc Mos 24)[2] verglichen werden. Soweit nötig, wird dabei auch das Fragment als Ganzes mit Aufmerksamkeit bedacht werden.

4Q423 2 ist – wie ein Blick auf die Photos zeigt – in der vorläufigen Ausgabe von Wacholder und Abegg weitgehend zuverlässig wiedergegeben[3]; es ist indes zu vermerken, daß es sich streng genommen um zwei Fragmente handelt, die allerdings nahtlos zueinander passen. Der Riß geht mitten durch den Satz, der hier besonderer Aufmerksamkeit gewürdigt werden soll; ich zitiere den Satz – mit Riß (/)

קוץ וד/רדר תצמיח לכה וכוחה לא תתן לכה

Dornen und Disteln soll sie [sc. die Scholle] dir sprießen lassen, und ihre Kraft soll sie dir nicht geben

---

1. Die Bezeichnung 4QSapiential Work V für 4Q423 stammt aus B.Z. WACHOLDER / M.G. ABEGG, *Preliminary Edition 2*, p. 166, die ältere Bezeichnung ist 4QTree of Knowledge. J. MAIER, *Texte* II, p. 497 nennt diesen Text 4QSapiential Work A (V) e; bei F. GARCÍA MARTÍNEZ / E.J.C. TIGCHELAAR, *Study Edition* II, p. 887 heißt er 4QInstruction^g.

2. Anstelle einer Edition wird hier für die Apc Mos die Synopse der Handschriften bei M. NAGEL, *Vie Grecque* (Tome III) benutzt. Die Edition D.A. BERTRAND, *Vie Grecque* ist problematisch wegen ihres eklektischen Umgangs mit der handschriftlichen Überlieferung.

3. Siehe B.Z. WACHOLDER / M.G. ABEGG: *Preliminary Edition 2*, p. 166, als Photo ist PAM 43.520 zu vergleichen, siehe hierzu die Mikrofilmedition: E. TOV, *Dead Sea Scrolls on Microfiche*, ferner R.H. EISENMAN / J.M. ROBINSON, *Facsimile Edition*, Plate 1470.

Um einer besseren Übersichtlichkeit willen repetiere ich im folgenden den Text des gesamten Fragments[4].

1	[｡[ב]⁵[כל פרי תנובה וכל עץ נעים נחמד להשכיל הלוא גן
2	[ג]⁶{ } [ל]ה]ש[כיל מ]｡[ה⁷ ובו המשילכה לעבדו ולשמרו
3	[קוץ ודרדר תצמיח לכה וכוחה לא תתן לכה]｡
4	[}{ במועלכה]
5	[ל] [הו]ר[⁹] ⁸ }ילדה וכל רחמי{
6	[בכל חפציכה כי כל תצמ[ח]¹⁰
7	[תם ה｡] [ובמ[ט]ע]

(1... Jede Frucht des Ertrags und jeden lieblichen Baum, begehrenswert zu erkennen. Ist [es] nicht ein Garten.... 2... Zu erkennen.... Und über ihn hat er dich zum Herrscher gemacht, daß du ihn bearbeitest und beschützest... 3... Dornen und Disteln soll sie [sc. die Scholle] dir sprießen lassen, und ihre Kraft soll sie dir nicht geben... 4... durch deine Untreue... 5 Sie hat geboren, und alles Erbarmen... 6... in all deinem Wohlgefallen, denn alles bringt sie hervor... 7... und in der Pflanzung...)

Zeile 1 scheint den in Gen 2-3 erwähnten Garten anzusprechen (dabei stammt נחמד להשכיל aus Gen 3,6); wie das Fragewort הלוא anzeigt, geschieht dies offenbar in diskursiver Form. Dieser Eindruck wird bestätigt in Zeile 2, wo erkennbar aus Gen 2,15 stammendes Material in Anredeform erscheint. Ist hier Adam angesprochen? Wird dem Adressaten der weisheitlichen Rede die Adamrolle zugedacht? Dies ist schwer zu bestimmen; eine schlichte Wiederholung des biblischen Textes liegt hier jedenfalls nicht vor.

---

4. Jeglicher editorischer Ehrgeiz ist vermieden. Grundlage ist B.Z. WACHOLDER / M.G. ABEGG, *Preliminary Edition 2*, p. 166; F. GARCÍA MARTÍNEZ / E.J.C. TIGCHELAAR, *Study Edition* II, p. 886 wird anhand des Photos (Anm. 2) verglichen. { } bezeichnet unbeschriebenen Schreibstoff, ｡ einen Buchstabenrest, [ ] einen Textverlust, ⌐ ⌐ eine unsichere Lesung.

5. F. GARCÍA MARTÍNEZ / E.J.C. TIGCHELAAR, *Study Edition* II, p. 886 lesen ג, eine Entscheidung fällt schwer (das Zeichen ist nur teilweise erhalten).

6. Das ג notieren F. GARCÍA MARTÍNEZ / E.J.C. TIGCHELAAR, *Study Edition* II, p. 886, B.Z. WACHOLDER / M.G. ABEGG, *Preliminary Edition 2*, p. 166 haben es übersehen.

7. F. GARCÍA MARTÍNEZ / E.J.C. TIGCHELAAR, *Study Edition* II, p. 886 lesen מו[א]דה, ich vermag nicht so viel zu erkennen.

8. B.Z. WACHOLDER / M.G. ABEGG, *Preliminary Edition* II, p. 166 notieren noch ה ש ｡ [ ], F. GARCÍA MARTÍNEZ / E.J.C. TIGCHELAAR, *Study Edition* II, p. 886 erkennen nichts, ich erkenne auch nichts.

9. F. GARCÍA MARTÍNEZ / E.J.C. TIGCHELAAR, *Study Edition* II, p. 886 notieren für das ר einen Buchstabenrest; es ist in der Tat nur unvollständig erhalten, scheint mir aber sicher zu sein.

10. F. GARCÍA MARTÍNEZ /E.J.C. TIGCHELAAR, *Study Edition* II, p. 886 notieren יח, aber der erhaltene Buchstabenrest scheint eher zu einem ח zu gehören.

Zu erwähnen bleibt, daß die biblische Vorlage in Zeile 2 auch insoweit verändert erscheint, als der in Gen 2,15 genannte Auftrag, den Garten Eden zu »bearbeiten« (לעבדה) und zu »behüten« (לשמרה)[11], hier offenbar vor einem spezifischen Deutehorizont verstanden wird, der im biblischen Text selbst zumindest nicht explizit wird: Er ist hier als ein *Herrschaftsauftrag* verstanden; den beiden Verben im Infinitiv wird die finite Form המשילכה (»er hat dich zur Herrschaft eingesetzt«) übergeordnet, die im biblischen Text nicht begegnet. Wird damit in 4Q423 II die Auffassung vertreten, die in Gen 2,15 erzählte Einsetzung des Menschen ins Paradies sei eine Einsetzung in ein Herrscheramt gewesen? Ist Adam im Paradies als Herrscher der Tiere aufgefaßt? Es gäbe für eine solche Auffassung eine Parallele in der Apokalypse des Mose (Apc Mos), Kapitel 15[12]. Angesichts der Tatsache, daß 4Q423 2 auf jeden Fall in Zeile 3 eine Parallele zu Apc Mos 24 aufweist, wirkt eine solche Vermutung durchaus plausibel.

Zeile 3 soll unten einer eingehenderen Besprechung gewürdigt werden; hier ist nur zu konstatieren, daß auch diese Zeile die Anredeform wahrt – freilich sind die ihr zugrundeliegenden biblischen Texte von jeher dialogisch gewesen. Dem Rest des Fragments ist nicht mehr viel zu ent-

---

11. Im hebräischen Text von Gen 2,15 sind die beiden o.g. Infinitive mit einem ה־ Suffix ausgestattet, das von den Masoreten als Possessivsuffix der 3. sg. fem. interpretiert wird (sie lesen לְעָבְדָהּ וּלְשָׁמְרָהּ). In 4Q423 2₂ stehen statt der ה־Suffixe ו־Suffixe (es heißt dort לעבדו ולשמרו). Der Grund für diese Differenz ist darin zu suchen, daß in Gen 2,15 eine scheinbare grammatische Irregularität vorliegt, die in 4Q423 2₂ korrigiert wird. Die beiden Suffixe weisen zurück auf die Wendung גן־עדן, wobei das Nomen regens גן regulär als das Bezugswort anzusetzen wäre, doch ergibt sich dabei das Problem, daß גן gewöhnlich masculin, die Suffixe nach der masoretischen Vokalisierung aber Feminina sind. Diese scheinbare Inkongruenz ist in 4Q423 2₂ vermieden. Der Text der Masoreten wird bei C. BROCKELMANN, *Hebräische Syntax*, §16g damit erklärt, daß sich hier das Genus des Regens גן ausnahmsweise nach dem femininen Rectum עדן richte, ähnlich B.C. WALTKE / M. O'CONNOR, *Biblical Hebrew Syntax*, §6,4,1d. Es ist allerdings die Frage zu stellen, ob sich die ה-Suffixe nicht eher auf עדן denn auf גן beziehen. Im übrigen kann 4Q423 2₂ auch als Beleg dafür genommen werden, daß in Gen 2,15 gegen die Masoreten *לְעָבְדָהּ וּלְשָׁמְרָהּ zu lesen ist. Mit der Differenz zwischen den Masoreten und 4Q423 2₂ kann auch ein Unterschied in der Aussage verbunden sein: Ganz gleich, ob man die ה־- Suffixe auf עדן oder auf ein sekundär unter dem Einfluß von עדן zum Femininum transformiertes גן beziehen will, in beiden Fällen liegt eine Auffassung der Wendung גן־עדן vor, derzufolge עדן eine Apposition zu גן, also der Name des Gartens ist. Gerade im Kontext (Gen 2,8.10) ist aber der Garten nicht mit עדן identisch, sondern vielmehr eine Gegebenheit innerhalb Edens (Gen 2,8: גן־בְּעֵדֶן). Es ist möglich, daß 4Q423 2₂ eine Interpretation der Wendung גן־עדן zugrundeliegt, die עדן im Lichte von Gen 2,8.10 als »Bereichsgenitiv« auffaßt, גן־עדן also im Sinne von »Garten Edens« versteht. Der eindeutige Rückbezug von לעבדו ולשמרו auf גן wäre dann leichter erklärbar. Auffassungsunterschiede zum Verhältnis von גן und עדן sind auch in der rabbinischen Literatur bezeugt, vgl. die Diskussion in Ber R 15,2 (zu Gen 2,8), wo erörtert wird, ob der Garten größer war als Eden oder Eden größer als der Garten.

12. In Apc Mos 15 ist Adam als Hüter der Tiere dargestellt; Mensch und Tier leben innerhalb des Paradieses in einer durch Distanz zwischen den Geschlechtern geprägten Lebensordnung, in der dem Menschen die Rolle der Ordnungsmacht zukommt – im Hintergrund steht wahrscheinlich die schon in altorientalischen Kulturen bezeugte Vorstellung vom König als Hirten.

nehmen. Insgesamt kann also mit Sicherheit nichts darüber hinaus festgestellt werden, daß 4Q423 2 zu den in Qumran seltenen Zeugen einer Rezeption von Gen 2-3 gehört – doch das ist aufsehenserregend genug. Es bleibt aber eine offene Frage, in welchen Argumentationszusammenhang der Autor das biblische Material letztlich gestellt hat.

2. 4Q423, FRAGMENT 2, ZEILE 3 UND APC MOS 24,2

Ist somit die Aussageabsicht von 4Q423 Fragment 2 kaum noch zu rekonstruieren, so läßt sich doch zumindest an Zeile 3 des Fragments zeigen, wie in dieser Weisheitsschrift biblische Texte verarbeitet werden konnten. Das heißt nicht, daß zu ermitteln wäre, zu welchem Zweck sie verarbeitet wurden, aber die Art der Verarbeitung läßt sich doch immerhin bestimmen. Es ist freilich nicht auszuschließen, daß der Autor hier Ergebnisse fremder Arbeit übernommen hat, daß also die hier zu beobachtende exegetische Technik Vorarbeit eines anderen ist. Die Tatsache, daß sich in Apc Mos 24 eine Parallele findet, macht dies sogar wahrscheinlich.

Die hier zur Untersuchung anstehende Phrase קוץ ודרדר תצמיח לכה וכוחה לא תתן לכה ist in ihrer ersten Hälfte eindeutig ein Bibelzitat; קוץ ודרדר תצמיח לכה entspricht Gen 3,18a 𝔐 bis auf die Plene-Schreibung bei לכה[13]. Etwas schwerer ist die zweite Hälfte zu identifizieren. Sie findet indessen eine sehr interessante Parallele in Apc Mos 24. Die Apc Mos ist eine frühjüdische Erzählung[14] über das Leben Adams und Evas nach der Vertreibung aus dem Paradies, die auch eine umfangreiche Erzählung über die Ereignisse im Garten aus dem Munde Evas (Apc Mos 15-30) enthält. In der Nacherzählung der Verfluchung Adams in Apc Mos 24 begegnet nun mit καὶ οὐ δώσει τὴν ἰσχὺν αὐτῆς »und sie wird nicht ihre Kraft geben« (Apc Mos 24,2) eine Wendung, die der

---

13. Das Sigel 𝔐 bezeichnet in diesem Artikel nicht die masoretische Überlieferung im engeren Sinne, zu der auch die Traditionen der Vokalisierung gehörten, sondern einen mit dem Konsonantenbestand des masoretischen Textes übereinstimmenden hebräischen Text.

14. Die Verortung der Apc Mos im frühen Judentum ist umstritten. Die handschriftliche Überlieferung setzt mit dem 11. Jh. ein, vgl. hierzu die Liste der Textzeugen bei M. NAGEL, Vie Grecque, Tome I, pp. X-XI. In der neueren Literatur wird bei M. DE JONGE / J. TROMP, Life of Adam, pp. 65-78 für christliche Herkunft der Schrift votiert, bei O. MERK / M. MEISER, Leben Adams, pp. 764-769 hingegen wird die Schrift als jüdisch angesehen und »eine Datierung der Apokalypsis Mosis etwa z.Zt. der Abfassung der paulinischen Briefe oder relativ kurz davor... favorisiert« (p. 769). Die in diesem Artikel angeführten Beobachtungen zu den exegetischen Grundlagen von Apc Mos 24 untermauern eher die Auffassung von MEISER und MERK.

zweiten Hälfte unseres Textes (וכוחה לא תתן לכה) beinahe wörtlich entspricht[15]. Sie steht dort ebenfalls im Zusammenhang mit Gen 3,18 (Apc Mos 24,2: ἀκάνθας καὶ τριβόλους), nur daß es diesem vorangeht, nicht – wie in 4Q423 II₃ – folgt.

In Apc Mos 24,2 geht καὶ οὐ δώσει τὴν ἰσχὺν αὐτῆς ein weiterer Satz voran, so daß die gesamte Wendung lautet: Ἐργάσῃ δὲ αὐτὴν καὶ οὐ δώσει τὴν ἰσχὺν αὐτῆς (»Du sollst sie bearbeiten, und sie wird nicht ihre Kraft geben«). Diese nun läßt sich aufgrund ihres großen Umfangs relativ leicht als eine nicht ganz wörtliche Zitation von Gen 4,12ab identifizieren. Dort wird zu Kain gesagt: »Wenn du die Erde bearbeitest, wird sie dir fürderhin nicht ihre Kraft geben«. 𝔊 liest ὅτι ἔργᾳ τὴν γῆν καὶ οὐ προσθήσει τὴν ἰσχὺν αὐτῆς δοῦναί σοι, 𝔐 in seinem Konsonantenbestand dagegen: כי תעבד את־האדמה לא תסף תת־כחה לך.

> Die nachfolgende Nebeneinanderstellung der aufeinander bezogenen Texte mag die Übersicht erleichtern. Eine synoptische Präsentation ist nicht möglich, da – wie bereits angesprochen – Apc Mos 24 und 4Q423 die einander entsprechenden Texte in unterschiedlicher Reihenfolge bieten. Im Folgenden sind die Entsprechungen zum ersten Teilsatz in 4Q423 2₃ jeweils kursiv, die Entsprechungen zum zweiten Teilsatz jeweils durch Unterstreichung gekennzeichnet. Es sind auch Passagen aufgeführt, die noch nicht erläutert wurden, jedoch für die nachfolgenden Erörterungen von Bedeutung sind:

Gen 3,17; 3,18; 4,12b	4Q423 2₃	Apc Mos 24,1-2
3,17 ארורה האדמה בעבורך...	*קוץ ודרדר תצמיח לכה*	24,1 ... ἐπικατάρατος ἡ γῆ
3,18 *וקוץ ודרדר תצמיח לך*	וכוחה לא תתן לכה	ἕνεκα σου
4,12a כי תעבד את־האדמה		24,2 ἐργάσει δὲ αὐτὴν
4,12b לא תסף תת־כחה לך		καὶ οὐ δώσει τὴν ἰσχὺν αὐτῆς
		ἀκάνθας καὶ τριβόλους ἀνατελεῖ σοι

Es kann also festgehalten werden, daß sowohl in Apc Mos 24 als auch in 4Q423 2₃ der Adamfluch durch eine mehr oder weniger deutliche Assoziation an Gen 4,12 erweitert wird – 4Q423 zitiert Gen 4,12b, Apc Mos 24,2 zitiert Gen 4,12ab. Dabei ist allerdings der Umstand zu beachten, daß 4Q423 2₃ und Apc Mos 24,2 in einem entscheidenden Punkt übereinstimmend vom biblischen Text – sei es nun 𝔐 in seinem Konsonantenbestand oder 𝔊 – abweichen: Es fehlt תסף (bzw. die griechische Entsprechung προσθήσει), dafür erscheint statt des Infinitivs eine finite Form; außerdem fehlt das Wort für Erde/Ackerboden (γῆ bzw. אדמה) - aus Kontextgründen, in Apc Mos 24 ganz sicher (vgl. Apc Mos 24,1!),

---

15. In Apc Mos 24,2 fehlt ein Korrelat zu לכה.

in 4Q423 2_3 mit einer gewissen Wahrscheinlichkeit. Es ist also in beiden Texten eine Abbreviatur von Gen 4,12b, durch welche die Verfluchung Adams amplifiziert wird.

Im folgenden sollen die beiden einander so nahe stehenden Texte auf ihre exegetischen Voraussetzungen untersucht werden, dabei wird zuerst Apc Mos 24 als der umfangreichere und besser erhaltene Text diskutiert (§3-4), zunächst im Hinblick auf die zugrundeliegenden Bibeltexte (§3), sodann im Hinblick auf die exegetische Methodik des Autors (§4). Anschließend soll auch der exegetische Hintergrund von 4Q423 2_3 zur Sprache gebracht werden; im Zusammenhang damit werden beide Texte in einen weiteren auslegungsgeschichtlichen Horizont eingeordnet (§5). Abschließend folgt ein Resumée, das den Ertrag dieser Untersuchung für die Erforschung der frühjüdischen Schriftexegese benennt (§6).

3. Apc Mos 24 und seine biblische Grundlage

Ich präsentiere zunächst den griechischen Text in einer eigenen – vorläufigen – Ausgabe, welche auf der Synopse der Handschriften basiert, die M. Nagel 1972 herausgegeben hat[16]:

24,1 Καὶ λέγει ὁ θεὸς τῷ ᾽Αδάμ·
ἐπειδὴ παρήκουσας τὴν ἐντολήν μου
καὶ ἤκουσας τῆς γυναικός σου,
ἐπικατάρατος ἡ γῆ ᵃἕνεκα σοῦ.
24,2 ᵇ'Εργάσῃᵇ17 ᶜδὲᶜ18 αὐτήν,

24,1 Und Gott sagt zu Adam:
»Weil du mein Gebot nicht beachtet
und auf deine Frau gehört hast,
soll die Erde um deinetwillen verflucht sein.
24,2 Du sollst sie bearbeiten,

---

16. Der von mir präsentierte Text ist Teil eines Lesetextes, den ich – mit textkritischem Kommentar versehen – meiner Dissertation zugrundelegen werde, ich verfolge nicht die Absicht, die Apc Mos zu edieren. Es soll aber demnächst eine Edition erscheinen, die von J. Tromp vorbereitet wird. Die Anmerkungen zum Text kommentieren auf der Grundlage der Synopse der Textüberlieferung bei M. Nagel, *Vie Grecque*, Tome III, pp. 174-179 v.a. die Abweichungen von der Ausgabe Bertrands; die dabei genannten Sigel der Handschriften entsprechen denen bei Nagel, *Vie Grecque*, vgl. insbesondere die Liste der Textzeugen in Vol. I, pp. X-XI, allerdings ersetze ich die von Nagel teilweise verwendeten griechischen Schriftzeichen durch lateinische. Die Sigel von D.A. Bertrand, *Vie Grecque* zu benutzen, halte ich nicht für geboten; es wird dadurch nur die Lektüre der Synopse von Nagel erschwert.

17. b-b: Bertrand liest ἐργάσει (Futur), doch der Konj. Aor. ἐργάσῃ ist naheliegender (das reguläre Futur wäre ἐργᾷ). Futurformen der 2. Sg. beginnen erst mit ἔσει in 24,3, das legt sich auch inhaltlich nahe: Dort geht es eher um Zustände, hier um Handlungen, die viel eher auch als Zustände angeordnet werden können.

18. c-c: Bertrand läßt δέ aus, aber dieses ist mit St AV (B) gut bezeugt, während auf der Seite der Auslassung nur die relativ schlechten Zeugen P² J² J³ verbucht werden können (A AC Ath formulieren den ganzen Satz um und zählen daher nicht, vgl. Anm. 19). B liest δή (Cod.: δη), vermutlich, um das der Partikel δέ inhärierende adversative Moment zu vermeiden, genau dies dürfte auch die Ursache für dessen Auslassung in Rez III sein.

καὶ οὐ δώσει τὴν ἰσχὺν αὐτῆς,[a19]	und sie wird dir nicht ihre Kraft geben,
ἀκάνθας καὶ τριβόλους ἀνατελεῖ σοι·	Dornen und Disteln wird sie dir hervorbringen;
καὶ ἐν [d]ἱδρώτητι[d20] τοῦ προσώπου σου	und im Schweiße deines Angesichtes
[e]φάγῃ[e21] τὸν ἄρτον σου.	sollst du dein Brot essen.
Ἔσει δὲ ἐν καμάτοις πολυτρόποις·	Du wirst unter vielfältigen Mühsalen leiden:
θλιβεὶς ἀπὸ πικρίας,	bedrängt von Bitternis –
καὶ μὴ γεύσει γλυκύτητος·	und du wirst Süße nicht schmecken;
24,3 θλιβεὶς ἀπὸ καύματος	24,3 bedrängt von Hitze
καὶ στενωθεὶς ἀπὸ ψύξεως.	und beengt von Kälte.
·'[f22] Καὶ [g]τῶν[g23] ἐκυρίευες θηρίων,	Und die du beherrschtest, die Tiere,
ἐπαναστήσονταί σοι ἐν ἀκαταστασίᾳ,	sie werden sich gegen dich unbotmäßig erheben,
ὅτι τὴν ἐντολήν μου οὐκ ἐφύλαξας.	denn du hast mein Gebot nicht gehalten.«

Es läßt sich an diesem Text einiges beobachten, was hier nur am Rande interessieren kann. In Apc Mos 24,4 scheint der Fluch über Adam um eine dem biblischen Text fremde Tradition amplifiziert: Adam wird der Aufstand der Tiere angekündigt; das Thema spielt in der Apc Mos auch sonst eine

19. a-a: An[II] Pa Br S[1] ersetzen den markierten Text durch ἐν τοῖς ἔργοις σου, bieten also einen auf Gen 3,17 𝔊 basierenden Kurztext. A AC Ath ergänzen ἐν τοῖς ἔργοις σου nach ἐπικατάρατος ἡ γῆ und formulieren ἕνεκα σοῦ zu *ἡνίκα γάρ um, wahrscheinlich mit der Absicht, ἕνεκα σοῦ auf diese Weise zu verdrängen. Beide Korrekturen verfolgen die gleiche Tendenz: Sie ersetzen das – wie sich zeigen wird (vgl. §4) – auf 𝔐 basierende ἕνεκα σοῦ durch dessen Septuagintakorrelat ἐν τοῖς ἔργοις σου und nehmen damit genau den biblischen Passus in den Text, auf dem das nachfolgende ἐργάσῃ δὲ αὐτήν, καὶ οὐ δώσει τὴν ἰσχὺν αὐτῆς beruht (vgl. §5), freilich mit dem Unterschied, daß An[II] Pa etc. diesen Passus durch seinen exegetischen Anknüpfungspunkt ersetzen, während A AC etc. ihn zur Explikation desselben machen. Beide Korrekturen jedoch zeigen durch ihr Vorgehen einen gewissen Einblick in die exegetischen Voraussetzungen des von ihnen bearbeiteten Textes; man kann daher annehmen, daß sie aus dem Milieu stammen, in dem dieser entstanden ist. Obgleich die Textzeugen aus später Zeit stammen, bieten sie doch alte Textüberlieferung – das gilt z.T. auch für die vom ältesten Stand der Überlieferung abweichenden Lesarten.

20. d-d: Bertrand liest ὑδρότητι, doch ἱδρώτητι ist vorzuziehen. Was die einzelnen Handschriften jeweils intendieren, ist schwer zu entscheiden, da die Aussprache beider Wörter in der Zeit der Kopisten identisch gewesen sein dürfte und sich die orthographischen Kenntnisse der Abschreiber in Grenzen hielten. Es ist jedoch zu beachten, daß immerhin 5 Handschriften (St AC P[2] J[2] J[3]) orthographisch korrekt ἱδρώτητι lesen, aber nur zwei (An[II] A) ὑδρότητι ohne Abweichungen bei der Orthographie der Vokale. Ἱδρώτητι ist auch als Variante zu ἱδρῶτι in Gen 3,18 𝔊 häufig belegt, ὑδρότητι hingegen nur in einem Zeugen zu Gen 3,18 𝔊 – der Minuskel 82. Wahrscheinlich handelt es sich um eine dittographische Variante zu ἱδρῶτι, die der Verfasser von Apc Mos 24 in seinem Septuagintatext vorfand. Ὑδρότητι hingegen ist sowohl in Gen 3,18 𝔊 als auch in Apc Mos 24,2 sekundäre Glättung – schon die Tatsache, daß ὑδρότης lexikalisch besser belegt ist als ἱδρώτης, weist in diese Richtung.

21. e-e: Gegen Bertrand ist wegen des vorhergehenden ἐργάσῃ der Konj. Aor. φάγῃ zu bevorzugen, vgl. Anm. 16. Auch in Gen 3,18 𝔊 begegnet φάγῃ.

22. f: An dieser Stelle setzt Bertrand gegen Nagel Apc Mos 24,4 an.

23. g-g: Bertrand liest mit B ὧν, doch alle Textzeugen außer B, das gerne konjiziert, lesen τῶν. In der volkssprachlichen Koine sind nicht selten Relativpronomina mit anlautendem τ- belegt (Angleichung an den Artikel in Analogie an die Übereinstimmungen im Anlaut bei den Nominativformen οἱ οἵ, αἱ αἵ), vgl. hierzu K. DIETERICH, *Untersuchungen*, p. 198.

Rolle, vgl. Apc Mos 10-12. In 24,2-3 begegnet eine durch Parallelismus membrorum auffallende Darstellung von »vielfältigen Mühsalen«, die Adam direkt im Anschluß an den biblischen Fluch, er werde sein Brot im Schweiß seines Angesichts essen müssen, angekündigt werden – wahrscheinlich eine Amplifikation eben dieses Motivs. In 24,1 fällt fernerhin eine Umstellung auf, die den Text von seiner biblischen Vorlage in Gen 3,17 unterscheidet: In Gen 3,17 wird zuerst darauf Bezug genommen, daß Adam auf seine Frau gehört habe, danach wird die eigentliche Tat referiert. In Apc Mos 24,1 hingegen wird zuerst die Tat genannt – vielleicht soll auf diese Weise einer Abwälzung der Schuld auf Eva vorgebeugt werden. Schließlich erscheint das Referat des Tathergangs im Vergleich zur biblischen Vorlage recht abstrakt: Dort wird konkret das Essen der verbotenen Frucht vor-geworfen, hier die Übertretung des Gebotes (ἐντολή). Dafür gibt es einen Anhaltspunkt in der biblischen Vorlage (𝔊: οὗ ἐνετειλάμην σοι, 𝔐: אשר צויתיך), doch ein gewisser Unterschied zwischen dem Pseudepigraph und dem Bibeltext bleibt bestehen: Apc Mos 24,1 wirkt vergleichsweise unanschaulich; an die Stelle des Vorgänglichen tritt theologische Deutung.

Wichtiger ist schon der Befund, daß in diesem Fluchwort eine Bezugnahme auf den Tod, wie er sich in Gen 3,19 findet, fehlt – ganz ähnlich wie wohl die Mehrheit der Exegeten heute, sieht dieser Autor die Erwähnung des Todes in Gen 3,19 nicht als Teil des Fluches; der Fluch über Adam kündigt für ihn nur die Mühen landwirtschaftlicher Tätigkeit an[24]. Das ist erstaunlich, denn eine der paulinischen Auffassung (vgl. Röm 5,12; 1 Kor 15,29) entsprechende Ansicht, daß der Tod Adams die Folge von dessen Gebotsübertretung sei, ist in der Apc Mos ansonsten durchaus anzutreffen (vgl. Apc Mos 14,2; 39,1) – vielleicht ist dies ein Anzeichen dafür, daß wir es an dieser Stelle mit einer älteren Tradition zu tun haben.

Entscheidend für das Untersuchungsziel ist der in Apc Mos zu beobachtende Umgang mit dem biblischen Text. Dabei ist zunächst einmal festzustellen, daß Apc Mos 24 wie die Apc Mos überhaupt in starkem Maße auf die Septuaginta[25] zurückgreift: Die Wendungen ἐπικατάρατος ἡ γῆ sowie ἀκάνθας καὶ τριβόλους ἀνατελεῖ σοι und φάγῃ τὸν ἄρτον σου sind wörtliche Zitate, καὶ ἐν ἱδρώτητι τοῦ προσώπου σου ist fast wörtlich. Dieser Befund überrascht etwas angesichts der Tatsache, daß in demselben Paragraphen eine fast wörtliche Übereinstimmung mit einem hebräischen Text aus Qumran vorzufinden ist – wie steht es denn nun mit der »Hebraitas« von Apc Mos 24?

Es gibt noch einen anderen Befund: An einer Stelle geht die Apc Mos nämlich mit 𝔐 zusammen, und dies betrifft eine Lesart, durch die sich der masoretische Konsonantentext signifikant von 𝔊 unterscheidet – in

---

24. Zur Auslegung von Gen 3,17-19 in der neueren Forschung vgl. C. WESTERMANN, *Genesis 1-11*, pp. 358-363. Für ihn hat Gen 3,17-19 die Funktion, eine Erklärung für die Mühen der Arbeit zu geben; die Frage, ob der Tod dort als Sündenstrafe aufgefaßt sei, verneint er: »Der Tod (...) ist also in 3,19 nicht Strafe für die Übertretung des Menschen, er ist die Grenze für die Mühsal der menschlichen Arbeit« (p. 363).

25. Als Edition der Septuaginta zur Genesis wird hier J.W. WEVERS, *Genesis* benutzt.

Gen 3,17: Im ursprünglichen Text von Apc Mos 24,1 heißt es: Ἐπικατάρατος ἡ γῆ ἕνεκα σοῦ. Das ist nicht der Text der Septuaginta, diese liest ἐν τοῖς ἔργοις σου[26]. Dagegen entspricht Ἕνεκα σοῦ in Apc Mos 24,1 wörtlich dem בעבורך von 𝔐. Wie ist dieses Nebeneinander von 𝔊- und 𝔐- Tradition in einem und demselben Text zu bewerten? Da Apc Mos 24 nachweislich von 𝔊 abhängig ist, legt sich natürlich der Gedanke nahe, daß der Verfasser auch hier von einem griechischen Bibeltext ausging – an dieser Stelle wäre seine Vorlage dann nach dem hebräischen Text revidiert. Gegen diese Sicht der Dinge erheben sich jedoch schwere Bedenken: Eine Revision der Septuaginta nach der hebräischen Überlieferung läßt sich nämlich gerade an dieser Stelle in den Handschriften nicht nachweisen, darüber hinaus lassen auch Symmachus (ἐν τῇ ἐργασίᾳ σου) und Theodotion (ἐν τῇ παραβάσει σου) die Auffassung des hebräischen Textes vermissen, nur bei Aquila (ἕνεκεν σοῦ) ist sie bezeugt. Die von 𝔊 bezeugte Lesart ist also derart unangefochten in der griechischen Überlieferung, daß sich die Annahme näherlegt, der Verfasser von Apc Mos 24 habe sowohl den griechischen als auch den hebräischen Bibeltext gekannt[27]. Daß dies gerade im weithin zweisprachigen Palästina keineswegs unmöglich war, ist u.a. seit der Auffindung eines revidierten Septuagintatextes zum Dodekapropheton[28] in der judäischen Wüste wohl kaum mehr bestreitbar – wie es sich damit in der Diaspora verhielt, ist eine andere Frage, der hier nicht nachgegangen werden kann.

4. Zur exegetischen Methode in Apc Mos 24

Läßt sich nun wahrscheinlich machen, daß der Verfasser von Apc Mos 24 sowohl 𝔊 als auch eine Frühform von 𝔐 gekannt hat, so muß dies freilich bedeuten, daß er beide Versionen nebeneinander benutzt und gewissermaßen synoptisch gelesen hat. Dies läßt sich in der Tat

---

26. Die Handschriften A AC Ath An^II Pa Br S¹ haben die Septuagintalesart sekundär wieder aufgenommen, vgl. Anm. 19.

27. Eine Abhängigkeit von Aquila ist an dieser Stelle zwar nicht auszuschließen, aber für die Apc Mos als Ganze unwahrscheinlich, hierzu ist auf meine in absehbarer Zeit erscheinende Dissertation zur Apc Mos zu verweisen. Auf hebräische Bibelüberlieferung im Hintergrund verweist mit großer Sicherheit Apc Mos 25, indirekt auch Vit Ad 18-21 als von der Apc Mos abhängiger Text (vgl. Anm. 31): In beiden Texten wird eine Bedeutung von תשובה realisiert, die nur dem hebräischen Wort eignet, nicht jedoch den in der griechischen Überlieferung belegten Korrelaten, vgl. hierzu §5.

28. Neue Edition: E. Tov, *Greek Minor Prophets Scroll*. Zur Hellenisierung Palästinas mag hier ein Hinweis auf M. Hengel, *Judentum und Hellenismus* genügen.

plausibel machen, und zwar von der bereits angesprochenen Beobachtung her, daß in Apc Mos der Fluch über Adam (Gen 3,17-19) durch einen Passus aus dem Fluch über Kain (Gen 4,11-12) erweitert wurde. Eine Assoziation von Gen 3,17-19 und Gen 4,11-12 legte sich gewiß inhaltlich nahe, immerhin geht es in beiden Erzählungen um Gottesflüche; es kommt hinzu, daß in beiden Flüchen das Stichwort Ackerboden (אדמה) Erwähnung findet. Doch das ist nicht alles, was Gen 3,17-19 und Gen 4,12 verbindet. Ein ganz entscheidender Anknüpfungspunkt für die Assoziation beider Texte ist nämlich an genau der Stelle zu suchen, die schon durch ihre Wiedergabe in Apc Mos 24,1-2 auffällig geworden ist: Es handelt sich um בעבורך in Gen 3,17 𝔐, dem in 𝔊 ἐν τοῖς ἔργοις σου entspricht²⁹ und das in Apc Mos mit ἕνεκα σοῦ Aufnahme findet.

An dieser durch die Apc Mos besonders markierten Stelle begegnet nämlich ein weiteres Stichwort, das den Fluch über Adam mit dem über Kain kompatibel macht, allerdings nur in 𝔊, das die Apc Mos, die im Kontext durchaus Septuagintakenntnis zeigt, ausgerechnet hier (scheinbar) unterdrückt. 𝔊 nimmt – anders als 𝔐 – mit ἐν τοῖς ἔργοις σου Bezug auf die Feldarbeit Adams, und von Feldarbeit ist auch in der Verfluchung Kains die Rede! Und genau das Motiv der Feldarbeit, das in dem an 𝔐 anlehnenden ἕνεκα σοῦ in Apc Mos 24,1 nicht verwirklicht ist, folgt nun direkt im Anschluß darauf – in einer freien Wiedergabe von Gen 4,12a (Apc Mos 24,2: ἐργάσῃ δὲ αὐτήν)! Eine solche Konstellation kann kaum zufällig sein. Eher ist anzunehmen, daß der Verfasser, indem er gerade an dieser Stelle von der gewöhnlich bevorzugten Septuaginta abwich, auf die exegetischen Hintergründe seiner Erzählung hinweisen wollte. Er wich hier, wo die Septuaginta sich von 𝔐 unterscheidet, auf seine hebräische Vorlage aus, um den kundigen Leser darauf aufmerksam zu machen, welches exegetische Spiel ihm hier gerade die Septuagintaversion ermöglicht. Auf diese Weise setzt er freilich auch die Septuagintaversion erzählerisch um, er verwirklicht also beide Versionen.

Ein solches exegetisches Verfahren setzt indes eine Hermeneutik voraus, die in Varianten etwas anderes sieht als schlichte Textverderbnisse. In der Tat spricht einiges dafür, daß es eine solche Hermeneutik gegeben hat. Schon das masoretische Kᵉtîb-Qᵉrê'-System zeigt ja, daß man mit

---

29. Ἐν τοῖς ἔργοις σου in 𝔊 basiert auf hebr. בעבוד(י)ך*, zugrunde liegt eine Verwechslung von ד und ר, verbunden mit der Annahme, daß *בעבוד(י)ך Plural sein müsse. Unsicher ist, ob der griechische Übersetzer בעבוד(י)ך* in seiner Vorlage fand oder aber diese Lesung dort willkürlich oder unwillkürlich identifizierte; weiteres zu Gen 3,17 𝔊 siehe unter §6.

Varianten äußerst behutsam umging; man hat sie gerade nicht via »Textkritik« getilgt, sondern tradiert – es waren Varianten mit geradezu kanonischem Ansehen. Doch nicht nur der »Verdacht auf Urtextfähigkeit« dürfte es gewesen sein, der Varianten eine besondere Wertschätzung einbrachte. Die hier zur Untersuchung anstehenden Texte, insbesondere Apc Mos 24, legen nahe, daß sie auch deshalb besonderes Ansehen genossen, weil sie das Bedeutungspotential eines Textes zu vermehren halfen³⁰.

Daß eine solche Lektürestrategie auch sonst in der frühjüdischen Exegese möglich war, zeigt eine besonders instruktive haggadische Exegese zu Gen 3,16 in Berê'šît Rabbâ (Ber R) 20,7³¹: Bekanntlich wird in Gen 3,16 der Fluch Gottes über Eva, sie werde nach ihrem Manne Verlangen haben (𝔐: ואל אשך תשוקתך), von 𝔊 mit καὶ πρὸς τὸν ἄνδρα σου ἡ ἀποστροφή σου wiedergegeben, dem liegt die hebräische Variante תשובתך* zugrunde. Diese Variante war offenbar auch außerhalb der Septuaginta bekannt; auch in Vita Adae et Evae (Vit Ad) 18-21³² scheint sie vorausgesetzt zu sein, nur daß dort תשובתך* im Sinne von »Buße« aufgefaßt wurde – ein deutlicher Beleg dafür, daß der Verfasser der Vit Ad hier nicht 𝔊, sondern deren hebräische Vorlage als Bezugstext hatte. Für die anstehende Untersuchung ist nun besonders wichtig, daß in Ber R 20,7 eine Haggada begegnet, die sowohl die Lesart תשוקתך als auch die Lesart תשובתך verwertet, indem sie diese in einer Art narrativem Kompromiß verbindet: Der Text lautet:

ואל אישך תשוקתך	Und nach deinem Manne wird dein Verlangen sein (Gen 3,16):
בשעה שהאשה יושבת על המשבר אומרת	*In der Stunde, da die Frau auf dem Gebärstuhl sitzt, sagt sie:*
איני נזקקת לביתי עוד מעתה	»Ich werde von nun an nicht mehr meinem Gatten beiwohnen.«
והקב"ה אומר לה	Und der Heilige, gepriesen sei er, sagt zu ihr:
תשובי לתשוקתך תשובי לתשוקך אישך	»Kehre zurück *zu* deinem Verlangen, kehre zurück *zu* deinem Verlangen, *deinem Mann*«.

---

30. Partiell vergleichbar ist das bei Autoren wie Arno Schmitt geübte Verfahren, den Aussagegehalt eines Textes durch bewußtes Spiel mit »Rechtschreibfehlern« zu erhöhen – auf diese Weise kann ein und derselbe Satz doppelte oder mehrfache Bedeutung bekommen.

31. Edition: J. THEODOR / CHR. ALBECK, *Bereschit Rabba*, Bd. 1, p. 191.

32. Unter der Bezeichnung Vita Adae et Evae (Vit Ad) bzw. Adamviten fasse ich die lateinische Vita Adae et Evae (Vit Ad [lat]), die armenische Penitence of Adam und das georgische Livre d'Adam zusammen; alle drei Texte (Sigel: Vit Ad [lat.arm.georg]) gehen auf ein griechisches Original (*Vit Ad) zurück, das M. NAGEL, *Vie grecque*, Tome I, p. 155-159 zufolge von einer leicht überarbeiteten Fassung der Apc Mos abhängig ist. Alle drei Texte finden sich zusammen mit der Apc Mos und einem Slavischen Adambuch, das ebenfalls auf die Apc Mos zurückgeht, in G.A. ANDERSON / M. STONE, *Synopsis*. Das Gesamt der dort nebeneinandergestellten Texte belege ich mit dem Terminus »Adamdiegesen«. Zu den speziell hebräischen exegetischen Hintergründen von Vit Ad 18-21 vgl. G.A. ANDERSON, *Penitence Narrative*, pp. 20-29.

Beide Lesarten stehen in der letzten Zeile auf engstem Raum nebeneinander. Darüber hinaus ist zu vermuten, daß die Reue der Frau in der Geburtsstunde vielleicht auch noch die dem Wort תשובה innewohnende Bedeutung »Buße« realisieren soll, so daß auch hier nach dem Prinzip der Mehrfachverwertung des Ausgangstextes verfahren wird, denn in der letzten Zeile wird die Variante תשובתך ja ganz anders eingesetzt.

Wir haben in Ber R 20,7 also den Fall vorliegen, daß eine durch 𝔊 bezeugte Variante mit einer durch 𝔐 bezeugten kombiniert wurde – gewissermaßen zu einer Mischlesart in Gestalt einer exegetischen Erzählung. Exegetische Kombinatorik ist ja des öfteren Ausgangspunkt der Haggada geworden, hier betrifft diese Kombinatorik Varianten. Es ist nicht auszuschließen, daß die Haggada in Ber R 20,7 unter Konsultation der Septuaginta abgefaßt wurde.

Nicht ohne Bedeutung für Apc Mos 24 ist, daß der Verfluchung Evas in Apc Mos 25 wahrscheinlich die gleiche Kombination wie in Ber R 20,7 zugrundeliegt, nur daß sie dort anders – im Sinne einer eher sexualitätsfeindlichen Einstellung – verstanden wird. Wir finden dort Korrelate zur Variante תשובתך (ἐπιστρέψω), möglicherweise aber auch zur Variante תשוקתך (Apc Mos 25,3: ἁμαρτίαν τῆς σαρκός), darüber hinaus scheint in ἐξομολογήσῃ auch die תשובה zusätzlich eignende Wortbedeutung »Buße« realisiert. Wenn eine solche auf Varianten beruhende Exegese also in Apc Mos 25 nachgewiesen werden kann, haben wir damit eine weitere Stütze für die These, daß Apc Mos 24 ein exegetisches Spiel mit Lesarten zugrundeliegt.

Es kann also für Apc Mos 24 festgehalten werden, daß die Assoziation der Verfluchung Adams mit der des Kain wesentlich mit einer kombinatorischen Lektüre zweier Übersetzungsvarianten zu Gen 3,17 zusammenhängt. Der Verfasser hat sowohl 𝔐 (בעבורך) als auch 𝔊 (ἐν τοῖς ἔργοις σου) narrativ verwirklicht, ersteres in Gestalt einer wörtlichen Übersetzung, letzteres in Gestalt einer exegetischen Assoziation: Er hat die Septuagintavariante als Anlaß genommen, Gen 4,12 in den Adamfluch zu »importieren«. Daß er dabei den Text von Gen 4,12b verkürzte, erklärt sich aus dem neuen Kontext: Kain konnte gesagt werden, daß die Erde ihm *fürderhin* ihre Kraft nicht mehr geben werde; bei Adam wäre das sinnlos: Dieser hatte ja die Erde zuvor noch gar nicht bearbeitet!

5. Die exegetischen Hintergründe von 4Q423 2₃ zur Auslegungsgeschichte von Gen 3,17

Eine Herleitung wie die soeben für Apc Mos präsentierte kann für 4Q423 2₃ nicht ausgeschlossen werden[33], sie läßt sich allerdings auch

---

33. Auch für Qumran ist Septuagintakenntnis bezeugt, vgl. die Septuagintafragmente 7Q1 und 7Q2.

kaum beweisen. Denkbar wäre freilich, daß dem Weisheitstext hier eine exegetische Überlieferung zugrundeliegt, die in ähnlicher Weise wie Apc Mos 24 mit der hebräischen Vorlage der Septuaginta zu Gen 3,17 spielte[34]. Doch dieser Annahme steht entgegen, daß die Wendung, die mit Gen 3,17 korreliert, in 4Q423 2_3 anders als in Apc Mos 24 nicht vor, sondern nach Gen 3,18 erscheint; wenn Gen 3,17 der exegetische Anknüpfungspunkt gewesen sein sollte, wären in 4Q423 2_3 die Spuren der exegetischen Arbeit verwischt worden. Auch dies ist möglich, doch liegt es näher, für die Amalgamierung der beiden Flüche in 4Q423 2_3 andere Ursachen zu benennen, am ehesten die bereits zu Beginn von §4 genannten: Gen 3,17-19 und Gen 4,11-12 sind beide durch das Thema Fluch sowie durch eine Stichwortassoziation (אדמה) verbunden. Daß 4Q423 2_3 dabei Gen 4,12b ganz ähnlich wie Apc Mos 24 in gekürzter Fassung übernommen hat, dürfte wie im Falle von Apc Mos 24 hinreichend durch die Notwendigkeiten der Kontextualisierung erklärt sein.

Apc Mos 24 und 4Q423 2_3 bezeugen also beide eine Tendenz, den Fluch über Adam mit dem über Kain zu assoziieren. Sie war offenbar weit verbreitet, und so gibt es durchaus Anlaß zu der Vermutung, daß sie auch den theologischen Hintergrund für die Übersetzungsvariante der Septuaginta zu Gen 3,17 darstellt. Wie bereits ausgeführt, liegt dem griechischen ἐν τοῖς ἔργοις σου in 𝕲 hebräisch *בעבודך zugrunde, statt ר ist also ד gelesen worden[35]. Dieses Wort kann der Übersetzer entweder in seiner Vorlage fälschlich identifiziert oder tatsächlich vorgefunden haben, denkbar ist auch, daß sie ihm als traditionelle Variante bekannt war. In jedem Falle kann eine alte Assoziation von Gen 3,17 mit Gen 4,12 die Funktion eines Katalysators gehabt haben.

> Daß hinter Apc Mos 24, 4Q423 Fragment 2 und Gen 3,17 eine alte kombinatorische Lektüre von Gen 3,17-19 und Gen 4,11-12 steht, legt eine Parallele nahe, welche die Verfluchung Evas und gleichfalls die Kain-Erzählung betrifft. In der Rede Gottes an Kain (4,6-7) begegnet ein Passus (4,7b: ואליך תשוקתו ואתה תמשל־בו »und nach dir ist sein Verlangen und du sollst über ihn herrschen«), der deutlich an Gen 3,16 (ואל אישך תשוקתך והוא ימשל־בך »und nach deinem Manne ist dein Verlangen, und er soll über dich herrschen«) anklingt. Wahrscheinlich ist irgendwann im Laufe der Textüberlieferung dafür gesorgt worden, daß beide Texte an dieser Stelle einander so stark ähneln, wohl mit dem Ziel, einen Querverweis zu schaffen.

---

34. Zur hebräischen Vorlage von ἐν τοῖς ἔργοις σου in Gen 3,17 𝕲 vgl. Anm. 29.
35. Vgl. Anm. 29.

6. Ertrag

4Q423 und Apc Mos 24 belegen auf ähnliche, aber doch unterschiedliche Weise eine alte exegetische Tradition zu Gen 3,17-19, die den Fluch über Adam mit dem über Kain in Verbindung brachte. Sie bezeugen damit eine exegetische Technik, die man als kombinatorische Lektüre bezeichnen kann; Bibeltexte werden durch Bibeltexte ausgelegt. Für die Apc Mos konnte darüber hinaus ein interessantes Spiel mit Textvarianten nachgewiesen werden, die gewissermaßen zu Mischlesarten in Gestalt eines narrativen Kompromisses zusammengeschweißt wurden. Dieses Verfahren wurde speziell dort angewandt, wo 𝔊 und 𝔐 voneinander abwichen. Die Apc Mos hat also hebräische und griechische Bibelüberlieferung parallel gelesen, damit stellt sie gewissermaßen ein narratives Seitenstück zu der Arbeit der Septuagintarevisoren dar. Während wir dort Zeugnisse einer philologischen Tätigkeit vorfinden, die moderner Textkritik zumindest nahekommt, stehen wir hier einer Art narrativer Philologie gegenüber: Aus Varianten werden Mischlesarten in Gestalt einer Erzählung gebildet. Varianten werden dabei nicht als ein die Einheitlichkeit der Textwahrnehmung störendes Ärgernis empfunden, sondern als Erweiterung des Bedeutungspotentials der kanonischen Schrift. Uneinheitlich überlieferte Texte sind also nicht verderbt, sondern bereichert.

Wolbecker Strasse 148a J. Dochhorn
48155 Münster
Deutschland

VI

THE WISDOM TEXTS FROM QUMRAN AND THE NEW TESTAMENT

FLESH AND SPIRIT IN THE PALESTINIAN JEWISH SAPIENTIAL TRADITION AND IN THE QUMRAN TEXTS

An Inquiry into the Background of Pauline Usage

The scholarly significance of the recently published sapiential texts from the Qumran library can hardly be overestimated[1]. They demonstrate that sapiential thought within Palestinian Judaism included a much wider variety of ideas and literary forms than previously available when only the canonical Wisdom texts, the Wisdom of Ben Sira and some later traditions from the diaspora could be analyzed. The new documents seem to provide an important "missing link" between earlier Biblical traditions and later ideas and help us to reconstruct some aspects of the semantic and literary development "between the testaments". Although most of the sapiential documents from the Qumran library are not "sectarian", but seem to have been composed within earlier "pre-Essene" circles, they might nevertheless shed light on the development of the later "Essene" or "sectarian" traditions.

In this article, I will show the importance of the new sapiential documents for the history of religions by means of an example which has also a great deal of significance for New Testament interpretation. The "pre-Essene" Wisdom texts are the earliest documents from Early Jewish tradition in which the term "flesh" is used in a strongly negative sense, linked with sin and disobedience to God and his will. Such a negative usage of "flesh" can also be seen in the Qumran "sectarian" texts and, then, in the letters of the Apostle Paul. Therefore, the new Wisdom texts from Qumran could provide the clue to the long-debated problem of the origin of the Pauline usage of "flesh" and his characteristic antithesis of "flesh" and "spirit". The religio-historical issue of the background of Paul's anthropological terms (or, at least, some of them) can be discussed afresh on the basis of the new sapiential texts from the Qumran library.

---

* Thanks to Dr. Charlotte Hempel (Washington) and to my assistants, Dr. Michael Becker and Mr. Enno Edzard Popkes, for corrections and helpful suggestions. Some passages of this paper are taken from my article *Notion of "Flesh"*; other aspects are discussed more extensively in my article *Paulinische Antithese*.
 1. Cf. D. J. HARRINGTON, *Reasons*.

1. THE PROBLEM: THE ANTITHESIS OF "FLESH" AND "SPIRIT" IN PAUL

In some passages of his letters, Paul uses the term "flesh" (σάρξ) in a sense which goes far beyond the range of meanings of בָּשָׂר in the Hebrew Bible. There, בָּשָׂר can denote the human body and its physical substance or, generally, the created human being in its weakness and mortality[2]. But in Paul, at least in some passages, the use of the term σάρξ is strongly associated with the notion of evil and iniquity. It even seems to denote a sphere or power opposed to God and his will, most obviously when it is used in contrast with the term "spirit" (πνεῦμα), e. g. in Gal 5,17 or Rom. 8,5ff:

> For the Flesh is actively inclined against the Spirit, and the Spirit against the Flesh. Indeed these two powers constitute a pair of opposites at war with one another, the result being that you do not actually do the very things you wish to do (Gal 5,17)[3].
> For those who exist in terms of the flesh take the side of the flesh, whereas those who exist in terms of the Spirit take the side of the Spirit. For the flesh's way of thinking is death, whereas the Spirit's way of thinking is life and peace. Because the flesh's way of thinking is hostility toward God, for it does not submit itself to the law of God; for it cannot. And those who are in the flesh are not able to please God (Rom 8,5-8)[4].

This dualistic use of "flesh" and "spirit" as opposed powers is unparalleled in Earliest Christianity[5], and when the terms are used in later

---

2. In other passages, בָּשָׂר can denote also a family relative, a part of the human body, e. g. genitals, or an animal body – dead or alive – or part of an animal body, e. g. meat or an offering; cf. D. J. A. CLINES (ed.), *Dictionary* 2, p. 277; L. KOEHLER, W. BAUMGARTNER & J. J. STAMM (eds.), *The Hebrew and Aramaic Lexicon of the Old Testament* 1, p. 164; see more extensively F. BAUMGÄRTEL, σάρξ, pp. 105-108; G. GERLEMAN, בָּשָׂר; N. BRATSIOTIS, בָּשָׂר.

3. Translation from J. L. MARTYN, *Galatians*, p. 479. Text: Ἡ γὰρ σὰρξ ἐπιθυμεῖ κατὰ τοῦ πνεύματος, τὸ δὲ πνεῦμα κατὰ τῆς σαρκός, ταῦτα γὰρ ἀλλήλοις ἀντίκειται, ἵνα μὴ ἃ ἐὰν θέλητε ταῦτα ποιῆτε.

4. Translation from J. D. G. DUNN, *Romans 1-8*, p. 414. Text: Οἱ γὰρ κατὰ σάρκα ὄντες τὰ τῆς σαρκὸς φρονοῦσιν, οἱ δὲ κατὰ πνεῦμα τὰ τοῦ πνεύματος. Τὸ γὰρ φρόνημα τῆς σαρκὸς θάνατος, τὸ δὲ φρόνημα τοῦ πνεύματος ζωὴ καὶ εἰρήνη· διότι τὸ φρόνημα τῆς σαρκὸς ἔχθρα εἰς θεόν, τῷ γὰρ νόμῳ τοῦ θεοῦ οὐχ ὑποτάσσεται, οὐδὲ γὰρ δύναται· οἱ δὲ ἐν σαρκὶ ὄντες θεῷ ἀρέσαι οὐ δύνανται.

5. The terms σάρξ und πνεῦμα are used in the pre-Pauline formula Rom 1,3f., but the usage in this early christological confession differs significantly from the usage of the antithesis by Paul himself. In Rom 1,3 σάρξ is used (as in Rom 9,5) to denote the earthly origin of Jesus ἐκ σπέρματος Δαυίδ. This corresponds completely with the Biblical usage of the term (cf. 2 Sam 7,12-14). The expression πνεῦμα ἁγιοσύνης (note the Semitic construction!) is used to characterize the resurrection of Jesus as a mighty work of the spirit. On the formula in Rom 1,3 cf. also M. HENGEL, *Sohn Gottes*, pp. 93-104; P. STUHLMACHER, *Biblische Theologie* 1, pp. 186-188. So, the pre-Pauline confession formula does not provide a real analogy to the Pauline usage of the terms such as, e. g., in Gal 5,17 or Rom 7-8 (cf. F. W. HORN, *Das Angeld des Geistes*, p. 278).

writings, their meaning differs significantly from the meaning in the aforementioned passages[6]. Thus, the peculiarities of the Pauline usage of the antithesis pose a number of theological, but also historical and religio-historical questions.

Theologically important is the issue of the precise meaning of the antithesis and its significance within the anthropology and soteriology of the Apostle: What is "flesh" in Paul? Does the term denote the human being as a whole, as a created being, or only its material or physical substance? And what is the "spirit", opposed to the "flesh"? Does Paul mean the Holy Spirit, or does he think of a spiritual dimension within the human being? And how can we understand that Paul sees "flesh" and "Spirit" actively inclined against each other (Gal 5,17)? Does he really mean that both powers enact some authority over the Christians, so that they "do not do the very things they wish to do"[7]? Or should we read the passage as a kind of abbreviation, i. e. in the sense that only one of the two powers has such an influence on believers[8]? And what is the

---

6. In Colossians and Ephesians, the terms are taken up in some passages, but, in contrast with Paul, the antithesis is toned down or used in the mere sense of the Hellenistic idea of different spheres (cf. E. SCHWEIZER, σάρξ, pp. 136f.). In the Pastorals, the antithesis is used only in the christological hymn 1 Tim 3,16 ἐφανερώθη ἐν σαρκί, ἐδικαιώθη ἐν πνεύματι where σάρξ and πνεῦμα are not viewed as opposed powers but also as two different spheres (cf. E. SCHWEIZER, *ibid.*, esp. 137f.; J. ROLOFF, *Der erste Brief an Timotheus*, p. 203). The Johannine use of the terms is completely different from Paul (cf. E. SCHWEIZER, *ibid.*, esp. pp. 138-140). In the Fourth Gospel and the Johannine Epistles, σάρξ characterizes the true humanity of the Logos-Son (Jn 1,14; cf. 1 Jn 4,2; 2 Jn 7 et al.). Besides, σάρξ is used to denote the human way of existence and thought (Jn 7,27; 8,15). In two passages, Jn 3,6 and Jn 6,63, there is an opposition of σάρξ and πνεῦμα. But even in these passages, σάρξ is not linked with sin, so the antithesis differs significantly from the Pauline use of the terms. In the Apostolic Fathers the use of σάρξ is even more hellenized (cf. E. SCHWEIZER, *ibid.*, esp. pp. 144-147). An early misunderstanding of the Pauline antithesis is also shown by the gloss in Rom 7,25b, cf. H. LICHTENBERGER, *Der Beginn der Auslegungsgeschichte von Römer 7*.
7. This is the interpretation by H. SCHLIER, *Der Brief an die Galater*, p. 249: "Das Gegeneinander von Fleisch und Geist, das im beiderseitigen feindlichen Begehren zum Austrag kommt, geschieht in der Absicht und hat das Ziel, das jeweilige Wollen des Menschen, das von dem Anspruch des Fleisches oder des Geistes provoziert ist, abzufangen und nicht zur Tat werden zu lassen." Cf. also P. ALTHAUS, *"...Damit ihr nicht tut, was ihr wollt"*, who interprets in the light of Rom 7,5. But most interpreters share the conviction that Rom 7 does not describe the existence of the Christian, but rather the existence of the non-Christian as it is viewed in the light of the Christian revelation (cf. R. BULTMANN, *Das Problem der Ethik bei Paulus*, p. 130; W. G. KÜMMEL, *Römer 7 und die Bekehrung des Paulus*, esp. p. 138).
8. Both possibilities to interpret the ἵνα μή ... in Gal 5,17 have been described precisely by R. BULTMANN, *Christus des Gesetzes Ende*, p. 46 n. 6: "Es ist entweder vom Gesichtspunkt des πνεῦμα aus gesprochen: das πνεῦμα kämpft gegen die σάρξ, damit der Mensch nicht tut, was er und d. h. die σάρξ will; oder vom Gesichtspunkt der σάρξ aus: die σάρξ kämpft gegen das πνεῦμα, damit der Mensch nicht das tut, was er *eigentlich* will, nämlich das, was auch das πνεῦμα will: daß er lebe (vgl. Rm. 7,14ff.)".

relation between God's or Christ's Spirit and the human self, or – even more complicated – between "flesh" and the physical existence of the created human being[9]? The answer to these theological questions depends on some historical and religio-historical issues.

Historically, there is the question whether we can interpret Gal 5,17 in terms of Rom 7-8 or not. Is the puzzling statement on the two "powers" a traditional formulation which is, then, modified in Gal 5,18 and later on worked out more thoroughly in Rom 7-8[10]? Or more generally: Did Paul's view on "flesh" and "spirit" undergo some development? What is the background of his antithetical use of "flesh" and "spirit" and of his strongly negative view of the "flesh" as the "breeding-ground for everything which is hostile to God"[11]? Are they relics of his pre-Christian past or a consequence of his conversion experience[12]? Or are they a result of his struggle with the churches in Galatia and Corinth[13]? In other words: Did Paul himself form the antithesis? Or could he have adopted it – or at least some aspects – from an earlier Christian, Jewish or even Pagan tradition? And if this is true, where do the terms or concepts come from?

Bultmann prefers the latter possibility. The former one is chosen by A. SUHL, *Der Galaterbrief*, p. 3124. A completely different view is taken by F. MUSSNER, *Der Galaterbrief*, pp. 377f., who suggests that the two powers neutralize each other so that the result is a new freedom for the Christian to choose between good and evil. But there is nothing in the text of Gal 5,17 in favour of such a suggestion, cf. the criticism by H. D. BETZ, *Galatians*, p. 281 n. 83. According to Gal 5,17, the struggle actually takes place.

9. In the background there is the question whether the Pauline use of σάρξ, e. g. in the phrase σάρξ ἁμαρτίας (Rom 8,3), does actually imply a devaluation of the bodily existence or, especially, human sexuality. It should be noted that some Pauline passages at least contributed to such a view. On the history of interpretation, e. g., of 1 Cor 6,12ff. and 1 Cor 7 s. W. SCHRAGE, *Der erste Brief an die Korinther* 2, pp. 38ff.74ff.113ff.183ff. 207ff.

10. Cf. the observation by H. D. BETZ, *Galatians*, p. 280: "It appears that in v 17 Paul submits his anthropological presuppositions in rather simple terms, but he leaves open the question how his soteriology affects his anthropology. In v 18 the soteriological presuppositions are brought in, but the theory in v 17 is left untouched. This situation forces us to conclude that the theory in v 17 is basically 'pre-Pauline'. It states the common anthropological doctrine on the basis of which Paul works out his own doctrine, but his own doctrine is much more complex. In Romans 7-8 we find an even more developed and more complex reworking of the elements which occur also in Galatians 5".

11. Cf. H. LIETZMANN, *An die Römer*, p. 81: "Nährboden alles Widergöttlichen".

12. This was supposed by some earlier interpreters, cf. e. g. P. FEINE, *Das gesetzesfreie Evangelium*, p. 223: "Die negativen Urteile über die σάρξ sind nur die Korrelate zu seiner Erfahrung und seinem Verständnis des πνεῦμα"; similarly A. JUNCKER, *Die Ethik des Paulus*, p. 75, who supposes that Paul's conversion caused a deeper moral judgement and, consequently, the negative view of σάρξ. Cf., on these authors, R. JEWETT, *Terms*, pp. 58f.93f.

13. Thus R. JEWETT, *Terms*, who explains the use of the Pauline anthropological terms on the background of the different situations underlying the various letters; a different explanation is given by F. W. HORN, *Das Angeld des Geistes*, pp. 278f.

The *religio-historical* problem of the origin of Paul's "dualistic" concept of σάρξ and πνεῦμα has occupied exegetes since the 19th century, and it seems to be an unresolved problem up to now. An adequate answer is significant not only for our view of the history of religions but also for the theological interpretation of the Pauline terms.

2. THE RELIGIO-HISTORICAL ISSUE IN THE SCHOLARLY DEBATE

In the present context, I can only give a brief account of the major suggestions and of the most important steps of the religio-historical discussion[14].

a) In a first period of research, since the middle of the 19th century[15], there was a discussion between the purely Biblical and a Hellenistic-Pagan explanation of the Pauline terms. It was inaugurated by the Tübingen School of Ferdinand Christian Baur and his pupils. According to their idealistic view of early Christian history, there was a fundamental antagonism between Paulinism and Jewish Christianity (as represented by James and others). Consequently, Paul and his thought were seen in a considerable distance from any kind of Jewish tradition and interpreted on the background of Hellenistic Paganism. On the basis of Rom 6,6, Baur had defined σάρξ in Paul as the material body[16]. The basic dilemma of the human being was, then, "that the good intentions of his νοῦς are immobilized by the sensual σάρξ"[17]. Thus, Carl Holsten, who wrote the first monograph on the issue, could interpret the antithesis of σάρξ and πνεῦμα as an influence of the Hellenistic dualism of matter and spirit[18]. Even though the simple identification of σάρξ with the material substance had to be abandoned[19], the view that Paul's use of σάρξ was influenced by Hellenistic thought was accepted by the majority of critical exegetes until the end of the 19th century[20]. It was also ad-

14. Cf. the more extensive accounts in C. H. LINDIJER, *Het begrip Sarx bij Paulus*, pp. 11-69; O. KUSS, *Der Römerbrief*, pp. 506-540; A. SAND, *Fleisch*, pp. 1-121, and R. JEWETT, *Terms*, pp. 49-94.
15. The first monograph on the issue was written by C. HOLSTEN in 1855 (*Die bedeutung des wortes σάρξ*).
16. R. JEWETT, *Terms*, p. 51; cf. F. CH. BAUR, *Vorlesungen*, p. 161.
17. R. JEWETT, *Terms*, p. 51.
18. C. HOLSTEN, *Die bedeutung des wortes σάρξ*, pp. 367.375f.392f. (cf., on this study, H. H. WENDT, *Begriffe*, pp. 80-83; O. KUSS, *Der Römerbrief*, pp. 521-524; A. SAND, *Fleisch*, pp. 15-19; R. JEWETT, *Terms*, pp. 51f.
19. Cf., especially, the study by H. LÜDEMANN, *Anthropologie*, on this study see W. G. KÜMMEL, *Das Neue Testament*, pp. 235f.; O. KUSS, *Der Römerbrief*, pp. 524-527; A. SAND, *Fleisch*, pp. 22-27; R. JEWETT, *Terms*, pp. 52-54.
20. Cf. R. SCHMIDT, *Christologie*, pp. 8-46; O. PFLEIDERER, *Urchristentum*, pp. 191f.; C. WEIZSÄCKER, *Zeitalter*, pp. 127f.

vocated by Heinrich Julius Holtzmann's New Testament theology, where Pauline anthropology is described as a result of the Hellenistic impact on Jewish thought, but the main focus is clearly on the Hellenistic side[21].

b) The idealistic view of σάρξ and πνεῦμα was then put aside by the works of the religio-historical school. Hermann Gunkel's early study on the spirit in Paul[22] turned attention to the dynamistic aspect of the early Christian understanding of the spirit. So, it was no longer possible to interpret the Pauline antithesis in terms of the dualism of matter and spirit. But the scholars of the religio-historical school maintained the view that the Pauline antithesis should be interpreted against the background of Hellenistic thought[23] or of the so-called Hellenistic-Oriental syncretism. Wilhelm Bousset and Richard Reitzenstein refer to the ancient mystery cults or to the mysticism of the Hermetic literature[24] which are both seen as a purely pagan kind of Gnosticism[25]. According to Bousset, Paul is influenced by this kind of thought in his pessimistic anthropology and his dualistic and supranatural type of soteriology[26]. Reitzenstein goes even so far as to call Paul "the greatest of all Gnostics"[27].

c) The influential school of Rudolf Bultmann[28] widely adopted the views of the religio-historical school. Even though Paul is not seen as a

21. H. J. HOLTZMANN, *Lehrbuch*, Vol. 2, p. 18. Cf. *ibid.*, p. 24: "daß innerhalb des Paulinismus aus dem Gegensatze physisch verschiedener Substanzen ein Dualismus ethisch sich widerstreitender Prinzipien geworden ist". Cf. also pp. 12ff.42ff. On Holtzmann's view, see A. SCHWEITZER, *Geschichte*, pp. 79ff., especially pp. 86-90; W. G. KÜMMEL, *Das Neue Testament*, pp. 239-242.

22. H. GUNKEL, *Wirkungen*. Cf., on this study, W. G. KÜMMEL, *Das Neue Testament*, pp. 307-309, and R. JEWETT, *Terms*, p. 61.

23. According to the compendium of W. BOUSSET and H. GRESSMANN, *Die Religion des Judentums*, p. 405, Paul's view of σάρξ is a strictly Hellenistic one. C. CLEMEN, *Religionsgeschichtliche Erklärung*, p. 133, hints at a Platonic background (Phaidon 66b – 67b). Cf., however, the insightful remark by H. GUNKEL, *Wirkungen*, p. 98, who asks at the end of his study: "Hatte die pessimistische Stimmung, welche zur Zeit Christi im hellenistischen Judentum herrschte, und nach welcher die Sinnlichkeit des Menschen, der Fleischesleib, welcher ihn an diese Sinnenwelt bindet, die eigentliche letzte Ursache der Sündhaftigkeit ist, hatte diese Stimmung auch im palästinensischen Judentum Eingang gefunden?". Gunkel leaves the question open, but he points already in the direction which would be opened up later on by the finds from the Qumran library.

24. W. BOUSSET, *Kyrios Christos*, p. 130: "Wir werden unsern Blick auf jene Mischbildungen zu richten haben, in denen sich Philosophie und orientalisch bestimmter Glaube, gedankliche Reflexion und antikes Mysterienwesen, Spekulation und religiösekstatische Mystik zu wundersamen neuen Gebilden verschlingen". Cf. also R. REITZENSTEIN, *Mysterienreligionen*, pp. 308ff.

25. W. BOUSSET, *Kyrios Christos*, p. 133: "hellenistische, rein heidnische 'Gnosis'".

26. W. BOUSSET, *Kyrios Christos*, p. 134.

27. R. REITZENSTEIN, *Mysterienreligionen*, p. 86: "den größten aller Gnostiker".

28. Cf. the important article by R. BULTMANN, *Paulus*, and the comprehensive account of Paul's theology in R. BULTMANN, *Theologie*, pp. 187-353.

Gnostic himself, Bultmann thinks that he is influenced by Gnostic terms, which he adopts to formulate his own Christian teaching[29]. These anthropological terms allow him to describe the structure of the human existence, which is basically maintained in the state of the believer as in the 'pre-Christian' state. According to Bultmann's interpretation, "flesh" in Paul is

> weder die Materie im griechischen Sinne als das Material, das vom Geist... gestaltet werden muß, noch im Sinne des gnostischen Dualismus... die Materie als die niedere, schlechte Stofflichkeit im Gegensatz zur Seele, sondern es ist die Welt des Vorhandenen, die durch die Haltung des Menschen zu ihr erst zur Sphäre der Sünde wird[30].

Theologically, Bultmann's existential interpretation of Pauline terms was quite fruitful. Historically, however, it was firmly based on the assumption that Paul had adopted his anthropological terms and also the antithesis of σάρξ and πνεῦμα from pre-Christian Gnostic thought[31]. Within the framework of this construction, the early Ernst Käsemann could even say that σάρξ in Paul is 'something like a Gnostic aeon'[32].

d) The next turning-point of the discussion was the discovery of the Qumran texts. Now, for the first time, Hebrew and Aramaic documents from Palestinian Judaism of Post-Biblical and Pre-Rabbinic times became available, and these finds could throw new light on the background of early Christianity. So, only a short time after the first discoveries, Karl Georg Kuhn pointed to the significance of the new finds[33] and suggested to understand the use of σάρξ and πνεῦμα in the New Testament against the background of Qumran[34]. He could demonstrate that in some passages of the new documents the connection between flesh and sin is much closer than in the Hebrew Bible. But since there is no full correspondence with the antithetical usage in Paul's letters[35], the

---

29. R. BULTMANN, *Paulus*, c. 1030.
30. R. BULTMANN, *Paulus*, c. 1035.
31. Cf. R. BULTMANN, *Paulus*, cc. 1030f.; ID., *Theologie*, p. 171. Cf., on Bultmann's construct of a pre-Christian Gnostic myth and its hermeneutical function for his theology J. FREY, *Eschatologie* 1, pp. 129ff. Notwithstanding the thorough criticism of this construction (cf. C. COLPE, *Schule*; M. HENGEL, *Sohn Gottes*, pp. 53ff.; ID., *Ursprünge der Gnosis*, pp. 203ff.; J. FREY, *Eschatologie* 1, pp. 133ff.), a Gnostic explanation of the Pauline terms is advocated by W. SCHMITHALS, *Gnosis in Korinth*, pp. 152 and 158; ID., *Anthropologie*, p. 84, and G. STRECKER, *Theologie*, p. 133.
32. E. KÄSEMANN, *Leib und Leib Christi*, p. 105: "so etwas wie ein gnostischer Aeon".
33. K. G. KUHN, *Zur Bedeutung*; ID., *Die in Palästina gefundenen hebräischen Texte*.
34. K. G. KUHN, *Πειρασμός – ἁμαρτία – σάρξ*, pp. 209ff. (English translation: *New Light on Temptation*); cf. ID., *Sektenschrift*, pp. 301f.; ID., *Jesus in Gethsemane*, p. 281. On the significance of Kuhn's early articles, see H. LICHTENBERGER, *Menschenbild*, pp. 49f.; R. JEWETT, *Terms*, pp. 82f.
35. Cf. H. LICHTENBERGER, *Menschenbild*, p. 50; cf. also H. HUPPENBAUER, *Fleisch*; F. NÖTSCHER, *Terminologie*, pp. 86f.; ID., *Geist und Geister*; H. BRAUN, *Selbstver-*

suggestion that the Pauline antithesis was developed under Qumranian influence[36] did not find wide acceptance within New Testament scholarship. Nevertheless, the Qumran discoveries have turned the eyes of New Testament exegetes back to the Biblical and post-Biblical traditions of Palestinian Judaism. They thus contributed to overcome the 'pan-Gnosticism' which was characteristic for the interpretation within the Bultmann school.

e) But soon after the subsidence of the first Qumran discussion, the focus of the religio-historical discussion seems to have turned again towards the side of Hellenism or, more precisely, of Hellenistic Judaism. Inspired by the study of Egon Brandenburger[37], the majority of scholars today explains the Pauline antithesis on the background of Hellenistic Jewish Wisdom[38]. In his comprehensive study, Brandenburger tries to give evidence for a dualistic type of Wisdom thought mainly from the *Book of Wisdom* and from the works of Philo. It is conjectured, then, that Paul came across such a concept in the circles of Hellenistic-Jewish Christians in Syro-Palestine[39] or – more precisely – at Antioch[40].

However, it must be inferred critically that the textual evidence for such a conception in Hellenistic Judaism is rather weak. Moreover, the lines from Palestinian Jewish traditions can be strengthened in the light of the recently published Wisdom texts from Qumran. Therefore, in my opinion, the development of the Pauline antithesis should be described in a different way.

3. FLESH AND SPIRIT IN THE HELLENISTIC-JEWISH TRADITION

In order to demonstrate this, we have to enter a critical discussion of the evidence for a Hellenistic Jewish background of the Pauline antithesis. In his pioneering study, Brandenburger tries to show the 'duali-

---

ständnis; ID., *Qumran und das Neue Testament*, vol. 1, pp. 178f.212-214, and vol. 2, p. 177; R. MEYER, σάρξ, pp. 109-118; J. PRYRKE, *Spirit*; R. E. MURPHY, *BŚR*, and A. SAND, *Fleisch*, pp. 253-273.

36. Cf. similarly S. JOHNSON, *Paul*, p. 161; W. D. DAVIES, *Paul and the Dead Sea Scrolls*; D. FLUSSER, *Dead Sea Sect*, pp. 252-263; O. BETZ, *Offenbarung*, pp. 120ff.; S. SCHULZ, *Rechtfertigung*; and J. BECKER, *Heil Gottes*, p. 243, who suggested, "daß Paulus in seinen Aussagen über die Sünde unter essenischem Einfluß steht". On the discussion see R. JEWETT, *Terms*, pp. 82ff; O. KUSS, *Römerbrief*, pp. 531-533.

37. E. BRANDENBURGER, *Fleisch und Geist*.

38. Cf. H. PAULSEN, *Überlieferung*, pp. 45-47; U. WILCKENS, *Römer* 2, pp. 67f.; U. SCHNELLE, *Anthropologie*, pp. 74f.

39. E. BRANDENBURGER, *Fleisch und Geist*, p. 228.

40. Antioch is mentioned by A. DAUER, *Antiochia*, pp. 77f.114f.; K. BERGER, *Theologiegeschichte*, p. 387; J. BECKER, *Paulus*, pp. 108f.

zation' of Hellenistic Jewish tradition primarily from two Alexandrinian witnesses, the *Book of Wisdom* and the works of Philo. Other Hellenistic Jewish works such as *4 Maccabees* are left aside, similarly other Alexandrinian authors and works such as Aristobulos, Demetrios, Ps.-Aristeas or the Third Book of the *Sibylline Oracles* where σάρξ and πνεῦμα are not used in an anthropological sense or – at least – not linked with each other.

a) The *Book of Wisdom* conveys Biblical traditions within the framework of Platonic and Stoic concepts[41]. In the centre of the book, there is the praise of wisdom (Wis 6,22-11,1) who, as God's throne-companion (9,4; cf. 8,3f.) and mediator of the creation (9,1f.), pervades the cosmos (8,1), orders the ways of Israel and grants virtue and understanding (8,7f.), salvation and immortality (8,17). But an examination of the anthropological terms in the *Book of Wisdom* causes scepticism against Brandenburger's suggestions: σάρξ is used only three times in the whole book, and there is only one passage, in which the term is used in an anthropological sense[42]: In Wis 7,1 the author in the royal garments of Pseudo-Solomon points out that he is a mortal man like all the rest, wrought into flesh (ἐγλύφην σάρξ) in his mother's womb. Then, six verses later he tells us that he prayed, and the "spirit of wisdom" (πνεῦμα σοφίας) was given to him (7,7; cf. 1 Kings 8,12-53). σάρξ and πνεῦμα do not have a predominant position in this passage: The term σάρξ, paralleled with αἷμα (7,2), denotes nothing else than the transitoriness of the human being[43], and in the composite term πνεῦμα σοφίας (7,7), the predominant element is σοφία, not πνεῦμα[44]. So, it is not possible to take this passage as an argument for any kind of fixed opposition between σάρξ and πνεῦμα[45] in *Wisdom* or in Hellenistic Jewish circles.

b) As primary witnesses to the tradition of dualistic wisdom within Hellenistic Judaism, Brandenburger quotes the works of Philo. But even

---

41. Cf. H. HÜBNER, *Die Sapientia Salomonis und die antike Philosophie*; on the origin and date of the work s. S. SCHROER, *Weisheit*. The origin from Alexandria is disputed, however, by D. GEORGI, *Weisheit Salomos*, pp. 395f.

42. In two passages (Wis 12,5 and 19,21) the plural is used in a completely different sense.

43. This is shown by εἰμὶ μὲν κἀγὼ θνητὸς ἄνθρωπος (Wis 7,1) which is followed by a series of phrases describing the ideal author's participation in human destiny.

44. This is confirmed by the fact that in Wis 7-9 σοφία is used 15 times, whereas πνεῦμα is used only 5 times. Cf. also B. L. MACK, *Logos und Sophia*, p. 64 n. 6: "Pneuma wird [nur] herangezogen, um das Wesen der Weisheit zu explizieren, und nicht umgekehrt".

45. Cf. E. BRANDENBURGER, *Fleisch und Geist*, p. 106 who wants to see a "Gegenüber von Fleisch und Geist" in this passage.

if it is true that there are numerous examples for the negative view on human corporality, there is no clear evidence for the dualistic antithesis of σάρξ and πνεῦμα.

Firstly, the term σάρξ is not very frequent in Philo. Compared with σάρξ, he uses σῶμα more than ten times as much[46]. When he uses σάρξ, he often takes the plural (αἱ σάρκες), and when he uses the singular, this is most frequently caused by the scriptural passage he interprets[47]. So we can conclude that Philo adopts his use of σάρξ from the Bible, but when he formulates freely, he prefers the term σῶμα which is of little significance in the Septuagint[48]. Moreover, we can observe that there is much variety in Philo's language. He is able to use σάρξ in numerous different phrases and put it in contrast to various other nouns such as ψυχή, νοῦς, πνεῦμα, λόγος, or σοφία, so that the result is a considerable number of different antitheses[49]. One of these is the word pair σάρξ – πνεῦμα which occurs in several passages[50]. I can only comment on two of them.

In *On the Giants* 29ff., both terms are taken from Gen 6,3: "My Spirit shall not abide forever among men, because they are flesh" (διὰ τὸ εἶναι αὐτοὺς σάρκας). In contrast to the Hebrew text, Philo applies the term πνεῦμα not to the Divine breath and the gift of life but to the spirit of pure insight (ἀκήρατος ἐπιστήμη), which is hindered by the fleshly nature of the human beings (ἡ σαρκῶν φύσις). In this passage, flesh is

---

46. Cf. J. LEISEGANG, *Index*, p. 703 (1 1/2 columns) and pp. 748-758 (about 20 columns). In Paul, σάρξ and σῶμα are used with roughly the same frequency; in the Septuagint, σάρξ is used more often than σῶμα.

47. Cf. on Gen 2,24: *On the Giants* 64; *Allegorical Interpretation* 2,49f.; on Lev 17,11: *The Worse attacks the Better* 84f.; *Who is the Heir* 55ff.; on Gen 6,12: *On the Unchangeableness of God* 140ff.; on Gen 6,3: *On the Giants* 19.29ff.; *On the Unchangeableness of God* 2; on Lev 18,6: *On the Giants* 32; etc.

48. Cf. E. HATCH / H. A. REDPATH, *Concordance*. In most instances, σάρξ is the translation of Hebrew בשר. On the contrary, σῶμα has no Hebrew equivalent. So, most of the passages where σῶμα is used are from the late books of the Septuagint which were written in Greek (Wis; 1-4 Macc) or from books where the Greek translation is quite free (e. g. Job).

49. See, e. g., the opposition of σῶμα – ψυχή: *On the Giants* 12; *On the Unchangeableness of God* 55, σῶμα – νοῦς: *On the Giants* 9; *Who is the Heir* 274, σῶμα - σοφία: *Allegorical Interpretation* 3,151f., σῶμα (and γῆ) – πνεῦμα· *Allegorical Interpretation* 161, σάρξ - ψυχή: *On the Giants* 40; *On Drunkenness* 69f; *On the Unchangeableness of God* 55f.; *Allegorical Interpretation* 3,158, σάρξ – νοῦς: *On the Giants* 40; *Allegorical Interpretation* 2,49f.; *Who is the Heir* 267f.274; *The Worse Attacks the Better* 84f.; *On the Special Laws* 4,122f., σάρξ - λόγος: *Allegorical Interpretation* 3,158 (cf. *On Drunkenness* 87), σάρξ – σοφία: *On the Unchangeableness of God* 141-143; *Allegorical Interpretation* 3,152.

50. Cf. *On the Giants* 19f.29, *On the Unchangeableness of God* 2, *The Worse attacks the Better* 84f., *On the Special Laws* 4,122f.; *Who is the Heir* 55ff.; see E. BRANDENBURGER, *Fleisch und Geist*, p. 116 n. 5.

even called "the chief cause of ignorance". But what Philo means by "flesh" he demonstrates in an enumeration which is obviously inspired by Platon's *Phaidon* (66b-67b)[51]: "Flesh" is a comprehensive term for the duties of daily life, marriage, rearing of children, provision of necessities and the business of private and public life which tie the human being to the earthly sphere and hinder the growth of wisdom. So, like σῶμα, the term σάρξ denotes the material and bodily life which burdens the soul and prevents it from its ascent to the divine sphere.

The only passage in which πνεῦμα and σάρξ are used in the same context to describe different ways of existence, is *Who is the Heir* 57. But even in this passage the terms are not used in a fixed opposition. Instead, the author switches between σάρξ and αἷμα[52] and, similarly, between πνεῦμα and νοῦς or λογισμός. His description of two opposed ways of existence has the purpose to admonish the readers not to remain in the servitude of the bodily life but to emigrate from sensuality and to become heirs of the spiritual things[53]. So, the "dualism" in this passage is embedded into the framework of an ascent mysticism. Therefore, the distinction between the lower and the upper sphere, the earthly things and the spiritual things seems to be the only kind of "dualism" in this passage. Of course, the earthly is inferior to the spiritual, and σάρξ belongs, like σῶμα, to the earthly sphere. But in contrast to Paul, σάρξ is considered neither to be the reason or occasion for sin, nor to be seen as a quasi-daemonic power with cosmic dimensions[54]. Even where Philo describes the flesh with personal images, he always withdraws them immediately and avoids any kind of mythic dualism[55]. Brandenburger's interpretation, instead, "tends to exaggerate the cosmic dimensions of the dualistic motifs, resulting in a picture of Hellenistic Judaism's wisdom speculation which is virtually manichaean"[56].

The religio-historical construction of the 'dualization' of sapiential tradition within Hellenistic Judaism can not be demonstrated strictly. Summarizing the religio-historical discussion, Robert Jewett correctly points out that "on the key issue of the precedent for Paul's cosmic σάρξ usage, the Qumran tradition offers a somewhat closer correlation than Hellenistic Judaism"[57]. These parallels shall be discussed in the following section.

51. More parallels are given in D. WINSTON / J. DILLON, *Two Treatises*, pp. 250f.
52. This is developed on the basis of Lev 17,11.14.
53. *Who is the Heir* 66; cf. 68ff.
54. Cf. G. SELLIN, *Der Streit*, p. 131: It is "eine Sphäre, in die der Mensch... sich verstricken kann, nicht aber... eine dämonische Potenz mit eigenem widergöttlichen Subjekt".
55. Cf. G. SELLIN, *Der Streit*, p. 131 n. 148.
56. R. JEWETT, *Terms*, p. 90.
57. R. JEWETT, *Terms*, pp. 92f.

4. The Classical Qumran Parallels

Some of the parallels for the Pauline usage of "flesh" from the manuscripts from Cave 1 are well known. They were discussed already in the 1950s by Karl Georg Kuhn, William D. Davies and others[58]. With the exception of these passages, the vast majority of occurences of בשר in Qumran remain firmly within the Biblical range of meanings[59]. For the present purpose, I can omit all of these passages and discuss only the few texts where בשר is strongly linked with the idea of sin and iniquity or even seems to represent a sort of cosmic power.

a) Firstly, there are some terminological parallels in the *War Rule* and in the concluding "psalm" in 1QS where בשר is used in connection with terms of sin, as in בשר עול (1QM IV 4; 1QS XI 9) and בשר אשמה (1QM XII 12[60]) which correspond to the Pauline expression σὰρξ ἁμαρτίας in Rom 8,3[61]. But the semantic differences should not be overlooked: In the *War Rule*, "sinful flesh" is used to denote "the wicked" (1QM IV 4), "Belial and all the men of his lot" (1QM IV 2), or the hostile "nations" (1QM XII 11; cf. XIV 7; XV 2), who will be destroyed in the eschatological war by the power of God. But in the phrases in 1QM IV 4 and XII 12 the notion of sin or guilt is conveyed by the words עול and אשמה. Therefore, strictly speaking, the meaning of בשר in these passages does not go beyond the Biblical range of meanings. בשר simply denotes a kind of human being[62], which is characterized more precisely only by the terms עול and אשמה. The composite terms בשר עול and בשר אשמה, then, refer to the nations as wicked and opposed to Israel or opposed to the sons of light[63]. But in spite of the semantic differences, phraseologically בשר עול is much closer to the term σὰρξ ἁμαρτίας (Rom 8,3) than any of the Greek parallels[64].

---

58. Cf. K. G. Kuhn, Πειρασμός – ἁμαρτία – σάρξ, pp. 209ff.; Id., *New Light on Temptation*; W. D. Davies, *Paul and the Dead Sea Scrolls*; Id., *Additional Notes*; D. Flusser, *The Dead Sea Sect*, pp. 252-263. On the early discussion, see H. Braun, *Qumran und das Neue Testament* 2, pp. 175-177.

59. This was already stated by H. Huppenbauer, *Fleisch*, and F. Nötscher, *Terminologie*, p. 85; cf. also R. Meyer, σάρξ, pp. 112-114.

60. Cf. the parallel passage without אשמה in 1QM XIX 4 from which some authors conjectured that אשמה in 1QM XII 12 is an interpretative addition, cf. J. Carmignac, *La Règle de la Guerre*, p. 182; J. van der Ploeg, *Guerre*, p. 148; J. Becker, *Heil Gottes*, p. 111.

61. Thus already K. G. Kuhn, Πειρασμός, p. 210 n. 2; cf. also J. Becker, *Heil Gottes*, p. 248; H. Braun, *Qumran und das Neue Testament* 1, p. 178.

62. H. Huppenbauer, *Fleisch*, p. 299.

63. Cf. J. Becker, *Heil Gottes*, p. 111.

64. The closest Greek parallel seems to be *Apocalypse of Moses* 25: ἁμαρτία τῆς σαρκός.

b) Even closer to the Pauline usage semantically are some passages in the *Hodayot* and, similarly, in the "psalm" attached to the *Community Rule* in 1QS. In these passages, the notion of sin is conveyed by the term בשר itself, not just by its complements. We should also note that some passages of the *Hodayot* even show a certain opposition of בשר and רוח, even if it is quite far removed from the Pauline antithesis.

α) In 1QH^a V 30-33 (= XIII 13-16 Sukenik)[65], one of the characteristic passages which Heinz-Wolfgang Kuhn has called "Niedrigkeitsdoxologien"[66], the author says:

> In the mysteries of your insight
> [you] have apportioned all these things,
> to make your glory known.
> [However, what is] the *spirit of flesh*[67]
> to understand all these matters
> and to have insight in [your wondrous] and great counsel?
> What is someone born of a woman among all your awesome works?
> He is a structure of dust fashioned with water,
> his counsel is the [iniquity] of sin, shame of dishonor and so[urce of] impurity,
> and a depraved spirit rules over him[68].

In this passage the term רוח בשר, "spirit of flesh"[69], refers to the human spirit[70], which is characterized as fleshly, i. e. not capable of grasping God's counsel and his wondrous deeds. בשר refers to the created existence of the human being, which is also described by ילוד אשה, "born of a woman", and מבנה עפר, "structure of dust", and finally characterized in terms of sin, impurity and depravation. But in this passage, the author chiefly stresses the incapability of the human being to understand God's counsel and to appreciate his glory. Humanity is unable to have

---

65. References to the manuscript 1QH^a are quoted according to the counting of columns and lines in H. Stegemann's reconstruction of the scroll. The reference according to the *editio princeps* by E. L. Sukenik is given in brackets. Cf. H. STEGEMANN, *Rekonstruktion der Hodajot*. I owe thanks to Prof. Stegemann for permission to use his unpublished dissertation and to quote according to his reconstruction of the *Hodayot*.

66. See the definition of this genre in H.-W. KUHN, *Enderwartung*, pp. 27f.; cf. also H. LICHTENBERGER, *Menschenbild*, pp. 73f., and J. BECKER, *Heil Gottes*, pp. 136f. The term is coined as a parallel to "Gerichtsdoxologie", which is a specific genre in the Biblical tradition (cf. Exod 9,27f.; Lam 1,18-22; Job 4f.; Ezra 9; Neh 9; Dan 3,31-4,34; 9); on this genre, see F. HORST, *Die Doxologien im Amosbuch*; G. v. RAD, *Gerichtsdoxologie*.

67. Cf. 4Q301 5 3; on this passage, see below.

68. English translation according to GARCÍA MARTÍNEZ & TIGCHELAAR, *Study Edition* I, pp. 150f., where the lines are counted differently (lines 19f.) Cf. the discussion of restorations in H. LICHTENBERGER, *Menschenbild*, p. 91.

69. See also 1QH^a IV 37 (= XVII 25 Sukenik). In 1QH^a XII 30 (= IV 29 Sukenik) the composite term is replaced by the single word בשר.

70. A. E. SEKKI, *The Meaning of ruaḥ*, p. 104 n. 24.

insight, ruled by a depraved spirit (רוח נעוה), and, consequently, acting in sin and impurity.

Having stated the human incapability of understanding, the hymn goes on to highlight the miracle of revelation and salvation. This is continued by the confession:

> And I, your servant, have known
> thanks to *the spirit* you have placed in me [...][71].

Whereas human nature is unable to appreciate the works of God, the author is led towards salvation by the divine spirit which provides knowledge. In some respects, the passage even plays with the contrast between "flesh" and "spirit" whereas the "fleshly" human nature, called רוח בשר, is unable to gain insight, the blindness of the flesh is healed by the gift of the spirit[72]. However, the contrast could also be expressed as the opposition of two different "spirits", the "spirit of depravation" ruling over the "fleshly" human being, and the spirit providing insight.

β) A contextual opposition of "flesh" and "spirit" can be found more clearly in 1QH[a] VII 34f. (= XV 21 Sukenik). The statement on the spirit in this passage is also preceded by a "Niedrigkeitsdoxologie" which uses בשר to denote human incapability of understanding the divine mysteries.

> What, then, is flesh, to understand [your mysteries]?
> How can dust direct its steps?

Then, the author continues:

> You have fashioned the spirit
> and have organised its task [before the centuries].
> From you comes the path of every living being[73].

In this passage, the human being, as a mere creature of dust, is contrasted with God, who has predestined the ways of every creature and "in his hand is the inclination (יצר) of every spirit (כול רוח)[74]." The context shows that the opposition of "flesh" and "spirit" in this passage must be understood in anthropological terms. Whereas "flesh" characterizes the nature of the created being, "spirit" denotes the predestined inclination, or even the predestined existence of every human being[75]. This usage is quite close to the way predestination is expressed in the pre-Essene doctrine of the two spirits in 1QS III 13 – IV 26[76].

---

71. 1QH[a] V 35f. (= XIII 18f. Sukenik).
72. Cf. H. LICHTENBERGER, *Menschenbild*, p. 91.
73. 1QH[a] VII 34f. (= XV 21f. Sukenik).
74. 1QH[a] VII 27 (= XV 14 Sukenik).
75. Cf. H.-W. KUHN, *Enderwartung*, pp. 120-130, esp. p. 123.
76. See esp. 1QS III 15-18. In this text, however, the main opposition is that of two

γ) In another passage, 1QHᵃ XII 30f. (= IV 29f. Sukenik), flesh is explicitly characterized as sinful:

> What is flesh compared to this?
> What creature of clay can do wonders?
> He is in sin (בעוון) from his maternal womb
> and in guilty iniquity (באשמת מעל) right to old age[77].

This passage can also be classified as "Niedrigkeitsdoxologie". It refers to the preceding praise of God's wondrous counsel and his powerful acts[78]. In contrast with this, the human being, called "flesh" and "creature of clay", is not only weak and frail, but even blind to God's glory and basically sinful and guilty. עוון and אשמה are part of the life of a human from the beginning to the end. In view of the construction with ב, Jürgen Becker has suggested that the author considers human beings within a sphere of sinfulness. Dominated by that sphere, they do evil deeds, and this characterizes them as בשר[79]. "Human beings, as such, are sinful from their conception to their old age, and they stand under the judgment of the God who alone is righteous"[80].

The passage is followed by a confession of salvation, introduced by the phrase ואני ידעתי כי[81]. Here the author states that it is God alone who provides salvation and insight, "by the spirit which he created" for the human being (ברוח יצר אל לו)[82]. Only his "spirit" can perfect the path of the sons of Adam. So, the opposition between "flesh" and "spirit" ex-

---

spirits governing human beings, not the opposition of "flesh" and "spirit". This is clearly visible in 1QS IV 20f. (transl. from GARCÍA MARTÍNEZ & TIGCHELAAR, *Study Edition* I, p. 79):
  "Then God will refine, with his truth, all man's deeds,
  and will purify for himself the structure of man,
  ripping out all spirit of injustice from the innermost part of his flesh,
  and cleansing him with the spirit of holiness from every wicked deed".
Even though there is a marked contrast between the human flesh and the two different spirits, the main opposition is between the spirit of deceit and the spirit of holiness, whereas the flesh is capable of being purified; cf. H.-J. FABRY, רוּחַ, p. 420, and already H. BRAUN, *Qumran und das Neue Testament* 1, p. 179. On the character and origin of the dualism expressed in the doctrine of the two spirits cf. J. FREY, *Dualistic Thought*, pp. 290-295; on the interpretation of this passage see generally A. LANGE, *Weisheit und Prädestination*, pp. 121-170. On the pre-Essene character of the text see also A. LANGE / H. LICHTENBERGER, *Qumran*, pp. 56f.

77. Translation according to GARCÍA MARTÍNEZ & TIGCHELAAR, *Study Edition* I, p. 169 (there lines 29f.).
78. 1QHᵃ XII 29 (= IV 28 Sukenik).
79. J. BECKER, *Heil Gottes*, p. 13.
80. G. W. E. NICKELSBURG, *The Qumranic Transformation*, p. 654; cf. ibid.: "This motif of universal judgment parallels *1 Enoch* 1:7, 9".
81. On the genre of "Heilsbekenntnis" and its characteristics, see H.-W. KUHN, *Enderwartung*, p. 26.
82. 1QHᵃ XII 32 (= IV 31 Sukenik).

pressed in this passage is chiefly formed by the contrast between human inability and God's saving power. Only through the "spirit" created by God can "flesh" grasp the power and glory of God, i. e., only through his predestination can a human being participate in salvation[83]. The praise of God's salvific acts is strengthened by the corresponding confession of human incapability.

1QH^a XII 30f. (= IV 29f. Sukenik) provides also the most explicit linkage between "flesh" and "sin" within the *Hodayot*. Here, בשר does not only express human weakness and frailty, but also a state of being characterized by inescapable sinfulness and basic opposition with the creator. And, in contrast with the passages mentioned above from the War Rule, the sinfulness of the "flesh" is not only related to the hostile nations or the "lot of Belial", i. e. to people outside the pious community; the author himself and the members of the community praying the *Hodayot* also confess that they are "flesh" and sinners – and as such they are called to have insight into God's wondrous counsel and to participate in salvation.

As Jürgen Becker has observed[84], this kind of negative usage of בשר can be found only in those passages of the *Hodayot* which are often called the hymns of the community, not in the individual Thanksgiving Hymns, the so-called hymns of the teacher. In the individual hymns, בשר is used only three times, firmly within the Biblical range of meaning, without any notion of sin or iniquity[85]. The use of the term as an expression of sin is confined to the communal hymns[86].

This observation might be an additional argument for the validity of the distinction between "Lehrerlieder" and "Gemeindelieder", developed in the early sixties by Gert Jeremias and Heinz-Wolfgang Kuhn[87].

---

83. In this passage, רוח is an expression of God's predestination, as in 1QH^a VII 34f. (= XV 21f. Sukenik; see above) and IX 10f. (= I 8f. Sukenik), cf. H.-W. KUHN, *Enderwartung*, pp. 120-130. The notion of God's predestination is also expressed in the following passage (1QH^a XII 39 [= IX 38 Sukenik]): "For you created the just and the wicked...".

84. J. BECKER, *Heil Gottes*, p. 67.

85. In 1QH^a XVI 32.34 (= VIII 31.33 Sukenik), בשר denotes the (weak) substance or power of the body (cf. J. BECKER, *Heil Gottes*, p. 67 n. 1), and in the expression מחסי בשר in 1QH^a XV 20 (= VII 17 Sukenik) it also conveys the notion of weakness, but not the slightest allusion to sin. Cf. *ibid.*, p. 67: "So ist der Mensch hier also noch nicht radikal als Sünder verstanden, der nichts anderes kann, als sündigen, so wie es später in der essenischen Gemeinde am בשר-Begriff... deutlich ausgesprochen ist".

86. 1QH^a XII 30ff. (= IV 29ff. Sukenik) was originally seen as part of the individual hymn 1QH^a XII 6 – XIII 6 (= IV 5 – V 4 Sukenik; cf. G. JEREMIAS, *Der Lehrer der Gerechtigkeit*, pp. 204ff.). But J. BECKER assumes more precisely that this passage (1QH^a XII 30b – XIII 6 [= IV 29b – V 4 Sukenik]) is a later expansion of the individual hymn 1QH^a XII 6-30a (= IV 5-29a Sukenik) by the community (cf. *Heil Gottes*, pp. 54f.). This view is also confirmed by H.-W. KUHN, *Enderwartung*, p. 23 n. 3.

87. On this distinction cf. generally G. JEREMIAS, *Der Lehrer der Gerechtigkeit*,

c) A passage similar to the communal hymns can be found in 1QS, in the psalm-like composition 1QS IX 26 – XI 22 which is attached to the Community Rule in that collective manuscript[88]. Within the final passage of that composition, בשר is used three times in a sense corresponding to the usage in the *Hodayot*.

In 1QS XI 7, the author says that he has been given knowledge which is hidden from the assembly of flesh (סוד בשר). In this phrase, בשר could refer to humanity as a whole, but the context suggests that the phrase "assembly of flesh" denotes the group of all people who do not belong to the "lot of the holy ones" (XI 7f.), i. e. to the community. Here, as in 1QM, בשר seems to be a mere characterization of the people remaining outside the Essene community.

But only a few lines later, in 1QS XI 9f., the confession of salvation is followed by a kind of "Niedrigkeitsdoxologie" which is quite similar to those in the communal hymns of the *Hodayot*. Here, the author confesses:

> However, I belong to evil humankind (ואני לאדם רשעה)
> to the assembly of unfaithful flesh (ולסוד בשר עול);
> my failings (עוונתי), my iniquities (פשעי), my sins (חטאתי)
> with the depravities of my heart (עם נעוית לבבי)
> let me belong to the assembly of worms
> and of those who walk in darkness[89].

In this passage, as in 1QHᵃ XII 30f (= IV 29f. Sukenik), the member of the community himself confesses sharing the lot of sinful humanity, because he is בשר. According to the preceding confession, he knows that he is predestined to participate in salvation, he also claims to have insight into God's wonders and into the "mystery of existence" (רז נהיה:

---

pp. 168ff.; H.-W. KUHN, *Enderwartung*, pp. 21ff.; cf. the formal distinction within the *Hodayot* in G. MORAWE, *Aufbau und Abgrenzung*. The distinction is primarily based on arguments of contents and language, cf. G. JEREMIAS, *Der Lehrer der Gerechtigkeit*, pp. 72ff. More recently, it seems to be confirmed by manuscript evidence as well. According to E. Schuller's reconstruction of the 4QH-manuscripts, the manuscript 4Q429 (4QHᶜ) only contained individual hymns, 4Q427 (4QHᵃ) only communal hymns, and 4Q432 (4QHᶠ) was also a copy which concentrated on individual hymns (cf. E. SCHULLER, *The Cave 4 Hodayot Manuscripts*, pp. 97f.). In 1QHᵃ the individual hymns are arranged in the middle part of the scroll, whereas the framework is made up of communal hymns. This shows, that at least during the stage of the collection of the *Hodayot*, the community was well aware of the specific character of the individual hymns (cf. H. LICHTENBERGER, *Menschenbild*, p. 31).

88. On the description of 1QS, see A. LANGE, *Weisheit und Prädestination*, pp. 121ff.; A. LANGE / H. LICHTENBERGER, *Qumran*, pp. 54-59. On the textual development of the material cf. S. METSO, *Textual Development*. The problems of the composition cannot be dealt with here.

89. Translation according to GARCÍA MARTÍNEZ & TIGCHELAAR, *Study Edition* I, pp. 97-99 (modified at the beginning of line 10).

1QS XI 3f.), even though he confesses that he belongs to the assembly of sinful flesh and shares the lot of evil humankind[90].

A few lines later (1QS XI 11f.) he confesses:

> As for me, if I stumble,
> the mercies of God shall be my salvation always,
> and if I fall by the sin of the flesh (בעוון בשר),
> in the justice of God which endures eternally, shall my judgment be[91].

The rendering of the phrase בעוון בשר is quite decisive. Many interpreters have tried to weaken the expression in order to keep it close to the Biblical usage of בשר[92], and the majority of the English translations lack clarity[93]. As Jürgen Becker has stated, in the phrase בעוון בשר the word בשר has the function of a *genetivus auctoris*: consequently, flesh is the cause of the evil deed and it is the power that provokes evil deeds[94].

d) Summarizing these passages, we can confirm the view of some earlier authors: whereas the vast majority of the Qumran passages use בשר within the range of meanings given in the Hebrew Bible, there are some instances which go beyond this range. Here, flesh is deeply linked with sin and impurity and in some way opposed to the spirit of God who gives insight and knowledge. Moreover, flesh seems to represent an evil sphere or even power that causes human sin and causes the pious to stumble.

But in contrast to the usage in the *War Rule*, the *Hodayot* and the final psalm in 1QS do not just consider 'the others', the enemies of the community or the sinful nations, to be flesh. Most interestingly, the people praying the *Hodayot* themselves confess to participation in the fleshly nature of human beings. They are flesh and sinners, and as such they are elected to participate simultaneously in revelation and salvation.

---

90. In the light of lines 9-10, the phrase סוד בשר in l. 7 also receives strong negative overtones.

91. Translation according to GARCÍA MARTÍNEZ & TIGCHELAAR, *Study Edition* I, p. 99 (modified in line 12).

92. Thus, e. g., F. NÖTSCHER, *Terminologie*, p. 86: "wenn ich fehle als schwacher Mensch"; H. HUPPENBAUER, *Fleisch*, p. 299: "wenn ich in meiner Eigenschaft als Mensch zu Fall komme", or R. MEYER, φαρισαῖος, p. 112: "sinfulness of the flesh". E. BRANDENBURGER, *Fleisch und Geist*, p. 101, gives a paraphrase which is also far too weak: "straucheln durch das der Sünde widerstandslos ausgelieferte Fleisch".

93. This holds true for the translation by F. GARCÍA MARTÍNEZ, *Dead Sea Scrolls Translated*, p. 18: "if I fall in the sin of the flesh" (= *Study Edition* I, p. 99), similarly the translation by J. H. CHARLESWORTH in ID. (ed.), *Dead Sea Scrolls* 1, p. 49. The best translation of the passage is in G. VERMES, *Dead Sea Scrolls*, p. 88: "If I stagger because of the sin of flesh".

94. J. BECKER, *Heil Gottes*, pp. 111f.: "Auf alle Fälle macht 11,12 ('wenn ich strauchle durch die Sünde meines Fleisches') deutlich, daß hier בשר die Ursache des Sündigens ist, die Macht, die zur Sünde verführt." Cf. also ibid. n. 8: "Man fällt vom Heil ab durch die konkrete Sündentat, die die בשר bewirkt".

In these passages, we have the closest parallels to the Pauline usage of flesh as a sphere or even power opposed to God and his Spirit. However, the suggestion that the apostle could have known and used the terms of the Qumran sect[95] has been far too bold to be accepted in the discussion. It is unlikely that Paul – even when he was a Pharisaic student of law – had close contacts with Qumranites or other Essene groups. Therefore, the question whether or not there is a historical or traditio-historical connection between the Qumranite and the Pauline usage of "flesh" has remained open and has caused many exegetes to explain Paul's language in terms of Hellenistic parallels instead.

5. THE NEW EVIDENCE FROM 1Q/4QINSTRUCTION AND 1Q/4QMYSTERIES

The publication of the hitherto unknown sapiential texts from cave 4[96] has opened up new perspectives on these semantic and religio-historical issues. These documents can help to understand the background of the use of בשר in the Qumran texts mentioned above. And, in my opinion, they confirm the view that the negative usage of σάρξ in Paul has its roots not in the theological developments of the Jewish diaspora, but in Palestinian Jewish sapiential traditions.

First of all we have to note that the new sapiential texts provide a great number of new attestations of בשר: of the 63 references in the index volume of Wacholder's and Abegg's edition[97], 22 are from additional manuscripts of the *Damascus Document*, the *Hodayot* or *Serek-ha-Yaḥad*. 21 of the 41 remaining references are found in sapiential texts[98], 16 of them in different manuscripts of a single work which was originally called *Sapiential Work A*[99] and is now renamed 1Q/4QInstruction (or *Musar lᵉ Mebin*, i.e., "Instruction for the Knowledge-

---

95. See, e. g., S. SCHULZ, *Rechtfertigung*, p. 184: "kein Zweifel..., daß Paulus die theologischen Anschauungen dieser Sekte gekannt und aufgegriffen hat"; J. BECKER, *Heil Gottes*, pp. 249f., who asserts an indirect Essene influence on the Pauline terminology of sin. Cf. also J. MURPHY O'CONNOR, *Truth: Paul and Qumran*, p. 179: "That there are traces of Essene influence in the Pauline corpus is now generally admitted". Recent scholarship has cautiously left open the question of the links between Qumranian and Pauline thought, cf., e. g., H.-W. KUHN, *Qumran und Paulus*, p. 244: "Darüber, wie Qumrantraditionen vor 70 n. Chr. Paulus erreicht haben können, läßt sich nur spekulieren".

96. The scholarly breakthrough was the release of computerized reconstructions of the texts from transcriptions made in the fifties and preserved in a preliminary concordance: B. Z. WACHOLDER & M. G. ABEGG, *Preliminary Edition*. The reconstruction of the sapiential texts was presented in fasc. 2, pp. 1-203. The official edition of these documents has appeared in 1997 and 1999 in vol. 20 and vol. 34 of the DJD-series.

97. B. Z. WACHOLDER & M. G. ABEGG, *Concordance*, pp. 95f.

98. 4Q301; 4Q306; 4Q411; 4Q416-418; 4Q426; 4Q525.

99. E. TOV & S. J. PFANN (eds.), *Companion Volume*, p. 43.

able")¹⁰⁰. One further important reference, 4Q301 5 3¹⁰¹ is from a manuscript which most probably represents the so-called *Book of Mysteries* (1Q/4QMyst)¹⁰² which is closely related to 1Q/4QInstruction in contents and terminology¹⁰³. The context of the four other references¹⁰⁴ remains unclear. I will, therefore, focus the discussion on the use of בשר and its relation with רוח in 4QInstruction and 4QMysteries.

a) Some introductory issues

In the context of the present volume, it is not necessary to discuss the complicated issues concerning the origin and character of 1Q/4QInstruction and the related texts¹⁰⁵. Only some most important observations can be mentioned briefly:

According to the editors, the work is preserved in seven or eight manuscripts (1Q26; 4Q415-418; 4Q418a; 4Q423)¹⁰⁶. They are all written in a Herodian hand (i. e. from the late first century BCE)¹⁰⁷. The number of copies and the relatively late date of copying show that the work was highly esteemed by the Qumranites. This is also confirmed by the fact that one of the copies was hidden in Cave 1 among the most important documents of the community¹⁰⁸. The terminological survey by John Strugnell and Daniel J. Harrington shows clearly that the work is a wisdom composition¹⁰⁹, and from the available evidence we can see that "it

---

100. Thus the official edition by J. STRUGNELL, D. J. HARRINGTON & T. ELGVIN, *Qumran Cave* 4. XXIV. Regrettably, the original Hebrew name of the text has not been preserved.

101. This passage might be quite important, because בשר seems to be used within a kind of "Niedrigkeitsdoxologie" similar to the passages in the communal hymns of the Hodayot discussed above. The text reads…]מ[ה בשר כיא…, "what is flesh, that…?"

102. For the arguments for the view that 4Q301 is one of three 4Q-manuscripts of the *Book of Mysteries* (4QMystᶜ), see A. LANGE, *Weisheit und Prädestination*, p. 93 n. 2; ID. *Physiognomie oder Gotteslob*, p. 283; but cf. the differing view in L. H. SCHIFFMAN, *Mysteries*, pp. 31 and 113f., who considers 4Q301 as a different composition resembling the Enochic literature.

103. On the thematic and terminological similarities between 1Q/4Q Mysteries and 1Q/4Q Instruction see A. LANGE, *In Diskussion mit dem Tempel*.

104. 4Q306 1 4; 4Q411 1 11; 4Q426 4 4; 4Q525 8 5.

105. Cf. the general introduction in the edition in J. STRUGNELL, D. J. HARRINGTON & T. ELGVIN, *Qumran Cave* 4. XXIV, pp. 1-40 and the article by A. LANGE in the present volume.

106. Cf. the cautious comments of the editors J. STRUGNELL, D. J. HARRINGTON & T. ELGVIN, *Qumran Cave* 4. XXIV, pp. 475-477 and 501, on the allocation of the fragments which were formerly collected unter the siglum 4Q418 but are now edited as 4Q418a (4QInstructionᵉ) and 4Q418c (4QInstructionᶠ?).

107. Cf. J. STRUGNELL, D. J. HARRINGTON & T. ELGVIN, *Qumran Cave* 4. XXIV, p. 21.

108. Cf. H. STEGEMANN, *Die Essener*, pp. 89f.

109. Cf. J. STRUGNELL, D. J. HARRINGTON & T. ELGVIN, *Qumran Cave* 4. XXIV, pp. 8ff. and 22ff.

was loosely structured at best"[110]. But although there are substantial passages preserved from the manuscripts 4Q416, 4Q417 and 4Q418 with some textual overlaps between the three, it is not yet possible to get certainty on the general outline or the redactional history of the composition.

> A sound judgement on these issues can only be reached on the basis of a material reconstruction of the manuscripts[111]. According to Annette Steudel and Birgit Lucassen, 4Q416 frg. 1 with its broad right margin was the beginning of that manuscript[112], whereas 4Q417 frg. 1 (formerly frg. 2) might have been the beginning of the manuscript 4Q417. If both suggestions are correct, the manuscripts 4Q416 and 4Q417 represent different stages of redaction. 4Q417, then, is a copy of an earlier version of the work, whereas 4Q416 represents a later stage of redaction which is also represented by 4Q418[113].

Obviously, the composition combines traditional types of instruction on practical issues like poverty and finances, social and family relations, with theoretical, theological reflections. The sapiential admonitions are presented within a cosmological and eschatological framework[114]. Consequently, 4QInstruction provides evidence of an early merging of sapiential with eschatological or even apocalyptic thought.

It should also be pointed out that there are no clear indications of Qumran "sectarian" origin[115]. The terminology differs markedly from that of the typical "sectarian" documents. There are no indications linking it to a specific religious community, let alone a community separated from the Temple, and the admonitions are concerned with daily life. Therefore, like most of the other sapiential texts from Qumran[116], the

---

110. Thus J. J. COLLINS, *Jewish Wisdom*, p. 118.

111. A first attempt was published by T. ELGVIN, *Reconstruction,* cf. also his doctoral thesis *Analysis* in which his reconstruction makes up the basis of his further analysis. Independently from Elgvin, A. STEUDEL and B. LUCASSEN have produced a material reconstruction which is about to be published in *RevQ*. Cf., until then, the short review by J. STRUGNELL, D. J. HARRINGTON & T. ELGVIN, *Qumran Cave* 4. XXIV, pp. 18f.

112. Thus already D. J. HARRINGTON, *Wisdom Texts from Qumran*, p. 41.

113. Cf. also A. LANGE, *In Diskussion mit dem Tempel*, pp. 127f., and his article in the present volume.

114. Cf. also T. ELGVIN, *Wisdom, Revelation and Eschatology*; ID., *Early Essene Eschatology*. On the eschatological dualism of the work, see also J. FREY, *Dualistic Thought*, pp. 298f.

115. See, most recently, the thorough terminological analysis by J. STRUGNELL, D. J. HARRINGTON & T. ELGVIN, *Qumran Cave* 4. XXIV, pp. 22ff.; cf. previously A. LANGE, *Weisheit und Prädestination*, pp. 48f.; D. J. HARRINGTON, *Wisdom at Qumran*, p. 148; ID., *Wisdom Texts from Qumran*, pp. 41, 85. T. ELGVIN also states that "our composition predates the *yaḥad* as an established community" (*Early Essene Eschatology*, p. 133). It is, therefore, somewhat bewildering that he nevertheless wants to call the work "a wider representative of the Essene movement, not of the *yaḥad*" (*ibid.*).

116. Thus already W. L. LIPSCOMB & J. A. SANDERS, *Wisdom at Qumran*, p. 278: "There are no true wisdom texts among the scrolls of undisputed Essene authorship"; cf.

work should be classified as a non-sectarian, or non-Essene, or – more precisely – pre-Essene work. This is valid although there may be different redactional stages. Even in the later version there are no clear traces of "sectarian" redaction or authorship.

As Armin Lange has shown from the treatment of cultic issues, the document seems to have originated in sapiential circles which were connected with and interested in the Temple[117]. So, 1Q/4QInstruction can be classified clearly as a product of the Palestinian Jewish sapiential tradition.

The suggested dates of composition vary from the 4th or 3rd century[118] to the middle of the 2nd century BCE[119]. Most plausible is a date at the end of the 3rd or in the first half of the 2nd century, i. e. roughly contemporary with the work of Ben Sira[120]. The composition is cited in the *Hodayot*[121], and the term רז נהיה which is characteristic of this work and of the *Book of Mysteries*[122] is used only in one more passage from Qumran, the final "psalm" of the manuscript 1QS[123]. Thus, the documents which take up some elements from the tradition of 1Q/4Q Instruction (or 1Q/4QMysteries) are obviously those texts which also use the term בשר in a very negative sense.

This observation leads to the question: Does the Qumran tradition derive its negative view of בשר from this pre-Essene sapiential tradition? Is a similar usage of בשר already visible in 1Q/4QInstruction and 1Q/4QMysteries?

b) *The Usage of* בשר *in 1Q/4QInstruction: An Overview*

α) Some of the 16 passages mentioned in the index of Wacholder and Abegg are uncertain or too fragmentary to be interpreted or classified semantically. This is true for the following instances:

---

also H. STEGEMANN, *Die Essener*, p. 143. A possible exception could be 4Q420-421 (4QWays of Righteousness), cf. T. ELGVIN, *Wisdom in the Yaḥad*, pp. 205f.

117. Cf. A. LANGE, *In Diskussion mit dem Tempel*, p. 131; ID., *Die Endgestalt des protomasoretischen Psalters*, p. 122. See also his article in the present volume.
118. H. STEGEMANN, *Die Essener*, p. 143.
119. T. ELGVIN, *Early Essene Eschatology*, p. 133.
120. Cf. A. LANGE, *Weisheit und Prädestination*, 47; ID., *In Diskussion mit dem Tempel*, pp. 129f.; ID., *Die Endgestalt des protomasoretischen Psalters*, p. 122. For the *terminus post quem*, Lange proposes linguistic arguments using, e. g., the Persian loan word רז and other words and constructions which occur only late; the *terminus ante quem* is given by the citation in the *Hodayot* which were composed within the second half of the 2nd century BCE.
121. 1QH^a XVIII 29f. (= X 27f. Sukenik) cites 4Q418 55 10, and 1QH^a IX 28f. (= I 26f. Sukenik) alludes to 4Q417 2 I 8; cf. A. LANGE, *Weisheit und Prädestination*, p. 46.
122. In the preserved fragments of 1Q/4QInstruction, it is used more than 20 times, in the preserved fragments of 1Q/4QMysteries it is documented 4 times.
123. 1QS XI 3.

- 4Q418 19 4: Only an uncertain ב[שרכה] is legible. The reading is questioned additionally by the DJD edition, where *dalet* is preferred over *reš* (the result is [שדכה]), but a *bet* is also thought to be possible[124].
- 4Q418 103 I 9: The reading בשר is certain, but without any context. The editors propose [הבשר], ו]בשר or הבשר。[125].
- 4Q417 3 4: Here we have the reading]בשר עם תעניתן[("flesh with fasting"), but the context remains totally unclear.
- 4Q417 1 II 14 (formerly 2 II 14)[126]: The term נבונות בשר "understanding of the flesh" is used in a series of prohibitions or warnings, not to be mislead or not to be lead astray. The editors propose that the text gives "a description of God's thoughts which are free of fleshliness"[127]. It should be noted, however, that in the context there is a reference to an evil יצר (4Q417 1 II 12), even if the precise sense to be given to יצר is uncertain[128]. Therefore, the passage remains quite unclear, but it may be suggested that the use of בשר within the phrase "understanding of the flesh" has a rather negative connotation.
- 4Q418 101 II 5: בשר is used in a context which probably deals with matters of property: The line reads בשרו לוא ימעל בבשרו[129]. The first בשרו could be the end of the foregoing phrase, which is lost. Then the text goes on: "He shall not do harm to (*or* act unfaithfully against) his *own kin*["[130]. So, even if the precise meaning of the passage remains unclear, it is probable that בשר is used in the sense of "kinsfolk". Thus, the use of בשר in this passage is within the range of Biblical usage.

β) There are seven other passages in which בשר is obviously used within the Biblical range of meanings:

- 4Q416 2 IV 4: לבשר אחד is a quotation of Gen 2,24.

---

124. Cf. J. STRUGNELL, D. J. HARRINGTON & T. ELGVIN, *Qumran Cave* 4. XXIV, pp. 242f.

125. Cf. J. STRUGNELL, D. J. HARRINGTON & T. ELGVIN, *Qumran Cave* 4. XXIV, p. 329.

126. It should be noted that the authors of the DJD edition have changed the numbering of the fragments of 4Q417. The former frg. 1 is now frg. 2; the former frg. 2 is now frg. 1. In the present article, I follow the new numbering.

127. J. STRUGNELL, D. J. HARRINGTON & T. ELGVIN, *Qumran Cave* 4. XXIV, p. 172. Cf. the similar interpretation of A. LANGE, *Weisheit und Prädestination*, p. 54, who renders בלוא נבונות בשר "ohne daß er Einsichten des Fleisches gebot".

128. J. STRUGNELL, D. J. HARRINGTON & T. ELGVIN, *Qumran Cave* 4. XXIV, p. 171.

129. Thus J. STRUGNELL, D. J. HARRINGTON & T. ELGVIN, *Qumran Cave* 4. XXIV, p. 326: "בשרך is to be excluded (unless much of the *kap* has been carried away), but *waw* or *yod* would also be very difficult".

130. Thus the translation by J. STRUGNELL, D. J. HARRINGTON & T. ELGVIN, *Qumran Cave* 4. XXIV, p. 326.

- 4Q416 2 III 21 (= 4Q418 10 6): In this passage, the addressee's wife is referred to as the עזר בשרכה, "the help of your flesh". The phrase seems to combine Gen 2,18 עזר כנגדו and Gen 2,23 בשר מבשרי.
- 4Q418 103 II 9 reads]הונכה עם בשרכה["your property with your flesh". The property of a person is taken together with his "flesh". Here, בשר might be used to denote the physical life of a person. The context is a halakha on mixed things. Another suggestion is made by Strugnell and Harrington: They propose to take בשר in the sense of "cattle" or "animal property", which is then contrasted with material wealth[131]. In any case, the usage of "flesh" in this passage remains fully within the Biblical range of meanings.
- In a passage which is preserved three times (4Q416 2 II 2f.; 4Q417 1 II 4 and 4Q418 8 1)[132], the phrase "if he shuts his hand, then there will be gathered the spirit of all flesh" takes up terms from Deut 15,7 ("you shall not close your hand") and Job 34,14 "if he were to... recall his life-giving spirit, all that lives would perish..."[133]. As in the Hebrew Bible, the phrase כל בשר denotes creation or humanity as a whole.

γ) Besides the passages mentioned above, there are three passages in 1Q/4QInstruction in which the term בשר is used clearly beyond the range of meanings in Biblical Hebrew. These passages show that already in this pre-Essene sapiential document "flesh" is closely associated with sin, upheaval and impurity. Most interestingly, all these passages use the term רוח בשר "spirit of flesh" which is also attested in the *Hodayot*[134]. In two of the passages, the term is used for a single human being, so that the expression כל רוח בשר can be formed. But in one passage, it seems to denote a collective spiritual entity, i. e. sinful humanity as a whole. The three passages deserve to be commented on in more detail.

c) *The Negative Usage of* בשר *in 1Q/4QInstruction*

α) The first passage where בשר has the meaning of "sinful flesh" is 4Q418 frg. 81. In this passage, the addressee is admonished to keep himself separate from all abomination, since God has separated him from all "spirit of flesh":

---

131. J. STRUGNELL, D. J. HARRINGTON & T. ELGVIN, *Qumran Cave* 4. XXIV, p. 334.
132. Translation according to J. STRUGNELL, D. J. HARRINGTON & T. ELGVIN, *Qumran Cave* 4. XXIV, p. 93. Cf. *ibid.*, p. 95: "Note that the whole phrase, protasis and apodosis, is found also in a different work, 4Q419 8 ii 7; it is more likely, historically, that 4Q419 came later and was quoting from 4Q415ff.".
133. Translation according to the *New English Bible*.
134. 1QH[a] V 30 (= XIII 13 Sukenik) and IV 37 (= XVII 25 Sukenik).

> "He has separated you from all spirit of the flesh; and you, keep separate from all that he hates and keep yourself apart from all abomination of the soul..."[135].

In this passage, כול רוח בשר is paralleled by "all that he [= God] hates", so the "all spirit of flesh" is a sphere or entity opposed to God and his will. The context is predestinarian: God has assigned a portion to every being, and he has placed the addressee, probably the student of Wisdom[136], in an outstanding position, to "rule over his treasure"[137]. He is, therefore, called to sanctify himself and to keep himself apart from the abominations that characterize the "spirit of flesh".

β) In 4Q416 frg 1 which was probably located at the very beginning of this manuscript[138] we find an announcement of the eschatological judgment. In 4Q416 1 10-13 we read:

> In the heavens he will judge every work of wickedness, but all sons of the truth he will favour [...] its end (scil. of iniquity?). And all those who wallow in it (= iniquity?) will tremble and shout, for..., the waters and the abysses will tremble and every spirit of flesh will be destroyed (יתערערו כול רוח בשר), but the sons of the heavens [...] his judgment, and all injustice will end...

In spite of the textual lacunae, the antithetic structure of the passage is obvious. Two groups of beings face an opposing eschatological fate. The first group is characterized by wickedness, iniquity and injustice, and its members will face judgment, they will tremble with fear and suffer final destruction. The other group is characterized by truth, and its members will be favoured by God. The members of the first group wallow in something (most probably iniquity), and are named by the collective term כול רוח בשר. The other group seems to comprise the sons of

---

135. 4Q418 81 1-2, translation according to F. GARCÍA MARTÍNEZ, *Dead Sea Scrolls Translated*, p. 391, but "keep yourself apart" instead of "keep yourselves apart" for the Imp. Sg. הבדל.

136. There is also the possibility that the addressee is Israel as a whole, but if the document was read and studied by individuals in a wisdom circle or school, they could simply consider themselves to be addressed.

137. 4Q418 81 9. The interpretation is uncertain. God's treasure could be wisdom, so that the insightful is a ruler over God's treasure. But it could also be the Tora.

138. Cf. D. J. HARRINGTON, *Wisdom Texts from Qumran*, p. 41. T. ELGVIN, *Wisdom, Revelation, and Eschatology*, pp. 456-459; ID., *Early Essene Eschatology*, pp. 146-164 interprets the fragment in accordance with his extensive textual reconstructions based on the alleged overlaps with fragments from 4Q418. But if it is true that 4Q416 1 is the beginning of the manuscript, Elgvin's reconstruction cannot be maintained. Therefore, the fragment is interpreted on the basis of the transcription by B. Z. WACHOLDER & M. G. ABEGG, *Preliminary Edition* 2, p. 54. In the DJD edition, J. Strugnell and D. J. Harrington cautiously accept only the overlaps with 4Q418 1-2, but not the overlap with 4Q418 201 suggested by T. ELGVIN, *Early Essene Eschatology*, pp. 146-153; cf. J. STRUGNELL, D. J. HARRINGTON & T. ELGVIN, *Qumran Cave 4. XXIV*, pp. 83f.

heaven and the sons of the truth, i. e. the angels together with the just human beings. The statement is quite clear: when God will enact his eschatological judgment and put an end to all kinds of injustice, every "spirit of flesh" will be destroyed[139]. Thus, the "spirit of flesh" is clearly opposed to the "sons of the truth" and the "sons of the heavens". It is characterized by wickedness and injustice, and will face eschatological destruction.

The use of בשר in this passage is clearly negative, and the context shows that רוח בשר is basically linked with iniquity and sin. It is obvious, however, that not all human beings are characterized as בשר. Apart from כול רוח בשר there are other human beings called "sons of the truth" who will not be destroyed, but favoured in the final judgment. Like in 4Q418 81 1f., בשר does not characterize humanity as a whole but *sinful* humanity. The author and the readers consider themselves separate from the "fleshly spirits". Therefore, the anthropological teaching of 1Q/4QInstruction is characterized by a kind of cosmic and eschatological dualism which has at least some similarities with the dualistic teaching in the doctrine of the two spirits in 1QS III 13 – IV 26[140].

γ) The cosmic background of the dualism in 1Q/4QInstruction is even more obvious in 4Q417 frg. 1 (formerly frg. 2). If the reconstruction of Annette Steudel and Birgit Lucassen is correct, the passage was the beginning of the earlier version of 1Q/4QInstruction[141] presenting a kind of epistemological introduction to the work as a whole. Here, the insightful (מבין) is admonished to study the רז נהיה, the "mystery of being" (or: "mystery that is to come")[142] in order to discern truth and iniquity, wisdom and folly (4Q417 1 I 6f. par. 4Q418 43 4).

A few lines later, there is mention of a heavenly book:

> Engraved is the ordinance, and ordained is all the punishment. For engraved is that which is ordained by God against all the iniquities of the children of Seth. And written in his presence is the book of memorial of those who keep his word. And the vision of Hago is the book of memorial. And he gave it as an inheritance to Enosh (אנוש) together with the people of

---

139. The verbal form יתערערו is probably a hitpalpel of ערר which is used in Jer 51,58 to denote the destruction of the city walls of Babylon. Therefore, it seems to be an expression for eschatological destruction. Cf. A. LANGE, *In Diskussion mit dem Tempel*, p. 143 n. 101.

140. Cf. J. FREY, *Dualistic Thought*, pp. 298f.; cf. also D. J. HARRINGTON, *Approaches*, p. 35: "The world view of Sapiential Work A seems midway between Ben Sira's timid doctrine of the pairs and the fully fleshed out dualistic schema of 1QS 3-4".

141. See above, n. 111; cf. A. LANGE, *In Diskussion mit dem Tempel*, pp. 127f.

142. On the interpretation of this term, cf. A. LANGE, *Weisheit und Prädestination*, pp. 57f.; J. J. COLLINS, *Jewish Wisdom*, pp. 121-125, and, most recently, T. ELGVIN, *The Mystery to Come*.

the spirit (עם רוח). For according to the pattern of the holy ones is his fashioning. But no more has meditation been given to the spirit of flesh (רוח בשר), for it knew not the difference between good and evil according to the judgment of its spirit (4Q417 1 I 15-18)[143].

The book of memorial[144] mentioned here is probably the Book of Hago which is known from some other Qumran texts[145]. Its contents might be an extract from heavenly tablets, comprising the ordinances of God, but also the coming judgment, i. e. the order of being. This book of heavenly knowledge is to be studied by the addressee of 1Q/4QInstruction. And the present passage gives a mythological explanation, why it can be studied, or why the insightful can gain heavenly insight.

The book, it is said, was given to אנוש. This word does not only denote humankind. Here, after the mention of the sons of Seth and their iniquities (l. 15), it seems to denote – as a proper name – Enosh, the son of Seth who is mentioned in Gen 4,26; 5,6.9-11; 1 Chron 1,1 and Sir 49,16, and who was, according to *Jubilees* 4,12, the first human being to invoke the name of the Lord[146]. The passage seems to refer to a mythological tradition of the fall of angels during the time of the sons of Seth, which presented Enosh and the עם רוח, the "people of the spirit", as the only pious of their time[147]. So this primeval father and the עם רוח, i. e. the obedient angels, gained the heavenly memorial as inheritance. In contrast, the book was not given to the רוח בשר, because it was not able to discern between good and evil (l. 17f.).

This passage on the רוח בשר is also clearly characterized by an ethical and eschatological dualism. The "spirit of flesh", i. e. sinful humanity, is characterized by opposition to God and the inability to discern between good and evil. As regards ethical behaviour and – even more importantly – the possibility of gaining heavenly wisdom, it is opposed to Enosh and the obedient angels. The addressee of 1Q/4QInstruction, who is admonished to study the "mystery that is to come"[148], can understand himself as an heir of the primeval father Enosh to whom the book of

---

143. Translation according to D. J. HARRINGTON, *Wisdom at Qumran*, p. 53 with minor alterations according to A. LANGE, *Weisheit und Prädestination*, p. 53.
144. Cf. Mal 3,16.
145. 1QSa I 6f.; CD X 6; XIV 6-8.
146. Cf. A. LANGE, *Weisheit und Prädestination*, pp. 87f. On the post-Biblical interpretation of Enosh, see also S. D. FRAADE, *Enosh and his Generation*, and P. SCHÄFER, *Der Götzendienst des Enosch*. Whereas Rabbinic traditions interpret Enosh as a representative of his idolatrous contemporaries, all non-Rabbinic traditions interpret Gen 4,26 as a positive statement on the individual patriarch. It is this line of interpretation to which 4Q417 1 I 16 belongs.
147. Cf. A. LANGE, *Weisheit und Prädestination*, p. 88.
148. 4Q417 1 I 6 (par 4Q418 43 4) and 1 I 18.

heavenly knowledge was given as an inheritance. So, the addressee is given an explanation as to why he is honoured with the gain of heavenly wisdom, which is not revealed to sinful humanity.

d) The Relation between בשר and יצר בשר

In 4Q416 1 16, at the end of the announcement of judgement which was discussed above, the term בשר occurs again. Between two *lacunae*, the reading י]צר בשר הואה ומבינו[ת is preserved, and from the parallel in 4Q418 2 8, it is possible to add כ]יא, so that the reading is כיא יצר בשר הואה[149]. However, the meaning of the phrase, and especially of the term יצר, remains unclear. Should it be translated by "[because] an object of flesh is he"? Or does יצר denote the "inclination", so that the translation is "[the in]clination of flesh is he"[150]? Cautiously, Strugnell and Harrington propose that, if יצר is preceded by a כיא, "הואה could refer to man or his sinful *yeṣer*"[151]. It can be asked whether the idea of the evil inclination (יצר הרע) which is quite frequent in later rabbinic literature is already present in 1Q/4QInstruction and whether it is related in any way to the idea of sinful flesh[152].

This may be confirmed by two other passages where the term יצר or even יצר רע is used: In 4Q417 1 II 12[153], within a series of warnings, it is said: אל תפתכה מחשבת יצר רע]: "Let not the thought of an evil inclination mislead thee..."[154]. Strugnell and Harrington note that the phrase is related to Gen 6,5 כל יצר מחשבות לבו רק תרע, but they leave the question open whether the phrase "indicated something ill-fashioned or something that plans, or intends, it evilly"[155]. In view of the term מחשבת, however, the latter seems to be more plausible.

The passage 4Q417 1 I 13ff. shows that יצר is conceived within a dualistic framework. In 4Q417 1 I 17 it is said that the יצר of Enosh was according to the pattern of the Holy Ones (i. e. the angels), so that he and the "spiritual people" (עמ רוח) received the "book of memorial". On the contrary, the "spirit of the flesh" (רוח בשר) was not able to dis-

---

149. Cf. J. STRUGNELL, D. J. HARRINGTON & T. ELGVIN, *Qumran Cave 4. XXIV*, p. 225.
150. Cf. J. STRUGNELL, D. J. HARRINGTON & T. ELGVIN, *Qumran Cave 4. XXIV*, p. 83.
151. J. STRUGNELL, D. J. HARRINGTON & T. ELGVIN, *Qumran Cave 4. XXIV*, p. 88.
152. The use of יצר in the Qumran literature and other pre-Rabbinic sources (e. g., *Jubilees*) can not be discussed here, but cf. R. E. MURPHY, *Yēṣer*.
153. Formerly 4Q417 2 II 12.
154. Translation from J. STRUGNELL, D. J. HARRINGTON & T. ELGVIN, *Qumran Cave 4. XXIV*, p. 170.
155. J. STRUGNELL, D. J. HARRINGTON & T. ELGVIN, *Qumran Cave 4. XXIV*, p. 172.

cern between good and evil, so that the heavenly revelation was not given to the רוח בשר. The passage shows that 1Q/4QInstruction shares the idea of two different "inclinations". The "good" one is associated with the ancestral hero, the angels and – probably – the students of wisdom. The "bad" inclination can be linked with the "fleshly spirit". This might also explain the notion of יצר רע in 4Q417 1 II 12 where the student is warned not to be misled by a "bad" יצר and the term נבונות בשר ("understandings of the flesh") is used in the subsequent line.

From these two passages, it is very probable that the term יצר בשר in 4Q416 1 16 must be understood within the same dualistic framework. Even if the precise meaning of the phrase can not be grasped, בשר carries the same negative connotation as a few lines above, in 4Q416 1 12.

e) רוח בשר and the Contextual Relation of בשר and רוח in 1Q/4QInstruction

A remarkable terminological feature of our sapiential tradition is the composite expression רוח בשר which is used in the three passages discussed above and in the *Hodayot*[156]. But even if the negative connotation of the composite term is quite clear, it is not easy to determine its meaning. Does רוח בשר denote a single human being characterized by "flesh"[157], or rather a collective, or spiritual or psychological phenomenon[158]? What is the semantic value of רוח within the composite term? And how is רוח בשר linked with other kinds of "spirit" in the present composition? Since it is not possible to present a comprehensive analysis of the use of רוח in 1Q/4QInstruction, I will limit my investigation to the three passages where the composite term occurs.

The expression כ(ול) רוח בשר in 4Q416 1 12 and 4Q418 81 1f. shows that the composite term רוח בשר can be used to denote any single human being who is characterized by flesh, so that the collective expression is formed by the addition of כל or כול. On the other hand, the usage without כול in 4Q417 1 I 17 (formerly 2 I 17) shows that the term can also be used for a collective or even for the evil part of humanity as a whole[159].

---

156. 1QH^a IV 37 (= XVII 25 Sukenik); V 30 (= XIII 13 Sukenik).

157. This could be suggested by the phrase כל רוח בשר.

158. This was suggested on the basis of the usage within the *Hodayot*, cf. A. E. SEKKI, *The Meaning of ruaḥ*, p. 104: "the spirit of man".

159. In their translation, the editors tentatively insert an indefinite article ("to a [?] fleshly spirit"; cf. J. STRUGNELL, D. J. HARRINGTON & T. ELGVIN, *Qumran Cave* 4. XXIV, p. 155.), but this seems to be a harmonizing interpretation. Their commentary is correct: "The statement,... concerning a group of the righteous... is contrasted with the collective רוח בשר, which describes not so much a psychological principle but the group of evil humanity" (*ibid.*, p. 165).

So, the use in 1Q/4QInstruction differs from the later use of רוח בשׂר in the *Hodayot* where the term seems to denote a kind of spiritual ability[160] or rather the lack of such an ability[161]. In 1Q/4QInstruction, however, the basic meaning is that of a "fleshly being", that is, a living creature (therefore רוח) which is governed by "flesh" in its thoughts and deeds.

In 1Q/4QInstruction, there is no clear terminological antithesis between בשׂר and רוח. Only in the passage 4Q417 1 I 15ff., there is a contextual opposition between רוח בשׂר, the *fleshly spirit* on the one side and the עם רוח, the *spiritual* people[162], on the other side. Within the dualistic framework of this passage, there is a contextual antagonism between the two terms, which are both used to qualify a specific group, a part of humanity or a group of heavenly beings. Of course, the term רוח is used not very precisely and has quite different meanings within this work[163]. But in spite of all differences in detail, it is not too bold to say that this passage is the earliest parallel to the later Pauline antithesis of "flesh" and "spirit".

f) Preliminary Conclusions

There are, of course, numerous passages in 1Q/4QInstruction, in which בשׂר is used within the Biblical range of meanings. In the Hebrew Bible, בשׂר may denote the frailty of the creature, but there is no clear connection with disobedience or sin[164]. The three passages mentioned above clearly go beyond the Biblical usage and use בשׂר – or more precisely רוח בשׂר – as a term to denote a *sinful* human being or *sinful* humanity. In these passages, "flesh" (בשׂר) is clearly characterized by its opposition to God and its inability to discern between good and evil. The chosen and wise have to be aware that they are separated from the "spirit of flesh", and all "spirit of flesh" will be destroyed in the eschatological judgement, when iniquity will finally cease.

---

160. Cf. A. LANGE, *Weisheit und Prädestination*, p. 87: "eine nicht näher beschriebene Form menschlicher Einsichtsfähigkeit".

161. The negative connotation of the רוח בשׂר in 1Q/4QInstruction suggests that the passages in the *Hodayot* have a similar negative connotation.

162. Cf. A. LANGE, *Weisheit und Prädestination*, p. 89: "ein himmlisches Geistvolk".

163. The same is true for the later Qumran usage, cf. H.-J. FABRY, רוּחַ.

164. This holds true even for the two passages, where בשׂר and רוח occur in contextual opposition, Isa 31,3 and Gen 6,3. In Isa 31,3 בשׂר denotes the weakness of the Egyptian horses compared with the saving power of God, and in Gen 6,3 it characterizes the frailty of the human being, who cannot last without God's life-giving breath. The passages mentioned by N. BRATSIOTIS, בָּשָׂר, cc. 863f., also express human weakness in contrast with God's power (Jer 17,5; Ps 56,5; 2 Chron 32,8), human frailty (Ps 78,39) or the human point of view compared with the divine one (Job 10,4). Cf. also H. D. PREUSS, *Theologie des Alten Testaments* 2, p. 117 with n. 73.

If it is correct to distinguish between two redactional stages of 1Q/4QInstruction, an earlier one represented by 4Q417 and a later one represented by 4Q416 and 4Q418, there is no difference between the two in respect of the negative usage of בשר and the dualistic framework in which בשר or רוח בשר is mentioned. Since 1Q/4QInstruction is a composition that predates the *yaḥad*, the passages mentioned above give evidence that the negative usage of בשר was not a Qumran sectarian development. The terminological development obviously predates the *yaḥad*. It rather originates in pre-Essene sapiential circles which might have been in close connection with the Jerusalem Temple. It is, therefore, definitely a Palestinian Jewish development, not an achievement of the diaspora[165].

6. Some Semantic and Traditio-Historical Trajectories

The observations in 1Q/4QInstruction open up new perspectives for the description of semantic developments. How was the range of meanings of the Hebrew word בשר widened beyond the borders which are documented within the Hebrew Bible? And how did other circles or later writings adopt the new kind of usage? Of course, the amount of sources is rather limited, but it is at least possible to give some suggestions.

a) The Development of the pre-Essene Sapiential View of בשר

The development of the negative usage of בשר can be explained by two observations, a generic and a traditio-historical one.

α) In the pre-Essene sapiential tradition, we can find the earliest examples of the genre "Niedrigkeitsdoxologie" which is widely used, later, in the *Hodayot*[166]. This new genre is normally viewed as a development from the Biblical genre "Gerichtsdoxologie"[167] in which a con-

---

165. This is true, even if it is an open question to what extent there were Hellenistic influences in the circles or schools of wisdom in Jerusalem. Such an influence can be seen in the work of Ben Sira or even earlier, in Qohelet. On Hellenistic influence in Palestine, see basically M. Hengel, *Judaism and Hellenism*; on Hellenism in the Qumran texts, s. Id., *Qumran und der Hellenismus*; most recently Id., *Jerusalem als jüdische und hellenistische Stadt*.

166. Cf. 4Q417 2 I 15-17 (formerly 1 I 16): "Who will be declared righteous when He gives judgement?..."; cf. 1QH^a XV 31 (= VII 28 Sukenik); see also 4QMyst^c = 4Q301 5 3: "What is flesh that... " (*m*]*h bśr ky'*[...), where בשר occurs for the first time in a "Niedrigkeitsdoxologie".

167. Cf. Exod 9,27f.; Lam 1,18-22; Job 4f.; Ezra 9; Neh 9; Dan 3,31-4,34; 9.

fession of human frailty is added to the confession of sin¹⁶⁸. However, both ideas are already related in the context of the earlier wisdom tradition, in Job 4,17-21; 14,1-4 and 15,14-16. The only element which is missing in these passages in Job is the term בשר¹⁶⁹, but this term is used in another passage in Job where human frailty is also expressed, in Job 34,14f.: "if he were to... recall his life-giving spirit, all that lives would perish, to the dust would man return." There is a clear reference to this tradition in 1Q/4QInstruction: 4Q416 2 II 2f. (paralleled by 4Q417 1 II 4 and 4Q418 8 1) reads: "If he shuts his hand, then they will be gathered in the spirit of all flesh"¹⁷⁰. Thus, we can see that 1Q/4QInstruction takes up and combines phrases of the earlier wisdom tradition, e. g. in Job. It is, then, only a small step to insert the term בשר into the traditional phrases and to link this term with the expressions on human injustice or sin which occur, e. g., in Job 4,17-21; 14,1-4 and 15,14-16. In 4QMyst^c (4Q301 5 3), then, the term בשר is used within the framework of a "Niedrigkeitsdoxologie". This shows that the sapiential circles responsible for 1Q/4QInstruction and 1Q/4QMysteries actually combined the two traditions.

β) A traditio-historical observation can be added. The earliest example of the negative usage of בשר in 4Q417 1 I 15ff. occurs within the framework of a mythological tradition on upheaval or apostasy in primeval times. In 4Q416 1 12 it is used within an announcement of eschatological judgment and of the final elimination of wickedness. Both passages show that in 1Q/4QInstruction, sapiential tradition is closely linked with apocalyptic elements. In the light of these apocalyptic traditions, the antagonism of the pious and the wicked acquires cosmic and eschatological dimensions. Only on the basis of the connection between traditionally sapiential ideas and cosmic-eschatological traditions, בשר or רוח בשר can be conceived as something hostile to God or, later, as a collective or a cosmic spiritual power.

γ) The mythological tradition adopted in 4Q417 1 I 15ff. on the primeval apostasy seems to be a parallel to the tradition of the fall of the watchers which is basically rooted in Gen 6,1f.4 and then expanded in 1

168. Cf. H.-W. KUHN, *Enderwartung*, p. 27; H. LICHTENBERGER, *Studien zum Menschenbild*, p. 73; J. BECKER, *Heil Gottes*, p. 136. On the Biblical genre "Gerichtsdoxologie", see F. HORST, *Die Doxologien im Amosbuch*; G. v. RAD, *Gerichtsdoxologie*.

169. Other terms are used: The human being is called "born by a woman" (ילוד אשה) Job 14,1; 15,4; there is mention of dust and mud (Job 4,19), of dying (Job 4,19.21), linked with terms of impurity (Job 4,17; 14,4; 15,14) and upheaval (עולה Job 15,16).

170. Translation according to J. STRUGNELL, D. J. HARRINGTON & T. ELGVIN, *Qumran Cave* 4. XXIV, p. 93. Cf. also the parallel in 4Q419 8 ii 7 which is possibly a quotation from 1Q/4QInstruction (thus J. STRUGNELL, D. J. HARRINGTON & T. ELGVIN, *Qumran Cave* 4. XXIV, p. 95).

En 15[171]. Anyhow, it should be noted, that in 1 En 15,4.6.8 there is also a development towards dualistic structures when the contrast between the "spiritual" angels and the "flesh" of the human wives and of the giants is distinctively stressed. One could even suppose that Gen 6,1ff. was the tradition that largely inspired the terminological development. In Gen 6,3 there is a contextual opposition between the divine "spirit" and the human "flesh"[172]. Even though the scriptural passage did not link the notion of "flesh" with sin or upheaval, the context could inspire such a view, because in Gen 6,5 reference is made to the wickedness of all human beings and to all the inclinations and thoughts of the human heart. Therefore, this passage could provide the basis not only for the connection of "flesh" and wickedness, but also for the combination of "flesh" and the "evil inclination". The (earliest) occurence of יצר רע in 4Q417 1 II 12 (formerly 2 II 12) is actually related to Gen 6,5. This might confirm the suggestion that Gen 6,1ff. together with other parallel traditions that are not preserved in the Bible could lead to the terminological developments described above.

b) The Reception in the Texts of the Yaḥad

The pre-Essene sapiential tradition, then, had an impact on the "sectarian writings" of the Essenes. 1Q/4QInstruction is cited in the communal hymns of the *Hodayot*[173], and the term רז נהיה which is so characteristic for 1Q/4QInstruction and 1Q/4QMysteries is taken up once in the final "psalm" in 1QS XI 3. Moreover, the literary genre "Niedrigkeitsdoxologie" which seems to originate in the pre-Essene sapiential tradition, is adopted quite frequently in *Hodayot* and in 1QS XI 9ff.

Given the impact of the pre-Essene sapiential tradition on the texts of the *yaḥad*, especially the communal hymns of the *Hodayot* and the final section of 1QS, we can assume that this is also the traditio-historical route on which the negative usage of the term בשר was passed on to the Essene community.

In the Essene texts, the pre-Essene terminology was adopted and further developed. In the *Hodayot*, we find again the term רוח בשר (1QH[a] IV 37 [= XVII 25 Sukenik] und V 30 [= XIII 13 Sukenik]). From the usage in 1Q/4QInstruction we can see now that the term is not quite as

---

171. The relations between 1Q/4QInstruction and the earlier Enochic tradition deserve serious consideration. Cf., however, the suggestions in T. ELGVIN, *Wisdom in the Yaḥad*, p. 448; and ID., *Early Essene Eschatology*.
172. Interestingly, Gen 6,3 is the only biblical passage where the Targumim interpret "flesh" in terms of sin.
173. Cf. A. LANGE, *Weisheit und Prädestination*, p. 46.

neutral as was often supposed[174], but was used also with a negative connotation. As in the pre-Essene sapiential tradition, "flesh" is now linked with the notion of both the human inability to grasp God's revelation and also human iniquity and sinfulness. In one passage it seems to be viewed even as a misleading power.

The most important difference between the pre-Essene sapiential tradition (and also the *War Rule*) and the Essene texts, such as the *Hodayot* and the final psalm in 1QS, is that in these documents בשר denotes not just people outside the community of the pious or the sinful nations facing final destruction. Indeed the members of the *yaḥad* praying the *Hodayot* are aware now that they are בשר themselves and share the sinful flesh. They are not merely separated from the רוח בשר (4Q418 81 1f.), but they are sinners themselves, and as such they are elect to serve God, to know his will and to keep his commandments. This view is a peculiarity of the Essene documents which is paralleled later in some respect by the Pauline view[175].

The new evidence from the pre-Essene sapiential documents shows that the negative usage of בשר as a term for human sinfulness does not originate in the Qumran sectarian group or the Essene circles but in sapiential circles of the late 3rd or early 2nd century BCE. The religio-historical background of the Essene usage of בשר is the ethical and cosmic-eschatological dualism which was formed within these pre-Essene sapiential circles. Their views were adopted and further developed by members of the Essene community, who also read and esteemed the pre-Essene sapiential texts[176].

c) The Reception outside the Essene Movement

It is, however, highly probable that the ideas of the pre-Essene sapiential tradition were not just adopted by the Essenes. We should rather assume that these texts, like Sirach, Jubilees or the Enochic traditions were read and discussed in wider circles, most probably in Jerusalem, in the context of the *Hakhamim* surrounding the Temple.

A trace of these traditions may be seen in the *Testaments of the Twelve Patriarchs* which generally seem to be a quite important line of

174. Cf. A. E. SEKKI, *The Meaning of* ruaḥ, p. 104, who refers to this view as a *communis opinio*.

175. There are, however, major differences depending on the different views of the Torah and its position (see below and, more extensively, my article: *Paulinische Antithese*, pp. 74f.).

176. There is also evidence for the suggestion that the "Doctrine of the Two Spirits" 1QS III 13 – IV 26 originated in the same pre-Essene sapiential circles; on this, cf. J. FREY, *Dualistic Thought*, pp. 295ff.; A. LANGE, *Weisheit und Prädestination*, pp. 127f.

transmission of dualistic thought. They attest not only the idea of the "Two Ways" (T. Asher 1,3-5), which can be found in the fragmentary sapiential document on the Two Ways (4Q473 1 3)[177], as well as the idea of the "two spirits" of truth and deceit (T. Judah 20,1ff.) resembling the pre-Essene "Doctrine of the Two Spirits" (1QS III 13 – IV 26), but also the notion of the sinful flesh, as shown in T. Judah 19,4:

> The prince of error blinded me, and I was ignorant as a human being, as flesh, corrupt in sins (ὡς σάρξ ἐν ἁμαρτίαις φθαρείς)[178].

Another passage in T. Zebulun 9,7f. reads:

> He does not bring a charge and wickedness against the sons of men, since they are flesh and err in their wicked deeds[179].

Contrary to earlier assumptions, these passages are not influenced by the Essenes, because all peculiarities of community terminology are lacking[180]. Nor do these passages show any clear traces of Christian reworking or glossing. There is nothing in them that could not be explained against the background of Early Jewish thought. Even the observation that the *Testaments of the Twelve Patriarchs* in their present form certainly were collected and reshaped in Christian circles[181] should not lead to the conclusion that they are not basically Jewish[182]. The evidence mentioned above suggests that they attest a wider influence of the sapiential traditions of Palestinian Judaism represented in 1Q/4QInstruction, 1Q/4QMysteries and also the "Doctrine of the Two Spirits".

Another piece of evidence for the wider influence of the pre-Essene view of sinful flesh is found in the *Life of Adam and Eve* 25,3. Here, Eve promises:

---

177. See the edition by T. ELGVIN, *473. 4QThe Two Ways*.
178. Transl. according to H. C. KEE, *Testaments*, p. 800. However, Kee's rendering "as flesh, in my corrupt sins", is incorrect.
179. H. C. KEE, *Testaments*, p. 807, translates according to another textual tradition: "they are flesh and the spirits of deceit lead them astray in all their actions". But cf. J. BECKER, *Testamente*, p. 90, where the shorter reading is chosen.
180. This theory was defended by M. PHILONENKO, *Les interpolations chrétiennes*, and A. DUPONT-SOMMER, *Les écrits esséniens*, pp. 310-318; cf. also A. DUPONT-SOMMER & M. PHILONENKO (eds.), *Ecrits intertestamentaires*, pp. LXXV-LXXVI. Cf., against this assumption, J. BECKER, *Studien zur Entstehungsgeschichte*, pp. 149-152; ID., *Testamente*, pp. 26f.
181. This is conceded also by J. BECKER, *Testamente*, p. 23. The view that the origin of the *Testaments of the Twelve Patriarchs* is generally Christian, was developed by M. DE JONGE, *Testaments*, pp. 117-128. Since then, de Jonge has modified his position several times, cf. especially ID., *Christian Influence*, and ID., *The Main Issues*.
182. On introductory issues, see generally J. BECKER, *Testamente*, pp. 23-27; A.-M. DENIS, *Introduction*, pp. 49ff; A. HULTGÅRD, *L'eschatologie* 2, pp. 214ff., and the balanced discussion in K.-W. NIEBUHR, *Gesetz und Paränese*, pp. 73-86.

Lord, Lord, save me and I will never again turn to the sin of the flesh (καὶ οὐ μὴ ἐπιστρέψω εἰς τὴν ἁμαρτίαν τῆς σαρκός)[183].

Even if the textual history of the Adam literature is quite complicated and the precise age of this passage must remain uncertain, the promise of Eve seems not to be dependent on Christian ideas or even on the Pauline view of sin. Rather it shows that the idea of sinful flesh was present in wider circles of Early Judaism and was not confined to the Essenes or the Qumran sectarian group. It could be translated into Greek terms as well. But even in the *Testaments of the Twelve Patriarchs* which represent a Diaspora setting, the idea is not shaped by the Hellenistic view of flesh as a material substance of minor value but by the Palestinian Jewish dualism as documented in the pre-Essene and Essene documents from the Qumran library.

7. THE SAPIENTIAL TRADITIONS AND THE PAULINE USAGE OF ΣΑΡΞ

Returning to the issue of the religio-historical background of the Pauline usage of σάρξ, especially in the characteristic antithesis of σάρξ and πνεῦμα, I can only comment on some of the most important issues[184].

a) An immediate literary influence of the Palestinian wisdom texts on the Pauline epistles cannot be proved. The problem is, however, a methodological one. Paul obviously adopts sapiential traditions. But it is hard to prove that he used traditions which are not documented in the Biblical wisdom literature or, perhaps in the *Wisdom of Solomon*, but which are peculiar to the tradition of 1Q/4QInstruction or 1Q/4QMysteries.

b) In the pre-Essene sapiential traditions and the Essene texts we can find the most interesting parallels to the Pauline notion of flesh as sinful and disobedient. Taken together, these traditions offer a much closer correlation to the Pauline views than all the parallels from Hellenistic Judaism.

c) 1Q/4QInstruction and 1Q/4QMysteries are not Qumran "sectarian" texts. They cannot be pushed aside, therefore, as products of an esoteric circle to which non-members could not get access. They rather originate from sapiential circles surrounding the Jerusalem Temple, and their ideas were discussed and further developed not only by the Essenes

---

183. Translation according to M. D. JOHNSON, *Life of Adam and Eve*, p. 283, who hints at close parallels in *b. Nid.* 31b and *Gen. Rab.* 20,7. On this text see the contribution by J. DOCHHORN in this volume.

184. For a more detailed discussion, cf. my article: J. FREY, *Paulinische Antithese*.

but also among the other groups of contemporary Judaism, especially the wise men (חכמים) in Jerusalem. There, in connection with the Temple, the transmission of Wisdom had an institutional framework, and it is likely that the early Pharisaic sages (who were also called חכמים[185]) knew and discussed these ideas as well. Their transmission is also documented in Greek by the *Testaments of the Twelve Patriarchs* and, perhaps, by the *Life of Adam and Eve*.

d) It is, therefore, quite probable that Paul, when he was a Pharisaic student in Jerusalem[186], also came across sapiential traditions such as 1Q/4QInstruction or 1Q/4QMysteries. In any case, an acquaintance with the traditions represented by these sapiential documents is more probable than a knowledge of Essene "sectarian" documents such as the *Hodayot* or the *Rule of the Community*.

e) Whatever the means by which Paul came across these traditions, semantically his view of σάρξ as a power hostile to God that rules and misleads human beings cannot be derived from Hellenistic ontology of the earthly and the spiritual sphere. It is much closer to the type of dualism of the Palestinian Jewish sapiential tradition, represented in works such as 1Q/4QInstruction or 1Q/4QMysteries and developed further in the Essene texts. Only in this tradition flesh is linked directly with sin and iniquity and viewed as a ruling and misleading power in a framework of predestinational thought. These are exactly the elements in which the Pauline usage of σάρξ goes beyond the Biblical usage of בשר.

f) Against the background of these parallels, we can assume that the apostle knew about the idea of sinful flesh from his Jewish background. Originally, this idea is not Christian, but was shaped in advance by traditions of contemporary Judaism which can be determined now with the publication of the non-Essene sapiential documents from Qumran Cave 4.

g) There is no fixed antithesis between "flesh" and "spirit" in early Jewish thought, neither in the *Wisdom of Solomon* nor in the works of Philo nor in Qumran. Some passages in the *Hodayot* and also the passage in 4Q417 2 I 15ff. attest a contextual opposition between בשר and רוח, but it is not yet fixed semantically. However, if Paul knew about the

---

185. Cf. R. MEYER, Φαρισαῖος, pp. 20-22.

186. The wide-spread scepticism against this information which is provided only by Luke (Acts 22,3; 26,4f.) seems unjustified, cf. already G. BORNKAMM, *Paulus*, p. 168, and more recently M. HENGEL, *The pre-Christian Paul*, pp. 18ff., and R. RIESNER, *Die Frühzeit des Apostels Paulus*, pp. 6-26. Apart from the notes on his provenance from Tarsus and his studies in Jerusalem there is a close correspondence between the Pauline and the Lucan testimony on Paul's religious origins. M. HENGEL correctly states that before 70 CE Jerusalem "was the only proper place for *strict* Jews – and Paul came from a strict Jewish family and was himself one – to study the Torah" (*The pre-Christian Paul*, p. 27).

negative usage of בשר or σάρξ from the Jewish tradition, he could, then, form such an opposition drawing on his own experience of the life-giving spirit in his vision near Damascus.

h) Paul's use of these terms is deeply rooted in Jewish tradition, or more precisely: in Palestinian Jewish tradition. The opposition of flesh against the spirit is not formed through an ontological distance between the created and the spiritual world but by the disobedience of humanity against God and his word. Human beings are flesh as a whole, not only in their material or sexual dimension, and this statement is not derogatory of their nature as created beings, but a verdict on their general direction of existence. Quite similarly, Paul always sees the human being as a whole. A human being wholly flesh and dominated by sin, if it is not dead to and directed by the spirit (Rom 7)[187].

i) Of course, there are major differences between the Jewish traditions and Paul, mainly in respect of the position towards the law. Whereas in Qumran the pious are elect to obey the Torah even more accurately, for Paul the call for circumcision in the Galatian communities is an attempt to be justified still according to the flesh (Gal 3,3). The reason is given in Gal 5,19 where Paul states that those who are "in Christ" have "crucified" their flesh and, consequently died to the law, so that they are no longer "under the law" (ὑπὸ νόμου). But even in these passages which seem to be so different from all kinds of "mainstream Judaism", Paul's usage of σάρξ as a striving opposed to God's will and to his salvific acts proves to be deeply rooted in the Palestinian Jewish tradition.

Ludwig-Maximilians-Universität   Jörg FREY
Institut für Neutestamentliche Theologie
Schellingstr. 3/V VG
D-80799 München
Deutschland

---

187. Cf. E. KÄSEMANN, *Zur paulinischen Anthropologie*, pp. 50-52.

WISDOM AS COGNITION
CREATING THE OTHERS IN THE BOOK OF MYSTERIES AND 1 COR 1-2

By publishing three important volumes on Christian and Jewish self-definition Sanders et al. have made a valuable contribution to our understanding of the self-knowledge of different religious groups and philosophical and medical schools in the Jewish and Greco-Roman culture of the Second Temple period[1]. The contributions attempt to describe the manner in which a given group defined itself. In continuation of the ideas of this impressive project the aim of this paper is to discuss two aspects of self-definition which are frequently neglected. The first pertains to the creation of others while the second relates to the cognitive dimensions of religious texts.

The paper has six sections. The first presents a brief theoretical introduction to the subject which in the second part is illustrated by a preliminary reading of Book of Mysteries and 1 Cor 1-2. The third section discusses briefly the reasons for comparing these very texts. Section four develops a theory of alterity which in the final sections is applied to the exegesis of the two texts.

An inherent part of self-definition involves the construction of an other. In order to understand one-self it is necessary to generate ideas of an other in relation to whom one's own identity can be defined. As Elizabeth Castelli has noted difference is necessary in order to define the same, and others are necessary in order to define the self[2]. Any ideology – religion included – is involved in such a hermeneutic double-movement. By constructing a trajectory of difference a self-identity is created which simultaneously breathes from the definition of the other. This means that to define itself a community has to engage in the construction of the others. Focusing on this aspect one approaches the cognitive roots of any religious discourse, because all religious discourses are spontaneously active constructors of religion.

By entitling this contribution *Wisdom as Cognition* I intend to emphasise a complementary aspect of religious texts of particular pertinence to the discussion of wisdom-texts. Religion may be defined in numerous

---

1. SANDERS (ed.), *Self-Definition*; SANDERS, BAUMGARTEN and MENDELSOHN (eds.), *Self-Definition* II; MEYER and SANDERS (eds.), *Self-Definition* III.
2. CASTELLI, *Imitating Paul*, p. 115.

ways but it is first and foremost constituted by a cognitive interpretative activity. It represents a particular frame of interpretation that constitutes and separates a given religion from other religions, ideologies, etc. Religion is a way of classifying the empirical world from the perspective of an extra-mundane world in which non-human actors play the decisive role. Like other taxonomies religious ones constitute a system through which the entire set of indiscriminate data and innumerable experiences of the world are organised in such a form that they become comprehensible and provide a basis for acting. The adherents of a given religion can not separate themselves from their constructed system, however, because they are objects as well as subjects of cognition. They are elements of the system because they themselves are categorised by their own taxonomies.

Bruce Lincoln has emphasised this aspect by claiming that "taxonomy is thus not only a means for organizing information, but also – as it comes to organize the organizers – an instrument for the classification and manipulation of society, something that is particularly facilitated by the fashion in which taxonomic trees and binary oppositions can conveniently recode social hierarchies..."[3]. By means of a number of cognitive structures and categories of meaning a semantic universe is developed assigning meaning to the different domains of religion: the spatial (heaven/earth); the temporal (this age/the age to come); the cognitive (the wise/the ignorant); the social-ethical (the righteous/the unrighteous) etc. Any semantic universe is constituted by a certain perception of the world and of human experience, and it is organised by a particular understanding of what is real and illusory, true and false, good and bad[4]. The semantic universe or world view provides meaning to the adherents of a given religion by establishing the veridictory (real vs. illusory) and the thymic (good vs. bad) categories by which they can familiarise themselves with the world.

According to Neil J. Smelser the world view may be seen as "... a system of patterned values, meanings and beliefs that give cognitive structure to the world, provide a basis for co-ordinating and controlling human interactions, and constitute a link as the system is transmitted from one generation to the next"[5]. A religious world view separates it-

3. LINCOLN, *Discourse*, p. 137.
4. Cf. PATTE, *Biblical Texts*, pp. 78f.
5. SMELSER, *Culture*, p. 11. SMELSER's definition is a definition of culture only. It does not tell against the approach taken in this article, however, as SMELSER is developing his definition by elaborating on older definitions of Clifford GEERTZ, Peter BERGER and Thomas LUCKMANN. Since they share an understanding of religion as a cultural entity, it is legitimate to extend SMELSER's definition to include religion, too. See GEERTZ, *Religion*, pp. 1-46; BERGER and LUCKMANN, *Construction*.

self from other cultural entities by including non-human actors and by alleging an extra-mundane world that decisively affects the order of the empirical world[6].

The aim of this contribution is to illuminate the two texts mentioned from this perspective. Revealed wisdom constitutes a particular act of cognition in both texts. Even though a cognitive aspect is vital to and an inherent part of any religious discourse it specifically distinguishes apocalyptic ones[7]. No matter how apocalyptic may be defined as an *etic* category[8], texts belonging to this line of thought are first and foremost characterised by their emphasis on a specific mode of transcendent knowledge different from the one contained in competing groups or the parent body. By accentuating the esoteric nature of the revealed knowledge the apocalyptic text – explicitly or implicitly – relegates the wisdom of other religious groups to the domain of the ordinary[9]. Revealed wisdom becomes the corner stone of a particular community united by a common frame of interpretation. The revealed wisdom is the criterion for inclusion in and exclusion from the community of the saved. By receiving the πνεῦμα of God (1 Cor 1-2) or the mysteries of God (Book of Mysteries) the faithful is – through the revelatory mediation of wisdom – granted a transcending perception. This very skill ensures that the believer is cognitively placed in the heavenly, spiritual world.

Book of Mysteries and 1 Cor 1-2: A Preliminary Reading

The opening of the preserved parts of 1Q27 characterises the ignorant as those who do not know of the future mystery or of ancient matters. They are ignorant of what is going to happen to them, and they will not save their souls from the future mystery. The wise on the contrary are summoned to take notice of the sign that is to come (1Q27 1 i 3-5; parallel 4Q300 3). In 4Q301 1, 1-2 God is speaking to the wise: "I will speak my mind and according to your kinds I will apportion my words to you. A parable and a riddle, and those who search the roots of understanding with those who hold fast to the wondrous mysteries".

---

6. Cf. PENNER, *Impasse*, p. 7.
7. Cf. GRUENWALD, *Mysticism*, pp. 14f.
8. For the problems of definition pertaining to the category of apocalyptic, see HELLHOLM (ed.), *Apocalypticism*, and the often cited definition by J. COLLINS, *Apocalypse*, p. 9; further developed and revised in J. COLLINS and J. CHARLESWORTH (eds.), *Mysteries*, p. 19.
9. See THOMPSON, *Location*, p. 2621: "The revealed knowledge about the world that comes from apocalyptic transcendence does not derive from public institutions, and it orients its knowers differently from public knowledge. The world it constructs, the orientation to that world, and the values shared by means of the revealed knowledge of an apocalypse create an alternative to those created by public knowledge".

Although fragmentarily preserved only, the text represents a common theme that pervades the two fragments. Because of God's revelation of wisdom to his chosen ones they are able to orientate themselves in the world and to fulfil his justice: "With great intelligence He opened our ears, so that we may hear" (4Q299 8, 6). Because of the fragmentary nature it is difficult to form an unambiguous understanding of the aim of the text. The emphasis given to the aspect of justice, however, beyond doubt demonstrates that the aim is to increase justice among its ideal readers: "There is nothing worse for a human being than evil, and nothing more exalted than righteousness" (4Q300 7, 1). When the sign promised to the wise by the opening of 1Q27 1 i 4 occurs "evil will disappear in front of justice as darkness disappears in front of light". "Justice will be revealed like a sun which regulates the world" (1Q27 1 i 6).

This brief survey suggests an intimate relation between a particular frame of interpretation and a corresponding set of acts within an ethical domain. By their ability to distinguish between falsehood and truth (the veridictory category) the wise are simultaneously capable of differentiating between good and evil (the thymic category), and, therefore, in a position to conduct their life in correspondence with the revelation of God. In this way Book of Mysteries is creating its own system of patterned values, meanings and beliefs that gives cognitive structure to the world and provides a basis for orientation and acting in the world.

1 Cor 1-2 similarly attributes a strong emphasis to a cognitive skill available to a select group of people only. This group has been endowed with a particular ability to interpret the hidden wisdom of God who simultaneously and continuously grants the cognitive skill to the believers. In the mediation of the heavenly world by the heavenly spirit the believer is cognitively related to the otherwise hidden or inaccessible heavenly world: "In the same way no one knows the thoughts of God except the Spirit of God. We have not received the spirit of the world but the Spirit who is from God, that we may understand what God has freely given us" (1 Cor 2, 11b-12). Through the revelatory mediation by the heavenly spirit of a transcending perception the believer is cognitively and hermeneutically placed in a transcendent reality, i.e. the heavenly world. This particular capability given to the believer by the spirit is constituted by a transcending rationality contrary to the rationality of this world. The believer is given a cognitive competence by means of which he is able to transcend the worldly perception: "He is a spiritual man that makes judgements about all things, but he himself is not subject to any man's judgement" (1 Cor 2, 15). This cognitive competence is so firmly anchored in the heavenly world that it can be described as an

attitude of mind shared with Christ: "For who has known the mind of the Lord that he may instruct him? But we have the mind of Christ" (1 Cor 2, 16).

Similar to the Book of Mysteries 1 Cor 1-2 is deeply engaged in creating a system of patterned values, meanings and beliefs that give cognitive structure to the world. This particular system of meaning by which the Corinthian Christians are encouraged to share the same attitude of mind (cf. 1 Cor 1, 10) provides the foundation for the exhortations in the following sections of the letter. The meanings and beliefs constitute the cognitive structures that simultaneously provide a basis for the description of how to orientate oneself and how to act in the world. They undergird the system of meaning by imbuing it with a cosmic structure that can be used and transferred into other religious domains as well: social, ethical, etc.

COMPARING BOOK OF MYSTERIES WITH 1 COR 1-2

By comparing Book of Mysteries with 1 Cor 1-2 I do not intend to suggest any historical-genealogical relationship between the two texts or the wisdom traditions expressed. The comparison is intriguing and obvious because the two texts display a number of structural similarities and resemblances regarding content[10]. In validating their claims to truth they both appeal to divine wisdom. The resemblance, however, is not limited to one motif only. In their discursive strategy both texts utilise a cluster of motifs and interrelated concepts common to many Jewish texts of the Hellenistic period. At a certain level of generalisation they may be seen as two different manifestations of what Martin Hengel has called a religious *koine* common to the Mediterranean world of antiquity[11]. Both mirror a taxonomic enterprise by reconfiguring the religious and cultural values of their age into their world view. They reflect a rhetorical game of redefining the marks of social, religious and cultural identity. In this sense both texts voice a process of social dissociation, reorganisation and ideological expropriation of the much-coveted traditions of their time. They express themselves as ideological entities promulgating a specific world view that involves extraordinary legitimation and war-

---

10. Since both texts reflect common structures of meaning characteristic of apocalyptic sapiential Jewish strains of thought of the Second Temple Period a *tertium comparationis* exists that makes the danger of *parallelomania* insignificant, see SANDMEL, *Parallelomania*, pp. 1-12.

11. HENGEL, *Judaica*, pp. 80, 82, 165, 275, 280.

rant for their contested structures of values and their contested system of beliefs and codes of behaviour. They are both utilising a strategy of polarisation to have their world view accepted. Within the sub-category of the religious and cultural *koine* that encompasses both texts cognition serves as the most important taxonomiser. Cognition establishes the basis for a differentiation of a given class into two sub-classes: those who share the revelation of the wisdom of God and those who do not. This cognitive domain is complemented by an ethical: the righteous and the unrighteous.

By the construction of a self-identity the others are relegated to the margins of religion being either religiously deviant or inferior. Simultaneously the in-group of both texts is placed in an authoritative superior position undergirded by the use of wisdom language and categories. According to this mode of organising the world conceptually and socially, only two options exist: inclusion or exclusion. Since both texts are directed towards the in-group, i.e. those who have a share in the hidden perception of God, they are mostly concerned with strengthening the cognitive categories of the adherents to ensure that they will remain within the interpretative frame of the text. The texts, indeed, may be seen as a conscious effort to delineate and to transfer a shared attitude of mind onto the readers.

Before introducing a theory of alterity it is important to stress that I do not try to provide a historical reconstruction of the others as characterised by the two texts. My analysis focuses on the discursive strategy of the single text. By emphasising the rhetoric of power by which the two texts create the others I intend to bracket the question of the 'real' opponents against whom the texts are polemising.

CREATING THE OTHERS

Robert Redfield has argued that the world view of any people essentially consists of two pairs of binary contrasts: man/not-man and we/they. Not surprisingly he also acknowledges that the contrasts are frequently correlated. We are men, and the others are not-men[12]. His claim is remarkably similar to the one found in Rodney Needham's book *Primordial Characters*. Needham notes that "it is a frequent report from different parts of the world that tribes call themselves alone by the arrogant title 'man', and that they refer to their neighboring peoples as mon-

---

12. REDFIELD, *World View*, p. 92.

keys or crocodiles or malign spirits"[13]. Obviously, one could be tempted to argue that this is a mere game of slander. Through the declaration of one's own authoritative and superior position one is separated from the surrounding peoples. The emphasis on the higher ethical status of one's own actions relegates the actions of the others to the margins of humanity. An aspect of 'mud-slinging' is evidently involved in the creation of the others, but other aspects manifest themselves, too. The necessity to affirm a self-identity and to establish boundaries to protect the identity is a social fact shared by all cultural entities, religious ones included[14]. James Boon has correctly noted that "any culture requires its actors to counterdistinguish themselves, irreducibly segmented from others: other worlds (divine, extraterrestrial), other eras (past idylls, future utopias), other languages, other cultures... Every discourse, like every culture, inclines toward what it is not, toward an implicit negativity"[15].

In order to develop one's own identity and to attain an idea of a self different from other selves it is crucial to categorise the others into classes different from one's own[16]. The construction of others is an inherent strategy of self-definition by which those who create or manipulate definitions of the other simultaneously invent, or re-invent, their own social group and its cultural identity. To speak of the other necessarily implies at least two terms, *a* and *b*, being different from each other. The two elements, however, become interesting only when they are integrated into the same system. Then a rhetoric of otherness may be developed by means of points of differentiation that are reflected upon and further expanded[17]. Just as informative as the naming of the others is

---

13. NEEDHAM, *Characters*, p. 5.
14. This is acutely noted by LIPPMANN, *Opinion*, pp. 63f.: "A pattern of stereotypes is not neutral. It is not merely a way of substituting order for the great blooming, buzzing confusion of reality. It is not merely a short cut. It is all these things and something more. It is the guarantee of our self-respect; it is the projection upon the world of our own sense of our own value, our own position and our own right. *The stereotypes are, therefore, highly charged with the feelings that are attached to them. They are the fortress of our tradition, and behind its defenses we can continue to feel ourselves safe in the position we occupy*" (my emphasis).
15. BOON, *Tribes*, p. 232.
16. LIPPMANN, *Opinion*, p. 83: "Thus we gradually paint portraits of each other. For the opponent presents himself as the man who says, evil be thou my good. He is an annoyance who does not fit into the scheme of things. Nevertheless he interferes. And since that scheme is based in our minds on incontrovertible facts fortified by irresistible logic, some place has to be found for him in the scheme".
17. Cf. LYOTARD referring to the work of SAUSSURE, *Discours*, p. 142: "La différence, écrit le commentateur, en soi, est bien un caractère négatif: si *a* est différent de *b*, cela revient simplement à dire que *a* n'est pas *b*, quel que soit le degré de non-coïncidence; mais dès l'instant qu'un rapport existe par ailleurs entre *a* et *b*, ils sont membres d'un même système, et la différence devient opposition".

for the manner in which a given religion or culture understands the others, just as significant is the naming as a source for the manner in which the religion or culture in question understands itself. In fact most labels adopted to express otherness – economic, generic, ethnic, religious, etc. – tell us far more about the people who use and deploy them than about the people they purport to describe. The different codes applied by a religion in describing the others are only plausible and powerful to the adherents if they have a reasonable grounding in their self-understanding. If the others are described as crocodiles or malign spirits the naming party presumably has a world view in which these taxa play a vital role. The symbols chosen by a particular culture or religion in order to express otherness are not arbitrary. To establish the decisive difference by which disparity is constructed the applied symbols must have a foundation in the self-understanding of the naming community. It is the ideas and sense of distinctiveness of the naming community that determine the choice of symbols. It is, after all, a person or a group of persons belonging to group *a* that tells other members of group *a* about *b*. The plausibility and power of the symbol chosen depends on its impact within the social-cultural foundation of the naming society. Terms like idol-worshippers or magicians have linguistic power only if they cover a social domain which the adherents of the religion in question grasp as significant in their construction of reality. William Scott Green has pointed to this fact: "A society does not simply discover its others, it fabricates them by selecting, isolating, and emphasizing an aspect of another people's life and making it symbolize their difference. To evoke the significant disparity of which otherness is composed, the symbol must correspond powerfully to the naming society's sense of its own distinctiveness"[18]. This points to another important aspect of the construction of the others. Otherness is not an absolute state of being, but a relative category exposed to continuous change. What in one case may be judged as other, is perhaps in another situation alike and therefore not other[19]. Just as sameness changes, so does otherness.

Scott Green has also emphasised that the creation of others reflects an exercise in caricature: "The neighboring peoples, after all, are not really crocodiles (any more than the ones who call them that are really "man"), but some trait of their collective life makes the label fitting and plausible to those who invent it"[20]. Green has further elucidated the manner in which the creation of the others is rhetorically constructed.

18. GREEN, *Otherness*, p. 50.
19. Cf. SMITH, *Difference*, p. 46.
20. GREEN, *Otherness*, p. 50.

The construction involves a double process consisting of an act of appropriation and a feat of exaggeration. The others do not construct themselves as others. They do not call themselves magicians or idol-worshippers. But they are perceived in this manner by the taxonomising society. The taxonomic enterprise by which otherness is constructed implies a double metonymy and a double distortion. First, in the process of being defined as other a part of the cultural or religious entity in question is confused with the entity in total. Second and simultaneously, an aspect of the taxonomisers is identified with the taxonomising party in total. A part of the others may be not-men, and, therefore, all the others are not-men. An aspect of the taxonomisers is men, and, therefore, all the taxonomisers are men. Each entity is construed in terms of the other.

In this manner the creation of others is not only a matter of keeping the others – the idol-worshippers and the magicians – at a distance. It is not only a matter of affirming one's own position and drawing boundaries to exclude the others and to keep them at a distance. By projecting a troublesome aspect of one-self onto the others this aspect is externalised making it possible to live with this very aspect[21]. In this sense the creation of others is also a way of managing own internal problems. Scott Green states that the correspondences between us and the others "can reshape the naming society's picture of itself, expose its points of vulnerability, and spark in it awareness of, or reflection about, the possibility or the reality of otherness within. The boastful proposition 'we are men and they are crocodiles' implies that 'we were, or could have been, or might yet be crocodiles too'"[22]. This is a phenomenon particularly pertinent to religious texts aimed at strengthening the identity of the in-group. Applying a strategy of polarisation the coherence of the internal world view is enhanced. This leads to a final aspect of a theory of alterity which is of the utmost interest for the texts under discussion.

---

21. This aspect particularly comes to the fore in the New Testament catalogues of vices. By means of symbolic generalisation the stereotype repetition of vices – always hyperbolically expressed – is projected onto the pagan world in order to maintain the purity and integrity of the Christian in-group. By the extension of internal peccadillos to the alleged sins of the external pagan world the aim is to overcome the internal problems. The exaggeration of the projection holds the readers to what they have already been granted and, thus to what they have obliged to live in accordance to, cf. 1 Cor 6, 9-11. Cf. LIPPMANN, *Opinions*, p. 78: "For when a system of stereotypes is well fixed, our attention is called to those facts which support it, and diverted from those which contradict".

22. GREEN, *Otherness*, p. 50. Cf. BOON, *Tribes*, p. 114: "Moreover, cultures, in positing notions of "other" as alternatives to themselves, motivate members of society both to maintain and to question their own social mechanisms. The conditions that produce either social maintenance or social change can be specified for particular instances but never for cultures as a whole, because it is in the nature of culture to be able to recondition the conditions. If this were not so, *we* could never identify *their* culture in the first place".

As suggested above otherness is a relative and not an absolute category, because difference is rarely a neutral class. Most often it is a matter in which one has a particular interest or something is at stake. Difference is a subject of interaction. For this reason the distant other is merely other, whereas the proximate other is the problematic other. Jonathan Z. Smith has pointed to the importance of this aspect in claiming that:

> While the 'other' may be perceived as being either LIKE-US or NOT-LIKE-US, he is, in fact, most problematic when he is TOO-MUCH-LIKE-US, or when he claims to BE-US. It is here that the real urgency of a 'theory of the other' emerges. This urgency is called forth not by the requirement to place the 'other', but rather to situate ourselves. It is here to invoke the language of a theory of ritual, that we are not so much concerned with the drama of 'expulsion', but with the more mundane and persistent process of 'micro-adjustment.' This is not a matter of the 'far,' but, preeminently, of the 'near'. The problem is not alterity, but similarity—at times, even identity. A 'theory of the other' is but another way of phrasing a 'theory of the self'[23].

By adopting the much-coveted codes of their time in order to have their world-view accepted Book of Mysteries and 1 Cor 1-2 expropriate the religious traditions from the parent body and the neighbouring religious movements. By their claim that they reflect the true revelation of God the two texts obviously imply a judgement concerning the obsolescence or even termination of previously valid norms and beliefs. They are expropriating the traditions of the parent body and adopting its marks of identity with the claim in mind that it has now come to an end. The use of this strategy indicates that the new religious community understands itself to be the true manifestation of that which the parent body was intended to be. The true embodiment of the revelation of God is not surprisingly the one voiced by the texts in question. One final point needs to be underlined before the textual analyses. Although slander may be used quite consciously as a rhetorical device by means of which chosen opponents can be denigrated[24], the creation of others is an unconscious ontological reality of human existence. As a rhetorical strategy slander may be used in the context of *pathos* to arouse the audience's feelings of disgust towards any selected opponents of the author or speaker in question. Thus, slander is an explicit and conscious strategy frequently used in rhetorics of otherness. The creation of others, however, takes place at a more basic level of human existence. The need to establish a 'group of we' different from a 'group of they' is intrinsic

---

23. SMITH, *Difference*, p. 47.
24. Telling examples are found in JOHNSON, *Slander*, pp. 419-441.

to cultural and social life. By means of such basic categorisations a foundation of meaning is developed which is fundamental for human thinking and acting. Neither Paul nor the author/authors of Book of Mysteries composed their texts with the conscious awareness of adopting a rhetoric of otherness.

Creating the Others in Book of Mysteries

Of the four preserved manuscripts of Book of Mysteries (1Q27; 4Q299-4Q301)[25] 1Q27 1 i includes text elements preserved in both 4Q299 and 4Q300. On the basis of 4Q300 frg. 3 it is, therefore, possible to reconstruct the lines preceding the preserved part of col. 1 in 1Q27. By applying a strategy of polarisation the author of Book of Mysteries portrays an eschatological scenario. The first part of the text provides the reason why the group accused is void of excuse. They can be held responsible for their actions since they have been granted the ability to discern between good and evil, truth and falsehood. Because of the wisdom they were given they were in a cognitive position in which they could have understood the mysteries of transgression (רזי פשע). But they knew neither the mystery of that which was coming into being (רז נהיה) nor did they know ancient matters. The רז נהיה, which is the basis for the designation of the text as Book of Mysteries, is apparently connected to the eschaton. It is used to designate the pre-existent order of the world that shall be realised in the eschaton[26]. It includes a body of teaching involving creation, ethical activity and eschatology[27]. Not grasping the significance of past events the members of this group obviously do not know what will befall them in the future. They are a group of people who will perish: "they will not save their lives from the mystery that is in the process of coming into being" (line 4). In line 5 the eschatological

---

25. In a number of publications SCHIFFMAN (*Reclaiming the Dead Sea Scrolls*, p. 206; *4QMysteries*ᵃ, p. 207; *4QMysteries*ᵇ, p. 205; *4QMysteries*, p. 199; *Mysteries*, pp. 31, 113) has argued that the fragments constituting 4Q301 do not belong to Book of Mysteries but to another composition which is related to the Hekhalot literature. Whereas there are a number of textual overlaps between 1Q27 and 4Q299-300 no overlaps exist between 4Q301 and the remaining fragments. A number of similarities between 4Q301 and the remaining fragments, however, concerning rare words and phrases render a belonging of 4Q301 to Book of Mysteries most probable, see LANGE, *Physiognomie oder Gotteslob*, p. 283. For this reason most commentators and translators have considered 4Q301 to be part of Book of Mysteries. See for instance WACHOLDER and ABEGG, *Preliminary Edition*, pp. 35-37.

26. Cf. LANGE, *Weisheit und Prädestination*, p. 99, and ELGVIN, *Mystery*, p. 150. I would stress, however, that ELGVIN's use of 'salvation history' – although in quotation marks – is misleading because of its connotations in contemporary theology.

27. Cf. HARRINGTON, *Wisdom Texts from Qumran*, p. 83.

prophecy regarding this group of people is sharply contrasted to another group of people.

The group now introduced possesses the adequate knowledge of the mystery of God. They are at least cognitively prepared for the visitation of God. They have the necessary skills making them capable of interpreting the sign that the end of days is dawning. To them a sign shall be given that the mystery of God is taking place. Lines 5-7 describe the signs by which the time of realisation of the eschatological prophecy in lines 3-4 can be identified: "the begotten of iniquity (מולדי עולה) will be delivered up, and wickedness will disappear before justice. Wickedness shall disappear forever in the same way as smoke disappears". Contrary to the present state justice shall then prevail like the sun regulates the world.

An interpretative crux appears in line 7. It is said that all the adherents of the wondrous mysteries (תומכי רזי פ[לא]) will perish. As the term mystery otherwise plays an important and positive role in Book of Mysteries the use in 1Q27 1 i 7 is enigmatic to say the least. For this reason a number of scholars have tried to evade the problem. Lawrence Schiffman for instance in his edition simply states that this designation is in contradiction with the context. He, therefore, proposes to emend the פלא and to substitute it by בליעל or some other synonym, thus translating the text: "And all the adherents of the mysteries of [Belial] will be no more"[28]. Similar solutions characterise the different translations. The תומכי רזי פלא is understood by many as an euphemism rendering either the "mysteries of sin"[29], "those who hold the marvellous mysteries (unjustly)"[30], or "those who curb the wonderful mysteries"[31].

A subtle solution has been proposed by Armin Lange who interprets the phrase in the context of the traditions of fallen angels in the Enoch literature. He argues that the תומכי רזי פלא "wohl alle jene innerhalb und außerhalb Israels bezeichnen, die ein Wissen um die der Welt zugrundeliegende kosmische Ordnung oder Teile dieser Ordnung mit Hilfe von Astrologie, Magie und Mantik, eben mit dem von den gefallenen Engeln den Menschen vermittelten Wissen und den dazugehörigen Fähigkeiten zu erlangen suchen oder erlangt haben"[32].

A parallel may be found in 4Q301 1, 2 which can be restored on the basis of the two seriously damaged fragments 4Q299 40, 2 and 4Q300 8,

---

28. SCHIFFMAN, *Mysteries*, pp. 36f., 106.
29. VERMES, *Dead Sea Scrolls*, p. 239.
30. DUPONT-SOMMER, *Essene Writings*, p. 327.
31. GARCÍA MARTÍNEZ, *Dead Sea Scrolls Translated*, p. 399.
32. LANGE, *Weisheit und Prädestination*, p. 119, see also p. 102.

5: "A parable and a riddle, and those who search the roots of understanding with those who hold fast to the wondrous mysteries"[33]. Apparently the true wisdom of God appears as a parable and a riddle to those who do not have the cognitive skills of interpreting it. Although they seek to grasp the roots of understanding (בשורשי בינה) they are doing it in an illegitimate way. Although only fragmentarily preserved it is obvious from the fragment that this group of people is strongly contrasted with the group to whom the introductory hortatory is directed: "I will speak my mind and according to your kinds I will apportion my words to you" (4Q301 1, 1). The world is divided into two groups: those who possess wisdom and those who do not. In 4Q299 6 ii 4 it is said that it is "hidden from all who hold fast to (נסתרה מכול תומכי)". The feminine form may suggest that it is wisdom or understanding which has been hidden from this group of people. Because of the fragmentary state of the texts it is impossible to be more precise in specifying the phrase תומכי רזי פלא. What can be said with certainty, however, is that תומכי in the context of 1Q27 1 i 7 designates a distinct group of people who are illegitimately trying to acquire a share in the wisdom of God. The author utilises a strategy of polarisation thus strengthening the identity of the in-group: the sense of being a we sharing a common interpretative frame in contrast to the others. Constitutive of this frame is the fact that the adherents have been granted access to the mysteries of God by being able to interpret the eschatological signs at the end of days. As suggested above the need to create others is not only a matter of self-affirmation and boundary drawing. It is also a means by which a community comes to reflect on its own internal problems, comes to cope with internal and, therefore, proximate otherness. The boastful proposition "we have received the divine wisdom of God and they are unrighteous" implies that "we were, or could have been, and perhaps even more important might yet be sinners, too".

By means of several rhetorical questions the last part of 1Q27 1 i intends to demonstrate the trustworthiness of the eschatological prophecies. They will eventually come true. As a consolation to the adherents of wisdom in their present state they are promised that in the end knowledge will pervade the world, and folly will come to an end. As a reliable sign that the end of days is imminent the adherents are asked to look for

---

33. LANGE, *Weisheit und Prädestination*, p. 101 has argued that because תומכי in Book of Mysteries "eine feststehende Bezeichnung einer Gruppe darstellt, darf aber angenommen werden, daß auch hier ein רזי bzw. רזים auf das תומכי gefolgt ist". If this is the case 4Q299 2 ii 9ff. becomes difficult to interpret. The exhortation in line 9 שמעו תומכי opens a hortatory speech addressed to the righteous to hold fast to justice.

the hypocrisy of the nations (lines 9-11). The eschatological scenario described in the first lines will occur when the hypocrisy of the nations becomes manifest. The nations pretend to hate iniquity but they do none the less practise it. Although they all object to oppression they do steal from other nations. Why the hypocrisy of the nations plays this important role in the eschatological scenario is uncertain. The code adopted is obviously informative for the social setting of the text but the fragmentary survival means that it remains a conundrum.

4Q299 2 ii is also marked by a strong polarisation between in-group and out-group. The passage begins with a number of rhetorical questions typical of sapiential literature. Apparently the passage is concerned with somebody who has a share in wisdom but acts contrary to his knowledge. This is the reason for the claim in line 3 that "every action of the righteous is impure". His wisdom, therefore, is likened to the "wisdom of evil cunning and the devices of Belial" (line 5). "He has violated the command of his Creator, for which reason his name shall be erased from the mouth of every" (line 8). Contrary to this type of person the adherents are summoned to hold fast to wisdom. In a hymnal praise the Lord is characterised as the one who "preordains every plan, and causes everything that comes into being" (line 11). He is qualified as eternal as "He is from before eternity and His name is the Lord for eternity". The qualities of God are mirrored anthropologically in his election of the adherents. A plan exists determining the house of the children which He opened before them (מחשבת בית מולדים פתח לפניהם) (line 13). He has tested their hearts and caused them to inherit (line 14). By claiming a moral superiority of the adherents compared to the outsiders a strong sense of an in-group is developed. The claim is substantiated by the concept of the predestination of the adherents, cf. 4Q301 frg. 3 lines 6-7: "And God is glorified by his holy people, He is exalted for his chosen ones".

The last fragment to be discussed from Book of Mysteries is 4Q300 1 ii. The text includes a polemic directed towards a group of people designated as wizards skilled in iniquity (החרטמים מלמדי פשע). They are described as uttering the parable and declaring the riddle before it is spoken. They are exemplifying folly, because the seal of the vision has been sealed for them, and they have neither considered the eternal mysteries, nor have they come to understand wisdom (line 2). The magicians have not considered the root of wisdom (בשורש חוכמה), and even if they open the vision the mysteries of God will remain hidden to them. Their self-acclaimed wisdom is null. Because of the fragmentary nature it remains unclear who the magicians are. Possibly it is a group of people applying mantic devices held to be illegitimate by the author of Book of Mysteries, or the term simply constitutes a pejorative category designated to externalise a particular group belonging to the same sapiential circles as Book of Mysteries. For this reason the magicians may be dangerous because they belong to a proximate group of people which is too much like the one relying on Book of Mysteries. So much can be seen from the text, however, that the group designated as magicians is in some way making a claim on the same truth as Book of Mysteries. Whether the magicians pertain to internal or external problems in the social setting of Book of Mysteries the author by way of designating them as cognitively unskilled makes a strong claim on behalf of his own world view. What the magicians are believing and practising is false and contrary to the truth revealed in the mystery of God included and explained in Book of Mysteries. In this manner Book of Mysteries is involved in the construction of power relations by means of which it is making claims to an all-encompassing and singular truth, i.e. the wisdom of God voiced by Book of Mysteries.

The exegetical results mean that the Book of Mysteries adopts a strategy of polarisation attempting to strengthen the identity of the in-group. Simultaneously with the creation of the others it offers its addressees an opportunity to reflect on internal problems. By means of a projection that externalises possible internal problems and transfers them onto the others the coherence of the in-group is reinforced. Book of Mysteries mirrors a taxonomic effort dividing the world into two realms in which cognition plays the decisive role. The adherents are united by a shared interpretative frame. The core of this frame is an alleged cleavage between those who have access to the mystery of God and those who have not. The contrast implied is reflected by two distinct categories of cognition determining the form of revelation: the רז נהיה and the רזי פלא. A similar polarisation manifests itself with regard to the objects of cognition. The adherents have a share in the wisdom of God or in the mystery that is to come. For them the objects of cognition are accessible and manifest, while for those holding fast to the wondrous mysteries the objects of cognition are inaccessible and hidden. The cognitive taxonomy is supported by a dualistic cosmic category. The first form of cognition is localised in heaven closely related to God, whereas the other is localised in this world related to Belial (4Q299 2 ii 5). In addition the cognitive taxonomy reflects a social taxonomy distinguishing between the righteous and the unrighteous. By validating its claims to truth by an appeal to divine wisdom Book of Mysteries is placing itself in a superior position rendering contradictory positions false and assigning them to the group of people who will not be saved. This is one of the reasons why the Qumranites at a later time included Book of Mysteries in their library[34].

Creating the Others in 1 Cor 1-2

The analysis of 1 Cor 1-2 is obviously different from the exegesis of Book of Mysteries because the text is completely preserved. This makes the exegesis more complex. The epistolary form of 1 Cor also makes a difference compared to the exegesis of the *Weisheitsrede* of Book of Mysteries. And finally, the knowledge of the social setting of 1 Cor is far more thorough than is the case concerning Book of Mysteries. In spite of the differences which I do not intend to minimise a number of similarities regarding the content and the argumentative structure, however, relate the two texts to each other.

Similar to Book of Mysteries 1 Cor depicts faith as constituted first and foremost by an act of cognition. Even a cursory reading of the first two chapters documents the extent to which cognitive terms and categories play a decisive role in the letter's founding structures of meaning: ἐν παντὶ λόγῳ καὶ πάσῃ γνώσει (1 Cor 1,5); ἵνα τὸ αὐτὸ λέγητε πάντες, ἦτε δὲ κατηρτισμένοι ἐν τῷ αὐτῷ νοΐ καὶ ἐν τῇ αὐτῇ γνώμῃ (1 Cor 1,10); οὐχὶ ἐμώρανεν ὁ θεὸς τὴν σοφίαν τοῦ κόσμου (1 Cor 1,20); ἐπειδὴ γὰρ ἐν τῇ σοφίᾳ τοῦ θεοῦ οὐκ ἔγνω ὁ κόσμος διὰ τῆς σοφίας τὸν θεόν (1 Cor 1,21); οὐ γὰρ ἔκρινά τι εἰδέναι (1 Cor 2,2); ἣν οὐδεὶς τῶν ἀρχόντων τοῦ αἰῶνος τούτου ἔγνωκεν, εἰ γὰρ ἔγνωσαν (1 Cor 2,8).

The brief section 1 Cor 2,10-16 provides a number of designations explaining what it means to be πνευματικός. The verbs used all have an exclusively cognitive content. They include: ἐραυνάω (2,10); γινώσκω (2,11); οἶδα (2,12); λαλέω ἐν διδακτοῖς πνεύματος λόγοις; συγκρίνω (2,13); δέχομαι; δύναμαι γνῶναι; ἀνακρίνω (2,14); γινώσκω νοῦν κυρίου; συμβιβάζω; νοῦν Χριστοῦ ἔχομεν (2,16). In addition to these semantically related verbs 'spiritual' is used to designate a particular mode of interpretation, cf. πνευματικῶς ἀνακρίνεται (2,14).

Corresponding to Book of Mysteries the problems pertinent to the Corinthian Christians are primarily hermeneutic by nature. The dispute concerns the right interpretation. This is not to say that social cleavages,

---

34. A number of scholars have in fact argued that Book of Mysteries even belongs to the sectarian texts composed by the Qumranites. See for instance RABINOWITZ, *Authorship, Audience, and Date*, p. 32; BETZ, *Offenbarung*, p. 57; TOV, *Scribal Markings*, pp. 57f.

ethical issues, etc. play a minor role only. They are important, indeed. Paul is certainly involved in the creation of community and the construction of identity by providing social-moral instructions[35]. My claim, however, that the issue at stake is primarily hermeneutic by nature is consistent with the chain of arguments of the letter. The first chapters document that Paul did understand the factionalism and the different abuses of the congregation as symptoms of a false mode of interpretation. This is clearly seen from the opening paragraphs of the letter. In 1,10 – the πρόθεσις of the letter stating the basic advice which Paul throughout his letter urges the Corinthians to accept – the congregation is addressed by a direct exhortation "in the name of our Lord Jesus Christ to agree with one another so that there may be no divisions among you and that you may be perfectly united in mind and thought"[36]. By establishing a fundamental epistemological taxonomy in the first paragraph 1,18-25 of the letter's proof sections[37] Paul provides an interpretative frame that supports proper conduct by delineating a world in which such conduct is only common sense[38].

Among other purposes the introductory greeting serves to consolidate the authoritative position of Paul's text. By directly linking himself to the main actors of the founding narrative voiced by the text Paul is speaking from a superior position. He has direct access to and knowledge of the will of God, because he has been called by God as an apostle of Jesus Christ. Serving as an introduction verses 5-7 proleptically indicate the problems pertinent to the Corinthians. They have in all ways been enriched in Christ: in speaking and in knowledge, because they approved of Paul's testimony. V. 7 draws a preliminary conclusion that simultaneously supports the argument developed in the succeeding sections: "Therefore you do not lack any spiritual gift as you eagerly await for our Lord Jesus Christ to be revealed". Apart from the eschatological reserve – consistent with Paul's stance throughout the letter – that the Corinthians are in a waiting position he praises them in lustrous terms. On the surface the passage appears as a *captatio benevolentiae*, but as will soon appear from the argument that follows the laudatory nature of the verses has a venomous sting of irony[39]. The Corinthians, in fact, do

---

35. This aspect has been elaborately elucidated by MEEKS in a number of publications. See for instance *Urban Christians* and *Origins*.

36. MITCHELL has convincingly documented that 1 Cor should be understood in the context of deliberative rhetoric. My own understanding of the structure of 1 Cor closely resembles the one found in MITCHELL, *Paul*, pp. 184-186.

37. Cf. MITCHELL, *Paul*, pp. 184-186; and in particular pp. 202-290.

38. Cf. GEERTZ, *Ethos*, p. 129.

39. See especially 4,6-13; 5,6; 6,1-8.

lack an important spiritual gift, because they are not in an adequate cognitive position regarding the gifts they have been granted already. They have been given baptism (chap. 10), communion (chap. 11) and a number of other spiritual gifts (chap. 12), but since they are still fleshly (3,3), they do not have the right mode of interpretation vis-à-vis the spiritual gifts. The fact that they do not share the same attitude of mind (1,10) is according to Paul the reason for the misdemeanours in the Corinthian community.

The paragraph 1,11-17 describes the present situation of the congregation haunted by problems causing internal divisions[40]. The reference to baptism in vv. 13-17 serves to emphasise the incompatibility of the Christian world view with the existing factions of the congregation. V. 17 substantiates the baptismal argument and introduces the theme of the succeeding section. The introduction of baptism in v. 13 is apparently ad hoc by nature intending only to demonstrate the absurdity of the Corinthian position[41]. Christ did not send Paul to baptise, but to preach the gospel. Again Paul is strengthening his position of authority by directly linking himself to the main actors of the world view voiced by the text. Paul's way of preaching the gospel is contrary to the word of wisdom ἐν σοφίᾳ λόγου. According to Paul this follows in principle from the decisive elements of the world view: "lest the cross of Christ be emptied of its power".

In 1,18-2, 5 Paul develops the σοφία λόγου contrary to the message of the cross. The chain of argument is developed in three separate, but interrelated sections. 1, 18-25 provides the fundamental cognitive taxonomy that defines the interpretative frame for the argument that follows. In 1,26-31 the basic categories of the taxonomy are adapted to the social composition of the Corinthian Christians. The *Umwertung aller Werte* provided by the rationality of the taxonomy is applied to the social setting of the community. Low status terms – most likely corresponding to the economic, social and cultural status of the majority of the community members – are elevated at the cost of high status terms[42]. In 2,1-5 Paul adapts the categories of the taxonomy to his own exist-

---

40. MITCHELL, *Paul*, pp. 200-202 designates it as the διήγησις that states the facts by describing the present situation of the Corinthian community and by correcting a possible misunderstanding that baptism may lead to factionalism.

41. This is evident from the rhetorical ductus of the argument since baptism does not play a particularly prominent role in the succeeding chapters.

42. Concerning the social composition of the Corinthian community see THEISSEN, *Soziale Schichtung*, pp. 232-272. MARTIN, *Body*, has persuasively pointed to the importance of status categories as intimately linked to the problems of the Corinthian community. Regarding status terminology in 1, 26-31 see MARTIN, *Body*, p. 61.

ence. Again low status terms are elevated at the cost of high status terms. Paul came to the Corinthians in weakness, fear and trembling. He did not preach to the Corinthians "with an excellence of wisdom" (2,1), nor did his gospel consist of "persuasive and skilful speeches" (2,4).

It is important to understand that the chain of argument is part of a highly contingent exchange of ideas. It is certainly not – as claimed by many exegetes – a theological treatise normatively outlining the discursive form of the gospel. The problems derived from a traditional *theologia crucis*-reading arise in the context of 2,6ff., which the supporters of this interpretation are unable to integrate into the epistolary argument[43]. The two lines of argument are conformable, however, when it is acknowledged that 1 Cor 1,18-2,5 has a contingent discursive nature and does not represent a theological, dogmatic theorem. In 2,2 Paul states his reason for exclusively preaching the gospel of the cross when he founded the congregation in Corinth: "For I resolved (ἔκρινά) to know nothing while I was with you except Jesus Christ and him crucified". In principle his preaching could have included other dimensions as well (such as the spiritually mediated knowledge referred to in 2,6ff.), but for hermeneutic reasons he decided to limit the gospel to the preaching of the cross. In 3,1f. Paul again refers to the time when he founded the congregation. At that time he could not address the Corinthians as spiritual, but only as fleshly, as mere infants in Christ. He could not give them solid food, but purposely had to reduce the proclamation of the gospel to a content and a form conforming to the Corinthians' ability to grasp it. In other words Paul's mode of preaching had hermeneutic cognitive reasons.

Paul's reasoning has the nature of a subsequent rationalisation designed to cope with the present situation of the community. As numerous scholars have emphasised 1 Cor is no apology but this does not exclude the possibility that apologetic motives are important for the argument of the letter. Paul is in a precarious position. The state of factionalism indicates to Paul that the Corinthians have fallen away from their initial acceptance of his gospel. The writing of 1 Cor is an attempt to have the Corinthians return to the foundation of the gospel which – not surprisingly – is identical with his version of it. There are quite a few things at stake. Granted that the Corinthians accept that Paul's accusation is reasonable (we do not know whether they or some of them did or did not) he must account for their deviation. Either he preached a deficient gospel that implied the possibility of deviation witnessed by the

---

43. E.g. CONZELMANN, *Korinther*, p. 87; FASCHER, *Korinther*, p. 118.

present state of the community or the problem lies with the Corinthians. In addition Paul must account for the particular notion of wisdom claimed by the Strong in the community. On the one hand, he has to convince them that they are conceited and acting contrary to the gospel by their alleged wisdom. On the other hand, to gain their continuous support he must in some way comply with their demands by pointing to something in his gospel functionally equivalent to their claim on wisdom. The only rhetorical option for Paul, therefore, is to convince them by asserting a wisdom of a higher nature. This precarious rhetorical situation accounts for the relationship between the two sections 1,18-31 and 2,1-16. The first section serves to undermine the alleged wisdom of the Strong, whereas the second section points to the particular wisdom Paul is about to reveal to the Corinthians through his discourse. In 3,1ff. he anticipates the obvious objection that can be raised (based on his argument in chapter two) against his initial preaching. If Paul possesses a wisdom which he did not promulgate to the Corinthians on his founding of the congregation then he can be held accountable for the present ruptures of the community. Paul's use of the well-known metaphor of milk and solid food is an attempt to ward off this accusation. Although being an ex-post explanation designed to account for the present situation of the community the overriding idea that pervades the first chapters of the letter is that Paul's mode of preaching had hermeneutic reasons.

In 1,18ff. Paul sharply contrasts the manner in which the word of the cross has been received by different interpretative communities. It is a foolishness to those who are perishing, but a power of God to the saved. Similar to Book of Mysteries a cognitive taxonomy determines the soteriological category. Inclusion into or exclusion from the group of the saved is determined by the quality of knowledge. As an inherent part of his attempt to construe an all-encompassing singular truth Paul utilises a strategy of polarisation that divides the world into two domains. In this manner he attempts to strengthen the cognitive categories of the adherents to ensure that they will remain within the interpretative frame of the text, i.e. sharing the same attitude of mind (1,10). According to this mode of organising the world conceptually and socially, only two options exist: being member either of the in-group or of the out-group.

V. 20 extends the argument to cosmic, temporal and spatial categories. Raising a number of rhetorical questions Paul introduces a dualism concerning this age in contrast to the coming age, this world in contrast to the heavenly world and God in contrast to this world. In the following verse the two modes of interpretation are socially specified. This world is contrasted to the believers. As documented by v. 22 the cosmological definition 'this world' in v. 21 designates a social entity. Ὁ κόσμος is a collective designation of the two ethnic entities Greeks and Jews, who are classified according to their mode of interpretation. Whereas Jews demand signs, Greeks seek wisdom. In spite of this difference they are classified within the same cognitive category, i.e. as sub-classes of the same category 'this world'. The community of believers, however, is sharply distinguished from the worldly interpretative communities. They have been chosen by an act of God (εὐδόκησεν ὁ θεός; αὐτοῖς δὲ τοῖς κλητοῖς) and have a share in the wisdom of God. The wisdom of God forms a strong contrast to the wisdom of the world. As suggested by v. 21 the wisdom of God cognitively appears as folly in the interpretative frame of this world. V. 23 explicitly states that the world view of the believers is folly to this world concretised by the Jews for whom it is a stumbling block, and by the Greeks for whom it is foolishness. To the elect, however, who have been granted the necessary cognitive skills Christ is the power and the wisdom of God (v. 24). V. 25 makes clear that the two opposing modes of interpretation are not equal. The one is cosmologically superior to the other, because it originates from God. This aspect is developed further in 1,26-30.

The cognitive and cosmological taxonomies correspond to a social. The group of people chosen by God to be saved is constituted by the ones, who are not fleshly wise, influential or of noble birth. Instead the believers are made up of those who appear foolish, weak or inferior to the world[44]. The Christian congregation consists of an interpretative community that according to the worldly mode of interpretation is characterised by a radical transformation of values. That which is μωρόν and σκάνδαλον in the interpretative frame of this world is in the interpretative frame of the Christians δύναμις and σοφία θεοῦ.

By the recapitulation of the theme of 1,17, the σοφία λόγου, the opening paragraph of chapter two exemplifies the argument of 1,18-31 on Paul's founding of the community in Corinth. When Paul came to Corinth he did not use eloquence or superior wisdom. In correspondence with the transformation of values characteristic of the Christian congregation Paul came in weakness, fear and trembling (2,3)[45]. His message and preaching were not based on persuasive words of wisdom, but rested on the Spirit's power (2,4). Again a cognitive dualism serves to enhance the plausibility of Paul's world view and to strengthen the inter-

---

44. See MARTIN, *Body*, p. 61 and THEISSEN, *Social Setting*, p. 72.
45. MARTIN, *Body*, pp. 47ff. has delineated the code behind the statement. In Greco-Roman rhetoric deprecations were a common topos, see for instance Dio Chrysostomos, *Discourse* 42; Isocrates, *Niocles, or the Cyprians* 45.

pretative categories of the adherents. Their frame of interpretation is not of this world. It belongs to the heavenly world to which they have gained access by the power of the Spirit. Their faith does not rest on the wisdom of men, but on the power of God (2,5). Paul's gospel indeed – perhaps not surprisingly – corresponds to the positive category of the founding taxonomy. It consists in the 'demonstration of the Spirit's power' in order that the faith of the Corinthians 'might not rest on men's wisdom, but on God's power'. Resuming the theme of the power of God (1,18.24) Paul relates it to the Spirit, thus paving the way for the succeeding section 2,6-16.

As stated above the argumentative aim of this section is highly disputed. The focus on the cognitive aspects of the text, however, makes the passage fit perfectly into the context. Indeed it is the argument of this section that provides the hermeneutic foundation of the entire letter[46]. The great exegetical problem pertains to the use of the πνευματικοί and the ψυχικός in the passage, and in connection with this problem the issue of the relationship between the message of the cross and the teaching of wisdom. Is the πνευματικοί an inclusive term designating all Christians or is it a designation of a particular group of Christians only? Does the ψυχικός designate the unbeliever only or does it also pertain to members of the Christian congregation? With regard to the second aspect, i.e. the relation of 2,6-16 to the message of the cross, Gerd Theißen acutely stated the nature of the problem:

> Grundsätzlich gibt es zwei Möglichkeiten, das Verhältnis von Kreuzespredigt zur Weisheitslehre zu bestimmen. Entweder faßt man die Weisheitslehre als höhere Stufe für Fortgeschrittene auf. Torheit und Weisheit verhielten sich dann wie Anfangslehre zur Lehre für Vollkommene, 2,6-16 wäre Überbietung der Kreuzespredigt. Oder aber man faßt beide als dialektische Einheit auf: Die Kreuzespredigt ist gegenüber der Welt Torheit, von Gott her gesehen jedoch Weisheit. Es handelt sich dann nicht um zwei aufeinanderfolgende Verkündigungsinhalte, sondern um denselben Inhalt unter zwei Aspekten: als Torheit für die Ablehnenden, als Weisheit für die Zustimmenden[47].

Since Paul in 3,1-4 distinguishes between different categories of Christians, the fleshly and the spiritual, spiritual is not an inclusive term encompassing all Christians. Some are spiritual, others are not. The problem of otherness is apparently pertinent to the in-group as well. The exegetical problems related to the passage are greatly reduced, however,

---

46. This is convincingly documented by TRONIER, *Transcendens*. See also the emphasis COUSAR attributes to the cognitive aspects of the passage, *Theological Task*, pp. 93-97.

47. THEISSEN, *Aspekte*, p. 342.

if it is acknowledged that they pertain to a cognitive aspect. Paul distinguishes between two groups of Christians. The one group may be termed Christians in the sense that they have been baptised, that they participate in the communion of the Lord, that they have received the message of the cross etc. They are so to say objectively related to Christianity[48]. But they lack the most important: faith occurring as a hermeneutic event mediated by the heavenly spirit, i.e. the subjective realisation of the spiritual act of cognition. In other words, it is a particular attitude of mind that according to Paul characterises faith. It is this very subjective cognitive element that distinguishes the one group from the other. The one group is characterised by a deficient mode of interpretation, they are σαρκικοί (3,3), whereas the other is described as having the true mode of interpretation originating from the Spirit, they are τέλειοι (2,6) or πνευματικοί (3,1). It is important to realise that Paul does not accuse the Corinthians of being ψυχικοί. In fact he refrains from applying this designation to the members of the community. On the surface this is odd because the argument of the last verses of chapter two suggests such a use. If Paul, however, had characterised the Corinthian Christians as natural humans, i.e. humans without the spirit, the distinction between in- and out-group would have collapsed. It would not be possible to maintain the strong boundaries between the world and the Christian community. The implications of the basic cognitive taxonomy would be nullified. Paul, on the contrary, distinguished between the perfect, spiritual Christians and the fleshly Christians who are objectively spiritual, but who lack the subjective realisation of the spiritual gifts specifically manifested in a particular spiritual mode of interpretation. Paul's adoption of this distinction simultaneously enables him to maintain the Corinthian Christians within the body of Christ and to acknowledge the existing differences of the members of the body. At the same time he succeeds in reaffirming the boundaries of the community and recognises the imperfection of the members within the community. By the differentiation between spiritual, natural and fleshly Paul attempts to overcome the internal problems of the Corinthian community by projecting them onto the pagan, natural world, thus, strengthening the identity of the in-group.

---

48. In the absence of an adequate terminology that corresponds to the distinction Paul draws between the mature and the immature relationship of the believers to the gracious gifts of God I have for the time being designated them by 'subjective' and 'objective'. Whereas the mature or the perfect are characterised by their objective and subjective spiritual realisation of God's gifts, the immature or fleshly are identified by their objective realisation only. Apart from the risk of projecting an anachronistic distinction onto the ancient texts I am well aware of the problems pertaining to the classification.

The dualistic theme of the preceding chapter pervades Paul's argument thematically linking the two lines of argument together⁴⁹. The wisdom Paul is proclaiming is directed at the perfect, the τέλειοι, but the Corinthians are not perfect. They are fleshly. By inserting 2,6-16 into his argument Paul is now revealing the wisdom of God to the Corinthians in order that they might become perfect. In this sense Paul's letter is a revelatory discourse manifesting the hidden wisdom of God. It is a wisdom contrary to this age and the rulers of this age who shall come to nothing. The temporal dualism of 1,20 is resumed in order to emphasise the concealment of wisdom in relation to the world. In this way it opens up for the introduction of the specific theme of revelation in 2,10ff. as the overarching idea.

Similar to Book of Mysteries the participation in the wisdom of God is described in predestinarian terms. God's hidden wisdom has been destined for the glory of the perfect before time began⁵⁰. Although the Christ event was manifest to everybody its meaning is not comprehended before it has been cognitively appropriated. If the rulers of this age had had a share in the mystery of God, they would not have crucified the Lord of glory. But since they lacked the cognitive skill that

---

49. Peter LAMPE is right at the point when he claims that 1 Corinthians 1,18-2,16 should be understood as a Trojan Horse, at first pleasing the listeners until they in 3,1ff. are shocked to discover that they themselves are criticized by the very same text, *Theological Wisdom*, pp. 128f. According to LAMPE Paul is applying the so-called *schema* of the rhetoricians purposely adopting a covert mode of speech. One problem, however, pertains to LAMPE's understanding. He does not sufficiently distinguish between the different content and argument of 1,18-2,5 and 2,6-16. When Paul in 1,26 emphatically admonishes the readers to look at their own call (Βλέπετε γὰρ τὴν κλῆσιν ὑμῶν, ἀδελφοί), how could the implied reader possibly think that the text did not concern him or her? Or in 1,30 where Paul pointedly underlines that the Corinthians are in fact in Christ Jesus. The deictic markers of the text strongly indicate that the content does involve the Corinthians (– not necessarily all, but at least some of them). In my view the Trojan Horse is found in 1,18-25. The successive sections 1,26-31 and 2,1-5 are a rudimental application of the argument on the Corinthian situation culminating in 2,6-16. Here Paul by consistently using first person plural emphatically renounces the gift to the Corinthians of the subjective realisation of the spiritual cognition. In 3,1ff. the consequences of the argument in 2,6-16 are explicitly drawn.

50. The concept of glory is an important code in Jewish texts of the Second Temple Period. Among other things it often designates the glory which Adam had before the fall. By the end of times the elect or holy of Israel shall obtain the prelapsarian Adamic status by achieving the glory of God. The presupposed soteriology, however, is not only one of restitution. The glory status of the end time is a final state in the sense that it is no longer possible to forfeit it. See for instance 1 QS IV, 23; 1 QH XVII, 15; CD III, 20; 2 Enoch 22,7; 4 Ezra 7,97; 2 Bar 51,10f.; Ascen. Is.7,33ff.; 9,6ff. The glory predestined for the believers is intimately linked to Christ who in 2,8 is described as the Lord of glory. Through baptism and the continuous growth in the cognition of Christ the believers are proleptically transformed into the glory of God, cf. 2 Cor 3,18; Phil 3,21; Rom 12,2. It is not until the end of times, however, that the Christians are bodily united with the glory of Christ, cf. 1 Cor 15,43.49.53. For Paul's understanding of glory see particularly JERVELL, *Imago Dei*, and SEGAL, *Paul the Convert*, pp. 58-71.

would have enabled them to recognise Jesus as the Lord of glory, they did crucify him. Paul shares with Book of Mysteries the idea that the elements of the heavenly world determine the course of the world and the idea that they are inaccessible to natural man (ὁ ψυχικὸς ἄνθρωπος) or natural cognition (τὸ πνεῦμα τοῦ κόσμου). This is emphatically stated in vv. 10ff.

The revelatory event occurs through an act of cognitive transformation by the heavenly Spirit. This event is understood to constitute the decisive soteriological category. It is not the historical Christ event but the cognitive transformation of the believers by the Spirit that is understood to be the fulfilment of the scriptural promises, cf. 2,9. Only the Spirit that originates from God can reveal the depths of God. Through the revelatory mediation of the Spirit the believers are linked to the Spirit, and are thus situated in a cognitive position which enables them to interpret the hidden mystery of God. They did not receive the spirit of this world but the Spirit of God in order to understand the gifts of God.

1 Cor utilises a structure of argument similar to Book of Mysteries which refers to creation as an indicative sign of the mystery of God (4Q299 frg. 4), but denies natural cognition the possibility of interpreting the signs. By their appearance in the world the signs are manifest but without the necessary interpretative frame they are hidden or void of meaning. Only the spiritual man who by an act of grace has been granted the cognitive skills by the Spirit is able to discern between truth and illusion, between God and this world. Natural man does not understand that which comes from the Spirit of God. To him it is foolishness (2,14). The authoritative position which Paul in the introductory greeting ascribes to the text by characterising himself as called to be an apostle of Christ Jesus is underlined by 2,13. The words of Paul belong to the heavenly mode of cognition. They are expressing spiritual truths in spiritual words contrary to the words taught by human wisdom. The impact of the argument that the spiritual humans judge spiritual things provides the 'indicative' founding for the subsequent moral exhortation. Through the discourse God's hidden wisdom has been revealed to the Corinthians so that they might become spiritual in order to discern and judge in social-moral matters. The conclusion of the section in 2,16 that the Christians have the mind of Christ (ἡμεῖς δὲ νοῦν Χριστοῦ ἔχομεν) implies that to Paul Christianity is first and foremost constituted by a particular mode of interpretation defined by the same νοῦς and the same γνώμη[51]. The unity

---

51. One can of course argue that the designation is intimately bound to the contingency of the Corinthian situation. As true as this may be one should not overlook the importance Paul attributes to cognition in his remaining letters. See for instance 2 Cor 3; Gal 2,16-21; Phil 3,19; Rom 12,1f.

of the community is manifested by a shared and transcending attitude of mind. Through the revelatory mediation of the Spirit that generates and constitutes the particular mode of cognition the community manifests the body of Christ, i.e. a particular interpretative community.

Indicatively the Corinthians became Christians at the time when Paul founded the community by being included in the objective revelatory work of the Spirit (baptism, communion, etc.). Objectively, they were united with the heavenly Christ, objectively constituting the σῶμα Χριστοῦ. But because of a deficient mode of interpretation numerous problems haunt the Corinthian community. Paul, therefore, imperatively admonishes the Corinthians also to implement the cognitive work of the Spirit, i.e. the adequate subjective, spiritual mode of interpretation that corresponds to the objective-spiritual gifts. It is in the conformity of these two aspects that the spiritual transformation occurs. The social constitutive work of the Spirit, the creation of the community as a spiritual and a social unity consisting of individual members is not realised until the cognitive transformation takes place. In the conformity of the objective-spiritual with the subjective-spiritual the spiritual interpretative community, which has been transferred from this world and the spirit of this world by being cognitively related to and identical with the transcendent spiritual world is firmly anchored in the heavenly world (although not bodily-substantially as documented by the discussion in 1 Cor 15). The distinction between an objective and a subjective embeddedness in the Christ event comes to the fore in Paul's differentiation of spiritual, natural and fleshly man. Natural man belongs to the out-group of the non-Christian world. Within the in-group, however, two classes exist, the perfect and the spiritual on the one hand and the fleshly on the other. The spiritual defines the ideal which the fleshly shall aspire to. If for a moment the two explanations of Gerd Theißen, the dialectic and the gradual, are recalled it appears that the gradual is the one that most adequately fits Paul's understanding.

It has been argued that 1 Cor 1-2 – similar to Book of Mysteries – adopts a strategy of polarisation attempting to strengthen the cognitive adherence of the in-group to a specified world view. 1 Cor 1-2 represents a taxonomic argument in which cognition plays the decisive role. The semantic universe of 1 Cor is constituted by a basic cognitive taxonomy dividing the world into two groups: those who have access to the hidden mystery of God, resp. share the spiritual interpretation mediated by the heavenly spirit, vs. those for whom it is a stumbling block and a foolishness. The contrast is constituted by two distinct categories of cognition determining the revelatory form: the spiritual and the natural.

Corresponding to this contrast 1 Cor 1-2 develops a sharp distinction regarding the objects of cognition. To the elect they are accessible and manifest, to the others they are inaccessible and hidden.

Parallel to Book of Mysteries the cognitive taxonomy is supported by cosmic, spatial and temporal categories. The true form of cognition is localised in heaven, whereas the other form is placed in this world and belongs to this age. The emphasis on this aspect places the over-all understanding of this contribution close to the increasing number of scholars who emphasise the apocalyptic nature of Paul's religious universe[52]. The cognitive taxonomy further reflects a social division of the world into the holy, the elect, the believers vs. the others who are relegated to the margins of culture and religion, cf. the catalogues of vices. 1 Cor validates its claims to truth by an appeal to divine wisdom, thus situating itself in a superior position rendering other positions false and assigning them to the group of people who shall perish.

Conclusion

Book of Mysteries and 1 Cor represent a taxonomic endeavour that creates a system of patterned values, meanings and beliefs that give cognitive structure to the world and provide a basis for co-ordinating and controlling human interactions. They adopt a cluster of wisdom motifs through which they divide the world conceptually and socially into two cognitive frames. In both texts two interpretative communities are sharply contrasted. Competing frames of interpretation determine the fundamental structures of meaning in both texts. The taxonomy is cosmically and spatially supported further mirroring a social taxonomy dividing the world into the righteous and the unrighteous. The construction of others plays a dominant role. The others serve to affirm the identity of the in-group, to draw boundaries towards the outside and to expose its points of vulnerability. In this manner an awareness of the proximate otherness within is created. This aspect is vital for 1 Cor which claims that an external and incompatible mode of interpretation has gained a footing in the in-group, thus creating the problems of the community.

Adopting sapiential traditions to enhance the plausibility of their world view the two texts are involved in a rhetorical game of redefining the marks of social, religious and cultural identity. In this manner they

---

52. See for instance BEKER, *Paul the Apostle*, p. 152: "Only a consistent apocalyptic interpretation of Paul's thought is able to demonstrate its fundamental coherence".

reflect a process of social dissociation, reorganisation and ideological expropriation of the much-coveted traditions of their time. They attempt to reconfigurate the religious and cultural codes of their age to make them compatible with and advocates of their world view. Although no direct historical link can be established between the two texts they do by virtue of their traditio-historical context, structural similarities regarding their argumentative strategy, content and their particular way of organising the world conceptually and socially belong to the same religious *koine*. Both texts pay witness to the impact of an apocalyptic transformation of sapiential motifs in a number of religious groupings in the last part of the Second Temple period. The wisdom which the two texts promulgate is not the one revealed and manifested in the Torah of God. On the contrary it is a hidden wisdom mediated by the heavenly world and accessible to the elect only.

Department of Biblical Exegesis   A. KLOSTERGAARD PETERSEN
University of Aarhus
Nrd. Ringgade 2-4
DK-8000 Århus C.
Denmark

APPENDIX

SYNOPSIS OF FRAGMENT NUMBERS EMPLOYED IN THE EDITIONS OF SAPIENTIAL MANUSCRIPTS FROM QUMRAN

Below the reader is provided with the differing fragment numbers in the editions of sapiential manuscripts published in the *DJD* series and in B.Z. Wacholder and M.G. Abegg, *A Preliminary Edition of the Unpublished Dead Sea Scrolls. The Hebrew and Aramaic Texts from Cave Four*. The latter is based on preliminary editions produced by the original international team of editors (i.e. J.T. Milik [4Q298; 4Q299-301], J. Strugnell [4Q415-418.423; 4Q424], J. Starcky [4Q525]) and incorporated into the card index compiled by R.E. Brown, J.A. Fitzmyer, W.G. Oxtoby, and J. Teixidor[1]. Recognized are only those manuscripts, which are identified in A. Lange's article in this volume (*Die Weisheitstexte aus Qumran – Eine Einleitung*) beyond any doubt as sapiential. An item typeset in round brackets, e.g. (4Q299 27), marks a fragment, which was not edited by B.Z. Wacholder / M.G. Abegg, but seems to have been included in their countings. A line marks a fragment of a given manuscript edited by B.Z. Wacholder / M.G. Abegg or in the DJD series, but not recognized in the corresponding edition, respectively.

Synopsis between the Preliminary Edition of B.Z. Wacholder / M.G. Abegg and the DJD series

4QCryptA Words of the Maskil to All Sons of Dawn		4QMysteries[a]	
Preliminary Edition	*DJD series*	*Preliminary Edition*	*DJD series*
		4Q299 2 i	4Q299 3a i
4Q298 1 i	4Q298 1-2 i	4Q299 2 ii	4Q299 3a ii
4Q298 1 ii (part of)	4Q298 2 ii	4Q299 2 ii (part of)	4Q299 3b
4Q298 1 ii (part of)	4Q298 3-4 i	4Q299 2 i (part of)	4Q299 3c
4Q298 1 iii	4Q298 3-4	4Q299 3	4Q299 2
ii		4Q299 11 (part of)	4Q299 13a
4Q298 2 i	4Q298 5 i	4Q299 11 (part of)	4Q299 13b
4Q298 2 ii	4Q298 5 ii	4Q299 12	4Q299 14

---

* For their help and support I am obliged to D.J. Harrington, C. Hempel and A. Lange.
1. H.-P. RICHTER, H. STEGEMANN & J. STRUGNELL (eds.), *A Preliminary Concordance to the Hebrew and Aramaic Fragments from Qumrân Including Especially the Unpublished Material from Cave IV*, vol. 1-5, Göttingen, privately printed, 1988.

4Q299 13	4Q299 15
4Q299 14	4Q299 16
4Q299 15 i	4Q299 17 i
4Q299 16	4Q299 18
4Q299 17	4Q299 19
4Q299 18	4Q299 20
4Q299 19	4Q299 21
4Q299 20	4Q299 22
4Q299 21	4Q299 23
4Q299 22	4Q299 24
4Q299 23	4Q299 25
4Q299 24	4Q299 26
4Q299 25	4Q299 27
4Q299 26	4Q299 27
4Q299 28	4Q299 30
4Q299 29	4Q299 32
4Q299 30	4Q299 33
4Q299 31	4Q299 34
4Q299 32	4Q299 35
4Q299 33	4Q299 36
4Q299 34	4Q299 37
4Q299 35	4Q299 38
4Q299 36	4Q299 39
4Q299 37	4Q299 40
4Q299 39	4Q299 42
4Q299 40	4Q299 43
4Q299 41	4Q299 44
4Q299 42	4Q299 45
4Q299 43	4Q299 46
4Q299 44	4Q299 47
4Q299 45	4Q299 48
4Q299 48	4Q299 51
4Q299 49	4Q299 52
4Q299 50	4Q299 53
4Q299 51	4Q299 54
4Q299 52	4Q299 55
4Q299 53	4Q299 56
4Q299 54	4Q299 57
4Q299 55	4Q299 58
4Q299 56	4Q299 59
4Q299 57	4Q299 60
4Q299 58	4Q299 61
4Q299 59	4Q299 62
4Q299 60	4Q299 63
4Q299 61	4Q299 65
4Q299 62	4Q299 66
4Q299 63	4Q299 67
4Q299 64	4Q299 68
4Q299 65	4Q299 69
4Q299 66	4Q299 70
4Q299 67	4Q299 71
4Q299 68	4Q299 72
4Q299 69	4Q299 73
4Q299 70	4Q299 74
4Q299 71	4Q299 75
4Q299 72	4Q299 76
4Q299 73	4Q299 77
4Q299 74	4Q299 78
4Q299 75	4Q299 79
4Q299 76	4Q299 80
4Q299 77	4Q299 81
4Q299 79	4Q299 83
4Q299 82	4Q299 86
4Q299 83	4Q299 87
4Q299 84	4Q299 88
4Q299 93	4Q299 97
4Q299 95	4Q299 99

4QMysteries[b]

Preliminary Edition	***DJD series***
4Q300 1 i	4Q300 1a i
4Q300 1 ii	4Q300 1a ii – 1b

4QMysteries[c]?

Preliminary Edition	***DJD series***
4Q301 2 (part of)	4Q301 2a
4Q301 2 (part of)	4Q301 2b
4Q301 3	4Q301 3a–b

4QInstruction[a]

Preliminary Edition	***DJD series***
4Q415 5	4Q415 5 + 3

4QInstruction[b]

Preliminary Edition	***DJD series***
4Q416 5	4Q416 5 i

4QInstruction[c]

Preliminary Edition	***DJD series***
4Q417 1 i	4Q417 2 i
4Q417 1 ii	4Q417 2 ii
4Q417 2 i	4Q417 1 i

4Q417 2 ii	4Q417 1 ii	4Q418 244	4Q418 275
4Q417 5	4Q417 11	4Q418 246	4Q418 259
4Q417 11	—	4Q418 247	4Q418 260
4Q417 18 (part of)	4Q417 5	4Q418 248	4Q418 261
4Q417 30	4Q417 26	4Q418 249	4Q418 278
4Q417 31	—	4Q418 250	4Q418 271
4Q417 32	—	4Q418 251	4Q418 272
		4Q418 252	4Q418 242

**4QInstruction^d, 4QInstruction^e,
4QText with Quotation from
Psalm 107?,
4QInstruction^f?**

		4Q418 253	4Q418 248
		4Q418 254	4Q418 249
		4Q418 255	4Q418 279
		4Q418 256	4Q418 251
		4Q418 259	4Q418 246
Preliminary Edition	*DJD series*	4Q418 261	4Q418 252
4Q418 2	4Q418 2,	4Q418 268	4Q418 241
	2a, 2b, 2c	4Q418 271	4Q418 244
4Q418 7	4Q418 7	4Q418 272	4Q418 245
	[=7a + 7b]	4Q418 274	4Q418 276
4Q418 9	4Q418 9 +	4Q418 275	4Q418 247
	9a + 9b + 9c	4Q418 276	4Q418 268
4Q418 10	4Q418 10a, b	4Q418 278	4Q418 243
4Q418 43	4Q418 43,	4Q418 279	4Q418 240
	44, 45i	4Q418 297	4Q418 250
4Q418 77	4Q418 77a, 77b		

4QInstruction^g

4Q418 81	4Q418 81 + 81a	*Preliminary Edition*	*DJD series*
4Q418 89	4Q418 91	4Q423 2 + 1 i	4Q423 1
4Q418 91	4Q418 89	4Q423 1 ii	4Q423 2
4Q418 102	4Q418 102a +b	4Q423 21	4Q423 3a
		4Q423 22	4Q423 21
4Q418 112	4Q418b 2	4Q423 23	4Q423 22
4Q418 115	4Q418b 1	4Q423 24	4Q423 23
4Q418 125	4Q418 116	4Q423 25	4Q423 24
4Q418 128	4Q418 128 + 129	4Q423 26	4Q423 5a

4QBéatitudes

4Q418 161	4Q418 161 [= 4Q418c]		
4Q418 161	4Q418c	*Preliminary Edition*	*DJD series*
4Q418 167	4Q418 167a + 167b	4Q525 8 - 9	4Q525 10
		4Q525 3	4Q525 2
4Q418 183	4Q418 183a + b	4Q525 4	4Q525 3
		4Q525 6	4Q525 4
4Q418 185	4Q418 185a + b	4Q525 7 ii	4Q525 6
		4Q525 10	4Q525 8
4Q418 240	4Q418 253	4Q525 12	4Q525 11-12
4Q418 241	4Q418 254	4Q525 17	4Q525 18
4Q418 242	4Q418 255	4Q525 18	4Q525 17
4Q418 243	4Q418 274	4Q525 22	4Q525 23

4Q525 23 ii	4Q525 24 ii	4Q299 3c	part of
4Q525 24	4Q525 25		4Q299 2 i
4Q525 25	4Q525 26	4Q299 11	—
4Q525 26	4Q525 27	4Q299 12	—
4Q525 27	4Q525 28	4Q299 13a	part of
4Q525 28	4Q525 29		4Q299 11
4Q525 29	4Q525 30	4Q299 13b	part of
4Q525 30	4Q525 31		4Q299 11
4Q525 31	4Q525 32	4Q299 14	4Q299 12
4Q525 32	4Q525 33	4Q299 15	4Q299 13
4Q525 34	4Q525 35	4Q299 16	4Q299 14
4Q525 35	4Q525 36	4Q299 17 i	4Q299 15 i
4Q525 37	4Q525 38	4Q299 18	4Q299 16
4Q525 38	4Q525 39	4Q299 19	4Q299 17
		4Q299 20	4Q299 18
		4Q299 21	4Q299 19
		4Q299 22	4Q299 20

Synopsis between the DJD series and the Preliminary Edition of B.Z. Wacholder/M.G. Abegg

4QCryptA Words of the Maskil to All Sons of Dawn

DJD series Edition	*Preliminary*		
4Q298 1-2 i	4Q298 1 i	4Q299 23	4Q299 21
4Q298 2 ii	part of	4Q299 24	4Q299 22
	4Q298 1 ii	4Q299 25	4Q299 23
4Q298 3 - 4 i	part of	4Q299 26	4Q299 24
	4Q298 1 ii	4Q299 27	4Q299 25
4Q298 3 - 4 ii	4Q298 1 iii	4Q299 27	4Q299 26
4Q298 3 - 4 iii	—	4Q299 29	(4Q299 27)
4Q298 5 i	4Q298 2 i	4Q299 30	4Q299 28
4Q298 5 ii	4Q298 2 ii	4Q299 31	—
4Q298 6	—	4Q299 32	4Q299 29
4Q298 7	—	4Q299 33	4Q299 30
4Q298 8	—	4Q299 34	4Q299 31
		4Q299 35	4Q299 32
		4Q299 36	4Q299 33
4QMysteries[a]		4Q299 37	4Q299 34
		4Q299 38	4Q299 35
DJD series Edition	*Preliminary*	4Q299 39	4Q299 36
		4Q299 40	4Q299 37
		4Q299 41	(4Q299 38)
		4Q299 42	4Q299 39
		4Q299 43	4Q299 40
		4Q299 44	4Q299 41
		4Q299 45	4Q299 42
		4Q299 46	4Q299 43
		4Q299 47	4Q299 44
		4Q299 48	4Q299 45
4Q299 2	4Q299 3	4Q299 49	(4Q299 46)
4Q299 3a i	4Q299 2 i	4Q299 50	(4Q299 47)
4Q299 3a ii	4Q299 2 ii	4Q299 51	4Q299 48
4Q299 3b	part of	4Q299 52	4Q299 49
	4Q299 2 ii	4Q299 53	4Q299 50

4Q299 54	4Q299 51	4Q299 102	—
4Q299 55	4Q299 52	4Q299 103	—
4Q299 56	4Q299 53	4Q299 104	—
4Q299 57	4Q299 54	4Q299 105	—
4Q299 58	4Q299 55	4Q299 106	—
4Q299 59	4Q299 56	**4QMysteries[b]**	
4Q299 60	4Q299 57		
4Q299 61	4Q299 58	*DJD series*	*Preliminary*
4Q299 62	4Q299 59	*Edition*	
4Q299 63	4Q299 60	4Q300 1a i	4Q300 1 i
4Q299 64	—	4Q300 1a ii – 1b	4Q300 1 ii
4Q299 65	4Q299 61	4Q300 14	—
4Q299 66	4Q299 62		
4Q299 67	4Q299 63	**4QMysteries[c]?**	
4Q299 68	4Q299 64		
4Q299 69	4Q299 65	*DJD series*	*Preliminary*
4Q299 70	4Q299 66	*Edition*	
4Q299 71	4Q299 67	4Q301 2a	part of
4Q299 72	4Q299 68		4Q301 2
4Q299 73	4Q299 69	4Q301 2b	part of
4Q299 74	4Q299 70		4Q301 2
4Q299 75	4Q299 71	4Q301 3a – b	4Q301 3
4Q299 76	4Q299 72	4Q301 8	—
4Q299 77	4Q299 73	4Q301 9	—
4Q299 78	4Q299 74	4Q301 10	—
4Q299 79	4Q299 75		
4Q299 80	4Q299 76	**4QInstruction[a]**	
4Q299 81	4Q299 77		
4Q299 82	(4Q299 78)	*DJD series*	*Preliminary*
4Q299 83	4Q299 79	*Edition*	
4Q299 84	(4Q299 80)	4Q415 3 (see 5)	(4Q415 3)
4Q299 85	(4Q299 81)	4Q415 5 + 3	4Q415 5
4Q299 86	4Q299 82	4Q415 10 ii	(4Q415 10 ii)
4Q299 87	4Q299 83	4Q415 14	(4Q415 14)
4Q299 88	4Q299 84	4Q415 17	(4Q415 17)
4Q299 89	(4Q299 85)	4Q415 26	(4Q415 26)
4Q299 90	(4Q299 86)	4Q415 29	(4Q415 29)
4Q299 91	(4Q299 87)		
4Q299 92	(4Q299 88)	**4QInstruction[b]**	
4Q299 93	(4Q299 89)		
4Q299 94	(4Q299 90)	*DJD series*	*Preliminary*
4Q299 95	(4Q299 91)	*Edition*	
4Q299 96	(4Q299 92)	4Q416 5 i	4Q416 5
4Q299 97	4Q299 93	4Q416 5 ii	—
4Q299 98	(4Q299 94)	4Q416 11	(4Q416 11)
4Q299 99	4Q299 95	4Q416 20	—
4Q299 100	—	4Q416 21	—
4Q299 101	—	4Q416 22	—

4QInstruction^c

DJD series Edition	*Preliminary*
4Q417 1 i	4Q417 2 i
4Q417 1 ii	4Q417 2 ii
4Q417 2 i	4Q417 1 i
4Q417 2 ii	4Q417 1 ii
4Q417 4 i	(4Q417 4 i)
4Q417 5	part of 4Q417 18
4Q417 8	(4Q417 8)
4Q417 11	4Q417 5
4Q417 17	(4Q417 17)
4Q417 18	—
4Q417 26	4Q417 30

4QInstruction^d

DJD series Edition	*Preliminary*
4Q418 2, 2a, 2b, 2c	4Q418 2
4Q418 7 [=7a + 7b]	4Q418 7
4Q418 8	(4Q418 8)
4Q418 9 + 9a + 9b + 9c	4Q418 9
4Q418 10a, b	4Q418 10
4Q418 27	(4Q418 27)
4Q418 30	(4Q418 30)
4Q418 40	(4Q418 40)
4Q418 41	(4Q418 41)
4Q418 43, 44, 45 i	4Q418 43
4Q418 50	(4Q418 50)
4Q418 61	(4Q418 61)
4Q418 62	(4Q418 62)
4Q418 63	(4Q418 63)
4Q418 67	(4Q418 67)
4Q418 69 i	(4Q418 69 i)
4Q418 72	(4Q418 72)
4Q418 77a, 77b	4Q418 77
4Q418 81 + 81a	4Q418 81
4Q418 89	4Q418 91
4Q418 91	4Q418 89
4Q418 93	(4Q418 93)
4Q418 98	(4Q418 98)
4Q418 99	(4Q418 99)
4Q418 102a + b	4Q418 102
4Q418 110	(4Q418 110)
4Q418 111	(4Q418 111)
4Q418 115	(4Q418 116)
4Q418 116	4Q418 125
4Q418 128 + 129	4Q418 128
4Q418 141	(4Q418 141)
4Q418 142	(4Q418 142)
4Q418 151	(4Q418 151)
4Q418 152	(4Q418 152)
4Q418 153	(4Q418 153)
4Q418 154	(4Q418 154)
4Q418 155	(4Q418 155)
4Q418 156	(4Q418 156)
4Q418 157	(4Q418 157)
4Q418 161 (= 4Q418c)	4Q418 161
4Q418 167a + 167b	4Q418 167
4Q418 183a + b	4Q418 183
4Q418 185a + b	4Q418 185
4Q418 187	(4Q418 187)
4Q418 194	(4Q418 194)
4Q418 195	(4Q418 195)
4Q418 203	(4Q418 203)
4Q418 215	(4Q418 215)
4Q418 226	(4Q418 226)
4Q418 231	(4Q418 231)
4Q418 232	(4Q418 232)
4Q418 233	(4Q418 233)
4Q418 240	4Q418 279
4Q418 241	4Q418 268
4Q418 242	4Q418 252
4Q418 243	4Q418 278
4Q418 244	4Q418 271
4Q418 245	4Q418 272
4Q418 246	4Q418 259
4Q418 247	4Q418 275
4Q418 248	4Q418 253
4Q418 249	4Q418 254
4Q418 250	4Q418 297
4Q418 251	4Q418 256
4Q418 252	4Q418 261
4Q418 253	4Q418 240
4Q418 254	4Q418 241
4Q418 255	4Q418 242
4Q418 259	4Q418 246
4Q418 260	4Q418 247
4Q418 261	4Q418 248
4Q418 268	4Q418 276
4Q418 270	(4Q418 270)
4Q418 271	4Q418 250
4Q418 272	4Q418 251

4Q418 274	4Q418 243	4Q423 23	4Q423 24
4Q418 275	4Q418 244	4Q423 24	4Q423 25
4Q418 276	4Q418 274		
4Q418 278	4Q418 249	**4QInstruction-like Composition B**	
4Q418 279	4Q418 255		
4Q418 288	—	*DJD series*	*Preliminary*
4Q418 289	—	*Edition*	
4Q418 293	—	4Q424 A	—
4Q418 294	—	4Q424 B	—
4Q418 296	—	**4QBeatitudes**	
4Q418 297	—		
4Q418 298	—	*DJD series*	*Preliminary*
4Q418 299	—	*Edition*	
4Q418 300	—	4Q525 2	4Q525 3
4Q418 301	—	4Q525 3	4Q525 4
4Q418 302	—	4Q525 4	4Q525 6
4Q418 303	—	4Q525 6	4Q525 7 ii
		4Q525 8	4Q525 10
4QInstruction^e		4Q525 9	—
		4Q525 10	4Q525 8-9
DJD series	*Preliminary*	4Q525 11 - 12	4Q525 12
Edition		4Q525 17	4Q525 18
4Q418a *all fragments*	—	4Q525 18	4Q525 17
		4Q525 22	—
4QText with Quotation from Psalm 107?		4Q525 23	4Q525 22
		4Q525 24 i	(4Q525 23 i)
		4Q525 24 ii	4Q525 23 ii
DJD series	*Preliminary*	4Q525 25	4Q525 24
Edition		4Q525 26	4Q525 25
4Q418b 1	4Q418 115	4Q525 27	4Q525 26
4Q418b 2	4Q418 112	4Q525 28	4Q525 27
		4Q525 29	4Q525 28
4QInstruction^f?		4Q525 30	4Q525 29
		4Q525 31	4Q525 30
DJD series	*Preliminary*	4Q525 32	4Q525 31
Edition		4Q525 33	4Q525 32
4Q418c	4Q418 161	4Q525 34	(4Q525 33)
		4Q525 35	4Q525 34
4QInstruction^g		4Q525 36	4Q525 35
		4Q525 37	(4Q525 36)
DJD series	*Preliminary*	4Q525 38	4Q525 37
Edition		4Q525 39	4Q525 38
4Q423 1	4Q423 2 + 1 i	4Q525 40	—
4Q423 2	4Q423 1 ii	4Q525 41	—
4Q423 3a	4Q423 21	4Q525 42	—
4Q423 5a	4Q423 26	4Q525 43	—
4Q423 21	4Q423 22	4Q525 44	—
4Q423 22	4Q423 23	4Q525 45	—

4Q525 46 —
4Q525 47 —
4Q525 48 —
4Q525 49 —
4Q525 50 —

Institut für antikes Judentum   A. BEHRINGER
und hellenistische Religionsgeschichte
Liebermeisterstr. 12
72076 Tübingen
Deutschland

BIBLIOGRAPHIES AND INDEX

LITERATURE ON THE WISDOM TEXTS FROM QUMRAN

Compiled by Charlotte HEMPEL and Armin LANGE

J.K. AITKEN, *Apocalyptic, Revelation and Early Jewish Wisdom Literature*, in C.T.R. HAYWARD & P.J. HARLAND (eds.), *New Heaven and New Earth. Prophecy and the Millennium* (Supplements to Vetus Testamentum, 77), Leiden, Brill, 1999, pp. 181-193. Short title: Apocalyptic

J.M. ALLEGRO, *Qumran Cave 4. I (4Q158-4Q186)* (Discoveries in the Judaean Desert, 5), Oxford, Clarendon, 1968. Short title: Qumran Cave 4. I

——, *"The Wiles of the Wicked Woman". A Sapiential Work from Qumran's Fourth Cave*, in *Palestine Exploration Quarterly* 96 (1964) 53-55. Short title: Wiles

I.D. AMUSSIN, *Un pamphlet antipharisien de Qumran*, in *Westnik Drevnei Stori* 178 (1986) 133-140. Short title: Pamphlet

D. BARTHÉLEMY & J.T. MILIK, *Qumran Cave 1* (Discoveries in the Judaean Desert, 1), Oxford, Clarendon, 1955. Short title: Qumran Cave 1

J.M. BAUMGARTEN, *On the Nature of the Seductress in 4Q184*, in *Revue de Qumran* 15 (1991-1992) 133-143. Short title: Seductress

——, *Some Notes on 4Q408*, in *Revue de Qumran* 18 (1997) 143-144. Short title: 4Q408

J. BECKER, *Das Heil Gottes. Heils- und Sündenbegriffe in den Qumrantexten und im Neuen Testament* (Studien zur Umwelt des Neuen Testaments, 3), Göttingen, Vandenhoek & Ruprecht, 1964. Short title: Heil Gottes

O. BETZ, *Offenbarung und Schriftforschung in der Qumransekte* (Wissenschaftliche Untersuchungen zum Neuen Testament, 6), Tübingen, Mohr Siebeck, 1960. Short title: Offenbarung

G. BRIN, *Wisdom Issues in Qumran. The Types and Status of the Figures in 4Q424 and the Phrases of Rationale in the Document*, in *Dead Sea Discoveries* 4 (1997) 297-311. Short title: Wisdom Issues

——, *Studies in 4Q424 1-2*, in *Revue de Qumran* 18 (1997) 21-42. Short title: 4Q424 1-2

——, *Studies in 4Q424 Fragment 3*, in *Vetus Testamentum* 45 (1996) 271-295. Short title: 4Q424 Fragment 3

G.J. BROOKE, *The Wisdom of Matthew's Beatitudes (4QBéat and Mt. 5:3-12)*, in *Scripture Bulletin* 19 (1988-89) 35-41. Short title: Matthew's Beatitudes

G.J. BROOKE, L.H. SCHIFFMAN, J.C. VANDERKAM (eds.), *Dead Sea Discoveries. A Journal of Current Research on the Scrolls and Related Literature, 4.3 Wisdom at Qumran*, Leiden, Brill, 1997.

M. BROSHI, *Beware the Wiles of the Wicked Woman. Dead Sea Scroll Fragment Reflects Essene Fear of, and Contempt for Women*, in *Biblical Archaeology Review* 9/4 (1983) 54-56. Short title: Wiles

H. BURGMANN, *"The Wicked Woman": Der Makkabäer Simon?*, in *Revue de Qumran* 7 (1972-1975) 323-359. Short title: Simon

A. CAQUOT, *Les textes de Sagesse de Qoumrân (Aperçu préliminaire)*, in *Revue d'histoire et de philosophie religieuses* 76 (1996) 1-34. Short title: Sagesse

J. CARMIGNAC, *Poème allégorique sur la secte rivale*, in *Revue de Qumran* 5 (1964-1966) 361-374. Short title: Poème allégorique

——, *Qu'est-ce que l'Apocalyptique? Son emploi à Qumran*, in *Revue de Qumran* 10 (1979-1981) 3-33. Short title: Qu'est-ce que l'Apocalyptique

J.J. COLLINS, *In the Likeness of the Holy Ones: The Creation of Humankind in a Wisdom Text from Qumran*, in D.W. PARRY & E. ULRICH (eds.), *The Provo International Conference on the Dead Sea Scrolls. Technological Innovations, New Texts, and Reformulated Issues* (Studies on the Texts of the Desert of Judah, 30), Leiden, Brill, 1999, pp. 609-618. Short title: Likeness of the Holy Ones

——, *Jewish Wisdom in the Hellenistic Age* (Old Testament Library), Louisville, Westminster/John Knox, 1997. Short title: Jewish Wisdom

——, *Seers, Sybils and Sages in Hellenistic-Roman Judaism* (Journal for the Study of Judaism in the Persian, Hellenistic and Roman Period Supplement, 54), Leiden, Brill, 1997. Short title: Seers, Sybils and Sages

——, *Wisdom, Apocalypticism and Generic Compatibility*, in L.J. PERDUE, B.B. SCOTT & W.J. WISEMAN (eds.), *In Search of Wisdom. FS John G. Gammie*, Louisville, Westminster/John Knox, 1993, pp. 165-185. Short title: Wisdom

——, *Wisdom Reconsidered in Light of the Scrolls*, in *Dead Sea Discoveries* 4 (1997) 265-281. Short title: Wisdom Reconsidered

W.D. DAVIES, *"Knowledge" in the Dead Sea Scrolls and Matthew 11:25-30*, in *Harvard Theological Review* 46 (1953) 113-139. Short title: Knowledge

A.-M. DENIS, *Les thèmes de connaissance dans le Document de Damas* (Studia Hellenistica, 15), Louvain, Publications Universitaires, 1967. Short title: Thèmes de connaissance

A. DUPONT-SOMMER, *Die essenischen Schriften vom Toten Meer*, Tübingen, Mohr Siebeck, 1960. Short title: Schriften

T. ELGVIN, *Admonition Texts from Qumran Cave 4*, in M.O. WISE, N. GOLB, J.J. COLLINS & D.G. PARDEE (eds.), *Methods of Investigation of the Dead Sea Scrolls and the Khirbet Qumran Site. Present Realities and Future Prospects* (Annals of the New York Academy of Sciences, 722), New York, Academy of Sciences, 1994, pp. 179-196. Short title: Admonition Texts

——, *An Analysis of 4QInstruction*, Jerusalem, Dissertation, 1998. Short title: Analysis

——, *Early Essene Eschatology: Judgement and Salvation according to Sapiential Work A*, in D.W. PARRY & S.T. RICKS (eds.), *Current Research and Technological Developments* (Studies on the Texts of the Desert of Judah, 20), Leiden, Brill, 1996, pp. 126-165. Short title: Early Essene Eschatology

——, *The Reconstruction of Sapiential Work A*, in *Revue de Qumran* 16 (1993-1995) 559-580. Short title: Reconstruction

——, *The Mystery to Come: Early Essene Theology of Revelation*, in F.H. CRYER & T.L. THOMPSON (eds.), *Qumran Between the Old and New Testaments* (Copenhagen International Seminar, 6 / Journal for the Study of the Old Testament Supplement Series, 290), Sheffield, Sheffield Academic Press, 1998, pp. 113-150. Short title: Mystery to Come

——, *4QWays of Righteousness*, in T. ELGVIN, M. KISTER, T. LIM, B. NITZAN, S. PFANN, E. QIMRON, L.H. SCHIFFMAN & A. STEUDEL, *Qumran Cave 4.*

XV. *Sapiential Texts. Part 1* (Discoveries in the Judaean Desert, 20), Oxford, Clarendon, 1997, pp. 173-202. Short title: 4QWays of Righteousness

——, *Wisdom and Apocalypticism in the Early Second Century BCE: The Evidence of 4QInstruction*, in L.H. SCHIFFMAN, E. TOV, J.C. VANDERKAM, & G. MARQUIS (eds.), *The Dead Sea Scrolls Fifty Years After Their Discovery. Proceedings of the Jerusalem Congress, July 20-25, 1997*, Jerusalem, Israel Exploration Society/The Shrine of the Book/The Israel Museum, 2000, pp. 226-47. Short title: Wisdom and Apocalypticism

——, *Wisdom in the Yaḥad. 4QWays of Righteousness*, in *Revue de Qumran* 17 (1996) 205-232. Short title: Wisdom in the Yaḥad

——, *Wisdom, Revelation, and Eschatology in an Early Essene Writing*, in *Society of Biblical Literature Seminar Papers* 34 (1995) 440-463. Short title: Wisdom, Revelation, and Eschatology

——, *Wisdom With and Without Apocalyptic*, in D. FALK, F. GARCÍA MARTÍNEZ & E. SCHULLER (eds.), *Sapiential, Liturgical and Poetical Texts from Qumran. Proceedings of the Third Meeting of the International Organization for Qumran Studies Oslo 1998* (Studies on the Texts of the Desert of Judah, 35), Leiden, Brill, 2000, pp. 15-38.

T. ELGVIN, M. KISTER, T. LIM, B. NITZAN, S. PFANN, E. QIMRON, L.H. SCHIFFMAN & A. STEUDEL in consultation with J.A. FITZMYER, *Qumran Cave 4. XV. Sapiential Texts. Part 1* (Discoveries in the Judaean Desert, 20), Oxford, Clarendon, 1997. Short title: Qumran Cave 4. XV

H.-J. FABRY, *Der Makarismus – mehr als nur eine weisheitliche Lehrform. Gedanken zu dem neu-edierten Text 4Q525*, in J. HAUSMANN & H-J. ZOBEL (eds.), *Alttestamentlicher Glaube und Biblische Theologie. FS H.D. Preuß*, Stuttgart, Kohlhammer, 1992, pp. 362-371. Short title: Makarismus

——, *Die Seligpreisungen in der Bibel und Qumran*, in: P. NAGEL et al. (eds.), *Dankesgabe für Heinrich Schützinger. Zum 75. Geburtstag dargebracht vom Orientalischen Seminar der Rheinischen Friedrich-Wilhelms-Universität Bonn* (Hallesche Beiträge zur Orientwissenschaft, 29/2000), Halle (Saale), Institut für Orientalistik, 2000, pp. 25-38.

J.A. FITZMYER, *A Palestinian Jewish Collection of Beatitudes*, in ID., *The Dead Sea Scrolls and Christian Origins*, Grand Rapids/Cambridge, Eerdmans, 2000, pp. 111-118. Short title: Beatitudes

J. FREY, *Different Patterns of Dualistic Thought in the Qumran Library. Reflections on their Background and History*, in M. BERNSTEIN, F. GARCÍA MARTÍNEZ & J.I. KAMPEN (eds.), *Legal Texts and Legal Issues. Proceedings of the Second Meeting of the International Organisation for Qumran Studies Cambridge 1995. FS J.M. Baumgarten* (Studies on the Texts of the Desert of Judah, 23), Leiden, Brill, 1997, pp. 275-335. Short title: Dualistic Thought

——, *The Notion of "Flesh" in 4QInstruction and the Background of Pauline Usage*, in D. FALK, F. GARCÍA MARTÍNEZ & E. SCHULLER (eds.), *Sapiential, Liturgical and Poetical Texts from Qumran. Proceedings of the Third Meeting of the International Organization for Qumran Studies Oslo 1998* (Studies on the Texts of the Desert of Judah, 35), Leiden, Brill, 2000, pp. 197-226. Short title: Notion of Flesh

J.G. GAMMIE, *Spatial and Ethical Dualism in Jewish Wisdom and Apocalyptic Literature*, in *Journal of Biblical Literature* 93 (1974) 356-385. Short title: Dualism

F. GARCÍA MARTÍNEZ, *Sapiential, Liturgical and Poetical Texts from Qumran*, in D. FALK, F. GARCÍA MARTÍNEZ & E. SCHULLER (eds.), *Sapiential, Liturgical and Poetical Texts from Qumran. Proceedings of the Third Meeting of the International Organization for Qumran Studies Oslo 1998* (Studies on the Texts of the Desert of Judah, 35), Leiden, Brill, 2000, pp. 1-11.

A.M. GAZOV-GINZBERG, *Double Meaning in a Qumran Work (The Wiles of the Wicked Woman)*, in *Revue de Qumran* 6 (1967) 279-285. Short title: Double Meaning

R. GORDIS, *The Knowledge of Good and Evil in the Old Testament and the Qumran Scrolls*, in *Journal of Biblical Literature* 76 (1957) 123-138. Short title: Knowledge of Good and Evil

D.J. HARRINGTON, Review of T. ELGVIN et al. (eds.), *Qumran Cave 4. XV*, in *Dead Sea Discoveries* 4 (1997) 357-360. Short title: Review of Qumran Cave 4. XV

———, *The Qumran Sapiential Texts in the Context of Biblical (OT and NT) and Second Temple Literature*, in L.H. SCHIFFMAN, E. TOV, J.C. VANDERKAM, & G. MARQUIS (eds.), *The Dead Sea Scrolls Fifty Years After Their Discovery. Proceedings of the Jerusalem Congress, July 20-25, 1997*, Jerusalem, Israel Exploration Society/The Shrine of the Book/The Israel Museum, 2000, pp. 256-62. Short title: Qumran Sapiential Texts

———, *The Raz Nihyeh in a Qumran Wisdom Text (1Q26, 4Q415-418, 423)*, in *Revue de Qumran* 17 (1996) 549-553. Short title: Raz Nihyeh

———, *Ten Reasons Why the Qumran Wisdom Texts are Important*, in *Dead Sea Discoveries* 4 (1997) 246-254. Short title: Reasons

———, *Two Early Jewish Approaches to Wisdom. Sirach and Qumran Sapiential Work A*, in *Journal for the Study of Pseudepigrapha* 16 (1997) 25-38. Short title: Approaches

———, *Wisdom at Qumran*, in E. ULRICH & J. VANDERKAM (eds.), *The Community of the Renewed Covenant. The Notre Dame Symposium on the Dead Sea Scrolls* (Christianity and Judaism in Antiquity Series, 10), Notre Dame, University of Notre Dame Press, 1994, pp. 137-152. Short title: Wisdom at Qumran

———, *Wisdom Texts*, in L.H. SCHIFFMAN & J.C. VANDERKAM et al. (eds.), *The Encyclopedia of the Dead Sea Scrolls*, Vol. 2, New York, Oxford University Press, 2000, pp. 976-980. Short title: Wisdom Texts

———, *Wisdom Texts from Qumran* (The Literature of the Dead Sea Scrolls), London/New York, Routledge, 1996. Short title: Wisdom Texts from Qumran

D.J. HARRINGTON & J. STRUGNELL, *Qumran Cave 4 Texts. A New Publication*, in *Journal of Biblical Literature* 112 (1993) 491-499. Short title: Qumran Cave 4 Texts

J.I. KAMPEN, *Aspects of Wisdom in the Gospel of Matthew in Light of the New Qumran Evidence*, in D. FALK, F. GARCÍA MARTÍNEZ & E. SCHULLER (eds.), *Sapiential, Liturgical and Poetical Texts from Qumran. Proceedings of the Third Meeting of the International Organization for Qumran Studies Oslo 1998* (Studies on the Texts of the Desert of Judah, 35), Leiden, Brill, 2000, pp. 227-239.

——, *The Diverse Aspects of Wisdom in the Qumran Texts*, in P.W. FLINT & J.C. VANDERKAM (eds.), *The Dead Sea Scrolls after Fifty Years. A Comprehensive Assessment*, Vol. 1, Leiden, Brill, 1998, pp. 211-243. Short title: Diverse Aspects

M. KISTER, *Commentary to 4Q298*, in *Jewish Quarterly Review* 85 (1994) 237-249. Short title: 4Q298

H. KOSMALA, *At the End of the Days*, in *Annual of the Swedish Theological Institute* 2 (1963) 27-37. Short title: End of the Days

——, *Maskil*, in D. MARCUS (ed.), *The Gaster Festschrift*, in *The Journal of the Ancient Near Eastern Society of Columbia University* 5 (1973) 235-241. Short title: Maskil

M. KÜCHLER, *Frühjüdische Weisheitstraditionen. Zum Fortgang weisheitlichen Denkens im Bereich des frühjüdischen Jahweglaubens* (Orbis biblicus et orientalis, 26), Freiburg (Schweiz), Universitätsverlag / Göttingen, Vandenhoeck & Ruprecht, 1979. Short title: Weisheitstraditionen

H.-W. KUHN, *The Wisdom Passage in 1 Corinthians 2:6-16 between Qumran and Proto-Gnosticism*, in D. FALK, F. GARCÍA MARTÍNEZ & E. SCHULLER (eds.), *Sapiential, Liturgical and Poetical Texts from Qumran. Proceedings of the Third Meeting of the International Organization for Qumran Studies Oslo 1998* (Studies on the Texts of the Desert of Judah, 35), Leiden, Brill, 2000, pp. 240-253.

A. LANGE, *The Determination of Fate by the Oracle of the Lot in the Dead Sea Scrolls, the Hebrew Bible and Ancient Mesopotamian Literature*, in D. FALK, F. GARCÍA MARTÍNEZ & E. SCHULLER (eds.), *Sapiential, Liturgical and Poetical Texts from Qumran. Proceedings of the Third Meeting of the International Organization for Qumran Studies Oslo 1998* (Studies on the Texts of the Desert of Judah, 35), Leiden, Brill, 2000, pp. 39-48.

——, *In Diskussion mit dem Tempel. Zur Auseinandersetzung zwischen Kohelet und weisheitlichen Kreisen am Jerusalemer Tempel*, in A. SCHOORS (ed.), *Qohelet in the Context of Wisdom* (Bibliotheca Ephemeridum Theologicarum Lovaniensium, 136), Leuven, Peeters, 1998, pp. 113-159. Short title: In Diskussion mit dem Tempel

——, *Die Endgestalt des protomasoretischen Psalters und die Toraweisheit. Zur Bedeutung der nicht essenischen Weisheitstexte aus Qumran für die Auslegung des protomasoretischen Psalters*, in E. ZENGER (ed.), *Der Psalter in Judentum und Christentum* (Herders Biblische Studien, 18), Freiburg i.B., Herder, 1998, pp. 101-136. Short title: Die Endgestalt des protomasoretischen Psalters

——, *Eschatological Wisdom in the Book of Qohelet and the Dead Sea Scrolls*, in L.H. SCHIFFMAN, E. TOV, J.C. VANDERKAM, & G. MARQUIS (eds.), *The Dead Sea Scrolls Fifty Years After Their Discovery. Proceedings of the Jerusalem Congress, July 20-25, 1997*, Jerusalem, Israel Exploration Society/The Shrine of the Book/The Israel Museum, 2000, pp. 817-25. Short title: Eschatological Wisdom

——, *Physiognomie oder Gotteslob? 4Q301 3*, in *Dead Sea Discoveries* 4 (1997) 282-296. Short title: Physiognomie oder Gotteslob

——, *Weisheit und Prädestination. Weisheitliche Urordnung und Prädestination in den Textfunden von Qumran* (Studies on the Texts of the Desert of Judah, 18), Leiden, Brill, 1995. Short title: Weisheit und Prädestination

——, *Wisdom and Predestination in the Dead Sea Scrolls*, in *Dead Sea Discoveries* 2 (1995) 340-354. Short title: Wisdom and Predestination
——, *1QGenAp XIX$_{10}$ – XX$_{32}$ as Paradigm of a Wisdom Didactive Narrative*, in: H.-J. FABRY, A. LANGE & H. LICHTENBERGER (eds.), *Qumranstudien. Vorträge und Beiträge der Teilnehmer des Qumranseminars auf dem internationalen Treffen der Society of Biblical Literature, Münster 25.-26. Juli 1993* (Schriften des Institutum Judaicum Delitzschianum, 4), Göttingen, Vandenhoeck & Ruprecht, 1996, pp. 191-204. Short title: Wisdom Didactive Narrative
E.W. LARSON, *Mysteries*, in L.H. SCHIFFMAN & J.C. VANDERKAM *et al.* (eds.), *The Encyclopedia of the Dead Sea Scrolls*, Vol. 1, New York, Oxford University Press, 2000, pp. 587-88. Short title: Mysteries
R.C. VAN LEEUWEN, *Scribal Wisdom and a Biblical Proverb at Qumran*, in *Dead Sea Discoveries* 4 (1997) 255-264. Short title: Scribal Wisdom
J. LICHT, כת מדבר יהודה רעתה של האשה "(4Q184)" שיר שנמצא בשרידי כתביה של לזכרו של יעקב ליוותר מחקרים במקרא ובספרות ימי בית שני In הזרה המקרא ותולדות ישראל. B. UFFENHEIMER (ed.), Tel Aviv, Tel Aviv University Press, 1971, pp. 289-296. Short title: 4Q184
H. LICHTENBERGER, *Eine weisheitliche Mahnrede in den Qumranfunden (4Q185)*, in M. DELCOR (ed.), *Qumrân. Sa piété, sa théologie et son milieu* (Bibliotheca Ephemeridum Theologicarum Lovaniensium, 46), Paris-Gembloux, Éditions Duculot / Leuven, University Press, 1978, pp. 151-162. Short title: Weisheitliche Mahnrede
W.L. LIPSCOMB & J.A. SANDERS, *Wisdom at Qumran*, in J.G. GAMMIE, W.A. BRUEGGEMANN, W. HUMPHREYS & J.M. WARD (eds.), *Israelite Wisdom*. FS S. Terrien, Missoula, Scholars Press, 1978, pp. 277-285. Short title: Wisdom at Qumran
J. MAIER, *Wiles of the Wicked Woman*, in L.H. SCHIFFMAN & J.C. VANDERKAM *et al.* (eds.), *The Encyclopedia of the Dead Sea Scrolls*, Vol. 2, New York, Oxford University Press, 2000, p. 976. Short title: Wiles of the Wicked Woman
H.G. MAY, *Cosmological Reference in the Qumran Doctrine of the Two Spirits and in Old Testament Imagery*, in *Journal of Biblical Literature* 82 (1963) 1-14. Short title: Cosmological Reference
R.D. MOORE, *Personification of the Seduction of Evil. The Wiles of the Wicked Woman*, in *Revue de Qumran* 10 (1979-81) 505-519. Short title: Personification
J. MUILENBURG, *A Qohelet Scroll from Qumran*, in *Bulletin of the American Schools of Oriental Research* 135 (1954) 20-28. Short title: Qohelet Scroll
G.-W. NEBE, *Lexikalische Bemerkungen zu* אושון, *"Fundament, Tiefe"*, in *4Q184, Prov 7,9 und 20,20*, in *Revue de Qumran* 8 (1972-75) 97-103. Short title: Lexikalische Bemerkungen
C. NEWSOM, *The Sage in the Literature of Qumran. The Functions of the Maskil*, in J.G. GAMMIE & L.G. PERDUE (eds.), *The Sage in Ancient Israel and the Ancient Near East*, Winona Lake, Eisenbrauns, 1990, pp. 101-120. Short title: Sage
——, *"Sectually Explicit" Literature from Qumran*, in W.H. PROPP, B. HALPERN & D.N. FREEDMAN (eds.), *The Hebrew Bible and its Interpreters*, Winona

Lake, Eisenbrauns, 1990, pp. 167-187. Short title: Sectually Explicit Literature

B. NITZAN, *Hymns from Qumran – 4Q510-4Q511*, in D. DIMANT & U. RAPPAPORT (eds.), *The Dead Sea Scrolls. Forty Years of Research* (Studies on the Texts of the Desert of Judah, 10), Leiden, Brill/Jerusalem, Magnes/ Yad Izhak Ben-Zvi, 1992, pp. 53-63. Short title: Hymns from Qumran

F. NÖTSCHER, *Zur Theologischen Terminologie der Qumran-Texte* (Bonner biblische Beiträge, 10), Bonn, Hanstein, 1956. Short title: Terminologie

G.B. OTZEN, *Old Testament Wisdom Literature and Dualistic Thinking in Late Judaism*, in *Congress Volume. Edinburgh 1974* (Vetus Testamentum Supplement Series, 28), Leiden, Brill, 1975, pp. 146-157. Short title: Wisdom Literature and Dualistic Thinking

S.J. PFANN, *4Q298. The Maskil's Address to All Sons of Dawn*, in *Jewish Quarterly Review* 85 (1994) 205-235. Short title: 4Q298

S.J. PFANN & M. KISTER, *4Q298. 4QcryptA Words of the Maskil to All Sons of Dawn*, in T. ELGVIN et al. (eds.), *Qumran Cave 4. XV. Sapiential Texts, Part 1* (Discoveries in the Judaean Desert, 20), Oxford, Clarendon, 1997, pp. 1-30. Short title: 4Q298

E. PUECH, *The Collection of Béatitudes in Hebrew and in Greek (4Q525 1-4 and Mt 5, 3-12)*, in F. MANNS & E. ALLIATA (eds.), *Early Christianity in Context. Monuments and Documents*, Jerusalem, Franciscan Printing Press, 1993, pp. 353-368. Short title: Beatitudes

——, *Un hymne essénien en partie retrouvé et les Béatitudes. 1QH V 12-VI 18 (= col. XIII-XIV 7) et 4QBéat*, in *Revue de Qumran* 13 (1988) 59-88. Short title: Un hymne essénien

——, *Qumrân grotte 4. XVIII. Textes hébreux (4Q521-4Q525, 4Q576-4Q579)* (Discoveries in the Judaean Desert, 25), Oxford, Clarendon, 1998. Short title: Qumrân grotte 4. XVIII

——, *4Q525 et les péricopes des béatitudes en Ben Sira et Matthieu*, in *Revue Biblique* 98 (1991) 80-106. Short title: 4Q525

E. QIMRON, *A Work Concerning Divine Providence: 4Q413*, in S. GITIN, M. SOKOLOFF & Z. ZEVIT (eds.), *Solving Riddles and Untying Knots. Biblical, Epigraphic, and Semitic Studies in Honor of Jonas C. Greenfield*, Winona Lake, Eisenbrauns, 1995, pp. 191-202. Short title: Divine Providence

——, *413. 4QComposition concerning Divine Providence*, in T. ELGVIN et al. (eds.), *Qumran Cave 4. XV. Sapiential Texts, Part 1* (Discoveries in the Judaean Desert, 20), Oxford, Clarendon, 1997, pp. 169-71. Short title: 4QComposition Concerning Divine Providence

I. RABINOWITZ, *The Authorship, Audience, and Date of the de Vaux Fragment of an Unknown Work*, in *Journal of Biblical Literature* 71 (1952) 19-32. Short title: Authorship, Audience, and Date

——, *Sequence and Dates of the Extra-Biblical Dead Sea Scroll Texts and "Damascus" Fragments*, in *Vetus Testamentum* 3 (1953) 175-185. Short title: Sequence and Dates

S.A. REED & M.J. LUNDBERG, *The Dead Sea Scrolls Catalogue. Documents, Photographs and Museum Inventory Numbers* (Society of Biblical Literature Resources for Biblical Study, 32), Atlanta GA, Scholars Press, 1994. Short title: Dead Sea Scrolls Catalogue

J.C.R. DE ROO, *4Q525 a Qumran Sectarian Document,* in S.E. PORTER & C.A. EVANS (eds.), *The Scrolls and the Scriptures. Qumran Fifty Years After* (Journal for the Study of the Pseudepigrapha Supplement Series, 26), Sheffield, Sheffield Academic Press, 1997, pp. 338-367. Short title: Qumran Sectarian Document

L.H. SCHIFFMAN, *Mysteries,* in T. ELGVIN, M. KISTER, T. LIM, B. NITZAN, S. PFANN, E. QIMRON, L.H. SCHIFFMAN & A. STEUDEL, *Qumran Cave 4. XV. Sapiential Texts. Part 1* (Discoveries in the Judaean Desert, 20), Oxford, Clarendon, 1997, pp. 31-123. Short title: Mysteries

———, *Reclaiming the Dead Sea Scrolls. The History of Judaism, the Background of Christianity, the Lost Library of Qumran,* Philadelphia/ Jerusalem, Jewish Publication Society, 1994. Short title: Reclaiming the Dead Sea Scrolls

———, *4QMysteries: A Preliminary Translation,* in D. ASSAF (ed.), *Proceedings of the Eleventh World Congress of Jewish Studies. Division A: the Bible and Its World,* Jerusalem, Magnes, 1994, pp. 199-206. Short title: Preliminary Translation

———, *4QMysteries^a. A Preliminary Edition and Translation,* in S. GITIN, M. SOKOLOFF & Z. ZEVIT et al. (eds.), *Solving Riddles and Untying Knots. FS Jonas C. Greenfield,* Winona Lake, Eisenbrauns, 1995, pp. 207-260. Short title: 4QMysteries^a

———, *4QMysteries^b. A Preliminary Edition,* in *Revue de Qumran* 16 (1993-1994) 203-223. Short title: 4QMysteries^b

E.J. SCHNABEL, *Law and Wisdom from Ben Sira to Paul. A Tradition Historical Enquiry into the Relation of Law, Wisdom, and Ethics* (Wissenschaftliche Untersuchungen zum Neuen Testament, II 16), Tübingen, Mohr Siebeck, 1985. Short title: Law and Wisdom

B. SHARVIT, *The Virtue of Wisdom in the Image of the Righteous Man in 1QS,* in *Beth Mikra* 19 (1974) 526-530. Short title: Virtue of Wisdom

H. STEGEMANN, *Die Bedeutung der Qumranfunde für die Erforschung der Apokalyptik,* in D. HELLHOLM (ed.), *Apocalypticism in the Mediterranian World and the Near East. Proceedings of the International Colloquium on Apocalypticism Uppsala, August 12-17, 1979,* Tübingen, Mohr Siebeck, ^{2}1989, pp. 495-530. Short title: Bedeutung

A. STEUDEL, *4Q408. A Liturgy on Morning and Evening Prayer. Preliminary Edition,* in *Revue de Qumran* 16 (1994) 313-334. Short title: 4Q408

———, *Sapiential Texts,* in T. ELGVIN et al. (eds), *Qumran Cave 4. XV. Sapiential Texts. Part 1* (Discoveries in the Judaean Desert, 20), Oxford, Clarendon, 1997, pp. 159-167, 203-224. Short title: Sapiential Texts

J. STRUGNELL, *More on Wives and Marriage in the Dead Sea Scrolls (4Q416 2 ii 21 [cf. 1 Thess 4:4] and 4QMMT §B),* in *Revue de Qumran* 17 (1996) 537-547. Short title: Wives and Marriage

———, *Notes en marge du Volume V des "Discoveries in the Judaean Desert of Jordan",* in *Revue de Qumran* 7 (1969-71) 163-276. Short title: Notes en marge

———, *The Sapiential Work 4Q415ff and pre-Qumranic Works from Qumran. Lexical Considerations,* in D.W. PARRY & E. ULRICH (eds.), *The Provo International Conference on the Dead Sea Scrolls. Technological Innovations, New Texts, & Reformulated Issues* (Studies on the Texts of the

Desert of Judah, 30), Leiden, Brill, 1999, pp. 595-608. Short title: Sapiential Work

J. STRUGNELL, D.J. HARRINGTON, & T. ELGVIN (eds.) in consultation with J.A. FITZMYER, *Qumran Cave 4. XXIV. Sapiential Texts, Part 2. 4QInstruction (Musar l^eMevin): 4Q415ff., with a Re-edition of 1Q26* (Discoveries in the Judaean Desert, 34), Oxford, Clarendon, 1999. Short title: Qumran Cave 4. XXIV

S.J. TANZER, *424. 4QInstruction-like Composition B*, in S.J. PFANN et al. (eds.), *Qumran Cave 4. XXVI. Cryptic Texts and Miscellanea, Part 1* (Discoveries in the Judaean Desert, 36), Oxford, Clarendon, 2000, pp. 333-346.

——, *The Sages at Qumran. Wisdom in the Hodayot*, Ph.D. Dissertation, Havard University, 1987. Short title: Sages at Qumran

E.J.C. TIGCHELAAR, הבא ביחד *in 4QInstruction (4Q418 64+199+66 par 4Q417 1 i 17–19) and the Height of the Columns of 4Q418*, in *Revue de Qumran* 18 (1998) 589–593. Short title: חבא ביחד

——, *The Addressees of 4QInstruction*, in D. FALK, F. GARCÍA MARTÍNEZ & E. SCHULLER (eds.), *Sapiential, Liturgical and Poetical Texts from Qumran. Proceedings of the Third Meeting of the International Organization for Qumran Studies Oslo 1998* (Studies on the Texts of the Desert of Judah, 35), Leiden, Brill, 2000, pp. 62-75.

——, *Sabbath Halakha and Worship in 4QWays of Righteousness: 4Q421 11 and 13+2+8 par 4Q264a 1-2*, in *Revue de Qumran* 18 (1998) 359-372. Short title: Sabbath Halakha.

P.A. TILLER, *The "Eternal Planting" in the Dead Sea Scrolls*, in *Dead Sea Discoveries* 4 (1997) 312-335. Short title: Eternal Planting

TH.H. TOBIN, *4Q185 and Jewish Wisdom-Literature*, in H.W. ATTRIDGE, J.J. COLLINS & TH.H. TOBIN, *Of Scribes and Scrolls. Studies on the Hebrew Bible, Intertestamental Judaism, and Christian Origins*, FS J. Strugnell (College Theology Society Resources in Religion, 5), Lanham/New York/London, University Press of America, 1990, pp. 145-152. Short title: 4Q185

E. TOV, *Letters of the Cryptic A Script and Paleo-Hebrew Letters Used as Scribal Marks in Some Qumran Scrolls*, in *Dead Sea Discoveries* 2 (1995) 330-339. Short title: Scribal Marks

——, *Scribal Markings in the Texts from the Judaean Desert*, in D.W. PARRY & S.D. RICKS (eds.), *Current Research and Technological Developments on the Dead Sea Scrolls. Conference on the Texts from the Judaean Desert, Jerusalem 30 April 1995* (Studies on the Texts of the Desert of Judah, 20), Leiden, Brill, 1996, pp. 41-77. Short title: Scribal Markings

E. TOV & S.J. PFANN, *Companion Volume to the Dead Sea Scrolls Microfiche Edition*, 2. Aufl., Leiden, Brill/IDC, 1995. Short title: Companion Volume

J.C. VANDERKAM, *Mantic Wisdom in the Dead Sea Scrolls*, in *Dead Sea Discoveries* 4 (1997) 336-353. Short title: Mantic Wisdom

R. DE VAUX, *La grotte des manuscrits hébreux*, in *Revue Biblique* 56 (1949) 586-609. Short title: La grotte des manuscrits hébreux

D.J. VERSEPUT, *Wisdom, 4Q185 and the Epistle of James*, in *Journal of Biblical Literature* 117 (1998) 691-707. Short title: 4Q185

B.T. VIVIANO, *Beatitudes Found Among the Dead Sea Scrolls*, in *Biblical*

Archaeology Review 18/6 (1992) 53-55.66. Short title: Beatitudes
——, *Eight Beatitudes at Qumran and in Matthew? A New Publication from Cave Four*, in *Svensk Exegetisk Årsbok* 58 (1993) 71-84. Short title: Eight Beatitudes
B.Z. WACHOLDER & M.G. ABEGG, *A Preliminary Edition of the Unpublished Dead Sea Scrolls. The Hebrew and Aramaic Texts from Cave Four*, Fasc. 2, Washington DC, Biblical Archaeology Society, 1992. Short title: Preliminary Edition 2
——, *A Preliminary Edition of the Unpublished Dead Sea Scrolls. The Hebrew and Aramaic Texts from Cave Four*, Fasc. 4: *Concordance of Fascicles 1-3*, Washington DC, Biblical Archaeology Society, 1996. Short title: Concordance
S. WHITE CRAWFORD, *Lady Wisdom and Dame Folly at Qumran*, in *Dead Sea Discoveries* 5 (1998) 355-366. Short title: Lady Wisdom
J.E. WORREL, *Concepts of Wisdom in the Dead Sea Scrolls*, PhD Dissertation, Claremont Graduate School, Claremont, 1968. Short title: Concepts of Wisdom
A.S. VAN DER WOUDE, *Wisdom at Qumran*, in J. DAY, R.P. GORDON & H.G.M. WILLIAMSON (eds.), *Wisdom in Ancient Israel*. FS J. A. Emerton, Cambridge, Cambridge University Press, 1995, pp. 244-256. Short title: Wisdom
Y. ZUR, *Parallels between Acts of Thomas 6-7 and 4Q184*, in *Revue de Qumran* 16 (1993-1994) 103-107. Short title: Parallels

OTHER LITERATURE

Compiled by Charlotte HEMPEL

E.A. ABBOTT, *The Interpretation of Early Christian Poetry*, in ID., *The Fourfold Gospel. The Beginning*, Cambridge, Cambridge University Press, 1914. Short title: Early Christian Poetry
——, *Light on the Gospel from an Ancient Poet*, Cambridge, Cambridge University Press, 1912. Short title: Light
M. ALBANI, *Zur Rekonstruktion eines verdrängten Konzeptes: Der 364-Tage-Kalender in der gegenwärtigen Forschung*, in M. ALBANI, J. FREY & A. LANGE (eds.), *Studies in the Book of Jubilees* (Texte und Studien zum antiken Judentum, 65), Tübingen, Mohr Siebeck, 1997, pp. 79-125. Short title: Verdrängtes Konzept
P.S. ALEXANDER, *Bavli Berakhot 55a-57b: The Talmudic Dreambook in Context*, in *Journal of Jewish Studies* 46 (1995) 230-248. Short title: Talmudic Dreambook
——, *From Son of Adam to Second God: Transformations of the Biblical Enoch*, in M.E. STONE & T.A. BERGREN (eds.), *Biblical Figures Outside the Bible*, Harrisburg PN, Trinity Press International, 1998, pp. 90-94. Short title: Second God
——, *"Hellenism" and "Hellenization" as Problematic Historio-graphical Categories*, in T. ENGBERG PEDERSEN (ed.), *Paul Beyond the Judaism/Hellenism Divide*, Louisville KY, Westminster/John Knox Press, 2001. Short title: Problematic Categories
——, *Physiognomy, Initiation, and Rank in the Qumran Community*, in H. CANCIK, H. LICHTENBERGER, & P. SCHÄFER (eds.), *Geschichte – Tradition – Reflexion. FS Martin Hengel*, Tübingen, Mohr Siebeck, 1996, Volume I, pp. 385-394. Short title: Physiognomy
——, *The Redaction-History of Serekh ha-Yaḥad: A Proposal*, in *Revue de Qumran* 17 (1996) 437-453. Short title: Redaction-History
P.S. ALEXANDER & G. VERMES, *Qumran Cave 4. XIX. Serekh Ha-Yaḥad and Two Related Texts* (Discoveries in the Judaean Desert, 26), Oxford, Clarendon, 1998. Short title: Qumran Cave 4. XIX
P. ALTHAUS, *"... Damit ihr nicht tut, was ihr wollt". Zur Auslegung von Gal 5,17*, in *Theologische Literaturzeitung* 76 (1951) 15-18. Short title: "...Damit ihr nicht tut, was ihr wollt"
F.I. ANDERSEN, *2 (Slavonic Apocalypse of) Enoch. (Late First Century A.D.). Appendix: 2 Enoch in Merilo Pravednoe. A New Translation and Introduction*, in J.H. CHARLESWORTH (ed.), *Pseudepigrapha I*, pp. 91-221. Short title: Slavonic Enoch
G.A. ANDERSON, *The Penitence Narrative in the Life of Adam and Eve*, in *Hebrew Union College Annual* 63 (1992) 1-38. Short title: Penitence Narrative
G.A. ANDERSON & M. STONE, *A Synopsis of the Books of Adam and Eve* (Society of Biblical Literature. Early Judaism and its Literature, 5), Atlanta GA, Scholars Press, 1994. Short title: Synopsis

H. ANDERSON, *4 Maccabees*, in J.H. CHARLESWORTH (ed.), *Pseudepigrapha II*, pp. 531-564. Short title: 4 Maccabees

J. ASHTON, *Understanding the Fourth Gospel*, Oxford, Clarendon, 1991, 1993. Short title: Fourth Gospel

J. ASSMANN, *Loyalismus, Frömmigkeit*, in E. HORNUNG & O. KEEL (eds.), *Studien zu altägyptischen Lebenslehren* (Orbis biblicus et orientalis, 28), Fribourg, Benzinger, 1979, pp. 12-72. Short title: Loyalismus

M. BAILLET, *Qumrân Grotte 4. III (4Q482-4Q520)* (Discoveries in the Judaean Desert, 7), Oxford, Clarendon, 1982. Short title: Qumrân Grotte 4

P. BATTIFOL, *Les Odes de Salomon*, Paris, Librairie Lecoffre, 1911. Short title: Odes

H. BAUER & P. LEANDER, *Grammatik des Biblisch-Aramäischen*, Tübingen, Max Niemeyer, 1927. Short title: Grammatik

J.M. BAUMGARTEN, *Qumran Cave 4. XIII. The Damascus Document (4Q266-273)* (Discoveries in the Judaean Desert, 18), Oxford, Clarendon, 1996. Short title: Qumran Cave 4. XIII

——, *The "Sons of Dawn" in CDC 13:14-15 and the Ban on Commerce among the Essenes*, in *Israel Exploration Quarterly* 33 (1983) 81-85. Short title: Ban on Commerce

——, *Studies in Qumran Law* (Studies in Judaism in Late Antiquity, 24), Leiden, Brill, 1977. Short title: Qumran Law

J.M. BAUMGARTEN et al., *Qumran Cave 4. XXV: Halakhic Texts* (Discoveries in the Judaean Desert, 35), Oxford, Clarendon, 1999. Short title: Qumran Cave 4. XXV.

F. BAUMGÄRTEL, σάρξ: *B. Flesh in the Old Testament*, in G. KITTEL & G. FRIEDRICH (eds.), *Theological Dictionary of the New Testament* VII, Grand Rapids MI, Eerdmans, 1971, pp. 105-108. Short title: σάρξ

W. BAUMGARTNER, *Hebräisches und aramäisches Lexikon zum Alten Testament*, Leiden, Brill 1967-1983. Short title: Lexikon

F.Ch. BAUR, *Vorlesungen über neutestamentliche Theologie*, Leipzig, Fues, 1864. Short title: Vorlesungen

J. BECKER, *Paulus. Der Apostel der Völker*, Tübingen, Mohr Siebeck, 1989. Short title: Paulus

——, *Studien zur Entstehungsgeschichte der Testamente der Zwölf Patriarchen* (Arbeiten zur Geschichte des antiken Judentums und des Urchristentums, 8), Leiden, Brill, 1970. Short title: Studien zur Entstehungsgeschichte

——, *Die Testamente der Zwölf Patriarchen* (Jüdische Schriften aus hellenistisch-römischer Zeit, III.1), Gütersloh, Mohn, 1974. Short title: Testamente

J.C. BEKER, *Paul the Apostle. The Triumph of God in Life and Thought*, Philadelphia, Fortress Press, 1980. Short title: Paul the Apostle

E. BEN YEHUDA, *Thesaurus totius hebraitatis et veteris et recentioris*, New York/London, Thomas Yoseloff, 1960. Short title: Thesaurus

K. BERGER, *Formgeschichte des Neuen Testaments*, Heidelberg, Quelle & Meyer, 1984. Short title: Formgeschichte

——, *Henoch*, in T. KLAUSER et al. (eds.), *Reallexikon für Antike und Christentum. Sachwörterbuch zur Auseinandersetzung des Christentums mit der antiken Welt*, Volume 14, Stuttgart, Anton Hiersemann,1988, pp. 474-545. Short title: Henoch

——, *Theologiegeschichte des Urchristentums*, Tübingen/Basel, Francke, 1994. Short title: Theologiegeschichte

P. BERGER & T. LUCKMANN, *The Social Construction of Reality. A Treatise in the Sociology of Knowledge*, Garden City NY, Doubleday, 1967. Short title: Construction

R. BERGMEIER & H. PABST, *Ein Lied von der Erschaffung der Sprache: Sinn und Aufbau von 1Q Hodayot I, 27-31*, in *Revue de Qumran* 5 (1965) 435-439. Short title: Lied

J.H. BERNARD, *The Odes of Solomon* (Texts and Studies, 8, 3), Cambridge, Cambridge University Press, 1912. Short title: Odes

D.A. BERTRAND, *La Vie Grecque d'Adam et Ève* (Recherches Intertestamentaires, 1), Paris, Maisonneuve, 1987. Short title: Vie Grecque

H.D. BETZ, *Galatians. A Commentary on Paul's Letter to the Churches in Galatia* (Hermeneia), Philadelphia, Fortress, 1979. Short title: Galatians

——, *Die Makarismen der Bergpredigt (Matthäus 5,3-12). Beobachtungen zur literarischen Form und theologischen Bedeutung*, in ID. (ed.), *Studien zur Bergpredigt*, Tübingen, Mohr Siebeck, 1985, pp. 21-33 (= *Zeitschrift für Theologie und Kirche* 75 [1978] 3-19). Short title: Makarismen

M. BLACK, *Apocalypsis Henochi Graece* (Pseudepigrapha Veteris Testamenti Graece, 3), Leiden, Brill, 1970. Short title: Apocalypsis

——, *The Book of Enoch or I Enoch. A New English Edition with Commentary and Textual Notes* (Studia in Veteris Testamenti Pseudepigrapha, 7), Leiden, Brill, 1985. Short title: Book of Enoch

G. BOCCACCINI, *Beyond the Essene Hypothesis. The Parting of the Ways Between Qumran and Enochic Judaism*, Grand Rapids MI, Eerdmans, 1998. Short title: Beyond the Essene Hypothesis

M. BOCKMUEHL, *Redaction and Ideology in the Rule of the Community (1QS/4QS)*, in *Revue de Qumran* 18 (1998) 541-560. Short title: Redaction and Ideology

J. BOON, *Other Tribes, Other Scribes. Symbolic Anthropology in the Comparative Study of Cultures, Histories, Religions and Texts*, Cambridge, Cambridge University Press, 1982. Short title: Tribes

G. BORNKAMM, *Paulus*, in K. GALLING et al. (eds.), *Die Religion in Geschichte und Gegenwart. Handwörterbuch für Theologie und Religionswissenschaft* 5, Tübingen, Mohr Siebeck, ^{3}1961, cc. 166-190. Short title: Paulus

Chr. BÖTTRICH, *Adam als Mikrokosmos. Eine Untersuchung zum slavischen Henochbuch* (Judentum und Umwelt, 59), Frankfurt u.a., Peter Lang, 1995. Short title: Mikrokosmos

——, *Astrologie in der Henochtradition*, in *Zeitschrift für die alttestamentliche Wissenschaft* 88 (1997) 222-245. Short title: Astrologie

——, *Beobachtungen zum Midrasch vom "Leben Henochs"*, in *Mitteilungen und Beiträge der Forschungsstelle Judentum an der Theologischen Fakultät Leipzig* 10 (1996) 44-83. Short title: Beobachtungen

——, *Das slavische Henochbuch* (Jüdische Schriften aus hellenistisch-römischer Zeit, V.7), Gütersloh, Gütersloher Verlagshaus, 1995, pp. 781-1040. Short title: JSHRZ V/7

——, *Weltweisheit – Menschheitsethik – Urkult. Studien zum slavischen Henochbuch* (Wissenschaftliche Untersuchungen zum Neuen Testament, 2/50), Tübingen, Mohr Siebeck, 1992. Short title: Weltweisheit

W. BOUSSET, *Kyrios Christos. Geschichte des Christusglaubens von den Anfängen des Christentums bis Irenaeus*, Göttingen, Vandenhoeck & Ruprecht, ^{6}1967. Short title: Kyrios Christos

W. BOUSSET & H. GRESSMANN, *Die Religion des Judentums im späthellenistischen Zeitalter*, Tübingen, Mohr Siebeck, ^{3}1926. Short title: Die Religion des Judentums

E. BRANDENBURGER, *Fleisch und Geist. Paulus und die dualistische Weisheit* (Wissenschaftliche Monographien zum Alten und Neuen Testament, 29), Neukirchen-Vluyn, Neukirchener Verlag, 1968. Short title: Fleisch und Geist

N. BRATSIOTIS, בָּשָׂר, in G.J. BOTTERWECK & H. RINGGREN (eds.), *Theologisches Wörterbuch zum Alten Testament* I, Stuttgart, Kohlhammer, 1973, cc. 850-867. Short title: בָּשָׂר

G. BRAUMANN, *Zum traditionsgeschichtlichen Problem der Seligpreisungen Mt 5, 3-12*, in Novum Testamentum 4 (1960) 253-260. Short title: Problem

H. BRAUN, *Qumran und das Neue Testament*, 2 vols., Tübingen, Mohr Siebeck, 1966. Short title: Qumran und das Neue Testament

——, *Römer 7, 7-25 und das Selbstverständnis des Qumran-Frommen*, in Zeitschrift für Theologie und Kirche 56 (1959) 1-18. Short title: Selbstverständnis

D. BREMER, *Pindar. Siegeslieder: Griechisch-deutsch*, München, Artemis und Winkler, 1992. Short title: Pindar

C. BROCKELMANN, *Grundriß der vergleichenden Grammatik der semitischen Sprachen*, Berlin, Reuther & Reichard, 1908-1913. Reprinted Hildesheim, Georg Olms, 1982. Short title: Grundriß

——, *Hebräische Syntax*, Neukirchen, Neukirchener Verlag, 1956. Short title: Syntax

I. BROER, *Die Seligpreisungen der Bergpredigt. Studien zu ihrer Überlieferung und Interpretation* (Bonner biblische Beiträge, 61), Bonn, Hanstein, 1986. Short title: Seligpreisungen

G.J. BROOKE, *4QTestament of Levi^d (?) and the Messianic Servant High Priest*, in M.C. DE BOER (ed.), *From Jesus to John. FS M. de Jonge* (Journal for the Study of the New Testament Supplement Series, 84), Sheffield, Sheffield Academic Press, 1993, pp. 83-100. Short title: 4QTestament of Levi^d (?)

——, *"The Canon Within the Canon" at Qumran and in the New Testament*, in S.E. PORTER & C.A. EVANS (eds.), *The Scriptures and the Scrolls. Qumran Fifty Years After* (Journal for the Study of the Pseudepigrapha Supplement Series, 26), Sheffield, Sheffield Academic Press, 1997, pp. 242-266. Short title: "The Canon Within the Canon"

W.H. BROWNLEE, *The Cosmic Role of Angels in the 11QTargum of Job*, in Journal for the Study of Judaism 8 (1977) 83-84. Short title: Cosmic Role of Angels

C. BRUSTON, *Les plus anciens cantiques Chrétiens*, Geneva, J.-H. Jeheber / Paris, Fischbacher, 1912. Short title: Cantiques

G. BUCCELLATI, *Tre saggi sulla sapienza mesopotamica III: La teodicea: Condanna dell'abulia politica*, in Oriens antiquus 11 (1972) 161-178. Short title: Teodicea

R. BULTMANN, *Christus des Gesetzes Ende*, in ID., *Glauben und Verstehen. Gesammelte Aufsätze* 2, Tübingen, Mohr Siebeck, ³1961, pp. 32-58. Short title: Christus des Gesetzes Ende

——, *Paulus*, in H. GUNKEL & L. ZSCHARNACK (eds.) *Die Religion in Geschichte und Gegenwart. Handwörterbuch für Theologie und Religionswissenschaft* 4, Tübingen, Mohr Siebeck, ²1930, cc. 1019-1045. Short title: Paulus

—, *Das Problem der Ethik bei Paulus*, in *Zeitschrift für die neutestamentliche Wissenschaft* 23 (1924) 123-140. Short title: Das Problem der Ethik bei Paulus
—, *Theologie des Neuen Testaments*, Tübingen, Mohr Siebeck, ⁹1984. Short title: Theologie
W. BURKERT, *The Orientalizing Revolution. Near Eastern Influences on Greek Culture in the Early Archaic Age*, trans. M.E. PINDER and W. BURKERT, Cambridge Mass., Harvard University Press, 1992. Short title: Orientalizing Revolution
—, *Kulte des Altertums. Biologische Grundlagen der Religion*, München, Beck, 1998. Short title: Kulte
F. CABROL & H. LECLERCQ, *Dictionnaire d'archéologie Chrétienne et de liturgie* 12/2, Paris, Letousey et Ané, 1936. Short title: Dictionnaire 12/2.
J. CARMIGNAC, *Un Aramaïsme biblique et qumranien: l'infinitif placé après son complément d'objet*, in *Revue de Qumran* 5 (1966) 503-520. Short title: L'infinitif
—, *Conjecture sur la première ligne de la Règle de la Communauté*, in *Revue de Qumran* 2 (1959) 85-87. Short title: Première ligne
—, *Qu'est-ce que l'apocalyptique? Son emploi à Qumran*, in *Revue de Qumran* 10 (1979-1981) 3-33. Short title: Apocalyptique
—, *Un Qumrânien converti au Christianisme: l'auteur des Odes de Salomon*, in H. BARDTKE (ed.), *Qumran-Probleme* (Deutsche Akademie der Wissenschaften zu Berlin, 42), Berlin, Akademie-Verlag, 1963, pp. 75-108. Short title: L'auteur des Odes
—, *La Règle de la Guerre*, Paris, Letouzey et Ané, 1958. Short title: La Règle de la Guerre
E. CASTELLI, *Imitating Paul. A Discourse of Power* (Literary Current in Biblical Interpretation), Louisville KY, Westminster/John Knox Press, 1991. Short title: Imitating Paul
H. CAZELLES, אשרי, in G.J. BOTTERWECK & H. RINGGREN (eds.), *Theologisches Wörterbuch zum Alten Testament* I, Stuttgart, Kohlhammer, 1973, pp. 481-485. Short title: אשרי
J.H. CHARLESWORTH, *Critical Reflections on the Odes of Solomon* (Journal for the Study of the Pseudepigrapha Supplement Series, 22), Sheffield, Sheffield Academic Press, 1998. Short title: Critical Reflections
—, *The Fourteen Literary Collections for Studying Early Judaism and Christian Origins: The Place of the Odes of Solomon*, in J. KEŘKOVSKY (ed.), *ΕΠΙΤΟΑΥΤΟ. FS Petr Pokorný*, Prague, Mlyn, 1998, pp. 185-207. Short title: Fourteen Literary Collections
—, *The Jewish Roots of Christology: The Discovery of the Hypostatic Voice*, in *Scottish Journal of Theology* 39 (1985) 19-41. Short title: Christology
—, *Les Odes de Salomon et les manuscrits de la mer morte*, in *Revue Biblique* 77 (1970) 522-49. Short title: Odes
—, *The Odes of Solomon*, Oxford, Clarendon, 1973. Reprinted in SBL Texts and Translations, 13, Pseudepigrapha Series, 7, Chico CA, Scholars Press, 1977. Short title: The Odes of Solomon
—, *The Old Testament Pseudepigrapha and the New Testament*, Harrisburg PA, Trinity Press International, 1998. Short title: Pseudepigrapha
—, *The SNTS Pseudepigrapha Seminars at Tübingen and Paris on the Books*

of Enoch (Seminar Report), in *New Testament Studies* 25 (1979) 315-323. Short title: Pseudepigrapha Seminars

J.H. CHARLESWORTH (ed.), *Caves of Enlightenment. Proceedings of the American School of Oriental Research Dead Sea Scrolls Jubilee Symposium (1947-1997)*, North Richland Hills TX, BIBAL, 1998. Short title: Caves

——, *Jesus and the Dead Sea Scrolls*, New York, Doubleday, 1992. Short title: Jesus

——, *The Old Testament Pseudepigrapha*, 2 Volumes, Garden City NY, Doubleday, 1983-1985. Short title: Pseudepigrapha I and II

J.H. CHARLESWORTH et al. (eds.), *The Dead Sea Scrolls. Hebrew, Aramaic, and Greek Texts with English Translations*. Volumes 1-4B, Tübingen, Mohr Siebeck / Louisville, Westminster John Knox, 1994-1999. Short title: Dead Sea Scrolls

C. CLEMEN, *Religionsgeschichtliche Erklärung des Neuen Testaments. Die Abhängigkeit des ältesten Christentums von nichtjüdischen Religionen und philosophischen Systemen*, Gießen, Töpelmann, ²1924. Short title: Religionsgeschichtliche Erklärung

D.J.A. CLINES (ed.), *The Dictionary of Classical Hebrew*, Sheffield, Sheffield Academic Press, 1994 -. Short title: Dictionary

J.J. COLLINS, *The Genre Apocalypse in Hellenistic Judaism*, in D. HELLHOLM (ed.), *Apocalypticism*, pp. 531-548. Short title: Genre Apocalypse

——, *The Scepter and the Star. The Messiahs of the Dead Sea Scrolls and Other Ancient Literature* (The Anchor Bible Reference Library), New York et al., Doubleday, 1995. Short title: The Scepter and the Star

J.J. COLLINS (ed.), *Apocalypse. The Morphology of a Genre* (Semeia, 14), Missoula MT, Scholars Press, 1979. Short title: Apocalypse

J.J. COLLINS & J.H. CHARLESWORTH (eds.), *Mysteries and Revelations. Apocalyptic Studies since the Uppsala Colloquium* (Journal for the Study of the Pseudepigrapha Supplement Series, 9), Sheffield, JSOT Press, 1991. Short title: Mysteries

R.F. COLLINS, *Beatitudes*, in D.N. FREEDMAN et al. (eds.), *Anchor Bible Dictionary* I, New York, Doubleday, 1996, pp. 629-631. Short title: Beatitudes

C. COLPE, *Die religionsgeschichtliche Schule. Darstellung und Kritik ihres Bildes vom gnostischen Erlösermythos* (Forschungen zur Religion und Literatur des Alten und Neuen Testaments, 78), Göttingen, Vandenhoeck & Ruprecht, 1963. Short title: Schule

F.C. CONYBEARE, J.R. HARRIS, & A.S. LEWIS, *The Story of Aḥikar from the Syriac, Arabic, Armenian, Ethiopic, Greek and Slavonic Versions*, Cambridge, Cambridge University Press, ²1913. Short title: Story

H. CONZELMANN, *Der erste Brief an die Korinther* (Kritisch-exegetischer Kommentar über das Neue Testament, 5), Göttingen, Vandenhoeck & Ruprecht, 1981. Short title: Korinther

C.B. COUSAR, *The Theological Task of 1 Corinthians. A Conversation with Gordon D. Fee and Victor Paul Furnish*, in D.M. HAY (ed.), *Pauline Theology*. Volume II: *1 & 2 Corinthians*, Minneapolis, Fortress Press, 1993, pp. 90-102. Short title: Theological Task

A. COWLEY, *Aramaic Papyri of the Fifth Century B.C.*, Oxford, Clarendon, 1923 = Osnabrück, Zeller, 1967. Short title: Aramaic Papyri

M. DAHOOD, *Canaanite-Phoenician Influence in Qoheleth*, in *Biblica* 33 (1952) 191-221. Short title: Canaanite-Phoenician Influence

J. DAN, *The Three Phases in the History of Sefer Yetzira*, in *Frankfurter Judaistische Beiträge* 21 (1994) 7-29. Short title: Three Phases

——, *The "Unique Cherub" Circle*, Tübingen, Mohr Siebeck, 1999. Short title: Unique Cherub

A. DAUER, *Paulus und die christlichen Gemeinden im syrischen Antiochia* (Bonner biblische Beiträge, 106), Weinheim, Philo, 1996. Short title: Antiochia

W.D. DAVIES, *Additional Notes*, in ID., *Paul and Rabbinic Judaism. Some Rabbinic Elements in Pauline Theology*, London, SPCK, ²1955. Short title: Additional Notes

——, *Paul and the Dead Sea Scrolls: Flesh and Spirit*, in K. STENDAHL (ed.), *The Scrolls and the New Testament*, New York, Harper, 1957, pp. 157-182, 276-282. Short title: Paul and the Dead Sea Scrolls

A.-M. DENIS, *Introduction aux Pseudépigraphes Grecs d'Ancien Testament* (Studia in Veteris Testamenti Pseudepigrapha, 1), Leiden, Brill, 1970. Short title: Introduction

P. DESELAERS, *Das Buch Tobit* (Orbis biblicus et orientalis, 43), Freiburg, Universitätsverlag / Göttingen, Vandenhoeck & Ruprecht, 1982. Short title: Buch Tobit

K. DIETERICH, *Untersuchungen zur Geschichte der griechischen Sprache. Von der hellenistischen Zeit bis zum 10. Jahrhundert n. Chr.* (Byzantinisches Archiv, 1), Leipzig, Teubner, 1898 [Nachdruck: Hildesheim, Georg Olms, 1970]. Short title: Untersuchungen

A. DIHLE, *Griechische Literaturgeschichte*, München, Beck, ²1991. Short title: Literaturgeschichte

D. DIMANT, *Dualism at Qumran: New Perspectives*, in J.H. CHARLESWORTH (ed.), *Caves*, pp. 55-73. Short title: Dualism

——, *"The Fallen Angels" in the Scrolls from the Wilderness of Judaea and among the Apocryphal and Pseudepigraphal Books Related to Them* (Hebrew), Jerusalem, Hebrew University PhD Dissertation, 1974. Short title: Fallen Angels

——, *The Qumran Manuscripts: Contents and Significance*, in D. DIMANT & L.H. SCHIFFMAN (eds.), *Time to Prepare a Way in the Wilderness. Papers on the Qumran Scrolls by Fellows of the Institute for Advanced Studies of the Hebrew University, Jerusalem, 1989-1990* (Studies on the Texts of the Desert of Judah, 16), Leiden, Brill, 1995, pp. 23-58. Short title: Qumran Manuscripts

C.H. DODD, *The Beatitudes: A Form-critical Study*, in ID., *More New Testament Studies*, Grand Rapids MI, Eerdmans, 1968, pp. 1-10. Short title: Beatitudes

J.D.G. DUNN, *Paul and the Dead Sea Scrolls*, in J.H. CHARLESWORTH (ed.), *Caves*, pp. 105-127. Short title: Paul and the Dead Sea Scrolls

——, *Romans 1-8* (Word Biblical Commentary, 38A), Dallas TX, Word Books, 1988. Short title: Romans 1-8

J. DUPONT, *"Béatitudes' égyptiennes*, in *Biblica* 47 (1966) 185-222. Short title: Béatitudes

A. DUPONT-SOMMER, *Les écrits esséniens découverts près de la Mer Morte*, Paris, Payot, ⁴1980. Short title: Les écrits esséniens

——, *The Essene Writings from Qumran*, English translation by G. VERMES, Oxford, Blackwell, 1961. Short title: Essene Writings

A. DUPONT-SOMMER & M. PHILONENKO (eds.), *Ecrits intertestamentaires*, Paris, Pléïades, 1982. Short title: Ecrits intertestamentaires

G. EICHHOLZ, *Auslegung der Bergpredigt*, Neukirchen-Vluyn, Neukirchener Verlag, ⁴1978. Short title: Auslegung

R.H. EISENMAN & J.H. ROBINSON, *A Facsimile Edition of the Dead Sea Scrolls*, Washington DC, Biblical Archaeology Society, 1991. Short title: Facsimile Edition

O. EISSFELDT, *Der Maschal im Alten Testament* (Beihefte zur Zeitschrift für die alttestamentliche Wissenschaft, 24), Gießen, Töpelmann, 1913. Short title: Maschal

T. ELGVIN, *4Q472. 4QEschatological Work B*, in S.J. PFANN *et al.* (eds.), *Qumran Cave 4. XXVI. Cryptic Texts and Miscellanea, Part 1* (Discoveries in the Judaean Desert, 36), Oxford, Clarendon, 2000, pp. 450-455. Short title: 4QEschatological Work B

——, *473. 4QThe Two Ways*, in G. BROOKE *et al.* (eds.), *Qumran Cave 4. XVII. Parabiblical Texts Part 3* (Discoveries in the Judaean Desert, 22), Oxford, Clarendon, 1996, pp. 289-294. Short title: 473. 4QThe Two Ways

——, *474. 4QText Concerning Rachel and Joseph*, in S.J. PFANN *et al.* (eds.), *Qumran Cave 4. XXVI. Cryptic Texts and Miscellanea, Part 1* (Discoveries in the Judaean Desert, 36), Oxford, Clarendon, 2000, pp. 456-463. Short title: 4QText Concerning Rachel and Joseph

——, *475. 4QRenewed Earth*, in S.J. PFANN *et al.* (eds.), *Qumran Cave 4. XXVI. Cryptic Texts and Miscellanea, Part 1* (Discoveries in the Judaean Desert, 36), Oxford, Clarendon, 2000, pp. 464-473. Short title: 4QRenewed Earth

——, *4QHalakha C*, in J. BAUMGARTEN *et al.* (eds.), *Qumran Cave 4. XXV. Halakhic Texts* (Discoveries in the Judaean Desert, 35), Oxford, Clarendon, 1999, pp. 155-156. Short title: 4QHalakha C

——, *Liturgical Works*, in E. CHAZON *et al.* (eds.), *Qumran Cave 4. XX. Poetical and Liturgical Texts, Part 2* (Discoveries in the Judaean Desert, 29), Oxford, Clarendon, 1999, pp. 437-446. Short title: Liturgical Works

F.M. FALES, *Riflessioni sull'Ahiqar di Elefantina*, in *Orientis Antiqui Miscellanea*, I, Rom, Istituto per l'Oriente, 1994, pp. 39-58. Short title: Riflessioni

H.-J. FABRY, רוּחַ *rûaḥ* VII-VIII in G.J. BOTTERWECK & H. RINGGREN (eds.), *Theologisches Wörterbuch zum Alten Testament* VII, Stuttgart, Kohlhammer, 1990, cc. 419-425. Short title: רוּחַ

——, *Seligpreisungen*, in W. KASPER *et al.* (eds.), *Lexikon für Theologie und Kirche* 9, Freiburg, Herder-Verlag, ³2000, cc. 442-444. Short title: Seligpreisungen

E. FASCHER, *Der erste Brief des Paulus an die Korinther. Erster Teil* (Theologischer Handkommentar zum Neuen Testament, 7/1), Berlin, Evangelische Verlagsanstalt, 1975. Short title: Korinther

P. FEINE, *Das gesetzesfreie Evangelium des Paulus nach seinem Werdegang dargestellt*, Leipzig, Hinrichs, 1899. Short title: Das gesetzesfreie Evangelium

L. FINKELSTEIN (ed.), *The Jews. Their History, Religion and Culture*, Vol. III, New York, Schocken, 1960. Short title: The Jews III

M. FISCH, *Rational Rabbis. Science and Talmudic Culture*, Bloomington/Indianapolis, Indiana University Press, 1997. Short title: Rational Rabbis

J.A. FITZMYER, *A Palestine Collection of Beatitudes*, in F. VAN SEGBROECK *et al.* (eds.), *The Four Gospels 1992*, FS F. Neirynck, Leuven, University Press/Peeters, 1992, pp. 509-515. Short title: Collection

D. FLUSSER, *Blessed are the Poor in Spirit...*, in *Israel Exploration Journal* 10 (1960) 1-13. Short title: Blessed

——, *The Dead Sea Sect and Pre-Pauline Christianity*, in Ch. RABIN & Y. YADIN (eds.), *Aspects of the Dead Sea Scrolls* (Scripta Hierosolymitana, 4), Jerusalem, Magnes Press, 1958, pp. 215-266. Short title: The Dead Sea Sect

S.D. FRAADE, *Enosh and his Generation. Pre-Israelite Hero and History in Postbiblical Interpretation* (Society of Biblical Literature Monograph Series, 30), Chico CA, Scholars Press, 1984. Short title: Enosh and his Generation

H. FRANKEMÖLLE, *Die Makarismen (Mt 5,1-12; Lk 6,20-23). Motive und Umfang der redaktionellen Komposition*, in *Biblische Zeitschrift* NF 15 (1971) 52-75. Short title: Makarismen

J. FREY, *Die johanneische Eschatologie I. Ihre Probleme im Spiegel der Forschung seit Reimarus* (Wissenschaftliche Untersuchungen zum Neuen Testament, 96), Tübingen, Mohr Siebeck, 1997. Short title: Eschatologie 1

——, *Die paulinische Antithese von "Fleisch" und "Geist" und die palästinisch-jüdische Weisheitstradition*, in *Zeitschrift für die neutestamentliche Wissenschaft* 90 (1999) 45-77. Short title: Paulinische Antithese

F. GARCÍA MARTÍNEZ, *The Dead Sea Scrolls Translated. The Qumran Texts in English*, English translation by W.G.E. WATSON, Leiden, Brill, 1994. Short title: Dead Sea Scrolls Translated

F. GARCÍA MARTÍNEZ & E.J.C. TIGCHELAAR, *The Dead Sea Scrolls. Study Edition. Volume One*, Leiden, Brill, 1997. Short title: Study Edition I

——, *The Dead Sea Scrolls. Study Edition. Volume Two*, Leiden, Brill, 1998. Short title: Study Edition II

——, *The Dead Sea Scrolls. Study Edition*, Grand Rapids MI, Eerdmans / Leiden, Brill, revised edition, 1999. Short title: Study Edition Revised

F. GARCÍA MARTÍNEZ & A.S. VAN DER WOUDE, *De rollen van de Dode Zee*, Kampen, Kok Pharos, 1994. Short title: Rollen

TH.H. GASTER, *The Dead Sea Scriptures. With Introduction and Notes*, Garden City, Anchor Press / Doubleday, ³1976. Short title: Dead Sea Scriptures

C. GEERTZ, *Religion as a Cultural System*, in M. BANTON (ed.), *Anthropological Approaches to the Study of Religion*, London, Tavistock, 1966, pp. 1-46. Short title: Religion

——, *Ethos, World View, and the Analysis of Sacred Symbols*, in ID., *The Interpretation of Cultures. Selected Essays by Clifford Geertz*, New York, Basic Books, 1973, pp. 126-141. Short title: Ethos

A.R. GEORGE & F.N.H. AL-RAWI, *Tablets from the Sippar Library. VII: Three Wisdom Texts*, in *Iraq* 60 (1998) 187-206. Short title: Sippar Library

D. GEORGI, *Weisheit Salomos* (Jüdische Schriften aus hellenistisch-römischer Zeit, III.4), Gütersloh, Mohn, 1980. Short title: Weisheit Salomos

G. GERLEMAN, בָּשָׂר *bāśār Fleisch*, in E. JENNI (ed.), *Theologisches Handwörterbuch zum Alten Testament* 1, München/Zürich, Kaiser/Theologischer Verlag, 1971, cc. 376-379. Kurzttitel: בָּשָׂר

E.S. GERSTENBERGER, *Der bittende Mensch. Bittritual und Klagelied des Einzelnen im Alten Testament* (Wissenschaftliche Monographien zum Alten und Neuen Testament, 51), Neukirchen-Vluyn, Neukirchener Verlag, 1980. Short title: Mensch

H. GESE, *Lehre und Wirklichkeit in der alten Weisheit. Studien zu den Sprüchen Salomos und zu dem Buche Hiob*, Tübingen, Mohr, 1958. Short title: Lehre und Wirklichkeit

———, *Wisdom Literature in the Persian Period*, in W.D. DAVIES & L. FINKELSTEIN (eds.), *The Cambridge History of Judaism*.Vol. I: *Introduction: The Persian Period*, Cambridge, Cambridge University Press, 1984, pp. 189-218. Short title: Wisdom Literature

L. GINZBERG, *An Unknown Jewish Sect*, New York, Jewish Theological Seminary of America, 1976. Short title: Jewish Sect

B. GLADIGOW, *Der Makarismus des Weisen*, in *Hermes* 95 (1967) 404-433. Short title: Makarismus

E. VON GLASERSFELD, *Einführung in den radikalen Konstruktivismus*, in P. WATZLAWICK (ed.), *Die erfundene Wirklichkeit*, München/Zürich, Piper, ⁵1988, pp. 16-38. Short title: Konstruktivismus

U. GLESSMER, *Der 364-Tage Kalender und die Sabbatstruktur seiner Schaltungen in ihrer Bedeutung für den Kult*, in D.R. DANIELS, U. GLESSMER, & M. RÖSEL (eds.) *Ernten was man sät*. FS Klaus Koch, Neukirchen-Vluyn, Neukirchener Verlag, 1991, pp. 379-398. Short title: Sabbatstruktur

J.W. VON GOETHE, *Zweiter Teil. Eintragung zum 20. Oktober 1828*, in J.P. ECKERMANN, *Gespräche mit Goethe in den letzten Jahren seines Lebens 1823 — 1832*, Jena, E. Diederichs, 1908. Short title: Eintragung

B. GOLDSTEIN, *The Jewish Contribution to Astronomy in the Middle Ages*, in L. FINKELSTEIN (ed.), *The Jews* III, pp. 270-75. Short title: Astronomy

F. GOLKA, *Die Flecken des Leoparden. Biblische und afrikanische Weisheit im Sprichwort*, in R. ALBERTZ (ed.), *Schöpfung und Befreiung*. FS C. Westermann, Stuttgart, Calwer Verlag, 1989, pp. 149-165. Short title: Flecken

———, *Die israelitische Weisheitsschule oder "des Kaisers neue Kleider"*, in *Vetus Testamentum* 33 (1983) 257-270. Short title: Weisheitsschule

———, *Die Königs- und Hofsprüche und der Ursprung der israelitischen Weisheit*, in *Vetus Testamentum* 36 (1986) 13-36. Short title: Ursprung

———, *The Leopard's Spots. Biblical and African Wisdom in Proverbs*, Edinburgh, T. & T. Clark, 1993. Short title: Spots

J. VAN GOUDOEVER, *Biblical Calendars*, Leiden, Brill, 1959, ²1961. Short title: Calendars

W.S. GREEN, *Otherness Within: Towards A Theory of Difference in Rabbinic Judaism*, in J. NEUSNER & E.S. FRERICHS (eds.), *"To See Ourselves As Others See Us"*, pp. 49-69. Short title: Otherness

J.C. GREENFIELD, *Ahiqar in the Book of Tobit*, in M. CARREZ, J. DORÉ & P. GRELOT (eds.), *De la Torah au Messie*. FS H. Cazelles, Paris, Desclée, 1981, pp. 329-333. Short title: Ahiqar

———, *The Wisdom of Ahiqar*, in J. DAY, R.P. GORDON, & H.G.M. WILLIAMSON (eds.), *Wisdom in Ancient Israel*. FS J.A. Emerton, Cambridge, Cambridge University Press, 1995, pp. 43-52. Short title: Wisdom

J.C. GREENFIELD & M.E. STONE, *The Prayer of Levi*, in *Journal of Biblical Literature* 112 (1993) 247-266. Short title: Prayer

——, *Remarks on the Aramaic Testament of Levi From the Geniza*, in *Revue Biblique* 86 (1979) 214-230. Short title: Remarks
P. GRELOT, *Documents araméens d'Egypte* (Littératures anciennes du Proche Orient, 5), Paris, Editions du Cerf, 1972. Short title: Documents
I. GRUENWALD, *Apocalyptic and Merkavah Mysticism* (Arbeiten zur Geschichte des antiken Judentums und des Urchristentums, 14), Leiden, Brill, 1980. Short title: Mysticism
R.A. GUELICH, *The Matthean Beatitudes: "Entrance-Requirements" or Eschatological Blessings?*, in *Journal of Biblical Literature* 95 (1976) 415-434. Short title: Beatitudes
H. GUNKEL, *Die Wirkungen des heiligen Geistes nach der populären Anschauung der apostolischen Zeit und nach der Lehre des Apostels Paulus*, Göttingen, Vandenhoeck & Ruprecht, ²1899. Short title: Wirkungen
W.K.C. GUTHRIE, *A History of Greek Philosophy*, Vols. I-II, Cambridge, Cambridge University Press, 1962-1965. Short title: Greek Philosophy
L.K. HANDY, *Among the Host of Heaven*, Winona Lake, Eisenbrauns, 1994. Short title: Host of Heaven
——, *Dissenting Deities or Obedient Angels. Divine Hierarchies in Ugarit and the Bible*, in *Biblical Research* 35 (1990) 18-35. Short title: Dissenting Deities
A. V. HARNACK and J. FLEMMING, *Ein jüdisch-christliches Psalmbuch aus dem ersten Jahrhundert* (Texte und Untersuchungen, 35.4), Leipzig, Hinrichs'sche Buchhandlung, 1910. Short title: Psalmbuch
D.J. HARRINGTON, *Sirach Research since 1965: Progress and Questions*, in J.C. REEVES and J. KAMPEN (eds.), *Pursuing the Text*. FS Ben Zion Wacholder (Journal for the Study of the Old Testament Supplement Series, 184), Sheffield, Sheffield Academic Press, 1994, pp. 164-176. Short title: Sirach Research
J.R. HARRIS & A. MINGANA, *The Odes of Solomon*, Manchester, Manchester University Press / London, Longmans, Green & Co., 1920. Short title: The Odes of Solomon
E. HATCH & H.A. REDPATH, *A Concordance to the Septuagint and the Other Greek Versions of the Old Testament (Including the Apocryphal Books)*, Grand Rapids MI, Baker Books, ²1998. Short title: Concordance
F. HAUCK & G. BERTRAM, μακάριος in G. KITTEL (ed.), *Theologisches Wörterbuch zum Neuen Testament* IV, Stuttgart, Kohlhammer, 1942, pp. 365-373. Short title: μακάριος
C.T.R. HAYWARD, *The Figure of Adam in Pseudo-Philo's Biblical Antiquities*, in *Journal for the Study of Judasim* 23 (1992) 1-20. Short title: Figure of Adam
D. HELLHOLM (ed.), *Apocalypticism in the Mediterranean World and the Near East. Proceedings of the International Colloquium on Apocalypticism Uppsala, August 12-17, 1979*, Tübingen, Mohr Siebeck, 1983. Short title: Apocalypticism
C. HEMPEL, *Comments on the Translation of 4QSd I,1*, in *Journal of Jewish Studies* 44 (1993) 127-128. Short title: Comments
——, *The Earthly Essene Nucleus of 1QSa*, in *Dead Sea Discoveries* 3 (1996) 253-267. Short title: Nucleus of 1QSa
——, *The Laws of the Damascus Document. Sources, Traditions and Redaction* (Studies on the Texts of the Desert of Judah, 29), Leiden, Brill, 1998. Short title: Laws of the Damascus Document

——, *Community Structures in the Dead Sea Scrolls: Admission, Organization, Disciplinary Procedures*, in P.W. FLINT & J.C. VANDERKAM (eds.), *The Dead Sea Scrolls After Fifty Years. A Comprehensive Assessment*, Leiden, Brill, 1999, Volume II, pp. 67-92. Short title: Community Structures

——, *The Laws of the Damascus Document and 4QMMT*, in J. BAUMGARTEN, E. CHAZON, & A. PINNICK (eds.), *The Damascus Document. A Centennial of Discovery: Proceedings of the Third International Symposium of the Orion Center* (Studies on the Texts of the Desert of Judah, 34), Leiden, Brill, 2000, pp. 69-84. Short title: Damascus Document and 4QMMT

M. HENGEL, *Jerusalem als jüdische und hellenistische Stadt*, in ID., *Judaica, Hellenistica et Christiana. Kleine Schriften 2* (Wissenschaftliche Untersuchungen zum Neuen Testament, 109), Tübingen, Mohr Siebeck 1999, pp. 115-156. Short title: Jerusalem als jüdische und hellenistische Stadt

——, *Judaism and Hellenism. Studies in their Encounter in Palestine in the Early Hellenistic Period*, English translation by J. BOWDEN, 2 vols., London, SCM / Philadelphia, Fortress, 1974. Short title: Judaism and Hellenism

——, *Judentum und Hellenismus. Studien zu ihrer Begegnung unter besonderer Berücksichtigung Palästinas bis zur Mitte des 2. Jh.s. v. Chr.* (Wissenschaftliche Untersuchungen zum Neuen Testament, 10), Tübingen, Mohr Siebeck, ³1988. Short title: Judentum und Hellenismus

——, *Qumran und der Hellenismus*, in M. DELCOR (ed.), *Qumrân. Sa piété, sa théologie et son milieu* (Bibliotheca Ephemeridum Theologicarum Lovaniensium, 46), Paris/Leuven, Peeters, 1978, pp. 333-372. Short title: Qumran und der Hellenismus

——, *The pre-Christian Paul*, London, SCM / Philadelphia PA, Trinity, 1991. Short title: The pre-Christian Paul

——, *Der Sohn Gottes. Die Entstehung der Christologie und die jüdisch-hellenistische Religionsgeschichte*, Tübingen, Mohr Siebeck, 1975. Short title: Sohn Gottes

——, *Die Ursprünge der Gnosis und das Urchristentum*, in J. ÅDNA et al. (eds.), *Evangelium – Schriftauslegung – Kirche*, FS Peter Stuhlmacher, Göttingen, Vandenhoeck & Ruprecht, 1997, pp. 190-223. Short title: Ursprünge der Gnosis

M. HENGEL unter Mitarbeit von R. DEINES, J. FREY, C. MARKSCHIES, A.M. SCHWEMER mit einem Anhang von H. BLOEDHORN, *Judaica et Hellenistica. Kleine Schriften 1* (Wissenschaftliche Untersuchungen zum Neuen Testament, 90), Tübingen, Mohr Siebeck, 1996. Short title: Judaica

J.G. HERDER, *Vom Geist der Ebräischen Poesie*, in B. SUPHAN (ed.), *Herders Sämmtliche Werke* 11, Berlin, Weidmannsche Buchhandlung, 1879. Short title: Geist

J. HOFTIJZER & K. JONGELING, *Dictionary of the North-West Semitic Inscriptions* (Handbuch der Orientalistik, I.21), Leiden, Brill, 1995. Short title: Dictionary

C. HOLSTEN, *Die bedeutung des wortes σάρξ im lehrbegriffe des Paulus*, 1855, republished in ID., *Zum Evangelium des Paulus und des Petrus*, Rostock, Stiller, 1868, pp. 365-447. Short title: Die bedeutung des wortes σάρξ

H.J. HOLTZMANN, *Lehrbuch der neutestamentlichen Theologie*, 2 vols., Tübingen, Mohr Siebeck, ²1911. Short title: Lehrbuch

W. HONRATH, O. RUBENSOHN & F. ZUCKER, *Bericht über die Ausgrabungen auf Elephantine in den Jahren 1906-1908*, in *Zeitschrift für Ägyptische Sprache und Altertumskunde* 46 (1909) 14-61. Short title: Bericht

F.W. HORN, *Das Angeld des Geistes. Studien zur paulinischen Pneumatologie* (Forschungen zur Religion und Literatur des Alten und Neuen Testaments, 154), Göttingen, Vandenhoeck & Ruprecht, 1992. Short title: Das Angeld des Geistes

F. HORST, *Die Doxologien im Amosbuch*, in *Zeitschrift für die alttestamentliche Wissenschaft* 47 (1929) 45-54, republished in ID., *Gottes Recht. Gesammelte Studien zum Recht im Alten Testament* (Theologische Bibliothek, 12) München, Kaiser, 1961, pp. 155-166. Short title: Die Doxologien im Amosbuch

F.L. HOSSFELD & E. ZENGER, *Die Psalmen. Psalm 1-50* (Neue Echter Bibel, 29), Würzburg, Echter Verlag, 1993. Short title: Psalmen

H. HÜBNER, *Die Sapientia Salomonis und die antike Philosophie*, in ID., (ed.), *Die Weisheit Salomos im Horizont Biblischer Theologie* (Biblisch-theologische Studien, 22), Neukirchen-Vluyn, Neukirchener Verlag, 1993, pp. 55-83. Short title: Die Sapientia Salomonis und die antike Philosophie

A. HULTGÅRD, *L'eschatologie des Testaments des Douze Patriarches*. Vol. 1: *Interprétation des textes* (Acta Universitatis Upsaliensis: Historia Religionum, 6), Uppsala, Almqvist & Wiksell, 1977. Short title: L'eschatologie 1

——, *L'eschatologie des Testaments de Douze Patriarches*. Vol. 2: *Composition de l'ouvrage, textes et traductions* (Acta Universitatis Upsaliensis: Historia Religionum, 7), Uppsala, Almqvist & Wiksell, 1982. Short title: L'eschatologie 2

H. HUPPENBAUER, בשר *"Fleisch" in den Texten von Qumran*, in *Theologische Zeitschrift* 13 (1957) 298-300. Short title: Fleisch

A. HURWITZ, *Shekye Hochmah be-Sefer Tehilim*, Jerusalem, Magnes Press, 1991. Short title: Hochmah

E. HUSSEY, *The Presocratics*, London, Duckworth, 1972. Short title: Presocratics

E. ISAAC, *1(Ethiopic Apocalypse of) Enoch*, in J.H. CHARLESWORTH (ed.), *Pseudepigrapha* I, pp. 5-89. Short title: 1 Enoch

H. JACOBSON, *Notes on 4Q303*, in *Dead Sea Discoveries* 6 (1999) 78-80. Short title: Notes

M. JASTROW, *A Dictionary of the Targumim, the Talmud Babli and Yerushalmi, and Midrashic Literature*, Brooklyn NY, P. Shalom, 1967. Short title: Dictionary

G. JEREMIAS, *Der Lehrer der Gerechtigkeit* (Studien zur Umwelt des Neuen Testaments, 2), Göttingen, Vandenhoeck & Ruprecht, 1963. Short title: Der Lehrer der Gerechtigkeit

J. JERVELL, *Imago Dei. Gen 1,26f. im Spätjudentum, in der Gnosis und in den paulinischen Briefen* (Forschungen zur Religion und Literatur des Alten und Neuen Testaments, 76), Göttingen, Vandenhoeck & Ruprecht, 1960. Short title: Imago Dei

R. JEWETT, *Paul's Anthropological Terms. A Study of Their Use in Conflict Settings* (Arbeiten zur Geschichte des antiken Judentums und des Urchristentums, 10), Leiden, Brill, 1971. Short title: Terms

L.T. JOHNSON, *The New Testament's Anti-Jewish Slander and the Conventions of Ancient Polemic*, in *Journal of Biblical Literature* 108 (1989) 419-441. Short title: Slander

M.D. JOHNSON, *Life of Adam and Eve*, in J.H. CHARLESWORTH (ed.), *Pseudepigrapha* II, New York NY, Doubleday, 1983, pp. 249-295. Short title: Life of Adam and Eve

S. JOHNSON, *Paul and the Manual of Discipline*, in *Harvard Theological Review* 48 (1955) 157-165. Short title: Paul

A. JOLLES, *Einfache Formen*, Tübingen, Niemeyer, ⁴1968. Short title: Formen

M. DE JONGE, *Christian Influence in the Testament of the Twelve Patriarchs*, in ID., *Studies on the Testaments of the Twelve Patriarchs. Text and Interpretation* (Studia in Veteris Testamenti Pseudepigrapha, 3), Leiden, Brill, 1975, pp. 193-246. Short title: Christian Influence

——, *The Main Issues in the Study of the Testaments of the Twelve Patriarchs*, in *New Testament Studies* 26 (1980) 508-524. Short title: The Main Issues

——, *The Testament of Levi and "Aramaic Levi"*, in *Revue de Qumran* 13 (1988) 367-385. Short title: Testament of Levi

——, *The Testaments of the Twelve Patriarchs. A Study of Their Text, Composition, and Origin*, Assen, van Gorcum, 1953. Short title: Testaments

M. DE JONGE & J. TROMP, *The Life of Adam and Eve and Related Literature* (Guides to Apocrypha and Pseudepigrapha), Sheffield, Sheffield Academic Press, 1997. Short title: Life of Adam

R. JOSPE, *Early Philosophical Commentaries on Sefer Yetzira: Some Comments*, in *Revue des études juives* 149 (1990) 369-415. Short title: Sefer Yetzira

P. JOÜON & T. MURAOKA, *A Grammar of Biblical Hebrew*, Rome, Editrice Pontificio Instituto Biblico, 1991.

A. JUNCKER, *Die Ethik des Apostels Paulus*, Halle a.d.S., Niemeyer, 1904. Short title: Die Ethik des Paulus

M.Z. KADDARI, *The Root TKN in the Qumran Texts*, in *Revue de Qumran* 5 (1965) 219-225. Short title: Root TKN

C. KÄHLER, *Studien zur Form- und Traditionsgeschichte der biblischen Makarismen*, Jena, Dissertation, 1974. Short title: Makarismen

E. KÄSEMANN, *Leib und Leib Christi. Eine Untersuchung zur paulinischen Begrifflichkeit* (Beiträge zur historischen Theologie, 9), Tübingen, Mohr Siebeck, 1933. Short title: Leib und Leib Christi

——, *Zur paulinischen Anthropologie*, in ID., *Paulinische Perspektiven*, Tübingen, Mohr Siebeck, 1969, pp. 9-60. Short title: Zur paulinischen Anthropologie

W. KÄSER, *Beobachtungen zum alttestamentlichen Makarismus*, in *Zeitschrift für die alttestamentliche Wissenschaft* 82 (1970) 225-250. Short title: Beobachtungen

H.C. KEE, *Testaments of the Twelve Patriarchs*, in J.H. CHARLESWORTH (ed.), *Pseudepigrapha* I, pp. 775-828. Short title: Testaments

O. KEEL, *Jahwes Entgegnung an Ijob* (Forschungen zur Religion und Literatur des Alten und Neuen Testaments, 121), Göttingen, Vandenhoeck & Ruprecht, 1978. Short title: Entgegnung

Chr. KLEIN, *Kohelet und die Weisheit Israels* (Beiträge zur Wissenschaft des Alten und Neuen Testaments, 132), Stuttgart, Kohlhammer, 1994. Short title: Kohelet

G.S. KIRK, *Heraclitus. The Cosmic Fragments*, Cambridge, Cambridge University Press, 1962. Short title: Heraclitus
G.S. KIRK & F.E. RAVEN, *The Presocratic Philosophers*, Cambridge, Cambridge University Press, 1957. Short title: Presocratic Philosophers
M.A. KNIBB, *The Ethiopic Book of Enoch. A New Edition in the Light of the Aramaic Dead Sea Fragments*. 2 Volumes. *Introduction, Translation, Commentary*, Oxford, Clarendon, 1978. Short title: Book of Enoch 1 and 2
——, *The Qumran Community* (Cambridge Commentaries on Writings of the Jewish & Christian World 200 BC to AD 200, 2), Cambridge, Cambridge University Press, 1987. Short title: Qumran Community
K. KOCH, *Gibt es ein Vergeltungsdogma im Alten Testament?*, in *Zeitschrift für Theologie und Kirche* 52 (1955) 1-42, (wieder abgedruckt in ID., *Um das Prinzip der Vergeltung in Religion und Recht des Alten Testaments* [Wege der Forschung, 125], Darmstadt, Wissenschaftliche Buchgesellschaft, 1972, pp. 130-180). Short title: Vergeltungsdogma
——, *Was ist Formgeschichte? Methoden der Bibelexegese*, Neukirchen-Vluyn, Neukirchener Verlag, ⁴1981. Short title: Formgeschichte
L. KOEHLER, W. BAUMGARTNER & J.J. STAMM (eds.), *The Hebrew and Aramaic Lexicon of the Old Testament* 1, Leiden, Brill, 1994. Short title: The Hebrew and Aramaic Lexicon of the Old Testament
I. KOTTSIEPER, *Die alttestamentliche Weisheit im Licht aramäischer Weisheitstraditionen*, in B. JANOWSKI (ed.), *Weisheit außerhalb der kanonischen Weisheitsschriften* (Veröffentlichungen der Wissenschaftlichen Gesellschaft für Theologie, 10), Gütersloh, Mohn, 1996, pp. 128-162. Short title: Weisheit
——, *El – ein aramäischer Gott? – Eine Antwort*, in *Biblische Notizen* 94 (1998) 87-98. Short title: El – ein aramäischer Gott?
——, *El – Ferner oder naher Gott?*, in R. ALBERTZ (ed.), *Religion und Gesellschaft* (Alter Orient und Altes Testament, 248), Münster, Ugarit-Verlag, 1997, pp. 25-74. Short title: El - ferner oder naher Gott?
——, *Die Geschichte und die Sprüche des weisen Achikar*, in O. KAISER (ed.), *Texte aus der Umwelt des Alten Testaments* III/2, Gütersloh, Mohn, 1991, pp. 320-347. Short title: Geschichte
——, *Die Sprache der Achikarsprüche* (Beihefte der Zeitschrift für die alttestamentliche Wissenschaft, 194), Berlin/New York, De Gruyter, 1990. Short title: Sprache
A. KROPAT, *Die Syntax des Autors der Chronik verglichen mit der seiner Quellen. Ein Beitrag zur historischen Syntax des Hebräischen* (Beihefte zur Zeitschrift für die alttestamentliche Wissenschaft, 16), Giessen, Töpelmann, 1909. Short title: Syntax
M. KÜCHLER, *Frühjüdische Weisheitstraditionen* (Orbis biblicus et orientalis, 26), Freiburg, Universitätsverlag / Göttingen, Vandenhoeck & Ruprecht, 1979. Short title: Weisheitstraditionen
W.G. KÜMMEL, *Das Neue Testament. Geschichte der Erforschung seiner Probleme* (Orbis Academicus, III.3), Freiburg/München, Karl Alber, 1958. Short title: Das Neue Testament
——, *Römer 7 und die Bekehrung des Paulus*, in ID., *Römer 7 und das Bild des Menschen im Neuen Testament* (Theologische Bücherei, 53), München, Kaiser, 1974, pp. 1-160. Short title: Römer 7 und die Bekehrung des Paulus

R. KUGLER, *A Note on 1QS 9:14: The Sons of Righteousness or the Sons of Zadok*, in *Dead Sea Discoveries* 3 (1996) 316-320. Short title: Note
——, *From Patriarch to Priest. The Levi-Priestly Tradition from Aramaic Levi to Testament of Levi* (SBL Early Judaism and its Literature, 9), Atlanta GA, Scholars Press, 1996. Short title: Patriarch
H.-W. KUHN, *Enderwartung und gegenwärtiges Heil. Untersuchungen zu den Gemeindeliedern von Qumran* (Studien zur Umwelt des Neuen Testaments, 4), Göttingen, Vandenhoeck & Ruprecht, 1966. Short title: Enderwartung
——, *Qumran und Paulus. Unter traditionsgeschichtlichem Aspekt ausgewählte Parallelen*, in U. MELL & U.B. MÜLLER (eds.), *Das Urchristentum in seiner literarischen Geschichte. FS J. Becker* (Beihefte zur Zeitschrift für die neutestamentliche Wissenschaft, 100), Berlin/New York, De Gruyter, 1999, pp. 227-246. Short title: Qumran und Paulus
K.G. KUHN, *Die in Palästina gefundenen hebräischen Texte und das Neue Testament*, in *Zeitschrift für Theologie und Kirche* 47 (1950) 192-211. Short title: Die in Palästina gefundenen hebräischen Texte
——, *Jesus in Gethsemane*, in *Evangelische Theologie* 12 (1952/53) 260-285. Short title: Jesus in Gethsemane
——, *New Light on Temptation, Sin, and Flesh in the New Testament*, in K. STENDAHL (ed.), *The Scrolls and the New Testament*, New York NY, Harper, 1957, pp. 94-113.265-270. Short title: New Light on Temptation
——, *Πειρασμός – ἁμαρτία – σάρξ im Neuen Testament und die damit zusammenhängenden Vorstellungen*, in *Zeitschrift für Theologie und Kirche* 49 (1952) 200-222. Short title: Πειρασμός – ἁμαρτία – σάρξ
——, *Die Sektenschrift und die iranische Religion*, in *Zeitschrift für Theologie und Kirche* 49 (1952) 296-316. Short title: Sektenschrift
——, *Zur Bedeutung der neuen palästinischen Handschriftenfunde für die neutestamentliche Wissenschaft*, in *Theologische Literaturzeitung* 75 (1950) 81-86. Short title: Zur Bedeutung
K.G. KUHN et al., *Konkordanz zu den Qumrantexten*, Göttingen, Vandenhoeck & Ruprecht, 1960. Short title: Konkordanz
O. KUSS, *Der Römerbrief. Zweite Lieferung*, Regensburg, Friedrich Pustet, 1959. Short title: Der Römerbrief
E.Y. KUTSCHER, *A History of the Hebrew Language*, Jerusalem, Magnes, 1982. Short title: History
W.G. LAMBERT, *Babylonian Wisdom Literature*, Oxford, Clarendon, 1960. Short title: Literature
P. LAMPE, *Theological Wisdom and the "Word About the Cross". The Rhetorical Scheme in 1 Corinthians 1-4*, in *Interpretation* 44 (1990) 117-131. Short title: Theological Wisdom
A. LANGE, *Vom prophetischen Wort zur Schriftauslegung. Studien zur Traditions- und Redaktionsgeschichte innerprophetischer Konflikte im Alten Testament*, Tübingen, Habilitationsschrift, 2000. Short title: Vom prophetischen Wort zur Schriftauslegung
A. LANGE & H. LICHTENBERGER, *Qumran*, in G. KRAUSE & G. MÜLLER (eds.), *Theologische Realenzyklopädie* 28, Berlin, De Gruyter, 1997, pp. 45-79. Short title: Qumran
Y.T. LANGERMANN, *Science, Jewish*, in J.R. STRAYER (ed.), *Dictionary of the Middle Ages* 11, New York, Scribner's, 1989, pp. 89-94. Short title: Science

T.-H. LEE, *Gattungsvergleich der akkadischen Šu-ila-Gebete mit den biblischen Lobpsalmen*, Münster, Dissertation, 1996. Short title: Gattungsvergleich

H. LEISEGANG, *Index ad Philonis Alexandrini Opera* (Philonis Alexandrini Opera, 7), Berlin, De Gruyter, 1926. Short title: Index

A.A. DILELLA, *The Wisdom of Ben Sira: Resources and Recent Research*, in *Currents in Research: Biblical Studies* 4 (1996) 161-181. Short title: Ben Sira

A. LESKY, *Geschichte der griechischen Literatur*, München, Francke, ³1971. Short title: Geschichte

J.R. LEVISON, *Portraits of Adam in Early Judaism. From Sirach to 2 Baruch* (Journal for the Study of the Pseudepigrapha Supplement Series, 1), Sheffield, JSOT Press, 1988. Short title: Portraits

J. LEVY, *Wörterbuch über die Talmudim und Midraschim*, Darmstadt, Wissenschaftliche Buchgesellschaft, 1963. Short title: Wörterbuch

H. LICHTENBERGER, *Der Beginn der Auslegungsgeschichte von Römer 7: Römer 7,25b*, in *Zeitschrift für die neutestamentliche Wissenschaft* 88 (1997) 284-295. Short title: Der Beginn der Auslegungsgeschichte von Römer 7

——, *Studien zum Menschenbild in Texten der Qumrangemeinde* (Studien zur Umwelt des Neuen Testaments, 15), Göttingen, Vandenhoeck & Ruprecht, 1980. Short title: Menschenbild

E. LIEBER, *Asaf's Book of Medicines: A Hebrew Encyclopedia of Greek and Jewish Medicine, Possibly Compiled in Byzantium on an Indian Model*, in J. SCARBOROUGH (ed.), *Symposium on Byzantine Medicine* (Dumbarton Oaks Papers, 38) Washington DC, Dumbarton Oaks Research Library and Collection, 1984, pp. 233-249. Short title: Asaf's Book

H. LIETZMANN, *An die Römer* (Handbuch zum Neuen Testament, 8), Tübingen, Mohr Siebeck, ⁴1933. Short title: An die Römer

T. LIM, *Meditation on Creation*, in T. ELGVIN et al. (eds.), *Qumran Cave 4. XV. Sapiential Texts. Part 1* (Discoveries in the Judaean Desert, 20), Oxford, Clarendon, 1997, pp. 151-158. Short title: Meditation on Creation

——, *307. 4QText Mentioning a Temple*, in S.J. PFANN et al. (eds.), *Qumran Cave 4. XXVI. Cryptic Texts and Miscellanea, Part 1* (Discoveries in the Judaean Desert, 36), Oxford, Clarendon, 2000, pp. 255-258. Short title: 4QText Mentioning a Temple

T.H. LIM in consultation with P.S. ALEXANDER (ed.), *The Dead Sea Scrolls Electronic Reference Library* Volume I, Oxford, Oxford University Press / Leiden, Brill, 1997. Short title: CD-ROM

B. LINCOLN, *Discourse and the Construction of Society. Comparative Studies of Myth, Ritual and Classification*, New York/Oxford, Oxford University Press, 1989. Short title: Discourse

J.M. LINDENBERGER, *The Gods of Ahiqar*, in *Ugarit-Forschungen* 14 (1982) 105-117. Short title: Gods

——, *The Aramaic Proverbs of Ahiqar*, Baltimore/London, Johns Hopkins University Press, 1983. Short title: Proverbs

——, *Ahiqar*, in J.H. CHARLESWORTH (ed.), *Pseudepigrapha* II, pp. 479-507. Short title: Ahiqar

C.H. LINDIJER, *Het begrip Sarx bij Paulus*, Assen, van Gorcum, 1952. Short title: Het begrip Sarx bij Paulus

E. LIPINSKI, *Macarismes et psaumes de congratulation*, in *Revue biblique* 75 (1968) 321-367. Short title: Macarismes

—, *Royal and State Scribes in Jerusalem*, in J.A. EMERTON (ed.), *Congress Volume: Jerusalem 1986* (Supplements to Vetus Testamentum, 40), Leiden, Brill, 1988, pp. 157-164. Short title: Scribes

W. LIPPMANN, *Public Opinion*, Worchester, Ebenezer Baylis and Son Ltd / London, Trinity Press, 1955. Short title: Opinion

U. LUCK, *Das Evangelium nach Matthäus* (Zürcher Bibelkommentare: NT, 1), Zürich, Theologischer Verlag Zürich, 1993. Short title: Matthäus

H. LÜDEMANN, *Die Anthropologie des Apostels Paulus und ihre Stellung innerhalb seiner Heilslehre. Nach den 4 Hauptbriefen dargestellt*, Kiel, Toeche, 1872. Short title: Anthropologie

U. LÜKE, *Evolutionäre Erkenntnistheorie und Theologie. Eine kritische Auseinandersetzung aus fundamental-theologischer Perspektive* (Edition Universitas), Stuttgart, Hirzel/Wissenschaftliche Verlagsgesellschaft, 1990. Short title: Erkenntnistheorie

U. LUZ, *Das Evangelium nach Matthäus* 1 (Evangelisch-katholischer Kommentar zum Neuen Testament I/1), Zürich/Neukirchen-Vluyn, Neukirchener Verlag, 1985. Short title: Matthäus

K. LORENZ, *Die Rückseite des Spiegels. Versuch einer Naturgeschichte menschlichen Erkennens*, München/Zürich, Piper, ³1973. Short title: Rückseite

G.E.R. LLOYD, *Early Greek Science. Thales to Aristotle*, London, Chatto & Windus, 1970. Short title: Science

W.J. LYONS, *Clarifications Concerning 4Q285 and 11Q14 Arising from Discoveries in the Judaean Desert 23*, in *Dead Sea Discoveries* 6 (1999) 37- 41. Short title: 4Q285 and 11Q14

J.F. LYOTARD, *Discours, figures* (Collection d'estetique, 7), Paris, Editions Klincksieck, 1971. Short title: Discours

B.L. MACK, *Logos und Sophia. Untersuchungen zur Weisheitstheologie im hellenistischen Judentum* (Studien zur Umwelt des Neuen Testaments, 10), Göttingen, Vandenhoeck & Ruprecht, 1973. Short title: Logos und Sophia

R. MACUCH, *Grammatik des samaritanischen Hebräisch*, Berlin, De Gruyter, 1969. Short title: Grammatik

C. MAIER & J. TROPPER, *El – ein aramäischer Gott?*, in *Biblische Notizen* 93 (1998) 77-88. Short title: El

J. MAIER, *Die Qumran-Essener. Die Texte vom Toten Meer* I-III (Uni-Taschenbücher, 1862-1863, 1916), München/Basel, E. Reinhardt, 1995. Short title: Texte

D. MARTIN, *The Corinthian Body*, New Haven/London, Yale University Press, 1995. Short title: Body

J.L. MARTYN, *Galatians* (The Anchor Bible, 33A), New York NY, Doubleday, 1998. Short title: Galatians

W. MCKANE, *Proverbs* (The Old Testament Library), London, SCM Press, ³1980. Short title: Proverbs

W.A. MEEKS, *The First Urban Christians. The Social World of the Apostle Paul*, New Haven/London, Yale University Press, 1983. Short title: Urban Christians

—, *The Origins of Christian Morality. The First Two Centuries*, New Haven/London, Yale University Press, 1993. Short title: Origins

O. MERK & M. MEISER, *Das Leben Adams und Evas* (Jüdische Schriften aus hellenistisch-römischer Zeit, II.5), Gütersloh, Gütersloher Verlagshaus, 1998. Short title: Leben Adams und Evas

H. MERKLEIN, *Jesu Botschaft von der Gottesherrschaft. Eine Skizze* (Stuttgarter Bibelstudien, 111), Stuttgart, Katholisches Bibelwerk, ³1989. Short title: Jesu Botschaft

———, *Die Jesusgeschichte – synoptisch gelesen* (Stuttgarter Bibelstudien, 156), Stuttgart, Katholisches Bibelwerk, 1994. Short title: Jesusgeschichte

S. METSO, *The Primary Results of the Reconstruction of 4QSe*, in *Journal of Jewish Studies* 44 (1993) 303-308. Short title: Primary Results.

———, *The Textual Development of the Qumran Community Rule* (Studies on the Texts of the Desert of Judah, 21), Leiden, Brill, 1997. Short title: Textual Development

D. METZLER, *Ahiqar in Trier*, in D. AHRENS (ed.), *ΘΙΑΣΟΣ ΜΟΥΣΩΝ*. FS J. Fink (Beihefte zum Archiv für Kulturgeschichte, 20), Köln/Wien, Böhlau, 1984, pp. 97-107. Short title: Ahiqar

B.F. MEYER & E.P. SANDERS (eds.), *Jewish and Christian Self-Definition*. Volume Three. *Self-Definition in the Greco-Roman World*, London, SCM, 1982. Short title: Self-Definition III

R. MEYER, *Φαρισαῖος*, in G. KITTEL & G. FRIEDRICH (eds.), *Theological Dictionary of the New Testament* IX, Grand Rapids MI, Eerdmans, 1974, pp. 11-36. Short title: Φαρισαῖος

———, *σάρξ* C. *Flesh in Judaism*, in G. KITTEL & G. FRIEDRICH (eds.), *Theological Dictionary of the New Testament* VII, English translation by G.W. Bromiley, Grand Rapids MI, Eerdmans, 1971, pp. 110-119. Short title: σάρξ

C. MICHAELIS, *Die π-Alliteration der Subjektsworte der ersten 4 Seligpreisungen in Mt 5,3-6 und ihre Bedeutung für den Aufbau der Seligpreisungen bei Mt., Lk. und Q*, in *Novum Testamentum* 10 (1968) 148-161. Short title: π-Alliteration

D. MICHEL, *Weisheit und Apokalyptik*, in A.S. VAN DER WOUDE (ed.), *The Book of Daniel in the Light of New Findings* (Bibliotheca Ephemeridum Theologicarum Lovaniensium, 106), Louvain, University Press, 1993, pp. 413-434. Short title: Weisheit und Apokalyptik

J.T. MILIK with the collaboration of M. BLACK, *The Books of Enoch. Aramaic Fragments of Qumran Cave 4*, Oxford, Clarendon, 1976. Short title: Aramaic Fragments

M. MITCHELL, *Paul and the Rhetoric of Reconciliation. An Exegetical Investigation of the Language and Composition of 1 Corinthians* (Hermeneutische Untersuchungen zur Theologie, 28), Tübingen, Mohr Siebeck, 1991. Short title: Paul

W.L. MORAN, *Notes on the Hymn to Marduk in Ludlul bēl nēmeqi*, in *Journal of the American Oriental Society* 103 (1983) 255-260. Short title: Notes

G. MORAWE, *Aufbau und Abgrenzung der Loblieder von Qumran. Studien zur gattungsgeschichtlichen Einordnung der Hodajoth*, Berlin, Evangelische Verlagsanstalt, 1960. Short title: Aufbau und Abgrenzung

J. MUILENBURG, *A Qohelet Scroll from Qumran*, in *Bulletin of the American Schools of Oriental Research* 135 (1954) 20-28. Short title: Qohelet Scroll

H.-P. MÜLLER, *Altes und Neues zum Buch Hiob*, in *Evangelische Theologie* 37 (1977) 284-304 (wieder abgedruckt in ID., *Mensch – Umwelt – Eigenwelt. Gesammelte Aufsätze zur Weisheit Israels*, Stuttgart, Kohlhammer, 1992, pp. 101-120). Short title: Altes und Neues

———, *Gottes Antwort an Ijob und das Recht religiöser Wahrheit*, in *Biblische Zeitschrift* 32 (1988) 210-231 (wieder abgedruckt in ID., *Mensch –*

Umwelt – Eigenwelt. Gesammelte Aufsätze zur Weisheit Israels, Stuttgart, Kohlhammer, 1992, pp. 121-142). Short title: Antwort
——, *Gottesfrage und Psalmenexegese. Zur Hermeneutik der Klagepsalmen des einzelnen*, in K. SEYBOLD & E. ZENGER (eds.), *Neue Wege der Psalmenforschung* (Herders biblische Studien, 1), Freiburg i. Br./Basel/ Wien, Herder, 1994, pp. 279-299 (wieder abgedruckt in ID., *Glauben, Denken und Hoffen*, Münster, Lit Verlag, 1998, pp. 81-101). Short title: Gottesfrage
——, *Hiob und seine Freunde. Traditionsgeschichtliches zum Verständnis des Hiobbuches* (Theologische Studien, 103), Zürich, EVZ–Verlag, 1970. Short title: Hiob
——, *Das Hiobproblem. Seine Stellung und Entstehung im Alten Orient und im Alten Testament* (Erträge der Forschung, 84), Darmstadt, Wissenschaftliche Buchgesellschaft, ³1995. Short title: Hiobproblem
——, *Die Hiobrahmenerzählung und ihre altorientalischen Parallelen als Paradigmen einer weisheitlichen Wirklichkeitswahrnahme*, in W.A.M. BEUKEN (ed.), *The Book of Job* (Bibliotheca Ephemeridum Theologicarum Lovaniensium, 114), Leuven, Peeters/University Press, 1994, pp. 21-39. Short title: Hiobrahmenerzählung
——, *Keilschriftliche Parallelen zum biblischen Hiobbuch. Möglichkeit und Grenze des Vergleichs*, in *Orientalia* 47 (1978) 360-375 (wieder abgedruckt in ID., *Babylonien und Israel. Historische, religiöse und sprachliche Beziehungen* [Wege der Forschung, 633], Darmstadt, Wissenschaftliche Buchgesellschaft, 1991, pp. 400-419; ID., *Mythos – Kerygma – Wahrheit. Gesammelte Aufsätze zum Alten Testament in seiner Umwelt und zur Biblischen Theologie* [Beihefte zur Zeitschrift für die alttestamentliche Wissenschaft, 200], Berlin/New York, De Gruyter, 1991, pp. 136-151). Short title: Parallelen
——, *Märchen, Legende und Enderwartung*, in *Vetus Testamentum* 26 (1976) 338-350. Short title: Märchen
——, *Plausibilitätsverlust herkömmlicher Religion bei Kohelet und den Vorsokratikern*, in B. EGO et al. (eds.), *Gemeinde ohne Tempel – Community Without Temple*, Tübingen, Mohr Siebeck, 1999, pp. 99-113. Short title: Plausibilitätsverlust
——, *Punische Weihinschriften und alttestamentliche Psalmen im religionsgeschichtlichen Zusammenhang*, in *Orientalia* 67 (1998) 477-496. Short title: Weihinschriften
——, *Die sogenannte Straußenperikope in den Gottesreden des Hiobbuches*, in *Zeitschrift für die alttestamentliche Wissenschaft* 100 (1988) 90-105. Short title: Straußenperikope
——, *Die weisheitliche Lehrerzählung im Alten Testament und in seiner Umwelt*, in *Welt des Orients* 9 (1977/ 78) 77-98 (wieder abgedruckt in ID., *Mensch – Umwelt – Eigenwelt. Gesammelte Aufsätze zur Weisheit Israels*, Stuttgart, Kohlhammer, 1992, pp. 22-43). Short title: Lehrerzählung
T.Y. MULLINS, *Ascription as a Literary Form*, in *New Testament Studies* 19 (1972/73) 194-205. Short title: Ascription
T. MURAOKA & B. PORTEN, *A Grammar of Egyptian Aramaic*, Leiden, Brill, 1998. Short title: Grammar
R.E. MURPHY, *BŚR in the Qumrân Literature and Sarks in the Epistle to the Romans*, in J. COPPENS et al. (eds.), *Sacra Pagina* 2, Paris – Gembloux, Duculot, 1959, pp. 60-76. Short title: BŚR

—, *The Tree of Life. An Exploration of Biblical Wisdom Literature* (The Anchor Bible Reference Library), New York NY, Doubleday, 1990. Short title: Tree of Life

—, *Yēṣer in the Qumran Literature*, in *Biblica* 39 (1958) 334-344. Short title: Yēṣer

J. MURPHY O'CONNOR, *Truth: Paul and Qumran*, in ID., (ed.), *Paul and Qumran*, London, Chapman, 1968, pp. 179-230. Short title: Truth: Paul and Qumran

F. MUSSNER, *Der Galaterbrief* (Herders theologischer Kommentar zum Neuen Testament, 9), Freiburg i. B., Herder, 1974. Short title: Der Galaterbrief

M. NAGEL, *La Vie Grecque d'Adam et d'Eve. Apocalypse de Moïse*, Tome I-III, Straßburg, Dissertation, 1972. Short title: Vie Grecque

F. NAU, *Histoire et Sagesse d'Aḥikar l'Assyrien*, Paris, Letouzey et Ané, 1909. Short title: Histoire

J. NEEDHAM, *Science and Civilization in China*, 6 vols., Cambridge, Cambridge University Press, 1954-1996. Short title: Science

R. NEEDHAM, *Primordial Characters*, Charlottesville VA, University Press of Virginia, 1978. Short title: Characters

O. NEUGEBAUER, *The Exact Sciences in Antiquity*, New York, Dover, ²1969. Short title: Sciences

—, *Appendix A: the "Astronomic" Chapters of the Ethiopic Book of Enoch (72-82)*, in M. BLACK, *The Book of Enoch or I Enoch*, Leiden, Brill, 1985, pp. 386-419. Short title: Appendix A

J. NEUSNER, *Jerusalem and Athens. The Congruity of Talmudic and Classical Philosophy*, Leiden, Brill, 1997. Short title: Jerusalem and Athens

—, *Judaism as Philosophy. The Method and Message of the Mishnah*, Baltimore/London, Johns Hopkins University Press, 1991. Short title: Philosophy

—, *Why No Science in Judaism?*, New Orleans, Jewish Studies Program of Tulane University, 1987. Short title: Science in Judaism

—, *Why No Science in the Mind of Judaism?*, in ID., *The Making of the Mind of Judaism. The Formative Age*, Atlanta, Scholars Press, 1987, pp. 139-60. Short title: Science in the Mind of Judaism

J. NEUSNER & E.S. FRERICHS (eds.), *"To See Ourselves As Others See Us". Christians, Jews, "Others" in Late Antiquity* (Scholars Press Studies in the Humanities, 9), Chico CA, Scholars Press, 1985. Short title: "To See Ourselves As Others See Us"

C.A. NEWSOM, *370. 4QAdmonition Based on the Flood*, in M. BROSHI et al. (eds.), *Qumran Cave 4. XIV. Parabiblical Texts, Part 2* (Discoveries in the Judaean Desert, 19), Oxford, Clarendon, 1995, pp. 85-97. Short title: 4QAdmonition Based on the Flood

C. NEWSOM & J.H. CHARLESWORTH with H.W.L. RIETZ & B.A. STRAWN, *Angelic Liturgy*, in J.H. CHARLESWORTH et al. (eds.), *Dead Sea Scrolls* 4B, pp. 1-189. Short title: Angelic Liturgy

G.W.E. NICKELSBURG, *Enochic Wisdom: An Alternative to the Mosaic Torah?*, in J. & S. GITIN (eds.), *Hesed ve-Emet*. FS E.S. Frerichs (Brown Judaic Studies, 320), Atlanta GA, Scholars Press, 1998, pp. 123-132. Short title: Enochic Wisdom

—, *The Qumranic Transformation of a Cosmological and Eschatological Tradition (1QH 4:29-40)*, in J. TREBOLLE BARRERA & L. VEGAS MONTANER (eds.), *The Madrid Qumran Congress. Proceedings of the International Congress on the Dead Sea Scrolls Madrid 18-21 March, 1991* (Studies on the Texts of the Desert of Judah, 11), Vol. 2, Leiden, Brill, 1994, pp. 649-659. Short title: The Qumranic Transformation

K.-W. NIEBUHR, *Gesetz und Paränese. Katechismusartige Weisungsreihen in der frühjüdischen Literatur* (Wissenschaftliche Untersuchungen zum Neuen Testament, 2. R. 28), Tübingen, Mohr Siebeck, 1987. Short title: Gesetz und Paränese

H. NIEHR, ערם, ערום, ערמה, in G.J. BOTTERWECK & H. RINGGREN (eds.), *Theologisches Wörterbuch zum Alten Testament* VI, Stuttgart, Kohlhammer, 1989, pp. 387-392. Short title: ערם

M. NILSSON, *Religion as Man's Protest against the Meaninglessness of Events* (Opuscula selecta, 3), Lund, CWK – Gleerup, 1960. Short title: Religion

B. NITZAN, *Admonitory Parable*, in T. ELGVIN *et al.* (eds.), *Qumran Cave 4*. XV. *Sapiential Texts. Part 1* (Discoveries in the Judaean Desert, 20), Oxford, Clarendon, 1997, pp. 125-149. Short title: Admonitory Parable

——, *4Q302/302a (Sap. A): Pap. Praise of God and Parable of the Tree. A Preliminary Edition*, in *Revue de Qumran* 17 (1996) 151-173. Short title: 4Q302/302a

E. VON NORDHEIM, *Die Lehre der Alten* I. *Das Testament als Literaturgattung im Judentum der hellenistisch-römischen Zeit* (Arbeiten zur Literatur und Geschichte des hellenistischen Judentums, 13), Leiden, Brill, 1980. Short title: Lehre

F. NÖTSCHER, *Geist und Geister in den Texten von Qumran*, in ID., *Vom Alten zum Neuen Testament. Gesammelte Aufsätze* (Bonner biblische Beiträge, 17), Bonn, Hanstein, 1962, pp. 175-187. Short title: Geist und Geister

——, *Zur theologischen Terminologie der Qumrantexte* (Bonner biblische Beiträge, 10), Bonn, Hanstein, 1956. Short title: Terminologie

G.S. OEGEMA, *Zwischen Hoffnung und Gericht. Untersuchungen zur Rezeption der Apokalyptik im frühen Christentum und Judentum* (Wissenschaftliche Monographien zum Alten und Neuen Testament, 82), Neukirchen-Vluyn, Neukirchener Verlag, 1999. Short title: Hoffnung und Gericht

N. OETTINGER, *Achikars Weisheitssprüche im Licht älterer Fabeldichtung*, in N. HOLZBERG (ed.), *Der Äsop-Roman* (Classica Monacensia, 6), Tübingen, Narr, 1992, pp. 3-22. Short title: Weisheitssprüche

S. OPPERMANN, *Paradoxa*, in W. SONTHEIMER (ed.), *Der Kleine Pauly. Lexikon der Antike* 2 (dtv, 5963), 1979, p. 500. Short title: Paradoxa

P. VON DER OSTEN-SACKEN, *Die Apokalyptik in ihrem Verhältnis zu Prophetie und Weisheit* (Theologische Existenz heute, 157), München, Kaiser, 1969. Short title: Apokalyptik

R. PATAI, *The Jewish Alchemists*, Princeton NJ, Princeton University Press, 1994. Short title: Alchemists

D. PATTE, *The Religious Dimensions of Biblical Texts. Greimas' Structural Semiotics and Biblical Exegesis* (Society of Biblical Literature Semeia Studies), Atlanta GA, Scholars Press, 1990. Short title: Biblical Texts

H. PAULSEN, *Überlieferung und Auslegung in Römer 8* (Wissenschaftliche Monographien zum Alten und Neuen Testament, 43), Neukirchen-Vluyn, Neukirchener Verlag, 1974. Short title: Überlieferung

H. PENNER, *Impasse and Resolution. A Critique of the Study of Religion* (Toronto Studies in Religion, 8), New York, Peter Lang, 1989. Short title: Impasse

M. PÉREZ FERNANDEZ, *An Introductory Grammar of Rabbinic Hebrew*, English translation by J.F. ELWOLDE, Leiden, Brill, 1997. Short title: Grammar

O. PFLEIDERER, *Das Urchristentum, seine Schriften und Lehren in geschichtlichem Zusammenhang*, Berlin, Reimer, 1887. Short title: Urchristentum

M. PHILONENKO, *L'apocalyptique qoumrânienne*, in D. HELLHOLM (ed.), *Apocalypticism in the Mediterranean World and the Near East. Proceedings of the International Colloquium on Apocalypticism Uppsala, August 12-17, 1979*, Tübingen, Mohr Siebeck, ²1989, pp. 211-218. Short title: L'apocalyptique qoumrânienne

———, *Les interpolations chrétiennes des Testaments des Douze Patriarches et les Manuscrits de Qumrân* (Cahiers de la Revue d'Histoire et de Philosophie Religieuses, 35), Paris, Presses Universitaires de France, 1960. Short title: Les interpolations chrétiennes

J. PIEPER, *Wahrheit der Dinge. Eine Untersuchung zur Anthropologie des Hochmittelalters*, München, Kösel, ⁴1966. Short title: Wahrheit

J. VAN DER PLOEG, *Le rouleau de la guerre* (Studies on the Texts of the Desert of Judah, 2), Leiden, Brill, 1959. Short title: Guerre

R. POLZIN, *Late Biblical Hebrew. Toward an Historical Typology of Biblical Hebrew Prose* (Harvard Semitic Monograph Series, 12), Missoula, Scholars Press, 1976. Short title: Late Biblical Hebrew

B. PORTEN & A. YARDENI, *Textbook of Aramaic Documents from Ancient Egypt* 3, Jerusalem/Winona Lake, Eisenbrauns, 1993. Short title: Textbook

H.D. PREUSS, *Theologie des Alten Testaments*, 2 vols., Stuttgart, Kohlhammer, 1991-1992. Short title: Theologie des Alten Testaments

J. PREUSS, *Biblisch-talmudische Medizin*, Berlin, S. Karger, 1911; repr. Farnborough Hants., Gregg International, 1969; English translation by F. ROSNER, New York/London, Sanhedrin Press, 1978. Short title: Medizin

J. PRYRKE, *"Spirit" and "Flesh" in the Qumran Documents and Some New Testament Texts*, in *Revue de Qumran* 5 (1965) 345-360. Short title: Spirit

E. PUECH, *Les deux derniers Psaumes davidiques du rituel d'exorcisme, 11QPsAp^a IV 4-V 14*, in D. DIMANT & U. RAPPAPORT (eds.), *The Dead Sea Scrolls. Forty Years of Research* (Studies on the Texts of the Desert Judah, 10), Leiden/Jerusalem, Brill/Yad Izhak Ben-Zvi, 1992, pp. 64-89. Short title: Psaumes

———, *Fragments d'un apocryphe de Lévi et le personnage eschatologique. 4QTestLévi^{c-d}(?) et 4QAJa*, in J. TREBOLLE BARRERA & L. VEGAS MONTANER (eds.), *The Madrid Qumran Congress. Proceedings of the International Congress on the Dead Sea Scrolls, Madrid 18-21 March, 1991* (Studies on the Texts of the Desert of Judah, 11), Leiden, Brill, 1992, pp. 449-501. Short title: Apocryphe de Lévi

———, *Qumran Grotte 4. XXII: Textes araméens, première partie (4Q529-549)* (Discoveries in the Judaean Desert, *31*), Oxford, Clarendon, 2001. Short title: Qumran Grotte 4. XXII

E. QIMRON, *The Hebrew of the Dead Sea Scrolls* (Harvard Semitic Studies, 29), Atlanta GA, Scholars Press, 1986. Short title: Hebrew

E. QIMRON & J. STRUGNELL, *Qumran Cave 4. V. Miqsat Ma'aśe ha-Torah* (Discoveries in the Judaean Desert, 10), Oxford, Clarendon, 1994. Short title: Qumran Cave 4. V

C. RABIN, *The Zadokite Documents*, Oxford, Clarendon, 1954. Short title: Zadokite Documents

G. V. RAD, *Gerichtsdoxologie*, in ID., *Gesammelte Studien zum Alten Testament* 2 (Theologische Bibliothek, 48), München, Chr. Kaiser, 1973, pp. 245-254. Short title: Gerichtsdoxologie

R. REDFIELD, *Primitive World View and Civilization*, in ID., *The Primitive World and Its Transformations*, Ithaca, Cornell University Press, 1967, pp. 84-110. Short title: World View

S.A. REED & M.J. LUNDBERG, *The Dead Sea Scrolls Catalogue. Documents, Photographs and Museum Inventory Numbers* (SBL Resources for Biblical Study, 32), Atlanta, Scholars Press, 1994. Short title: Catalogue

J.C. REEVES, *What Does Noah Offer in 1QapGen X,15?*, in *Revue de Qumran* 12 (1986) 415-419. Short title: Noah

R. REITZENSTEIN, *Die hellenistischen Mysterienreligionen: nach ihren Grundgedanken und Wirkungen*, Leipzig/Berlin, Teubner, ³1927. Short title: Mysterienreligionen

H.-P. RICHTER (ed.), *A Preliminary Concordance to the Hebrew and Aramaic Fragments from Qumrân Caves II-X Including Especially the Unpublished Material from Cave IV*. Printed from a card index prepared by R.E. BROWN, S.S., J.A. FITZMYER, S.J., W.G. OXTOBY, J. TEIXIDOR. Prepared and arranged for printing by H.-P. RICHTER. Volumes I-V. Editorum in Usum, Göttingen, privately printed, 1988. Short title: Preliminary Concordance

W. RICHTER, *Recht und Ethos* (Studien zum Alten und Neuen Testament, 15), München, Kösel-Verlag, 1966. Short title: Recht

R. RIESNER, *Die Frühzeit des Apostels Paulus* (Wissenschaftliche Untersuchungen zum Neuen Testament, 71), Tübingen, Mohr Siebeck, 1994. Short title: Die Frühzeit des Apostels Paulus

D. RÖMHELD, *Die Weisheitslehre im alten Orient* (Biblische Notizen Beihefte, 4), München, Manfred Görg, 1989. Short title: Weisheitslehre

J. ROLOFF, *Der erste Brief an Timotheus* (Evangelisch-katholischer Kommentar zum Neuen Testament, 15), Zürich/Neukirchen-Vluyn, Benziger/Neukirchener Verlag, 1988. Short title: Der erste Brief an Timotheus

D.B. RUDERMAN, *Jewish Thought and Scientific Discovery in Early Modern Europe*, New Haven/London, Yale University Press, 1995. Short title: Jewish Thought

L. RUPPERT, *Zur Funktion der Achikar-Notizen im Buch Tobias*, in *Biblische Zeitschrift* 20 (1976) 232-237. Short title: Funktion

D.S. RUSSELL, *The Method and Message of Jewish Apocalyptic: 200 BC – AD 100* (Old Testament Library), London, SCM, 1964. Short title: Method and Message

E. SACHAU, *Aramäische Papyrus und Ostraka aus einer jüdischen Militär-Kolonie zu Elephantine*, Leipzig, Hinrichs, 1911. Short title: Papyrus

M. SÆBØ, אשר *'šr pi. glücklich preisen*, in E. JENNI (ed.), *Theologisches Handwörterbuch zum Alten Testament* 1, München/Zürich, Kaiser/Theologischer Verlag, 1971, cc. 257-260. Short title: אשר

A. SAENZ-BADILLOS, *A History of the Hebrew Language*, English translation by J.F. ELWOLDE, Cambridge, Cambridge University Press, 1993. Short title: History

A. SAND, *Der Begriff "Fleisch" in den paulinischen Hauptbriefen* (Biblische Untersuchungen, 2), Regensburg, Friedrich Pustet, 1967. Short title: Fleisch

E.P. SANDERS (ed.), *Jewish and Christian Self-Definition*. Volume One. *The Shaping of Christianity in the Second and Third Centuries*, London, SCM, 1980. Short title: Self-Definition I

——, with A.I. BAUMGARTEN & A. MENDELSON (eds.), *Jewish and Christian Self-Definition*. Volume Two. *Aspects of Judaism in the Graeco-Roman Period*, London, SCM, 1981. Short title: Self-Definition II

J.A. SANDERS with J.H. CHARLESWORTH and H.W.L. RIETZ, *Hymn to the Creator*, in J.H. CHARLESWORTH et al. (eds.), *Dead Sea Scrolls* 4A, pp. 198-199. Short title: Hymn to the Creator

S. SANDMEL, *Parallelomania*, in *Journal of Biblical Literature* 81 (1962) 1-12. Short title: Parallelomania

G. SARTON, *Introduction to the History of Science*, 5 vols., Baltimore, Williams and Wilkins, 1927-1948. Short title: Introduction

G. SAUER, *Jesus Sirach [Ben Sira]* (Jüdische Schriften aus hellenistisch-römischer Zeit, III.5), Gütersloh, Mohn, 1981. Short title: Sirach

W. SCHADEWALDT, *Die frühgriechische Lyrik* (Tübinger Vorlesungen, 3), Frankfurt a. M., Suhrkamp, 1989. Short title: Lyrik

P. SCHÄFER, *Der Götzendienst des Enosch*, in ID., *Studien zur Geschichte und Theologie des rabbinischen Judentums* (Arbeiten zur Geschichte des antiken Judentums und des Urchristentums, 15), Leiden, Brill, 1978, pp. 134-152. Short title: Der Götzendienst des Enosch

S. SCHECHTER, *Documents of Jewish Sectaries*. Vol. 1. *Fragments of a Zadokite Work*, Cambridge, Cambridge University Press, 1910. Short title: Documents

A. SCHERER, *Vielfalt und Ordnung. Komposition in den biblischen Proverbien und in den aramäischen Achikarsprüchen*, in *Biblische Notizen* 90 (1997) 28-45. Short title: Vielfalt

H. SCHLIER, *Der Brief an die Galater* (Kritisch-exegetischer Kommentar über das Neue Testament, 7), Göttingen, Vandenhoeck & Ruprecht, [13]1965. Short title: Der Brief an die Galater

J. SCHMID, *Seligpreisung*, in J. HÖFER & K. RAHNER (eds.), *Lexikon für Theologie und Kirche* 9, Freiburg, Herder, [2]1964, pp. 639-642. Short title: Seligpreisung

R. SCHMIDT, *Die paulinische Christologie in ihrem Zusammenhange mit der Heilslehre des Apostels dargestellt*, Göttingen, Vandenhoeck & Ruprecht, 1870. Short title: Christologie

W. SCHMITHALS, *Die Gnosis in Korinth. Eine Untersuchung zu den Korintherbriefen* (Forschungen zur Religion und Literatur des Alten und Neuen Testaments, 48), Göttingen, Vandenhoeck & Ruprecht, [2]1965. Short title: Gnosis in Korinth

——, *Die theologische Anthropologie des Paulus*, Stuttgart, Kohlhammer, 1980. Short title: Anthropologie

U. SCHNELLE, *Neutestamentliche Anthropologie: Jesus – Paulus – Johannes*, (Biblisch-theologische Studien, 18), Neukirchen-Vluyn, Neukirchener Verlag, 1991. Short title: Anthropologie

A. SCHOORS, *The Preacher Sought to Find Pleasing Words* (Orientalia Lovaniensia analecta, 41), Leuven, Peeters, 1992. Short title: The Preacher

W. SCHRAGE, *Der erste Brief an die Korinther. 2. Teilband 1 Kor 6,12-11,16* (Evangelisch-katholischer Kommentar zum Neuen Testament, 7.2), Solothurn, Benziger / Neukirchen-Vluyn, Neukirchener Verlag, 1995. Short title: Der erste Brief an die Korinther 2

E. SCHRÖDINGER, *Naturwissenschaft und Religion*, in H.-P. DÜRR (ed.), *Physik und Transzendenz*, Bern/München/Wien, Scherz, ³1986, pp. 171-183. Short title: Naturwissenschaft

S. SCHROER, *Weisheit*, in E. ZENGER et al., *Einleitung in das Alte Testament*, Stuttgart, Kohlhammer, 1995, pp. 277-284. Short title: Weisheit

E. SCHULLER, *The Cave 4 Hôdāyôt Manuscripts: A Preliminary Description*, in H.-J. FABRY, A. LANGE, & H. LICHTENBERGER (eds.), *Qumranstudien* (Studien des Institutum Judaicum Delitzschianum, 3), Göttingen, Vandenhoeck & Ruprecht, 1995, pp. 87-100. Short title: The Cave 4 Hôdāyôt Manuscripts

S. SCHULZ, *Zur Rechtfertigung aus Gnaden in Qumran und bei Paulus*, in *Zeitschrift für Theologie und Kirche* 56 (1959) 155-185. Short title: Rechtfertigung

A. SCHWEITZER, *Geschichte der paulinischen Forschung von der Reformation bis auf die Gegenwart*, Tübingen, Mohr Siebeck, ²1933. Short title: Geschichte

E. SCHWEIZER, *Formgeschichtliches zu den Seligpreisungen Jesu*, in *New Testament Studies* 19 (1972) 121-126. Short title: Formgeschichtliches

——, *Art. σάρξ*, in G. KITTEL & G. FRIEDRICH (eds.), *Theological Dictionary of the New Testament* VII, Grand Rapids MI, Eerdmans, 1974, pp. 119-151. Short title: σάρξ

A.F. SEGAL, *Paul the Convert. The Apostolate and Apostasy of Saul the Pharisee*, New Haven/London, Yale University Press, 1990. Short title: Paul the Convert

M.H. SEGAL, *A Grammar of Mishnaic Hebrew*, Oxford, Oxford University Press, 1958. Short title: Grammar

E. SEKKI, *The Meaning of ruaḥ at Qumran* (Society of Biblical Literature Dissertation Series, 110) Atlanta GA, Scholars Press, 1989. Short title: The Meaning of ruaḥ

G. SELLIN, *Der Streit um die Auferstehung der Toten. Eine religionsgeschichtliche und exegetische Untersuchung von 1 Korinther 15* (Forschungen zur Religion und Literatur des Alten und Neuen Testaments, 138), Göttingen, Vandenhoeck & Ruprecht, 1986. Short title: Der Streit

C. SINGER, *Science and Judaism*, in L. FINKELSTEIN (ed.), *The Jews* III, pp. 216-65. Short title: Science

N.J. SMELSER, *Culture: Coherent or Incoherent*, in R. MÜNCH & N.J. SMELSER (eds.), *Theory of Culture* (New Directions in Cultural Analysis), Berkeley/Los Angeles/Oxford, University of California Press, 1992, pp. 3-28. Short title: Culture

J.Z. SMITH, *What A Difference A Difference Makes*, in J. NEUSNER & E.S. FRERICHS (eds.), *"To See Ourselves As Others See Us"*, pp. 3-48. Short title: Difference

W. VON SODEN, *Die babylonische Theodizee – Ein Streitgespräch über die Gerechtigkeit der Gottheit*, in O. KAISER (ed.), *Texte aus der Umwelt des Alten Testaments* III/1, Gütersloh, Mohn, 1990, pp. 143-157. Short title: Babylonische Theodizee

——, *Der leidende Gerechte. Ludlul bel nēmēqi. "Ich will preisen den Herrn der Weisheit"*, in O. KAISER (ed.), *Texte aus der Umwelt des Alten Testaments* III 1: *Weisheitstexte* I, Gütersloh, Mohn, 1990, pp. 110-135. Short title: Leidender Gerechter

——, *Die Schutzgenien Lamassu und Schedu in der babylonisch-assyrischen Literatur*, in *Baghdader Mitteilungen* 3 (1964) 148-156. Short title: Schutzgenien

M.I. SOKOLOV, *Materialy i zametki po starinnoj slavjanskoj literature. Vypusk tretij. VII. Slavjanskaja Kniga Enocha Pravednago. Teksty, latinskij perevod i izledovanie. Posmertnyj trud avtora prigotovil k izdaniju M. Speranskij* (ČOIDR, 4), Moskow, Sinodalnaja Tipografija, 1910. Short title: Slavjanskaja Kniga Enocha

H. SPIECKERMANN, *Die Satanisierung Gottes. Zur inneren Konkordanz von Novelle, Dialog und Gottesreden im Hiobbuch*, in I. KOTTSIEPER et al. (eds.), *"Wer ist wie du, HERR, unter den Göttern?" Studien zur Theologie und Religionsgeschichte Israels*. FS O. Kaiser, Göttingen, Vandenhoeck & Ruprecht, 1994, pp. 431-444. Short title: Satanisierung

M. STADLER & P. KRUSE, *Über Wirklichkeitskriterien*, in V. RIEGAS (ed.), *Zur Biologie der Kognition*, Frankfurt a. M., ³1993, pp. 133-158. Short title: Wirklichkeitskriterien

H. STEGEMANN, *Die Bedeutung der Qumranfunde für die Erforschung der Apokalyptik*, in D. HELLHOLM (ed.), *Apocalypticism in the Mediterranean World and the Near East. Proceedings of the International Colloquium on Apocalypticism Uppsala, August 12-17, 1979*, Tübingen, Mohr Siebeck, ²1989, pp. 495-530. Short title: Bedeutung

——, *Die Essener, Qumran, Johannes der Täufer und Jesus*, Freiburg i. B., Herder, 1993. Short title: Die Essener

——, *ΚΥΡΙΟΣ Ο ΘΕΟΣ und ΚΥΡΙΟΣ ΙΗΣΟΥΣ, Aufkommen und Ausbreitung des religiösen Gebrauchs von ΚΥΡΙΟΣ und seine Verwendung im Neuen Testament*, Bonn, Habilitation Masch., 1969. Short title: ΚΥΡΙΟΣ

——, *The Library of Qumran. On the Essenes, Qumran, John the Baptist, and Jesus*, Leiden, Brill, 1998. Short title: Library of Qumran

——, *Rekonstruktion der Hodajot. Ursprüngliche Gestalt und kritisch bearbeiteter Text der Hymnenrolle aus Höhle 1 von Qumran*, Heidelberg, Philological Dissertation (typoscript), 1963. Short title: Rekonstruktion der Hodajot

——, *Religionsgeschichtliche Erwägungen zu den Gottesbezeichnungen in den Qumrantexten*, in M. DELCOR (ed.), *Qumrân. Sa piété, sa théologie et son milieu* (Bibliotheca Ephemeridum Theologicarum Lovaniensium, 46), Paris, Gembloux, 1978, pp. 195-217. Short title: Gottesbezeichnungen

——, *Zu Textbestand und Grundgedanken von 1QS III,13-IV,26*, in *Revue de Qumran* 13 (1988) 95-113. Short title: Textbestand und Grundgedanken

A. STEUDEL, *408. 4QApocryphon of Moses^c?*, in S.J. PFANN et al. (eds.), *Qumran Cave 4. XXVI. Cryptic Texts and Miscellanea, Part 1* (Discoveries in the Judaean Desert, 36), Oxford, Clarendon, 2000, pp. 298-315. Short title: 4QApocryphon of Moses^c?

——, *410. 4QVision and Interpretation*, in S.J. PFANN *et al.* (eds.), *Qumran Cave 4. XXVI. Cryptic Texts and Miscellanea, Part 1* (Discoveries in the Judaean Desert, 36), Oxford, Clarendon, 2000, pp. 316-319. Short title: 4QVision and Interpretation

——, *Assembling and Reconstructing Manuscripts*, in P.W. FLINT & J.C. VANDERKAM (eds.), *The Dead Sea Scrolls After Fifty Years. A Comprehensive Assessment.* Volume 1, Leiden, Brill, 1998, pp. 516-534. Short title: Assembling

M.E. STONE, *Enoch, Aramaic Levi and Sectarian Origins*, in ID., *Selected Studies in Pseudepigrapha and Apocrypha. With Special Reference to the Armenian Tradition* (Studia in Veteris Testamenti Pseudepigrapha, 9), Leiden, Brill, 1991, pp. 247-258. Short title: Sectarian Origins

——, *Ideal Figures and Social Context: Priest and Sage in the Early Second Temple Age*, in ID., *Selected Studies in Pseudepigrapha and Apo-crypha. With Special Reference to the Armenian Tradition* (Studia in Veteris Testamenti Pseudepigrapha, 9), Leiden, Brill, 1991, pp. 259-270. Short title: Ideal Figures

G. STRECKER, μακάριος, in H. BALZ & G. SCHNEIDER (eds.), *Exegetisches Wörterbuch zum Neuen Testament* II, Stuttgart, Kohlhammer, 1981, pp. 925-932. Short title: μακάριος

——, *Theologie des Neuen Testaments* (ed. by F.W. HORN), Berlin/New York, De Gruyter, 1996. Short title: Theologie

J. STRUGNELL, *Le travail d'édition des fragments manuscrits de Qumrân: Communication de J. Strugnell*, in *Revue biblique* 63 (1956) 64-66. Short title: Travail d'édition

L.T. STUCKENBRUCK, *Angel Veneration and Christology* (Wissenschaftliche Untersuchungen zum Neuen Testament, II.70), Tübingen, Mohr Siebeck, 1995. Short title: Angel Veneration

P. STUHLMACHER, *Biblische Theologie des Neuen Testaments* 1, Göttingen, Vandenhoeck & Ruprecht, 1992. Short title: Biblische Theologie 1

A. SUHL, *Der Galaterbrief – Situation und Argumentation* (Aufstieg und Niedergang der römischen Welt, II 25.4) Berlin/New York, De Gruyter, pp. 3064-3134. Short title: Der Galaterbrief

S. TALMON, *The Sectarian* יחד *— a Biblical Noun*, in *Vetus Testamentum* 3 (1953) 133-140. Short title: יחד

S. TANZER, *419. 4QInstruction-like Composition A*, in S.J. PFANN *et al.* (eds.), *Qumran Cave 4. XXVI. Cryptic Texts and Miscellanea, Part 1* (Discoveries in the Judaean Desert, 36), Oxford, Clarendon, 2000, pp. 320-332. Short title: 4QInstruction-like Composition A

G. THEISSEN, *Psychologische Aspekte paulinischer Theologie* (Forschungen zur Religion und Literatur des Alten und Neuen Testaments, 131), Göttingen, Vandenhoeck & Ruprecht, 1983. Short title: Aspekte

——, *The Social Setting of Early Christianity*, Philadelphia, Fortress Press, 1982. Short title: Social Setting

——, *Soziale Schichtung in der korinthischen Gemeinde. Ein Beitrag zur Soziologie des hellenistischen Urchristentums*, in *Zeitschrift für die neutestamentliche Wissenschaft* 65 (1974) 232-272. Short title: Soziale Schichtung

J. THEODOR & Ch. ALBECK, *Bereschit Rabba mit kritischem Apparat und Kommentar*, 3 vols., Jerusalem, Shalem Books, ²1996. Short title: Bereschit Rabba

L.L. THOMPSON, *Social Location of Early Christian Apocalyptic*, in W. HAASE (ed.), *Religion. Vorkonstantinisches Christentum: Neues Testament* (Sachthemen [Forts.]) (Aufstieg und Niedergang der römischen Welt, II.26.3), Berlin/New York, De Gruyter, 1992, pp. 2615-2656. Short title: Location

L. THORNDIKE, *A History of Magic and Experimental Science*, 8 vols., New York, Macmillan, 1923-1958. Short title: History

E.J.C. TIGCHELAAR, *Working with Few Data: The Relation Between 4Q285 and 11Q14*, in *Dead Sea Discoveries* 7 (2000) 49-56. Short title: Few Data

——, *294. 4QSapiential-Didactic Work C*, in S.J. PFANN et al. (eds.), *Qumran Cave 4. XXVI. Cryptic Texts and Miscellanea, Part 1* (Discoveries in the Judaean Desert, 36), Oxford, Clarendon, 2000, pp. 247-248. Short title: 4QSapiential-Didactic Work C

K. VAN DER TOORN, *Seth*, in B. BECKING, P. VAN DER HORST & K. VAN DER TOORN (eds.), *Dictionary of Deities and Demons in the Bible*, Leiden, Brill, ²1998, pp. 748-749. Short title: Seth

F. TOPITSCH, *Vom Ursprung und Ende der Metaphysik*, Wien, Springer, 1958. Short title: Ursprung

E. TOV, *The Rabbinic Tradition concerning the "Alterations" Inserted into the Greek Pentateuch and their Relation to the Original Text of the LXX*, in *Journal for the Study of Judaism* 15 (1984) 65-89. Short title: Greek Pentateuch

——, *The Orthography and Language of the Hebrew Scrolls Found at Qumran and the Origin of these Scrolls*, in *Textus* 13 (1986) 31-57. Short title: Orthography

——, *The Greek Minor Prophets Scroll from Nahal Ḥever (8ḤevXII gr). The Seiyâl Collection* I (Discoveries in the Judaean Desert, 8), Oxford, Clarendon, 1990. Short title: Greek Minor Prophets Scroll

——, *Letters of the Cryptic A Script and Paleo-Hebrew Letters Used as Scribal Marks in Some Qumran Scrolls*, in *Dead Sea Discoveries* 2 (1995) 330-339. Short title: Letters

——, *List of the Texts from the Judaean Desert*, in P.W. FLINT & J.C. VANDERKAM (eds.), *The Dead Sea Scrolls after Fifty Years. A Comprehensive Assessment*, Vol. 2, Leiden, Brill, 1999, pp. 669-717. Short title: List

——, *Scribal Markings in the Texts from the Judean Desert*, in D.W. PARRY & S.D. RICKS (eds.), *Current Research and Technological Developments on the Dead Sea Scrolls. Conference on the Texts from the Judean Desert, Jerusalem, 30 April 1995* (Studies on the Texts from the Desert of Judah, 20), Leiden, Brill, 1996, pp. 41-77. Short title: Scribal Markings

——, *The Significance of the Texts from the Judean Desert for the History of the Text of the Hebrew Bible: A New Synthesis*, in F.H. CRYER & T.L. THOMPSON (eds.), *Qumran Between the Old and New Testaments* (Copenhagen International Seminar, 6 / Journal for the Study of the Old Testament Supplement Series, 290), Sheffield, Sheffield Academic Press, 1998, pp. 277-309. Short title: Significance

——, *The Unpublished Qumran Texts from Caves 4 and 11*, in *Biblical Archaeologist* 55 (1992) 94-104. Short title: Unpublished Qumran Texts

——, *The Unpublished Qumran Texts from Caves 4 and 11*, in *Journal of Jewish Studies* 43 (1992) 101-136. Short title: Unpublished Qumran Texts

E. Tov with the collaboration of S.J. Pfann (eds.), *The Dead Sea Scrolls on Microfiche. A Comprehensive Facsimile Edition of the Texts from the Judean Desert*, Leiden, Brill/IDC, 1993. Short title: Microfiche Edition

E. Tov with the collaboration of S.J. Pfann, *Companion Volume to the Dead Sea Scrolls Microfiche Edition*, Leiden, Brill, 1995. Short title: Companion Volume

G. Tronier, *Transcendens og transformation i Første Korintherbrev* [Transcendence and Transformation in 1 Corinthians] (Tekst og Tolkning, 10), København, Akademisk Forlag, 1994. Short title: Transcendens

J. Tropper, *Die Inschriften von Zincirli* (Abhandlungen zur Literatur Alt-Syrien-Palästinas, 6), Münster, Ugarit-Verlag, 1993. Short title: Inschriften

S. Uhlig, *Das äthiopische Henochbuch* (Jüdische Schriften aus hellenistisch-römischer Zeit, V,6), Gütersloh, Mohn, 1984. Short title: Henochbuch

A. Vaillant, *Le livre des secrets d'Hénoch. Texte slave et traduction française* (Textes publiés par l'Institut d'Études slaves, IV), Paris, Institut d'Études slaves, 1952, ²1976. Short title: Le livre

J.C. VanderKam, *Enoch. A Man for all Generations*, Columbia SC, University of South Carolina Press, 1995. Short title: Enoch

G. Vermes, *The Complete Dead Sea Scrolls in English*, London, Penguin, 1997. Short title: Complete Dead Sea Scrolls in English

——, *The Dead Sea Scrolls in English*, Sheffield, JSOT Press, 1987. Short title: Dead Sea Scrolls

——, *The Dead Sea Scrolls in English*, London, Penguin, ⁴1995. Short title: Dead Sea Scrolls 4th edition

——, *The Leadership of the Qumran Community: Sons of Zadok – Priests – Congregation*, in H. Cancik, H. Lichtenberger, & P. Schäfer (eds.), *Geschichte – Tradition – Reflexion*, FS Martin Hengel, Tübingen, Mohr Siebeck, Volume I, 1996, pp. 375-384. Short title: Leadership

——, *Preliminary Remarks on Unpublished Fragments of the Community Rule from Qumran Cave 4*, in *Journal of Jewish Studies* 42 (1991) 250-255. Short title: Preliminary Remarks

B.Z. Wacholder & M.G. Abegg, *A Preliminary Edition of the Unpublished Dead Sea Scrolls. The Hebrew and Aramaic Texts from Cave Four*, Fasc. 3, Washington DC, Biblical Archaeology Society, 1995. Short title: Preliminary Edition 3

M. Wagner, *Die lexikalischen und grammatikalischen Aramaismen im alttestamentlichen Hebräisch* (Beihefte zur Zeitschrift für die alttestamentliche Wissenschaft, 96), Berlin, De Gruyter, 1966. Short title: Aramaismen

N. Walter, *Die Bearbeitung der Seligpreisungen durch Matthäus*, in F.L. Cross (ed.), *Studia Evangelica* IV (Texte und Untersuchungen zur Geschichte der altchristlichen Literatur, 102), Berlin, Akademie Verlag, 1968, pp. 246-258. Short title: Bearbeitung

B.C. Waltke & M. O'Connor, *An Introduction to Biblical Hebrew Syntax*, Winona Lake, Eisenbrauns, 1990. Short title: Biblical Hebrew Syntax

W.G.E. Watson, *The Ahiqar Sayings: Some Marginal Comments*, in *Aula Orientalis* 2 (1985) 253-261. Short title: Ahiqar Sayings

H. Wehr, *Arabisches Wörterbuch für die Schriftsprache der Gegenwart*, Wiesbaden, Harrassowitz, 1956. Short title: Arabisches Wörterbuch

C. WEIZSÄCKER, *Das apostolische Zeitalter der urchristlichen Kirche*, Freiburg i. B., Mohr, ²1892. Short title: Zeitalter

H.H. WENDT, *Die Begriffe Fleisch und Geist im biblischen Sprachgebrauch*, Gotha, Perthes, 1878. Short title: Begriffe

P. WERNBERG-MØLLER, *The Manual of Discipline. Translated and Annotated with an Introduction* (Studies on the Texts of the Desert of Judah, 1), Leiden, Brill, 1957. Short title: Manual of Discipline

M.L. WEST, *Early Greek Philosophy and the Orient*, Oxford, Clarendon, 1971. Short title: Greek Philosophy

C. WESTERMANN, *Der Aufbau des Buches Hiob* (Calwer theologische Monographien, 6), Stuttgart, Calwer Verlag, ²1977. Short title: Aufbau

——, *Forschungsgeschichte zur Weisheitsliteratur 1950-1990* (Arbeiten zur Theologie, 71), Stuttgart, Calwer Verlag, 1991. Short title: Forschungsgeschichte

——, *Der Gebrauch von* אשרי *im Alten Testament*, in ID., *Forschung am Alten Testament. Gesammelte Studien* II (Theologische Bücherei, 55), München, Kaiser, 1974, pp. 191-195. Short title: Gebrauch von אשרי

——, *Genesis 1-11* (Biblischer Kommentar zum Alten Testament, 1,1), Neukirchen-Vluyn, Neukirchener Verlag, ³1983. Short title: Genesis 1-11

— *Weisheit im Sprichwort*, in K.-H. BERNHARDT (ed.), *Schalom. Studien zu Glaube und Geschichte Israels.* FS A. Jepsen (Arbeiten zur Theologie, 46), Stuttgart, Calwer Verlag, 1971, pp. 73-85, (wieder abgedruckt in ID., *Forschung am Alten Testament* II [Theologische Bücherei, 55], München, Kaiser, 1974, pp. 149-161). Short title: Weisheit

——, *Wurzeln der Weisheit. Die ältesten Sprüche Israels und anderer Völker*, Göttingen, Vandenhoeck & Ruprecht, 1990. Short title: Wurzeln

J.W. WEVERS, *Genesis* (Septuaginta. Vetus Testamentum Graecum Auctoritate Academiae Scientiarum Gottingensis Editum, 1), Göttingen, Vandenhoeck & Ruprecht, 1974. Short title: Genesis

U. WILCKENS, *Weisheit und Torheit. Eine exegetisch-religionsgeschichtliche Untersuchung zu 1. Kor. 1 und 2* (Beiträge zur historischen Theologie, 26), Tübingen, Mohr Siebeck, 1959. Short title: Weisheit und Torheit

——, *Der Brief an die Römer 1-3* (Evangelisch-katholischer Kommentar zum Neuen Testament, VI/1-3), Zürich, Benzinger/Neukirchen-Vluyn, Neukirchener Verlag, 1978-1982. Short title: Römer

D. WINSTON & J. DILLON, *Two Treatises of Philo of Alexandria. A Commentary on De Gigantibus and Quod Deus sit immutabilis* (Brown Judaic Studies, 25), Chico CA, Scholars Press, 1983. Short title: Two Treatises

M. WISE, M. ABEGG, & E. COOK, *The Dead Sea Scrolls. A New Translation*, London, Harper Collins, 1996. Short title: Dead Sea Scrolls

Y. YADIN, *Megillat Ha-Miqdash*, Jerusalem, Israel Exploration Society/Institute of Archaeology of the Hebrew University/Shrine of the Book, 1977. Short title: Megillat Ha-Miqdash

——, *The Temple Scroll*, 3 Volumes, Jerusalem, Israel Exploration Society, 1983. Short title: Temple Scroll

——, *The Ben Sira Scroll from Masada*, in ID., *Masada VI. Yigael Yadin Excavations 1963-1965, Final Reports*, Jerusalem, Israel Exploration Society/The Hebrew University of Jerusalem, 1999, pp. 151-252. Short title: Masada VI

E. ZELLER, *Die Philosophie der Griechen in ihrer geschichtlichen Entwicklung*, Bd. I/ 1, Leipzig, O. R. Reisland, ⁷1923. Short title: Philosophie

——, *Gnome*, in W. SONTHEIMER (ed.), *Der Kleine Pauly. Lexikon der Antike* 2 (dtv, 5963), München, Deutscher Taschenbuch Verlag, 1979, pp. 822-829. Short title: Gnome

E. ZENGER cf. F.L. HOSSFELD.

W. ZIMMERLI, *Ezechiel. I. Teilband. Ezechiel 1-24* (Biblischer Kommentar, Altes Testament, 13.1), Neukirchen, Neukirchener Verlag, 1969. Short title: Ezechiel

F. ZORELL, *Lexicon hebraicum Veteris Testamenti*, Roma, Pontificium Institutum Biblicum, 1984. Short title: Lexicon

INDEX OF REFERENCES

HEBREW BIBLE

Genesis			*Exodus*	
1	215, 228, 232, 240		9,27-28	397
			20,12	269
1-3	306		32,16	19, 272
2	215			
2-3	213		*Leviticus*	
2,8	353		5,18	15
2,9	250		16	15
2,15	250, 353		19,19	24, 210, 269
2,18	390			
2,23	390		*Numbers*	
2,24	213, 269, 389		24,17	185
3,14	250		30,6-15	211, 269
3,16	213, 250, 269, 361, 363		31,26	280
3,17	355, 358-359, 362-363		*Deuteronomy*	
			5,16	209, 269
3,17-19	358, 360, 363-364		13,7	209
			15,7	390
3,18	250, 355, 363		22,9	210
3,18 (LXX)	357		22,9-11	24, 269
3,18a	354		27,15	209
4,6-7	363		27,16	209
4,11-12	360, 363		28,54	209
4,12	362			
4,12ab	355		*Joshua*	
4,12b	355		1,8	5
4,25-26	186			
4,26	213, 393		*1 Kings*	
5,6	393		8,12-53	375
5,6-11	213			
5,9-11	393		*1 Chronicles*	
5,21-24	233		1,1	393
6	236			
6,1ff.	399		*2 Chronicles*	
6,1-2	398		32,8	396
6,3	376, 396, 399			
6,4	398		*Ezra*	
6,5	394, 399		9	397
14	307		10,13	146

Nehemiah

9	397
10,30	218

Job

1,5	215
1,6-12	169
1,9	157, 162
1,20-21	157-158, 162
1,21	169
1,22	154
2,1-7	169
2,3	157, 162
2,9-10	158, 160
2,10	154
2,10b	154, 160
3,2-10	169
3,11-19	160
4-5	160
4,17	397
4,17-21	398
4,19	398
4,21	398
5,8	398
5,9-14	160
8,5-7	162
9,5-10	160
9,8-10	160, 162
10,4	160, 162
11,6bff.	396
11,7-11	162
14,1	162-163
14,1-4	398
14,4	398
15,4	398
15,14	398
15,14-16	398
15,16	162, 398
22,4ff.	162
28	39, 160, 219
34,14	390
34,14-15	398
37,14	215
38-41	236
38,1ff.	162
38,1-6	237
38,7	206-207
38,8-11	163
38,12-17	163
38,16-30	163
39,13-18	160, 167
40,15-41, 26	160
42,1-6	163
42,7-9	163
42,10	158
42,10ff.	162, 169
42,12-17	158

Psalms

1	26
1,1	195
1,1-2	218
1,2	5, 29, 330
2	26
15,2-3	29
22	164-165
22,4	165
22,4-6	165
22,21-22	164
22,22bß	164
22,23-32	165-166
22,24	164
22,24-32	165-16
56,5	396
78,39	396
84,10	330
104,24	18
119,1	218
145	26
146	26
147	26
148	26
149	26
150	26

Proverbs

1-6	39
1-9	219
3,19	18
7	10
8	229, 237-238, 240
8-9	39
8,1	337
8,2	337-338
8,4	338
8,17	338
8,22	338-339

8,29-33	237-238	61,1ff.	197
9,13-18	39	60,21	257
10-29	155	61,3	257
10-31	155		
19,17	169	*Jeremiah*	
22,17-24, 22	219	17,5	396
Qoheleth		*Lamentations*	
3,11	237	1,18-22	397
4,2-3	161		
5,5	208	*Ezekiel*	
6,8	208	13,10-11	28
6,11	208	13,10-12	28
7,19	206		
8,5-6	26	*Daniel*	
11,9c	26	3,31-4, 34	397
12,12-14	26	9	397
		11,5	146
Isaiah			
5,7	257	*Micah*	
9,5	121	6,8	294
11,3	7		
13,13	115, 117	*Zephaniah*	
14,4	84	2,3	294
30,18	194		
31,3	396	*Malachi*	
40,3	329	3,2-3	147
51,1	294	3,15-16	19
53,3-4	218	3,16	393
59,20	280	3,16-18	214, 286

EARLY JEWISH LITERATURE (EXCEPT QUMRAN)

Apocalypse of Moses		1-36 *(Book of Watchers)*	301
15	353	1,2	247
24	351, 356-359	1,3	247
24,1-2	355	2-5	123
24,4	357	2,1	121-122, 341
25	359, 362	5,2	341
		5,6	247
Baruch		5,7	249
3-4	327	5,8	247
3,9	39	5,8 (Cod. Pan.)	247
4,4	39	7,1	235
		8,1	235
2 Baruch (Syriac Baruch)		8,1 (Kebran 9/II)	235
48,9	341	10,3	249-250, 253-256
1 Enoch	51, 236, 261	10,3 (Syncellus)	253

10,15-16	253	2,2	300
10,16	249-250, 256	7,1-5	319
10,16-17	254	12,1	301
10,17	253	15,2	301
12,4	308	18,1-9	319
13,4-6	309	19,1-6	309
14,4-7	309	22	301
15	398-399	22,8-10	309
15,1	308	22,11	297, 309
15,4	399	23,1	311
15,6	399	23,1-2	310
15,8	399	23,3	310
33,3-4	309	23,4	311
37-71 *(Book of Parables)*		24,3	313-314
42,1-3	339	24,3-28, 4	315
43	39	25,1	301
69,20-21	121	30,6	311
70-71	301	30,8	313
71	301	30,8-14	306, 315
71-72	301	30,15-16	307
72-82 *(Astronomical Book)*	238, 240, 301, 315	30,16	312
		31,7	307
72	231	33,1-2	310
75,8	120	33,3	314
81,1-2	308	33,11-12	314
83-90 *(Book of Dreams)*		33,4	313
84,6	249-250, 254-255	35,2	314
		37,1-2	309
91-108 *(Epistle of Enoch)*		39-67	303
91-105	257, 259-261, 301	40-67	305
		40,3	313
91,12-17; 93	257	40,9	311
92,2-5	259	40,13	309
92,3	258-259	42,6-14	311-312
92,4	257-259	43,1	309
92,4 (Kebran 9/II)	258	43,1-3	318
92,4b	259	43,2	313
92,5a	259	44,2-3	312
93,2	255, 260, 308	48,2	300
93,5	249-250, 254-256	48,7-9	315
		50,1	309
93,10	249-250, 254-256, 259-260	52,1-14	311-312
		52,15	301, 309
103,2	260, 308	53,2-3	309, 311
106	307	54,1	310
106,19	308	56,1-2	309
107,1	308	59,3	301
		61,4-5	300
2 Enoch (Slavonic Enoch)		62,2-3	300
1-38	303, 305	64,5	309

65,2	310	12,13	349
65,5	309	15,4	345
54,34	310	16	341
66,8	309	16,1	325
68-69	300	16,11	343
68-73	303, 306	16,12-14	340
68,2	309	16,19	343
71-72	307	18,6	346
		18,11-13	345, 347
Jubilees	51	20,6	347
1,16	250	24,1	329
4,12	393	24,10-11	331
16,26	250	28,20	331
21,24	250	29,6	329
36,6	250	30,1	340
		30,4	340
Life of Adam and Eve		33	336
18-21	359, 361	33,5-13	337-338
25,3	401	34,1-3	332
		36,1-2	343
4 Maccabees		38	335
1,16	332	38,1-3	333
1,16-17	326	38,4-6	333
		38,7-15	334
Odes of Solomon		38,16-22	334
3,3-5	332	38,17	340
3,5	332	41	330
3,10	331	41,3-4	329
3,11	332	41,6	330
4,5	330	42,8	348
6,1-2	326		
7,7-8	331	*Philo*	
7,8	338-339	*On the Cherubim*	
7,13-14	344	40-48	307
7,20	344	*On Giants*	
7,26	344	29ff.	376
8,8-11	346	*Who is the Heir*	
8,10-11	347	57	377
9,1	345	66	377
11	336		
11,4-5	348	*Psalms of Solomon*	
11,12	340	18,12-14	121, 341
11,18	340		
11,23	343	*Sirach*	50, 52, 264
12,2	339	3,7	209
12,4	339	8,18	13, 23
12,7	339	12,11	13, 23
12,11	339	14,20-27 [-15, 2]	29
12,12	339	14,20-15, 1	193

14,20-15, 2	197	*Testament of Judah*	
16	341	19,4	401
16,26-28	340-341	20,1ff.	401
24	39, 219, 327, 339		
		Testament of Naphtali	42
24,2	339		
24,3	339-340	*Testament of Zebulon*	
24,8	339	9,7-8	401
24,9	339		
24,11	339-340	*Tobit*	176-177
24,13	340	1,21-22	177
24,20	340	2,10	177
24,21	340	4,17	177
24,25-27	339	11,19	177
24,30	339	14,10	177
24,32	339		
25,7-11	193	*Wisdom of Solomon*	
25,8-9	197	3,9	339
33,7-15	318	4,15	339
49,9	158	6,22-11, 1	375
49,16	393	7-9	39, 327
51	219	7,1	375
		7,2	375
Testament of Asher		7,7	375
1,3-5	401		

QUMRAN

1QH^a (Hodayot)	29, 33	*1QM (War Scroll)*	
IV 37 (Sukenik XVII 25)	395, 399	IV 4	378
V 30 (Sukenik XIII 13)	395, 399	XII 7-16	112
V 30-33 (Sukenik XIII 13-16)	379	XII 12	378
V 35-36 (Sukenik XIII 18-19)	380	XIX 1-8	112
VI 2-3 (Sukenik XIV 2-3)	195		
VII 34-35 (Sukenik XV 21)	380	*1QS (Community Rule)*	29, 33
IX 11 (Sukenik I 9)	125	I 1	289
IX 13 (Sukenik I 13)	125	III-IV	271, 273
X 28-29 (Sukenik I 26-27)	23	III 5	331
XII 30-31 (Sukenik IV 29-30)	381-383	III 13	25, 289
XII 32 (Sukenik IV 31)	381	III 13-IV 26	13, 25-26, 289, 380, 392, 400-401
XIV 12b-16a (Sukenik VI 12-16)	253		
XV 31 (Sukenik VII 28)	397		
XVIII 29-30 (Sukenik X 27-28)	23, 246	III 15	25
		III 17	125
1QpHab (Pesher Habakkuk)	214	IV 4	25
II 8-9	214	IV 15ff.	25
VII 4-5	214	IV 20-21	381
		IV 22	26

INDEX OF REFERENCES

V 1	292	1 i 5-7	15-16
VI 3-4	285-286	1 i 5-6	15
VI 13ff.	291, 293	1 i 6	71, 408
VIII 15	291	1 i 6-7	16
IX 11	329	1 i 7	26, 93, 416-417
IX 12	288-289, 291	1 i 10	70
IX 12-26	289-290, 292	1 i 11	69
IX 14	290	1 ii 3	208
IX 15-16	291	3 2	14
IX 17-18	290	6 2	14, 15
IX 18-19	291	6 2-3	14, 208
IX 21	289		
IX 26-XI 22	383	*1Q28a (Rule of the Congregation)*	
X 4	121, 125	I 7	285
X 20	280	I 6-7	19, 393
XI 3	399		
XI 3-4	284, 384	*4Q109 (Qohelethᵃ)*	206
XI 7-8	383		
XI 7-9	253	*4Q163 (Pesher Isaiahᶜ)*	194
XI 9	378		
XI 9ff.	399	*4Q184 (Wiles of the Wicked Woman)*	
XI 11-12	384		9-10, 56-60, 75-76
CD (Damascus Document)	29	1	9, 10
II 5	280	1 2	82
X 6	19, 285, 393	1 5	86
XII 20b-22a	288	1 7	40
XIII 2	285	1 13	69
XIII 2-3	19	1 14	75
XIII 14-15	293	2	40
XIII 22	289	3	40
XIV 8	285		
XIV 6-8	19, 393	*4Q185 (Sapiential Work)*	11, 32, 37, 39, 41-42, 53, 56-60, 65-66, 94, 194, 219
XVI 10-12	211		
XX 17	280		
1Q26 (Instruction)	17-26, 66, 346-348, 386	1-2 i 7-8	85
		1-2 i 12	85
1 2	86	1-2 i 13-15	211
2 4	24	1-2 i 13 – ii 3	11
		1-2 ii 3	81
1Q27 (Mysteries)	12-16, 48, 66, 94, 215-216, 281-283, 319	1-2 ii 4	212
		1-2 ii 8	194
		1-2 ii 1	3, 194
1 i	14, 17, 415, 417	1-2 ii 14	76
1 i 3	86-87		
1 i 3-5	407	*4Q204 (Enochᶜ ar)*	
1 i 4	68, 73, 86-87, 408	1 i 19	121
		1 v 4	253
1 i 5	68-69, 71	1 v 5	253

4Q212 (Enoch^g ar)		4Q267 (Damascus Document^b)	
1 iv 12-13	255-256	9 v 12	285
1 iv 13	260		
		4Q270 (Damascus Document^e)	
4Q213 (Levi^a ar)	26	6 iv 17	285
4Q213a (Levi^b ar)	26	4Q294 (Sapiential Didactic Work C)	
		4	5
4Q213b (Levi^c ar)	26		
		4Q298 (cryptA Words of the Maskil to All Sons of Dawn) new or unchanged fragment numbers	
4Q214 (Levi^d ar)	26		
4Q214a (Levi^e ar)	26		12, 32, 43, 44, 53, 56-60, 216, 292-295, 344
4Q214b (Levi^f ar)	26		
		1-2 i 1	12
4Q215a (Time of Righteousness)*		1-2 i 1-2	344
	42-43, 56-60	1-2 i 1-3	12
		1-2 i 2	294
4Q256 (Rule of the Community^b)		1-2 i 2-3	12
IX 1	289	1-2 i 3	43
XVIII 4-5	289	3-4 ii 3-4	12
		3-4 ii 4-9	12
4Q257 (Rule of the Community^c)		3-4 ii 5	43
V 1-8	25	3-4 ii 7-10	344
4Q258 (Rule of the Community^d)		4Q299-301 (Mysteries^{a-c}) new or unchanged fragment numbers	
I 1	289		
VIII 5-6	289		
		4Q299-301	12-16, 48, 53-54, 56-60, 66, 94-95, 215-216, 281-283, 345
4Q259 (Rule of the Community^e)			
III 6	291		
III 6-7	289		
III 6-8	288		
IV 2-3	289	4Q299 (Mysteries^a)	66-67, 94, 415
		3a ii - b 3	14
4Q260 (Rule of the Community^f)		3a ii - b 5	89
IV 10	280	3a ii - b 9	14
		3a ii - b 12	82
4Q264a (Halakha B)	7, 45, 284	3a ii - b 14	74
		4	429
4Q266 (Damascus Document^a)		5	215
2 ii 5	280	6 i	14
8 iii 5	285	6 i 5	92, 121
9 ii 7-8	288	6 ii	14
		6 ii 4	417

* In his contribution to this volume J. Strugnell identifies a separate manuscript which he designates with the siglum 4Q215b, cf. pp. 32-33 n. 5.

6 ii 8	280	2 ii 9ff.	417
8 5	76	24 2	67
8 6	279, 408	40 2	416
10	280	65 2	67
10 3	280		
10 5	280	*4Q300 (Mysteries^b)*	
10 7	280	1 ii	418
55 5	14	1 ii 1	73, 74
59 1-5	16		
60 4	280	*4Q301 (Mysteries^c)*	
69	15	3 6-7	418
69 1	14		
69 2	14	*4Q302 (Admonitory Parable)*	
70	15		5, 44, 53, 56-60, 212
70 3	14		
71 1	280	1 i 7	212
76 3	280		
79	15	*4Q303-305 (Meditation on Creation A-C)*	
79 6-7	14		5, 37, 53, 56-60, 215
4Q300 (Mysteries^b)	66-67, 94	3	21
1a ii - b	14		
1a ii - b 1	13	*4Q307 (Text Mentioning Temple)* 6	
1a ii - b 2-5	13		
3	407, 415	*4Q308 (Sapiential frags.?)* 6	
3 4-6	15		
5 4	14	*4Q370 (Admon Flood)*	
5 5	13	ii 5-9	11
7 1	408		
8 4	90	*4Q392 (Works of God)*	66 94
8 5	416-417	1, 5	68
		1, 8	68
4Q301 (Mysteries^c)	66, 94	1 9	68
1	14		
1 1	417	*4Q394-399 (MMT^{a-f})*	
1 1-2	407	B 75-79	210
1 2	93, 416		
1 3	90	*4Q408 (apocrMoses^c?)* 6	
2b	14		
3a-b 6ff.	16	*4Q410 (Vision and Interpretation)*	
3a-b 8	281		6, 33
5 3	397-398		
		4Q411 (Sapiential Hymn)	6, 37, 52-53, 55-60, 81-82, 215
4Q299-301 (Mysteries^{a-c}) old fragment numbers			
		1 ii 2	82
4Q299 (Mysteries^a)		1 ii 10	40
2 ii	418	1 ii 11	82
2 ii 5	419	1 ii 12	82

1 ii 13	82	1 10	103, 116, 254
1 ii 17	82	1 10-13	391
		1 10-14	126
4Q412 (Sapiential-Didactic Work A)		1 11	110, 118, 124
	6, 38, 52-53, 55-60	1 11-12	119
		1 11-13	114-115
1 3	79-80	1 11-14	106, 115, 118
1 4	38	1 12	68, 110, 114, 124, 395, 398
1 6	38		
		1 13	103, 117, 124
4Q413 (Composition concerning Divine Providence)		1 14	124
	6-7, 38-39, 53, 55-60, 66, 212	1 15	124
		1 16	394-395
1-2 1	65, 74	1 16-17	115
		1 17	103, 116
4Q415-418.418a.418c.423 (Instruction$^{a\text{-}g}$*) new or unchanged fragment numbers*		2	265
		2 i - iv	18
		2 i 5	25, 86, 251
4Q415-418.418a.418c.423	17-26, 31, 39-40, 43, 44, 47-49, 51-55, 216-217, 219, 257, 259-260, 261, 263-264, 266, 274-275, 346-348, 386	2 ii 2-3	390, 398
		2 ii 17-18	346
		2 ii 18	70
		2 ii 19-20	77
		2 ii 21	82, 209
		2 iii	283
		2 iii 9	70, 86
		2 iii 10	79
4Q415 (Instruction^a*)*	66	2 iii 12	77
2 i	100	2 iii 14	86, 251
2 ii 1-9	184	2 iii 14-15	347
6 4	86	2 iii 15	69
		2 iii 16-19	209
4Q416 (Instruction^b*)*	66, 77, 94, 266	2 iii 17-18	251
1	17, 20, 100-126, 185, 265	2 iii 18	86, 283
		2 iii 19- iv 6	269
1 1	103	2 iii 20	77
1 1-2	107, 123, 125	2 iii 20-21	283
1 1-3	106, 123	2 iii 20 – iv 5	213
1 1-4	109	2 iii 21	41, 390
1 1-8	119	2 iv 4	389
1 1-9	20-21	2 iv 5	23
1 1-18	123-124	2 iv 6-9	211
1 2	120, 126	2 iv 6-13	269
1 3	24, 125	2 iv 8-9	24
1 4	103, 121	7 3	86
1 5	105		
1 6	125	*4Q417 (Instruction*^{c}*)*	66, 317
1 9	117, 125-126	1	17
1 9-10	115-116	1-2	265
1 9-18	118	1 i	17, 18-19, 100

INDEX OF REFERENCES

1 i 6	393	5 1	86
1 i 6-7	392	7-10	18
1 i 1-18	17	8 1	390, 398
1 i 8-12	19	10a+b 9-10	24
1 i 13ff	. 394	19 4	389
1 i 15	19	20 2	24
1 i 15ff.	396, 398	21 2	287
1 i 15-16	19	24 1	80
1 i 15-18	19, 393	43-45 i	17-19
1 i 16	19	43-45 i 4	251
1 i 17	19, 394-395	44 1	100
1 i 18	393	44 2	100
1 i 18 – ii 5	17	55	18, 252
1 i 25	123	55 3	82-83
1 ii 4	390, 398	55 4	69
1 ii 12	389, 394-395, 399	55 6	90
		55 8	252
1 ii 14	389	55 10	23, 246, 249
2 i - ii	18	55 11	252
2 i 10-11	25	55 12	249, 252
2 i 12	25	69	20, 258
2 i 15ff.	403	69 ii	17, 21-22
2 i 15-17	397	69 ii 4-9	22
2 i 24	25	69 ii 10	254, 258
3 4	389	69 ii 11-12	258
4 ii 2	24	69 ii 12-13	252, 258
5	17	69 ii 13	73, 249, 258
		69 ii 13-14	258
4Q418 (Instruction^d)	66, 94, 265	69 ii 14	257-259
1	100-101, 104-105, 108, 112-113	73	106-107, 117
		73 1	117
		73 3	117
1-2	109-112, 125	73 4	117
1 2	105	73 5	117
2	104, 105, 108, 110-113	73 9	117
		77	18
2 3	110, 124	77 2	25
2 3-5	110	81+81a	17
2 4	110, 124	81+81a 5	24
2 5	124	88	18
2 7	124	101 ii 5	389
2a	104, 112, 116-117	103	269
		103 i 9	389
2a 1	112	103 ii	17
2a 2	112	103 ii 7-9	210
2b	104, 112-113	103 ii 9	210, 390
2c	117	103 iii 6-9	24
3	104-105, 113	118 3	24
4	113	123 ii 2-8	251

Reference	Page
123 ii 4	86, 251
123 ii 45	83
126 ii	17
126 ii 5	18
172 1	86
184 2	86, 215
199	122
201	107-109
201 1	107
208	114, 116-117
208 2	117, 124
208 3	117
209	116
208 2	114
209	115, 117, 126
209 1	126
209 6	126
210	106
211	119-120
211 2	119-120
211 3	120
212	106-108, 110, 115, 117-118
212 1	117, 124
212 2	117
213	105-108, 110-112, 115-117
213 2	124
213 3	117
217	115-117
218	116-117
224	116-117
224 2	117
229	120, 122, 126
229 3	121-122
234	116
236	100
238	122-123, 126
238 1	287
286	108

4Q418*

Reference	Page
1	112-113, 125 118-120, 122, 126
2	118
2 3	114
2 4	114

Reference	Page
4Q418a (Instruction^e)	66, 111
24	111
25	111
4Q418c (4QInstruction^f?)	66

4Q423 (Instruction^g) new or unchanged fragment numbers 17-26, 31, 39-40, 43, 44, 47-49, 51-55, 66

Reference	Page
1-2 i 1	250
1-2 i 2	250
1-2 i 3	250
1-2 i 4	250
1-2 i 5	250
1-2 i 7	249-250
3 4	24
9 2	70

4Q415-418.418a.418c.423 (Instruction^{a-g}) old fragment numbers

4Q417 (Instruction^c)

Reference	Page
1 i	185
1 i 1-5	177
1 i 11	84-86
1 i 21-22	177
1 i 23	64
1 i 25	86
2 i 1	83
2 i 2	251
2 i 6-9	347
2 i 8	86
2 i 14	71, 251
2 i 15	185-186
2 i 15-16	286
2 i 16	213
2 i 17	286
2 i 18	83, 86, 251
2 i 19	248
2 i 21	86
2 i 25	251, 287
2 ii 3	86
2 ii 9	86
2 ii 14	76

* 4Q418* is identified by E. Tigchelaar's contribution to this volume as a separate manuscript.

INDEX OF REFERENCES

4Q418 (Instruction^d)	
2 8	394
7 10	86
9 8	70
9 17	69
10 6	390
43	100
43 4	392-393
43 14	86
43 16	86
77 2	86
77 4	86
81	251
81 1-2	391-392, 395, 400
81 1-3	248
81 4	248
81 4-5	248
81 6	71
81 9	251
81 11	248, 252
81 12	248 251-252
81 13	249-253
81 14	247-249
81 15	251
81 17	70, 287
81 18	70

4Q423 (Instruction^g)	
2	351
2 3	351-364

4Q418b (Text with Quotation from Psalm 107?)	
	108

4Q419 (Sap. Work B)	7, 66, 94
1 6	65

4Q420 (Ways of Righteousness^a)	
	7, 34, 44-45, 47-48, 52-53, 56-60, 202, 217, 220, 283
1a ii-b 1	68

4Q421 (Ways of Righteousness^b)	
	66, 219
1-10	45

1a i	217
1a i 2-3	45
1a ii – b 10	288
1a ii – b 12	288
9 2	81
11	45
11-13	45
12	45
13	45

4Q424 (Instruction-Like Work)	
	26-28, 34, 46-48, 52-53, 56-60, 66, 94
1 3-4	27, 28
1 4	84
1 4-5	27
1 6	69, 78, 91
1 7	93
1 8	83
1 9	27
1 10	69
2 2	27
2 3	70
3 1	27
3 2	27
3 3	80-81
3 4	27
3 4-5	348
3 6	82-83
3 7	81
3 8	27

4Q425 (Sapiential-Didactic Work B)	
	8, 34, 46-48, 52-53, 56-60, 66

4Q426 (Sapiential-Didactic Work A)	
	8, 34, 46-48, 52-53, 55-60, 66
1 ii 5	81
2, 1	80
9 1	88
12 3	48

4Q472 (Eschatological Work B)	8	14 ii 20	70
4Q473(The Two Ways)	8	14 ii 21	92
1 3	401	14 ii 23	85
		14 ii 27	72
4Q474 (Text Concerning Rachel and Joseph)	8	21 6	89
		23 1-6	50
		24 3-5	50
4Q475 (Renewed Earth)	8-9	254	52
4Q476 (Liturgical Work B)	9	*4Q525 (Beatitudes) old fragment numbers*	
		2 ii + 3 2	78
4Q476a (Liturgical Work C)	9	2 ii + 3 3-4	74
		2 ii + 3 5	70
4Q486 (papSap A?)	9	6 3	84
4Q487 (papSap B?)	9	*4Q528 (Hymnic or Sapiential Work B)*	9, 33
4Q498 (papSap/Hymn)	9		
		4Q541 (Apocryphe de Lévi[b?]ar)	218
4Q525 (Beatitudes) new or unchanged fragment numbers	28-29, 40, 49-51, 53-60, 65, 94, 190, 198, 218-219, 320	4Q541 6 3	218
		4Q541 9	218
		11Q5 (Psalms^a)	
		XVIII	38, 39, 40, 53, 56-60
2 ii 1-2	348		
2 ii 1-4	194-195	XVIII 5-15	219
2 ii 2-9	219	XVIII 7-10	41
2 ii 6	196	XXVI	37-38, 56-60
2-3 ii	29	XXVI 9-15	342
4 6-13	219		
5 5	70	*11Q10 (TgJob)*	206-207
5 12	69	XXXVIII 7-8	207
5 13	91		
14 ii	29	*11Q19 (Temple^a)*	111-112
14 ii 16	70, 74	V 6-11	111-112
14 ii 19	70	VI 2-8	111-112

NEW TESTAMENT

Matthew		6, 63	369
5, 3-12	189, 196-199	14, 6	336
5, 11-12	195	14, 21	338
25, 31-46	197	15, 16	338
Luke		*Acts*	
6, 20-22	196-199	22, 3	403
6, 20b-23	189	26, 4-5	403
John		*Romans*	
1, 14	369	1, 3-4	368
3, 6	369	5, 12	358

INDEX OF REFERENCES 501

6, 6	371	2, 11	420
7	404	2, 12	420
7-8	370	2, 13	420
7, 5	369	2, 14	420
7, 25b	369	2, 16	420
8, 3	370, 378	2, 10-16	420
8, 5-8	368	2, 11b-12	408
		2, 15	408
1 Corinthians		2, 16	409, 429
1-2	405-432	3, 1ff.	424, 428
1, 5	420	3, 1-4	426
1, 10	409, 420-421, 424	6, 9-11	413
		15	430
1, 11-17	422	15, 29	358
1, 18ff.	424		
1, 18-25	421	*Galatians*	
1, 18-31	424	3, 3	404
1, 18-2, 5	422, 423	5, 17	368-370
1, 18-2, 16	428	5, 18	370
1, 20	420	5, 19	404
1, 21	420		
1, 26-30	425	*1 Timothy*	
2, 1-16	424	3, 16	369
2, 2	420		
2, 6ff.	423	*James*	158
2, 6-16	426, 428		
2, 8	420	*1 John*	
2, 10	420	4, 10	338

RABBINIC LITERATURE

Babylonian Talmud		*Genesis Rabbah*	
b.Ber. 55a-57b	227	1, 1	229
b.Nid. 31b	402	15, 2	353
b.Sanh. 67b	228	20, 7	361-362, 402
b.Taʿan. 26b	300		
		Sefer Yetzirah	227-229
Palestinian Talmud			
j.Taʿan. 68c	300		

GREEK AND LATIN LITERATURE

Anaximander	169	*Fragments*	
		1	237
Artemidorus Daldianus		2	237
Oneirocritica	227	50	237
		114	237
Heraclitus	237		

Pindar	155	*Solon*	155
Plato		*Phocylides*	155
Phaedo			
66b-67b	377	*Theognis*	155

ANCIENT NEAR EASTERN LITERATURE

Ahiqar		*Ludlul bēl nēmeqi*	164-165
43	177	I 1-31	165
126	184	III 9	165
142	177	III 9-47	165
		IV 99-100	165
Babylonian Theodicy	166-169	IV 112	165
279-286	167		
295	166	*Poor Man from Nippur*	159
295-297	166	L. 71	159
296	166		
Frg. KAR 340=VAT 9943	166		

ISLAMIC SOURCES

Koran		38, 41-44	158
21, 83-84	158		

BIBLIOTHECA EPHEMERIDUM THEOLOGICARUM LOVANIENSIUM

Series I

* = Out of print

- *1. Miscellanea dogmatica in honorem Eximii Domini J. Bittremieux, 1947.
- *2-3. Miscellanea moralia in honorem Eximii Domini A. Janssen, 1948.
- *4. G. Philips, La grâce des justes de l'Ancien Testament, 1948.
- *5. G. Philips, De ratione instituendi tractatum de gratia nostrae sanctificationis, 1953.
- 6-7. Recueil Lucien Cerfaux. Études d'exégèse et d'histoire religieuse, 1954. 504 et 577 p. Cf. infra, n°s 18 et 71 (t. III). 25 € par tome
- 8. G. Thils, Histoire doctrinale du mouvement œcuménique, 1955. Nouvelle édition, 1963. 338 p. 4 €
- *9. Études sur l'Immaculée Conception, 1955.
- *10. J.A. O'Donohoe, Tridentine Seminary Legislation, 1957.
- *11. G. Thils, Orientations de la théologie, 1958.
- *12-13. J. Coppens, A. Descamps, É. Massaux (ed.), Sacra Pagina. Miscellanea Biblica Congressus Internationalis Catholici de Re Biblica, 1959.
- *14. Adrien VI, le premier Pape de la contre-réforme, 1959.
- *15. F. Claeys Bouuaert, Les déclarations et serments imposés par la loi civile aux membres du clergé belge sous le Directoire (1795-1801), 1960.
- *16. G. Thils, La «Théologie œcuménique». Notion-Formes-Démarches, 1960.
- 17. G. Thils, Primauté pontificale et prérogatives épiscopales. «Potestas ordinaria» au Concile du Vatican, 1961. 103 p. 2 €
- *18. Recueil Lucien Cerfaux, t. III, 1962. Cf. infra, n° 71.
- *19. Foi et réflexion philosophique. Mélanges F. Grégoire, 1961.
- *20. Mélanges G. Ryckmans, 1963.
- 21. G. Thils, L'infaillibilité du peuple chrétien «in credendo», 1963. 67 p.
   2 €
- *22. J. Férin & L. Janssens, Progestogènes et morale conjugale, 1963.
- *23. Collectanea Moralia in honorem Eximii Domini A. Janssen, 1964.
- 24. H. Cazelles (ed.), De Mari à Qumrân. L'Ancien Testament. Son milieu. Ses écrits. Ses relectures juives (Hommage J. Coppens, I), 1969. 158*-370 p. 23 €
- *25. I. de la Potterie (ed.), De Jésus aux évangiles. Tradition et rédaction dans les évangiles synoptiques (Hommage J. Coppens, II), 1967.
- 26. G. Thils & R.E. Brown (ed.), Exégèse et théologie (Hommage J. Coppens, III), 1968. 328 p. 18 €
- *27. J. Coppens (ed.), Ecclesia a Spiritu sancto edocta. Hommage à Mgr G. Philips, 1970. 640 p.
- 28. J. Coppens (ed.), Sacerdoce et célibat. Études historiques et théologiques, 1971. 740 p. 18 €

29. M. DIDIER (ed.), *L'évangile selon Matthieu. Rédaction et théologie*, 1972. 432 p. 25 €
*30. J. KEMPENEERS, *Le Cardinal van Roey en son temps*, 1971.

SERIES II

31. F. NEIRYNCK, *Duality in Mark. Contributions to the Study of the Markan Redaction*, 1972. Revised edition with Supplementary Notes, 1988. 252 p. 30 €
32. F. NEIRYNCK (ed.), *L'évangile de Luc. Problèmes littéraires et théologiques*, 1973. *L'évangile de Luc – The Gospel of Luke*. Revised and enlarged edition, 1989. X-590 p. 55 €
33. C. BREKELMANS (ed.), *Questions disputées d'Ancien Testament. Méthode et théologie*, 1974. *Continuing Questions in Old Testament Method and Theology*. Revised and enlarged edition by M. VERVENNE, 1989. 245 p. 30 €
34. M. SABBE (ed.), *L'évangile selon Marc. Tradition et rédaction*, 1974. Nouvelle édition augmentée, 1988. 601 p. 60 €
35. B. WILLAERT (ed.), *Philosophie de la religion – Godsdienstfilosofie. Miscellanea Albert Dondeyne*, 1974. Nouvelle édition, 1987. 458 p. 60 €
36. G. PHILIPS, *L'union personnelle avec le Dieu vivant. Essai sur l'origine et le sens de la grâce créée*, 1974. Édition révisée, 1989. 299 p. 25 €
37. F. NEIRYNCK, in collaboration with T. HANSEN and F. VAN SEGBROECK, *The Minor Agreements of Matthew and Luke against Mark with a Cumulative List*, 1974. 330 p. 23 €
38. J. COPPENS, *Le messianisme et sa relève prophétique. Les anticipations vétérotestamentaires. Leur accomplissement en Jésus*, 1974. Édition révisée, 1989. XIII-265 p. 25 €
39. D. SENIOR, *The Passion Narrative according to Matthew. A Redactional Study*, 1975. New impression, 1982. 440 p. 25 €
40. J. DUPONT (ed.), *Jésus aux origines de la christologie*, 1975. Nouvelle édition augmentée, 1989. 458 p. 38 €
41. J. COPPENS (ed.), *La notion biblique de Dieu*, 1976. Réimpression, 1985. 519 p. 40 €
42. J. LINDEMANS & H. DEMEESTER (ed.), *Liber Amicorum Monseigneur W. Onclin*, 1976. XXII-396 p. 25 €
43. R.E. HOECKMAN (ed.), *Pluralisme et œcuménisme en recherches théologiques. Mélanges offerts au R.P. Dockx, O.P.*, 1976. 316 p. 25 €
44. M. DE JONGE (ed.), *L'évangile de Jean. Sources, rédaction, théologie*, 1977. Réimpression, 1987. 416 p. 38 €
45. E.J.M. VAN EIJL (ed.), *Facultas S. Theologiae Lovaniensis 1432-1797. Bijdragen tot haar geschiedenis. Contributions to its History. Contributions à son histoire*, 1977. 570 p. 43 €
46. M. DELCOR (ed.), *Qumrân. Sa piété, sa théologie et son milieu*, 1978. 432 p. 43 €
47. M. CAUDRON (ed.), *Faith and Society. Foi et société. Geloof en maatschappij. Acta Congressus Internationalis Theologici Lovaniensis 1976*, 1978. 304 p. 29 €

*48. J. KREMER (ed.), *Les Actes des Apôtres. Traditions, rédaction, théologie*, 1979. 590 p.
49. F. NEIRYNCK, avec la collaboration de J. DELOBEL, T. SNOY, G. VAN BELLE, F. VAN SEGBROECK, *Jean et les Synoptiques. Examen critique de l'exégèse de M.-É. Boismard*, 1979. XII-428 p. 25 €
50. J. COPPENS, *La relève apocalyptique du messianisme royal. I. La royauté – Le règne – Le royaume de Dieu. Cadre de la relève apocalyptique*, 1979. 325 p. 25 €
51. M. GILBERT (ed.), *La Sagesse de l'Ancien Testament*, 1979. Nouvelle édition mise à jour, 1990. 455 p. 38 €
52. B. DEHANDSCHUTTER, *Martyrium Polycarpi. Een literair-kritische studie*, 1979. 296 p. 25 €
53. J. LAMBRECHT (ed.), *L'Apocalypse johannique et l'Apocalyptique dans le Nouveau Testament*, 1980. 458 p. 35 €
54. P.-M. BOGAERT (ed.), *Le livre de Jérémie. Le prophète et son milieu. Les oracles et leur transmission*, 1981. Nouvelle édition mise à jour, 1997. 448 p. 45 €
55. J. COPPENS, *La relève apocalyptique du messianisme royal. III. Le Fils de l'homme néotestamentaire*. Édition posthume par F. NEIRYNCK, 1981. XIV-192 p. 20 €
56. J. VAN BAVEL & M. SCHRAMA (ed.), *Jansénius et le Jansénisme dans les Pays-Bas. Mélanges Lucien Ceyssens*, 1982. 247 p. 25 €
57. J.H. WALGRAVE, *Selected Writings – Thematische geschriften. Thomas Aquinas, J.H. Newman, Theologia Fundamentalis*. Edited by G. DE SCHRIJVER & J.J. KELLY, 1982. XLIII-425 p. 25 €
58. F. NEIRYNCK & F. VAN SEGBROECK, avec la collaboration de E. MANNING, *Ephemerides Theologicae Lovanienses 1924-1981. Tables générales. (Bibliotheca Ephemeridum Theologicarum Lovaniensium 1947-1981)*, 1982. 400 p. 40 €
59. J. DELOBEL (ed.), *Logia. Les paroles de Jésus – The Sayings of Jesus. Mémorial Joseph Coppens*, 1982. 647 p. 50 €
60. F. NEIRYNCK, *Evangelica. Gospel Studies – Études d'évangile. Collected Essays*. Edited by F. VAN SEGBROECK, 1982. XIX-1036 p. 50 €
61. J. COPPENS, *La relève apocalyptique du messianisme royal. II. Le Fils d'homme vétéro- et intertestamentaire*. Édition posthume par J. LUST, 1983. XVII-272 p. 25 €
62. J.J. KELLY, *Baron Friedrich von Hügel's Philosophy of Religion*, 1983. 232 p. 38 €
63. G. DE SCHRIJVER, *Le merveilleux accord de l'homme et de Dieu. Étude de l'analogie de l'être chez Hans Urs von Balthasar*, 1983. 344 p. 38 €
64. J. GROOTAERS & J.A. SELLING, *The 1980 Synod of Bishops: «On the Role of the Family». An Exposition of the Event and an Analysis of its Texts*. Preface by Prof. emeritus L. JANSSENS, 1983. 375 p. 38 €
65. F. NEIRYNCK & F. VAN SEGBROECK, *New Testament Vocabulary. A Companion Volume to the Concordance*, 1984. XVI-494 p. 50 €
66. R.F. COLLINS, *Studies on the First Letter to the Thessalonians*, 1984. XI-415 p. 38 €
67. A. PLUMMER, *Conversations with Dr. Döllinger 1870-1890*. Edited with Introduction and Notes by R. BOUDENS, with the collaboration of L. KENIS, 1985. LIV-360 p. 45 €

68. N. LOHFINK (ed.), *Das Deuteronomium. Entstehung, Gestalt und Botschaft / Deuteronomy: Origin, Form and Message*, 1985. XI-382 p.   50 €
69. P.F. FRANSEN, *Hermeneutics of the Councils and Other Studies*. Collected by H.E. MERTENS & F. DE GRAEVE, 1985. 543 p.   45 €
70. J. DUPONT, *Études sur les Évangiles synoptiques*. Présentées par F. NEIRYNCK, 1985. 2 tomes, XXI-IX-1210 p.   70 €
71. *Recueil Lucien Cerfaux*, t. III, 1962. Nouvelle édition revue et complétée, 1985. LXXX-458 p.   40 €
72. J. GROOTAERS, *Primauté et collégialité. Le dossier de Gérard Philips sur la Nota Explicativa Praevia (Lumen gentium, Chap. III)*. Présenté avec introduction historique, annotations et annexes. Préface de G. THILS, 1986. 222 p.   25 €
73. A. VANHOYE (ed.), *L'apôtre Paul. Personnalité, style et conception du ministère*, 1986. XIII-470 p.   65 €
74. J. LUST (ed.), *Ezekiel and His Book. Textual and Literary Criticism and their Interrelation*, 1986. X-387 p.   68 €
75. É. MASSAUX, *Influence de l'Évangile de saint Matthieu sur la littérature chrétienne avant saint Irénée*. Réimpression anastatique présentée par F. NEIRYNCK. *Supplément: Bibliographie 1950-1985*, par B. DEHANDSCHUTTER, 1986. XXVII-850 p.   63 €
76. L. CEYSSENS & J.A.G. TANS, *Autour de l'Unigenitus. Recherches sur la genèse de la Constitution*, 1987. XXVI-845 p.   63 €
77. A. DESCAMPS, *Jésus et l'Église. Études d'exégèse et de théologie*. Préface de Mgr A. HOUSSIAU, 1987. XLV-641 p.   63 €
78. J. DUPLACY, *Études de critique textuelle du Nouveau Testament*. Présentées par J. DELOBEL, 1987. XXVII-431 p.   45 €
79. E.J.M. VAN EIJL (ed.), *L'image de C. Jansénius jusqu'à la fin du XVIIIe siècle*, 1987. 258 p.   32 €
80. E. BRITO, *La Création selon Schelling. Universum*, 1987. XXXV-646 p.   75 €
81. J. VERMEYLEN (ed.), *The Book of Isaiah – Le livre d'Isaïe. Les oracles et leurs relectures. Unité et complexité de l'ouvrage*, 1989. X-472 p.   68 €
82. G. VAN BELLE, *Johannine Bibliography 1966-1985. A Cumulative Bibliography on the Fourth Gospel*, 1988. XVII-563 p.   68 €
83. J.A. SELLING (ed.), *Personalist Morals. Essays in Honor of Professor Louis Janssens*, 1988. VIII-344 p.   30 €
84. M.-É. BOISMARD, *Moïse ou Jésus. Essai de christologie johannique*, 1988. XVI-241 p.   25 €
84A. M.-É. BOISMARD, *Moses or Jesus: An Essay in Johannine Christology*. Translated by B.T. VIVIANO, 1993, XVI-144 p.   25 €
85. J.A. DICK, *The Malines Conversations Revisited*, 1989. 278 p.   38 €
86. J.-M. SEVRIN (ed.), *The New Testament in Early Christianity – La réception des écrits néotestamentaires dans le christianisme primitif*, 1989. XVI-406 p.   63 €
87. R.F. COLLINS (ed.), *The Thessalonian Correspondence*, 1990. XV-546 p.   75 €
88. F. VAN SEGBROECK, *The Gospel of Luke. A Cumulative Bibliography 1973-1988*, 1989. 241 p.   30 €

89. G. THILS, *Primauté et infaillibilité du Pontife Romain à Vatican I et autres études d'ecclésiologie*, 1989. XI-422 p. 47 €
90. A. VERGOTE, *Explorations de l'espace théologique. Études de théologie et de philosophie de la religion*, 1990. XVI-709 p. 50 €
*91. J.C. DE MOOR, *The Rise of Yahwism: The Roots of Israelite Monotheism*, 1990. *Revised and Enlarged Edition*, 1997. XV-445 p.
92. B. BRUNING, M. LAMBERIGTS & J. VAN HOUTEM (eds.), *Collectanea Augustiniana. Mélanges T.J. van Bavel*, 1990. 2 tomes, XXXVIII-VIII-1074 p. 75 €
93. A. DE HALLEUX, *Patrologie et œcuménisme. Recueil d'études*, 1990. XVI-887 p. 75 €
94. C. BREKELMANS & J. LUST (eds.), *Pentateuchal and Deuteronomistic Studies: Papers Read at the XIIIth IOSOT Congress Leuven 1989*, 1990. 307 p. 38 €
95. D.L. DUNGAN (ed.), *The Interrelations of the Gospels. A Symposium Led by M.-É. Boismard – W.R. Farmer – F. Neirynck, Jerusalem 1984*, 1990. XXXI-672 p. 75 €
96. G.D. KILPATRICK, *The Principles and Practice of New Testament Textual Criticism. Collected Essays*. Edited by J.K. ELLIOTT, 1990. XXXVIII-489 p. 75 €
97. G. ALBERIGO (ed.), *Christian Unity. The Council of Ferrara-Florence: 1438/39 – 1989*, 1991. X-681 p. 75 €
98. M. SABBE, *Studia Neotestamentica. Collected Essays*, 1991. XVI-573 p. 50 €
99. F. NEIRYNCK, *Evangelica II: 1982-1991. Collected Essays*. Edited by F. VAN SEGBROECK, 1991. XIX-874 p. 70 €
100. F. VAN SEGBROECK, C.M. TUCKETT, G. VAN BELLE & J. VERHEYDEN (eds.), *The Four Gospels 1992. Festschrift Frans Neirynck*, 1992. 3 volumes, XVII-X-X-2668 p. 125 €

SERIES III

101. A. DENAUX (ed.), *John and the Synoptics*, 1992. XXII-696 p. 75 €
102. F. NEIRYNCK, J. VERHEYDEN, F. VAN SEGBROECK, G. VAN OYEN & R. CORSTJENS, *The Gospel of Mark. A Cumulative Bibliography: 1950-1990*, 1992. XII-717 p. 68 €
103. M. SIMON, *Un catéchisme universel pour l'Église catholique. Du Concile de Trente à nos jours*, 1992. XIV-461 p. 55 €
104. L. CEYSSENS, *Le sort de la bulle Unigenitus. Recueil d'études offert à Lucien Ceyssens à l'occasion de son 90e anniversaire*. Présenté par M. LAMBERIGTS, 1992. XXVI-641 p. 50 €
105. R.J. DALY (ed.), *Origeniana Quinta. Papers of the 5th International Origen Congress, Boston College, 14-18 August 1989*, 1992. XVII-635 p. 68 €
106. A.S. VAN DER WOUDE (ed.), *The Book of Daniel in the Light of New Findings*, 1993. XVIII-574 p. 75 €
107. J. FAMERÉE, *L'ecclésiologie d'Yves Congar avant Vatican II: Histoire et Église. Analyse et reprise critique*, 1992. 497 p. 65 €

108. C. BEGG, *Josephus' Account of the Early Divided Monarchy (AJ 8, 212-420). Rewriting the Bible*, 1993. IX-377 p. 60 €
109. J. BULCKENS & H. LOMBAERTS (eds.), *L'enseignement de la religion catholique à l'école secondaire. Enjeux pour la nouvelle Europe*, 1993. XII-264 p. 32 €
110. C. FOCANT (ed.), *The Synoptic Gospels. Source Criticism and the New Literary Criticism*, 1993. XXXIX-670 p. 75 €
111. M. LAMBERIGTS (ed.), avec la collaboration de L. KENIS, *L'augustinisme à l'ancienne Faculté de théologie de Louvain*, 1994. VII-455 p. 60 €
112. R. BIERINGER & J. LAMBRECHT, *Studies on 2 Corinthians*, 1994. XX-632 p. 75 €
113. E. BRITO, *La pneumatologie de Schleiermacher*, 1994. XII-649 p. 75 €
114. W.A.M. BEUKEN (ed.), *The Book of Job*, 1994. X-462 p. 60 €
115. J. LAMBRECHT, *Pauline Studies: Collected Essays*, 1994. XIV-465 p. 63 €
116. G. VAN BELLE, *The Signs Source in the Fourth Gospel: Historical Survey and Critical Evaluation of the Semeia Hypothesis*, 1994. XIV-503 p. 63 €
117. M. LAMBERIGTS & P. VAN DEUN (eds.), *Martyrium in Multidisciplinary Perspective. Memorial L. Reekmans*, 1995. X-435 p. 75 €
118. G. DORIVAL & A. LE BOULLUEC (eds.), *Origeniana Sexta. Origène et la Bible/Origen and the Bible. Actes du Colloquium Origenianum Sextum, Chantilly, 30 août – 3 septembre 1993*, 1995. XII-865 p. 98 €
119. É. GAZIAUX, *Morale de la foi et morale autonome. Confrontation entre P. Delhaye et J. Fuchs*, 1995. XXII-545 p. 68 €
120. T.A. SALZMAN, *Deontology and Teleology: An Investigation of the Normative Debate in Roman Catholic Moral Theology*, 1995. XVII-555 p. 68 €.
121. G.R. EVANS & M. GOURGUES (eds.), *Communion et Réunion. Mélanges Jean-Marie Roger Tillard*, 1995. XI-431 p. 60 €
122. H.T. FLEDDERMANN, *Mark and Q: A Study of the Overlap Texts. With an Assessment* by F. NEIRYNCK, 1995. XI-307 p. 45 €
123. R. BOUDENS, *Two Cardinals: John Henry Newman, Désiré-Joseph Mercier.* Edited by L. GEVERS with the collaboration of B. DOYLE, 1995. 362 p. 45 €
124. A. THOMASSET, *Paul Ricœur. Une poétique de la morale. Aux fondements d'une éthique herméneutique et narrative dans une perspective chrétienne*, 1996. XVI-706 p. 75 €
125. R. BIERINGER (ed.), *The Corinthian Correspondence*, 1996. XXVII-793 p. 60 €
126. M. VERVENNE (ed.), *Studies in the Book of Exodus: Redaction – Reception – Interpretation*, 1996. XI-660 p. 60 €
127. A. VANNESTE, *Nature et grâce dans la théologie occidentale. Dialogue avec H. de Lubac*, 1996. 312 p. 45 €
128. A. CURTIS & T. RÖMER (eds.), *The Book of Jeremiah and its Reception – Le livre de Jérémie et sa réception*, 1997. 331 p. 60 €
129. E. LANNE, *Tradition et Communion des Églises. Recueil d'études*, 1997. XXV-703 p. 75 €

130. A. DENAUX & J.A. DICK (eds.), *From Malines to ARCIC. The Malines Conversations Commemorated*, 1997. IX-317 p. 45 €
131. C.M. TUCKETT (ed.), *The Scriptures in the Gospels*, 1997. XXIV-721 p. 60 €
132. J. VAN RUITEN & M. VERVENNE (eds.), *Studies in the Book of Isaiah. Festschrift Willem A.M. Beuken*, 1997. XX-540 p. 75 €
133. M. VERVENNE & J. LUST (eds.), *Deuteronomy and Deuteronomic Literature. Festschrift C.H.W. Brekelmans*, 1997. XI-637 p. 75 €
134. G. VAN BELLE (ed.), *Index Generalis ETL / BETL 1982-1997*, 1999. IX-337 p. 40 €
135. G. DE SCHRIJVER, *Liberation Theologies on Shifting Grounds. A Clash of Socio-Economic and Cultural Paradigms*, 1998. XI-453 p. 53 €
136. A. SCHOORS (ed.), *Qohelet in the Context of Wisdom*, 1998. XI-528 p. 60 €
137. W.A. BIENERT & U. KÜHNEWEG (eds.), *Origeniana Septima. Origenes in den Auseinandersetzungen des 4. Jahrhunderts*, 1999. XXV-848 p. 95 €
138. É. GAZIAUX, *L'autonomie en morale: au croisement de la philosophie et de la théologie*, 1998. XVI-760 p. 75 €
139. J. GROOTAERS, *Actes et acteurs à Vatican II*, 1998. XXIV-602 p. 75 €
140. F. NEIRYNCK, J. VERHEYDEN & R. CORSTJENS, *The Gospel of Matthew and the Sayings Source Q: A Cumulative Bibliography 1950-1995*, 1998. 2 vols., VII-1000-420* p. 95 €
141. E. BRITO, *Heidegger et l'hymne du sacré*, 1999. XV-800 p. 90 €
142. J. VERHEYDEN (ed.), *The Unity of Luke-Acts*, 1999. XXV-828 p. 60 €
143. N. CALDUCH-BENAGES & J. VERMEYLEN (eds.), *Treasures of Wisdom. Studies in Ben Sira and the Book of Wisdom. Festschrift M. Gilbert*, 1999. XXVII-463 p. 75 €
144. J.-M. AUWERS & A. WÉNIN (eds.), *Lectures et relectures de la Bible. Festschrift P.-M. Bogaert*, 1999. XLII-482 p. 75 €
145. C. BEGG, *Josephus' Story of the Later Monarchy (AJ 9,1–10,185)*, 2000. X-650 p. 75 €
146. J.M. ASGEIRSSON, K. DE TROYER & M.W. MEYER (eds.), *From Quest to Q. Festschrift James M. Robinson*, 2000. XLIV-346 p. 60 €
147. T. RÖMER (ed.), *The Future of the Deuteronomistic History*, 2000. XII-265 p. 75 €
148. F.D. VANSINA, *Paul Ricœur: Bibliographie primaire et secondaire - Primary and Secondary Bibliography 1935-2000*, 2000. XXVI-544 p. 75 €
149. G.J. BROOKE & J.D. KAESTLI (eds.), *Narrativity in Biblical and Related Texts*, 2000. XXI-307 p. 75 €
150. F. NEIRYNCK, *Evangelica III: 1992-2000. Collected Essays*, 2001. XVII-666 p. 60 €
151. B. DOYLE, *The Apocalypse of Isaiah Metaphorically Speaking. A Study of the Use, Function and Significance of Metaphors in Isaiah 24-27*, 2000. XII-453 p. 75 €
152. T. MERRIGAN & J. HAERS (eds.), *The Myriad Christ. Plurality and the Quest for Unity in Contemporary Christology*, 2000. XIV-593 p. 75 €
153. M. SIMON, *Le catéchisme de Jean-Paul II. Genèse et évaluation de son commentaire du Symbole des apôtres*, 2000. XVI-688 p. 75 €

154. J. VERMEYLEN, *La loi du plus fort. Histoire de la rédaction des récits davidiques de 1 Samuel 8 à 1 Rois 2*, 2000. XIII-746 p. 80 €
155. A. WÉNIN (ed.), *Studies in the Book of Genesis. Literature, Redaction and History*, 2001. XXX-643 p. 60 €
156. F. LEDEGANG, *Mysterium Ecclesiae. Images of the Church and its Members in Origen*, 2001. XVII-848 p. 84 €
157. J.S. BOSWELL, F.P. MCHUGH & J. VERSTRAETEN (eds.), *Catholic Social Thought: Twilight of Renaissance*, 2000. XXII-307 p. 60 €
158. A. LINDEMANN (ed.), *The Sayings Source Q and the Historical Jesus*, 2001. XXII-776 p. 60 €
159. C. HEMPEL, A. LANGE & H. LICHTENBERGER (eds.), *The Wisdom Texts from Qumran and the Development of Sapiential Thought*, 2002. XII-502 p. 80 €
160. L. BOEVE & L. LEIJSSEN (eds.), *Sacramental Presence in a Postmodern Context*, 2001. XVI-382 p. 60 €
161. A. DENAUX (ed.), *New Testament Textual Criticism and Exegesis. Festschrift J. Delobel*, 2002. XVIII-391 p. 60 €
162. U. BUSSE, *Das Johannesevangelium. Bildlichkeit, Diskurs und Ritual. Mit einer Bibliographie über den Zeitraum 1986-1998*, 2002. IX-572 p. 70 €
163. J.M. AUWERS & H.J. DE JONGE (eds.), *The Biblical Canons*. Forthcoming.
164. L. PERRONE (ed.), *Origeniana Octava. Origen and the Alexandrian Tradition*, 2002. Forthcoming.
165. R. BIERINGER, V. KOPERSKI & B. LATAIRE (eds.), *Resurrection in the New Testament. Festschrift J. Lambrecht*, 2002. XXXI-551 p. 70 €
166. M. LAMBERIGTS & L. KENIS (eds.), *Vatican II and Its Legacy*, 2002. Forthcoming.